*Education
and
Culture*

Education and Culture ——Anthropological Approaches

GEORGE D. SPINDLER

Stanford University

Holt, Rinehart and Winston
New York · *Chicago* ·
San Francisco · *Toronto* · *London*

TO THE WOMEN IN MY LIFE

WINIFRED
CORABELLE
LOUISE
SUE

*who have influenced everything
I have done
or ever will do.*

Preface

Education and Culture is a purposeful exploration of a frontier area—the application of anthropology to education. The focus of this exploration is the transmission of culture, and particularly the values that are activated by educational events and in educational settings. Education is conceived as goal oriented in a particular cultural context. The approach is therefore cross-cultural and, by implication, comparative. Our educational system is seen in the perspective of educational systems in very different cultures. So the suburban elementary school described by Jules Henry in one of the chapters in this book can be viewed as one variant among many possibilities, such as a West African "Bush" School, a Japanese youth group, Hopi education and culture, or a Tiwi initiation ceremony. And education is interpreted functionally and holistically. The interdependence of educational systems and functions, teacher roles, cultural norms and values, and cultural process is stressed.

The twenty-five chapters included in *Education and Culture* were either written especially for the volume or were carefully selected on the basis of the following criteria: each one must represent some dimension of a process particularly significant within the scope of emergent anthropological applications to analysis of the educative process in our own society or in other societies; the chapters selected must interrelate to provide a manageable consistency of focus within a very large scope of possibilities; with a very few exceptions where the role of the chapter as a "think-piece" is especially significant, the chapters must be based upon analysis of empirical data.

The book is divided into a logical sequence of three parts. Part I presents the scope of the problems comprised in the realized and potential relationships of anthropological concepts, methods, and data to education, and specifies the area of contribution of each of the subsequent chapters. Part II focuses on the educational process and implements many of the propositions about education in our own society (and how to study them) that are surveyed in the first section. Part III provides cross-cultural perspective by presenting analyses of education in non-Western cultural contexts. An editorial preview is given at the beginning of each part to clarify its purpose and that of each of the chapters comprising it.

G. D. S.

January 1963

Acknowledgments

Every author or editor accumulates many debts owed to people and organizations that have helped him to produce his book. I gratefully acknowledge mine to:

My father, Frank Nicholas Spindler, who was professor of education, philosophy, and psychology in the Teachers College at Stevens Point, Wisconsin. He made me feel that education was a crucial human activity and that the role of the teacher should be among the most exalted. And to my mother, Winifred Hatch Spindler, whose house and heart were always full of young people whom she helped through school and into life.

The students in the two high schools where I taught before World War II. In these schools I learned how thoroughly frightened a new, young teacher can be, facing vigorous, active young people who are not asking to learn but daring someone to try to teach them. As we got over our misconceptions of each other and I learned that they had little commitment to learning because what they were being asked to learn was quite unrelated to those things that were important to them, then they began to teach me about education.

The Carnegie Foundation for a grant that made it possible to hold a seminar-conference of twenty-four prominent educators and anthropologists in 1954 under the combined auspices of the School of Education and Department of Anthropology at Stanford University, and the American Anthropological Association. This conference resulted in the book, *Education and Anthropology*, from which five of the chapters included in the present volume have been drawn. The results of this conference are also represented indirectly in other chapters included in *Education and Culture*, since many of the authors participated in the conference.

The Wenner-Gren Foundation for Anthropological Research and the Social Science Research Council which provided financial support for Dr. Louise Spindler and myself for the field work with the Menomini; the Ford Foundation Supplementary Research Grant that enabled me to organize my collected case materials on teachers, administrators, and their communities; and the Center for Advanced Study in the Behavioral Sciences, where I had an opportunity to think and talk about many of the problems represented in this volume.

My colleagues in the School of Education and the Department of Anthropology at Stanford University for their active support, and particularly to Dr. I. James Quillen, now Dean of the School of Education, and Dr. John Bartky, formerly Dean, and Dr. Felix M. Keesing, chairman of the Department of Anthropology, for their vigorous commitment to the working principle of a joint appointment in education and anthropology. And to the graduate students in both I owe a very sincere expression of gratitude. They keep asking questions and doubting the answers in such a way that complacency is impossible.

Dr. Robert N. Bush of the School of Education and the multidisciplinary research project he headed at Stanford and with which I worked intermittently from 1950 to 1958. Our object was to study teachers and administrators in interaction with each other and with students, in the natural setting of the school and community—a purpose thoroughly congruent with the anthropological approach. The project was supported by the Rosenberg Foundation in its early phases.

And to my wife Louise I owe a very special debt of gratitude. During the development of this book, as with everything else in

which we have been involved, she has played the potentially conflicting roles of professional colleague and loving wife with ex-
quisite sensitivity. It would be quite impossible for me to say where
her influence and help begins and ends, for they are represented
everywhere in this book.

G. D. S.

The Authors

THEODORE BRAMELD is Professor of Educational Philosophy at Boston University. He is author of many books and articles on the philosophical foundations of educational theory, and since the midfifties has become established as a foremost synthesizer of cultural and educational theory. He has recently finished an extensive field study in Puerto Rico. His *Cultural Foundations of Education* and *The Remaking of a Culture: Life and Education in Puerto Rico* are particularly significant from the perspective of his chapter in this book.

DOROTHY EGGAN started making major contributions to knowledge and understanding of the psycho-cultural aspects of behavior in 1943, with her paper on "The Problem of Hopi Adjustment" in the *American Anthropologist*. She has become particularly interested lately in the significance of dreams for an understanding of the psycho-social aspects of behavior, and has published (among other material) "Dream Analysis" in Bert Kaplan, ed., *Studying Personality Cross-Culturally* and "The Personal Use of Myth in Dreams," in Thomas Sebeok, ed., *Myth: A Symposium.*

JOHN L. FISCHER is currently teaching in the Department of Sociology and Anthropology, Tulane University, New Orleans. He is especially interested in the relationships between socialization, social structure, and expressive culture (art, recreation, religion), and linguistics. He received his graduate and undergraduate training in anthropology at Harvard University. His principal field work, conducted jointly with his wife, Ann, has been in Truk and Ponape, Caroline Islands, where he served as district anthropologist and native affairs officer for four years; in a semirural village in New England; and most recently, in the Japanese city of Fukuoka.

C. W. M. HART is Professor of Social Sciences at the University of Istanbul, Turkey. He has been President of the Society for Applied Anthropology, Professor of Anthropology at Toronto University and the University of Wisconsin, and is a native of Australia, who did his advanced studies under the tutelage of the great Radcliffe-Brown in England. He has written *The Tiwi of North Australia* and numerous articles on Australian ethnology and social organization and on industrial communities in Canada. He has done field work in northern Australia, Ontario, and Windsor, Canada, besides his current work in Turkey.

JULES HENRY is Professor of Anthropology at Washington University at St. Louis and has been a Research Associate at the Sonia Shankman Orthogenic School at the University of Chicago. He is one of the few anthropologists that has done field research in education in our own society as well as in others. In the perspective of this book, one of his most significant publications is "An Outline for the Study of Education," in *Current Anthropology*, Volume I. He has done field work among the Apache Indians, the Kaingang of Brazil, the Pilaga of Argentina, the Tarahumara of Mexico, and in public elementary schools in the United States.

SOLON T. KIMBALL is Professor of Education, Department of Social and Philosophical Foundations at Teachers College, Columbia University, and former Chairman of the Department of Sociology and Anthropology, University of Alabama. He has published many articles on cultural dimensions in education and books on community studies. He has done field work in Newburyport, Massachusetts; County Clare, Ireland; rural Michigan; Talladega, Alabama; and among the Navaho Indians.

DOROTHY LEE now divides her year between Iowa State University and San Fernando Valley State College, is consultant in Teaching at the Merrill-Palmer School, Detroit, was formerly Professor of Anthropology at Vassar College, and recently worked with the Harvard Undergraduate Study project. She is author of many articles on the conceptual and value aspects of culture, and other publications in ethnology. She has done field work in Melanesia, among the Wintu Indians of California, and in public schools in the United States.

MARTIN B. LOEB is Professor of Social Work at the University of Wisconsin and previously taught social work at the University of California, Berkeley. He has also taught in the School of Education at the Universities of Chicago and Kansas City. He has his doctorate in Human Development from the University of Chicago where he specialized in social anthropology. His field work has been primarily among people in American cities (he sometimes refers to his people as the "Amerurbs"). He has done research on children, adolescents, the middle aged, and the aged. His publications include: *Who Shall Be Educated: The Challenge of Unequal Opportunities* with W. Lloyd Warner and Robert I. Havighurst; three books coauthored with Jurgen Ruesch and others on psycho- and sociosomatic illnesses; and many articles on such topics as adolescence, social class, and adoption.

MARGARET MEAD is Associate Curator of Ethnology, American Museum of Natural History, and Adjunct Professor of Anthropology, Columbia University. She has made comparative studies of education in eight different cultures during the past thirty years, and has been continuously interested in the contribution of anthropology to education. From among the long list of distinguished books, monographs, and articles she has authored, some of those particularly relevant for the purposes of this volume include *Coming of Age in Samoa, Growing up in New Guinea, The School in American Culture*, and *New Lives for Old.*

RHODA MÉTRAUX is Associate Director, Studies in Allopsychic Orientation, American Museum of Natural History, and lecturer on cultural aspects of psychotherapy at the Postgraduate Center for Psychotherapy. Her graduate work in anthropology was done at Columbia University. She has been a member of the Planning Staff, Office of Strategic Services, and the Columbia University research staff in studies in contemporary cultures. She has done field work in Haiti, Mexico, Argentina, and Montserrat, British West Indies. Her current studies in allopsychic orientation focus on the learning and conceptualizing of space, time, and the unknown in modern and primitive cultures.

WALTER J. ONG, S.J., is Professor of English at Saint Louis University and is known as a scholar in both the Renaissance field and the field of contemporary literature, and as a prolific writer on problems of contemporary civilization. In 1961–1962 he was a Fellow at the Center for Advanced Studies at Wesleyan University, Middletown, Connecticut. He has been a lecturer at the Center for Advanced Renaissance Studies at Tours, France, at the Georgetown Conference on New Criticism, and at the Michigan State University Conference on Modern Literature, and has served as Visiting Professor of English at the University of California. Father Ong has published many distinguished books, among them *American Catholic Crossroads* and *Darwin's Vision and Christian Perspectives.*

I. JAMES QUILLEN is Professor of Education and Dean of the School of Education at Stanford University. His major interests are in the social foundations of education and in the development of social studies in the public schools. He has been President of the National Council for the Social Studies and an official of the UNESCO Secretariat in Paris. His publications include, among others, *The Social Studies in General Education* (with others); *Textbook Improvement and International Understanding;* and *Education for Social Competence* (with Lavone Hanna).

BERNARD J. SIEGEL is Professor of Anthropology and Executive Head of the Department of Anthropology at Stanford University. His major interests are in peasant societies, social organization, and culture change. His publications include "Suggested Factors of Culture Change at Taos Pueblo" (Proceedings Twenty-ninth International Congress of Americanists), "Implications of Social Structure for Economic Change in Brazil" (*Economic Growth,* J. Spengler, ed.), "Pervasive Factionalism" (with A. R. Beals, *American Anthropologist,* Vol. 62). He has done field work in a Syrian community in Boston; at Taos Pueblo, New Mexico; in Brazil; in Portugal; and was Visiting Professor, Faculty of Education, Tokyo University in 1960–1961.

MELFORD E. SPIRO is Professor of Anthropology at the University of Washington. His interests are broad and include such diverse areas as the theory of social systems and personality functioning, comparative religion, and the cultures of Southeast Asia. His *Children of the Kibbutz* is a major contribution to the literature of culture and personality and education. He was a Fellow at the Center for Advanced Study in the Behavioral Sciences in 1958–1959, and is on the Board of Directors of the Social Science Research Council. He has done field work in Ifaluk (Micronesia), in Kiryat Yedidim (Israel), and most recently, in Southeast Asia.

MARK HANNA WATKINS is Professor of Anthropology, Head of the Department of Sociology and Anthropology, and Director of the African Language and Culture Center, at Howard University, Washington, D.C. He is particularly interested in descriptive linguistics and has published a number of articles on African languages. At present he is both analyzing and teaching (under the National Defense Education Act) two African Bantu languages and one Kwa language. He has done field work in Haiti, Guatemala, and in South Africa.

FRED H. WERNER was a graduate student in the Department of Anthropology at Stanford University and is now at Columbia University. He has done research on the adaptation of undergraduate students to the university and college milieu at one western and several eastern institutions. His interests are in communication, cultural transmission, and the psychocultural aspects of behavior.

Contents

Part I

The Articulation
of Anthropology
and Education

Preview

The purposes of Part I, "The Articulation of Anthropology and Education," are to survey the kinds of relationships that have occurred between anthropology and education, to suggest ways that these and other relationships could profitably be developed, and to present the rationales for the various phases and types of relationship. Part I places what follows in a broad framework and provides a wider frame of reference than the papers in Parts II and III can implement, since it reviews an exploratory and emergent field that has many dimensions and moves in many different directions.

"The Character Structure of Anthropology" provides a synoptic statement of the characteristic features of the approaches employed by the anthropologists who describe and interpret the educative process. The reader will see that this profile is shared unevenly and with different emphases in the various papers, but there is an underlying consistency that makes the anthropological contribution to better understanding of education distinctive.

"Current Anthropology" performs a different function. Its purpose is to describe anthropology as it exists today, without regard for the kinds of applications that have been made or could be made to educational problems. In view of the very complex, far-flung nature of the "study of man and his works," this aim may seem unrealistic. But it must be attempted, for many readers will have had little exposure to anthropology, and a general comprehension of the field is essential if one is to conceive in broad perspective its nature and potential. The theme of the chapter is human nature in cultural diversity.

Dean Quillen writes from the educator's position in "Problems and Prospects." He describes what appear to him to be the most immediate and relevant problem areas in education with which he believes anthropology can help. In doing so, he does not infer that anthropology's interests in the educational process must be limited to what educators define as the problem areas of education. Formulations of problems will necessarily be drawn from anthropology's internal framework as well. Dean Quillen's statement provides a useful way of measuring the convergences and divergences of educators' and anthropologists' concerns, for most of the papers in this volume were generated from within the anthropological system. The reader will see that the degree of convergence is remarkably high.

"Anthropology and Education: An Overview" provides an analytic survey of the accomplishments and possibilities of the anthropology-education relationship in a number of different dimensions. In it the problem areas within education are viewed from the perspective of the anthropologist, and the resources of anthropology are probed to see what relevant products have been developed and what may yet be developed. This chapter also has the important function of specifying the place of each chapter to follow in this volume within the framework of the anthropology-education relationship.

In "The Meeting of Educational and Anthropological Theory," Theodore Brameld places the capstone on the structure of relationships between anthropology and education that the other chapters have built. He analyzes the theoretical articulations that lie behind the programmatic specificities of the other chapters. He deals with the implicit assumptions about human goals, and the nature of culture and cultural process that influences the thinking of anthropologists and educators as they formulate problems, research them, and write about them.

1—— *George D. Spindler*

The Character Structure
of Anthropology

The chapters to follow in this part demonstrate that anthropology goes in a number of directions and utilizes a number of approaches. It is a sprawling and diversified field. The anthropology of education, though it is only one area of application, exhibits the same characteristics. It is therefore unrealistic to describe one anthropological approach that will also characterize an anthropology of education.

Careful examination of the chapters included in this volume and particularly in Parts II and III will reveal, however, certain consistencies in the selection and interpretation of phenomena. None of these points of similarity in approach are shared in the same degree or in the same way by each of the papers, but they permit an inexact profiling of the shared character structure of anthropology as it is represented in this book. A description of this character structure is the business of this first paper.

ECLECTICISM

Anthropologists are willing to learn from anybody—including their colleagues in other disciplines. Most papers in this volume borrow extensively from other disciplines in their conceptualization and interpretation, and borrow less extensively but still considerably in the use of research techniques. Psychological concepts are heavily represented. Most of the papers in the Part II utilize psychodynamic formulations in interpretation of observed phenomena. The more behavioristic forms of psychological conceptualizing tend to be underrepresented, perhaps because they are more limited in scope than those formulations derived originally from psychoanalytic theory. Anthropologists will, however, use any theory or concept, that proves useful. Psychology, philosophy, and sociology have all made obvious contributions to the armamentarium of anthropology as it is applied in this volume to the observation and analysis of the educational process.

The concept that is most frequently represented is that of *culture* and its processes. Culture is conceived in most instances in these papers as a patterned system of tradition-derived norms influencing behavior. The fact that culture is seen as traditionally derived does not mean, however, that it is conceived as unchanging. Cultural norms are in a constant state of flux. They are traditional in the sense that they exist prior to behavioral events in which people are involved, but they are affected and changed by these events. This dynamic character of culture is seen in the attention to conflicts in values (those cultural definitions of the desirable in which people have the greatest emotional investment), and to the processes of acculturation and cultural transmission in many of the analyses.

The areas of particularly strong eclecticism on the part of anthropologists are the concepts of social structure (the interaction of people through the organization of their statuses, roles, and group affiliations) and of personality (the organization of the individual's bio-emotional and intellectual resources formed through adaptation to environment determined in part by culture). Although all of these concepts have a respectable tradition in anthropological usage, they have been heavily influenced by the works of sociologists and psychologists. The special character of anthropological usage is that these concepts are combined in analyses to whole situations. This eclectic and combinatory quality is appropriate to a discipline that takes as its subject matter the study of man and his works.

RESEARCH TECHNIQUES

Anthropologists are willing to learn from anybody in yet another sense. No bit of behavior is too simple or too unimportant to escape observation. No person is too lowly in status or too uninformed to be worthy of attention. No society is too "primitive" to provide useful data and useful insights into the sources of human behavior. Anthropologists respect their "informants" and anybody, anywhere, can be an informant.

Most anthropological reports are based upon direct observation of behavior in situations in which the anthropologist is at least a marginal participant, and upon personal documents collected from a sample of persons representing different age groups, sexes, statuses, and roles. Anthropologists are aided in the field work by cameras and tape recorders, but the basic instrument is the highly complex observer, who is "programmed" with a cognitive map derived from his training and professional experience and who can write down and later sort out what he sees and hears. Anthropology is one of the few sciences of human behavior where direct, uninstrumented, experience is held to be of primary value.

Structured and unstructured interview techniques, questionnaires, psychological tests, socioeconomic inventories, census reports, sociometric techniques, value-projective techniques, the whole range of procedures used in the social and behavioral sciences are utilized at times by some anthropologists. But underlying all of these usages is the constant attention to the flow of life around the participant-observer, the anthropologist, that gives meaning to the results of the specialized techniques. This basic approach to research in the field is very apparent in many of the chapters in this book. Jules Henry's two chapters in Part II are models for what needs to be done in the application of anthropology to the analysis of educational process in our own society. Most of the chapters in Part III demonstrate clearly what the commitment of the anthropologist to direct observation means. The fact that this commitment is more apparent in the papers that deal with educational process in nonwestern societies than in those in our own is an indication that anthropologists have only begun their work in our own society. Probably the most substantial contribution that anthropology could make to education would be the building of a body of case materials based upon direct observation in a variety of educational situations, but most of this work remains to be done.

BEHAVIOR AND BELIEF

The anthropologist assumes that people cannot tell the observer why they do things or even what they do. He assumes that what people consistently say they do and what they say about why they do it is a product of culturally provided rationalizations —the expression of a belief system. What people say when they are expressing their beliefs are important, factual data, but what they do and why they do it bears no necessary direct relationship to their stated beliefs.

The fact that there is no necessary correspondence between behavior and belief is not a reflection of the inherent dishonesty of the human species. Behavior and cognition are extremely complex, both within their respective spheres and in their interaction. The total configuration of belief and patterned behavior characterizing a society is infinitely more complex than any participant can understand, and perhaps even more complex than the relatively detached and intellectually objective observer can understand. The relationship between belief and behavior in the system of even a single individual is more than the individual himself can understand. This is partly so because one is never an exact replication of anyone else, so one can never see oneself clearly mirrored in the behavior and verbalization of others, and partly because the belief system of the individual about his own behavior prevents him from viewing his behavior objectively.

There are always several levels of communication involved in social interaction. The manifest content of any interaction set may be quite clear to participants within it, but the latent, or implicit content may be virtually undetected in a direct, conscious sense. It is the anthropologist's job to try to expose this implicit level in his interpretation of behavior and its consequences. One of the clearest examples is to be seen in the way a linguist works with an unstudied language. He finds that most of the people speaking the language adhere to common, standardized usages, but that no one can tell him what the general rules for these usages really are. So he must continue to record and analyze utterances until he discovers them, and then continually try them out on new forms.

So it is also with all other areas of culturally influenced behavior. The anthropologist records and analyzes his data in a continuous search for the underlying principles of organization, the undeclared meaning and functions of behavior in both verbal and nonverbal dimensions.

This part of the profile of the character structure of anthropology is quite clear in the papers in this book. It becomes particularly clear in the analysis of the behavior of teachers engaged in the educational act. Their declared intentions are frequently discrepant with the actual outcomes of their actions because latent content and functions of the student-teacher interaction are unknown. If there were no unanticipated results, no implicit meanings to behavior, and no discrepancy between belief and behavior, there would be little reason for any study of education, by anthropologists or others, to be undertaken at all. Everything would be linear and known without the help of an outside observer armed with specialized techniques of observation and a conceptual framework to guide interpretation that transcends "common sense."

The other social and behavioral sciences also begin with the assumption ascribed to the anthropologist. The significant differences between the anthropological approach and those of others are that the anthropologist relates his interpretations and observations to the cultural process, even when studying individual behavior, and attempts to take into account as broad a range of behavior as is feasible within the setting in which he is working.

HUMANISTIC INCLINATIONS

Anthropologists are concerned with the improvement of the human condition and with the improvement of our own society. Though these values are not always apparent in the immediate focus of a specific piece of research, they are usually ultimate purposes. Anthropologists are vitally concerned with humanistic issues. They believe that this humanistic contribution can best be made through empirical study of the human condition in all its varieties. Generalizations that lead on the one hand to systematic, complex, and therefore useful theory and method, and on the other hand to the direct improvement of the human condition through sharper insights into the dynamics of behavior that can be used in applied anthropology must be based upon hard cases. Anthropologists are not given to armchair philosophizing about human behavior.

Anthropologists try to keep the essentially human qualities in their descriptions and analyses of culture case materials and behavior. Highly formalistic models or analytic procedures are not dominant in the discipline, although there are movements in this direction at present. But even the anthropologist who uses formalistic models and abstract categories of analysis for particularistic issues within the framework of the behavior of a given society usually also at some point in his reporting of the materials he has collected shows evidence of deep concern with the very human qualities of his observation and experience with the people. Anthropologists are committed to the real life models furnished by living cultures.

These qualities of concern with the improvement of the human condition and concern with the human characteristics of their substantive cases are very apparent in the writings of anthropologists collected for this volume. The first is most clear in Part II, where almost every chapter makes a case for some area of the educative process in our society that needs improvement. The latter is clearest in Part III, where all of the papers present humanized analyses of behavior as relevant to the particular issues with which the writer is concerned. The two concerns overlap and appear in various degrees of emphasis in all the papers.

CONFIGURATIVE THINKING

Anthropologists approach their case materials with a commitment to analyze the interdependent functions of apparently separate aspects of behavior. Education at puberty is seen in an interdependent relationship with education before puberty. The behavior of the teacher in the classroom is seen as influenced by the life experience of the teacher outside of the classroom. The interactions of pupils and teachers are seen as asymmetrically interdependent. The educational process is perceived as reflecting the value conflicts current within the cultural milieu surrounding the school. The role of the school administrator is conceived as a function of the formal organization of the school system, the expectations of various groups in the community, the history of changes in the community, his interaction with the staff, and the personality of the administrator.

This configurative, functional approach militates against the application of controlled experimental research designs. These designs, employing rigorous selection of limited variables and their observation under controlled conditions, can probably best be left to our colleagues in the other behavioral sciences—at least for the present. This is not where the strength of anthropology as a contributor to the understanding of behavior lies. It rests in the ability of the anthropologist to interrelate phenomena that may otherwise never be perceived as functionally interdependent. The contribution of anthropology to education will consist of the building of a body of careful, empirical cases of educative process in the sociocultural milieu, and their functional analysis. This body of cases, collected and interpreted by skilled observers, is lacking today, and this is a serious lack because the basic, organic processes and interrelationships in educational settings are left unknown. Without these basic case materials the more controlled and necessarily more limited kinds of research on educative process lack direction and therefore make less of a contribution to the development of useful educational theory than they should.

COMPARATIVE EDUCATION AND CROSS-CULTURAL PERSPECTIVE

Most statements made by anthropologists in their analyses of culturally bounded phenomena are implicitly comparative statements. An anthropologist observing and interpreting any situation is sorting out his recorded impressions with a cognitive structure that is coded with other cultural norms—those of his own society, those of the societies in which he has done field work, and those of the societies he has learned about from ethnographies written by others. Frequently the comparative, cross-cultural perspective is not made explicit, but each culture case is seen as one variety of human behavior among many possibilities. This cross-cultural perspective gives the anthropologist a certain objectivity in his examination of behavior in our own society that is very difficult to attain otherwise. This does not mean that the anthropologist is free from bias; more could be done to make the biases apparent. It does mean that the anthropologist has the advantage of a very broad perspective on human affairs that prevents him from making culturally limited generalizations about human nature and brings him to include alternative possibilities in his interpretations of behavior. These qualities are apparent in the chapters in Part II, particularly because they are concerned with the educative process in our own society, where the objectivity of a cross-cultural perspective is so important if the analyst is to avoid being trapped by the singular prejudices of our own culture about education and the nature of man.

In the chapters in Part III the cross-cultural perspective on education is the major focus. In many of the papers in this section there are explicit references to education in our own society in comparison to others. Basic social, cultural and psychological processes in educational situations are analyzed, rather than the formal dimensions of institutional structuring or the economic resources of education in various settings. A truly comparative educational discipline would capitalize on this kind of potential, with the purpose of developing a universally applicable theory of education through systematic comparisons of the same categories of educational experience in different cultures and the exploration of functional interdependencies within and between these categories. The relationships between educative process, social structure, and cultural values, between prepubertal and postpubertal education; between economic and educational structuring, for example, could be studied cross-culturally.

A comparative approach of this type must be, at least in its first stages of development, essentially case-oriented. Rigorously controlled comparisons across cultural boundaries are extremely difficult to make, since the anthropologist must accept reality as it is expressed in the uniqueness of each culture and each educational system that functions within it. Some control is possible through observation and analysis of the same categories of phenomena, but no set of categories should be seen as binding since new categories may appear. The comparative approach of the anthropologist should demonstrate the range of possibilities in educational structure and process as displayed in existing cultures. It should contribute to a comprehensive theory of education that accounts for this range of demonstrated possibilities.

Eventually it may prove possible to set up hypotheses about antecedents and consequences in educational action that can be tested in cross-cultural studies using accumulated case materials and that will guide the collection of new case materials. We may expect attempts to study education cross-culturally with a rigorous comparative methodology, using semiexperimental designs. The chapters in Part III of this book, however, are explicitly oriented to the task of providing basic case materials demonstrating the range of possibilities in educative process, and providing insight into the interdependent relationships of potentially comparable dimensions of that process.

CONCLUSION

The parts of the character structure of anthropology, as they are displayed in this volume on education and the cultural process, are: (1) the eclecticism in the use of concepts from other disciplines and the eclectic quality of anthropological research methodology (but tempered with a fundamental commitment to direct observation); (2) the assumption that behavior and belief are not necessarily correspondent and that social interaction involves both manifest and implicit levels of communication and meaning; (3) the interest of anthropologists in improving the human condition and the concern of anthropologists with the living reality of human behavior in different cultural settings; (4) the case study, configurative approach, which permits analytic connections to be made among what might otherwise appear to be unrelated phenomena; (5) the perspective and objectivity inherent in cross-cultural study based upon the recording and analysis of culture case studies; (6) the comparative approach that is implicit at times and explicit at others in most of what anthropologists write.

The rest of the chapters in Part I perform different functions than this first one. The next chapter, "Current Anthropology," describes anthropology as it is today and some of its major concerns, many of which fall outside the framework of this book. Such an introductory acquaintance seems necessary if the reader is to get a fair picture of the resources of anthropology. Dean Quillen in the third chapter succinctly defines the possible contributions of anthropology to education from an educator's point of view. "Anthropology and Education: An Overview" is a review of the formal and programmatic relations between the two fields. It, too, provides a wider frame of reference than the chapters in this volume can utilize, but it should be useful because it demonstrates a wide range of possibilities and concerns that could be mutually profitable to education and to anthropology. Dr. Brameld's chapter performs its functions at a different level—the metacultural—where the relevance of anthropological theory for the development of educational theory is explored.

The full flowering of the anthropological profile that has been sketched in this first chapter will not be fully perceived until the reader has gone well into Part II and Part III, for it is in these parts of the book that the substantive, field-oriented, culture case materials are presented.

2——— *George D. Spindler*

Current Anthropology*

Current anthropology is concerned with human ecology, genetics, biological evolution and adaptation; behavioral and anatomical links with the lower primates; the structure of language, changes in language through time, the influence of language on forms of thought and feeling; systems of clan, kinship, and the emergence of political and legal structures, old and new world culture history and their inter-relationships; social evolution, cultural change and acculturation; national character; mental illness and culture; child training and the development of personality types; cultural values; the analysis of small groups and the study of whole communities; and the study of economic and educational systems. These are some, not all, of the many problem areas with which anthropologists are currently concerned.

Anthropology is not a neat division of interests and problems; it is a sprawling and diversified field. The usual divisions include: cultural or social anthropology (the study of cultures and social systems around the world); linguistics (the study of language); archeology (the study of material traces of man's past existence); and physical anthropology (the study of human races, human evolution, and biological maturation).

As Professor Alfred Kroeber has said:

It is evident that anthropology—however specific it may be in dealing with data—aims at being ultimately a co-ordinating science, somewhat as a legitimate holding corporation co-ordinates constituent companies. We anthropologists will never know China as intensively as a Sinologist does, or prices, credit, and

* Reprinted, with extensive revision, from *New Viewpoints in the Social Sciences,* Roy A. Price, 1958, where it appears under the title "Trends and Applications in Anthropology," with permission.

15

banking as well as the economist, or heredity with the fulness of the genetic biologist. But we face what these more intensive scholars only glance at intermittently and tangentially, if at all: to try to understand how Chinese civilization and economics and human heredity, and dozens of other highly developed special bodies of knowledge, do indeed interrelate in being parts of "man"—flowing out of man, centered in him, products of him (Kroeber, 1953:xiv).

This is, to be sure, an irritating pipe dream to many of our colleagues in the other social and natural sciences. But "generalists" are badly needed today to understand man and why he behaves as he does. Scientific interests have become more and more highly specialized and circumspect—to the extent that at times it seems that we are losing sight of our ultimate and common goal. No one student of human behavior can hope to master this great and heterogeneous mass of interests centered on man. But an anthropologist carries with him the obligation to be *aware* of these interests, even in the pursuit of his specialty, and this awareness affects the way he deals with his realistically limited studies.

It is by virtue of this very generalizing, holistic breadth that anthropology is particularly relevant to education. Suitable to this mutual breadth, the theme of this chapter, if there can be said to be a single theme, is human nature in cultural diversity.

EVOLUTION

Anthropologists have long been concerned with the evolution of physical man. While the broad relationships of *Homo sapiens* to extinct species of the human family and to the lower primates become clearer with the discovery of new fossils, and with further work on the physical structure, social life, and psychology of monkeys and apes, this new knowledge raises as well as answers questions. (Eisely, 1955; Howells, 1959; Washburn, 1961). These problems cannot be discussed here, except to point out that one of the most vexing problems is the definition of what is human. This is not so difficult until one encounters the intermediate forms of human-apelike creatures whose skeletal remains have recently been added to the collection in man's evolutionary closet. Some, like the "South-African Man Apes" are so intermediate between human and ape that they can literally be classed as either. Distinctions on purely morphological grounds must be quite arbitrary. Some anthropologists have turned in a different direction and have said that the distinguishing criteria of man must be based on *culture*—the use of tools and the communication of tradition with language (Hallowell, 1956).

The eminent biologist, Julian Huxley, holds that the transformation and transmission of cultural tradition, evolved *by* man, makes fundamental improvements at the merely biological level unlikely, or even impossible (Huxley, 1955). At the same time many anthropologists and some biologists have been focusing attention on the fact that even the most primary and rude human inventions, such as the use of fire to cook and weapons to kill, have had much to do with the biological evolution of man. A train of biological consequences has been set in motion by every primary invention of this sort—more food became available because more game was secured and was more digestible because it was cooked—so population expanded and the possibilities of biological changes from which selection could be made increased (Washburn, 1960). But eventually, as Dr. Huxley has noted, the tradition accumulates to the point where new adaptations to the conditions of life, however extreme they may be, are made on and within cultural terms, and not by biological adaptations transmitted in genes.

Yet another step seems necessary for a full consideration of the relationships between biological man and culture. We must understand more fully the physical adaptation of man to the environment he has created through his technology. The industrial revolution, the urbanization of human populations, and the presence of radioactive pollutants that find their way into the foods we eat as well as the air we breathe are creating a new environment for survival. The ecological relationships between man and his self-created environment are only very dimly understood at present.

HUMAN NATURE

An undercurrent running through much of what is being done in the study of man is the problem of human nature—the biological and bio-emotional preconditions to human status (LaBarre, 1954). From the viewpoint of the non-anthropologist, this must appear to be an obvious and logical concern. From the viewpoint of the anthropologist the problem has been complicated by certain long-range developments within the field. The nineteenth-century anthropologists, like Lewis Henry Morgan, Edward Tylor, and practically all others of the period, were so impressed by Darwin's evolutionary theories, and so caught up in the rosy glow of nineteenth-century progress that they overgeneralized. They saw human social evolution as a straight and ascending line, marked by major stages, such as "savagery," "barbarism," and "civilization," and ending with the status quo of Victorian society. They forced the classification of all living people into one or another of these categories, and generalized for the whole of human culture. The essential element of human nature in their thinking was *progress,* narrowly defined in terms of their own society.

A new perspective emerged rather quickly as expeditions into the field became more common, and descriptions of the exotic and dramatically different ways of life practiced and defended by human populations about the world began to be gathered on a less casual and biased basis than that afforded by the traveler and trader. What impressed the student of human behavior like Franz Boas (the "Dean" of American anthropology) was the *diversity* of human cultures. And so Boas and his colleagues stressed the uniqueness of every human society. Another kind of extremity was created. Every culture had to be studied separately, in terms of its own unique history. Commonalities and regularities were obscured, and the insight that every culture is a complex solution to a set of common problems by a sentient animal with a universal sharing of biological and intellectual propensities was temporarily lost. But the pendulum of study and thought reached full swing in the direction of exclusive interest in the uniqueness of culture during the thirties, and now the search for regularities in human culture as solutions to common problems, preconditioned by the bio-emotional brotherhood of man, is clearly underway.

Culture History and Human Nature

This theme will appear in various guises elsewhere in the discussion to follow. For the moment let us examine the implications of certain current trends in the study of culture history. V. Gordon Childe has probably done more than any other contemporary writer to clarify and communicate the major outline of social, cultural, and political sequences in the prehistoric development of the old world (Childe, 1946, 1951). In his works the outlines of the western world in which we live today emerge clearly in the sweeping changes in the modes of human existence set in motion by the "Neolithic revolution." The invention and adoption of agriculture with the domestication of grains like wheat and millet, and animals like cattle, sheep, and goats; the emergence of a sedentary village pattern, with the consequential development of formalized and hierarchical political leadership; and eventually the invention of writing and numerical notation, possibly to record the transactions of busy markets and trading expeditions in the increasingly interdependent and urbanizing world; all these basic creations of man spread slowly from the southern Mediterranean lands to Europe, Asia, and Africa. Man has never been the same since. (See also Braidwood, 1961.)

Of dramatic interest to the conception of human nature is the question of whether New World developments paralleling those apparent in the detailing of the Neolithic revolution of the Old World were independent and convergent with those of the Old World, or whether they are the consequence of cultural diffusion from the old to the new. Knowledge of the ancient civilizations of the Maya, Aztec, and Inca Indians of the Americas, increasing rapidly at present, makes it obvious that an impressive list of basic features are held in common: domesticated plants and animals, irrigation, cities and towns, metallurgy, states and empires, social classes, priesthoods, calendars and writing, mathematics and even pyramids. Were these the inventions of men with common human endowments facing similar problems of human existence —like those of the men of the old world? Or are these striking parallels in human resourcefulness the result of copying the inventions of older, and by implication, *uniquely* inventive man? The weight of considered opinion appears to be on the side of common human endowment and problem solution. Each of the great Neolithic revolutions is unique in character in the sense that quite different plants and animals were domesticated, different relations between priests, warriors, and common people emerged, and the calendars and writing are based upon different principles of notation and combination. The content of these great revolutions in the relations of man to habitat and man to man are different, but the outlines and sequences, even the timing, are approximately the same (Steward, 1955; Howells, 1954; Coon, 1955).

This long view of human development holds promise that man's adaptive capacities are too great to be destroyed, even by his own inventions. The sense of crisis is indeed with us, but man has faced crises before and has mastered them. It is important to know that this capacity for mastery is not the unique possession of one or another specific kind of man, but a propensity shared by all men; that it is, indeed, *human nature*.

Cultural Values

It is not only in the grand perspective of human history that we can see the forces of human nature at work. Anthropologists have become increasingly interested in analyzing the values characteristic of each culture. They see that no way of life is a meaningless and goalless jumble of odd behaviors. It is clear that each culture selects certain conditions of living, certain objects of possession, certain characteristics of personality, as more desirable than others (Mering, 1961; Kluckhohn and Strodtbeck, 1961). And these *desirables* are seen as motivating people to behave in acceptable and worthwhile ways, as underlying complex and highly specific manners and customs. The philosopher Northrop conceives of cultures as philosophies, and values as ". . . the fruits of living according to the basic philosophical assumptions used by a people in conceptualizing the raw data of their experience [Northrop, 1953]."

Alfred Kroeber points out that although the explicit theoretic formulation of values is a trend established during the last decade within the field of anthropology, every broad and integrative description of a culture presents a picture of characteristic values (Kroeber, 1955). The single largest step in the direction of systematic comparison of values in different cultures has been taken in the long-term project of the Harvard University Laboratory of Social Relations known as "The Comparative Study of Values in Five Cultures." The field for this study is the region south of Gallup, New Mexico, where communities of five different cultural traditions—Zuni and Navaho Indians, Mormons, Catholic Spanish-Americans, and Protestant-American homesteaders from Texas—all contend with the same high-altitude semiarid environment (Vogt and Roberts, 1956; Kluckhohn and Strodtbeck, 1961).

For the members of the Spanish-American community the present is what counts, with its drama, color, and spontaneity—as expressed in the traditional fiesta. There is no point in working too hard or worrying about the future; one can do little but accept what comes. But the transplanted Texans do not feel this way about things. The future is what counts, and passive acceptance of what comes is seen as a lazy way out. Nature can be mastered, they believe, so they buy tractors, adopt the latest farming methods, and work unceasingly to overcome the harsh, semiarid environment. The Mormons are more like the Texans than they are like the Spanish-Americans, but they work not so much for economic development as for progress toward godhood. The Zuni are different from any of these three. They live in the present, to be sure, in a beautifully coordinated and complex cooperation with nature, but also look towards the past more than the other three cultures—to a glorious past in mythological time when their ancestors came out of the wombs of the earth to settle down and form the heritage of a way of life revered and kept distinct by ritual and belief to the present time. The Navaho are much like the Zuni in their attitude toward time and nature. But they see nature as more profoundly threatening and dangerous than do the Zuni, and highly value curing ceremonials that can keep things from getting any worse by restoring harmony to the balance of man in nature.

It is clear that basic values of this sort express much of the distinctive character of a culture. At this point it may seem that we have again lost sight of human nature in this diversity. But this is not the case. It is apparent that in each of these cultures man is a *valuing* creature. This, by itself, is a most significant attribute of human nature.

Universals

Anthropologists, while impressed by the diversity of human cultures and the character definition given each by its core values, have not neglected to point out the essential similarities among them. Dr. George Murdock, for instance, has given us a list of over one hundred items that are found in every culture known to history and ethnography (Murdock, 1945). Sports, ethics, feasting, ethnobotany, games, gift-giving, folklore, family, hospitality, kinship nomenclature, magic, mourning, obstetrics, puberty customs, sexual restrictions, weaning, and weather control are a few of the cultural properties we humans all share. And not only do these far-reaching cross-cultural similarities appear, but, more impressive, all languages can be resolved into comparable kinds of components, such as phonemes (conventional sound units), morphemes (meaningful elements of language), and grammar (standard rules for combining words in sentences). Even the kinds of sounds that can be produced by the human vocal mechanisms are limited; therefore the range of vowels and consonants, the kinds of glottal stops (as when a Brooklynite says "bottle"), even the noises made with lips and clicks of tongue and teeth, are resolvable into comparatively few categories.

In a closely related approach reviewing the attempts to deal with the underlying regularities of culture and values, Clyde Kluckhohn asks the question: "Are there fairly definite limits within which cultural variation is constrained by panhuman regularities in biology, psychology, and the processes of social interaction?" He refers to various and tentative limits and cultural results, such as the existence of two sexes, the ordinary human life-span, reactions to stress situations, the limitations imposed by group composition and by territoriality, the functioning of the self-concept, and others (Kluckhohn, 1953).

For our purposes it is important to realize that students of the study of man are concerned with the problem and are striking out in an attempt to go beyond the remarkable and dramatic diversity of the hundreds of human cultures to the broader consideration of human nature.

Culture Change

Attention to the processes of culture change and acculturation is another current trend in the study of anthropology that is of particular relevance. This focus on change reflects the context in which anthropologists work. Only a few years ago the major preoccupation among social and cultural anthropologists was to salvage the fast-disappearing nonliterate cultures scattered about in jungles, deserts, and forests around the world. This task is still with us and, indeed, it is more pressing that ever in some ways, because the remaining strongholds of the "primitive" peoples of the world are rapidly being opened to the impact of industrialized civilization. But precisely because this progressive and dramatically rapid expansion of the industrial-urban societies is bringing hundreds of small, technologically and politically emergent societies under the impact of heretofore unfelt influences that create new and upsetting problems of adaptation, anthropologists have also become more and more interested in these very problems. The consequences of this impact and the causes of demoralization and disintegration versus the causes of successful adaptations are the focus of attention (Spindler and Spindler, 1959).

The earlier systematic attempts to deal with the events set in motion by the contact of cultures with each other tended to center on the diffusion of culture traits from one society to the other; and usually from Euro-American culture to others. The substitution of iron tools for stone, corrugated roofs for thatch, European clothing for grass skirts, new agricultural techniques for old, these were the focus of interest.

A. Irving Hallowell was one of the first anthropologists to call attention to the fact that there were *people* involved in the process of culture change. He designed and carried out a study of the Ojibwa Indians of Ontario and northern Wisconsin that related psychological changes occurring in peoples to changes in their culture as their way of life was brought increasingly under the impact of Euro-American culture. He used projective psychological tests (Rorschach and Thematic Apperception Tests) plus the usual techniques of the cultural anthropologist to study three different "levels" of cultural adaptation among the Ojibwa. His least acculturated (most unchanged) group, far back in the woods and largely out of contact with white men and their civilization, spoke only Ojibwa, hunted and trapped for a living, and carried on the traditional religion. His intermediate group, more in contact with the white man, and more dependent upon western material goods and economic techniques, spoke both Ojibwa and English and were mostly Christianized. His most acculturated group, in Wisconsin reservations, had lost nearly all of the traditional culture and its members were mostly living as poor whites (Hallowell, 1945; 1956).

His conclusions are dramatic: that despite great changes that occurred in dress, speech, religion, and economic techniques, the Ojibwa at all three levels of acculturation remained, psychologically speaking, Ojibwa Indians. There were no radical changes in personality structure, in spite of large changes in the more obvious aspects of culture. The changes that did occur were psychologically disorganizing and regressive. The basic outlines of the personality were badly corroded by the partial adaptation to our culture, but its outlines were still clear at even the most acculturated level of the Wisconsin reservation.

The Spindlers did a somewhat similar study of the Menomini Indians living in what is now a separate county in Wisconsin (G. Spindler, 1955; L. and G. Spindler, 1958; L. Spindler, 1962). This afforded unique opportunities for this type of research because there were four levels of acculturation present in this single tribe and location. There was a native-oriented group where the patterns of the traditional way of life were still alive; a Peyote Cult (Native American Church) group which had made an adjustment to the impact of our civilization by adopting a religion that combines Indian and white beliefs; an intermediate, or transitional, group whose members had experienced the old way of life but had moved towards Catholicism and western culture during their lifetimes; and an acculturated group, some of whose members lived and thought like the middle-class Americans in towns near the Menomini. We found also that the Indian personality structure was surprisingly refractive to change in depth. The least acculturated group exhibited a highly controlled, unaggressive, stoic, and well-organized personality. The Peyotists exhibited an almost schizoid self-involvement within the outlines of the native-oriented personality structure. The transitionals exhibited various types of psychological disorganization within this same persistent personality type, reflecting the marginal position they occupy with respect to both the old and the new ways of life. But the majority of the most highly acculturated exhibited a personality that is nearly indistinguishable from that of the "ideal" of the American middle class. There are differences. Their personalities and their world outlook are not "standard middle class." But they are psychologically controlled around different psychological pivots than the least acculturated. They are success and achievement-oriented on American cultural terms and show it in their psychological structure.

In short, the Menomini study showed where and when a positive psychological adaptation takes place to accompany the manifest cultural transformation involved in being committed to a wage economy and success achievement on American terms. What is extremely important about this is the fact that it was only when certain Menomini were able to achieve success on our terms, *so that they became acceptable within our system,* that a positive psychological adaptation could occur. And this success was made possible by the existence of a lumber industry in the community that permitted some of the Menomini to earn good incomes, buy houses and cars, get an education, interact on an equal social footing with whites, and control their own destinies in a self-governing system. The lesson in this is that until a people in the process of adapting to entirely new conditions of life are accepted within the framework of those new conditions there is no reason why the personality appropriate to the traditional way of life should undergo anything but regressive and demoralizing changes.

And this brings us to another recent study of culture change. Margaret Mead returned after twenty-five years to study the people of Manus, who live in the Admiralty Islands of the South Pacific. Her earlier study is reported in *Growing up in New Guinea* (1930) and the most recent in *New Lives for Old* (1956). Her recent study and the conclusions that she draws from it are of impelling importance.

The Admiralty Islands are a small, remote and isolated part of the world. When Margaret Mead was there twenty-five years ago, she lived in and studied a community built on stilts out in the shallow salt lagoons and between the islands; a community constituted of a people who had no comprehension of the world outside, knew no writing, handled the problems of social interaction and reciprocal obligation in terms of kinship, who wore G-strings and grass skirts, and whose economic life she described as a "treadmill." The way of life had distinction and style, but much of its distinctiveness was false, in the sense that most of the material objects that gave this impression of style were not made by the people using them. They were secured in trade with the land peoples, a trade that kept the Manus engaged in unremitting labor to secure the products of the sea with which to trade.

When she returned, twenty-five years later, she was ". . . greeted by a man in carefully ironed white clothes, wearing a tie and shoes, who explained that he was the 'council,' one of the elected officials of the community" (Mead, 1956:22). She was handed a letter, signed by the locally chosen school teacher, a man that had been a baby in arms when she was there before, who asked her if she would help him teach the children. A few days after her arrival she was asked, by another elected official, to help work out a list of rules for modern child care—feeding, discipline, sleeping, and so on. When she explained that her comments would be based on the latest thinking of the International Seminar on Mental Health and Infant Development held at Chichester, England, in 1952, under the auspices of the World Federation for Mental Health and the World Health Organization of the United Nations, this man, who was born into what was at the time of his birth a primitive "stone age" society, *understood what she was saying*. Dr. Mead declares that until that moment she had not really known what the word *literacy* meant.

So much was changed in Manus society and culture, and even in the character of the people, that it would be futile to try to summarize here. She left a primitive, isolated, nonliterate people. She returned to find a people moving rapidly, and with self-conscious, purposeful energy, into the stream of modern world culture. She found a people striving to act in the best tradition of democracy and searching for education that would permit them and their children to participate more fully in the modern world. And this occurred in one lifetime!

How did this happen? Over a million American men poured through the Admiralty Islands during World War II. They set up sawmills in the bush to make lumber to build barracks. They knocked down mountains, leveled airstrips. And they treated the Manus men who worked for and with them like individuals, not "natives." While it may seem strange that the Manus could see us this way, in view of our racial prejudices and anti-integration riots at home, it is not so strange in that particular context. What the Manus men saw was our basic American preference, ". . . overlaid as it is with the residue of slavery and the scars of immigration of peoples with markedly lower standards of living . . . to treat every man on his merits, regardless of creed or color or national origin. . . [Mead, 1956:170]."

So the Manus modeled themselves in the image of what they conceived ourselves and our society to be. And they did not do a partial job of it. They literally threw away their old culture, and have attempted to recreate the way of life in terms of the perceived model.

To those who are flattered because this particular group of "little brown brothers" chose to "imitate" us, I can only say that they have not sensed the implications of what has been said. The Manus believe that by doing as they have done they can participate fully in a world dominated by the western way of doing things and receive benefits from this participation. If they find that this is not the case, as so many other peoples have discovered in the last century, they too will become discouraged, demoralized, and full of hatred for us. Successful adaptation to the impact of industrial-urban literate civilization on the part of the underdeveloped societies of the world can only occur when the fruits of participation are made freely and fully available to them. This is not merely a sanctimonious generalization. It is a conclusion based on good evidence.

CULTURAL PERSISTENCE

The nature of human nature is revealed as much in the persistence of cultural forms as in their change. A recent study by Arthur Rubel (1960) of a Mexican-American subcultural group near the Texas-Mexican border is apropos in this regard. The title "Concepts of Disease in Mexican-American Culture" is not too appealing, but its implications are intriguing.

There are four illnesses common in "Mecca," the mixed Mexican-American and Anglo community. I will mention only one, "caida de la mollera" (fallen fontanel). This condition is restricted to infants. The people believe that the skull is virtually egg-shell fragile, and that the frontal portion of the upper skull (the fontanel) is easily depressed by a fall or bump. It is also believed that this portion of the skull is counterpoised by pressure from the upper palate, which depresses when the fontanel sinks, in turn blocking the oral passage. Frequently the mother does not, nor does anyone else, witness the fall. The first sign of trouble is inability to suckle properly, loose bowels, or unusual crying or restlessness. And what babies do not exhibit such "symptoms" at times?

When these signs are noted, the child is usually taken to a curer. Prayers are recited—the Catholic Credo, Ave Maria, and Padre Nuestro. The child is dipped headfirst in a pan of water. A raw egg is rubbed on the supposedly depressed portion of the skull to form a patch to draw upward the fallen fontanel and palate. The child is held upside-down by the ankles and brusquely shaken toward the head. If this treatment is not performed it is believed the child will die.

It is significant that only people of Mexican background are afflicted by this and the other three illnesses; and that it is believed that no technically trained physician can diagnose or treat them. Members of the Mexican-American group will seize upon every opportunity to vouch for the authenticity of the condition and its treatment by a native curer. They tell of cases where a person suffering from one of the four maladies goes to a physician and is told nothing is wrong, then goes to a curer and is diagnosed and cured. This is offered as proof of the efficacy of traditional medical practice. It also "proves" the validity of traditional concepts of disease.

It is apparent that this is a self-sustaining pattern of belief. It serves to reinforce and maintain the identity of the Mexican-American group. It is symbolic of the traditional way of life. It also helps to reduce anxiety about health and illness, since curers are readily available, inexpensive and are familiar people with a friendly, understood role.

Self-sustaining patterns of belief are found in all cultures and serve approximately the same functional needs. In our own culture, for example, the pattern of water witching (locating underground water using a forked twig or other object) has persisted since colonial days and has its roots in late medieval Europe. Today there are at least 25,000 active water witches in the United States. A vast amount of anecdotal support exists for water witching— much like that supporting Mexican folk concepts of disease and treatment. There is not one shred of scientifically acceptable evidence to support this belief. Anthropologists Evon Vogt and Ray Hyman in their fascinating book *Water Witching, U.S.A.* analyze the whole problem (1959).

But water witching reduces anxiety. A nationwide survey indicates that the greatest proportion of water witches are called upon in counties where the sources of underground water are uncertain and information inadequate. The water witch relieves the individual of responsibility for deciding where to put down his well. Witching fees are much lower (some water witches make no charges) than those of technically trained ground-water specialists, and the latter are usually strangers with formidable official status and are less readily available.

So both water witching and traditional concepts of disease and treatment persist within the structure of our own society. Many other examples of such patterned, self-sustaining belief systems existing in our society could be described. Most readers would not accept any analysis of their patterns of belief in child rearing, education, or religion as "self-sustaining." This would be too threatening. Who wants proof of something he "knows"—especially when this "knowing" serves the purposes of reducing uncertainty and maintaining cultural identity?

This is the nature of man, and it is the nature of his culture. Culture, seen from this perspective, is a traditionally patterned, shared system of beliefs about reality that reassures the individual that life is worthwhile, that he knows the truth, and that by following the truth as he knows it he will be protected by his group and by his gods.

This is why cultures do not change quickly—why traditional patterns of behavior, and particularly of belief and world outlook, adapt through transformation only when the pressures are enormous.

Our world will be pluralistic for a long time—probably for as long as it exists. Technological, material, and political aspects of life may change, and the tendency for these manifest aspects of culture to become more and more uniform all over the globe is pronounced, at least for the present. But the cultural level we have just been discussing—the level of cherished beliefs, core values, world outlook—seems to be transmitted from generation to generation, and reinforced in each generation, with different mechanisms than those involved at the manifest level.

We must prepare ourselves to get along with others in a rapidly contracting world. And we must learn to get along with each other where the illusion of similarity will be as persistent as the reality of diversity. Perhaps our basic problem is *communication*—complicated by several levels of discourse. But would we really want it otherwise? Diversity is so much more interesting than uniformity!

RESEARCH METHODS AND APPROACHES

The specific ways in which anthropologists gather and analyze their data may be of less interest than some of the other topics that have been discussed. Non-anthropologists are usually more interested in the results of anthropological research methods than they are in the research methods themselves. And yet the alert user of these results will want to know how reliable they are; how much he can depend on the conclusions drawn by anthropologists as they interpret the raw data of their field experience.

In some respects the anthropologist who goes into the field to study and report upon the whole way of life of a people, however "simple" they may be, sets for himself an impossible task. In the first place he usually has to adjust to a totally new and very strange environment. It can almost be said that he has to learn to think, as well as speak differently, in order to communicate effectively with the subjects of his study. And then having learned to do this, with what is always a partial degree of success, he has to observe, question, experience until he is able to make sense out of patterns of behavior and motivation that are never simple and are always strange when seen from the perspective of his own culture. So he has to, in part, impose order upon the raw data of his experience, and this order must constitute a translation that is communicable to his audience, which will be constituted of his own kind and not of the people he has been studying.

These conditions of data gathering and interpretation have many implications. For one thing, they mean that however free from specific hypotheses the anthropologist may be as he approaches the field, he gathers data in terms of some frame of reference, however implicit it may be. One of the frustrating results of this is the fact that studies done at one period in the development of anthropology do not provide data for the answering of questions that we did not know enough to ask then but do now. For instance, most of the reports of cultures written before the mid-thirties did not include data on child rearing. Now it is too late in many cases to gather the information, but there are many significant questions being asked now that require such data. So no report of a whole culture is really total, whatever its pretensions.

Another result of the particular conditions under which the anthropologist works is that the problem of controlling personal bias is even more pressing for him than for his colleagues in some of the more "scientific" disciplines. It is an anthropological commonplace that the same situation is experienced and interpreted differently by different field workers. Perhaps the classic case is that of the parade of field workers who have studied the Southwestern Pueblo societies. Some of these workers see the Pueblo Indians as cooperative, unhostile, nonaggressive folk. Others see them as people who cooperate and have strict rules for conformity to the cooperative norm because they are covertly hostile. In a sense both interpretations are correct, but perhaps one goes further into the covert life of the people—the life behind the cultural ideals. But covert hostility is not something that everyone can see with the same ease, and some people, including anthropologists, doubtless make a point to look for it, while others would prefer not to see it at all (Bennett, 1946).

It seems clear that no anthropological report dealing with the feelings, outlook, and values of a people, as well as the more obvious aspects of culturally determined behavior, can be completely "objective." The anthropologist's personality and personal past experience will color the report in some degree if it is to have any color at all. And a description of a way of life without color is like a bloodless man—it is cold and dead. Even worse, it is inaccurate, because all human societies are composed of living, breathing, feeling people, and this vitality must be communicated.

Users of anthropological reports of human cultures should be aware of this coloring effect, and realize that they are seeing a different way of life through someone else's eyes. Educators should find this a comfortable stance, because they realize that the same classroom and the same students are not the same to any two different teachers. They have learned to make allowances for the participant-observer in the situation.

But anthropologists have become increasingly aware of this

problem, and this awareness is reflected in the attempt to become more "scientific." Research designs are being made explicit. Hypotheses are being stated. Some research designs that control the conditions of data gathering are being developed and applied. Some anthropologists are formulating specific hypotheses about the possible relations between variables before they go to the field or use the reports based on the field work of others in cross-cultural surveys. The studies by Hallowell and the Spindlers use a type of research design that can be called "comparative," and in both there is attention to covariance between processes—the defined levels of acculturation constitute what may be regarded as the "independent" variable. The personality structure is the "dependent" variable. They are comparative because the several levels of acculturation are compared with each other to observe differences.

Margaret Mead's Manus study is representative of the trend toward a more scientific approach in the sense that a single situation is restudied after a lapse of time so that changes can be traced with greater accuracy than is possible otherwise. Oscar Lewis has done a rigorous restudy of the Mexican village studied some years before by Robert Redfield (Lewis, 1951). This work contributes to increased objectivity not only through restudy after time lapse but sheds some light on the differences in interpretation resulting from divergencies between one field worker's points of view and approach and those of another. The five-culture values project at Harvard University discussed previously is explicitly comparative in its whole design, and many of the specific studies, like John Roberts' comparison of Navaho households, utilize highly objective, comparative research and interpretive techniques (Roberts, 1951). There are many other anthropologists whose recent studies give substance to the trend toward greater objectivity and control in research. The recent article by Anthony Wallace, "Culture and Cognition" (1962), demonstrates, for example, how the logical structure of culturally organized behavior may be analyzed using componential analysis and symbolic logic. It is highly probable that we will be hearing more about this approach, since logical mathematical models are being applied in all of the behavioral sciences, as they have been in the natural sciences.

But anthropologists are not all agreed that this trend towards a more scientific status for their discipline is altogether a benefit. Some point out that anthropology is as much a part of the humanities as of the social sciences; that some of the works having the greatest impact on the development of the study of man, like Ruth Benedict's *Patterns of Culture* (1934), are clearly within the fold of the humanities; and that the holistic, empathetic, intuitive values apparent in good anthropological reporting and interpretation could be lost if extremes in "scientism" should prevail. Their concern is not to be taken lightly, and anthropologists, it is hoped, will try to continue to combine objectivity with insight.

CULTURE AND PERSONALITY

The current anthropological interest in the relationships between culture and personality assumed the proportions of a fad during the mid-forties, to the point where some anthropologists wholeheartedly rejected the whole approach as a form of "reductionism." They felt that the useful things we had learned about culture and social structure were being neglected, and all processes were being interpretively reduced to the level of the psychology of the individual. If this was ever true it has ceased to be a problem, for extremes in psychological interpretation are uncommon now. This field of interest has come of age now, as indicated by recent publications that present a sophisticated and balanced point of view (Honigmann, 1954; Kaplan, 1961; Hsu, 1961).

Though there were various antecedents in the works of others, Edward Sapir's article in 1932 triggered the joining of anthropology and psychology to a greater degree than any other. He showed how important it was to understand the individual in order to understand the culture, and how the insights and methods of psychoanalytic psychiatry could be joined with those of anthropology in this effort (Sapir, 1932).

Ruth Benedict, with her *Patterns of Culture* (1934), demonstrated something else—that it made sense to see cultures in terms of their dominant patterns, and that these patterns could be translated into psychological terms. She interpreted the cultures and psychological characteristics of the Zuni Indians (a southwestern pueblo people), the Kwakiutl Indians (who represent a type of culture that was spread along a narrow coastal strip from Oregon to Alaska), and the Dobuans (who live on a small island off the eastern shore of southern New Guinea). There is no need to concern ourselves with the specifics of these interpretations here. What is important is that Ruth Benedict portrayed how closely joined the most important aspects of the culture and the most striking aspects of the personality could be. She did not demonstrate this scientifically and she used no psychological techniques to gather data not already provided by a study of the culture. She demonstrated it intuitively and descriptively, and by turning culture over as though it were a coin to see the psychological face on the other side.

Her book stimulated a great deal of thinking, research, and writing, not only in anthropology but in sociology and social psychology. As books and articles with a psychological point of view on the Alorese, Sioux Indians, Samoans, and many other peoples came into print, it became clearer that the organization of emotional forces and moral character exhibited by the peoples studied reflected at every turn the determinant force of cultural patterning. The people were clearly products of their culture (Kluckhohn, Murray, and Schneider, 1953; Haring, 1956).

This to be sure is not such a surprising finding. We know that human beings achieve human status by learning, and this learning must take place in a social environment that is never wholly unique and is always structured in some degree by whatever cultural norms govern the behavior of the people in their society. But it also became clear as more psychologically oriented studies were done that cultures function as they do in part, because some of the psychological characteristics are shared within the society that are congruent with and appropriate to the culture. Erich Fromm has pointed out that the culture has to be built into the personality structure of the people so that they will *want* to act as they *have* to act (Fromm, 1949). The goals, the motivations to secure and express the goals, and the ways of attaining them are internalized by the individual as they are transmitted to him by the agents of the culture (parents, teachers, elders, and so on) so that he supports the norms of the culture as *though they were his own*. In view of other formulations of the relationship between culture and personality, Fromm may have overstated his case. But it seems true that without this kind of relationship between people and their cultures, the social order would not be maintained for long. This becomes clear in the anthropological studies of societies that have no policemen, courts, or strong authority figures. In these politically simple societies the personality structure has to assume a greater share of the controls than in a society that has external controls of these types highly developed. But even in this latter kind of society, as in our own, the internalized controls are extremely important, and disorganization results when the controls are not built into the personality structure very firmly.

At the same time it has become increasingly apparent that there is rarely a one to one correspondence between culture and personality. They are two different levels of abstraction drawn from the observation of behavior. Culture is normative and shared. Personality is a reactive product of the relationship between each individual and his culture, and it is unique in some degree to each person. The individual shares some motivations and some patterns of thought with other members of his group. He has knowledge of motivations and thought patterns on the part of others in his society that he does not share. The culture may be regarded as, in part, a complex set of contracts for regulating interaction between people with like and unlike motivations and thought patterns. Personality structures maintain cultures but not necessarily by being identical with each other, or with culture. Anthony Wallace has discussed this problem in his recent book, *Culture and Personality* (1961). Ralph Linton, using the concept of "status personality" (1945), and Gregory Bateson (1936), using the concept of schizmogenesis (behavior leading progressively to differentiation), anticipated some of the more recent thinking.

With these two propositions established—that personalities are in a large (but not total) degree culturally determined, and the reverse, that personality structures maintain culture—the next step was to find out how culture was transmitted, and learned.

Anthropologists turned to psychoanalytic theory for help, because it provided a way of thinking about personality formation and function that accounted for more of the behaviors that anthropologists saw in their studies of other societies around the world than did any other available theory. The focus of attention became child rearing and the development of personality. Child rearing techniques were seen to vary with the culture, as did the adult personality structure, and the linkages between the two made sense in terms of psychoanalytic theory. The focus of attention was naturally on events that had to be dealt with in some way in every society, such as weaning and toilet training, and that occurred early in life. The first systematic analysis of this sort occurred as the result of the collaboration of the anthropologist Ralph Linton, and the psychoanalyst Abram Kardiner, using data supplied by Dr. Linton and by two other anthropologists on three cultures—the Comanche Indians, the Alorese (residents of a small island off New Guinea), and "Plainsville," United States (Kardiner and Linton, 1945).

This analysis of the three cultures was a most important attempt, and one that was largely successful in its aims, but seen in the perspective of more recent work, its sample of societies is too limited and its attention is too exclusively focused on events of narrow scope in infancy and early childhood. The approach is being enlarged and enriched by some of the most vigorous anthropological work being done today. John Whiting and Irvin Child's study using the Human Relations Area Files (an elaborate organization of cultural materials on hundreds of cultures, abstracted and filed according to a complex and detailed outline) is an example (Whiting and Child, 1953). This study is notable for its sample—it uses data from seventy-six societies (including our own)—and for its originality. The purpose is to find out what relationship there is between culturally accepted explanations of illness, and the kind of child rearing practices maintained in a society. The child rearing practices are grouped into five categories, such as training for independence and sexual training. The seventy-six societies are then rated on scales related to these categories, such as relative age of independence training, and these ratings are then correlated against various classifications of explanations of illness. The purpose is to test whether or not the explanations of illness can be interpreted as projections through the adult personality structure of basic attitudes acquired in early childhood as the result of specific forms of rearing.

Important aspects of certain recent trends in anthropology are apparent in the Whiting and Child study. It uses a comparatively wide sample of the world's cultures—so there is a better basis for generalization. It uses comparatively rigorous criteria for definition of variables to be related to each other. It uses statistical tests to establish or reject hypotheses. It draws hypotheses from a body of theory. In short, it is representative of the more scientific trend. It is also representative of the renewed and increased interest in human nature that has appeared in various guises throughout this chapter. Insofar as regularities of connection between two things as remote to each other as child rearing and explanations of disease (seen from the common-sense point of view) appear predictably, and on the basis of a psychological mediation within the personality structure, common human features of "human nature" seem to be operating.

These few comments on culture and personality do no more than serve to indicate something of the general character of the field. There are many other approaches and interests, such as the problem of relations between mental disease and culture, and mental health and culture, that are of significance.

NATIONAL CHARACTER AND CULTURE

The continuing study of national character can be seen as a special focus within the culture and personality framework. Many of the same basic ideas, such as the mutually supportive relationship between personality structure, culture, and the social order, are used as points of departure in research and interpretation of the facts gathered. This special focus has its distinctive problems, however, in that complex national groupings of population are the object of study. Brazil, India, Japan, England, Germany, China, Israel, Puerto Rico, Iran, Norway, Russia, and the United States have been subjected to analyses of a national character or national culture type. Some of these studies have been done on small communities within the nation or have been limited in scope in some other way, while others represent attempts to extract the least common denominators of culture and character for a nation as a whole.

Many of the studies have been criticized from both within and outside anthropology as being based on inadequate sampling, for ignoring subcultural differences within the national whole, for treating communities within the nation but ignoring the wider social and political context, for attempting to explain a complex civilization in terms of weaning, toilet training, or swaddling, for dealing with ideal patterns but not the real distribution of behavior, for ignoring history, for being static, and so on (Mandelbaum, 1955).

Many of the criticisms seem justified, but some of the critics make the anthropologists seem to say things they did not intend to say. They also forget that the study of national character emerged under pressure of the conduct of war propaganda and occupation during and after World War II. Many of the studies even had to be done without the anthropologist actually visiting the country studied. Instead, "informants" (the anthropological term for living representatives of a culture) were interviewed and life histories taken from them as sources of data. Margaret Mead and Rhoda Metraux present and defend this approach in *The Study of Culture at a Distance* (1953). Some of these studies at a distance are now being followed up by field work, but the iron and bamboo curtains are effective barriers against this being done in some places where it needs to be done the most.

Whatever their defects, the national character studies have furnished us with depictions of contemporary, complex cultures that seem to show more meaningful aspects of human relations than do many more strictly historical, formal economic, or political science approaches. They deal with the feelings, values, and outlook of the people rather than with sequences of events or formal institutions. If they are used with the proper correctives in mind they can be very useful.

One of the current approaches to American culture th

combines concepts and various disciplinary strategies is the study of changing American character and values (Mead, 1942; Kluckhohn and Kluckhohn, 1948; Gillin, 1955; Lantis, 1955). David Riesman has told us how the American character is changing from inner-direction to other-direction (Riesman, 1953). The first type is self-actualized and relatively independent of situational or group pressures. The latter type is continually readjusting to those pressures with a built-in psychological radar. I have included in this book a chapter about the distinction between a "traditional" and an "emergent" values pattern on the basis of data from an extensive Stanford example. The traditional pattern includes the values of individualism and independence, absolute, nonsituational morality of the puritan variety, future-time orientation, and strong emphasis on achievement through hard work. The emergent pattern stresses participation in and harmony with groups, a relativistic morality, a present-time orientation, a lessening of emphasis on achievement for its own sake. I have stated that our core values may be moving in the emergent direction, as indeed the term implies.

Talcott Parsons and Winston White (1961) in a joint paper have recently contested this interpretation. They see the core American values as decidedly persistent. They do not see strong achievement drive, the "hard work leads to success" pattern, diminishing. They say that American values center around "instrumental activism"—the individualistic achievement of a good life in a supportive society, which in turn imposes an obligation on the individual to achieve successfully by helping to build a good society. Personal gratification must be deferred to successful achievement. This focus, they say, has persisted in American culture. What has changed are the specific ends by which achievement is validated, once gained, and the specific means by which success is achieved, not the core of "instrumental activism." Entrepreneurial profit, for example, is replaced as a goal by specialized and highly skilled performance in a specialized role within a large organization. Occupational roles have become more thoroughly professionalized. "Success" is measured by the degree of approval one meets in carrying out the role responsibly.

I think Parsons and White are essentially correct. If they are, some of our current thinking about American culture, and the new generation, will have to be revised, even though one can perceive other-directedness and emergent values in the "instrumental activism" they ascribe to the system. This is decidedly to the good. I need not point out that understanding of such processes is of great relevance to education, since the core vaues of a society must be the core goals of its educational system.

ANTHROPOLOGY AND EDUCATION

Among the newer developments in anthropology is the application to education. It is, indeed, what this book is about. This application takes two general forms: the use of anthropological concepts and data in courses of study in the elementary and secondary school and in teacher-training institutions; and the application of anthropological concepts and methods to the analysis of the educative process—an anthropology of education.

A few school systems are making self-conscious efforts to develop such utilizations of anthropological materials. The California State Central Committee on Social Studies, for instance, has taken the first steps to include some contributions from anthropology in the construction of instructional programs (California State Department of Education, 1954). While this is a praiseworthy effort and a thoughtful one, an inspection of progress reports to date reveals that the concepts considered most relevant stress culture history, social development, and problems of race. Concepts and materials from comparative social anthropology, personality and culture, and culture change studies are not stressed or are absent. Another programmatic and experimental development in the public schools of Dearborn, Michigan, focuses on the materials of comparative social anthropology and culture change, with the purposes of developing in students an understanding of the ways in which the component parts of a culture interrelate, how these component parts and their interrelationships are affected in rapid culture change, and an ability to be objective in viewing their own and other cultures (Hoffenbacher, 1954).

The important principle in planning designed to achieve such objectives is that concepts like the interrelationship of the parts of a culture cannot be taught abstractly. Demonstrations are needed. Anthropological materials provide many such demonstrations in the culture case materials found in descriptions of cultures and societies around the world. Such useful case materials are available, for instance, on the Samoans, Pueblo Indians, Andamanese, Eskimo, Plains Indians, Japanese, many African tribes, villages in Mexico and the Yucatan, to name but a few. Some of the case material can be read and understood by high school students. The Spindlers have recently developed a series of short, nontechnical books written especially for college freshmen and sophomores (Spindler, G. and L., 1960). Some of this case material must be reinterpreted by the teacher. I will not attempt to cue readers of this article further on the relevant literature. They will need to consult with anthropologists in nearby colleges and universities, and take some of the introductory anthropology courses available to them in summer school programs in teacher training institutions.

Another important principle in the design of such programs of instruction is that the living vitality of a culture can be communicated by case materials supported by films and dramatizations that also present the way of life being considered in the case study. Such materials have become increasingly available during recent years (Vogt, 1955). Many universities have film services for instructional programs, and their offerings usually include films on Hopi and Navaho Indians, the Eskimo, African peoples, and others. A new series of radio programs, now on records, provide exceptionally useful materials. There are two series of thirteen each of such records, entitled "Ways of Mankind," including dramatizations of cultural case materials on values, technology, language and culture, status and role, religion, law, ethics, education, family and other topics (Goldschmidt, 1953). Discussions can be built around these records and they can be used to illustrate both specific cultural solutions to problems and general concepts. They are not too difficult for even seventh and eighth graders, and yet are sufficiently substantial to be rewarding fare for college freshmen and sophomores. It seems apparent that when teachᴇrs become motivated to incorporate anthropological materials into their instructional programs there will be appropriate materials for them to use.

The anthropology of education is an attempt to understand better what the teacher is doing and of what the educational process consists, by studying the teacher as a cultural transmitter and education as a process of cultural transmission. Some interesting results appear from such analyses. For instance, it becomes clear that even the most fair-minded teachers are highly selective of the values they communicate to students and are equally selective with respect to what values they screen out from what students might potentially communicate to them. It also seems clear on the basis of such approaches that teachers, in fact whole educational programs, frequently communicate assumptions and outlooks about human relations that are not in agreement with their declared goals. This is a theme that will be expanded in several papers in the next part.

Another area of an anthropology of education is being developed as anthropologists study education as cultural transmission cross-culturally. Margaret Read, a British anthropologist, has written one of the best treatments in her book *Children of Their Fathers*, on the Ngoni, a West-African tribe (1960). Jules Henry has written an article in the international journal *Current Anthropology* entitled a "Cross-Cultural Outline for the Study of Education," which is based on anthropological field work done by himself and others in many cultures, and also field work in American elementary schools (1960). The outline is a useful contribution to a truly comparative education—a field to which anthropology has just begun to make contributions. Part III of this book develops this area of application further.

CONCLUSION

The major trends in current anthropology that appear to be particularly relevant are these: (1) The redevelopment of interest in the evolution of man, seen in both its biological and sociocultural dimensions. (2) The new interest in the character of human nature, with the pursuit of this interest in the study of culture history, cultural values, universal categories of culture, culture and personality, and by implication, in the study of culture change. (3) The persistence of core values and world outlook in the face of manifest transformation. (4) The attempt to become more scientific in the study of man and his works, but at the same time retaining dedication to a humanistic outlook. (5) The focus on extracting cross-cultural regularities in human behavior—a focus that combines both the scientific and humanistic commitments of anthropology. (6) Finally, some dimensions of anthropology in the curriculum and of an anthropology of education.

Many of these dimensions will appear, in various guises, in the chapters to follow. It will become apparent, however, that anthropology has many more potentially useful concepts, approaches to the interpretation of data, and substantive information than has even begun to be utilized in applications to education. Each of the chapters in this book illustrates how some of these dimensions of current anthropology are applicable. Much remains to be done.

The next two chapters will survey the relationships between anthropology and education in greater detail, with the assumption that this chapter on the condition of anthropology today will provide the reader with a broad frame of reference, a preliminary understanding of many of the concepts that will be referred to in the survey and applied later in the other chapters, and a useful bibliography to turn to for further information and insight.

References

Bateson, Gregory, 1936, *Naven*. New York: Oxford University Press (Revised edition, 1958, Stanford University).

Benedict, Ruth, 1934, *Patterns of Culture*. Boston: Houghton Mifflin Company.

Bennett, John W., 1946, "The Interpretation of Culture: A Question of Values." *Southwestern Journal of Anthropology*, 2:361–374.

Braidwood, Robert J., 1961, *Prehistoric Man*, Chicago Natural History Museum Popular Series, No. 37, 3rd edition.

California State Department of Education, 1954, *Progress Report on Social Studies*. Sacramento, Calif.: California State Printing office.

Childe, V. Gordon, 1946, *What Happened in History*. New York: Pelican Books.

———, 1951, *Social Evolution*. London and New York: Abelard-Schuman, Ltd.

Coon, Carleton S., 1955, *The Story of Man*. New York: Alfred A. Knopf, Inc.

Eisely, Loren C., 1955, "Fossil Man and Human Evolution," in W. L. Thomas, Jr., ed., *Yearbook of Anthropology*. New York: Wenner-Gren Foundation for Anthropological Research.

Fromm, Erich, 1949, Psychoanalytic Characterology and its Application to the Understanding of Culture," in S. Stanfield Sargent, ed., *Culture and Personality*, proceedings of an interdisciplinary conference held under the auspices of the Viking Fund. New York: Viking Fund Inc.

Gillin, John, 1955, "National and Regional Cultural Values in the United States." *Social Forces*, 34:107–113.

Goldschmidt, Walter, ed., 1953, *Ways of Mankind*, Series I & II. National Association of Educational Broadcasters, distributed from 14 Gregory Hall, University of Illinois Press, Urbana, Ill.

Hallowell, A. Irving, 1945, "Sociopsychological Aspects of Acculturation," in Ralph Linton, ed., *The Science of Man in the World Crisis*. New York: Columbia University Press.

———, 1956, *Culture and Experience*. Philadelphia: University of Pennsylvania Press.

———, 1956, "The Structural and Functional Dimensions of Human Existence." *The Quarterly Review of Biology*, 31:88–101.

Haring, Douglas G., ed., 1956, *Personal Character and Cultural Milieu*. Syracuse, N.Y.: Syracuse University Press.

Henry, Jules, 1960, "Cross-cultural Outline for the Study of Education." *Current Anthropology*, 1:267–305.

Hoffenbacher, Harold B., 1954, "Putting Concepts from Anthropology into the Secondary School Program" (mimeographed).

Honigmann, John J., 1954, *Culture and Personality*. New York: Harper & Row, Publishers.

Howells, William, 1954, *Back of History*. New York: Doubleday & Company, Inc.

————, 1959, *Mankind in the Making*. New York: Doubleday & Company, Inc.

Hsu, Francis, ed., 1961, *Psychological Anthropology*, Homewood, Ill.: Dorsey Press.

Huxley, Julian, 1955, "Evolution, Cultural and Biological," in W. L. Thomas, Jr., ed., *Yearbook of Anthropology*. New York: Wenner-Gren Foundation for Anthropological Research.

Kaplan, Bert, 1961, *Studying Personality Cross-culturally*. New York: Harper & Row, Publishers.

Kardiner, Abram, and Ralph Linton, 1945, *The Psychological Frontiers of Society*. New York: Columbia University Press.

Kluckhohn, Clyde, 1953, "Universal Categories of Culture," in A. L. Kroeber, ed., *Anthropology Today: An Encyclopedic Inventory*. Chicago: University of Chicago Press.

————, and Florence Kluckhohn, 1948, "American Culture: Generalized Orientations and Class Patterns," in *Conflicts of Power in Modern Culture*, Seventh Symposium of the Conference on Science, Philosophy, and Religion. New York: Harper & Row, Publishers.

————, Henry Murray, and David Schneider, 1953, *Personality in Nature, Culture, and Society*. New York: Alfred A. Knopf, Inc.

Kluckhohn, Florence, and F. Strodtbeck, 1961, *Variation in Value Orientations*. New York: Harper & Row, Publishers.

Kroeber, Alfred L., ed., 1953, *Anthropology Today: An Encyclopedic Inventory*. Chicago: University of Chicago Press.

————, 1955, History of Anthropological Thought," in W. L. Thomas, Jr., ed., *Yearbook of Anthropology*. New York: Wenner-Gren Foundation for Anthropological Research.

LaBarre, Weston, 1954, *The Human Animal*. Chicago: University of Chicago Press.

Lantis, Margaret, ed., 1955, "The U.S.A. as Anthropologists See

It." *American Anthropologist,* 57, No. 6 (Special Issue), 1113–1295.

Linton, Ralph, 1945, *The Cultural Background of Personality.* New York: Appleton-Century-Crofts, Inc.

Lewis, Oscar, 1951, *Life in a Mexican Village: Tepoztlan Restudied.* Urbana, Ill. University of Illinois Press.

Mandelbaum, David, 1955, "The Study of Complex Civilizations," in W. L. Thomas, Jr., ed., *Yearbook of Anthropology.* New York: Wenner-Gren Foundation for Anthropological Research.

Mead, Margaret, 1930, *Growing Up in New Guinea.* New York: William Morrow & Company, Inc.

———, 1942, *And Keep Your Powder Dry.* New York: William Morrow & Company, Inc.

———, 1956, *New Lives for Old.* New York: William Morrow & Company, Inc.

———, and Rhoda Metraux, eds., 1953, *The Study of Culture at a Distance.* Chicago: University of Chicago Press.

Mering, Otto von, 1961, *A Grammar of Human Values.* Pittsburgh.

Murdock, George P., 1945, "The Common Denominators in Cultures," in Ralph Linton, ed., *The Science of Man in the World Crisis.* New York: Columbia University Press.

Northrop, F. S. C., 1953, "Cultural Values," in A. L. Kroeber, ed., *Anthropology Today: an Encyclopedic Inventory.* Chicago: University of Chicago Press.

Parsons Talcott, 1961, and Winston White, "The Link Between Character and Society," in S. M. Lipset and Leo Lowenthal, *Culture and Social Character. The Work of David Riesman Reviewed.* Glencoe, Ill.: Free Press.

Read, Margaret, 1960, *Children of Their Fathers: Growing Up among the Ngoni of Nyasaland.* New Haven, Conn.: Yale University Press.

Riesman, David, Nathan Glazer, and Reuel Denney, 1953, *The Lonely Crowd, a Study of the Changing American Character.* New Haven, Conn.: Yale University Press.

Roberts, John M., 1951, *Three Navaho Households.* Papers of the Peabody Museum of American Archaeology and Ethnology, Harvard University, Vol. 40, No. 3. Cambridge, Mass.: The Museum.

Rubel, Arthur J., 1960, "Concepts of Disease in Mexican-American Culture." *American Anthropologist*, 62:795–814.

Sapir, Edward, 1932, "Cultural Anthropology and Psychiatry." *Journal of Abnormal and Social Psychology*, 27:229–242.

Spindler, George D., 1955, *Sociocultural and Psychological Processes in Menomini Acculturation*. Culture and Society Series, Vol. 5. Los Angeles; University of California Press.

———, and Louise S. Spindler, eds., 1960, *Case Studies in Cultural Anthropology*. New York: Holt, Rinehart and Winston, Inc.

Spindler, Louise S., 1962, *Menomini Women and Culture Change*, Memoir 91, American Anthropological Association, Vol. 64, No. 1, Part 2.

———, and George D. Spindler, 1958, "Male and Female Adaptations in Culture Change." *American Anthropologist*, 60:217–233.

———, and ———, 1959, "Culture Change," in B. J. Siegel, ed., *Biennial Review of Anthropology*, Stanford: Stanford University Press.

Steward, Julian H., 1955, *Theory of Culture Change*. Urbana, Ill.: University of Illinois Press.

Vogt, Evon, 1955, "Anthropology in the Public Consciousness," in W. L. Thomas, Jr., ed., *Yearbook of Anthropology*. New York. Wenner-Gren Foundation for Anthropological Research.

Vogt, Evon, and Ray Hyman, 1959, *Water Witching, U.S.A.* Chicago: University of Chicago Press.

———, and John M. Roberts, 1956, "A Study of Values." *Scientific American*, 195:25–31.

Washburn, Sherwood, 1960, "Tools and Human Evolution," *Scientific American*, 203:62–75 (available as separate reprints from *Scientific American*).

———, ed., 1961, *The Social Life of Early Man*. New York: Viking Fund Publications in Anthropology, No. 31.

Whiting, John W. M., and Irving L. Child, 1953, *Child Training and Personality: A Cross-cultural Study*. New Haven, Conn.: Yale University Press.

Wallace, Anthony F. C., 1961, *Culture and Personality*. New York: Random House, Inc.

———, 1962, "Culture and Cognition." *Science* 135:351–357.

3———J. James Quillen

Problems and Prospects[*]

Professional educators today face many problems. These problems are produced by such factors as the complexity and heterogeneity of American culture, the rapidity and inco-ordination of cultural change, the effort to provide equality of educational opportunity for all children and youth, the explosive increase of population, the competition for the tax dollar, current ideological conflict, and conflicting theories of education. Educational problems center in such areas as the cultural role and objectives of education, the organization and administration of the school, the content of education, methods of teaching and learning, the evaluation and guidance of the student, and public relations and the provision of adequate financial support.

In the solution of school problems, professional educators have for some time utilized knowledge from such disciplines as biology, psychology, history, philosophy, and sociology. More recently increasing attention has been directed toward anthropology as a resource for conceptual knowledge and research methods which can contribute directly to the improvement of education. Anthropologists and educators have recognized areas of common interest and concern and have begun to work together on common problems. These cooperative efforts have been limited thus far, but this volume is an indication both of the significant progress that has been made and of future possibilities. This introductory chapter defines some of the problem areas in education where anthropology can make a contribution. The overview by George Spindler, following, maps out some areas in anthro-

* Reprinted, with revisions, from *Education and Anthropology*, George D. Spindler, Editor, with permission of the Publishers, Stanford University Press; copyright 1955 by the Board of Trustees of Leland Stanford Junior University.

pology that are relevant to these problems and surveys the articulation and historical contacts of the two fields.

Education is the instrument through which cultures perpetuate themselves. It is the process through which the members of a society assure themselves that the behavior necessary to continue their culture is learned. Since education is a cultural process, it is important for educators to have a clear conception of the meaning of culture. Confusion over this meaning is an important factor in confusion and conflict concerning the proper role of the school. Here is a basic area where anthropologists can make a significant contribution.

The school is concerned with the transmission, conservation, and extension of culture. Cultural transmission and personality formation are perhaps the two most important functions of the school. A knowledge of these processes as they occur in a variety of cultures can help educators to secure a clearer conception of their roles and provide them with a reservoir of tested experience from which they can draw ideas and techniques that may be useful in American schools.

For some time there has been considerable conflict in the United States concerning the role of education in the extension and improvement of American culture. This conflict became acute during the depression period and has been intensified by the current concern about communism. George Counts dramatized the issue when he wrote *Dare the School Build a New Social Order?* The problem here concerns the role of the school in cultural innovation. This is another area where the interests of anthropologists and educators converge.

The school is only one educative agency in American culture, and perhaps not the most important. The family, church, young people's organizations, and the media of mass communication all play important roles in the education of the child. In many instances, out-of-school agencies, particularly the mass media, compete with the school for the attention of the child and produce behavioral changes which are contradictory to those which the school is trying to establish. In other instances, out-of-school agencies reinforce the efforts of teachers and other school personnel. If formal education is to be effective, teachers need to understand the role and influence of nonschool educational experiences. Content from anthropology can help greatly toward this end.

Education involves the changing of behavior in a desirable direction. The school is an educational institution specifically established to produce desirable changes in behavior. Educational objectives consist of descriptions of behavior which the school seeks to produce. The over-all objectives of the school are defined by a description of the behavior of the ideal citizen, including his knowledge, values, skills, and abilities. In a heterogeneous culture such as ours, the description of the ideal citizen is difficult, and confusion and conflict concerning educational objectives result. Anthropologists can help educators to develop a conception of the ideal cultural man and can assist in identifying the core values which Americans seek to preserve and perpetuate in an age of conflict.

The school program of study consists of those areas of experience and content which are essential to the development of the desired characteristics of behavior which have been chosen as objectives. The contents and experiences included in the school program are selected from the total range of possibilities which exist in the culture. Intelligent selection can be based only on considerable cultural insight and understanding. If those who make the school curriculum do not understand the changing culture of which they are a part, deadwood will be carried indefinitely in the school program, and there will be important gaps in what is taught and learned. Harold Benjamin showed the proneness of schools to perpetuate outmoded content and experiences in his satire, *The Saber-Tooth Curriculum*.

The complexity and rapidity of change in modern culture make the selection of curriculum content particularly difficult. Anthropologists can help educators to understand better their community, nation, and world. The techniques of community study developed by anthropologists can be used by teachers to study their own community.

Methods of teaching and learning are perpetual problems in education. How can methods be used in the classroom that will transfer directly to effectiveness in living outside of the school? Anthropologists can help teachers understand how informal methods are used to further enculturation in other cultures. Here the study of societies where there are no formal schools, in the strict sense of the word, is particularly instructive. Anthropologists can also contribute to an understanding of the relationship between cultural motivation and learning.

A number of educators and social scientists have been concerned recently about the effects of the cultural experiences of an individual on his performance in intelligence tests. This has resulted in an effort to develop a "culture fair" intelligence test. Teachers need to be helped to see the significance of such activities in the furtherance of equality of educational opportunity.

Closely related to the question of the meaning of the I.Q. is the question of grouping. To what extent is homogeneous grouping in the school compatible with the values of democracy? What is the significance of the variety of cultural backgrounds of American children and youth for grouping and educational methods generally? The heterogeneity of American culture provides an excellent opportunity for the development of intergroup understanding and the improvement of human relations. In this area the concept of race is of special importance. Anthropologists can help clarify the meaning of race and the relationship (or lack of it) between race, intelligence, and culture.

Finally, educators have become increasingly concerned about the development of intercultural and international understanding. A number of educators and anthropologists have participated in UNESCO's activities in this area. Educators need to be helped to develop more effective techniques for the study of the ways of living of people of other cultures. In many instances comparative culture studies in the school tend to reinforce prejudice rather than to increase understanding and appreciation. In addition to intercultural and international understanding, educators are concerned with the role of education in the international technical assistance programs. American educational methods are now being exported to other nations. To what extent is this possible and desirable? How can American educators aid in the transition from isolated, nonliterate status to literacy, national status, and world participation that is taking place in so many former underdeveloped and hinterland areas of the world today?

4——— *George D. Spindler*

Anthropology and Education: An Overview[*]

INTRODUCTION

Some educational theorists cite the concept of culture as most crucial in their systematic thinking. Text books used in the training of teachers contain references to anthropological literature. Elementary school teachers include projects on "Peoples in Other Lands" or "Our Indian Friends" in social studies units. A growing number of departments of anthropology are offering courses with the specific needs of teachers-in-training in mind. Anthropology has been applied to educational problems since at least 1904, when Hewett wrote his first pieces on education for the *American Anthropologist* (1904, 1905). The *Yearbook of Anthropology* contains a substantial review of the work by anthropologists on education (Hoebel, 1955). An important lecture series in 1961, the Martin G. Brumbaugh lectures on education, is devoted exclusively to anthropology and education (Gruber, 1961).

But education was not even listed as an area of application for anthropology in the encyclopedic inventory, *Anthropology Today* (Kroeber, 1953). Education is not in the subject index of the *Decennial Index: 1949–1958* to the *American Anthropologist* and *Memoirs* of the American Anthropological Association. Only a handful of joint appointments in education and anthropology exist in American colleges and universities. Very few anthropologists have attempted to study the educational process in our society.

* Reprinted, with extensive revision, from *Education and Anthropology*, George D. Spindler, Editor, with the permission of the Publishers, Stanford University Press; copyright 1955 by the Board of Trustees of Leland Stanford Junior University.

Despite the steady increase of interest, anthropology and education still maintain a tenuous relationship as Brameld has pointed out (1961). It is a frontier area.

The purpose of this overview paper is to survey this frontier area—to outline the parts of both anthropology and education as they relate to mutual interests, to indicate those points where the anthropologist can help formulate meaningful educational research and theory, mention what anthropologists have written about education and what educators have used of what anthropologists have written, describe some special problems that exist in the relationships between the two fields, and provide useful bibliographic citations for those who may wish to read further. The rest of the papers in this volume are examples of some of the most significant ways in which anthropological approaches can illuminate educational process. Their places in the articulation of education and anthropology will be indicated as this survey proceeds.

RELEVANT FIELDS AND INTERESTS IN ANTHROPOLOGY

Anthropology as a Resource for General Education

Anthropology as the "study of man and his works," with its traditional interests in cultural process and in language, race, and human evolution, is a potential contributor to a good general education at all levels of educational experience. This potential contribution of anthropology as a source of data and of concepts to be used in the development of curricula will be discussed first, though this is not what most of the book is about. While no claim is made here that anthropology should become the core of a complete social studies program in the secondary school, or in the liberal arts (or "general studies") program at the college level, it seems clear, as pointed out in Chapter 2, that no other existing discipline provides an integration, however loose, of so much that is so important concerning man and his behavior.

The study of man thus broadly conceived makes it possible to bridge the gap between the animal and the human being, to conceive of both the relativity and universality of human behavior and propositions about it, to project human affairs upon a time plane that stretches far into the past and future, and turns the focus upon the basic round of life and man's relation to nature.

The implication is clear that anthropology should be used as a contribution to general education more widely than it is. It should not be taught as it must be to graduate students training to become professional anthropologists. Nor should it be taught as an introduction to a scholarly discipline, as it often is at the college level, even in the beginning course. It should be taught as an introduction to a new perspective on human life, as a way of thinking that we might call "humanistic objectivity." This is not merely a personal opinion. It is a value judgment, but one shared widely by professional anthropologists who are teaching introductory courses in colleges and universities. The overwhelming majority of anthropologist respondents from thirty-seven colleges and universities placed humanistic purposes first and training in the "science" of anthropology second (Bruner and Spindler, 1961). The anthropologist has a point of view and wants to communicate it.

Anthropology should probably also be taught in the secondary school (Lee, 1960; Mandelbaum, 1961), possibly under some already existing rubric (Spindler, 1946). As Mandelbaum has pointed out, most American anthropologists would agree that ". . . modern concepts of culture, cultural similarities and differences, race, and evolution should properly be a part of the high school curriculum," (Mandelbaum, 1961b). But at the same time anthropologists will agree that these concepts are easily misinterpreted. Uninformed teachers will make serious errors that are all the more serious because the concepts are so powerful. It is crucial that teachers who are going to use anthropological concepts and data get good training in anthropology. The summer institutes in anthropology for high school teachers that are being set up in a few colleges and universities under the Course Content Section of the National Science Foundation will provide more opportunities for appropriate training during the next few years than have been available until now. The National Science Foundation has also made a substantial grant to the Committee on Anthropology in Secondary Schools for the American Anthropological Association. This committee, headed by Malcolm Collier, working out of the Department of Anthropology at the University of Chicago, is surveying existing uses of anthropological material in secondary schools and will develop appropriate materials for future use, including films, museum facilities, pamphlets, and bibliographies.

Anthropology is being taught at the elementary school level when teachers develop lesson units or activities centering on American Indian tribes or peoples in other lands—but sometimes badly because the teachers have had little or no exposure to anthropology as such and consequently contravene their primary goals. A teacher who has had no direct exposure to another way of life, particularly a primitive way of life, and who has had no instruction in how to objectify perceptions of other cultures or how to control value judgments, is very likely to communicate prejudicial views when he or she teaches a unit on the Hopi, the Navaho, or the village peoples of India. It is hoped that teachers in elementary schools will be able to obtain training in anthropology as a part of their preparation in social studies.

Anthropologists have been aware of the potential contributions of their field to general education and have written about it (Ehrich, 1947; Howells, 1952), but they have until recently rarely done anything about it. That this will change is clear. The Educational Resources in Anthropology Project, headed by David Mandelbaum, and supported by the National Science Foundation, with help from the Wenner-Gren Foundation, has engaged the attention of scores of anthropologists in this country and abroad for the last three years (Mandelbaum 1960; Mead, 1960; Whiteford, 1960). We can expect these efforts to have an important direct effect on the teaching of anthropology in colleges and universities, and an equally important, but less direct effect, on the use of anthropological resources in the secondary school. The *Teaching of Anthropology*, to be published as a Memoir of the American Anthropological Association, edited by David Mandelbaum, Gabriel Lasker, and Ethel Albert, out of the many conferences held, will include papers on most phases of the use of anthropology as an educational resource for higher education, and supplements on teaching aids and recommended bibliography will either be included or published separately (Mandelbaum, 1961a).

As a source of materials to be used in general education all of anthropology is relevant. Selections need not be made only from the sociocultural side of the discipline. The most important contribution of physical anthropology to education has been on the subject of race and the relationships—or rather lack of them—between race, culture, and intelligence. Anthropological perspectives on the meaning of race and the myth of racial superiority have been popularized by Ethel Alpenfels in her capacity as staff anthropologist for the Bureau for Intercultural Education, and have become familiar to many social studies teachers through this and other agencies. Otto Klineberg has given us the classic treatment on relationships between race, culture, and I.Q. (1935), that has had wide circulation in an encapsulated form in a UNESCO pamphlet (1951) and in a symposium edited by Linton (1947). Teachers will find G. Lasker's introduction to physical anthropology (1961) and the articles by Washburn, Deevey, Dobzhansky, Howells from the September, 1960, *Scientific American*, useful for information on various aspects of physical anthropology and human evolution.

Anthropology as a Resource in the Analysis of Educational Process

So far the relevance for anthropology as a body of knowledge and way of thinking to the development of curricula and programs in general education has been discussed. Now attention shifts to the contributions of anthropology as a frame of reference for analysis of the educative process. This is a different kind of utilization of the resources of anthropology. It is not, however, an attempt to create an "educational anthropology." Though they demonstrate some unique properties, the processes and structures of education are not fundamentally different in kind from the processes and structures involved in other areas of human life. Anthropology can help shed light on human behavior in educational situations just as it has on behavior in factories, hospitals, peasant communities, air force installations, Indian reservations, New England towns, and various primitive societies. All of the papers in Parts II and III in this volume are examples of anthropological analyses of the educational process in a broad spectrum of educational contexts, including our own.

Directly relevant are the concepts and data of specialized and relatively new fields in anthropology, such as personality and culture ("psychological anthropology"), and cultural dynamics (culture change and acculturation). In fact, when use of anthropology as an analytic frame of reference in education is considered, this is usually where people in both fields begin to look first (Kimball, 1956; Taba, 1957; Rosenstiel, 1959). These areas of anthropology are discussed in the previous chapter, but certain points particularly relevant to the educational context need to be emphasized here.

For certain purposes it is useful to view education of the child to human, group-accepted status as a total process of growth and adaptation. The center of the process is the child—adapting to an environment structured by culture, as well as by group size, climate, terrain, ecology, and the personalities of his always unique parents or parental surrogates. Education may also be thought of as a more limited process—what is done to and for a child, by whom, in what roles, under what conditions, and to what purpose. Jules Henry has given us the first substantial cross-cultural outline for the study of education from this point of view (Henry, 1960). Education in this focus is the process of transmitting culture—including skills, knowledge, attitudes, and values, as well as specific behavioral patterns. It is the culture of the human being, —where culture is used as a verb.

There are many books, monographs, and articles by anthropologists on socialization of the child—education in the total sense—in different cultures. One of the most significant problem-oriented comparative researches is Whiting and Child's *Child Training and Personality* (1953). Spiro provides us with a very interesting analysis of socialization and education in Israel, in his *Children of the Kibbutz* (1958), one aspect of which is developed in the chapter by him, "Education in a Communal Village in

Israel" included in this book. A recent survey by the Whitings provides reference to many of the relevant publications (Whiting, 1960). There are relatively few studies on education in the more strict sense of the word. British anthropologists, with their functionalistic predilections, have provided relevant analyses (*e.g.*, Read, 1960). Pettit has provided one of the most useful studies by an American anthropologist on the who, what, when, and where questions of educational process seen cross-culturally, as he summarizes education in North American Indian cultures (Pettit, 1946). Solon Kimball provides a provocative perspective on the cultural influences shaping the role of the child in his chapter in Part II.

The data used by Whiting and Pettit were provided by ethnographies written by others. The fact that such analyses could be carried out despite the fact that the people who did the actual studies in the field could not have anticipated their use is a tribute to the inclusiveness of a good ethnography. But only too often, Whiting, Pettit, and others who have attempted similar analyses, have looked for the pertinent facts in ethnographies and have not been able to find them, or find them partially or ambiguously stated. Most often anthropologists will describe the *results* of education but not the *process*. There is a great deal more to be done with the materials furnished by ethnographies and other field studies already completed, but it is crucial that future studies in the field be done with a good cross-cultural outline of education in mind. Henry's (1960) outline will doubtless prove very useful in this respect. What is lacking, however, even in Henry's excellent attempt, is a consistent, underlying theory that can give coherence and organization to the categories of behavior to be observed and their interpretation. Culture theory, personality theory, and social interaction theory must be joined. When such an "outline" for the cross-cultural study of education is developed, with a comprehensive and consistent theoretical structure behind it, we will be on our way towards a truly *comparative* education. The indispensable, basic requirement for the development of a comparative education is that there be a systematic frame of reference, with consistent theoretical underpinnings, to guide the collection and interpretation of relevant data cross-culturally, so that meaningful processual comparisons can be made. Anthropology can provide a significant part of the frame of reference needed. The chapters in Part III, *Education Viewed Cross-culturally*, provide a substantial indication of the categories of phenomena that operate and must be taken into account as a cross-cultural, potential comparative frame of reference is developed.

Anthropological work in cultural dynamics is concerned primarily with those processes of cultural change and stability that are frequently included under the heading "acculturation." For our purposes we can define acculturation as subsuming those processes that occur as a society (or a group of people) with a distinctive culture adapts to changes in the conditions of life brought about by the impact of another population and its culture. Much of the work done so far on acculturation has been characterized by a lack of penetrating interpretation—most of the issues are left at the descriptive level—and very little attention has been paid to the role of cultural transmission and education in culture change. Cultural change as well as stability must be mediated by what is transmitted from parents and teachers to children. Unless these variables intervening between changes in the conditions of life and the adaptations of people to them are understood, much of the "dynamic" part of cultural dynamics is left unilluminated. Anthropologists have done little here. All of the studies by anthropologists of the socialization and enculturation of children in different cultural settings are contributions to our knowledge of how education functions to preserve cultural continuity, but few of them have focused on cultural transmission or have been explicitly concerned with the problems of cultural change. Herskovits has supplied one of the few explicit statements of some relationships between education and cultural change in his "Education and Cultural Dynamics" (1943). Dorothy Eggan's analysis of education and cultural continuity among the Hopi Indians and the author's analysis of the Menomini in Part III of this book give us insight into the stability-maintaining functions of education in situations where external pressure for change is great. In her chapter in Part III on "Our Educational Emphases in the Perspective of Primitive Societies," Margaret Mead shows us how our educational process is geared to change—to the creating of discontinuities in experience for the child. She provides an illuminating analysis of the role of education in in-duced cultural change in the chapter on "Cultural Factors in Community Education," also in Part III, and Jack Fischer (Part III) shows us that many of the same processes are activated even when the inducing or "donor" culture is non-western. Bruner (1956a, 1956b) has provided pertinent analyses of the influence of experience in the primary group on cultural transmission in culture change situations. Fred Werner has analyzed a culture conflict situation in college experience in his paper in Part II. Other relevant writings include Frank (1959) and Mead (1959, 1960), which are less explicit in their use of concepts and data from the field of cultural dynamics but illuminating in their atten-tion to cultural change as the context of modern education.

One field of interest in anthropology that has realized rela-tively more of its potential in relation to educational problems is that of social structure. If the interests here are conceived as broadly relating to group alignments, prestige ranking, status and role interrelationships, and social control in the community con-text, all of the very useful work of the Warner group and other closely related efforts may be regarded as a contribution from this area. The contributors include, besides Warner, such workers as Davis, Gardner, Dollard, Loeb, Withers, Useem, and many non-anthropologists who have been strongly influenced therein, such as Havighurst, Hollingshead, the Lynds, Taba, and so on. The relevance of this field to education, particularly with respect to a concept of social class that has been regularized by Warner and his associates, is indicated by two special issues of the *Harvard Educational Review* on the subject (1953). Recent textbooks on the social foundations of education, such as Mercer (1957), Cox and Mercer (1961) use these materials extensively. No claim is made that this is exclusively an anthropological domain or con-tribution, but one of the mainsprings driving the interest and its application is fastened to an anthropological pivot.

In this instance the situation as it exists otherwise in the various potential or emergent articulations with education is re-versed. More is known about how the educative process is af-fected by social class and community structure in Jonesville and Elmtown than in the nonliterate societies that are the accustomed habitat of the anthropologists. To be sure, nonliterate societies rarely have social classes in the same sense that Jonesville has, but some do, and all have groups structured into a social organization. Whether a social structure is formalized by a widely ramifying kinship system, or by inherited statuses, or by a complex political-social power system, or is atomistic and individuated—the who, what, when, and why of education—will reflect this structure at every turn, since education must produce the men and women to function in the structure. For the sake of a clearer concept of education as a sociocultural process something more should be known about these functional interrelationships between educational goals, educative process, and social structure in nonwestern societies. The chapters on the Hopi and Menomini in this book are steps in this direction, and Bernard Siegel provides a penetrating analysis of these interrelationships in two Japanese village areas in his chapter in Part III.

Other uses for the anthropological frame of reference in analyses of educational process will be discussed below, as fields and interests in education are surveyed.

RELEVANT FIELDS AND INTERESTS IN EDUCATION

When we view education as a field with its own problems and institutional structure, it becomes clear that there are more relevant problems and interests than anthropologists could begin to bear appropriate gifts to—even if they were so motivated. Some of the particularly significant problems have been succinctly described by James Quillen. The discussion below will approach some of these same problems from a different perspective and describe certain interests and fields in education in which these problems occur.

The Foundation Fields and Professional Education

The first part of the discussion will be concerned with the institutional context called "Professional Education"—programs where teachers, administrators, counseling and guidance personnel, educational psychologists, and others are trained, usually in schools of education or teachers colleges. That part of these programs that most clearly provides a suitable context for anthropology is that of the "foundation" fields. The general rubrics are social, psychological, philosophical, historical, comparative, and biological. They represent what is drawn into education as a professional field from the behavioral and social sciences, the humanities, and natural sciences, as their data and concepts are used in educational research, the building of educational theory and philosophy, and in the training of teachers. It is important to understand how anthropology as a contributing discipline and the anthropologist as a contributing professional can function appropriately in this context. The fact that few anthropologists hold positions in Schools of Education and that there are few joint appointments in education and anthropology despite a professed interest on both sides suggests that the institutional arrangements do not function satisfactorily in some cases. The organization of courses and their purposes will be discussed now. Later on, the roles of the anthropologist in the milieu of professional education will be described.

Anthropology has only recently begun to make a significant contribution to the social foundations of education. Educational psychology has clearly dominated the scene, partly because of a historical accident that institutionally wedded psychology and education rather early in America and partly because the need for tests and measurements and applied principles of learning have been particularly obvious in the educational milieu of American schools and have been appropriate for psychological applications. In many teacher-training institutions psychology is still the only behavioral science explicitly recognized in the organization of professional education courses.

Education as a professional field has also drawn from political science, economics, and jurisprudence, but particularly from sociology. Educational sociology has its own house organ, numerous texts bearing its name, and an impressive pile of research to its credit. Most foundation courses in professional education in the social area are called "educational sociology."

In a few places where teachers are trained in America—particularly at Teachers College at Columbia University under the leadership of Lyman Bryson and now Solon T. Kimball; at New York University under Ethel Alpenfels; at Washington University, St. Louis, through Jules Henry's influence; and at Chicago, Harvard, Yale, and Stanford—an explicit anthropological contribution is integrated with those of other social sciences in the foundation program. Hunter College, New York City, has seen the development of a curriculum of "foundational" education and anthropology (Rosenstiel, 1954), and New York University's School of Education has a long-standing development of this sort. Ruth Landes has been working on a particularly interesting project focusing on cultural factors in teacher education, sponsored by the Rosenberg Foundation, in the Teacher Education Division of the Claremont Graduate School (1961). San Francisco State College has a wide-ranging social foundations curriculum in which anthropology is well represented. Courses in anthropology are required of teachers-in-training at some universities and colleges where there is no formalized integration of anthropological contributions with the foundation fields in education.

At Stanford University, as an illustration of the ways in which anthropology can contribute to the foundation fields in education, relevant materials are presented in two courses: "Social Foundations in Education"; "Cultural Transmission"; and one seminar, "Social Anthropology in Education." They are given under the aegis of a joint appointment in the School of Education and the Department of Anthropology. Credit is given to students in both fields in their respective undergraduate majors or advanced degree program and the courses are cross-listed in the course announcements of both the School of Education and Department of Anthropology.

"Social Foundations in Education" is required of all upper division education students and all candidates for the Master of Arts degree in education, as well as for the various professional credentials. It combines selected materials from sociology, anthropology, and social psychology. The anthropological contribution lies mainly in a systematic analysis of American cultural patterns and values as they bear directly upon the role and functions of the teacher and public school system. Cross-cultural data are used here for illustrative purposes. Other topical areas covered include social class and education, problems in student-teacher communication, group stereotypes and prejudice in schools, the community context of the school, and the school as a social system.

"Cultural Transmission" is offered as a course at Stanford for advanced degree candidates and is presented jointly within the advanced social foundations sequence in education and the advanced offerings in the Department of Anthropology. In this course a frame of reference for viewing transmission and enculturation processes is constructed. This frame of reference is then used in the analysis of these processes in nonliterate societies, European societies, and American society. The course ends with case studies of selected types of teachers in their classrooms and schools in our society. Sociometric, autobiographic, socioeconomic, observational, and community "social base" data are included in the case study materials.

"Social Anthropology in Education" at Stanford is a seminar taken by advanced graduate students in education, anthropology, and psychology. It is likewise listed as part of the advanced course offerings in both the school of Education and the Department of Anthropology. It has been devoted so far to an analysis of the educative process in nonliterate societies, using ethnographic references and the Human Relations Area Files. Special problems in cultural transmission are explored, such as explicit and implicit transmission of values in the education of adolescents, and the application of learning theory to the analysis of educational situations and events reported for other cultures by ethnographers.

These courses accomplish different things in different ways. An important point in relation to the problem of an education-anthropology articulation is that the frame of reference is not exclusively anthropological; in all of the courses it seems essential to include selected aspects of sociology and psychology. When the educative process is the focus, and particularly in our own society, the anthropological frame of reference is not sufficient by itself. But it is essential. The core of the contribution is in the attention to culture as an influence on behavior, as a perception-mediating set of patterns, and in the attention to the variable forms these patterns take. *Cultural awareness* is one vital aim of each course, but not merely generalized cultural awareness; the aim is to create in the teacher an awareness of how his own culture influences specifically what he does as a teacher and how his students' cultures influence what they do, and how to think about, observe, and analyze these influences. Cultural awareness as one goal in professional preparation with which the anthropologist can help is also particularly important for the administrator, since he manipulates the setting in which the teacher interacts with students and parents. He must not only display cultural awareness but must also understand the mechanics of culture change, the cultural expectations affecting the leader's role, the concrete as well as idealistic meaning of cultural values, and the social system of the school in the setting of the encompassing community and national social structure. Chapter 12 on the role of the school administrator in Part II is directly concerned with these problem areas.

Courses in conventional anthropology do not serve this same purpose directly, even though they are necessary as a phase of professional educational training. By the time the student is preparing to be a professional educator, or is improving his already established proficiency, he should have had an introduction to the materials of at least cultural anthropology as a part of his general education, though he should also have some experience in intermediate and advanced course work in anthropology as a graduate student. Many graduate students majoring in the social foundations of education, comparative education, educational administration, and elementary education at Stanford take advanced degree minors in anthropology. The anthropology a student gets in his *professional* education within the college or school of education should be integrated with the other foundational offerings and applied to analysis of educative process. Otherwise we are asking him to provide this integration and make this application; and most students—in education or otherwise—simply cannot do it without expert help. The chapters in Part II of this book dealing with education in American society are all analyses of significant dimensions of education in our society and are therefore directly relevant to this purpose.

Educational Research

Education as a professional field is not only concerned with teacher training, teaching, curriculum design, and administra-

tion of schools; it has a research base. Probably no social or behavioral science has as great a backlog of research nor encompasses
such a high degree of variability of quality of research. The reason
for the first fact is obvious. The reason for the second one is
partly that education cuts across every phase of human activity,
and it is impossible to do good research without specialization in
the science or discipline treating with selected dimensions within
this range. This is very difficult when so much has to be done
all at once.

There are many phases of research within the framework of
education that call for anthropological attention. There has been
an incorporation of anthropologically based concepts and methods
in the studies of social class influences on learning (Davis, 1952),
social class and community structures in relation to the social
organization of the school and educational opportunities (Warner,
Loeb, *et al.*, 1944), and problems of adolescence (Havighurst and
Taba, 1949), in the extensive study of the relationships between
intelligence and cultural differences by the Chicago group (Eells,
et al., 1951), and in the studies of social class differences in socialization with their implication for education (Davis and Havighurst, 1947). This interest in social class and learning, and social
class and school organization, has been the main stream of influence on research directly relevant to education and stemming
from anything that can be regarded as an anthropological source.
The main contribution of anthropology, other than in the form
of some of the personnel involved, has been in the notion of cultural relativity and in a functional total-community approach.

Thus a definite and extensive contribution to research on educational problems, in American society at least, has yet to be made
by anthropology. This reflects the fact that until quite recently
anthropologists have not been very interested in our own society.
Their proper object of study has been the nonliterate peoples, in
their pure or reconstructed form, or as these peoples have struggled to adapt to the impact of the industrial-based civilizations.

Anthropologists have been interested in and involved with the
problem of education in dependent, trust and colonial territories,
and Indian reservations, where nonliterate or recently nonliterate
indigenes have been exposed to a Western-mediated education. But

the involvement has been largely in terms of an applied anthropology in various administrative and consultative capacities, and actual research reports on the processes involved are quite scarce, Felix Keesing has described some of the interesting problems that arise in these contexts in a summary of a seminar conference, including educators, anthropologists, sociologists, and government officials, on the problems of education in Pacific countries (Keesing, 1937). Margaret Mead has provided a provocative analysis of the feasible educational objectives and the major factors to be taken into account in the post-World War II education of "dependent" peoples (1946), and has brought this analysis up to date in the chapter included in this volume. J. Fischer, in his description of Japanese schools on Truk in Chapter 24, provides insights into the problems of a non-Western power.

There are many areas of potential application of anthropologically based concepts and methods in educational research in our own society to which more attention should be directed. The roles of teacher and school administrator in American society call for treatment from a cultural point of view that will focus on some of the paradoxes projected in the role expectations. The discussion of the school administrator's role in this book makes some of them explicit. The effect of culturally based values upon teacher perceptions of behavior and personal qualities of students needs to be dealt with in a way that the positionally oriented social class studies do not. The Burton Lecture by Spindler (1959) on "The Transmission of American Culture", a revised version of which is included in this book, deals with this process. The informal transmission of value orientations and covert culture by teachers and in peer groups has received very little attention. The chapters by Dorothy Lee and Jules Henry in Part II are significant contributions in this area. New approaches to the study of the school as a social system need to be devised—perhaps in the manner of the factory system studies that were in part anthropologically inspired. James Coleman (1961) has provided a most significant analysis of the social climates in high schools and the development of a separate teen-age culture. American culture as a specific context of the goals, expectations, and functions of education needs exploration—possibly in the vein of national character approaches. Rhoda Metraux makes a useful contribution in this direction with her chapter on implicit and explicit values in education in Part II. Martin Loeb gives us a challenging and disturbing insight into the dynamics of learning the male role in a social system (ours) that provides few male models for growing boys. The conceptual categories and symbolic referents of speech in communication between teacher and child called for a psycho-linguistic, language-in-culture application.

Particularly appropriate to anthropological interests is the need for cross-cultural research in education. Culture is idealized in the educative process. Every teacher, whether mother's brother or Miss Humboldt of Peavey Falls, re-enacts and defends the cultural drama. As the culture is passed on from one generation to the next in the hands of the teacher, it assumes a patent and rationalized shape. The world view is somehow encapsulated in each gesture, admonition, indoctrination, or explanation. And this seems true whether physics or sacred origin myths are being taught. Cross-cultural research on education puts our own educational process in new perspective. Education is a pan-human process, but one that varies sharply from culture to culture. Each of the chapters in Part III of this book is a contribution to some new dimension of the cross-cultural perspective on education. The chapters by C. W. M. Hart, Mark Watkins, and Reverend Walter J. Ong provide a particularly dramatic and compelling focus on cultural transmission during adolescence, at which time in many cultures the value system is most vigorously presented to members of the generation changing identity from child to adult.

THE ROUTES OF DIFFUSION

Anthropological Routes

The institutional and research routes of diffusion of knowledge between education and anthropology have been described. The routes of diffusion through anthropological and educational literature exhibit certain characteristics that have affected the articulation of the two fields and will be analyzed briefly.

Maria Montessori's influence is of particularly long standing (1913). Her principal assumptions have been integrated into the framework of modern education through the progressive "school." She saw clearly the need for stressing the "organic" relation of the whole child to the environment; emphasized the developmental process so that the child was not seen as a "diminutive adult"; anticipated the problem of the differential meaning of school experience to children from various social classes and ethnic groups in her concept of a "regional ethnology" and study of local conditions; called for respect for individual differences in growth and function; demanded that a "scientific pedagogy" concern itself with normal individuals primarily; and developed a "biographical chart" that took the place of the report card and included "antecedents"—vocation of parents, their aesthetic culture, their morality and sentiments and care of children—as well as reports of physical and psychological examinations and on-going observations in the form of "diaries."

Educators may contest the characterization of this work as an anthropological influence, since Montessori is so clearly a part of the educationist's heritage, but she called her approach a "Pedagogical Anthropology," and used what were regarded as anthropological concepts, methods, techniques, and data. Though her cultural anthropology is guilty of what today would be regarded as certain racist errors, and her physical anthropology is now outmoded, her farsighted anticipation of much of the best of the contemporary art and science of education is impressive. Whether this is true because she had genius or because she had an anthropological orientation cannot be divined. She had both.

A history of anthropology-to-education diffusion cannot omit the early contributions of Edgar L. Hewett (1904, 1905). His articles "Anthropology and Education" (1904) and "Ethnic Factors in Education" (1905) in the *American Anthropologist* were the first and almost the last contribution of their kind in that journal. He argued for an "enrichment of the course of study of every public school in the land" through the incorporation of ethnological materials, particularly on culture history not confined to the Western world; called for joint meetings of the national education and anthropology societies to discuss mutual problems; scored culture historians for misuse and lack of use of ethnological data; claimed the clear relevance of an "ethnic psychology" that would contribute to the teacher's understanding of the fact that ". . . Italian and Bohemian, Celt and Hebrew, Anglo-Saxon and African look upon questions of honor, morality, and decency out of separate ethnic minds. . . ."; asked educators to realize that "a civilization imposed from without is usually harmful, often destructive, always undesirable," because the "development of a race must be from within"; and suggested that for all these reasons "normal schools and other institutions for the training of teachers should give a prominent place to the anthropological sciences." The fact that none of his calls was implemented reflects partly an ethnocentrism of American culture, partly the peculiar conservatism of American public education, and particularly the fact that American anthropologists did not have time for much of anything but ethnographic and culture history salvage until the 1930's.

Franz Boas, the dean of American anthropology, clearly saw the relevance of anthropological and educational interests. In his *Anthropology and Modern Life* (1928) he devotes one whole chapter to these interests. He points out that "anthropological research offers, therefore, a means of determining what may be expected of children of different ages, and this knowledge is of considerable value for regulating educational methods." He talks of "normative data for development," sex differences, ethnic differences, and differences in environmental conditions that should be taken into account. He treats of some of the problems of cultural transmission, and points out that "our public schools are hardly conscious of the conflict" between democratic ideas of freedom and flexibility, and coercion; "they instill automatic reactions to symbols by means of patriotic ceremonial, in many cases by indirect religious appeal, and too often through the automatic reactions to the behavior of the teacher that is imitated." He suggests that tradition-based transmission of values and ethics is particularly strong among intellectuals and that the "masses" respond "more quickly and energetically to the demands of the hour than the educated classes. . . ."

Articles by anthropologists on education have turned up persistently in educational journals and elsewhere for the past twenty-five years. The place of anthropology in a college education, the contributions of anthropology to the training of teachers, the place of primitive education in the history of education are the favorite themes. The articles add to what Montessori, Hewett, and Boas spelled out, but few of them produce clear innovations. Exceptions to this general rule include Mead's suggestive article on education in the perspective of primitive cultures (1943) and her Inglis Lecture, under the title, *The School in American Culture* (1950); Kluckhohn's comments in *Mirror for Man* (1949); Opler's "Cultural Alternatives and Educational Theory" (1947); Goldenweiser's "Culture and Education" (1939); and Herskovits' stimulating discussion in his text, *Man and His Works* (1950). The whole issue of the *American Journal of Sociology* (1943) devoted to "Education and Cultural Dynamics," including articles by Johnson, Redfield, Malinowski, Mekeel, Benedict, Herskovits, Powdermaker, and Embree is an especially outstanding contribution. Fred Eggan (1957, 1959) and Dorothy Lee (1957) provide useful perspectives on the relevance of anthropology to education. T. Brameld (1961) reviews recent contributions.

It seems clear, upon examination of what has been done, that anthropologists have not been able to say much more than was said fifty years ago by Hewett when they talk about the general relevance of anthropology to general education. This is primarily because there is not much else to say. When the anthropologists have either analyzed their own intimately understood cross-cultural data or have analyzed the educative process in our society, using empirical data, they have made a definite contribution.

Educational Routes

Irrespective of the attentions by anthropologists to education, the educators have gone ahead on their own to search out and utilize what seemed relevant to them of the anthropological products. An examination of representative and substantial texts in the psychological, sociocultural, philosophical, and comparative historical foundations of education used in professional teacher-training institutions about the country reveals a clear shift toward appropriation of social and cultural concepts and data produced by anthropologists.

In educational psychology, for example, the text by Pressey and Robinson (1944) mentions no anthropological references, and uses no cross-cultural data for illustrative purposes. Cronbach, in his model for educational psychology texts (1954) draws upon Mead, Davis, Warner, Benedict, and Kluckhohn, among others, and makes considerable reference to cultural pressures, different cultural settings influencing personality development and learning, and formation of social attitudes and values. Martin and Stendler's text, *Child Development*, intended for use by educators and noneducators both, and already used widely in elementary education and other professional education courses, places a very heavy emphasis on culture-personality relationships. Culture case data are cited for the Alorese, Balinese, Comanche, Japanese, Kwoma, Mentowie, Navaho, Samoans, Sioux, Tanala, Tepoztecans, Yurok, Zuñi, and others. Cultural relativism has found its way into the heart of this book. McDonald in his popular text (1959) depends less heavily upon cultural concepts but does cite numerous works by anthropologists. Of the seven textbooks in educational psychology examined, published between 1958 and 1961, five cite anthropological works, but mostly the same works by Mead, Benedict, and Linton.

In educational sociology—a field that is rapidly being expanded into a sociocultural foundation of education—a like trend is occurring. The Cooks' book (1950, revised edition), a text of long standing and wide use in educational sociology and social foundations, cites cross-cultural materials infrequently but draws much from the anthropologically influenced community studies on Middletown, St. Denis, Yankee City, and Plainsville. Robbins' *Educational Sociology* (1953) uses many of the same references and refers to writings by Mead, Benedict, Murdock, and Linton for the notion of cultural relativity. Brown's 1954 edition of *Educational Sociology* uses extensive references to cultural data on the Navaho, Australian tribes, Zuñi, and the Acoma Pueblo, and cites

anthropological pieces—by Gillin, Kluckhohn, Wagley, Herskovits, Goldfrank, Redfield, Tylor, Stirling, Warner, Rivers, Linton,
Hewett, Mead, Powdermaker, Benedict, and Montague—approximately twice as often as in the 1947 edition. Twelve textbooks in
the social foundations of education published between 1956 and
1961 were examined. All but one cited anthropological works.

The trend is not as noticeable in the philosophical and comparative foundations of education—in so far as the limits of the
sample of texts permit generalizations. The tendency in these
fields has apparently been to utilize highly generalized and West-
ern-limited concepts of culture as an important part of the frame
of reference, but to draw relatively little from any of the work by
anthropologists in cross-cultural contexts. Brameld has made one
of the strongest arguments for a culture base for educational philosophy, but even he cites only a few anthropological works—
namely, some by Davis, Kluckhohn, Benedict, Warner, and Herskovits in his earlier text (1950). But he has made the most consistent and substantial contribution to a thorough articulation of
educational and anthropological theory (1957) since then, and
he has tested out this integrated theory in a field situation (1959).
These recent important works have been reviewed by Siegel
(1959) and Spindler (1961), and the gist of his point of view is
expressed in his paper "The Meeting of Educational and Anthropological Theory" in this part.

An over-all summation of the anthropological concepts and
data utilized in the contemporary texts in the foundations of education reveals certain general trends. It is clear that educators interested in childhood education, elementary curriculum, school-
community interrelations, and all of the social and behavioral
foundations of education have arrived at the point where an anthropological point of view and, particularly, cross-cultural materials
have a positive value for them. They indicate an awareness of
culture concepts and cultural data produced by anthropologists by
fairly extensive documentations with appropriate literature. They
include anthropological references in their recommended reading
lists. They consider it desirable to qualify generalizations about
learning, cultural transmission, human nature, the functions of
education, child growth and development, by invoking the notion
of cultural relativity. Some of them incorporate a cultural per-

spective into their thinking—beyond using cultural relativity as a valued check.

The number of concepts used by educators relating to the cultured process is impressive. Anthropologists have no copyright but certainly some possessory rights over these concepts. To the anthropologist the terms values, acculturation, cultural normalcy, cultural diffusion, cultural change, cultural transmission, subcultures, peer culture, folk culture, enculturation ring with authentic familiarity as they are used by educationist authors.

But it is also clear that the range of materials being diffused through educationist channels from anthropological sources is in actuality quite limited. The same names and same references keep turning up constantly. Kluckhohn, Mead, Benedict, Davis, West (Carl Withers), and Warner are cited in great disproportion to all others. This suggests that the purveyance of anthropological thinking to education has at most two main disciplinary vehicles— personality and culture, and community studies—and that the mediation of data and concepts is inevitably given an indelible impress by these particular workers. Particularly significant is the fact that it is the relatively most popularized works of these contributors that are cited most frequently. These two tendencies indicate that however useful the contributions and however able the contributors, the educators are not getting a fair and substantial diet of anthropological materials. It is up to them to actively search out, with anthropological help, the richly relevant materials that await them.

THE ROLES OF THE ANTHROPOLOGIST IN THE EDUCATIONAL CONTEXT

One clear implication in this overview has been that if anthropology is actually going to contribute to education, the anthropologists will have to act at times within the setting of professional education. This is no argument that all anthropologists should. Anthropology has many dimensions and interests, and nothing should be permitted to happen in relations with other fields that draws many anthropologists away from its central purposes. But anthropologists have always been marked with a certain versatility. If there is a job to do in education some anthropologists will, for one reason or another, be bound to do it. Therefore an explication of some of the roles possible in the context of professional education is in order.

The anthropologist may act as a consultant. Ideally, he should be able to contribute ideas to every division of educational specialization—elementary, secondary, higher education, health, guidance, administration. He contributes, ideally, a widened perspective on human behavior. He sees the educative process as a cultural process, and thus not bounded by formalized, or ritualized, lines of specialization or conceptual compartmentalization. He devotes some of his attention to breaking down ethnocentric biases. He is, ideally, not time-bound. He provides objectification of cultural values and, if he is successful, brings educational objectives into appropriate congruence with them. He contributes some useful analytic-descriptive categories, the foremost of which is culture, followed by a train of constructs like cultural transmission, enculturation, role and status, and social organization. To do these things he has to act as a participating member of the groups for which he acts as a consultant, for it is necessary for him to grasp the point of view and problems of those with whom he is consulting. He has already had experience in doing this in his field research.

The anthropologist may do research in education or act as a consulting member of a team that is doing research. He does so with the same perspectives and capabilities that have been outlined above and in attacks upon problems that fall into areas described previously in this chapter. His major contribution lies in the molar approach that characterizes anthropological method. His greatest problem is one of relevance. His problems, definitions, and research values cannot remain exactly the same as they would if he were doing anthropological field research in a nonliterate, or even an acculturating community. He must understand what it is that educators need to know in order both to build better educational theory and to solve problems of immediate applied relevance. In the research team developed at Stanford under the direction of Robert Bush and known as the Stanford Consultation

Service, it was found that a good *modus operandi* was achieved when the educator, psychiatrist, and anthropologist exchanged roles for a time so that each could achieve insight into the other's problems. In this project, also, a unique combination of ameliorative case consultation goals and pure research goals has been achieved, so that neither end-point of the value pendulum in educational research is lost. There are frustrations inherent in this procedure, to be sure.

The anthropologist need not work within the framework of immediate education interests in his research. He may confine himself to his own cross-cultural field, chasing down questions on educative process in non-Western societies, as John Whiting has done in his Laboratory of Human Development in the graduate school of education at Harvard University. Possibly the most significant contributions of anthropology to education through research channels actually lie here.

The anthropologist may also act as a teacher in the setting of professional education. Certain propositions concerning this role have already been explicated. His obligation lies mainly in making explicit the cultural assumptions and values that are a substratum of every move in educational action or theorizing. His contribution is particularly critical because education is a sensitive part of the total cultural process, and because in its very nature as an art and science of human cultivation it is loaded with a heavy burden of values. To achieve this contribution he goes to cross-cultural variability first, then turns to our own cultural modes as they bear directly upon the educative process—from the viewpoint of both the learner and the teacher. His aim is to create cultural awareness, which is even more important than self-awareness in the teacher's sphere of activity and which is pedagogically much more attainable.

LIMITATIONS AND RESERVATIONS

The list of particulars for the roles the anthropologist may assume in the context of professional education is stated in ideal terms. No one anthropologist could do all of these things equally well. Choices have to be made on the basis of personal inclination and unique situations.

But other limitations on his functions call for statement. One danger is that the "study of man" can sometimes seem so total that it becomes *the* study of man. One ethnocentrism is substituted for another. The anthropologist's comments seem to glitter like gold—to him at least—because for a time they are new and fresh. He becomes a kind of cultural oracle. But when his stock of illuminating asides on the Upper Pukapuka on the Lower Zambesi runs low he will be forced to take another stance. Then he may be reduced to making broad, conjectural statements that he may confuse as final judgments or substantial generalizations rather than a potential source of hypotheses. He may fool some of the educators some of the time, but he can't fool them all.

Further, the anthropologist's experience with small and relatively integrated societies sometimes gives him an extraordinary naïveté about the complex relations in our own society—a society that he himself may have escaped from—into anthropology. He fails to see complications and looks for integrating features, consistencies, and values where there are none. And as a consequence he may make outlandish pronouncements as to what educators should or should not do.

Beyond this, the anthropologist is not always particularly sophisticated intellectually. He is often not sufficiently familiar with the social and intellectual histories of the great civilizations—including his own. He may have become an anthropologist in order to become an explorer (subconsciously, of course), or buried himself so thoroughly in ethnographies that he has no room in his head for other thoughts. If so, his suggestions to educators would fall short of the mark when he talks about cultural transmission, since he would not know the culture to be transmitted.

And there are limitations inherent in the culture concept. Though no anthropologist would limit his conceptual repertoire to it exclusively, most are heavily influenced by it. Though the great utility of this construct cannot be denied, it is not a theory in itself. It is not sufficiently dynamic, or field-oriented, but tends to contain itself around patterning phenomena that provide form but not function as variables for analysis. The anthropologist will usually find in the educational context that he has turn to other disciplines, along with his anthropological armamentarium, for concepts and methods.

Despite these reservations, it does appear that anthropology has a new and needed perspective on education. This volume is an exploration of this perspective.

References

Boas, Franz, 1928, *Anthropology and Modern Life*. New York: W. W. Norton & Company, Inc.

Brameld, Theodore, 1950, *Patterns of Educational Philosophy*. New York: Harcourt, Brace & World, Inc.

————, 1957, *Cultural Foundations of Education: An Interdisciplinary Exploration*. New York: Harper & Row, Publishers.

————, 1959, *The Remaking of a Culture—Life and Education in Puerto Rico*. New York: Harper & Row, Publishers.

————, and E. B. Sullivan, 1961, Anthropology and Education. *Review of Educational Research*, 70–79.

Brown, Francis J., 1954, *Educational Sociology*, 2d ed. Englewood Cliffs, N.J.: Prentice-Hall, Inc.

Bruner, Edward M., 1956*a*, "Cultural Transmission and Cultural Change." *Southwestern Journal of Anthropology*, 12:191–199.

————, 1956*b*, "Primary Group Experience and the Process of Acculturation." *American Anthropologist*, 58:605–623.

————, and George D. Spindler, 1962, "The Introductory Course in Anthropology." Paper prepared for the Conference on Teaching of Anthropology, University of California, Berkeley, March, 1961. To be published with other papers in the *Teaching of Anthropology*, edited by D. Mandelbaum, E. Albert, G. Lasker as Memoir 94, American Anthropological Association.

Bryson, Lyman, 1939, "Anthropology and Education," in D. D. Brand and Fred Harvey, eds., *So Live the Works of Men*. Albuquerque, N.M.: University of New Mexico Press.

Coleman, James S., 1961, *Social Climates in High Schools*. Co-operative Research Monograph No. 4, U.S. Dept. of Health, Education and Welfare.

———, 1961, *Adolescent Society*. New York: The Free Press of Glencoe, Inc.

Cook, L. A., and Elaine F. Cook, 1950, *A Sociological Approach to Education*. New York: McGraw-Hill Book Company, Inc.

Cox, P. W., B. E. Mercer, 1961, *Education in Democracy*. New York: McGraw-Hill Book Company, Inc.

Cronbach, Lee J., 1954, *Educational Psychology*. New York: Harcourt, Brace & World, Inc.

Davis, Allison, 1952, *Social Class Influences on Learning*. Cambridge, Mass.: Harvard University Press.

Davis, A., and R. J. Havighurst, 1947, *Father of the Man*. Boston: Houghton Mifflin Company.

Deevey, E. Jr., 1960, "The Human Population." *Scientific American* 203, No. 3, 194–204.

Dobzhansky, Theodore, 1960, "The Present Evolution of Man." *Scientific American Reprints*, 203, No. 3, 206–217.

Eells, Kenneth, Allison Davis, Robert J. Havighurst, Virgil E. Herrick, and Ralph W. Tyler, 1951, *Intelligence and Cultural Differences*. Chicago: University of Chicago Press.

Eggan, Fred, 1957, Social Anthropology and the Educational System. *School Review*, 65:247–259.

———, 1959, "An Anthropologist Looks at Discipline." *Grade Teacher*, 76:93–95.

Ehrich, Robert W., 1947, "The Place of Anthropology in a College Education." *Harvard Educational Review*, XVII:57–61.

Frank, Lawrence K., 1959, *The School as Agent for Cultural Renewal*. Cambridge, Mass.: Harvard University Press.

Gruber, Fred C., ed., 1961, *Anthropology and Education*, The Martin G. Brumbaugh Lectures in Education. Philadelphia: University of Pennsylvania Press.

Harvard Educational Review, 1953, "Social Class Structure and American Education." Parts I and II, XXIII, 149–338.

Havighurst, Robert J., and Hilda Taba, 1949, *Adolescent Character and Personality*. New York: John Wiley & Sons, Inc.

Henry, Jules, 1960, "A Cross-cultural Outline of Education." *Current Anthropology*, I:267–305.

Herskovits, Melville J., 1943, "Education and Cultural Dynamics." *American Journal of Sociology*, XLVIII:109–21.

————, 1950, *Man and His Works*. New York: Alfred A. Knopf, Inc.

Hewett, Edgar L., 1904, "Anthropology and Education." *American Anthropologist*, VI:574–75.

————, 1905, "Ethnic Factors in Education." *American Anthropologist*, VII:1–16.

Hoebel, E. Adamson, 1955, Anthropology in Education in W. L. Thomas, Jr., ed., *Yearbook of Anthropology*. New York: Wenner-Gren Foundation for Anthropological Research.

Howells, W. W., 1952, "The Study of Anthropology." *American Anthropologist*, 54:1–7.

————, 1960, "The Distribution of Man." *Scientific American* 203, No. 3, 113–130.

Johnson, Charles S., ed., 1943, "Education and the Cultural Process." *American Journal of Sociology*, XLVIII, 1–136.

Keesing, Felix M., 1937, *Education in Pacific Countries*. Shanghai, China: Kelly and Walsh.

Kimball, Solon T., 1956, "Anthropology and Education." *Educational Leadership*, 13:480–483.

Klineberg, Otto, 1935, *Racial Differences*. New York: Harper & Row, Publishers.

————, 1947, "Racial Psychology," in Ralph Linton, ed., *The Science of Man in the World Crisis*. New York: Columbia University Press.

————, 1951, *Race and Psychology*. New York: UNESCO.

Kluckhohn, Clyde, 1949, *Mirror for Man*. New York: McGraw-Hill Book Company, Inc.

Kroeber, A. L., ed., 1953, *Anthropology Today*. Chicago: University of Chicago Press.

Landes, Ruth, 1960, *Tools of Desegregation*. Paper read before the American Association for the Advancement of Science, Section H (Anthropology), in December, New York City. (mimeographed)

Lasker, Gabriel, 1961, *The Evolution of Man, A Brief Introduction to Physical Anthropology*. New York: Holt, Rinehart and Winston, Inc.

Lee, Dorothy, 1957, "Anthropology and American Secondary Education," in P. M. Halverson, ed., *Frontiers of Secondary Education*. Syracuse: University of Syracuse Press.

Mandelbaum, David, 1960, *The Teaching of Anthropology in the U.S.A., A Review of the Symposia of the Project in Edu-*

cational Resources in Anthropology. New York: Wenner-Gren Foundation for Anthropological Research. (mimeographed)

————, 1961*a*, "Progress Report on Educational Resources in Anthropology Project." *Fellow Newsletter,* American Anthropological Association, 2:2–3.

————, 1961*b*, "Anthropology in the High Schools." *Fellow Newsletter,* American Anthropological Association, 2:2–3.

Martin, William E., and Celia Stendler, 1953, *Child Development.* New York: Harcourt, Brace & World, Inc.

McDonald, Fred, 1959, *Educational Psychology.* San Francisco: F. Wadsworth Publishing Co.

Mead, Margaret, 1943, "Our Educational Emphasis in Primitive Perspective." *American Journal of Sociology,* XLVIII:633–39.

————, 1946, "Professional Problems of Education in Dependent Countries." *The Journal of Negro Education,* XV:346–57.

————, 1950, *The School in American Culture.* Cambridge, Mass.: Harvard University Press.

————, 1959, "A Redefinition of Education." *NEA Journal,* 48:15–17.

————, 1960*a*, "Anthropology as Part of a Liberal Education." Paper prepared for symposium No. 5, Summer 1960, Burg Wartenstein, Austria, sponsored by Wenner-Gren Foundation for Anthropological Research.

————, 1960*b*, The High School of the Future. *California Journal of Secondary Education,* 35:360–69.

Mercer, B. E., E. R. Carr, 1957, *Education and the Social Order.* New York: Holt, Rinehart and Winston, Inc.

Montessori, Marie, 1913, *Pedagogical Anthropology.* New York: J. B. Lippincott Company.

Opler, Morris, 1947, "Cultural Alternatives and Educational Theory." *Harvard Educational Review,* XVII:28–44.

Pettit, George, A., 1946, "Primitive Education in North America." *University of California Publications in American Archeology and Ethnology,* XLIII:1–182.

Pressey, Sidney, and Francis Robinson, 1944, *Psychology and the New Education.* New York: Harper & Row, Publishers.

Read, Margaret, 1960, *Children of Their Fathers: Growing Up among the Ngoni of Nyasaland.* New Haven, Conn.: Yale University Press.

Robbins, Florence G., 1953, *Educational Sociology*. New York: Holt, Rinehart and Winston, Inc.

Rosenstiel, Annette, 1954, "Educational Anthropology: A New Approach to Cultural Analysis." *Harvard Educational Review*. XXIV:28:36.

———, 1959, "Anthropology and Childhood Education." *School and Society*, 87:482:83.

Siegel, Bernard, 1959, Review of *Cultural Foundations of Education* by T. Brameld. *American Anthropologist*, 61:118–120.

Spindler, G. D., 1946, "Anthropology May Be an Answer." *Journal of Education*, CXXIX:130–31.

———, 1959, *The Transmission of American Culture*, Third Burton Lecture. Cambridge, Mass.: Harvard University Press.

———, 1961, Review of T. Brameld, *Remaking of a Culture*, with reply by T. Brameld. *Harvard Educational Review*, 31:345–353.

Spiro, Melford, 1958, *Children of the Kibbutz*. Cambridge, Mass.: Harvard University Press.

Stanley, William O., *et al.*. 1956, *Social Foundations of Education*. New York: Holt, Rinehart and Winston, Inc.

Taba, Hilda, 1957, "Educational Implications in the Concepts of Culture and Personality." *Educational Leadership*, 15: 183–86.

Warner, W. Lloyd, *et al.*, 1949, *Democracy in Jonesville*. New York: Harper & Row, Publishers.

———, Robert J. Havighurst, and Martin B. Loeb, 1944, *Who Shall Be Educated?* New York: Harper & Row, Publishers.

Washburn, Sherwood, 1960, "Tools and Human Evolution." *Scientific American Reprints*, Vol. 203, No. 3, 12pp.

Whiteford, Andrew H., ed., 1960, *Teaching Anthropology*. Logan Museum Publications in Anthropology, No. 8, Beloit, Wisconsin: Beloit College Press

Whiting, John, and Irvin L. Child, 1953, *Child Training and Personality*. New Haven, Conn: Yale University Press.

Whiting, John, and B. B. Whiting, 1960, "Contributions of Anthropology to the Methods of Studying Child Rearing," in Paul H. Mussen, ed., *Handbook of Research Methods in Child Development*. New York: John Wiley & Sons, Inc.

5——Theodore Brameld

The Meeting of Educational and Anthropological Theory[*]

I

Although both educators and anthropologists have always been more or less aware of the theoretical underpinnings of their respective fields, it is probably true that never have they been as acutely concerned with the import of those underpinnings as at the present time. In both fields one finds growing attention to the assumptions upon which research and practice inevitably, if precariously, rest. In both fields, also, one detects not only an abundance of fermentation and fresh insight in the area of theory, but perhaps an equal abundance of uncrystallized thinking and unrefined terminology.

The reasons for this heightened concern are no doubt themselves cultural. Melville Herskovits (1948, pp. 314f.), one of the few anthropologists who has thus far paid sustained attention to education as an institution of culture, suggests that one may easily distinguish between the way it functions for a people like the Zuñi and for a more complex civilization because the one is relatively stable by comparison with the other:

The homogeneity of the [Zuñi] culture makes for a unity of teaching objectives that reflect unity of cultural aims and methods of inculcating them in the young, and thus leaves little room for

* Reprinted, with revision, from *Education and Anthropology*, George D. Spindler, Editor, with the permission of the Publishers, Stanford University Press; copyright 1955 by the Board of Trustees of the Leland Stanford Junior University.

conflict between the directives given by different preceptors. . . .
This conflict in directives is perhaps the source of the most
serious difficulties in larger, less homogeneous societies, where
the total educational process includes schooling as well as training in the home. Serious conflicts and deep-seated maladjustments
may result from education received at the hands of persons whose
cultural or sub-cultural frames of reference differ.

Although Morris Opler (1947) has pointed to the danger of
oversimplifying this distinction, as Herskovits does also, it does
seem obvious that today the divergence of educational methods
and objectives in complex civilizations in widespread indeed—a
divergence that is reflected not only in growing attention to and
refinement of educational theory as a specialized discipline, but in
deep-seated conflicts among its own spokesmen. Schools of all
sorts are found to operate upon what I may call "meta-educational" assumptions, quite as fully as cultural beliefs and practices
operate upon what the anthropological theorist, David Bidney
(1935a) aptly terms metacultural assumptions.

Indeed, as might be expected in view of the ultimate if far
from sufficiently delineated interdependence of education and
culture, the same types of traditional philosophic categories may
be utilized to characterize both fields of theory. Thus realism is an
influential educational doctrine (Frederick Breed is a representative), but it is also influential in anthropology (Robert H. Lowie
has been so classified). So too, among other doctrines, are idealism, historical materialism, neo-Thomism, and pragmatism. To be
sure, these terms are not always manipulated with equal refinement, nor do the two fields always reveal exactly comparable
meanings. Bronislaw Malinowski, to choose but one anthropologist,
is undoubtedly closer to pragmatism than to any other current
philosophic outlook; yet, as the philosopher Horace Friess (1950)
has reminded us, his special way of adapting that doctrine to culture theory would scarcely satisfy the most influential American
pragmatist and educational philosopher, John Dewey.

The difficulty with much of this kind of metacultural and
meta-educational thinking, however, is that it claims more by way
of explanation of the present struggles besetting both fields than
it can justify. Bidney (cf. 1953a, pp. 25, 37 f.), for example, some-

times leaves the impression that he has satisfactorily interpreted, say, Alfred L. Kroeber when he labels this anthropologist as an objective idealist. The philosopher of culture, F. S. C. Northrop (1946), attempts a not dissimilar feat on a grand scale when he tries to explain Western civilization in terms of the philosophy of modern science, and Eastern culture in terms of aesthetic intuition. Similarly, various educational theorists seem to think they have finally understood Robert M. Hutchins when they classify him as an Aristotelian, or Alexander Meiklejohn as a Kantian.

Where such explanations fall short is in failing to inquire carefully whether or not they have reached the limits of interpretation when they have noted that educators and anthropologists, or even whole cultures, rest upon presuppositions that can be defined according to more or less established philosophic categories. Helpful, indeed indispensable, as these categories are, the problem that still remains is the intricate linkages between them and the cultural experiences with which they are properly associated. It is one thing, for example, to underscore the pragmatic premises upon which, to some extent, the work of Ruth Benedict among other anthropologists undoubtedly rests. It is another thing to infer that we have thereby sufficiently revealed the origin, role, or practical significance of these premises. We still need to ask, after we have articulated them as clearly as possible, how and why pragmatism developed as it has in America. And we need to do so, I suggest, not merely by careful conceptualization or even by tracing it to earlier philosophies, such as the Hegelian, but by considering it as the symbolic corollary of a constellation of natural and cultural phenomena that are, in numerous respects, indigenous to the American milieu. In short, the crucial problem is the venerable but far from solved one of the interlacing of ideas, concepts, categories, on the one hand, with nature, human experience, culture, on the other hand. If another instance of reductionism is not to be committed, we must avoid what I may term here the "philosophic fallacy"—a fallacy to which some anthropological and educational theorists seem vulnerable.

Just how far anthropologists have thus **far become** sensitive to the context of political, economic, moral, and other influences upon their own frames of reference I am not qualified to say. It is, I confess, surprising to note such relative paucity of attention paid to the bearing of that context upon anthropological theory in such an imposing overview of the field as *Anthropology Today*. And it is at least plausible to ask if there has been anything like enough interdisciplinary effort thus far to incorporate into anthropology the perspectives of such diverse nonanthropological interpreters of American cultural assumptions as Charles Beard, Harold Laski, Max Lerner, Vernon Parrington, Merle Curti, Thorstein Veblen, or even John Dewey.

It would be, of course, a gross exaggeration to contend that educational theory has proceeded much, if any, further in such an effort. Here, too, the disregard of or at least insensitivity to the reciprocity of "inarticulate major premises" and environmental influences is far more typical than not. At the same time, the dim outlines of a more adequate approach are at least discernible—an approach no doubt due in considerable part to the immense influence of Dewey, who insisted throughout his long professional life upon the interaction of ideas and events, and in part also to the practical character of schooling as an on-going institution in everyday American life. Thus, the conflicts rampant in education today—conflicts now commanding frequent attention even in mass-circulation magazines—are occasionally assessed by theorists in terms of what may in general be called, after Karl Mannheim (1936), the sociology of knowledge. Here the aim is always to explore the environmental motivations of social theory as essential to the meaning of that theory: the conditions of economic and social tension and crisis, for example; the technological and political revolutions sweeping our century; the abnormal rate of change from, say, the "inner-directed" to the "outer-directed" types of character analyzed by David Riesman (1950); and numerous other factors that are approachable only through a multidimensional interpretation in which conventional philosophic categories are a necessary but certainly not sufficient explanation of present educational bewilderments and struggles.

Granting that we have hardly begun to develop this kind of approach to any area of experience and knowledge, I wish nevertheless to illustrate what it might begin to mean in effecting a closer rapprochement between the two fields with which we are here primarily concerned. More particularly, I propose to select four among many more problematic concepts from anthropology and to suggest not only how these may be helpful to the tasks of American education, but how their consideration by educational theory viewed in the wider context referred to above may enhance their own importance and fruitfulness for anthropology. These four are: (1) the reality of culture, (2) process in culture, (3) values in culture, and (4) the integration of culture. In view of my purpose, it is obvious that I shall find it necessary to mention various facts and principles which, though familiar to members of one field, may be unfamiliar to the other. It is obvious, also, that each of these problematic concepts embraces so huge a territory that one can only hope at best to emphasize aspects of major relevance.

The frame of reference, if I may take the liberty of extending Mannheim's term, is an as yet embryonic methodology—the "metaculturology of knowledge"—metaculturology here being redefined provisionally as that encompassing discipline concerned with the assumptions of culture theory, and which accordingly includes not only the assumptions of anthropology, sociology, and all other sciences of man, but of the history and philosophy of cultures as well.

II

The problem of the reality of culture refers to the disputes waged over its locus, autonomy, and substance. The impression a layman receives from reviewing recent anthropological discussion is that, while in general there is now widespread agreement that culture connotes a level of human experience clearly distinguishable from although related to all other levels of nature and humanity, there continues to be disagreement over its ontological status. If the anthropologist, Leslie White (1949a), is right in his historic survey, early pioneers such as Emile Durkheim were closer to the correct position than many recent theorists—the position that culture is a unique, objective level of reality, self-sustaining and self-generating (*sui generis*). White deplores, therefore, what he considers to be a retreat from this position by the majority of American anthropologists—Ralph Linton and Edward Sapir, to name but two—who, he feels, have reduced culture chiefly to psychological phenomena. Ironically, perhaps the two most vigorous American defenders of cultural objectivism are at opposite poles in their interpretation of what the "substance" of culture is: White himself, who is sometimes called a historical materialist, and the sociocultural theorist, Pitirim A. Sorokin, who is a metacultural idealist. In passing, it should be noted that the *sui generis* position, however, subtle its ramifications, must also be assumed finally both by Marxian anthropologists (who consider the fountainhead of their doctrine to be Friedrich Engels' *Origin of the Family*), and by those subscribing to the metaphysics of Thomism (Father W. Schmidt no doubt being the most prominent).

Kroeber's long meditation upon the problem has led him to modify in crucial respects his own original *sui generis* view of culture (1952, pp. 22 ff.). At least two recent statements (Kroeber, 1952, p. 121; Kroeber and Kluckhohn, 1952, pp. 148 f.) appear to take a clear-cut operational approach by holding that culture is not a reified substance but a functional abstraction by which certain kinds of human experience are delineated and interpreted. Despite certain inconsistencies, this is likewise the main direction pursued by Malinowski (1944), as it is of such diverse figures as the "philosophical anthropologist," Ernst Cassirer (1944), and the anthropological theorist-practitioner, Clyde Kluckhohn (1949).

Now it is surely interesting, though not really surprising, that much the same type of dispute runs through educational philosophy (cf. Brameld, 1955, 1956). Although culture is seldom precisely defined, the meta-educational attitude presupposed by the two groups of theorists often called essentialists and perennialists is that it is largely an objectively posited level of reality. Despite important differences among them (perennialists are Aristotelians and Thomists, secular or ecclesiastic, while essentialists usually are modern realists or idealists), both groups incline toward a pre-established, predetermined cosmos, and therefore of the world of social institutions and events as part of that cosmos.

The consequences of this attitude for education are enormous. Learning becomes chiefly a process of stimulus-response, mental discipline, or some similar practice devoted mainly to absorption of and/or training for unity with the already given cultural environment. The notion entertained by some anthropologists that education is established to guarantee transmission of the cultural heritage is welcomed by essentialists and perennialists as confirming their own predilections as to the relation of the learner to the reality that is learned.

Against this general orientation, educational philosophy in America is characterized today by at least two other viewpoints, occasionally termed progressivism and reconstructionism. Like their counterpositions, these also have a great deal in common amidst genuine distinctions. While reconstructionism, for example, tends to emphasize more strongly the need for clearly enunciated cultural goals, both accept the operational way of interpreting nature and culture. Therefore both emphatically reject a *sui generis* position. Being concerned with educational methods as instruments of social control, they tend to deny that education, formal or informal, is properly characterized as an agent merely of cultural transmission. Since they are deeply respectful of science they do not ignore, of course, the anthropological evidence for such transmission. They do question whether the evidence is thus far complete enough to warrant the hasty generalizations frequently made, and especially so in view of the scarcity of systematic investigations by anthropology of education as a distinct institution of culture.

The conception of learning developed by this second pair of philosophies also departs from the first pair. Malinowski's anthropological functionalism, for example, is by no means foreign to the educational functionalism now widely taught under such a label as organismic psychology. Here learning centers in the activity of mediating the immediacies of experience, to use the language of Dewey (cf. 1916, 1939). That these immediacies are, if you please, the "givens" of nature and culture, and that they are very real, very stubborn, and sometimes overpowering, is recognized. The inference from these characteristics that they are *sui generis* existences in which man must either acquiesce or perish is, however, considered to be false—an inference plausible enough, in the face of long-standing unscientific habits and attitudes, but not therefore either logical or moral.

Education, in this framework, becomes normatively creative and recreative rather than primarily reflexive or reproductive. The major assumption is that habits of variation and exploration are cultivable, indeed that some cultures (our own most notably, perhaps) have to a considerable degree acquired amenability to habits of this kind at least as self-consciously as others have acquired alternative kinds. It follows that, since culture is entirely learned, education deliberately geared to modification or reconstruction can also be learned. The sociologist, Charles S. Johnson (1943, p. 4), speaking of "education and the cultural process," epitomizes the general view: "Education, thus, is more than the transmission of culture from one generation to another. It is this transmission and it is also transformation of people who are more or less in conflict."

Although further examination would reveal certain overlappings between all four of the theories mentioned, just as there are overlappings between, say, White and Linton, a more important consideration here is whether we can detect any still wider significance for the problem of cultural reality as it bears upon both education and anthropology. Here, then, we approach the question of what a metaculturology of knowledge might reveal as to the more pervasive reasons for the dispute.

One clue to an answer lies in the conflict within Western culture between what I shall call, in widest possible compass, an absolute-transcendental approach to nature, man, and society, on the one side, and an experimental-empirical approach, on the other side. This conflict is, of course, both ancient and multiple. While its most sophisticated formulation is philosophic, it is by no means merely or even primarily so either in origin or expression. Rather, it is religious, legal, industrial, familial, political, moral—indeed, one would have difficulty in sifting out any phase of Western experience that it has not invaded. Usually, we think of the Middle Ages as representing the dominance of the absolute-transcendental alternative, although we appreciate that this was by no means purely the case any more than modern civilization is purely experimental-empirical.

As a matter of fact, one of the most striking features of modern culture is that it has never emancipated itself from the heritage of medieval habits, beliefs, and practices—certainly not to anything like the extent suggested by Sorokin (1941) in condemning our "sensate" culture. Not only do most contemporary religious institutions perpetuate that heritage; so, too, do political institutions, including even American democracy with its anchorage of *a priori* axioms concerning equality, freedom, and the dignity of man.

Nor would we be wrong in recalling that modern science is far from immunized. On the contrary, as Jerome Frank (1945) among many others has shown, the mechanistic philosophy of science (perhaps oftenest associated with Newton), which views the universe as an objective system of pre-established law, is not only widely taken for granted even by some relativity physicists of our own day; it is, to an astonishing degree, assumed as the model to be emulated by social scientists as well. Recently, in those parts of the world controlled by communism, the absolutist outlook rationalized by dialectical materialism is officially espoused and enforced in all departments of life: in the natural and social sciences, in political indoctrination, and in every type of school.

The relevant conclusion here is that the problem both of cultural reality and of education's response to that reality is integral with the much wider problem of alternative ways of believing and acting in cultural experience. To be sure, these ways are made clearer both by anthropological and educational theories, just as they are by formal philosophies. One additional measure of such theories, however, derives from perception of the underlying currents of influence, ideological and otherwise, which play upon them at the same time that theories share in expressing and molding the influences themselves. In the problem under discussion, this may well mean, first of all, that the unresolved issue of the *sui generis* versus operational views of cultural reality, and likewise the unresolved issue of the essentialist-perennialist versus progressivist-reconstructionist views of education, are finally integral with absolutist versus experimentalist institutions, attitudes, and habits that both precede and follow those views.

We need hardly be reminded, however, that any brief attempt

to sketch the significance of our first problematic concept on such a huge canvas inevitably ignores innumerable qualifying factors. It should be borne in mind that this attempt is itself strictly operational. The test of its value lies in the extent to which it assists us in mapping a very large territory with a greater degree of potential and actual meaning, in developing greater consciousness of the network of interrelations of the two fields with which we are concerned, and in constructing the beginnings of a framework through which to approach our three remaining concepts.

III

By the concept of process I refer, in general, to the cluster of questions centering in "the dynamics of culture change." That these are intimately connected with the concept of reality is evident, but not at all in the sense that the absolutist orientation denies change while the experimentalist accepts it. No anthropologist, regardless of his premises, would defend any notion of completely static culture; and no competent educator would defend any notion of completely static education. To be sure, the perennialist and certain essentialists regard time as subordinate to the timeless forms of reality, and this regard affects their final outlook upon the responsibilities of education. Even they, however, typically provide curricula and techniques that include recognition of changing events and needs with which students must be prepared to cope during their lives.

And yet, in an important sense, the absolutist view of culture approaches the problem of process from assumptions that tend to encourage consequences divergent from those of the operational interpretation; so, too, do conflicting philosophies of education. White, for example, still retains important features of the "evolutionary" thesis developed by such immortals of anthropology as Henry B. Tylor, Lewis H. Morgan, and Herbert Spencer—a thesis that presumes to detect in human history a unilinear progress from "savagery" through "barbarism" to "civilization." Despite differences, this is also broadly the Marxian doctrine—civilization in its highest form becoming the classless society of pure communism. In the history of American educational theory, the classical "evolutionary" position has never been more consistently expounded than by the neo-Hegelian philosopher and early United States Commissioner of Education, William T. Harris (1901), who, while scarcely hoping for the final emergence of a classless society, does find a melioristic trend in culture which it is the first business of the schools to reflect and reinforce. As Curti (1935) has shown, the Harris theory of education is accordingly traditionalistic in its cultural role. Change is not for an instant denied. But, as with the great majority of other essentialists and perennialists, the schools are charged with the first obligation to follow, not to modify or redirect, whatever course the institutions and practices of man as a member of society are destined to pursue.

As we have already seen, progressivists and reconstructionists are unwilling to settle for the Harris variety of policy and program. This is not to say that they conceive of education as *the* agency of cultural change—certainly not without broadening the concept of education to embrace much more than formally organized learning and teaching. Their organismic psychology, however, plus their normative picture of democracy as a social laboratory engaged in continuous experimentation with every sort of human problem, enables them to argue that cultural change is not a mere epiphenomenon to which schools must passively adjust but is, in significant degree, a controllable process for human growth.

But operationalists in education could benefit by further attention to some of the insights and discoveries of anthropology with regard to the meanings of process. For one thing, considerable evidence could be produced to show that progressivism, particularly, has underestimated or simply failed to cope squarely with the powerful resistances to consciously directed change that are typical of cultures. The frequent criticism leveled against Dewey, and even more against his educational disciples, that they have inherited too generous a residue of faith in progress and rationality characteristic of the Enlightenment, contains more than a grain of truth.

Thus, while it would be inaccurate to assert that they have ignored the weaknesses of this traditional faith, progressivists do not appear to have given direct, careful attention to the importance of, for example, cultural patterns—to the kind of intensive investigations conducted by Kroeber (1944) and others to demonstrate the recurrence and persistence of such patterns throughout history. Greater awareness of this phenomenon would compel educational theorists to take into consideration a hypothesis such as cultural curves of upswing and downswing, and so to assess far more realistically their own sometimes overconfident if not naïve belief in the novelty, flexibility, and continuity of organized human development.

It is even possible that greater appreciation of anthropological theory and research would force progressivists to take a new look at their favorite concept of "creative intelligence." While they have never accepted anything like the "great man theory of history," neither have they adequately scrutinized the limitations of individual capacity to effect change. The "child-centered school," although sometimes a distortion in practice of progressivism in theory, and although now partly overshadowed by the notion of "community-centered schools," is still held up to thousands of teachers in training as an educational ideal. It is an ideal, I suggest, which to some extent is governed by individualistic and tender-minded biases that are in fact incompatible with anthropological knowledge of cultural structures and persistences.

Contributions to the problem of cultural process have been so numerous that it is difficult to resist the temptation to explore their educational bearings further. Here I am able to select only two concepts of unusual provocation. The first, neglected thus far by education, is "cultural focus"—the tendency, if Herskovits (1948, pp. 542 ff.) is correct, for cultures to organize certain variable clusters of traits in terms of dominant interests (aesthetic, economic, social, or others) of which members are likely to be especially aware, and hence which are more pliable. Assuming that the focus of our own culture, for example, is technological, it does seem true that in this domain we are readier to examine methods and devices, to strive for improvement and innovation, than in more peripheral domains such as organized religion. Granting that the concept is debatable, it suggests to educators that if they are to play any sort of creative role in cultural process, one of their first duties must be to determine as clearly as possible the precise character of the focus or foci of given cultures and subcultures, and then to construct strategies of change geared to this character.

The second concept is derived not immediately from anthropology, which is apparently unaware of it, but from educational philosophy—the theory of "practical intelligence" developed by Bruce Raup (1950) and a group of associates in the progressivist camp. Utilizing numerous principles from anthropology as well as other social sciences, they have sought to sharpen the function of intelligence as an instrument of cultural change by dissecting several components which they contend are neglected by those who define it in typically scientific terms. Thus they find that practical intelligence consists of three "moods"—the indicative, optative, and imperative—expressing respectively the surveying, normative, and programmatic phases of the total function. The major methodology of action emerging from their analysis is expressed in the discipline of an "uncoerced community of persuasion." It is this discipline which they hope can be put into widespread educational and social operation, as a way both to reduce tensions between and within cultural groups and to accelerate change in directions found to be desirable in the course of testing that methodology. The potential reciprocity of the concepts of practical intelligence and cultural focus in affecting educational change is rich. Beginnings are, indeed, discernible in the greater perceptiveness of some educational leaders to the structures of local communities where schools operate.

Raup and his colleagues proceed from a crucial assumption that is by no means as carefully considered by either educational or anthropological theory as it ought to be—the assumption that the present period of history is beset by abnormal strain, confusion, and a pervading sense of crisis. I select the concept of crisis for a moment of special attention because it is here perhaps most revealingly that one may place the problem of cultural process in the setting of a metaculturology of knowledge. Returning for a moment to the four philosophies of education in order to explicate the point, it is at least a legitimate hypothesis that these philosophies may be viewed not merely as significant symbolizations but as alternative diagnoses and prognoses of the present crisis in political, moral, economic, and other forms of national and international relations.

In very general terms, the perennialist formula aims to change culture by reacting against what it considers to be the ailment of materialistic and experimental habits and beliefs. Therefore it favors the restoration of aristocratic and/or theocratic principles and practices prevailing at a much earlier time in Western history —the Greek and Medieval periods, especially. The essentialist formula, exemplified by Harris, tends to utilize the *sui generis* ontology of modern idealism or realism in order to cultivate adjustment to the moving stream of history. Progressivism, symbolized by such concepts as practical intelligence, is committed to a democratic methodology that encourages gradual but deliberately planned cultural change with secondary regard for commitment to future goals. The reconstructionist, finally, builds his case upon the premise that progressivism, however potent, is no longer satisfactory to cope with the deep-seated maladjustments of a crisis-age such as ours. Hence he contends that if the democratic values and institutions in which he believes are to survive, flourish, and expand, fresh and challenging designs for culture-and-education must now be constructed as well as implemented upon an audacious scale, with the fullest possible recognition of the obstacles and pressures which anthropology and other social sciences enable him to estimate.

It is only fair to admit that this metaculturological interpretation of American theories of education is not as yet widely influential. Also, one ought to note that it is a way of organizing diffused masses of theory and practice that overlap in numerous ways, and therefore resist such neat classifications. Nevertheless, if we remember that the attempt is entirely operational, this kind of approach may prove meaningful not only for the field of education but also for other fields.

It is interesting, for example, to examine the extent to which the concept of crisis in its peculiar relevance for the twentieth century is central to anthropological theory. Of course the concept is by no means ignored. Not only is it crucial to the work of such philosophers of culture as Oswald Spengler, Arnold Toynbee, Lewis Mumford, and Ortega y Gassett, but one also finds it receiving occasional attention by Franz Boas (especially in his writings for the layman), and by other leaders in anthropology. At the same time, one is struck by the fact that *as an explicitly treated concept* it is conspicuously absent from the index and content of *Anthropology Today*, from the recent technical "review of concepts and definitions of culture" by Kroeber and Kluckhohn (1952), from more than one widely read textbook in anthropology (e.g., Kroeber, 1948; Herskovits, 1948), and even from the invitingly titled symposium, *The Science of Man in the World Crisis* (Linton, ed., 1945).

I do not pretend to guess all the reasons for such striking omissions or peripheral treatments. Yet it would seem fair to inquire why a considerable section of anthropological theory finds the concept of crisis so uncongenial to its own systematic investigations. Surely, if it is held that we are now in the throes of world-wide cataclysm, one would expect both its general meaning and bearing upon specific issues to receive sustained attention from anthropology. As is true of educational theory, I do not find this, by and large, to be the case. Perhaps even more than in educational theory, however, I fail to find careful attention paid to the question of why those theorists of culture who have explicitly dealt with the problem of crisis tend to react to it in alternative ways.

The issue here, in other words, is whether it is possible that anthropologists and allied scholars themselves vary both in their critiques and proposals according to their various locations on what might be called the continuum of a metaculturology of knowledge. To what degree if at all, for example, is Sorokin's anticipation of a new "ideational" culture motivated by his own metaculturological preferences rather than detached scientific judgments? Again, might further investigation show that the approach of functionalism in anthropology reflects, more or less, the same sociopolitically liberal orientation toward cultural change as does the educational methodology of practical intelligence? Similarly, is the *sui generis* position (cf. White, 1949*b*, pp. 344–47) likely to reveal or at least inadvertently to bolster attitudes and actions somewhat analogous to the conservative predilections of most educational essentialists? Is it even possible, finally, that those anthropologists, like those educators, who largely disregard the concept of crisis do so partly, at any rate, because it remains outside the range of their own ideological orientation—their own personal and professional status in the culture of their time?

The answer to such questions is far from self-evident. A meeting, however, of anthropological and educational theory at this juncture might benefit both fields in their endeavor to articulate and cope with the concept of process from their more deep-seated, pervasive assumptions.

IV

The problem of cultural values (anticipated, of course, in the issue just raised) is, if anything, still more hazardous. One reason is that philosophers who specialize in axiology are themselves profoundly at odds. Another reason is that anthropologists have not until recently paid careful attention to values. Educational theory is affected by both of these reasons. Its own widely varying theories support an equally wide range of opposing views of the role of values, but attempts to relate these views to the live issues of teaching and learning in real cultures have frequently been sterile. Still, it is my impression that today both education and anthropology are increasingly eager to tackle the problem.

In anthropological theory, one of the most promising approaches may prove to be through the personality-and-culture movement. The contributions of such diverse experts in the psychological sciences as Geza Roheim, Abram Kardiner, Lawrence K. Frank, Harry Stack Sullivan, Gardner Murphy, and of anthropologists such as Margaret Mead, A. Irving Hallowell, Anthony F. C. Wallace (1961), and others earlier mentioned, have widened and deepened the concept of cultural values even when they have not always sought to single them out for sustained examination. The immediate explanation, no doubt, is that values for all of these scholars tend, on the one hand, to be grounded in the energies of human beings—in what are variously referred to as needs, wants, drives, interests, desires—and, on the other hand, to be molded by the environment of nature and culture. Thus despite disagreement and uncertainty at many points, the personality-and-culture movement serves to locate the problem where educational theory is, in turn, only starting to cope seriously with it—in scientifically ascertainable realms of discourse and investigation.

So far as I have been able to pursue the concept of values in contemporary anthropological sources, two statements have impressed me most. The first, by Kluckhohn (1952) with the help of others, is weakened by terms like "somehow" and "in some senses" which often threaten to beg the precise points at issue. Nevertheless, the statement attempts painstakingly to formulate a theory of values based upon recent investigations both by philosophers and social scientists. I select only a few highlights.

Kluckhohn's key definition, in the context of a "general theory of action," is this: "A value is a conception, explicit or implicit, distinctive of an individual or characteristic of a group, of the desirable which includes the selection from available modes, means, and ends of action" (p. 395). He analyzes this definition to mean, among other things, that (1) values are constructs involving both cognitive and cathectic factors; (2) they are potentially but not always actually verbalized; (3) while primarily cultural products they are uniquely expressible by each individual and each group; (4) because particular desires may be either disvalued or valued, it is essential to make sure that values are equated rather with the desirable, defined according to the "requirements of both personality and sociocultural system for order, the need for respecting the interests of others and of the group as a whole in social living" (p. 399); (5) selection among available alternative values are attachable to both the means and ends of action. This general conception has unusual significance for educators unwilling to settle for the easy notion of education as transmission of values: it invites them to treat value determination and implementation as, at least partially, also a conscious, selective, and creative enterprise of man in culture.

In trying to classify values, Kluckhohn finds that they may be grouped into such dimensions as modality, content, intent, generality, intensity, explicitness, extent, and organization. Of all these dimensions, perhaps the most pertinent for educational theory is that of "extent," which grapples with the old but lively issue of the relativity versus universality of values. Kluckhohn is dubious of the position, popularized by Benedict (1934) and others, that values are purely relative to the particular culture which supports them. While recognizing that the problem of universal values has not as yet been attacked at all adequately by social scientists, he nonetheless contends that some values—reciprocity, control of mere impulse, respect for human life, for example—are in general considered desirable by all known cultures. His review with Kroeber (1952, pp. 174 ff.) is careful to insist that neither universality nor relativity is a sufficient category: "Both perspectives are true and important, and no false either-or antinomy must be posed between them." Nevertheless, "the phrase 'a common humanity' is in no sense meaningless." Judgments about value can be "based both upon cross-cultural evidence as to the universalities in human needs, potentialities, and fulfillments and upon natural science knowledge with which the basic assumptions of any philosophy must be congruent."

The importance of this view of the dimension of "extent" is made clearer by the second statement, prepared by Bidney (1953b). While there is much here, too, that cannot be summarized, I call particular attention to his repudiation of extreme relativism. After tracing "the concept of value in modern anthropology" all the way from Rousseau and other philosophers of the Enlightenment down to the present day, Bidney develops his own position (p. 698):

> The choice is no longer between a romantic cultural pluralism and a fixed evolutionary absolutism but rather between a world in perpetual crisis and a world order based on rational principles capable of winning the adherence of the nations of the world. . . . So long as anthropology remains at the descriptive stage, which is the first stage of empirical science, anthropologists may rest content with cultural pluralism, on the ground that they do not wish to overstep the bounds of scientific fact. But if anthropology is to attain the stage of making significant generalizations . . . then comparative studies of cultures must be made with a view to demonstrating universal principles of cultural dynamics and concrete rational norms capable of universal realization.

These words might have been written by an educational re-constructionist. Borrowing much from progressivism as always, he too rejects absolutist theories of value held by essentialist-peren-nialist educators and widely indoctrinated today both by secular and parochial schools. He too, however, denies that relativism is the only possible alternative to these theories. With Bidney, the reconstructionist searches for a way to build empirical and hence temporal universals amidst the admitted relativity of values—universals emerging with the help of cross-cultural investigations such as those of G. P. Murdock (1945) that search for the "com-mon denominator of cultures."

While reconstructionism is a decidedly unfinished theory, I should like to select four features of its emerging conception of values (cf. Brameld, 1956, 1957, 1959, 1961) where close co-opera-tion with anthropological theory would conceivably benefit both sides. It should be emphasized, however, that these features are selected not to proselytize for a particular outlook but solely to illustrate further how the two disciplines of anthropology and education may converge around a common issue. Other theories than reconstructionism might have been chosen to make the same point.

One feature is the effort of reconstructionists to define values as, in essence, "want-satisfactions"—an effort reflecting the in-fluence of, among others, W. L. Thomas, Ralph Barton Perry, and Bronislaw Malinowski. Here Kluckhohn's treatment of the role of the "desirable" and of "selection" would, I am sure, greatly re-fine the reconstructionist conception. Also, the negative answer of Dorothy Lee (1948) to her own question, "Are basic needs ultimate?" should contribute further to its refinement by calling attention to the cultural values that underlie needs and wants themselves. One might then argue (to paraphase Veblen's amusing dictum, "Invention is the mother of necessity") that values are the mother of needs. Perhaps still more precise formulation, however, would recognize the polarity of the two terms. For, as Kluck-hohn (1952, p. 428) observes, "the relationship between a value system and a need or goal system is necessarily complex. Values *both* rise from and create needs."

A second feature is the normative generalization, "social-self-realization"—a high-level abstraction for the most encompassing universal value. This term might meet Lee's objection that needs are given merely as a list. Suggesting a Gestalt of want-satisfactions in which both personal and group values interpenetrate, it epitomizes much of the same affirmative viewpoint to be found in the culturally oriented psychoanalyst, Erich Fromm (1947).

Third, reconstructionism emphasizes the role of "social consensus" in value formulation. Social-self-realization, for example, always involves tacit or open agreement among participants in a culture that here, indeed, is the guiding norm of their conduct. The necessity of such agreement as intrinsic to the process and product of valuation is insufficiently considered either by anthropology or by education. It is only mentioned in Kluckhohn's statement, for example; and although consensus as an explicit concept enters into the writings of Herskovits (1948, e.g., p. 575), even he does not appear to have profited widely from the research of Kurt Lewin (1948) and other "field" theorists in the social sciences who are concerned more or less directly with the import of that concept. Yet, any effort to establish a defensible conception of universal values is, I suggest, singularly in need of the consensus principle. If Bidney is right in his demand for values "capable of winning the adherence of the nations of the world," anthropology and education will have to concern themselves with how and to what degree such adherence can be attained. Implicit in the concept is also, of course, the necessity and privilege of dissent.

Fourth, reconstructionism asks whether the concept of "myth" may not carry unassessed significance for a mature theory of cultural values. Here philosophers like Cassirer as well as anthropologists could provide additional guidance. Not only might they point to the dangers and limitations of mythical values in past and present cultures; they might help also to clarify the issue of whether there is still not a legitimate place for affectively toned, poetically expressed, but rationally defensible dramatizations of twentieth-century culture—dramatizations that could serve to magnetize the humane goals now so urgently required to neutralize the fascination of totalitarian mythologies.

Little further need be said here of the relevance of a metaculturology of knowledge for the problem of values. It is implicit throughout the discussion above. Yet, as in the case of cultural process, it is difficult to believe that either anthropological or educational theorists are frequently concerned with the questions of how far and in what ways ideological motivations, for example, may be operating surreptitiously upon their own value judgments and commitments. One of Bidney's (1953b, pp. 688 f.) too rare comments on this crucial point illustrates the kind of needed interpretation to which I refer. Speaking of Benedict, Boas, and cultural relativists in general, he says:

> In retrospect, it appears that American anthropologists continued to reflect the prevailing attitude of their democratic society. As liberals and democrats, they merely accentuated tendencies inherent in their culture but professed to have derived their "higher tolerance" from a comparative study of primitive cultures. They uncritically assumed the value of cultural differences and their mutual compatibility. . . . Had they thought in terms of the possible incompatibility and conflict of ideologies . . . they would not have labored under the naïve optimism of cultural laissez-faire. It has taken the impact of the second World War to shake this romantic cultural optimism and to awaken anthropologists to the reality of cultural crises and to the need for cultural integration on a world scale.

Cultural relativism, no less than cultural absolutism or any other theory of values held by educators and anthropologists, is itself conditioned by the cultural matrix of patterns and forces within which it is expressed, rejected, or espoused.

V

For the concluding problem, I have chosen cultural integration, referred to by Bidney above, mainly because it serves to tie together numerous strands earlier considered.

Although "integration" is itself a term of diverse meanings, the focal problem it generates is evident enough. On what demonstrable grounds, if any, can we hope to fashion a theory and program of education-and-culture that will organize, unify, harmonize the bewildering multiplicities of knowledge, values, practices, and beliefs that characterize an age of overspecialization, cross-purposes, and strife?

The concern of educators with this question is illustrated today by the current debate over "general education." There is widespread agreement that something must be done about the chaos of departments, techniques, courses, and standards that clutter both the lower and higher levels of the schools. Yet when one scans the specific proposals for curing the evils that flow from this eclecticism and confusion, one is struck by equally widespread disagreement as to what kind of general education is most desirable. Perennialists advocate classical curricula based largely on "great books," a faculty psychology, and a more or less freely admitted metaphysics derived from Aristotle. Essentialists, rearrange traditional classifications and tone them up with a few cautious concessions to recent trends in curricula and techniques. Progressivists and reconstructionists advocate various forms of the "core curriculum" which reflects the Gestalt influence: central concern is with clusters of problems regarded as vital to young people living in a period of rapid transition. None of these positions, however, seems to have inquired at all thoroughly into what anthropological theory might offer by way of fresh criteria, and this despite the fact that various educational theorists would agree that cultural experience should provide some or all of those criteria.

It is helpful, I believe, to consider the problem in two main dimensions—integration as spatial order and as temporal order—each of which is, of course, polar to the other. By spatial order, I mean the holistic relations of cultures and subcultures viewed in horizontal and vertical cross-sections. By temporal order, I mean those same relations viewed as historical and sequential continuities and discontinuities.

Of several possible concepts, two—"pattern" and "social class"—may be chosen to illustrate the spatial dimension of culture. Kroeber's (1952, pp. 92 f.) definition of patterns is authoritative: they are "nexuses of culture traits which have assumed a definite and coherent structure, which function successfully, and which acquire major historic weight and persistence." They may either cut across cultures, as in the case of "Hebraic-Christian-Mohammedan monotheism" and "plow agriculture"; or, as in

Benedict's models, they may coincide with indigenous, whole cultures (pp. 90–92). The other term, social class, refers to status levels as developed most conspicuously by W. L. Warner (1941) —a social class being defined in major part as "the largest group of people whose members have intimate access to one another. . . . Class is present in a community when people are placed by the values of the group itself at general levels of inferiority and superiority. . . ." (Cf. Mayer 1953; Warner, Havighurst, Loeb, 1944, p. 19.)

Although educational theory has undoubtedly been influenced more by the second of these two concepts, one may doubt whether either pattern or social class has been considered seriously by educators to exemplify a fresh and productive approach to the problem of integration itself. Yet the need for this approach must surely seem axiomatic to any anthropologist: an ordered general education must first of all incorporate, cope with, and evaluate the orders discernible in cultures. Thus these two concepts, combined of course with others, could help to crystallize new curricular designs dependent, first of all, upon the observable relations of real people living in real cultures—designs cutting both horizontally through groups and national boundaries (cf. Mead, 1953), and vertically through layers such as status, class, and caste (cf. Davis, Gardner, 1941).

The polar dimension, temporal order, points to the dynamic factor of integration. It is a factor that demands recognition of the endless flow of cultural events through the past, into the present, and toward the future. Most anthropologists today reject any semblance of inherent progress in this flow, as indeed they have rejected the earlier "evolutionary" theory of culture. Few if any, however, have ever denied the indispensable value of history. The understandable reaction of Boas and his school against the speculative character of "evolutionary" anthropology is now being qualified in the direction of more balanced views, such as those of the English archaeologist, V. Gordon Childe (1951) and the historical theories of Kroeber (cf. 1952, pp. 118 ff). The latter has, indeed, gone so far as to cite approvingly the opinion of Eduard Meyer that anthropology, being "the study of the general . . . forms of human life and development," is a more proper term for that study than the philosophy of history (p. 76). Kroeberian contributions of great value include the effort to synchronize history and science on a "sliding-scale," as opposed to the traditional dichotomy of the two disciplines, and the hypothesis that one may profitably concentrate upon "cross-sectional moments" of history in such a way as to subordinate time for purposes of characterizing the forms and patterns of a given period of culture.

Both education and anthropology itself could, nevertheless, benefit from the possibilities of enriching the concept of integration afforded by recent philosophies of history. Some attention, to be sure, has been paid to Spengler and others mentioned above. Also, it is interesting to note that Kroeber, in holding that history is properly interpretative and reconstructive, expresses much the same general view as the English philosopher of history, R. G. Collingwood (1946), among others. On the whole, however, interdisciplinary explorations of this sort remain in the future. In terms of general education, the need for such explorations to revitalize the function of history in high-school and college curricula is acute indeed. The sterile courses now littering typical programs should be discarded in favor of creative, comparative interpretations of the great movements and struggles of cultures through time—interpretations that utilize Kroeber's (1944) "configurations of culture growth," Northrop's (1946) "undifferentiated esthetic continuum" of Oriental cultures, Mumford's (1941) pendulum of "renewal," Toynbee's (1939) "challenge-and-response," and many other galvanizing and synthesizing concepts that could invigorate and stretch the youthful mind.

One final concept from anthropology—"configuration"—highlights the dialectical character of spatial and temporal order. While the term is often used synonymously with "pattern," it more often tends now to connote culture as a "way of life" or, as Sapir (1949, pp. 548 ff.) puts it, "deep-seated culture patterns" that "are not so much known as felt, not so much capable of conscious description as naïve practice . . ." A configuration is the implicit aesthetic design, the theme, of a culture. Clearly, also, it relates to "value-orientations" discussed in Kluckhohn's (1952, p. 411) statement on values mentioned earlier; there they are defined as "a generalized and organized conception, influencing behavior, of nature, of man's place in it, of man's relations to man, and of the desirable and nondesirable as they relate to man-environment and interhuman relations."

Configurations then embrace and deepen, on the one hand, both the horizontal and vertical interrelations of culture, and, on the other hand, their historical interrelations. They apply either to a fairly homogeneous subculture, such as the Navaho Indian, or to a heterogeneous culture, such as the Japanese. That configurations are one of the chief reasons both for the stubbornness and ubiquity of ethnocentricism is fairly obvious. With all their subtleties and complexities, however, they point to a new concept of integration for educational theory. For one thing, they enable us to perceive that cultural reality, process, and value are all encompassed by that concept. For another, they suggest a possible fusion of the traditionally honorific notion of culture, laden as it is with the values of the "cultivated" carrier, and the scientific conception of culture as the inclusive view of the environment fashioned by man. For still another, they complement the concept of myth as a cautious aid in envisaging the needed goals of modern life.

But perhaps the most exciting of all implications in the concept of configuration is the likelihood that it can eventually assist anthropologists and educators in the formulation of an operationally incisive metaculturology of knowledge. The insistence of Sapir upon the unconscious or covert meanings inherent in culture as a way of life calls our attention in a different way to the elusive assumptions that govern all attempts to express those meanings. In our time, the problem of adequate expression is especially difficult. All of us are likely to be caught in the whirlpools of fear and uncertainty generated, in turn, by the speed of acculturation and the threat of totalitarian power, of moral disintegration, and of planetary war. But few of us are sufficiently aware of the grim contradictions between those explicit credos endorsed by governments and schools, and those implicit values and similar beliefs expressed in overt conduct (cf. Myrdal, 1944).

The question still remains, of course, (a) whether education is able to do anything fundamental about such contradictions, and (b) if it is able, whether it should. The first part of this question was anticipated in discussing the reality of culture. If one tends to hold a *sui generis* view of culture, then one is likely also to hold that education can accomplish little except to conform with and endorse already given cultural configurations. If, however, one holds an operational view, then it is entirely plausible to contend that education can play a constructive part in enunciating and acting upon the problems generated by those configurations.

The second part of the question brings us back to the statement by Sapir with which our discussion of configurations began. After delineating the meaning of "the unconscious patterning of behavior" in culture, he concludes with the following passage:

> No matter where we turn in the field of social behavior, men and women do what they do, and cannot help but do, not merely because they are built thus and so, or possess such and such differences of personality . . . but very largely because they have found it easiest and aesthetically most satisfactory to pattern their conduct in accordance with more or less clearly organized forms of behavior. . . . It is sometimes necessary to become conscious of the forms of social behavior in order to bring about a more serviceable adaptation to changed conditions, but I believe it can be laid down as a principle of far-reaching application that in the normal business of life it is useless and even mischievous for the individual to carry the conscious analysis of his cultural patterns around with him. That should be left to the student whose business it is to understand these patterns. A healthy unconsciousness of the forms of socialized behavior to which we are subject, is as necessary to society as is the mind's ignorance, or better, unawareness, of the workings of the viscera to the health of the body. . . . We must learn to take joy in the larger freedom of loyalty to thousands of subtle patterns of behavior that we can never hope to understand in explicit terms . . . [pp. 588 f.].

Now this is a disturbing argument, certainly, to anyone who takes a transformative view of culture and of education as an instrument of culture. It can be construed as an invitation to relegate efforts to examine and express the premises of any culture solely to experts. It can be construed as an invitation, also, to leave the rest of us blissfully ignorant of what our culture most deeply means, and hence insensitive to its disparities, its lags, its obsolescences. If Sapir were merely to mean that we cannot and should not always, at every moment, be conscious of cultural configurations he would, of course, be right. Cultural like individual experience is, in Dewey's terms, immediate as well as mediate or reflective. But it is clear that Sapir does not mean this merely. Rather, he implies a dualistic thesis: on the one side, there are the few who are alone competent to delve into the mysterious depths of unconscious culture and on the other side, the many who are incompetent.

Such a position, the motivations of which might themselves benefit by exposure to a metaculturology of knowledge, is untenable in a democratic culture—or even in one that might become democratic. However, gigantic the task, however frequent the failures, a culture of this kind is one that must be understood, genuinely understood, by the largest possible proportion of those who carry its burdens, who hold ultimate responsibility for its failures and achievements, its means and ends. Hence utmost consciousness of configurational order is likewise their responsibility.

There are, I suggest, at least five norms by which education must be guided if it is to be seriously concerned with that kind of order. The first is for the schools of each culture to formulate as clearly and explicitly as they are able their present implicit premises—premises which are, of course, more or less precisely those of their respective cultures. The second is to consider wherein their resultant formulations appear outworn, inconsistent, or otherwise wanting in view of the transformations now occurring in economic, religious, and other spheres of life. The third is to experiment with restatements that more honestly enunciate their actual as against traditionally professed configurations, and to implement these restatements through integrated policies and programs. The fourth is to provide for comparative studies of the results, by as many informal as well as formal educational agencies of as many cultures as possible. The final aim is to achieve not only a whole array of educational formulations that have profited by critical interaction, but also a unified international formulation that accepts common principles, common objectives, and common tasks for education everywhere on earth.

These five norms, difficult and gigantic though they are, may not be as remote as at first they seem. Sporadic and fumbling efforts along similar lines are already under way, both in the schools of various countries and in commissions of the United Nations Educational, Scientific, and Cultural Organization. One trouble with many of these efforts has been, that they have often been superficial because unwilling or unable to penetrate to the covert level where the real problem of configuration lies. Moreover, partly because of a dearth of close co-operation between educators, on the one side, and anthropologists, on the other, there has been a failure to perceive that any successful effort to reformulate a unified conception of education for our age must incorporate what we may now call three dimensions of cultural order. These are: the horizontal-vertical dimension of culture in space, the historical dimension of culture in time, and the "qualitative" dimension of configuration which compounds the first two into an integrated whole—an aesthetic design for a modern philosophy of education-and-culture.

References

Benedict, Ruth, 1934, *Patterns of Culture*. Boston: Houghton Mifflin Company.

Bidney, David, 1953*a*, *Theoretical Anthropology*. New York: Columbia University Press.

———, 1953*b*, "The Concept of Value in Modern Anthropology," in A. L. Kroeber, ed., *Anthropology Today*. Chicago: University of Chicago Press, pp. 682–99.

Brameld, Theodore, 1955, *Philosophies of Education in Cultural Perspective*. New York: Holt, Rinehart and Winston, Inc.

———, 1956, *Toward a Reconstructed Philosophy of Education*. New York: Holt, Rinehart and Winston, Inc.

———, 1957, *Cultural Foundations of Education*. New York: Harper & Row, Publishers.

———, 1959, *The Remaking of a Culture: Life and Education in Puerto Rico*, New York: Harper & Row, Publishers. Part Four.

————, 1961, *Education for the Emerging Age.* New York: Harper & Row, Publishers. Part Two.

Cassirer, Ernst, 1944, *An Essay on Man.* New Haven, Conn.: Yale University Press.

Childe, V. Gordon, 1951, *Man Makes Himself.* New York: Mentor Books.

Collingwood, R. G., 1946, *The Idea of History.* New York: Oxford University Press.

Curti, Merle, 1953, *The Social Ideas of American Educators.* New York: Charles Scribner's Sons.

Davis, Allison, Gardner, B. B., and Gardner, Mary R., 1941, *Deep South.* Chicago: University of Chicago Press.

Dewey, John, 1916, *Democracy and Education.* New York: The Macmillan Company.

————, *Freedom and Culture,* New York: G. P. Putnam's Sons.

Frank, Jerome, 1945, *Fate and Freedom.* New York: Simon and Schuster, Inc.

Friess, Horace, 1950, "Philosophies of Culture," in Vergilius Ferm, ed., *A History of Philosophical Systems.* New York: Philosophical Library, Inc., pp. 588–97.

Fromm, Erich, 1947, *Man for Himself.* New York: Holt, Rinehart and Winston, Inc.

Harris, William T., 1901, *Psychological Foundations of Education.* New York: Appleton-Century-Crofts, Inc.

Herskovits, Melville J., 1948, *Man and His Works.* New York: Alfred A. Knopf, Inc.

Johnson, Charles S., 1943, "Education and the Cultural Process: Introduction to the Symposium," in Charles S. Johnson, ed., *Education and the Cultural Process.* Chicago: University of Chicago Press, pp. 1–4.

Kluckhohn, Clyde, 1949, *Mirror for Man.* New York: McGraw-Hill Book Company, Inc.

————, 1952, "Values and Value-Orientations in the Theory of Action: An Exploration in Definition and Classification," in Talcott Parsons and Edward L. Shils, eds., *Toward a General Theory of Action.* Cambridge, Mass.: Harvard University Press, pp. 338–433.

Kroeber, Alfred L., 1944, *Configurations of Culture Growth.* Berkeley, Calif.: University of California Press.

————, 1948, *Anthropology.* New York: Harcourt, Brace & World, Inc.

————, 1952, *The Meaning of Culture*. Chicago: University of Chicago Press.

————, ed., 1953, *Anthropology Today*. Chicago: University of Chicago Press.

Kroeber, Alfred L., and Clyde Kluckhohn, 1952. *Culture: A Critical Review of Concepts and Definitions*. Cambridge, Mass.: Peabody Museum.

Lee, Dorothy, 1948, "Are Basic Needs Ultimate?" *Journal of Abnormal and Social Psychology*, XLIII: 391–95.

Lewin, Kurt, 1948, *Resolving Social Conflicts*. New York: Harper & Row, Publishers.

Linton, Ralph, ed., 1945, *The Science of Man in the World Crisis*. New York: Columbia University Press.

Malinowski, Bronislaw, 1944, *A Scientific Theory of Culture and Other Essays*. Chapel Hill, N.C.: University of North Carolina Press.

Mannheim, Karl. 1936. *Ideology and Utopia*. New York: Harcourt, Brace & World, Inc.

Mayer, Kurt, 1953, "The Theory of Social Classes." *Harvard Educational Review*, XXIII: 149–69.

Mead, Margaret, 1953, "National Character," in A. L. Kroeber ed., *Anthropology Today*. Chicago: University of Chicago Press, pp. 642–67.

Mumford, Lewis, 1941, *The Condition of Man*. New York: Harcourt, Brace & World, Inc.

Murdock, George P., 1945, "The Common Denominator of Cultures," in Ralph Linton, ed., *The Science of Man in the World Crisis*. New York: Columbia University Press, pp. 123–42.

Myrdal, Gunnar, 1944, *An American Dilemma*. New York: Harper & Row, Publishers.

Northrop, F. S. S., 1946, *The Meeting of East and West*. New York: The Macmillan Company.

Opler, Morris, 1947, "Cultural Alternatives and Educational Theory," *Harvard Educational Review*, XVII: 28–44.

Raup, Bruce, George E. Axtelle, Kenneth D. Benne, and B. Othanel Smith, 1950, *The Improvement of Practical Intelligence*. New York: Harper & Row, Publishers.

Riesman, David, 1950, *The Lonely Crowd*. New Haven, Conn.: Yale University Press.

Sapir, Edward, 1949, "The Unconscious Patterning of Behavior in Society," in David B. Mandelbaum, ed., *Selected Writings of*

Edward Sapir. Berkeley: University of California Press, pp. 544–59.

Sorokin, Pitirim A., 1941, *The Crisis of Our Age*. New York: E. P. Dutton & Co., Inc.

Toynbee, Arnold, 1939, *A Study of History*. New York: Oxford University Press.

Wallace, Anthony F. C., 1961, *Culture and Personality*. New York: Random House, Inc.

Warner, W. L., R. J. Havighurst, and M. B. Loeb. 1944. *Who Shall Be Educated?* New York: Harper & Row, Publishers.

Warner, W. L., and P. S. Lunt, 1941. *The Social Life of a Modern Community*. New Haven: Yale University Press.

White, Leslie. 1949a, "Ethnological Theory," pp. 357–84, in R. W. Sellars, V. J. McGill and Marvin Farber, eds., *Philosophy for the Future*. New York: The Macmillan Company.

———, 1949b, *The Science of Culture*. New York: Farrar, Straus and Cudahy, Inc.

Part II

Education in
American Culture

Preview: This section, "Education in American Culture," focuses on the educational process in our own society. It implements some of the most significant propositions developed in Part I. Contemporary American society might seem an inappropriate subject for anthropologists, whose customary field is usually thought to be a remote tribe or folk community. But these papers are authentic anthropological approaches to problems that would be meaningful to most professional cultural anthropologists. They are decidedly meaningful in the educator's frame of reference.

One of the themes in this section that gives it unity and focus is that of cultural transmission in a context of conflicting values. Rhoda Métraux sets the stage with her chapter on values, which she sees as very pervasive in educational action and theory because they are central themes in American culture and thus give education in our society some degree of unity. In "Education in a Transforming American Culture" I attempt to show how very different, in fact virtually antithetical values may exist side by side in our culture, partly because our way of life is undergoing very rapid change, and how this situation affects educational action. Métraux's interpretation and mine are not at odds despite the fact that one stresses unity and the other conflict. I am dealing with values that divide people and groups interacting within the very broad framework of agreement that Métraux discusses. Both of these papers attempt to define the value context in which cultural transmission occurs in our society. Little is known on an empirical basis about American value systems, but these interpretations appear to be steps in the right direction and provide a useful backdrop for considerations to follow.

My paper on "The Transmission of American Culture" follows logically from the position established in the first two. It sharpens the focus on cultural transmission by showing how the teacher activates certain educational channels and neglects or shuns others as a consequence of his own cultural background, educational experience, and value set, and how this unintended selectivity may defeat his professed educational goals. Dorothy Lee's analysis of the teaching of American culture in home economics programs reinforces this theme by showing how the implementation of these programs, as described in manuals, may contradict the stated purposes of the Home Economics experience for young girls, where the feminine roles in our society are explicitly taught. Jules Henry advances the theme that has by now emerged—that the unintended consequences of educational action may be entirely divergent, in fact antithetical, to the intended goals of the action and that this paradox is a function of the cultural setting in which education takes place. He shows how a well-intended teacher in an elementary school classroom manipulates the situation in such a way that a witch-hunt syndrome ordinarily latent in our culture is activated in the classroom.

To many readers the papers just previewed may prove disturbing. It is important to remember that they all deal with specific situations that were selected for study because they were interesting. What is interesting to the anthropologist observer is not always most pleasing to others. The self-defeating dualities in cultural transmission reflect value conflicts and discrepancies between real behavior and ideals in the social and cultural environment of the schools. They are of compelling interest to the observer interested in cultural dynamics and the relations of individuals, social institutions, and cultural patterning. And by achieving awareness of the problem the educator may gain some intelligent control over the consequences of education.

In his second chapter, "Spontaneity, Initiative, and Creativity in Suburban Classrooms," Jules Henry describes with the objectivity of the anthropologist a very different kind of situation than that described in his first chapter. The teachers in the classroom he describes control individual and group activity by skillful play upon affect. It is clear that Henry regards the cultural milieu of the suburban school as the source of this pattern of control. So the cultural context provides both the "witch-hunt syndrome" and the "control by affect" pattern. It also provides many others, some of which balance these two, and education as a process of cultural transmission projects them all into the classroom at some time or another.

The papers on the role of the school administrator by Spindler and on cultural shock and student transition by Werner might seem because of their topics to constitute a sharp break with the others. This is not the case. My paper starts with the dualities and conflicting value patterns in American culture and projects them into the expectations of various audiences that view and judge the performance of the school administrator. It shows how the performance of the administrator is a function of these expectations and of other forces in his environment, such as the formal, bureaucratic organization of the school, and how his individual personality must also be taken into account. Fred Werner applies some principles of cultural dynamics to an analysis of the experience of the college student who is drawn from a social environment that is discontinuous with the culture and values of higher education. His approach is consistent with the emphasis on conflict in cultural patterning and its resolution.

The last two chapters in Part II by Solon Kimball and Martin Loeb are in a calculated respect divergent from the others in their emphases. They focus more on the social and cultural environment of the educational process in our society than they do on educational activity in the classroom. They provide illumination of selected aspects of the setting of education. Kimball uncovers cultural assumptions about childhood and growing up in our society that are congruent with those independently described by Rhoda Métraux in the first paper in this section, but his emphasis is quite different and significant dimensions are added to the profile of these assumptions. Martin Loeb also deals with the cultural milieu in his documented contention that adolescent boys in our society, particularly those from middle-class homes, lack adequate masculine models and approved means of growing into the masculine role. This interpretation has most significant implications for education, since one of the primary responsibilities of education in any society, as Part III makes clear, is to transmit and reinforce models of the sex-linked roles that are functional in the society.

6 ———— *Rhoda Métraux*

Implicit and Explicit Values in Education and Teaching as Related to Growth and Development[*]

In this preface to our discussion, I shall do no more than to suggest certain values which are inherent in our attitudes toward education and, because it would seem to fit in best with our intentions, I shall refer mainly to American attitudes. Nevertheless, because much of what I shall say is so familiar as to be nearly invisible, I shall begin with an illustration from another culture, which may sharpen, through contrast, our view of ourselves.

The values of a culture are reflected in all its aspects, and each detail can be seen in its relationship to the larger whole. In traditional Chinese culture, for instance, calligraphy is much more than a means of setting down ideas—of writing history or making out a household marketing list or teaching the good life—it is also an art form, and some of the great classical scholars have also been poet-painter-writers. The training was a very long one. A little boy whose family might hope that one day he would be a scholar—a learned man, an artist, and perhaps the governor of a province—began to learn calligraphy when he was five or six years old. Even younger, he might have learned to recognize a few characters, made for him with bold brush strokes on bright red cards by his grandfather. Then he was taught to sit at a table, very straight—his head, his body, his feet, his left hand exactly placed, the brush poised in his right hand; and every day he copied models, the meaning of which no one explained to him, which he

* Reprinted from *The Merrill-Palmer Quarterly*, 2, 1955, 27–34, with permission.

did not "understand" perhaps for many years. This teaching was more than a skill; it was also a way of forming his moral character. If he continued to practice for ten years, twenty years, thirty years, if he mastered the styles of the great calligraphers, he might one day produce something of his own, original because of its strength and vigor. In traditional Chinese culture, not spontaneity but maturity was valued. This was reflected in the belief that learning and artistry took long years to come to flower, and in the linking of creativeness to mature strength and vigor. Moreover, the training of the classical writer was reflected in body movement; today, as one watches a Chinese man sitting and speaking, one can tell what kind of education he has had. The man who in his youth had a classical education, and who still values it, sits upright and easily poised, his hand gestures moving out from the center of his body. The rebel against classical education leans away from this central poise, his movements often out of balance. The young man who has attended only modern schools lounges like any other undergraduate. In these postural alterations we can see more than individual learning experience. We are given clues also to the effects of culture change, of changing values in education, upon the life of the individual.[1]

With this in mind, let us turn to an American situation. For the past several months I have attended a teaching clinic in a hospital in New York City. This has been part not of my research but of my own learning experience of work in a hospital setting. We meet once a week, a small group around a long table, and at each of the sessions one of the participants—it may be an internist, or a psychiatrist, or a medical student, presents a case. The patient comes in and is interviewed, so we can see for ourselves what manner of person this is, who has been described to us. Later any of us, participants or visitors, may ask questions or make suggestions to the physician who has the final responsibility. This clinic is part of a pioneering effort in the teaching of psychosomatic medicine, and the explicit emphasis is upon the wholeness of the individual. With great pride I was told that here the doctors are concerned not with isolated symptoms located somewhere in the body of a "36 year old white female," but with a person, a young woman with parents and brothers, a husband and children, and a unique life history including stressful experiences that have affected adversely her physical, mental, and emotional well-being. Here, in the presence of a group of specialists, the patient—by the shared knowledge of a life history, known and understood— is reconstituted as a whole living person. This is the expressed intention of the teaching. Implicit in it is our American valuation of the uniqueness of the individual and our sense that the total personality—capabilities and experiences, strengths and weaknesses— must be taken into account if we are to understand who someone is.

But listening and watching in that clinic I, who was a novice in a hospital, learned something quite different that also was implicit in the situation: namely, that such teaching can lead to the development of a multiple conscience in each of the participants. For there sat the students and with them around the table perhaps a dozen specialists, *simultaneously* focusing their trained attention upon the complicated problems of one sick person. So the medical student (as perhaps each of us for our work also) is learning for his future practice to hear not one voice of one teacher nor successively the voices of different teachers, but voices arranged in a kind of polyphony. Explicitly, this method of teaching gives back to the student understanding of the wholeness of the person he is observing. Implicitly it gives him also a sense of the wholeness of the approach. Ideally, it gives him a way to thinking, a way of placing his particular aptitudes and knowledge and experience in an inclusive context. And this too is one of the things we value in our kind of education. So, for instance, no matter how lost we may get in the maze of departmental specializations, we continue to trust, at the undergraduate level, the liberal arts type of education. Or at a much younger age level, with our first graders who are just learning to learn formal knowledge, we try to make this not a fragmented but a total experience in which counting and reading and writing and self-expression and social relationships and play and work are all interwoven. Or, in another context, anyone who has worked on an interdisciplinary research project and who has taken part in the struggle really to share materials, to fit all the bits into a meaningful whole, will understand—however different the superficial aspects—the patterning of teaching and learning in the clinic I have so briefly described.

Now I have given this illustration, taken from a rather unfamiliar setting, for two reasons. First, because this attempt to do a new kind of teaching in a medical school—to modify the relationship between teacher and student, to incorporate new knowledge into a method of work, to overcome difficulties that grew out of previous new knowledge, that is, the difficulties resulting from intense specialization—is shaped by ideas and beliefs inherent in our most general thinking about education. This sense of the uniqueness of the individual and of the need for integration is something we may temporarily lose in our attempts to solve other problems, and then we struggle to find it again.

Secondly, I have used this illustration because it places me as a kind of person thinking about and discussing values in education. One thing the anthropogist has learned is to place himself—for himself and others—inside the observations made. And, of course, I speak here as a cultural anthropologist, not as an educator. For, aside from my own training, my main connection with education has been as an indirect participant in the education of my children and some younger colleagues and as an observer, sometimes in American life, sometimes doing field work abroad, sometimes working with informants on a distant culture. So what I can do here is to point out what seem to be certain regularities in our thinking about education and to suggest how these are linked up to our thinking about human growth and development.

It should be said, however, that it is highly artificial to separate our ideas about education and our ideas about growth and development. For one of the most remarkable achievements in our thinking about human beings in the last 50 years or so has been a recognition of the systematic circularity of the learning and teaching processes and of the processes of growth and development. What is new is not the understanding that personality and character are shaped by learning—we have only to turn to any of the old utopias to see that—but that learning and growth are related aspects of man's biological nature. Our new knowledge of maturation and our new understanding of character formation—whether based on our own culture or more broadly on compari-

sons of cultural materials—have transformed the questions asked
and the answers given about learning and teaching; and re-inter-
pretations of educational problems have led us to refine our knowledge of growth. So we have one kind of circularity imposed on
another. No less remarkable has been the speed with which we
have incorporated this new knowledge into our educational thinking and, though often superficially and unevenly, into educational practice. Some years ago we could feel as an intensely
dramatic climax in an autobiography the moment when Helen
Keller's teacher managed to establish communication with her.[2]
Now a large movie audience can feel the dramatic excitement of
the moment when, in the movie version of *The Blackboard Jungle*,
the young teacher catches the imagination of a classroom group
of young hoodlums.[3] Some awareness of the relationship between
growth and learning is essential to our recognition of both of
these situations as dramatic climaxes.

One thing which this linking up of teaching and learning and
growth and development has meant for us is a new sense of the
continuity of experience throughout life. In the cultures from
which our own traditions are derived, it has been usual to break
up education into two main aspects that can be called "up-bring-
ing" and "schooling." In German the terms are *Erziehung* and
Unterricht; in French they are *formation* and *instruction.*[4] Though
in fact they overlap, both aspects of education, so viewed, are
highly compartmentalized. There is little need, for example, for
French or German parents and teachers to have contact or communication with one another. And both aspects of education are
essentially time-limited, although the time span may be different
for the two. But in American culture—despite struggles at different times to separate or to bring together home and school—
the lines between upbringing at home and education in school have
long been blurred. And now, thinking in terms of growth and
development—when we have to include pre-natal influences at
least on the child's constitution and when we move from the new-
born infant's response to the ways it is wrapped, held, and fed to the
six-year-old's response to the school environment, to the student's
learning of skills, to the young mother's and father's responses to
their own six-year-old's learning in school—formal education

is even more fully incorporated into the whole experience of growing and learning. And, although we have very strong peer group feelings about education—so that we tend to feel that the proper place for a ten-year-old is in the fifth grade with other ten-year-olds—we also in American culture do not think of formal education as age-limited. So, in New York City, we have special adult education classes for foreigners who are barely literate, and we have places in our grade room classes for them: and we also have certificates of equivalence for adults who have not completed a stage of formal education, so that a mother can, so to speak, graduate from high school together with her eighteen-year-old daughter. What this means is that we do have a notion that "education" is something a person can get at any time of life. Furthermore, with the development of our understanding of growth and maturation, with its emphasis upon the child, upon things beginning, we have also begun to consider the possibilities of special kinds of learning for the aged, for those who have already retired. And therefore, however we approach the problem, it is difficult to visualize "education" as a separate entity.

But from another point of view, education, as we see it, is not at all circular but linear: education is progress, it takes us where we have never been before. Describing what we think higher education has done for us or should do for our children, we are likely to use such images as "new ways" and "open doors" and to picture the liberal arts college as a house with many doors *all* opening out onto the world; or we speak of "broad paths" or "new vistas" or "wider horizons."[5] Considering such images, we can recognize two things. Education is movement—movement forward and outward. And all these images express openness. We are no more willing to shut ourselves up in an ivory tower of learning than, in other circumstances, we are willing to be fenced in. Our conception of education is open-ended. We do not value learning or skills for their own sake, nor the scholar for the sake of his scholarship. We value education for the opportunities learning opens up, for the multiplicity of new directions. So, for example, the studies of American servicemen in World War II written up in *The American Soldier*[6] indicate that while educational status was a factor in a man's promotion, the servicemen themselves did not regard education in itself as an important means to advancement in the services. We think of education as open-ended because it gives the individual tools and skills and trained capacities and a reservoir of knowledge—and perhaps a little "know-how"; we think of the *lack* of education as a real limitation upon what a man can be, but we do not think education determines who a man can be. This open-endedness provides us with a kind of optimism about man's possibilities for development, both the individual and mankind. It fits in with our belief that we should work with an individual's particular strengths in his education and that we can, given special means, overcome at least in part the difficulties of the poorly endowed, the slow, the incapacitated.

When we think of education in American terms, teaching and learning are bound up in our minds not only with values and performance and dreams, with enriching our heritage, with developing skills that will shape a future as yet unknown, but also, continuously, with the making of new Americans. For we have believed that any individual, by wanting to do so, could become an American and, to a greater or lesser degree, could learn a whole new cultural orientation in a lifetime—a highly unusual belief. Implicit in this is our faith in—for we "believe in"—education and in the human being's continuing powers of adaptation that enable him, if he will, to learn and re-learn, to change from his past to a new present in which he continues as an individual. Partly for this reason, we have been extraordinarily self-conscious about our educational successes and failures and, on the whole, more articulate about more aspects of education than any other people I know about.

And just as we have felt that the individual could learn and re-learn without a break in continuity, without necessarily ever losing a sense of his personal identity (though we recognize as possibilities for those who get caught between two worlds—second generation Americans who do not know where they stand—either loss of identity or some kind of over-rigid identification that is not complete),[7] so too we have kept a kind of flexibility in thinking about education, a willingness to change content and method often and rapidly without fearing that those who have learned one kind of thing one way will necessarily be out of communication with those who have learned another kind of thing another way. We are ready and even eager to look around the world and select, whatever their original context, ways of learning that might add to the enjoyment of our children. We do not expect children to learn as their elders did, or even younger siblings as did their elder ones. Instead, we expect elders to make new adaptations and we expect a great deal of learning to take place within the peer group. This has had several consequences for education and for our interpretations of growth and development. For one thing, it means that our present has very shallow roots in the past. In fact, we are even losing the ability to think and feel with the imagery of natural growth that is appropriate to a sense of organic continuity. We are unlikely to think of a new flowering, a new harvest from an old tree. Change is more easily thought of in terms of a new version—this year's model of auto, a new model parent, a new model child, a phrasing which is more congenial to our whole preference for motor imagery.

It also means that we are, in a very real way, perpetual amateurs trying out new things because they are new to us in our own generation as well as because they are genuinely new, and exceedingly dependent on the experiments of our peers in making judgments about success. It is in this light that we must see our tremendous valuation of professionalized skills and of professionalized standards as guides. The importance of standards of excellence may not be so apparent when we think only about ourselves or compare ourselves to a people like the French with their high valuation of individual craftsmanship. But it becomes very clear when we look at some other people whose amateurism—if one may call it that—is not combined with an over-all conception of skill. So for instance, one could consider the culture of Montserrat, a small island in the Leeward Islands Colony of the British West Indies. The peasants of Montserrat have attempted, rather haphazardly, to jettison their whole past, to get rid of their folk tradition and to move into the modern world, at whose outer edge they feel they live. But there, in a sense, each man has been his own innovator and each attempts to interpret and place bits and pieces, to argue with all others about the reality of fragments seen this way or that. There is much emphasis upon "trying it out" and upon "doing your best," but as there is little sense of style in performance or of excellence, these people have come to accept fragmentation, uncertainty and amateurism as themselves making up a style of living which they cannot—and about this they are quite articulate—alter without going away from their island.[8]

There is also another consequence of our valuation of change and of flexibility in teaching and learning, and that is that we have a very continuous need for information, for facts about a new situation or a new idea or a new ethic. We can only act and act responsibly when our understanding is shaped by facts which we share with one another. This has deeply affected our ideas about the dissemination of news. It has influenced our programs of "learning by doing" in progressive education. It is important in any new national situation—such as we faced when rationing became necessary in World War II—when, in the beginning, people see the new in terms of an enormous variety of images; then it is possible to get responsible acceptance only when people are carefully briefed—are not merely told, "Be good, be good" or "Do this, do that," but are given facts on the basis of which they can make a choice and a commitment.[9] This insistence upon the importance of facts is basic in our particular valuation of reality testing, whether we are meeting a crisis, working out a research problem, or encouraging a toddler to move, to reach out, to taste and smell and touch the objects that make up his world.

In this brief paper I have attempted to indicate what some American values are in education. Looking at education not as an educator but as a cultural anthropologist, I have thought of these different things—our valuation of the uniqueness of the individual, our sense of the whole, our sense of continuity which does not necessarily imply continuity of content, our sense of the open-endedness of learning, our belief in the possibility of change and in its beneficence—as important themes in American culture which are expressed in various ways in education as in other aspects of living. I have not attempted to differentiate between what is made explicit and what remains implicit because in different contexts the same value may be expressed in one or the other way. Rather what I have tried to do is to suggest to you certain themes, certain values which we share as Americans and which are relevant to our thought and feeling and action whether we are concerned specifically with problems of education and teaching or with problems of growth and development or with the relationships of growth and education to our whole style of life.

References

1. For background material on Chinese child training and education, cf. Ruth Bunzel, 1950, *Explorations in Chinese Culture*. New York: Columbia University Research in Contemporary Cultures, dittoed. For an autobiographical description of classical education, cf. Chiang Yee, 1952, *A Chinese Childhood*. New York: John Day. The material on posture is taken from unpublished research in the Study Program on Human Health and the Ecology of Man: China, Cornell Medical College New York Hospital.
2. Keller, Helen, 1954 (First edition, 1902), *The Story of My Life*, New York: Doubleday & Company, Inc.
3. Hunter, Evan, 1955, *The Blackboard Jungle*. New York: Pocket Books. Screen version, Metro-Goldwyn-Mayer (1955). The screen version has picked up and amplified this theme, altering the whole emphasis of the story.
4. On German attitudes towards upbringing and education, cf. three articles by Rhoda Métraux in Margaret Mead and Martha Wolfenstein, 1955, *Child Rearing in Contemporary Cultures*. Chicago: University of Chicago Press. For France, cf. Rhoda Métraux and Margaret Mead, 1954, *Themes in French Culture, A Preface to a Study of French Community*. Stanford, Calif.: Stanford University Press.
5. Cautley, Patricia W., 1949, *AAUW Members Look at College Education, An Interim Report*. Washington, D.C.: American Association of University Women.
6. Stouffer, S. A., *et al.*, 1949–1950, *Studies in Social Psychology in World War, II*. 4 vols. Princeton, N.J.: Princeton University Press.
7. This is always a factor to be considered in understanding the American material on prejudice and on "the authoritarian

personality" as described, e.g., in the several volumes of *Studies in Prejudice*, edited by Max Horkheimer and Samuel H. Flowerman, 1949–50, New York: Harper & Row, Publishers.

8. Based on unpublished field work in Montserrat, B.W.I., 1953–1954, by Rhoda Métraux and Theodora M. Abel.

9. Based on qualitative attitude analyses made for the Committee on Food Habits, National Research Council, 1942–1943.

7——George D. Spindler

Education
in a Transforming
American Culture*

The American public school system, and the professional educators who operate it, have been subjected to increasingly strident attacks from the public and from within its own ranks. My premise is that these attacks can best be understood as symptoms of an American culture that is undergoing transformation—a transformation that produces serious conflict. I shall discuss this transformation as a problem in culture change that directly affects all of education and everyone identified with it.

The notion of social and cultural change is used persuasively, if carelessly, by too many writers to explain too much. Generalized allusions to technological change, cultural lag, the atomic age, the mass society, are more suggestive than clarifying. We must strike to the core of the change. My argument is that this core can best be conceived as a radical shift in values.

The anthropologist, and I speak as one but not for all, sees culture as a goal-oriented system. These goals are expressed, patterned, lived out by people in their behaviors and aspirations in the form of values—objects or possessions, conditions of existence features of personality or character, and states of mind, that are conceived as desirable, and act as motivating determinants of behaviors. It is the shifts in what I believe to be the core values in American culture, and the effect of these shifts on education today, that I wish to discuss. These shifts in values will be seen as the conditions of life to which education and educators, whether progressives, experimentalists, conservatives, or in-betweens, must

* Reprinted, with revision, from The Harvard Educational Review, XXV, 1955, 145–156, with permission.

adapt—and to which they are adapting, albeit confusedly. My emphasis within the value frame-work will be upon shifts in the conception of the desirable character type, since education can never be freed from the obligation to support, if not produce, the features of personality and social character deemed desirable in society.

There is a body of literature on American culture. M. Mead (1942), C. and F. Kluckhohn (1947), C. Kluckhohn (1949), L. Warner (1953, 1959), G. Gorer (1948), D. Riesman (1950), M. Lantis (1955), S. Lipset and L. Lowenthal (1961). These writings range from the highly intuitive to the observation-based. Though there is consensus, and a surprising degree of it, on the part of these students of American culture, little they say can be or is intended by them to be taken as empirically demonstrated. These writings are useful as a starting point but most emphasize static patterning in values more than change in values. To extend the factual baseline I have been collecting relevant data from college students for the past eight years. The sample consists of several hundred students, ranging in age from 19 to 57 years, mainly participants in professional education courses, and representing socio-economic strata describable as lower-middle to upper-middle class. The sample is as representative of this professional group and these economic strata as any regionally biased sample can be. I have used two simple value-projective techniques. The aim has been to find out what features of social character (the term I will use to designate those personality elements that are most relevant to social action) the students in the sample hold as being valuable and that presumably influence their behavior in classrooms. The first of these techniques is a series of 24 open-ended statements; such as "The individual is ———", "Intellectuals should ————", "All men are born ———". The second of these techniques is to require each student to write one brief paragraph describing his (or her) conception of the "Ideal American Boy".

I have subjected the responses of the students in the sample to a straight-forward content analysis—counting numbers of responses that fall into certain categories appearing from the data themselves. Perhaps some examples will illustrate both the techniques and the kinds of materials from which I am going to draw in the rest of this article.

From the open-ended sentence value-projective technique, results like these have been obtained: "All men are born ———", "equal" (70% of all responses), "wolves", "stupid", "dopes", "hot-blooded" (a miscellaneous negative category of 28%—provided mainly by females in the sample); "Artists are ———", "queer", "perverted", "nuts", "effeminate" (a negative-hostile category of 38% of all responses), "different", "people", "few", (a neutral category of 35%), "creative", "smart", "original", "interesting" (a positive category of 25%); "Intellectuals should ———", "be more sociable", "be more practical", "get down to earth" (a mildly derogative category of 36%), "keep it under cover", "drop dead", "shut up" (an openly hostile category of 20%), "apply their intellect", "study", "create", "think" (a neutral to positive category of 40%); Nudity is ———, "vulgar", "obscene", "profane", "repulsive" (a negative-moralistic category of 43%), "pleasant", "self-expressive", "beautiful", "healthy" (an enthusiastic-positive category of 20%), "depends on how interpreted", "alright in some places", "depends on who is looking" (a relativistic category of 30%).[1]

The values are self-evident, and do not call for discussion, as such, for the moment. What is more important is that this fairly homogeneous sample of students provides a wide range of response to each of these statements, excepting for the purposefully stereotyped "All men are born———." And not only is there a wide range of response evidenced, but many of the categories of response to a single statement can be considered as contradictions with respect to each other. This suggests that although there are clear modalities of values in this sample, there are also differences between people and groups of people in respect to what they believe is good.

The material gathered together as results from the "Ideal American Boy" technique are even more suggestive. A sentence-content analysis reveals that the desirable features of character are ranked in the following order, from highest number of mentions, to lowest number: He should be *sociable*, like people, and get along well with them; he must be *popular*, be liked by others; he is to be *well-rounded*, he can do many things quite well, but is

---

[1] Where percentages do not total 100 it is because various miscellanea are omitted.

not an expert at anything in particular; he should be *athletic* (but not a star), and *healthy* (no qualifications); he should be *ambitious* to succeed, and have clear goals, but these must be acceptable within limited norms; he must be *considerate of others*, ever-sensitive to their feelings about him and about events; he should be a *clean-cut Christian*, moral and respectful of God and parents; he should be *patriotic;* and he should demonstrate *average academic ability*, and *average intellectual capacity.*

These are the characteristics of the ideal American boy seen as most important by a modal number (about 40%) of the students in the sample. Leadership, independence, high intelligence, high academic ability, individuality, are mentioned relatively infrequently (in about 20% of the descriptive paragraphs). But individuals do vary in the pattern of characteristics that are combined in the paragraph. Some emphasize the high achievement and individualized characteristics just mentioned. Some include elements from the modal list and combine them with these latter items. There have also been some shifts in the modal features of the ideal type over the eight years of data collection. But the characteristics listed above are mentioned most frequently.

The implications seem clear. The keynote to the character type regarded as most desirable, and therefore constituting a complex of values, is *balance, outward-orientedness, sociability*, and *conformity* for the sake of adjustment. Individuality and creativity, or even mere originality, are not stressed in this conception of values. Introspective behavior is devaluated (intellectuals are suspicioned by many). Deviancy, it seems, is to be tolerated only within the narrow limits of sociability, of general outwardness, of conformity ("Artists are perverts"). The All-American boy is altogether adjusted.

The materials just cited not only serve to illustrate the technique, but more important for present purposes, indicate rather clearly the fabric of the value pattern that seems to be emerging as the dominant core of the social character values in American culture (providing one can assume, as I am here, that the middle-class culture is the core of our way of life—the pattern of norms against which lower and upper class cultures are seen as deviations). From this point on, I shall use the implications of these data without further explication of the factual baseline. The purpose is to sketch in bold strokes the major dimensions of culture change in our American society and relate them to the contretemps of modern public education and educators.

The statements to be made now about American values, their shift, and the effect on education, are based upon the varying responses of different age groups in the sample, upon person-to-person variation in responses, and upon variations in response and particularly contradictions of response within single individual protocols (the total set of responses for a single individual). On the basis of these kinds of data, in the context of wider observations on institutions and culture patterns in the United States, it appears that a major shift in American values is taking place.[2] I find it convenient to label this shift as being from *traditional* to *emergent,* though no basic cultural change of this kind is actually linear. The values thus dichotomized are listed under their respective headings below, with explanatory statements in parentheses.

TRADITIONAL VALUES	EMERGENT VALUES
Puritan morality (Respectability, thrift, self-denial, sexual constraint; a puritan is someone who can have anything he wants, as long as he doesn't enjoy it!)	*Sociability* (As described above. One should like people and get along well with them. Suspicion of solitary activities is characteristic.)
Work-Success ethic (Successful people worked hard to become so. Anyone can get to the top if he tries hard enough. So people who are not successful are lazy, or stupid, or both. People must work desperately and continuously to convince themselves of their worth.)	*Relativistic moral attitude* (Absolutes in right and wrong are questionable. Morality is what the group thinks is right. Shame, rather than guilt is appropriate.)

[2] In my formulation of value trends and the interpretation of my data I have been particularly influenced by the writings of David Riesman.

Individualism (The individual is sacred, and always more important than the group. In one extreme form, the value sanctions egocentricity, expediency, and disregard for other people's rights. In its healthier form the value sanctions independence and originality.)

Achievement orientation (Success is a constant goal. There is no resting on past glories. If one makes $9,000 this year he must make $10,000 next year. Coupled with the work-success ethic, this value keeps people moving, and tense.)

Future-time orientation (the future, not the past, or even the present, is most important. Time is valuable, and cannot be wasted. Present needs must be denied for satisfactions to be gained in the future.)

Consideration for others (Everything one does should be done with regard for others and their feelings. The individual has a built-in radar that alerts him to others' feelings. Tolerance for the other person's point of view and behaviors is regarded as desirable, so long as the harmony of the group is not disrupted.)

Hedonistic, present-time orientation (No one can tell what the future will hold, therefore one should enjoy the present—but within the limits of the well-rounded, balanced personality and group.)

Conformity to the group (Implied in the other emergent values. Everything is relative to the group. Group harmony is the ultimate goal. Leadership consists of group-machinery lubrication.)

American culture seems to be undergoing a confused transformation, producing many disjunctions and conflicts, from the traditional to the emergent value systems outlined above. It is probable that both value systems have been present and operating in American culture for some time. But recently, and under the impetus of World Wars, the pressures exerted by the "radical right" and the "radical left," the external communist threat, atomic insecurities, and a past history of "boom and bust", the tendencies in the emergent direction have gathered strength and appear to be on the way towards becoming the dominant value system of American culture. At the same time, there is a minority resurgence of extreme versions of the traditional values as some people reaffirm allegiance to them as a reaction to the threat of rapid culture change.

Like all major shifts and schisms in culture, this one has consequences for people. Culturally transitional populations, as anthropologists know from their studies of acculturating Indian tribes, Hindu villages, and Samoan communities (among others), are characterized by conflict, and in most severe form—demoralization and disorganization. Institutions and people are in a state of flux. Contradictory views of life are held by different groups and persons within the society. Hostilities are displaced, attacks are made on one group by another. And this applies as well to the condition of American culture—the context of American education.

The traditionalist may view the emergentist as "socialistic," "communistic," "spineless and soft-headed," or "downright immoral." The emergentist may regard the traditionalist as "hidebound," "reactionary," "selfish," or "authoritarian."[3] Most of what representatives of either viewpoint do may be regarded as insidious and destructive from the point of view of the other. The conflict goes beyond groups or institutions, because individuals in our transitional society are likely to hold elements of both value systems concomitantly. This is characteristic, as a matter of fact, of most students included in the sample described previously. There are few "pure" types. The social character of most is split, calling for different responses in different situations, and with respect to different symbols. So an ingredient of personal

---

[3] Irrespective of this kind of name-calling, the dichotomy of values employed in this analysis is not the same as "conservative" and "liberal" or politically "left" and "right." It is certainly very probable, for example, that some political liberals are traditionalists in respect to core cultural values.

confusion is added that intensifies social and institutional conflict.

I hypothesize that the attacks upon education, which were our starting point, and the confusion and failure of nerve characterizing many educators today, can be seen in clear and helpful perspective in the light of the conflict of traditional and emergent values, and particularly in the extremes of both forms that have been described. It is the heart of the matter. The task then becomes one of placing groups, institutions, and persons on a continuum of transformation from the one value system to the other. A simple diagram will aid comprehension of what is meant.

The diagram conveys the information that different groups operating in the context of relations between school and community, educator and public, occupy different positions on the value continuum, with varying degrees and mixtures of traditional and emergent orientations. It should be understood that the placements indicate hypothecated tendencies, that no one group representing any particular institution ever consists of "pure" value types, but that there is probably a modal tendency for the groups indicated to place on the transformation, or continuum line, in the way expressed in the diagram.

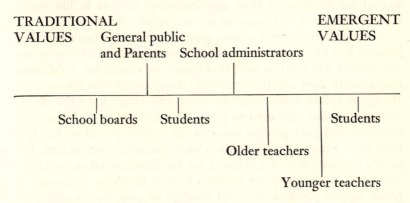

TRADITIONAL VALUES — General public and Parents — School administrators — EMERGENT VALUES

School boards — Students — Students — Older teachers — Younger teachers

School boards are placed nearest the *traditional* end of the continuum because such boards are usually composed of persons representing the power, *status-quo*, elements of the community, and of persons in the higher age ranges. They are therefore people who have a stake in keeping things as they are, who gained their successes within the framework of the traditional value system and consequently believe it to be good, and who, by virtue of their age, grew up and acquired their value sets during a period of time when American culture was presumably more tradition-oriented than it is today. They may be driven to extreme forms of traditionalism as a response to the pressures mentioned previously.

The general public and parent group, of course, contains many elements of varying value predilection. It is therefore unrealistic to place this public at any particular point in the value continuum. But I hypothesize that the public *tends* to be more conservative in its social philosophy than professional educators are. The placement to the left of center of the continuum takes on further validity if it is seen as a placement of that part of the public that is most vocal in its criticism of educators and education—since many of the criticisms made appear to spring out of value conflicts between traditionalist and emergentist positions. Parents complain that their children are not being taught the "three R's" (even when they are), that educators want to "socialize" the competitive system by eliminating report cards, that children are not taught the meaning of hard work. These all sound, irrespective of the question of their justification or lack of it, like traditionalist responses to change in an "emergent" direction.

Students are placed at two points on the transformation line because it is clear that those coming from traditionalist family environments will tend to hold traditionalistic values, but hold them less securely than will their parents (if our hypothesis for over-all change is valid), while other students who come from emergent-oriented families will tend to place even further, as a function of their age and peer groups, towards the emergent end of the line than their parents would. This is only partially true, indeed, for such a rationale does not account for the fact that offspring in revolt (and many American children from 6 to 16 are in a state of revolt against parental dictums) may go to extremes in either direction.

School administrators, older, and younger teachers, place at varying points on the emergent half of the transformation line. I have placed them there because I believe that the professional education culture (every institution has its own way of life, in this sense) that they have acquired in the schools and colleges of education has a clear bias towards an emergent-oriented ethos. Many of my educationist colleagues will reject this interpretation, and indeed, such interpretations are always guilty of over-generalization. Others will welcome such a characterization, but still question its validity. My case must rest on contemporary educational philosophy, theory, and practice. The emphasis is on the "social adjustment" of the individual, upon his role as a member of the group and community. Most of the values listed under the *emergent* heading are explicitly stated in educational literature as goals. Some of them, such as conformity to the group, are implicit. This value, in particular, grows out of the others, is more or less unintended, and constitutes a *covert* or *latent* value, by definition. This is, admittedly, a little like accusing a man of hating his mother, but not knowing it, and such accusations are usually rejected, or rationalized out of existence. But I believe that it is literally impossible to hold the other values in this system and avoid placing a strong emphasis on group harmony, and group control of the individual. My data, at least, gathered largely from students in professional education courses, indicate that this is the case.

But educators and schools do not all come off the same shelf in the supermarket. Older teachers will tend, I hypothesize, to hold relatively traditionalist views by virtue of their age, and time of their childhood training (when they acquired their basic values)— a period in American culture when the traditionalist values were relatively more certain and supported than they are at present. Younger teachers were not only children and acquired their personal culture during a relatively more emergent-oriented period of American history, but they have been (I hypothesize) exposed to a professional education culture that has become emergent-oriented in its value position. They are therefore placed near the extreme of the transformation line in the emergent direction.

School administrators came from a different shelf in the same section of the supermarket. They, to be sure, range in age from young to old, come from different family backgrounds, and have been exposed in varying degrees to the professional education culture. But sociological and anthropological studies of the influence of status and role on behavior and perception indicate that these factors tend to over-ride others, and produce certain uniformities of outlook. The school administrator's role is a precarious one—as any school principal or superintendent knows. He faces towards several different audiences, each with different sets of demands—school boards, parents, power groups, teachers, and students—as well as other administrators. He has to play his role appropriately in the light of all these demands. The fact that many cannot, accounts for the increasingly short tenure of personages like school superintendents. But to the extent that he plays *across the board* he will place somewhere towards the center of the line of transformation. Furthermore, his dependence upon the school board, and the power groups in the community, in many cases will tend to make his outlook relatively more conservative, and probably more traditionalistic, than that of his teachers—at least the younger ones. There are many exceptions, of course. I am only claiming *tendencies*.

My thesis, I hope, is clear by now. I am attempting to explain, or help explain, the increasingly bitter and strident attacks on schools and educators, and the conflict and confusion within the ranks. I have claimed that this situation can better be understood in the context of conflicts in core values. And I have tried to show the direction of the values shift in American culture and place the various actors in the drama upon a transformation line within this shift.

In this perspective, many conflicts between parents and teachers, school boards and educators, parents and children, and between the various personages and groups within the school system (teachers against teachers, administrators against teachers, and so on) can be understood as conflicts that grow out of sharp differences in values that mirror social and cultural transformation of tremendous scope—and for which none of the actors in the situation can be held personally accountable. This is the real, and perhaps only contribution of this analysis. If these conflicts can be seen as emerging out of great sociocultural shifts—out of a veritable transformation of a way of life—they will lose some of their sting. To understand, the psychiatrist says, is to forgive.

But now, though it seems indeed improper at this point, permit me to add another complication to an already complicated picture. I have tried to make it clear that not only are there variations in values held by groups and different parts of the social body and school institutions, but that there are also various values, some of them contradictory, held by single individuals as diverse streams of influence in their own systems. This is always true in rapid culture-change situations, as the anthropologist and philosopher know.

This means that the situation is not only confused by groups battling each other, but that individuals are fighting themselves. This has certain predictable results, if the anthropological studies of personal adaptation to culture change have any validity. And I believe that those results can be detected in the behaviors of most, if not all, of the actors in the scene. Let me try to clarify this.

I will deal only with teachers, as one of the most important sets of actors on this particular stage. I hypothesize that the child training of most of the people who become teachers has been more tradition than emergent value-oriented. They are drawn largely from middle to lower-middle social class groups in American society, and this segment of the class structure is the stronghold of the work-success ethic and moral respectability values in our culture (even in a culture that is shifting away from these values). Furthermore, it seems probable that a selective process is operating to draw a relatively puritanistic element into the public school teaching as an occupation. Self-denial, altruism, a moralistic self-concept, seem to be functional prerequisites for the historically-derived role of school teacher in American society (I might have said "school-marm").

If this can be granted, then only one other ingredient needs to be added to explain several persistent types of personal adaptation to value conflicts observable among school teachers. That ingredient is one already spelled out—the relatively heavy emphasis, within the professional education culture, on the emergent-oriented value system. Teachers-to-be acquire their personal culture in a more tradition-oriented family environment, but they encounter a new kind of culture when in training to become school teachers—in the teacher-training institutions. This is a particular kind of culture-conflict situation that anthropologists have recently begun to study, but mostly in non-western societies undergoing acculturation under the impact of the western way of life.[4]

On the basis of observations of teachers in coastal communities and in the middle west, I hypothesize that three types of adaptation to this personal culture-conflict situation and experience are characteristic.

Ambivalent: This type is characterized by contradictory and vacillating behavior, particularly with respect to the exercise of discipline and authority. The type tends to be *laissez-faire* in some classroom situations, and authoritarian in others, depending upon which behavior is called into being as a defense against the threat of loss of control of self or of the classroom.

Compensatory: This type is characterized by one of two modes of behavior. The teacher overcompensates consistently either in the direction of the emergent or the tradition-centered values. In the first mode he (or she) tends to become a member of a *group-thinkism* cult—a perversion of progressive educational philosophy in action. The total stress is placed on social adjustment. Individuality is not sanctioned to any significant degree. Conformity to the group becomes the key to success. The type, in its extreme form, is a caricature of the emergent-centered value set. The second type compensates for internal culture conflict in the opposite direction, and becomes an extreme traditionalist. Tight dominance is maintained over children. Relationships with them are formalized and rigid. No deviation is allowed, so curiously enough, in this reactionary caricature of the tradition-centered values set there is convergence in the demand to conform—in one instance to the group, in the other to the teacher.

Adapted: This type can be either traditional or emergent value-oriented. But the compensatory and ambivalent mechanisms operating in the first two types are much less intense, or absent. The teacher of this type has come to terms with the value conflict situation and experience, and has chosen (consciously or unconsciously) to act within the framework of one or the other value

---

[4] *Acculturation* is used here to refer to the changes brought about in the culture of groups or individuals as adaptation to a culture different from their own takes place.

set, or has achieved a workable synthesis of both. There is consequently a consistency of behavior, and the mode of classroom management and teacher-student relationship is not a caricature of either value system.

No one is in a position to say which of these types is represented in greatest numbers among American public school teachers today, and there are few "pure" types. Certainly there are many traditional and emergent-oriented teachers who have adapted successfully to the personal culture-conflict situation and discontinuity of enculturative experience described. But equally certainly there are many school teachers who fall more clearly into one or the other typologies. It would be asking too much to suppose that a cultural values-conflict situation as intense as the one transforming American culture could be handled without strain by a key agent of the culture-transmission process—the school teacher. But again, to understand is to forgive.

In any event, it seems clear that if conditions are even partially of the nature described, the group culture-conflict situation resulting in attacks by representatives of those groups upon each other is intensified and at the same time confused by the personal culture-conflict problem. Both processes must be seen, and understood, as the results of a larger culture-transformation process.

In conclusion to this incomplete analysis, let me make it clear that I am not attacking either the emergentists, or the traditionalists. Value systems must always be functional in terms of the demands of the social and economic structure of a people. The traditional mode has been functional in our society, and there is a staunchness, and a vitality in it that many of us view with considerable nostalgia. But rugged individualism (in its expedient, ego-centered form), and rigid moralism (with its capacity for displaced hate) become dysfunctional in a society where people are rubbing shoulders in polyglot masses, and playing with a technology that may destroy everything with a pushing of buttons. The emergentist position seems to be growing in strength. Social adaptability, relativistic outlooks, sensitivity to the needs and opinions of others, and of the group, seem functional in this new age. We need, as citizens, educators, anthropologists, and parents, to examine our premises more closely. The emergentist can become a group conformist—an average man proud of his well-rounded averageness—without really meaning to at all.

And lastly, I would like to reiterate the basic theme of this article. Conflicts between groups centering on issues of educational relevance, and confusions within the rank and file of educators, can be understood best, I believe, in the perspective of the transformation of American culture that proceeds without regard for personal fortune or institutional survival. This transformation, it is true, can be guided and shaped to a considerable degree by the human actors on the scene. But they cannot guide and shape their destiny within this transformation if their energies are expended in knifing attacks on each other in such a central arena as education, or if their energies are dissipated in personal confusions. I am arguing, therefore, for the functional utility of understanding, and of insight into the all-encompassing transformation of American culture and its educational-social resultants.

References

Gorer, Geoffrey, 1948, *The American People*. New York: W. W. Norton and Company, Inc.

Kluckhohn, Clyde, 1949, *Mirror for Man*. New York: McGraw-Hill Book Company, Inc.

————, and Florence Kluckhohn, 1947, "American Culture: Generalized Orientations and Class Patterns", in *Conflicts of Power in Modern Culture, Seventh Symposium of the Conference on Science, Philosophy, and Religion*. New York: Harper & Row, Publishers.

Lantis, Margaret, ed., 1955, "The U.S.A. as Anthropologists See It." Special issue of the *American Anthropologist 57:* 1113–1295.

Lipset, Seymour, and Leo Lowenthal, eds., 1961, *Culture and Social Character: The Works of David Riesman Reviewed*. New York: The Free Press of Glencoe.

Mead, Margaret, 1942, *And Keep Your Powder Dry*. New York: William Morrow & Company, Inc.

Riesman, David, Nathan Glazer, and Reuel Denney, 1950, *The Lonely Crowd*. New Haven, Conn.: Yale University Press.

Ruesch, Jurgen, and Gregory Bateson, 1951, *Communication: The Social Matrix of Psychiatry*. New York: W. W. Norton and Company, Inc.

Warner, W. Lloyd, 1953, *American Life: Dream and Reality*. Chicago: University of Chicago Press.

————, 1959, *The Living and the Dead: A Study of the Symbolic Life of Americans*. New Haven, Conn.: Yale University Press.

8———*George D. Spindler*

The Transmission of
American Culture*

The transmission of American culture and the teacher as a cultural transmitter are the subjects of this chapter. Within this framework the analysis will center on the unintended, unanticipated consequences of cultural transmission in schools in our society that are at variance with the intended goals of transmission.

This is one of the less well illuminated areas of educational practice and conceptualization. Discrepancies between intended educational goals and what is actually transmitted are present in curriculum design, in the literature of textbooks and teaching aids, and in classroom procedure. They permeate all phases of the student-teacher relationship, the professional education of teachers, and the very subculture of education.

The treatment of processes within this focus must be exploratory and incomplete, for there is so much that is unknown. But the problem is important. With more knowledge of the ways in which the goals of education can be defeated in the very process of education, we may achieve better control over the results of education.

THE TRANSMISSION OF CONFLICTS
IN AMERICAN CULTURE

The discrepancies and conflicts between intent and outcome, between ideal and real that the teacher transmits to

* Adapted with revisions and abridgment from *The Transmission of American Culture,* copyright 1959 by the President and Fellows of Harvard College, and reprinted by permission of the publisher, the Harvard Graduate School of Education.

children in any classroom must originate in the culture. As Theodore Brameld has demonstrated so well in his book, *The Cultural Foundations of Education,* the educator must look beyond the schools and the people in them to the cultural context of education, in order to understand the problems and aspirations of education.

The American culture is dynamic and is composed of many once-separate streams of cultural influence. It is adapting to radical changes in the human environment. It is now, and for some time has been, a culture notable for the conflicts woven into the very fabric of its value system. We place a traditional value upon thrift, but we appear to believe even more strongly in the value of keeping up good appearances that depend upon mortgages and installment payments, which make thrift impossible as we play the game according to the rules of the American Dream. We believe in deferring satisfactions to the future but want the benefits of deferment now. We believe that success is to be won by hard work, but emphasize "personality" and social contacts as means to getting ahead. We laud honesty as a virtue but acknowledge the primacy of pragmatic expediency in real life. We are egalitarian in ideal and in much of our practice, but indulge in wide-ranging and destructive expressions of invidious prejudice. We deny sexuality but titillate ourselves with sex in our mass media, dress, and imagery. Our culture is patterned in conflicts that in part mirror the struggle between the puritan ethic and the demands and opportunities of an industrializing society of abundance. And we are undergoing the confused transformation from traditional to emergent values that I have already described and will apply further in this analysis.

When I discuss the transmission of conflicts and discrepancies in our classrooms I am not, therefore, simply blaming the teacher. If the teacher is a cultural transmitter and if teachers have experienced and, in some degree, internalized the conflicts in values described, it is probable they will transmit them to children. But it is equally important to avoid the error of assuming that because these conflicts and discrepancies are present in our culture they *should* be transmitted. If we accept this proposition, we accept the defeat and contradiction of many of our declared goals.

To illustrate concretely what is meant, permit me to describe certain educational situations in which discrepancies are transmitted. In doing so I will borrow from examples afforded by two of my anthropological colleagues as well as from my own research. I have reinterpreted what my colleagues have written to fit the format of my analysis, and they can be held responsible only for the observations that provide the data.

The first example is provided by Jules Henry's "Attitude Organization in Elementary School Classrooms," included in this book. He points out that one of the most striking characteristics of American culture is the phenomenon of intragroup aggression, which finds its most pure expression in "witch hunts." This "witch's brew," he declares, consists of destructive criticism of others, docility, feelings of vulnerability, fear of internal (intragroup) hostility, confession of evil deeds, and boredom.

He describes a number of specific situations in elementary school classrooms where elements of this pattern are inadvertently transmitted by teachers. He does not find the full-blown pattern in the majority of classrooms in which he conducted research observations. But he found it in a few and was able to identify elements and tendencies in this direction in more.

For example, he describes one classroom situation where the teacher organized a Vigilance Club. The purpose of this club was to teach children to be better citizens. The club functioned as a means by which the "good deeds" and "bad deeds" of the children could be recorded in a booklet kept by the teacher for each child. Every child was required to report the wrongs and rights of his own conduct during the week, and the class was asked to contribute information about his behavior. Miscreants were placed in an "isolation ward" in the back of the room until their record was favorably balanced. In the recorded observations of this procedure it becomes abundantly clear that intragroup aggression, docility in conforming to external pressure of the group and to teacher authority, feelings of vulnerability and fear of detection, and the value of spying and confession were activated and encouraged and, therefore, transmitted. These must be regarded as unintended consequences of the teacher's purposeful action, since the intended purpose was to encourage good citizenship. These unintended consequences did not appear out of a vacuum. The pattern was already available in the culture, was present in varying degrees of latency in the children, but was activated in the behavioral setting created by the teacher.

This is admittedly an extreme example, and is cited as almost a caricature of what normally happens in many classrooms. Let me extract another less extreme illustration from those provided by his work. In one fifth grade classroom the period was devoted to short reports and stories by the children. The class was requested by the teacher to criticize each report. Children responded by pointing out that the sentences were too short, there was too much detail, there was too little expression, and so on. No positive criticisms emerged, nor did the teacher seek out any. Probably many teachers would do so, since they would realize that criticism by one's peers, particularly at that age level, is more likely to be destructive than constructive. But the net effect of this procedure was to support children in their tendency to be carpingly critical of their fellows and, therefore, to contribute to the development of patterns of intragroup aggression that were already internalized in some degree by the children from their culture. The experience was organized by the teacher, however, for the purpose of increasing skill in writing and reporting, and also, I infer, to contribute to learning to "take criticism"—one of the frequently cited criteria for good adjustment. The contradiction of ends and means is apparent.

Another documentation of the processes involved in transmitting cultural discrepancies in educational situations is provided by Dorothy Lee's chapter in this book. She has attempted to answer this question: "What covert attitudes and concepts are communicated through the home economics program in public schools?" She makes it explicit that the study is concerned with what is communicated implicitly, unintentionally, and contrary to the intention of the program. Her work has been particularly influential in the development of my own thinking on the matter.

Professor Lee used state and city manuals for teachers of home economics, representing different regions, and one textbook in common use as sources of data. Admittedly, teachers deviate from manuals in actual instruction. This study therefore provides illustration of the fact that cultural discrepancies are found in the design of classroom procedures and not only in their implementation.

These programs, it is stated in the manuals, are designed to help the student develop a healthy personality through participation in human relations in the home, and to help students mature into adults who will establish democratic, happy, cooperative homes, as well as to pass on the skills necessary for homemaking.

She cites a number of instances where the design of the manuals can be interpreted as introducing contradictions to this purpose. For example, in one manual, presumably not atypical, the lesson on family relationships states other objectives: to realize the purpose of restrictions, to realize one's contributions to family conflict, and to help the student to learn ways of reducing conflict. The student is to relate herself to a family life that is full of conflict and restriction. "Why do parents always say 'no'?" "What can a boy or girl do about a 'pesky' sister or brother?"— these are some of the questions posed for the student.

Other examples drawn from those she provides include the contradiction between the declared goal of learning to share meaningful experiences in the home and an implementation of this goal in curriculum design that provides great detail on selecting recipes, nutritional needs, finishing seams and doing laundry, but nothing on who shares these activities or who is being helped. Another dualism is conveyed by the declared emphasis on creative enjoyment of the home and of family living but an implementation in design that characterizes housekeeping as work that needs to be done efficiently so that one can have more leisure time away from it all. Only escape has value. Ordinary home life seems to provide little emotional nourishment. And, lastly, another declared goal is to develop mature personalities (that development, presumably, requires some sustenance for the inner self), but it is solely the external characteristics of good grooming, pleasant manners, being popular and making friends, being efficient about one's expenditure of time that are stressed.

It is only fair to point out that Dorothy Lee felt that her interpretation might have been biased by certain personal values that she holds because she was a Greek before she was an American. Apparently a happy life, sharing family activities, enjoying the ordinary routine of family living, and developing a self-actualized personality are valued in Greek culture. But I have always thought they were valued in American culture as well. What is important for our purposes here is that the design of the manuals for home-making includes these values as goals but also includes designs for implementation that are in varying degrees of contradiction to them. In one sense this design is therefore an accurate projection of American culture. This makes it all the more important that the contradictions be analyzed and perhaps in some instances reduced or eliminated.

For a last example of direct transmission of obvious but culturally patterned contradictions, I would like to use one of my own case studies of teachers and their classrooms.

The cultural transmitter in this case was a highly respected teacher in a large elementary school, who had certain duties as a counselor. He originated from a respectable immigrant family and had improved his social status during his lifetime by becoming a schoolteacher. The particular situation from which I have extracted certain verbatim records to follow was one of the "rites of passage" that occur now and then throughout the educational life cycle of children. The students in the eighth grade were being prepared for the choice of programs in high school and were making out proposed study lists under his guidance. The class group consisted of thirty-five children, twenty-four of whom were Mexican-Americans. The range of scores on the California Mental Maturity test was 80 to 120, with a median of 102. There was a broadly corresponding variety of reading and academic achievement represented in the group. I will present a few items from the verbal interaction of the teacher-counselor and the students.

T: You must be a good citizen, or they won't accept you. Now, what do you need to get into Orthodox State College? (*Children raise hands, repeat answers previously learned.*) What do you need to get into Junior College?" (*Students respond likewise.*)

T: In arranging your programs for next year, there are certain things that everyone must take, so we'll just put them down. You will all take P.E., English, and Social Studies. (*Teacher writes these down on the board opposite numbers 1, 2, and 3.*) Now you have to decide whether you want to take Algebra or not. You have to take math all the way through high school if you want to be an engineer. Now, if you've gotten B's and C's all the way through eighth grade, what are your chances of doing well in ninth grade Algebra? (*Students murmur various things.*) That's right! Not so good! So what can you do?

S: Try to raise your grade.

T: Yes.

S: Work harder.

T: That's one thing. But what else? . . . Do like I did when I wanted to be a singer but found I couldn't sing. What did I do? Yes . . . that's right; I changed my plans. . . . With respect to language, how many here speak Spanish? (*Six of the Mexican-Americans raised their hands, but all speak some Spanish.*) It will help you if you do. But you have to realize that there is some work to do—homework! It is good to take Spanish if you want to go on to college and need a language. But you can't take Spanish and General Business. They come at the same period. Now, one of the things you have to do is to be neat and orderly. If you aren't good at that it might be hard for you until you learn to do it better.

T: Now here we have Mechanical Drawing. This is exclusively a boy's class. I don't know why some girls couldn't take it if they wanted to. But only boys take it. Now Home-making is for girls, so you can take that.

T: Now when you come to see me, if I tell you to take General Business instead of Spanish, it should be understood that you don't have to take it. You can do as you wish. But it means that I think you will do better in General Business. (*Several more subject choices are covered.*)

T: And here is typing. It looks interesting when you pass the typing room, doesn't it? But do you know there aren't any letters on those keyboards? You have to watch a chart at the front of the room, and if you look at the keyboard, you fail!

Of course a great deal more went on during this hour of counseling. I have purposefully selected those verbal items that constitute the most clear indications of bias in cultural transmission. And this is always unfair to the cultural transmitter. But I believe the extracted items accurately reveal persistent trends in his counseling of the mixed Mexican-American and Anglo-groups in the eighth grade.

After this particular class session, the teacher-counselor said,

"This is a passive group. There is no spark in there. The better groups get quite excited about this. Of course, most of the better groups are college-preparatory and perhaps only three or four of these students will go to college." Previous to the session, in his statement of educational philosophy, he had commented, "I believe that our job is to make the most of the potential of each child. Of course there is a wide range of ability among our students. A good many of them will never go on to college. And we have to do the best we can to help them on to a satisfactory adjustment."

He was defeating his own aims in the way he handled this crucial rite of passage, this point of compression in the relation of the child and his culture where choices made affect future development decisively. He opened the gates to valued channels of development and then shut them in the children's faces. And he did not open the gates to any alternative channels. What he transmitted, it seems to me, was that the only worthwhile goal was to go to college so that one could become an engineer or something equivalent, that if the child did not have the necessary qualifications there was no other dignified and worthy choice, and that most of the members of this class group did not have the necessary qualifications.

If this person were a small, mean individual with explicit prejudices, and if he were not concerned with making the most of the potential of each child I would be less concerned. But he is not small and mean. He is a generous, well-intended person, and believes in democratic opportunity. In his counseling he projects his own struggle to improve his status, mirrors the discrepancy in our culture between ideal and real in the definition of opportunity, and inadvertently defeats his own professed aims.

THE ACCULTURATION OF THE SCHOOL TEACHER

What has been established so far is that our culture is one in which conflicts in values, and between goals and the means to them, are present and patterned. And that teachers, as cultural transmitters, convey these patterned conflicts to children in their classrooms, with the consequence that many professed goals are defeated, or at least obscured. It should also be clear that I have not been castigating teachers. They are the agents of their culture.

A further step must be taken if we are to see the full meaning and scope of the problem. Teachers are a special group. They are not selected at random as official culture transmitters; they are trained and accredited to that status and role. They must take courses in educational psychology, the social foundations of education, curriculum design, philosophy and history of education, the methods of education, and must do supervised practice teaching. In short, they must attend teacher-training institutions and graduate with the stamp of approval from the established professional cadre. But professional educational instruction and training consist not only of courses and training in techniques. Every institution with a history and internal organization and a specialized personnel has a culture or, more properly, a subculture. Certain values, symbols, beliefs, and certain basic premises are patterned into the structure and process of the institution. The institutions of professional education—the teacher-training schools and the literature of education—are no exception.

At this point it is necessary to refer back to the traditional and emergent value patterns. The traditional pattern includes emphasis on thrift, self-denial, faith in the future, a strong emphasis on success and a belief that hard work was the means to it, absolute moral norms, and a strong value placed upon the individual. The emergent pattern includes value placed upon sociability, sensitivity to the feelings of others, a relativistic attitude, a present-time orientation, and high value placed upon the group.

The dynamic process of greatest relevance to us at the moment is the relationship between the culture that the school teacher brings to the professional teacher-training institution subculture and the patterning of that subculture, the adaptation that the teacher-in-training makes to this patterning and the consequences in selective culture transmission in the classroom.

This is a complex relationship with many subtle ramifications. I have outlined it in the preceding chapter. Since an understanding of it is essential to the logic of the analysis to follow, I will restate and expand the argument. It is well established that the majority of public school teachers originate from a middle and lower-middle social class culture. The value pattern that I have termed "traditional" is probably found in this cultural context in its most pure form. To the extent this is so, it means that whatever selective processes are operating tend to bring many people of traditionalistic value orientation into teacher-training.

The question that the anthropologist raises is—what are the characteristics of the subculture of the teacher-training institution to which these students bring their traditionalist orientations? Analysis of a sample of some of the influential literature of curriculum design for elementary education reveals that there is present a strong values bias that fits in general terms the "emergent" pattern. The literature of child development and educational psychology reveals some of the same trends. Interpretations of the social behavior of boys and girls, intended for educational consumption, provide both implicit and explicit value judgments in the same pattern. The popularity of sociometric techniques is diagnostic of this orientation. The topical content of many of our teacher-training courses suggests it as well.

The basic premise underlying the specific emergent values is that what is most important is the social adjustment of the child. His place in the group, the responses of his peers to him, his ability to get along well, to work and play with others are penultimate concerns. This is not all bad by any means. The emphasis on social adjustment is the educator's attempt to meet the demands of a new kind of society, where this kind of adjustment is of vital importance. When balanced by a concern for individual differences, by support for the deviating child, the creative student, intellectual development, and the acquisition of cognitive skills, and when it does not become a form of "groupism," this emphasis on social adjustment is a possible compensatory process for some of the more harshly competitive anxiety-arousing patterns of our culture.

But the point is that however understandable and useful the emphasis may be, this pattern of values incorporated in the ethos of professional education is frequently at variance with what the new teacher-in-training brings into the situation. The neophyte in training must reorient his value system wherever the conflict in values is encountered.

When neophyte teachers in training or people in any other acculturating group adapt to sharply disjunctive value systems, their adaptations assume predictable forms. The individual meets the new value system and feels threatened because it challenges his established, familiar, and comfortable values. He does not, of course, necessarily interpret the experience in these terms. He is more likely to see it as a personal conflict, which heightens the intensity of the threat. After some exploration in the new dimensions of feeling and belief offered to him by the opposing system, his feeling of threat overcomes him and he seeks refuge in the comforting shelter of his established values. But something has changed. He has been driven back to his "native state" by threat. Therefore he overcompensates, and rigidifies the original system in what may be psychologically termed a reaction formation, or culturally termed a "nativistic reaffirmation." I will term him a "reaffirmative traditionalist" in the framework of this analysis. The teacher of this type will tend to be rigid in his uncompromising projection of traditional values in his classroom behavior.

An alternative adaptive response is represented by the person who encounters the new value system which is sharply disjunctive with his own, likewise feels threatened by the conflict in personal terms, but adapts by overcompensating in the direction of the new system. Perhaps he is more threatened by the possibility of being out of step than he is by the demand to change. He uncritically appropriates the new values in their entirety and frequently becomes a strident proselytizer for them. This kind of teacher I term a "compensatory emergentist." His channels of communication with children, and his criteria for their behavior, become narrowed to individual-in-harmony-with-the-group. "Groupism" reigns in his classroom. Individualistic differences and deviations become smothered by group conformity.

A third alternative adaptive response is exhibited by the person who encounters the conflict of value systems and superficially internalizes segments of both but does not rework them into any coherent synthesis. He is a mixed type but quite different from a type that I shall describe shortly. He is usually not particularly thoughtful about the conflicts he encounters and leaves them unresolved, but still a part of his acquired culture. This person as a teacher is likely to vacillate between different modes of group leadership and different modes of interaction with individual children. Obvious discontinuities in his classroom management cause trouble for both him and his students. We can call him the "vacillator."

The fourth alternative is a happier one than any of the others. This person comes into the acculturative situation with a capacity for adjustment to differences in values and conflicts between them. Usually he is thoughtful or philosophic-minded and has the ability to combine useful features from more than one system of belief on a rational basis. He does not need to overcompensate as a defense against conflict because he is not threatened by it. He is a mixed type but does not internalize the mixture segmentally. He recombines the aspects from both systems into a creatively coherent synthesis. I have labeled this an "adjusted" type.

As a matter of fact I believe that increasing numbers of students are of this latter type. They exhibit workable combinations of what seem to be the best of both the emergent and traditional values. For instance, they accept the need of the individual to be a member of the group but believe that the individual should also be self-possessed and self-actualized. They believe that hard work is necessary for success but that there is no point in being unpleasantly puritanic about it. They take a relativistic, tolerant view of differences between individuals and between groups, but they have a personal moral code that governs their own behaviors within broad but definite limits. Whether they represent a shift in the kind of training they receive or whether they represent a change in the culture of generations, or both, is not clear. In any event, I am happy to see them and hope their numbers increase, for I am convinced that large numbers of teachers, at least new ones, are reaffirmative traditionalists, compensatory emergentists, or vacillators.

A value judgment is made here because it seems clear that teachers falling into the first two adaptive categories tend to exhibit highly selective biases as culture transmitters. They transmit in narrow channels with few alternatives due to their rigidity. Without intending to do so, they open some doors to self-cultivating developments for some children but close them for many others. And the vacillator, though he is not rigid and transmits along many channels, issues only weak signals and produces little but static as a result.

A CASE STUDY ILLUSTRATION

To illustrate further what is meant, another case study that is representative of others we have made of elementary school teachers and their classrooms will be presented.[1] The salient features of this case classify him as a reaffirmative traditionalist. This type may be encountered more frequently in other parts of the country than it is on the West Coast where my observations were made, and the analysis should, therefore, have wide applicability.

This fifth-grade teacher is a young man of twenty-five. He originates from a clearly traditionalistic middle-class family. His father is an executive of middle rank in a wholesale business organization and belongs to the usual service and fraternal organizations. His mother is college educated and active in the League of Women Voters. His father is not college educated and achieved his position by hard work. Both parents like to play bridge. They belong to the country club and own a summer cottage where the subject spent many happy hours as a boy. Twice during the subject's lifetime the family moved to more expensive homes in better neighborhoods.

The subject likes to play golf, drinks socially but moderately, attends the Methodist church, and reads the local newspaper, *Reader's Digest,* and the *Saturday Evening Post*. He aspires to be a school administrator and regards his teaching experience as preparation for that role. He is a pleasant, good-looking young man who appears somewhat constrained but not visibly anxious. He is well

---

[1] The case study was done when the author was a member of a research team operating out of the School of Education at Stanford University.

liked by his colleagues and is rated as one of the outstanding young teachers in the school system.

His professed aims in teaching, beyond the management of instruction so that his students acquire the requisite knowledge, are to bring out creativity to the maximum ability of each child, help children to express themselves clearly and help children to learn how to get along with each other. He states that he tries to give every student in his class a chance to participate. He prides himself particularly on being fair and just with all the children. He says explicitly that every student gets a "fair break" in his classroom. He feels that he is very concerned about the problems of his students and always tries to understand them. His statements about his aims and his relations with his students are consistent with what his principal, his supervisor, and the members of the central staff of the school system say about him.

He told me that many of his teacher-training courses were "a waste of time." In probing this blanket indictment of professional educational preparation as he experienced it I discovered that he was dismayed and upset by certain points of view that he perceived as consistently appearing in his course work. He felt that his preceptors were trying "to give the school to the children," that they were more concerned with how children adjusted than what they learned, and that his instructors stressed cooperation, or at least group harmony, at the expense of competition. All of this he lumps together under the label "progressive education," which he rejects with feeling, but which he is content to leave as an unanalyzed abstraction.

He fits the criteria for the reaffirmative-traditionalist teacher type. He originated from a family culture where the traditional values previously described apparently existed in virtually pure form. He encountered the emergent-oriented values of the professional teachering subculture. He sensed the conflict, felt the threat, rejected the threatening alternatives, and sought refuge in the shelter of his original values.

The further presentation of data on this teacher and his classroom will include a few items selected from a considerable mass of information. We worked together for many months, and his file is extensive. But these few items will establish the pattern that permeated many of the interrelationships between him and his students.

One of our standard practices in case studies is to ask the teacher to fill out a form titled "Information Concerning the Student." It includes items on academic and social adjustment in the child's previous school, his home situation, approximate I.Q. test performance, special interests, hobbies, health history, his ambitions and plans for the future. The teacher is requested to fill out this form for each student without recourse to written records. He is scored on the number of items of information. A perfect score, indicating highest knowledge, would be ten.

This teacher averaged 3.2 for the forms filled out on all of his thirty-three students, which is lower, on the average, than the score attained by other teachers in our sample. The mean of his knowledge concerning children in his group originating from families of highest socio-economic status was 4.9. His mean score for those of lowest status was 2.8. It is apparent that some bias is operating that tends to contradict his professed aims.

He was asked to list the names of those students in his class that he considered to be the best adjusted—emotionally and socially. Of the seven children he listed as best adjusted only one child was included who originated from a family of less than middle-class status, and this child exhibited strong status-achievement drives. He was also asked to list the names of those students whom he considered least well adjusted. Of these seven children, only one came from a middle-class setting. The other six were from families of lower-class or special ethnic status. It is possible, of course, that he was correct in his appraisal, even from a psychiatric point of view. Other evidence concerning the behavior of these children indicates that he was not accurate in a number of instances. For our purposes at the moment what is significant is that the same bias in perception is revealed in this as was exhibited in his knowledge about students.

He was asked to list the 25 percent of his class group with whom he thought he had the most effective relationship. He listed eight children, and of these eight, five were from families of middle-class social status. He was also asked to list the 25 percent of his group with whom he felt he had the least effective relationship. All but one of these children were from families of lower-class status. Other evidence indicates that in this instance he appraised the situation more or less accurately. The pattern of selective perception, of differential bias in his interrelationships with children in his class group is, however, strengthened.

He was requested to name those children who were the most popular with or most accepted by their classmates. He listed eight, only one of whom represented a lower-class position. In only three instances did he name the same children that the students themselves did, according to sociometric information collected from the class. He was also asked to name those children to whom nobody in the class paid much attention. He listed six children, two of whom were middle-class in origin. The other four were from families of lower-class status. In four instances his perceptions matched those of the classroom group, but there were ten comparatively isolated children in that group, according to the sociometric data collected from the class. Of these ten, five were children originating from middle-class backgrounds, four of whom he missed in his appraisal. Again, there is a clear pattern of selective bias in his perception of the children in his classroom. It is difficult for him to implement his professed aims in the context of this pattern.

A few excerpts from anecdotal and verbatim records will strengthen the interpretation. One boy, who was quite isolated in the interaction among the boys in the class and who chose only girls in his own responses to a sociometric questionnaire was described by the teacher as a "real go-getter, one of the most magnetic personalities of any young child I have ever known. He has a very warm personality—truthful, sincere, with a good sense of humor. Tom gets along well with anyone, anywhere." This boy sometimes brought sample bottles of hair tonic, shoe polish, simple toys and gadgets to class in a small suitcase and tried to sell them to the other children. One day when I was observing, he was allowed to "make his pitch" before the class. He was, indeed, a motivated, magnetic, salesman, and probably will go far. The teacher apparently perceived only this attribute—one that is congruent with some of his own achievement drives and their prec-

edents in his family models. There is much else about this child
that he needed to know in order to guide his development effectively.

In another instance of the same type the teacher described
one girl as having a "horrible personality . . . egoistic, insincere,
false. She never has a nice word to say about anyone but herself.
I don't particularly care for Charlotte." She was the friendship
choice of the "star-of-attraction"—the girl most frequently chosen
as a friend by the other girls in their sociometric responses. She
was observed to interact effectively with most of the other girls.
She had a high rating in status-reputation data collected from the
class. She came from a broken home in a lower-class setting.

In his response to oral reports by the children about what
they were reading in their spare time, his gestures, facial expression, bodily postures, comments and silences were all patterned
in the framework of the same selective bias. He communicated
approval of most of what the children of middle-class origins said,
and of what they were reading. He communicated lack of interest, or suppressed distaste for what the children of lower-class
origins said, how they said it, and of what they were reading.

I have almost too much data on this teacher and his classroom, and have had to struggle against the inclination to continue
with examples that all substantiate the same pattern of bias and
selective perception in his relationships with his students. He
interacted effectively with only a minority segment of his classroom group—that segment which matched his own aspirations
and values, derived from his own cultural setting. He opened doors
for this selected group to channels of development they were already heading toward, and he sped them on their way. But for
the larger number of his students, those who did not match his
values and aspirations, he closed doors and left them waiting in the
foyer of our culture.

Analysis of all of the data collected about this teacher and
his operations in the classroom leads to the conclusion that his
consistent selective bias was in part due to his own cultural background. But this pattern was accentuated by his reactive adjustment to the conflict between the culture he brought with him

when he entered professional training to become a teacher and the special subculture he encountered there.

His exercise of the role of cultural transmitter was in contradiction to his own professed aims, and even to his own beliefs about what he actually did in the classroom. He was not giving all children an opportunity to participate; he did not understand their problems; he was not being fair and just to all his students; they were not all getting a "fair break." All these aims and beliefs were contradicted by his highly selective positive interaction with a small segment of his class. He was wearing cultural blinders that limited his perceptions to a single channel. His transmitting apparatus was sending out positive signals only to that segment responding within the frequency of that single channel.

A CROSS-CULTURAL PERSPECTIVE

Now I would like to apply a cross-cultural perspective to this case and some of the inferences drawn from it. In one of my seminars we have been reviewing the available literature on the educative process in a wide variety of nonliterate, so-called "primitive" societies. One of the concepts we have found particularly useful is one we have termed "cultural compression." The meaning of the term is simple. It refers to any period of time in the life cycle of the individual when he encounters a culturally patterned reduction of alternatives for behavior, usually through restrictive cultural definitions of new roles appropriate to his particular stage of maturation. During these periods, culturally normative restrictions are placed upon him. They are the points in his development as a creature of culture when the norms of his group and society bear in upon him with the greatest intensity and where, as a consequence, he undergoes a change in social identity. I will apply this concept to the educational process in cultures other than our own, and then return to a brief reconsideration of the educative process in our society and the case of our teacher in this broadened perspective.

Cultural compressions may be detected in the life cycle in

any society at a number of developmental stages. Toilet training and weaning are forms of cultural compression. So is induction to work. Culturally patterned preparations for assumption of adult roles are particularly critical points in the compressive sequence. In our examination of the literature available on forty non-literate societies we have isolated a number of types of cultural compression sequence. We find that we can even draw graphs of them. Imagine two horizontal lines of equal length, one above the other. Place the newborn infant at one end between the lines and start him through his developmental stages. Contract the lines in such a way as to portray the points in his progressive experience where cultural restrictions are placed upon him in any specific cultural context. Expand them so as to portray the points in his experience where cultural restrictions are lifted as they no longer become appropriate to his age and status. This imagery should serve to indicate the kinds of models we have constructed. The specific types for different cultures are not relevant for our purposes here.

We find that the types differ sharply from each other in the sequence of cultural compressions during the prepubertal years. We find in all of them, however, that the channels of self and cultural development become progressively narrowed as time goes on. Eventually most alternative channels are eliminated, and only a single major one (but possibly several secondary ones) is provided for each sex in the more homogeneous societies. In order to insure that the cultural boundaries of this channel are internalized by the developing individual many societies introduce dramatically compressive restrictions at the time of puberty in the form of initiation ceremonies. In these societies this period is a time of very intensive training and of very severe restriction. Dramatic rituals, isolation from home and familiar surroundings and people, the use of forbidding strangers as instructors, heighten the effect of the restrictions and cultural transmissions that occur at this time. And there is only one correct major channel into which the initiate is compressed. The paper by C. W. M. Hart included in this book has stimulated my thinking in this direction. He describes the initiation experience among the Tiwi of North Australia.

So far his life has

been easy; now it is hard. . . . The boy of twelve or thirteen, used to noisy, boisterous irresponsible play, is expected and required to sit still for hours and days at a time, saying nothing whatever but concentrating upon and endeavoring to understand long intricate instructions and "lectures" given him by his hostile and forbidding preceptors. Life has suddenly become real and earnest and the initiate is required literally to 'put away the things of a child,' even the demeanor. The number of tabus and unnatural behaviors enjoined upon the initiate is endless. He mustn't speak unless he is spoken to; he must eat only certain foods and often only in certain ways; at certain fixed times and in certain fixed positions. All contact with females, even speech with them, is rigidly forbidden, and this includes mother and sisters. He cannot even scratch his head with his own hand, but must do it with a special stick, and so on, through a long catalogue of special, unnatural, but obligatory behaviors covering practically every daily activity and every hour of the day and night.

Professor Hart continues in his description, but this will communicate what is meant by the notion of compression to a single channel.

This technique of cultural transmission apparently works very well in many small, non-literate societies. They are comparatively homogeneous in value systems, there being a limited framework of values to which members of the society are committed. Specialization in roles and statuses is at a minimum compared to the situation in our society.

There are personality differences between members of any society, however "simple" it may be, but they cluster around the cultural promontories afforded by traditional values and prescribed roles. The society and its culture are tradition-oriented and unchanging, compared to ours. The highly compressive techniques are effective because the cultural boundaries and barriers imposed upon the growing individual are consistent with the character and limitations of the culture as a whole. Alternative channels for development are not needed as long as the equilibrium of the social system and the culture is not seriously disturbed.

It is easy to make the mistake of assuming that because these techniques of cultural transmission work well in comparatively

simple non-literate societies they will work for us also. Our society is extraordinarily complex with respect to the specializations required of individuals and the multiple roles and statuses
provided for these specializations. And although our value system
has some coherence, the alternatives and conflicts within it are
impressive.

A single-channel type of cultural transmission is dysfunctional in our society. It is dysfunctional because we need variety of
outlook, skills, and personality types in order to maintain our
internal complexity. And if we are to adapt successfully to the
rapidly changing conditions of existence forecast by the opening
events of the atomic age and the first tentative steps towards the
exploration of outer space and other worlds, we must provide,
in our cultural transmission, for innovative channels of self and
cultural development.

I think my point is clear. This teacher not only defeated
some of his own educational aims in his classroom management,
but he transmitted within only a single channel. He did not intend to do so, to be sure. This is precisely why his case is of interest to us. None of the illustrations of cultural transmission described were examples of wilful, intentional, misconstruing of the
teacher's role. It is because cultural processes of this sort are difficult to perceive, particularly when one is caught up in them, that
this topic is worthy of analysis.

CULTURAL THERAPY

So that we do not lose focus, the major points that I
have tried to communicate will be summarized briefly. I will then
go on to a consideration of steps we might take towards a solution,
and conclude with a statement of some unresolved dilemmas.

This chapter started with an analysis of conflicts in the patterning of American culture, and attempted to illustrate, through
examples borrowed from the writings of Jules Henry and Dorothy
Lee, and extracted from my own case records, how these conflicts were transmitted in our schools, with emphasis on the elementary years. I also tried to show how in the act of transmission,

the professed aims of teachers were sometimes defeated and contradicted. I then moved on to an analysis of the conflict between the cultural values many teachers bring with them into professional training and those subsumed in the culture of the teacher-training institutions, and of the adaptive consequences of this conflict. The case study of the fifth-grade teacher was used to demonstrate the selective and goal-defeating process of cultural transmission that I believe to be characteristic of one of the adaptive types. I then shifted the emphasis from the transmission of culture conflicts to the problem of single-channel transmission and tried to demonstrate that this process is not only contradictory to the teacher's professed aims, but is also dysfunctional in our complex, changing society. Throughout, it has been maintained that as an agent of culture the teacher is not to be personally blamed for the consequences described.

We cannot let the matter rest there. It is true that the teacher is activating a precedent cultural condition in the process of transmission. It is also true that because this is so, changes are difficult to bring about, since the problem is of extraordinary scope. The total structure of our society and the patterning of our culture is involved. But because this is a problem in cultural process, I am going to propose a first step in solution that I will term "cultural therapy."

I did not describe my role in the teacher case studies used for illustrative purposes. This role has a direct bearing upon the notion of "cultural therapy." I was a member of a team that had a dual purpose—to collect case study data on the basic processes of education and to work in a close relationship with our teacher cases to improve their professional competence. We made no effort to select "problem" cases, and neither of these I have cited were defined as such. We merely operated on the assumption that all teachers were interested in improving their professional competence. Each member of the team took responsibility for certain cases, but we consulted with each other throughout both the research and consultative phases of the studies.

In the consultative phase of all cases we fed back to the teacher the data we had collected in the research phase. The completeness, timing, sequence, and interpretation of this "feedback" differed for each case. Some teachers can tolerate their objective image more easily than others. The fifth-grade teacher case was one who had a surprising capacity for such objective feedback. He was very interested in improving his professional competence, partly because he was an ambitious man, and partly because he was a person who sincerely wanted to do the best he could for the children in his classes.

Over a period of several months I presented data to him and tried to guide him more or less gently to a broadened cultural perspective on himself, his students, and his teaching. At times, this being a mutual and cooperative relationship, he guided me, and in doing so contributed to my understanding of process in cultural transmission. We explored together his cultural background, his experience in the teacher-training institution, and the specific ways in which the dynamics resultant from this combination of cultural influences were expressed in his selective response to his students. Sometimes he was chagrined, sometimes depressed and self-doubting, sometimes angered, but always intensely interested and frequently very surprised. As a result, his perspective and understanding were broadened significantly, and he was able to interact more effectively with the broad cultural range represented by his students. He was able to do so because he had acquired a knowledge of his own cultural position, its influence upon him, the cultural range of his students, and his selective relationships within this range. I do not think he underwent a significant change in personality. It was not my intent, at least, to effect such a change. He did undergo a change in his cultural scope.

The use of the values-projective techniques in my education classes, and the analysis of data revealed by them in those classes, is an attempt to provide cultural therapy before the cultural patterns are activated in the classroom. I have no direct measure of their effectiveness. Students tell me, and give evidence in their behavior, of having experienced "cultural shock." They are able to place themselves in the matrix of values revealed in the analysis, and presumably are able to anticipate some of the ways in which their position may be a determinant in their exercise of the teacher's role, since this process is treated at length in class discussions and documented with many illustrations.

In both procedures—the "feedback" process in cooperative case studies and in the cultural analysis in the social foundations courses—the essential feature is that culture is treated as a third person. What I mean by this is that we are not dissecting the teacher's or the student's personalities; we are dissecting *culture*. The teacher's culture varies from the culture of others, but all variations reflect and are a part of the larger cultural context in which we all function. This makes a certain objectivity possible, which is usually impossible when the issue becomes more personal and the individual's emotional defenses are more directly aroused. The object of cultural therapy sees that his problem is not unique to him. It is shared in some degree with all of his colleagues—as a matter of fact, with everyone in his society. The "therapist" and the subject thus have the problem in common of understanding better how culture operates in and through all of us.

Cultural therapy is one direct measure we can take in our teacher-training programs to help reduce the self-defeating effect of cultural transmission in American schools. I hesitate to suggest the case study method as a direct measure because it takes a great deal of work to produce an effect on a single case. I am not optimistic about the probability that either approach will become widespread in the immediate future. We do not have the trained personnel to act as therapists. At this point I am not about to suggest that every teacher training institution start hiring anthropologists. Most anthropologists do not want to become therapists, even cultural therapists; they have other necessary and pressing work to do, and there are not enough to go around anyhow. With some help, the trainers of teachers can perform this function themselves, and the growing literature contributed by educators on the social and cultural process in American schools is an indication that this is already taking place.

SOME UNRESOLVED DILEMMAS

Any highly schematic but exploratory analysis of the kind I have presented should be concluded with some unresolved dilemmas. In one sense I have had to attack an important source of some of the values I am trying to promote. I have argued for multiple channels of cultural transmission, and against single-channel transmission. I have also tried to show how conflicts in our culture are communicated to children, to the defeat of many of the professed aims of teachers. Until we understand the dynamics of cultural transmission more fully than we can hope to now, one of the insurances against single-channel transmission is conflict transmission. Of course, the pursuit of this point of view would eventually lead us to a position at dead center, where we acknowledge the defeat of our declared educational goals as desirable. But assuredly it is true that much of the healthy variation in personalities in our society, and certainly some of the innovations that are produced in our culture, issue from the conflicts patterned into it.

Perhaps the way out of this dilemma is to acknowledge the conflicts in our culture more explicitly, even in the act of transmitting them. Some day we may reach the point in our self-knowledge where we can at least be selective of the kinds of conflicts we transmit, and control better than we do the negative and unanticipated results of our transmission.

But there is another dilemma. Presuming that we somehow learn to control the results of our intended transmissions with increased knowledge of the relationship between the teacher and his culture, and between the teacher, his culture, the students and theirs, another order of question is raised—an ethical question.

The danger in knowledgeable and purposeful control is that this control could be used for purposes of inducing conformity, for purposes of transmitting values and patterns of behavior within a single channel. And with the trends toward conformity that seem well established in our culture, this seems highly possible.

We must exercise extreme care that a growing awareness of the cultural dimension, and particularly of the values dimension and its transmission is not misused, by accident or intent. What I am arguing for here is that the teacher, as a cultural transmitter, achieve sufficient awareness of the multidimensional processes involved so that fewer potentially creative channels of communication, of transmission, be blocked, with the consequence that more children can be effectively caught up in the educative process. But the ethical problem raised is unresolved. Here we must turn to the philosophers for help.

9——Dorothy Lee

Discrepancies
in the Teaching
of American Culture[*]

The study on which this paper is based was initiated in an attempt to discover what cultural values, concepts, and attitudes are presented to the growing generation in the school.[1] The subject matter included in the Home Economics program, and occasionally under Family Life Education, was chosen because this includes generally most of what anthropologists cover under the term culture. It is concerned with helping the student to develop a healthy personality through participation in human relations in the home and the community and to develop into a mature and healthy adult, who will establish a home where democratic, happy co-operative living will prevail. Skills and understanding and knowledge necessary for homemaking are taught under this program. Behavior at home and outside the home is discussed, as well as personal ethics, social intercourse, friendship, and marriage.

The study was made through an analysis of teachers' manuals and guides;[2] and early in the study it became apparent that often there was a wide discrepancy between the objectives of the program and their implementation. A similar discrepancy was present

* Reprinted from *Education and Anthropology*, George D. Spindler, Editor, with permission of the Publishers, Stanford University Press; Copyright 1955 by the Board of Trustees of the Leland Stanford Junior University.

1 This paper is a by-product of a pilot study on American values and concepts made possible by a grant from the Humanities Division of the Rockefeller Foundation.

2 The manuals and guides used for this study are referred to by code number. The list will be supplied by the author of this paper on request.

173

esentation of areas of culture, as, for example, between ... skills of homemaking and the relations and values in home-making, or between the self and society. The family of one's birth and the family to be made through marriage appeared to contain discontinuous values. Work and leisure, duty and fun, the given and the chosen were presented in an exclusive dualism of opposition.

It is these discrepancies which form the subject of this paper. I believe that none of them are intended, since sometimes the implementation runs counter to the explicitly stated objective, and sometimes what is presented is obviously at odds with the general principles of the manual. The discrepancies are there apparently as a result of the revolutionary change in the function of the Home Economics program, as well as of the enormity of the task it has undertaken. In the early part of the century, and often even in the mid-'thirties, Home Economics concerned itself only with the skills and operations of housekeeping. Home economics books, dealing with "home management" and "housewifery," referred to husband and children only by implication, as when they spoke of cleaning the "master bedroom" or when they spoke of the "children's room." Human relations, in the earlier books, were recognized only in the administration of maids. People trained in this subject matter were suddenly confronted with the need to include in their teaching material on personality development, community responsibility, personal ideals, human relations. The other element was already there; it was the basic core. To this was added the social, affective, value aspect of the home; and if there is discrepancy at present, it is because this new addition has not yet been fully incorporated.

In addition, Home Economics has now undertaken to teach not only a woman's skills but also a woman's role to the growing girl; and the courses in Family Life may teach the adult role to both boys and girls. In this era of social mobility and second-generation immigrants it has proved excessively difficult to avoid an implication of discontinuity between the student's present family and the one he hopes to make through marriage, between family values and the ones he is taught in school.

As *A Guide to Planning Units in Home Economics* states:

The success of the family is dependent upon spiritual values as well as material things. Attitudes and beliefs originate in the home. . . . *When home influences are not what they should be, the teacher has double responsibility.* [The italics are added.] [2]

Again, the school cannot guide a girl to learn to become a woman through sharing the life and work of her mother, even if the factor of social mobility did not make this difficult. In the main, the school itself makes it impossible to teach the student in this way. The girl is required by law to absent herself from the home during the time when the everyday work of the home is carried on. The mother, well taught, has learned to wash dishes, clean the house, make beds, bathe and sun the baby, market, and even start dinner, before the daughter returns from school. Home-work—whether given to the student by way of involving the parents in her schooling, or by way of keeping her occupied and out of mischief, contributes to this cutting off from the life of the home. In rural areas where schools are consolidated, the child may be absent from home for ten or eleven hours daily. Clubs in the school encourage the student to further absent herself from the home and its life. In addition, technological progress, the new time-saving devices, the new theories of human relations and personality make it necessary for the girl to learn in school about the home, the family, and herself. As a textbook in common use puts it:

We cannot assume that we shall learn all that we need to know merely because we grew up in a family. We cannot afford to over-look that part of our school training which contributes to suc-cessful home living. . . . Home Economics gives us improved techniques for home living. . . . We need training in homemaking if we are to be successful homemakers.

To make the study, I analyzed some fifteen state and city manuals and guides for the teaching of Home Economics or the related field of Family Life Education. One textbook used as basic in one of the programs was also analyzed. The manuals come from the West Coast, the Middle West, the Southwest, the South, the East; they were written for teachers in these areas, although the writers may come from other regions and may thus represent certain cultural variations. I have analyzed the latest manuals I could find from each region; these cover a span of nine years. Since this is a study of discrepancy in the manuals, and not an investigation of what is taught today, no attempt was made to find out exactly how the manuals are used, how much freedom of interpretation a teacher has in using them, and to what extent she is free to use them only as guides suggesting procedure.

The writers of these manuals have undertaken, to a large extent effectively, the enormous task of clarifying human relations in a society of unclear roles; of maintaining belief in the dignity of work in an era of mass production; of presenting the American way with simplicity and conviction to a generation coming from a variety of cultural, social, religious backgrounds. My paper gives no indication of the great extent of what has been already achieved. Again, in presenting the material, I suspect that I often pass judgment on what I find, instead of giving an objective statement of fact. If I do so, I am subject to the same criticism which I make of the manuals: I do not implement my objective adequately. My intention is to be merely descriptive, and to draw conclusions without bias. When I speak of externality as dominant, I intend this to be sheer statement of fact. If I state it with dismay, it is because, as a Greek by birth and rearing, I regard externality as deplorable. I give this autobiographical item, because I believe it may be a factor in my perception and selection, as well as in the tone of my presentation.

I

The discrepancy existing between theory and implementation, as well as between the areas of home living and of homemaking skills, is expressed variously in discontinuities and dualisms, which, though more pronounced in the older manuals, are still present to an extent in the newer ones. A discussion of family life and marriage from a course of study designed for high school, published in 1950, will illustrate this point. This course is offered because:

We are living now in a changing society. The family patterns and traditions of yesterday no longer hold true in the world of to-day. . . . Plainly, people do need help in understanding the real values of life; in appreciating the very real treasure of the family . . . they need help in preparing for marriage in order to live fully, richly, and satisfyingly. The justification for the teaching of courses in the schools in human relationships is found in that last sentence.[3]

The main objective of the course is stated as follows: "To promote the founding of . . . ideal homes. . . ." For this the individual needs a healthy personality; and the basic social needs for the personality are best met in the family unit. The family is of "immense importance in the emotional development" of the individual; therefore, the course includes units which are to help the student develop his personality through the human relations in the home. The lesson on Family Relationships has as its first objective to "help the student to understand the meaning of the co-operative, the sharing; the democratic home. . . ."

How is the student's home life actually to be used in helping him found an "ideal home"? In the lesson on Family Relationships there are three more objectives stated:

2. . . . To realize the purpose of restrictions.
3. . . . To realize his contribution to family conflict.
4. . . . To help the student know ways of improving family life, of reducing conflict.

And the name of the lesson has as subtitle: "Family Relationships: Conflicts—Ways of Improving."

The lesson apparently attempts here to teach its material in terms of specific problems to be solved, specific things to do. And the problematic material is characteristically negative: not something had, to be enjoyed, but something to be achieved or solved or ameliorated. To teach in terms of problems has long been considered an effective method; the problem delimits, makes concrete, clarifies. But in selecting this method the manual necessarily suggests the presentation of family life as negative, thus going counter to its avowed intention. Family life is presented as not good and there is no suggestion that the student is to be helped to indulge in it and be emotionally nourished. He is to relate himself to it in terms of adjusting to it, correcting its evils, improving it, rather than enjoying it. Home life is full of conflict and restriction. In this lesson, the question posed as: "Why do parents act as they do?" is spelled out as "Why do they 'always' say no?" The brother-sister relationship is covered in one question, "What can a boy or girl do about a 'pesky' sister or brother . . . ?" and under one subheading, "Sister-sister, brother-brother, brother-sister conflicts." This is the picture which the course presents of "the very real treasure of the family" which it is to help the student to appreciate.

In using his family experience to develop into an adult who can found an ideal home, the student is to be urged to learn "to get along." He is to recognize restriction, improve relations, resolve conflicts so that he can "get along" with others and himself. Of the six "immediate and specific objectives" given for the course, four are to help the student "to get along." It is a negative objective, satisfied with a minimum which lacks positive values; it does not go beyond the elimination of the undesirable. It is corrective rather than creative. The most dynamic and positive phrasing in which this "getting-along" sphere of human relations is expressed is represented by statements such as the following: "A substitute for that tried and true method of getting along—desire and effort—has never been found. . . . Try to attain the live-and-let-live attitude, and see . . . the achievement in maturity it will mean, even its relationship to preparation for marriage." This minimal phrasing of goals is certainly not what this course of study wants to convey to the growing generation as American culture.

The American ideal of the maximum is expressed only when speaking of the future, of the homes which the students themselves will establish with a chosen mate. This future family life is presented in positive value terms, full of creativity. In the one lesson on Family Relationships, the term "get along" occurs seven times; in the eight lessons on dating, courting, engagement, and marriage, it occurs, I think, only once. And what is impressive here is the large number of times when the "get along" attitude is absent, replaced by terms implying spontaneity and value (the italics throughout the following are added): "You *enjoy* the thought of being his wife." "You work out disagreements as they appear, for your relationship is more *important* than being right." "You are *willing to do personally anything* to make it [the marriage] succeed." "You are *willing and eager* to share with him in everything." Now the student is to be helped to establish an "ideal home" where happy family life is maintained, by being helped to develop emotionally and mature through experiencing human relations in his family. How can the meager and stingy soil of the "get-along" relationships bring forth anything so vital?

"Family living" in the present and "marriage" in the future also differ in the way "sharing" is presented. "To be willing to share" is one of the signs of maturity listed in the course, and sharing is mentioned often throughout the course; the student is to be helped to understand "the meaning of the cooperative, the sharing." However, only in the marriage relationship is it *sharing in,* as in the last quotation given. In the life which develops the attitudes that would make this possible, it is always a *sharing*. And sharing, without the *in*, is diminishing and dividing; it is concerned with fairness, atomistically pitting one individual against another. It is in this respect the opposite of *sharing in,* which enhances in the very act of sharing.

The writers of this guide, faced with the task of presenting good marriage, give a picture of a warm, positive, creative, agentive relationship, full of value and without utilitarianism. But in trying to show the student how to relate himself with his present family, they face a dilemma. They would like to show him how to find emotional nourishment, value, and security here. Yet often this is a situation in which he is not accorded an agentive role, where he has no opportunity to create; it is a given, and often for him its predominant quality is one of dissonance and conflict. So the solution is to guide the student in resolving this conflict, understanding the basis of the restrictions, "getting along" with the least possible friction.

As a result, the course suggests that creativity in human relations be taught through the medium of situations which allow only of correction, and a positive attitude, through relations which are phrased as negative and restrictive. It has to teach the American ideal of the maximum—"willing to do . . . anything," "eager to share in everything"—through experiences phrased as minimal.

This type of unresolved dualism is found generally between the given and the chosen, the areas of the *must do* and the *free to do*. The skills used in homemaking are presented as a *must*, to be recognized and accepted. For example, a textbook tells the student "We must have a working knowledge of nutrition. We must know what foods. . . . We must apply what we know. . . . [1]"

The following are stated objectives for the "Clothing Unit" in one of the manuals:

> Recognition that some seams need no finish.
> Recognition of order of work as important.
> Recognition of effect of laundry and pressing on appearance.
> Realization of need for fixing good habits.
> Appreciation of need for good habits. [7]

This, like the family of one's birth, is in the area of the given, to which the student is to be led to adjust minimally and not necessarily with joy. There is no social value in this, there are no "good times." Value and freedom lie in the chosen, the leisure-time activity, the hobby, the special occasion (the italics are added):

> Problem 4: *Discuss* values of remembering family birthdays, other *special* days.
> Problem 5: Discuss the *problems* of brother-sister relations. [4]

The chosen is something that I *can* do (I am free to do or not do) rather than something I *should* do (I am not free not to do). For example we have (italics added), "What responsibility in my home *should* I share?" and, farther down in the same section, "How *can* I help my family *enjoy leisure* time? [8]"

It is in the area of the chosen that value lies. During leisure time, one is free to choose one's occupation; this then may contain "fun" or other value. Consequently, there is a dualism between work and leisure. The word "enjoy" is used rarely, if ever, in connection with the regular work or life of the home. In one manual I found it used only once, when "to enjoy work [3]" is given in a list as one of the characteristics of maturity. In one guide, which suggests courses, lessons, and units for six grades, the word "enjoy [9]" is used twice to my knowledge, both times in speaking of hobbies. This guide suggests that the unit entitled Food for Family Fun be correlated with the unit on Family Relations; a year-long unit called Food for Family Health precedes this, but no suggestion is made as to its being connected in any way with family relations. In another manual, only leisure occupations are called "enriching [5]"; and only in connection with leisure did I find the words "joy" and "satisfaction" used.

The one value, apart from "nutritional value," implemented through the teaching of the skills needed for routine work in homemaking is "the value of saving time and energy," or the "value of time and money management." And this value is negative, tending not toward deriving satisfaction from the process, but toward the opposite. It helps shorten the process, which has been called a "meaningful experience" in the list of objectives, but is actually presented as preoccupation with the meaningless. In doing their work girls are urged to "perform housekeeping duties using both old and new equipment; compare results of experiment as to time, energy, and efficiency [8]." Relative enjoyment is apparently not to be considered as a factor is the evaluation. The human relations differential between the mechanical dishwasher and the family dishpan is not discussed. What is important is that the *must* be diminished, leaving more time and energy for the chosen.

It is so important, in fact, to diminish this *must* of everyday living that many of the manuals urge the "sharing" of work not as a good and rewarding experience in itself, but as a means of increasing leisure time, particularly, of course, for the mother. In one manual, the objective of "sharing responsibility" is implemented as "sharing household duties to allow for leisure [10]." In another we read,

> *Appreciation of fact that sharing home tasks means some leisure time for all.* Problem: Report on sharing care of rooms in homes and on sharing mother's special tasks.
> a. How mother used that extra free time.
> b. Good times made possible by working together. [7]

Another way to escape from the valueless given is to make a special occasion of what is otherwise a routine task, for example, to prepare a picnic instead of the usual lunch. Instead of following established procedure passively, the individual can, in this way, exercise initiative and spontaneity, and be agentive in creating the special.

In all the writing there is repeatedly this suggested escape from the routine to the special, from work to leisure, when the good is to be introduced:

> *Housekeeping is an important part of the spirit that makes a home.* . . . The end product of effective housekeeping is comfortable living. Comfortable living affords time for leisure. . . . [1]

Being without value the work of ordinary home life is not dynamic and provides no emotional nourishment, no feedback. This, like all the good, comes through leisure:

> Happy family life is essential to the welfare of individuals and nations as well. . . . Total health, mental and physical, has its foundations in the habits established in home living. . . . Recreation is doing things for fun. Out of fun comes relaxation and renewal of energy for all we must do.

It is in the special that social values lie, and through these are they implemented. The section on Thinking of Others, in the seventh-grade homemaking course given in one of the manuals, states the following objectives:

> 1. An interest in doing things for others.
> 2. To learn ways girls can do thoughtful things for others.
> [These are implemented through the following means:]
> 1. Events that call for special thoughtful attention to others.
> 2. Ways of remembering special times.
> 3. Simple refreshments for an "afternoon at home."
> 4. Decorations and favors for special occasion. [4]

The list continues through eleven objectives all dealing with the special. Another manual teaches "consideration for others and willingness to compromise," entirely through the problem. "Sharing facilities for entertainment: 1. Radio, 2. Other entertainment [7]." In one high-school course "Good Citizenship" is presented as "positively practiced [5]" only during one's leisure.

Family feeling, unity, loyalty, come through sharing occasions of fun. "The strong feeling of love and respect in a modern family is the result of playing together more often than working together," according to one textbook.

> The greatest satisfaction is derived from the companionship of the people who live there [the family] and the pleasures they enjoy together. . . . It would be wise to adopt the slogan: "The family . . . that plays together stays together." . . . Good times shared by the family group result in a better understanding of each other and therefore promote family unity. [1]

At no time are the operations involved in everyday home-making presented as areas where spontaneity might be given range. Initiative and creativity are listed, in one manual, only in the section on Fun with the Family, under the subtitle "Cultivating Hobbies [10]." In another manual, there is a leisure-time unit listed under "Clothing [7]" and only here is the development of originality mentioned.

"Work can be fun" but only in the context of the "special," or when one adds fun to it externally; in itself, it contains no good. The manual suggests that the family "hang a bulletin board over the sink and put jokes and messages on it; discuss plans together. This will add fun to the job of family dishwashing [7]." The work of homemaking will further be made bearable if you plan carefully so that it can be made as brief as possible and can thus give you leisure for creativity, fun, and the exercise of co-operation, consideration for others, and allied social traits. Working with others is good, because the work can then be completed faster. Working for others is drab, but you can adorn it with special acts of your own choice and initiative. Everyday life is grim because it is the given, and value lies only in private freedom of choice; but you can always escape from routine work into the freedom of the special if you master your skills and learn to plan wisely.

The last manual, quoted above, states that one of its general objectives is "to develop an appreciation of homemaking as a valuable and enjoyable occupation." But it finds it impossible to show how homemaking in itself can be valuable. It attempts to teach "the value of a plan providing for . . . cleaning in which re-sponsibilities are shared. . . ." One must "understand . . . the value of planning one's work" and the "value of planning for the care of the house." I think these are the only occasions when the word "value" is used. Several times the word "enjoy" is used, all except one in connection with leisure-time "Fun with the Family," as might be expected from the slogan quoted above. The exception is a "special" occasion, when girls were urged to prepare Sunday breakfast as a "surprise for daddy" and to "give mother a chance to stay in bed an extra half-hour [10]." The girls reported that they "enjoyed" this.

II

One reason why there is no value in the given operations of everyday homemaking is that the dualism between social relations and socially oriented operations is still unresolved, although much progress has been made since the two (family life and housework) have been put together under one program. There is an explicit attempt to merge the two, but so far it has not been entirely successful. "Both [skills and arts] are interwoven into what we mean by homemaking"; yet nowhere are housekeeping skills and operations presented as implementing the making of a home, which is "an emotional climate . . . [where] we are loved and wanted for ourselves. We find security and safety." Social value, warmth, love, human relations, or the inculcating of attitudes and values in the young child are not yet presented as implemented through any of the operations of housekeeping. One manual states the following in its introduction:

> Learning to live, to share, to work and play together through wholesome and meaningful experiences in home and school living develops attitudes, abilities, appreciation and a sense of values essential for a democratic society. . . . The primary purposes [of Home Economics education] are satisfaction and efficiency in home living . . . [4]

The manual then proceeds to describe a unit on Family Meals for eighth-grade students. In this section the girl is taught what is appropriate kitchen dress, what are the nutritional needs of an individual, and how to save time, have an orderly kitchen, judge the results of her work, serve attractively, and select recipes. No "learning to live, to share, to work . . . together through . . . meaningful experiences" here: there is "efficiency," but no "satisfaction." The girl is "helping with the family meals," but the helped does not appear at all. She is asked to "serve family style"; but apart from these two instances, the "family" is not present or implied in any of the activities except when a girl is urged to "help younger brother or sister with eating habits." In all the manuals examined, home living as presented lacks value when proceeding on its usual way. For example, one brings up the subject under the following title: "Some Understanding of Factors Which Affect the Family: Friction and Strain in the Modern Family [7]."

The home economists are well aware of the need of introducing value into their picture of family living and homemaking. They speak of family values in their general statements. Out of twenty-four subjects suggested for discussion in one manual, two mention value:

> Suggest round table discussion on: What values families cherish and how some values persist and others are modified as families grow up. . . . Find out how children and youth contribute to family's cash income. List values gained by such contributions.

Yet the very nature of the situation, the teaching of home life away from its context of social warmth, so far has presented an insuperable obstacle. When skills and attitudes are taken directly from the mother, while the child participates in her life, they contain the value of the social context. But Home Economics is given the task of adding value, human relations, and ethics of everyday living, to mechanically defined skills taught within the context of the sterile Home Economics laboratory. And even when the laboratory is a house or an apartment, it is one in which there is no pulsing life, where no one loves and grieves and rages, where none of the significant work of living is carried on. There is no continuity of daily living here; the acts performed fulfill no function apart from that of the teaching of an operation. Here we may find muffins baked at 1:00, to be consumed by girls replete with lunch at 1:35, because they have to learn not to waste food. The very situation demands that value be added afterward, externally, necessarily through the special. And when the skills and operations are discussed in their family context, this extraneous view of value persists, as it has been so firmly established.

What is striking here is that the consistent characteristic of the valueless, which apparently accounts for its lack of meaning, is that it is the *given*. All that the girl can do with the given in family relations is to improve them, adjust to them, correct them so as to make them bearable; or she can use them as an exercise in human relationship, by way of developing her personality. They are not nourishing in themselves or to be enjoyed for themselves. And she is not expected to find a creative role within the given. One manual mentions as one of its general objectives "helping the student appreciate freedom within the law [3]." But, as a matter of fact, nowhere here or in any of the manuals and textbooks examined is this objective carried out. It is never suggested that the student be given guidance in finding freedom *within* the law, the given relations, the routine of homemaking. To be free, to be creative, to exercise initiative and originality, to enjoy spontaneously, she is to be invited to escape into the chosen: into leisure-time activities, into the special occasion, the nonpatterned Sunday supper, the birthday party, the picnic, and away from the family of her birth into the chosen relationship of marriage. And here, also, it is only the relationship as wife which contains freedom and spontaneity; the mother's life then reverts to the routine procedures of the must.

III

Another dualism implicit in the manuals is that between self and society. The student is urged to develop herself by acquiring and developing, in the main, traits which meet with the approval of others: to achieve "a pleasing voice, a pleasant expression [5]," to find an answer to the question, "How can I be popular with others? [4]" This means that standards and criteria for personality and conduct are to be sought outside the self. The emphasis seems to be on the development of the "other-directed," to use Riesman's term. One manual lists a unit which "might be called personality and good grooming [7]"; and, in general, personality is defined largely in terms of manners, grooming, and adherence to accepted conduct:

> Personality Development. Objectives: Desire and ability to know and use approved social customs and good manners. Make and keep friends. Possess good personality traits. Problems:
>
> *a.* Get along with people by having good manners.
> *b.* How to develop good manners at home.
> *c.* Careful grooming to make you pleasing at first sight.
> *d, e, f, g, h* deal with being a good guest and a good hostess and having a good voice.
> *i.* How to be popular, and make and keep friends. Five points listed under this deal with good manners, two with dating procedures, five with how to behave in public. [4]

Such a person, who has good manners and behaves acceptably on social occasions, has "the ability to get along with people [which] not only increases your chances of having a good time but also contributes to success in every phase of living [4]." Another manual lists.

> *General Objectives:* [of unit which "might be called personality and good grooming."]
> 1. Realization of the importance of good personal appearance and the development of a good personality for successful living.
> 2. Knowledge of how to behave in a socially acceptable manner. [7]

One manual lists seven objectives for the unit which helps the individual in personality development. Of these, two are:

> 1. Understands the importance of knowing current customs.
> 2. Practices some ways of acting which are socially accepted. [6]

Another manual states as one of its objectives "Appreciation of and a desire for a pleasing personality." A "pleasing" personality is not necessarily good, or strong, or mature, or relaxed, one which satisfies an internal standard; it is an externally directed one, which succeeds when it pleases another. This stress on the teaching of good grooming and acceptable manners comes, to some extent, in response to a felt need and reflects the social mobility of this society; it will probably remain, even after the disparity between a good personality and a pleasing personality has been overcome.

There is another way in which society is presented as external to the self: it is to be used for the meeting of the needs of the self. A unit for the eighth grade, entiled "Being a Likeable Person in Your Own Home," states as one of its objectives the teaching of the student to look "for ways in which family life contributes to success." In the same manual, in a unit for the ninth grade, entitled "Feeling Successful in High School Years," the students are to become aware of "ways in which school and community are contributing to their success [6]." In another manual, relationships within the family, "contacts," and "cooperation" are urged on the student for the development of a "truly effective personality [5]." Consistent with this conception of the self, as external to society, a course is divided into sections on: *helping myself*, and *helping others*.

IV

The goals and values of the self are also phrased in terms of externality. Its qualities and traits are spoken of as possessed and acquired. Time and energy and even habits are mentioned as "managed" or "used" by the self. One manual states as its first objective

> Ability to use wisely available human and material resources such as time, energy, health, money, attitudes, and understandings. [8]

It follows that the self, as presented here, is not an internally growing unit, but one which increases through accretion, so that personal development is a matter of "acquiring desirable traits."

In one manual, the unit on "Growing Up" lists the following among seventeen "needs and interests" (italics are added):

To *better* understand one's self and others.
Make *more* of own decisions.
Buy *more* of own things.
Assume *more* responsibility for behavior.
Find ways to *improve* personality.
Be *more* popular. [10]

Much of this is, of course, abetted by a language which makes it extremely difficult to refer to growth and development except in terms of accretion, increase, and improvement. Thus even emotional maturity itself may be phrased as external, a goal to be achieved, not a becoming. One manual which uses the phrase, "the child *grows into* [italics added] adult situations," nevertheless presents maturity as "a goal that pays the highest dividends." It speaks of the individual who "pays too high a price for the security he gains by withdrawal or by aggression," thus giving the impression that security, also, is something external to be bought at a price. Continuing this phrasing of externality it tells how some individuals maintain a discrepancy between the goals they set for themselves and "the energy they are willing to expend." An individual who has "a sense of values" knows that "there is a price to pay and is willing to pay for value received [11]."

The self is clearly conceived as external to its life process when we come to the discussion of planning. Managing the time and energy of the self by planning one's work is presented as one of the main objectives in a variety of areas. Out of forty-eight "behavior changes sought" through the unit on "Clothing" in one manual, seven mention "planning and the management of time [9]." In another manual, out of five objectives to be met in four to six weeks of teaching, one is "learn to save time [4]." In a unit on "Foods for Special Occasions," covering two pages, a manual mentions "plan" eighteen times and "time management" three: "Plan work efficiently, and manage time well" . . . "the value of planning" . . . "plan and carry out" . . . "plan time schedules" . . . "plan market order [7]" . . . and so forth. "Careful planning helps make the task easier," states another manual;

"Value of Planning Care of the House: 1. Saving time, 2. Saving energy [10]."

In general, planning is taught in connection with the given, the required work. Here there is to be no wasted motion or wasted time; no exploring and no randomness of operation. Time saved from this area is time for leisure and fun; energy saved means energy for leisure-time activity, and this may be used for exploring. One manual, however, carries planning into the chosen: leisure time itself can be planned and managed to the advantage of the self. A student can use leisure time to earn money, for example, and, in this way, meet three objectives:

1. Realization that what she does today is important to tomorrow's success.
2. Realization that success in the school, home, and community are related.
3. Finding out what are opportunities for part-time jobs.

The student is told, in effect, that if she wants to succeed tomorrow she should plan carefully so that even the leisure time of today may contribute toward this end. This manual quotes students' reports on how their free time was used, and lists some of the answers giving "satisfactory" ways (italics added):

Drove out in the country *in order to see the sunset.*
Read a book that *has been recommended.*
Did some typing for a neighbor for pay to build up a fund *for a definite purpose.*

No random driving in the country, nor exploring in lanes, no exploring in the realm of books, no building up a fund and then discovering something to spend it on. No exploration, no adventure is quoted as desirable, even in this "free" time. Time is "wasted" when one is "day-dreaming instead of attending to the present"; when "one talks idly for long times." It is "not wasted" when "talking idly to someone in order to be better acquainted." Yet when does one discover that one wants to be better acquainted? Planning beforehand would save time, as "knowing what radio program you would like to listen to and when they come." Yet how does one discover the unknown and unpredictable?

V

The discrepancies, discontinuities, and unresolved dualisms listed in this paper are implicit in a program which is the result of accretion. The program is in constant process of revision and integration; when it becomes a unit some of these discrepancies will probably disappear. Others, however, are inherent in the very structure of a mobile society and in a culture which values change. It is possible, then, that in presenting the adult role in terms of discontinuity and exclusive dualism the writings examined here are merely faithfully presenting American culture.

10———Jules Henry

Attitude Organization in Elementary School Classrooms[*]

The word *organization* in this paper is used to stand for order and determinateness as distinguished from disorder and randomness. The emotions and attitudes of prepubertal children in our culture are not, on the whole, directed toward generalized social goals, but focused rather on the peer group and parents. From the point of view of an observer who has in mind the larger social goals, like the maintenance of stable economic relations, common front against the enemy, maintenance of positive attitudes toward popular national symbols, and so on, the emotions and attitudes of prepubertal children in our culture may be viewed as lacking order. The adult, on the other hand, is supposed to have so organized his tendencies to respond to the environment that his emotions, attitudes, and activities subserve over-all social goals. While it is true that attitudes and feelings are bent toward social goals even from earliest infancy, (Henry and Boggs, 1952), many institutions combine to organize these attitudes and feelings so that ultimately a social steady state will be maintained. The elementary school classroom in our culture is one of the most powerful instruments in this effort, for it does not merely sustain attitudes that have been created in the home, but reinforces some, deemphasizes others, and makes its own contribution. In this way it prepares the conditions for and contributes toward the ultimate

[*] Reprinted from *The American Journal of Orthopsychiatry*, XXVII, January, 1957, 117–133, with permission. The material in this article and the one following is developed more fully in a book by Professor Henry, *Culture Against Man*, Random House, 1963.

organization of peer- and parent-directed attitudes into a dynamically interrelated attitudinal structure supportive of the culture.

This organizing process is comparable to, though not identical with, the *re*organization of attitudes and resources that takes place as a society shifts from a peacetime to a wartime footing. During a period of peace in our society, adult hostility and competitiveness may be aimed at overcoming competition in business or social mobility, while love and cooperation are directed toward family and friends, and toward achieving specific social economic ends *within* the society. With the coming of war the instruments of government seek to direct hostility and competitiveness toward the enemy, while love and cooperation are directed toward the armed forces, civilian instruments of war (price controls, rationing, civilian officials, etc), and national symbols. From the point of view of an observer *within the war machine*, the civilian attitudes at first seem random and unorganized. He wants to change them so that from *his point of view* they will seem organized. The situation is similar, though not identical, with respect to the child: to an observer inside the head of even some psychotic children, attitudes and behavior may seem organized. But to the observer on the outside, whose focus is on social goals, the child seems *un-* or *dis*-organized. The prime effort of the adult world is *to make child attitudes look organized to adults.* The emphasis in this paper is on the description of the process of organizing child attitudes as it can be observed in some middle-class urban American classrooms.

THE WITCH-HUNT SYNDROME

One of the most striking characteristics of American culture since the settlement has been the phenomenon of intragroup aggression, which finds its pathological purity of expression in witch hunts (Starkey, 1949). It comes as a frightening surprise to democratic people to find themselves suddenly in terror of their neighbors; to discover that they are surrounded by persons who carry tales about others while confessing evil of themselves;

to perceive a sheeplike docility settling over those whom they considered strong and autonomous. The *witch-hunt syndrome* therefore, as constituting one of the key tragedies of democracy, is selected for the elucidation of the organization of attitudes in our culture. In this witch's brew *destructive criticism* of others is the toad's horns; *docility* the body of the worm; *feelings of vulnerability* the chicken heart; *fear of internal (intragroup) hostility* the snake's fang; *confession of evil deeds* the locust's leg; and *boredom and emptiness* the dead man's eye. The witch-hunt syndrome is thus stated to be a dynamically interrelated system of feelings and actions made up of destructive criticism of others, docility, feelings of vulnerability, fear of internal aggression, confession of evil deeds, and boredom.

The witch-hunt syndrome in full panoply was observed in but one of the dozen classrooms in four schools studied in the research which I discuss here. Thus it seems a relatively rare phenomenon. But the question I set myself to answer is, How could it occur at all? What are the attitudes, present in the children, that were organized by this teacher into the syndrome? How could she do it? With what materials did she work? She did not create out of nothing the attitudes she manipulated in her "Vigilance Club" in this fourth-grade classroom in a middle-class American community. She had to have something to start with. The argument of this paper will be that the feelings and tendencies to action which this teacher organized into the witch-hunt syndrome in her class are present in an *un*organized state in other classrooms. Given a certain type of teacher, he or she will be able to develop into a highly specialized, tightly integrated system in his classroom those attitudes which are present in differently organized state in the children in all classrooms. Let us now look at a meeting of the Vigilance Club.

1. In the extreme back of the room is a desk called the "isolation ward." A child has been placed there for disciplinary reasons. The Vigilance Club of the class is holding a meeting. . . . Officers are elected by the group. The purpose of the club is to teach children to be better citizens. The order of procedure is as follows: the president . . . bangs her gavel on the desk and . . . says, "The meeting of the Vigilance Club will come to order."

Each child then takes from his or her desk a booklet whose title is *All About Me . . .* and places it on top of his desk. The vice-president calls the name of a child, gets the child's booklet, and places it on the teacher's desk. The president then calls on the child and asks, "———, have you been a good citizen this week?" The president says, "Name some of the good things you have done," and the child tries to recall some, like opening doors for people, running errands, etc. Next the president asks the class if it remembers any good things the child has done. Each point is written in the child's booklet by the teacher. The president then . . . says to the child, "Name the bad things you have done. . . ." The child reports the wrongs he has committed during the week, and the class is asked to contribute information about his behavior. This too is written in the booklet by the teacher, who also reprimands the student, registers horror, scolds, etc. . . . When one child reports a misdemeanor of another the teacher asks for witnesses, and numerous children sometimes volunteer. . . . The child in the "isolation ward" reported some good deeds he had done; the children reported some more, and the isolated child was told he would soon be released. . . . [During this meeting some children showed obvious pleasure in confessing undesirable behavior. One child, by volunteering only good things of the students, seemed to be using the situation to overcome what seemed to the observer to be her unpopularity with the class.][1]

Before analyzing this protocol for the attitudes present in it, it will be well to look at some events that occurred in this classroom on another day.

2. During the game of "spelling baseball" a child raised her hand and reported that Alice and John had been talking to each other. This occurred when neither child was "at bat." The teacher asked Alice if this was so, and she replied that it was, but John denied having spoken to Alice. The teacher said that John must have listened to Alice, but he denied this too. Then the teacher asked whether there had been any witnesses, and many hands were raised. Some witnesses were seated on the far side of the room, and hence could not have seen Alice and John from their location in the room. All those testifying had "seen" Alice talking, but

---

[1] In order to prevent identification of teachers and children, the names of my student observers are not used.

denied John's guilt. Alice was sent to the "bull pen," which meant that she had to sit on the floor behind the teacher's desk, and could no longer participate in the game. . . .

3. Mary raised her hand and said, "It hurts me to say this. I really wish I didn't have to do it, but I saw Linda talking." Linda was Mary's own teammate, had just spelled a word correctly, and had gone to first base. The teacher asked Linda if she had talked, and Linda said, "No, I just drew something in the air with my finger. . . ." She was sent to the "bull pen."

In these examples we see intragroup aggression; docility of the children in conforming, with no murmur of protest, to the teacher's wishes; and confession of "evil." In such a situation children develop feelings of vulnerability and fear of detection. Let us now look for these phenomena in classrooms presided over by teachers who seem to represent the more normal American type, in comfortable, middle-class, white communities: teachers who are conscientious and reasonably gentle, but creatures of their culture, and humanly weak. We begin not with internal aggression as expressed in spying and talebearing, but with the milder, though closely related phenomenon of carping, destructive criticism. While this occurs throughout the sample, I give here examples only from a fifth-grade classroom in the same school system.

4. Bill has given a report on tarantulas. As usual the teacher waits for volunteers to comment on the child's report.
Mike: The talk was well illustrated, well prepared. . . .
Bob: Bill had a piece of paper [for his notes], and teacher said he should have them on cards. . . .
Bill says he could not get any cards.
Teacher says that he should tear the paper next time if he has no cards.
Bob: He held the paper behind him. If he had had to look at it, it wouldn't have looked very nice.

5. Betty reports on Theodore Roosevelt.
A child comments that it was very good but she looked at her notes too much.
Teacher remarks that Betty had so *much* information.
Bob: She said "calvary" [instead of "cavalry"].

6. Charlie reads a story he made up himself: "The Unknown

Guest." One dark, dreary night . . . on a hill a house stood. This house was forbidden territory for Bill and Joe, but they were going in anyway. The door creaked, squealed, slammed. A voice warned them to go home. Spider webs, dirty furniture . . . Bill wanted to go home. They went upstairs. A stair cracked. They entered a room. A voice said they might as well stay and find out now; and their father came out. He laughed and they laughed, but they never forgot their adventure together.

Teacher: Are there any words that give you the mood of the story? . . .

Lucy: He could have made the sentences a little better. . . .

Teacher: Let's come back to Lucy's comment. What about his sentences?

Gert: They were too short. . . .

Charlie and Jeanne are having a discussion about the position of the word "stood."

Teacher: Wait a minute, some people are forgetting their manners. . . .

Jeff: About the room: the boys went up the stairs and one "cracked"; then they were in the room. Did they fall through the stairs or what?

Teacher suggests Charlie make that a little clearer.

Lucy: If he fell through the step. . . .

Teacher: We still haven't decided about the short sentences. Perhaps they make the story more spooky and mysterious.

Gwynne: I wish he had read with more expression instead of all at one time.

Rachel: Not enough expression.

Teacher: Charlie, they want a little more expression from you. I guess we've given you enough suggestions for one time. (Charlie does not raise his head, which is bent over his desk as if studying a paper.) Charlie! I guess we've given you enough suggestions for one time, Charlie, haven't we? (Charlie half raises his head, seems to assent grudgingly.)

The striking thing about these examples is that the teacher supports the children in their carping criticism of their fellows. Her performance in this is not, however, consistent; but even where, as in Example 6, she seems at one point to try to set herself against the tide of destruction, by calling attention to the possible artistry in Charlie's short sentences, she ends up supporting the class against him, and Charlie becomes upset. Thus teacher, by rewarding the children's tendencies to carp, reinforces them. Teachers, however, are able to make their own contributions to this tendency. The single example given below will serve as illustration:

> 7. Joan reads us a poem she has written about Helen Keller . . . which concludes with the couplet:
> "Helen Keller as a woman was very great;
> She is really a credit to the United States."
> Teacher (amusedly): Is "states" supposed to rhyme with "great"? When Joan murmurs that it is, the teacher says, "We'll call it poetic license."

From time to time one can see a teacher vigorously oppose tendencies in the children to tear each other to pieces. The following example is from the sixth grade:

> 8. The Parent-Teachers Association is sponsoring a school frolic, and the children have been asked to write jingles for the publicity. For many of the children the experience of writing a jingle seems painful. They are restless, bite their pencils, squirm around in their seats, speak to their neighbors, and from time to time pop up with questions like, "Does it have to rhyme, Mr. Smith?" . . . At last Mr. Smith says, "All right, let's read some of the jingles now." Child after child says he "couldn't get one"; but some have succeeded. One girl has written a very long jingle, *obviously the best in the class*. However, instead of using Friday as the frolic day she used Tuesday, and several protests were heard from the children. Mr. Smith defended her. "Well, so she made a mistake. But you are too prone to criticize. If *you* could only do so well!"

It will be observed that all the examples are taken from circumstances in which the child's self-system is most intensely involved; where his own poetry or prose is in question, or where he has worked hard to synthesize material into a report. It is precisely at the points where the ego is most exposed that the attack is most telling. The numerous instances in the sample, where the teachers, by a word of praise or a pat on the head, play a supportive role, indicate their awareness of the vulnerability of the children. Meanwhile, as I have pointed out, the teachers often fall into the trap of triggering or supporting destructive impulses in the children.

The carping criticism of one's peers is a form of intragroup aggression, which can be quite threatening and destructive. Tale-bearing, however, countenanced by some teachers more than by others, can be an overwhelming threat to autonomy. While telling on others can be organized into the patrol-monitor complex (prestige through controlling and telling), useful perhaps in maintaining order in large school populations, its operation within the classroom may have serious consequences. Let us look at a couple of examples.

> 9. Second grade. As teacher asked the children to clear their desks one boy raised his hand, and when called on said, "Jimmy just walked by and socked me on the head."
> Teacher: Is this true?
> Jimmy: He hit me first.
> Teacher: Why don't you both take seats up here (in front of the room). I'm not sure people like you belong in the second grade.
> 10. Sixth grade special class for bright students.
> The children are working on their special nature study projects. Joseph passes where Ralph is working. Ralph (to teacher): Joseph is writing too much on his birds.
> Teacher: Joseph, you should write only a few things.

In our sample, telling on other children in the classroom is infrequent outside the class in which the Vigilance Club was formed. Destructive criticism is the preferred mode of attack in most classrooms. The ease with which tendencies to attack peers can be organized into telling on others, however, is illustrated by the monitor-patrol complex, and by the Vigilance Club (Example 3).

Competition

Competition is an important element in the witch-hunt syndrome. Since witch hunts involve so often obtaining the attention and approval of some powerful central figure, the examples of competitiveness that I shall cite illustrate how approval and attention seeking occur as the child attempts to beat out his peers for the nod of the teacher. It would be easy to cite examples from protocols of the merciless laughter of children at the failures or gaucheries of their classmates. I am interested, however, more in showing the all-pervading character of the phenomenon of competition, *even in its mildest forms*. The first example is from a fourth-grade music lesson:

> 11. The children are singing songs of Ireland and her neighbors from the book *Songs of Many Lands*. . . . Teacher plays on piano while children sing. . . . While children are singing some of them hunt in the index, find a song belonging to one of the four countries, and raise their hands before the previous song is finished in order that they may be called on to name the next song. . . .

Here singing is subordinated, in the child, to the competitive wish to have the song he has hunted up in the index chosen by the teacher. It is merely a question of who gets to the next song in the index first, gets his hand up fast, and is called on by the teacher.

The following examples also illustrate the fact that almost any situation set by the teacher can be the occasion for release of competitive impulses:

> 12. The observer enters the fifth-grade classroom.
> Teacher: Which one of you nice polite boys would like to take [observer's] coat and hang it up? (Observer notes: From the waving hands it would seem that all would like to claim the title.) Teacher chooses one child . . . who takes observer's coat. . . .
> Teacher: Now children, who will tell [observer] what we have been doing?
> Usual forest of hands . . . and a girl is chosen to tell. . . .
> Teacher conducted the arithmetic lesson mostly by asking, "Who would like to tell . . . the answer to the next problem?"
> This question was usually followed by the appearance of a large and *agitated* forest of hands; apparently *much competition to answer*.

Thus the teacher is a powerful agent in reinforcing competition.

It has already been pointed out that carping criticism helps to settle in the child a feeling of vulnerability and threat. In this connection it is significant that *the failure of one child is repeatedly the occasion for the success of another.* I give one illustration below from the same class as the one from which I have taken Example 12.

> 13. Boris had trouble reducing $^{12}\!/_{16}$ to lowest terms, and could get only as far as $^6\!/_8$. Much excitement. Teacher asked him quietly [note how basically decent this teacher is] if that was as far as he could reduce it. She suggested he "think." Much heaving up and down from the other children, all frantic to correct him. Boris pretty unhappy. Teacher, patient, quiet, ignoring others, and concentrating with look and voice on Boris. She says, "Is there a bigger number than 2 you can divide into the two parts of the fraction?" After a minute or two she becomes more urgent. No response from Boris. She then turns to the class and says, "Well, who can tell Boris what the number is?" Forest of hands. Teacher calls Peggy. Peggy gives 4 to be divided into $^{12}\!/_{16}$, numerator and denominator.

Where Boris has failed Peggy has been triumphant; *Boris's failure has made it possible for Peggy to succeed.*

This example and also Example 6 are ones in which the discomfort of the child was *visible*, and such instances may be multiplied. They illustrate how vulnerable the children feel in the presence of the attacks of the peer group in the classroom. But since these are children who face the world with serious anxiety to begin with, the classroom situation sustains it. Let us look at some stories created by these very children, and read by them to their classmates. We have already seen one, Example 6, Charlie's story of "The Unknown Guest." Here are *all* the stories read to their classmates by these children during an observation period.

> 14. (a) Charlotte's story: "Mistaken Identity." One day last year my family and I went to the hospital to visit somebody. When we were coming out and were walking along my father hit me. I came up behind him to hit him back, but just as I was about to do it I looked back and he was behind me! I was going to hit the wrong person!
> (b) Tommy's story: "The Day Our House Was Robbed." [Observer has recorded this in the third person.] He was coming

home from school one afternoon. He knew his Mom was away that afternoon. He started to go in the side door, but decided, he doesn't know why, to go round the back. He found the door open, went into the kitchen, looked into the front room where he saw a thief. Tommy "froze stiff" (chuckle of appreciation from the class), ran out, shouted, "Stop thief" as the man ran out after him. He went to a neighbor, rang the bell, called his mother at the store. The cops came, asked questions, but the man had gotten away with $99 and his mother's watch. If he had gone in the side door he would not have had a chance to see the man. Changing to the back door "may have saved my life." [Teacher's only remarks about this story were: 1) instead of having said "froze stiff," Tommy should have said, "froze stiff as something"; 2) he should have left out the word "then" in one place; 3) he could have made the story clearer; 4) he changed from the past to the present tense.]

(c) Polly's story: "Custard the Lion." Custard the Lion was the most timid animal in Animal Town. The doctors couldn't cure him. Then they found a new medicine. It had strange effects, but Custard wanted to try it. When he did he felt very queer. (Child gives details of queer feeling.) But he soon realized he wasn't afraid of anything. [Teacher's first remark: "You didn't let us hear the last sentence."]

(d) Dan's story: "The Boy Hero." Bill wanted to be a fireman, so he went to the firehouse. The Chief was telling him to go home when the bell clanged. While the Chief was getting into the engine, he didn't see that Bill was getting on too. (Class or teacher picks up flaw in sentence and it is reread correctly.) The Chief said O.K. as long as Bill was aboard, "But you're not to get into no mischief." (Class choruses, "Any. . . .") Everyone was out of the fire except a little girl and her doll. The firemen cannot figure out what to do, but Bill, seeing a tree near the house, climbs it over the protests of the firemen. He misses the girl on his first try, but gets her on the second. While sliding down the tree she slips and almost falls, but grabs Bill's pants, and they make it to safety. . . . [Children's remarks center on position of "clang, clang, clang" in the story. Teacher talks about how to use direct quotations, which, it seems, Dan had not used properly.]

(e) Bertha's story: Title not recorded. The story is about Jim who was walking home past the Smith's house one night and heard a scream. Penny Smith came out and said there was a robber in the house. When the cops came they found a parrot flying around in there, and Penny's parents told her to shut the parrot up before she read mystery stories again. [This story was followed by much carping criticism, which was terminated by the teacher's telling Bertha to change the story to suit the class.]

These stories contain elements of anxiety and even of terror. As each child finishes, the carping criticism of students and teacher then reminds him of his vulnerability. As the child sends out his cloud of fear, it returns with the leaden rain of hostility.

Docility

It comes as a somewhat shocking surprise, perhaps, to middle-class parents, to find their children described as "docile." Yet we have already seen the perfection of docility in the Vigilance Club, and we shall presently see its manifold forms in more normal classrooms.

15. First grade. The children are to act out a story called "Pig Brother," which is about an untidy boy. The teacher is telling the story. One boy said he did not like the story, so the teacher said he could leave if he did not wish to hear it again, but the boy did not leave.

16. In gym the children began to tumble, but there was much restless activity in the lines, so the teacher had all the children run around the room until they were somewhat exhausted before she continued the tumbling.

17. Second grade.
The children have been shown movies of birds. The first film ended with a picture of a baby bluebird.
Teacher: Did the last bird ever look as if he would be blue?
The children did not seem to understand the "slant" of the question, and answered somewhat hesitantly, yes.
Teacher: I think he looked more like a robin, didn't he?
Children, in chorus: Yes.

Item 17 is one of a large number of instances, distributed throughout all grades, in which the children exhibit their docility largely through giving the teacher what he wants. Thus in the elementary schools of the middle class the children get an intensive eight-year-long training in hunting for the right signals and giving the teacher the response wanted. The rest of the examples of docility document this assertion.

18. Fourth grade.
(a) An art lesson.
Teacher holds up a picture.
Teacher: Isn't Bob getting a nice effect of moss and trees?
Ecstatic Ohs and Ahs from the children. . . .
The art lesson is over.
Teacher: How many enjoyed this?
Many hands go up.
Teacher: How many learned something?
Quite a number of hands come down.
Teacher: How many will do better next time?
Many hands go up.
(b) Children have just finished reading the story "The Sun Moon and Stars Clock."
Teacher: What was the highest point of interest—the climax?
The children tell what they think it is. Teacher is aiming to get from them what *she* considers the point of climax, but the children seem to give everything else but.
Bobby: When they capture the thieves.
Teacher: How many agree with Bobby?
Hands, hands.

19. Fifth grade.
This is a lesson on "healthy thoughts," for which the children have a special book depicting, with appropriate illustrations, specific conflictful incidents among chldren. The teacher is supposed to discuss each incident with the children in order to help them understand how to handle their emotions.
One of the pictures is a follows: A sibling *pair* is illustrated by *three* boys: 1) One has received a ball. 2) One is imagined to react with displeasure. 3) One is imagined to react benignly and philosophically, saying, "My brother couldn't help being given the football; we'll use it together."
Teacher: Do you believe it's easier to deal with your thoughts if you own up to them, Betty?
Betty: Yes it is, if you're not cross and angry.
Teacher: Have you any experience like this in the book, Alice?
Alice tells how her brother was given a watch and she envied him

and wanted one too; but her mother said she wasn't to have one until she was fifteen, but now she has one anyway.

Teacher: How could you have helped—could you have changed your thinking? How could you have handled it? What could you do with mean feelings?

Alice seems stymied. Hems and haws.

Teacher: What did Susie (a character in the book) do?

Alice: She talked to her mother.

Teacher: If you talk to someone you often then feel that "it was foolish of me to feel that way. . . ."

Tommy: He had an experience like that, he says. His cousin was given a bike and he envied it. But he wasn't "ugly" about it. He asked if he might ride it, and his cousin let him, and then, "I got one myself; and I wasn't mean, or ugly or jealous."

Before continuing it will be well to note that since the teacher does not say Alice was wrong the children assume she was right and so copy her answer.

Two boys, the dialogue team, now come to the front of the class and dramatize the football incident.

Teacher (to the class): Which boy do you think handled the problem in a better way?

Rupert: Billy did, because he didn't get angry. . . . It was better to play together than to do nothing with the football.

Teacher: That's a good answer, Rupert. Has anything similar happened to you, Joan?

Joan can think of nothing.

Sylvester: I had an experience. My brother got a hat with his initials on it because he belongs to a fraternity, and I wanted one like it and couldn't have one; and his was too big for me to wear, and it ended up that I asked him if he could get me some letters with my initials, and he did.

Betty: My girl friend got a bike that was 26-inch, and mine was only 24; and I asked my sister what I should do. Then my girl friend came over and was real nice about it, and let me ride it.

Teacher approves of this, and says, Didn't it end up that they both had fun without unhappiness?

Here we note that the teacher herself has gone astray, for on the one hand her aim is to get instances from the children in which they have been yielding, and capable of resolving their own jealousy, etc.; yet, in the instance given by Betty, it was not Betty who yielded, but her friend. The child immediately following Betty imitated her since Betty had been praised by the teacher:

> Matilde: My girl friend got a 26-inch bike and mine was only 24; but she only let me ride it once a month. But for my birthday my mother's getting me a new one, probably (proudly) a 28. (Many children rush in with the information that 28 doesn't exist.) Matilde replies that she'll probably have to raise the seat then, for she's too big for a 26.

As we go on with this lesson, we shall continue to see how the children's need for substitute gratification and their inability to accept frustration are the real issues, which even prevent them from getting the teacher's point. We shall see how, in spite of the teacher's driving insistence on her point, the children continue to inject their conflicts into the lesson, while at the same time they gropingly try to find a way to gratify the teacher. *They* cannot give the "right" answers because of their conflicts; teacher cannot handle their conflicts, even perceive them, because *her* underlying need is to be gratified by the children! The lesson goes on:

> Teacher: I notice that some of you are only happy when you get your own way. You're not thinking this through, and I want you to. Think of an experience when you didn't get what you want. Think it through.
>
> Charlie: His ma was going to the movies and he wanted to go with her, and she wouldn't let him; and she went off to the movies, and he was mad; but then he went outside and there were some kids playing baseball, so he played baseball.
>
> Teacher: But suppose you hadn't gotten to play baseball? You would have felt hurt, because you didn't get what you wanted. We can't help feeling hurt when we are disappointed. What could you have done; how could you have handled it?
>
> Charlie: So I can't go to the movies, so I can't play baseball, so I'll do something around the house.
>
> Teacher: Now you're beginning to think! It takes courage to take disappointments. (Turning to the class) What did we learn? The helpful way . . .
>
> Class: is the healthy way!

Before entering the final section of this paper, we need to ask: Why are these children, whose fantasies contain so many hostile elements, so docile in the classroom; and why do they struggle so hard to gratify the teacher and try in so many ways to bring themselves to her attention (the "forest of hands")? We might, of course, start with the idea of the teacher as a parent figure, and the children as siblings competing for the teacher's favor. We could refer to the unresolved dependency needs of children of this age, which make them seek support in the teacher, who manipulates this seeking and their sibling rivalry to pit the children against each other. Other important factors, however, that are inherent in the classroom situation itself, and particularly in middle-class classrooms, ought to be taken into consideration. We have observed the children's tendency to destructively criticize each other, and the teachers' often unwitting repeated reinforcement of this tendency. We have taken note of the anxiety in the children as illustrated by the stories they tell, and observed that these very stories are subjected to a carping criticism, whose ultimate consequence would be anything but alleviation of that anxiety. Hence the classroom is a place in which the child's underlying anxiety may be heightened. In an effort to alleviate this he seeks the approval of the teacher, by giving right answers and by doing what teacher wants him to do under most circumstances. Finally, we cannot omit the teacher's need to be gratified by the attention-hungry behavior of the children.

A word is necessary about these classrooms as middle class. The novel *Blackboard Jungle* describes schoolroom behavior of lower-class children. There we see the children *against the teacher*, as representative of the middle class. But in the classes I have described we see the *children against each other*, with the teacher abetting the process. Thus, as the teacher in the middle-class schools directs the hostility of the children toward one another and away from himself, he reinforces the competitive dynamics within the middle class itself. The teacher in lower-class schools, on the other hand, appears to become the organizing stimulus for behavior that integrates the lower class, as the children unite in expressing their hostility to the teacher (Hunter, 1954).

Confession

The Vigilance Club would have been impossible without confession, and the children's pleasure in confession. But, as with the other parts of the syndrome, confessing occurs in other classrooms also; it can be elicited when the proper conditions are present, and the children can be seen to enjoy it—to vie with one another in confessing. Let us follow the lesson on "healthy thoughts" a little further. We will see how confession occurs as the children seek to give teacher *precisely* what she wants.

20. Teacher asks if anyone else has had experiences like that [of two children who have just recited], where they were mean and angry.
Dick: He has a friend he plays baseball with, and sometimes they fight; but they get together again in a few minutes and apologize.

In this first example we note one of the important aspects of the confession element in the syndrome: the culprit must have given up his evil ways, and now be free of impurities.

In response to Dick's story, teacher says: You handled it just right. Now let's hear about someone who had a similar experience and didn't handle it just right.
Tom: His little brother asked for the loan of his knife, but it was lost, and he got angry with his little brother for asking. [This knife story follows a sequence of several stories about knives told by other children. The exuberance of knife stories following immediately on the teacher's approval of the first one suggests that some of them are made to order and served up piping hot for teacher's gratification.]
Teacher: Now Tom, could you have worked it out any differently? (Observer notes that Tom seems to enjoy this confession; certainly he is not abashed or ashamed.)
Tom: Later he asked me if he could help me find it. He found it in a wastebasket, and then I let him borrow it.
Harry: Sometimes I get angry when my friends are waiting for me and . . . (observer missed some of this) and my little sister asked if she could borrow my auto-racing set, and I hit her once or twice (Class laughs.)

Here we see another factor so important to the flourishing of the syndrome: the audience gets pleasure through the confessor's telling about deeds the audience wishes to commit: who among Harry's listeners would not like to have hit his sister, or anyone, "once or twice"?

> The teacher then goes on: What would you do now—would you hit her?
> Harry: Now I'd probably get mad at first, but let her have it later.

Thus Harry has mended his ways—in teacher-directed fantasy at least—and returned to the fold.

So far we have had confession of mean and angry thoughts and violence. We shall now see confession to unacceptable fear. In all cases the teacher says what type of confession she wishes to hear, and what the resolution should be of the unacceptable behavior; and the children vie with one another to tell commensurable tales, as they derive pleasure from the total situation—through approval of the teacher, expression of their own real or fantasied deviations, and the delight of their peers. In these situations the pleasure of the peer group is seen to derive not so much from the "happy ending" the children give their stories but rather from the content of the story itself. It is interesting that no carping criticism appears; rather the entire situation is a jolly one. It seems that within unspoken limits the children permit one another to boast of "evil" behavior because of the deep pleasure obtained from hearing it. Thus impulse expression becomes a device for role maintenance in the classroom.

The lesson proceeds:

> Two children enact a little skit in which they have to go to the principal to ask him something. One of them is afraid of the principal, the other is not. The moral is that the principal is the children's friend, and that one should not be shy.
> Gertrude: Well, anyway, the principal isn't a lion, he's your friend; he's not going to kill you.
> Teacher: That's right, the principal is a friend, he says hello and good morning to you. . . . Have you ever felt shy?
> Meriam: The first year I sold Girl Scout cookies I didn't know how to approach people; and the first house I went to I didn't know the lady; and I stuttered and stammered, and didn't sell any cookies. By the second house I had thought it all out before I rang the bell, and I sold two boxes. (Triumphantly.)

Teacher: It helps to have self-confidence.

Ben now tells a story, with a happy ending, of being afraid of a principal. Then Paul tells a story, amid gales of laughter, about his being scared on a roller coaster. By this time there is so much excitement among the children that the teacher says: Wait a minute—manners!

John: He was scared to go on the Whip-the-Whirl (scornful laughter from the class); but after he went he liked it so much that he went eight times in a row. (This is well received.)

Many hands go up. Teacher waits. . . .

Michael: He was at Pleasure Park on the ferris wheel (scornful Aw from the class) and a girl kept rocking it, and I started to get green (roar of laughter).

Teacher: Now we'll have to stop.

Certain phenomena not emphasized before appear in this section. Confession is used by the authoritative figure, the teacher, to strengthen attachment to significant but potentially terrifying figures like school principals, and to polish up cultural shibboleths like "self-confidence." For the child storytellers confession becomes an opportunity for bathing in the emotional currents of the peer group, as the child stimulates the group's approval through presentation of group standards, and awakens group pleasure as the peer group responds to its own anxiety about weakness, and experiences resolution of the anxiety through the happy ending. With a perfect instinct for what is right, each child provides catharsis for his peers. By presenting himself as weak, he enables his peers to identify with him; and then, as he overcomes his weakness, he enables his companions too to feel strong.

What this lesson on healthy thoughts may have accomplished by way of creating a permanent reservoir of "healthy thoughts" is difficult to say, but that it helped create solidarity among the students, and between them and the teacher is clear from the fact that when she suddenly shifted ground to say, "Do you think you are wide enough awake for a contest in subtraction of fractions?" the children responded with a unanimous roar of "Yes," as if she had asked them whether they were ready for cookies and ice cream!

Thus in this lesson, in which all have participated more with their *unconscious* than with their conscious emotions, solidarity has been achieved. Teacher thought she was teaching the children to have healthy thoughts, but she was showing them how to gratify her. The children sensed this and struggled to gratify her, while they sought acceptance by their peers also. The essential difference between this teacher and the one who perpetrated the Vigilance Club is that though the latter tended to demolish solidarity among the children while placing the teacher in supreme command, the lesson on healthy thoughts tended to a dubious solidarity among all. *Both teachers organize some of the same elements in the children, but into different configurations, of total feeling and behavior.*

Boredom

It seems unnecessary to document the fact that children become bored in class, for much of modern thinking and curriculum arrangement is aimed at eliminating it. The shifts at 15-minute intervals from one subject to the next in the elementary school classrooms is one example of this effort. Boredom, which means emotional and intellectual separation from the environment, is an insupportable agony, particularly if the emotional vacuum created by such separation is not filled by gratifying fantasies, or if it is filled by terrifying ones. To fill this vacuum people in our culture will throw themselves into a great variety of even relatively ungratifying activities. Since in this situation, bored children attack almost any novel classroom activity with initial vigor, the witch-hunt syndrome or any modification thereof helps to overcome boredom: better to hunt than be bored. In a full and satisfying life there is no place for witch hunts. The school system that can provide a rich program for children has no need of Vigilance Clubs, nor even of lessons on "healthy thoughts."

DISCUSSION AND CONCLUSIONS

In this paper I have used suggestions from communications theory in an effort to order the data obtained from direct observation of elementary school classrooms. Information, the central concept of communications theory, refers to measurable differences in states of organization. In human behavior, as seen in the classroom under discussion, we observe *qualitative shifts in state*, for *different teachers organize the same underlying emotional characteristics of the children to achieve different organizations of the emotions*. One teacher so organizes the children's emotions as to accomplish an intensification of the fear of intragroup aggression, while she turns the children's hostility toward one another. A different teacher may organize the emotions of the children so that a euphoria in which students and teacher are bathed in a wave of emotional gratification is achieved. The great skill in being a teacher would seem to be, therefore, a *learned* capacity to keep shifting states of order intelligently as the work demands. This does not mean the traditional classroom order, where you can hear a pin drop, but rather the kind of order in which the *emotions of the children are caught up and organized toward the achievement of a specific goal*. It is not necessary, perhaps, that even the most prominent emotions of the children, like competitiveness, for example, form part of the organized whole. Yet, on the other hand, it is difficult to see how, in the present state of our culture, competitiveness can be overlooked. It would seem, perhaps, that the important outcome to avoid is that the competitiveness should become destructive of peers, while reinforcing dependence on the teacher.

The phenomenon I have labeled "docility" occurs because of the absolute dependence for survival of the children on the teacher. That is to say success in school depends absolutely on the teacher, and self-respect, as a function of the opinion of others, in the home or among peers, is in part a function of success or failure in school. In these circumstances the child's capacity to respond automatically to the signals he gets from the teacher is bound to acquire somewhat the appearance of instinctive behavior. Although it occurs at a much higher level of integration than instinct, the child hunts for the proper signals from the teacher, and the child's responses take on instinctual quality. They *must;* otherwise, like the nestling who does not open its mouth when the mother arrives with a worm, he will never eat the ambrosia of teacher's approval, so necessary to his survival. In this situation both children and teacher easily become the instruments of their own unconscious processes, as they, like Joseph and his brethren, fall on each other's necks in a shared ecstasy of exuberant dependence. Teacher and pupil will have gratified each other, but it remains an open question whether the children will have learned what the curriculum committee planned.

We see in the organization of the components of the witch-hunt syndrome an important phase in the formation of American national character, for tendencies to docility, competitiveness, confession, intragroup aggression, and feelings of vulnerability the children may bring with them to school, are reinforced in the classroom. This means that independence and courage to challenge are observably played *down* in these classrooms. It means, on the other hand, that tendencies to own up rather than to conceal are reinforced—a development which, in proper hands, might become a useful educational instrument. It means, further, that while many teachers do stress helping others they may inadvertently develop in the children the precise opposite, and thus undermine children's feelings of security. One could come from a very secure and accepting family and yet have one's feelings of security and acceptance threatened in these classrooms. On the other hand, what seems most in evidence from the stories they make up is that the children come to school with feelings of vulnerability which are intensified in the classroom.

Meanwhile we should try to understand that all the teachers in the sample were probably trying to be good teachers,[2] and all the children were trying to be good pupils. Their unconscious needs, however, naturally dominated their behavior. The teacher who organized the Vigilance Club probably thought she was teaching her children to be upright and honest, and to perform good deeds, but her unconscious tendencies caused these worthy inclinations to seek the wrong expression. All teachers need conformity in the classroom in order that the children shall absorb a respectable amount of academic knowledge. But the teacher's (often unconscious) need for acceptance by the children, and her fear (sometimes unconscious) of her inability to control free

---

[2] I am indebted to B. Bettelheim for this suggestion.

discussion, compel her to push the children into uncritical docility at times, while they seek her approval.

The creation of stories, and their discussion by the class, are accepted principles of progressive education. But the teacher's own (at times unconscious) need to carp and criticize gets in the way of her adequately developing the creative and supportive possibilities in her charges. Thus these are not "bad," "vicious," or "stupid" teachers, but human beings, who express in their classroom behavior the very weaknesses parents display in their dealings with their children. The solution to the problem of the contradiction between the requirements of a democratic education on the one hand, and the teachers' unconscious needs on the other, is not to carp at teachers, and thus repeat the schoolroom process, but to give them some insight into how they project their personal problems into the classroom situation.

References

Henry, Jules, and Joan Whitehorn Boggs, 1952, "Child Rearing, Culture, and the Natural World." *Psychiatry*, 15:261–271.

Hunter, Evan, 1954, *The Blackboard Jungle*. New York: Simon and Schuster, Inc.

Starkey, Marion L., 1949, *The Devil in Massachusetts*. New York: Alfred A. Knopf, Inc.

11———Jules Henry

Spontaneity, Initiative, and Creativity in Suburban Classrooms[*]

Nowadays much of the preoccupation with creativity seems to stem not so much from interest in artistic and scientific originality as from anxiety about preserving any human impulse toward spontaneity and initiative. Fundamentally, our contemporary concern about creativity is a culturally acceptable rationalization of our own fear of loss of Self. In our expressed anxiety over creativity in our children, we are really saying that we are frightened that our culture has wrested our Selves from us and is selling them down the river. The present paper, reflecting the current fear, deals, therefore, with factors affecting initiative and spontaneity in elementary public school classrooms in middle-class suburbs.[†]

This paper is based on direct observations by my students and me over a three-year period.[1] We owe a debt of deepest grati-

[*] Reprinted from The American Journal of Orthopsychiatry, XXIX, April, 1959, 266–279, with permission.

[†] To the teachers and principals who have so tolerantly accepted me and my students as observers in their classrooms I am most grateful. The need to protect the identity of teachers, principals, and children makes it impossible for me to thank them or my observers by name. Nevertheless, I can thank them all anonymously for their thoughtfulness and help, but above all for their contribution to this work.

[1] Other publications on this research are: J. Henry, "Culture, Education, and Communications Theory," in George D. Spindler (Ed.), Education and Anthropology (Stanford, Calif.: Stanford Univ. Press, 1955); J. Henry, Docility, or Giving Teacher What She Wants, J. Soc. Issues, 11:33–41, 1955; J. Henry, Attitude Organization in Elementary School Classrooms, Am. J. Orthopsychiatry, 27:117–133, 1957; J. Henry, Working Paper on Creativity, Harvard Educ. Rev., 27:148–155, 1957.

tude to the teachers who voluntarily put up with our intrusions into their classrooms. There is no doubt that an objective description of anyone's behavior in our culture would have in it much that might appear on superficial examination to be strange or bizarre. Our observations show teachers as normal and dedicated human beings struggling with massive problems the culture has dropped in their lap, and if anything in these studies of them were to be construed as absurd or bizarre, it would be a gross injustice.

DIRECT OBSERVATIONS

The root of life is impulse; and its release in the proper amounts, at the proper time and place, and in culturally approved forms, is one of the primary concerns of culture. Day after day in the classroom, the public school teacher faces the surging impulses of the children and she resists them in order not to be overwhelmed; in order to do her duty as a cultural surrogate; and in order that the whelming impulse life of her charges—normal as well as sick—may not get in the way of their learning the materials prescribed in the curriculum. The contemporary public school teacher is thus faced with the following paradox: in line with current educational philosophy she must foster initiative and spontaneity in her children and at the same time maintain order and teach according to school requirements. In the middle-class suburban classrooms we have studied, however, the emphasis on initiative and spontaneity fosters a "permissiveness" which, in some rooms, sweeps the class to the brink of chaos. In these circumstances it became an empirical requirement of our research to develop a rough rating for noise; and it is still an unsolved problem as to whether such classrooms can be said at certain times to have any social structure at all. Indeed, it would almost appear as if the pivot of order were no longer, as under more traditional discipline, the teacher, but rather had become lodged in the egos of the children; as if responsibility for the maintenance of order had been shifted from the teacher to the children. Meanwhile, it is

important to bear in mind that these are not delinquent children, tearing the social structure from its hinges by brute force, but nice, clean middle-class suburban boys and girls who are merely given their heads.

The impulses of the children are always a serious matter to teachers, and one of the most important problems of our day is to discover the variety of devices they use to control or evade them. Since, quite without our requesting it, principals have selected for us classrooms having what they consider outstanding teachers, the examples I give here of classroom control represent forms considered best by the principals. The first example is from a second-grade classroom in school A, with 37 children. Rather full excerpts are taken from one typical day, and very brief materials from one day a month later.

> The Observer arrives in the classroom at 12:45 and remarks, "As has been the case in past observations, the noise rating was 2."
> There are about seven children walking around, apparently doing nothing. There are about nine children sitting on the floor on the left side of the teacher's desk. Teacher is passing back some papers the children worked on yesterday. She says, "If you missed more than one of the questions on the board, it means that you either aren't reading carefully or that you aren't thinking enough. Betty, will you sit over here, please. Thank you."

This teacher, like most of the teachers in the area, uses "honey" and "dear" a great deal in interaction with the children. Some of the examples recorded on this day are:

> 1. Could you talk a little louder, Johnny dear?
> 2. I'll have to ask you to go to your seat, honey.
> 3. Honey, where were you supposed to go if you didn't have your paper?
> 4. Bill, I think George can do that by himself, honey.
> 5. Susie, honey, what's the name of it?
> 6. It's up here, dear.

The record continues:

> 1:10. The reading period is over. Children return to their seats. Teacher begins to write four words on the board. As she does this the talking and moving around the room increase to a

mild uproar. Noise rating 3. Teacher says, "May I have your eyes this way, please? Bill, will you and Tommy please watch?"

1:20. "May I suggest that the people in John Burns' group, instead of doing this work with the vowels, read in *The Family Village*."

1:40 Teacher is sitting at desk. Children seem to be busy at work. Everyone seems to be doing something different. Noise rating has dropped to 2. Fifteen out of 34 of the children present are not doing the assigned work. Most of the children in this group are doing absolutely nothing in the line of schoolwork. Some are merely staring into space; some are playing with rubber bands, hankies, etc.

1:56. Presently there are ten children out of their regular seats and seated in the rockers at the bookcase, at the library table, or just aimlessly walking around the room. Two little girls in the back of the room are showing each other their scarves. There is a great deal of footshuffling; everyone looks as if he is preparing to go home. Teacher comments, "Boys and girls, we do not go home at two o'clock, so please continue with your work. Doug, may I talk to you a minute?" Doug goes up to Teacher, who says, "We're going to let you stay five minutes after school because of this talking."

A month later the record reads as follows:

12:40. When the teacher reprimands the children, her voice in all instances is soft, almost hesitant. She informed me (the Observer) later that when she scolds she wants the children to feel she is disappointed in them. I can see how the sad tone of her voice would convey this message.

12:50. Teacher says, "May I have you in your seats, please." During the collection of papers the noise rate had increased to 2, and 12 people were out of their seats.

A few minutes later the teacher left the room and the noise rate approached 3. Six children were walking around the room, most of them chatting with their neighbors. Roger says to Observer, "Kind of noisy, isn't it?"

1:04. Teacher returns and says, "Annie, would you sit down honey, and get busy. Whose feet are making so much noise?" One child says, "Pam's!" and the teacher says, "Pam, that's very annoying, please don't. Observer remarks, "It's odd that this small noise should bother Mrs. Olan. I didn't even hear it." Teacher

says, "Doug, will you turn around, please? Billy, do you understand the process—how to do it? I thought maybe Jimmy was
helping you. Stephen, are you finished? Murray and Mickey! Boys
and girls, let's tend to our own work, please."

1:55. Five minutes before recess. Teacher says, "Put your
work away quietly." She sits back and with a completely expressionless face waits for the five minutes to pass. The number of
children out of their seats increased to 17. Three boys were
bouncing balls on the floor; one was throwing his against the wall
of the cloakroom; three children were killing each other with
imaginary guns.

Regardless of their age, our observers became tired and ir-
ritated by the noise in this type of classroom. During any 1½-hour
observation period, Mrs. Olan was in and out of the classroom
several times, sometimes for as long as 10 minutes. It will be observed that at one point she merely sat and stared into space.
Meanwhile, her repeated withdrawal results in an intensification of
the noise, which mounts toward the third level when she leaves,
so that when she returns, an effort must be made to re-establish
the previous lower noise level. Probably the reason why the social
structure of the room does not disintegrate is that the teacher
warms the atmosphere with "honey" and "dear" and by occasionally fondling a child; and because by saying she is "disappointed"
in them she makes the children afraid of loss of love. Actually,
Mrs. Olan plays the role of the tired, overburdened, entreating
mother, who attempts to control her children by making them
feel guilty. Her sweetness and elaborate politeness—she even says
"honey" and "dear" when she reprimands a child—are really saying to the children, "Look how sweet and courteous I am; how
could you be otherwise?"

In all of this the children's egos seem remarkably firm, and
Mrs. Olan's capacity to do an all-but-impossible job is striking.
Although the noise rating is never zero in this room, it is sometimes recorded as 1 or approaching 2, which suggests that the
children have inner resources of control which are skillfully mobilized by the teacher. When one understands, however, the pressure toward "permissiveness" in these schools, the fact that the
children do learn something is a tribute to Mrs. Olan's fortitude

and to her dedication to teaching, as well as to the ego strength of the children.

The contemporary American idea that good elementary school teachers should be accepting, giving parents has resulted, as we have seen, in the teachers' using affection as a defense against other impulses of the children: the teacher stimulates their love by calling them "honey" and "dear" and by fondling, while at the same time she awakens fear of loss of her love if they get out of line. Though in our sample, caressing is common, its full possibilities in the classroom can be evaluated best by studying minutely the behavior of one teacher who obtains deep pleasure from fondling the children. Mrs. Thorndyke is affectionate, sensitive, and alert, and, as usual, is considered one of the best by her principal. In the observation record we are present at a reading lesson in her third-grade class on a day when the children are asking each other questions about the story instead of being asked questions by her. There are 25 children in the class, but the group to be described is made up of the dozen or so best readers, and they are sitting facing each other in two rows of little chairs placed in front of the room. The rest of the children are working at their desks on their exercise books. This paper picks up the lesson when it been in progress about 15 minutes, during which excitement has mounted and the children tend to erupt in noisy argument. At 10:27 Mrs. Thorndyke is standing behind one row:

> She pats Alfred to restrain him and he shows a slight tendency to withdraw. There is a loud burst of noise. Mrs. Thorndyke's hand is on Alfred and he seems to wish to get out. Now her hand is on Arty, who makes no move. Teacher pats and strokes Matty, who also makes no move to withdraw. Now Teacher is standing behind Arty, lightly passing her finger tips over his neck. She goes back to Arty, puts a hand on Alfred to restrain him. He makes withdrawal signs. Alfred and Arty are now interlocking their hands in the air and Alfred is talking to Arty. At 10:32, Teacher stops behind Otto to restrain him. Her hands are on his cheeks; his tongue goes in the direction of his right cheek and pushes it out as he closes his eyes. When Mrs. Thorndyke withdraws her hands, his eyes pop open as if he had suddenly awakened. Mary, who previously was holding onto Mrs. Thorndyke

as the teacher stroked the child's arm, has now slumped in her seat. Teacher goes to her, puts her arms around her and pulls her back. Mary takes Teacher's hand. Alfred is talking and Mrs. Thorndyke pats and strokes him. He does not withdraw this time. Alfred is now talking to Arty and Teacher is stroking Alfred. Again he does not withdraw. Now Alfred caresses Otto and Arty caresses Alfred. Malcolm asks questions now (10:38) and all the children say his questions have been asked. Mrs. Thorndyke says, "My only objection to that question is that it can be answered by either yes or no." She strokes Matty. All this time the questions are being asked and there is great excitement among the children. Sherry asks question and Teacher says, "We've gone over that." She strokes Matty and he does not resist. She touches Mary flutteringly with her finger tips.

Now Mrs. Thorndyke terminates the lesson, and the papers with the questions are collected. Suddenly she becomes very grave and silent. She later told me that Mary had answered a snippety "no" to something Teacher had said. Now Mrs. Thorndyke says, "*My, I'm terribly disappointed.*" There is absolute silence, and Mrs. Thorndyke says, "Matty, you're excused to go to your seat." She later told me it was because he's a general all-round talker and wouldn't quiet down. Matty goes to his seat looking very unhappy, his lips compressed. The room is silent now.

Now Group 2, the poorer readers, occupy the seats deserted by Group 1. Teacher seems very tired now, and goes through the lesson mechanically. Her voice is weak and she leans against the blackboard. Time, approximately 10:50.

The interesting thing about erotization is that *it substitutes one impulse or one impulse pattern for another:* The children's excitement, whatever its effective components, is narcotized by releasing other, namely libidinal, emotional resources in the children. What is so striking in Mrs. Thorndyke is her skill in so stimulating these resources that contagion occurs: the affectivity of the teacher is spread by some children to others. Otto is a somewhat different case: he simply went into a regressive trance while enjoying the teacher's stroking.

Put in the broadest possible way, what we have seen here is Mrs. Thorndyke's effort to master, by means of narcotization, powerful *spontaneous* impulses of the children which had been placed at the service of their intellects. Thus, in the very act of releasing spontaneity, the teacher, in order not to be overwhelmed by it, narcotizes it. Obviously the effort was exhausting, for when the lesson was over, Mrs. Thorndyke was tired and listless and leaned against the blackboard for support.

While women teachers in our sample of middle-class suburban schools seem repeatedly to control the children's impulses by awakening affection and fear of loss of it, as would almost any normal middle-class mother, the question arises as to what the male teacher does in the same situation. Over the years we have been able to get good observations on only one man teacher, Mr. Jeffries, who teaches a sixth-grade class of 35 in the same school as Mrs. Thorndyke. In the classroom Mr. Jeffries takes the role of a type of contemporary middle-class American father: a Puck-ish imp-of-fun, buddy of the boys and sweetheart of the girls, he addresses the latter with endearments and uses nicknames and diminutives for the former as he pats them on the head or puts an arm around their shoulders. His room is a rough-and-tumble, happy-go-lucky, brink-of-chaos sort of place, much less controlled than Mrs. Thorndyke's and less overtly erotized. Mr. Jeffries calls it a "rat race" and; says, "We get tired and ready to drop by the time it is over." Let us then have a look at Mr. Jeffries' room:

11:05. The class is having a reading lesson. Teacher says, "Galapagos means tortoise. Where are 300-pound turtles found?" A boy says, "In the zoo," and Teacher says, "Where are they native in this country?" A girl says, with a grimace of disgust, "We saw them in Marine Land in Florida. They were slaughtered and used for meat. Ugh!" John has raised his hand and Teacher calls on him. "We saw one in Wisconsin about the size of Bob's head." Teacher says, "That's plenty big." and the class laughs. Teacher asks, "What was Douglas [a boy in the story] doing on the island? Have you ever been scared, John?" "Yes," replies John. "So have I," says the teacher, and the class laughs. Teacher says, *"That's what I like about buddies."*

11:25. Teacher says, "Let's read the story silently." He says to a girl. "Do you mind putting your beads away for the rest of the morning instead of tearing them apart?"
The room is now very quiet. He walks around the aisles as the children read.

Mr. Jeffries obviously runs a "democratic" classroom, and his pupils are spontaneous and effervescent. He tells the children that he is their "buddy"; he is no aloof figure, pretending to invulnerability, but like them he is capable of fear; he is "scared" *with* them. He is right down there on the floor with the kids, so to speak: like a contemporary American *buddy-daddy*, he has leveled the distance between himself and the children. Yet by command he can suddenly get quiet when he wants it, though rarely for long. A sound curve of his class would have a relatively constant high noise plateau with occasional narrow valleys of relative quiet.

10:15. The class is discussing types of nouns. Teacher says, "If I had lots of Ritas, she'd be a type. Maybe we're lucky we have only one." Class laughs. A girl raises her hand and Teacher says, "What is it, honey?"

10:25. The room has grown noisy during the lesson and Teacher says, "Can't hear you, Shirley. You're not going to find out a thing by looking in that direction." His voice has risen, getting louder in order to be heard above the classroom noise.

10:40. Clatter is increasing. Eight or nine pupils are walking around the room. One boy throws a paper wad at another. Four pupils are at the pencil sharpener. Noise grows louder but *teacher ignores it*.

10:45. Teacher says, "It would seem to me that in the past five minutes you haven't accomplished a thing; you've been so busy wandering around." This creates complete silence. Then two boys stand to look at neighbor's work. Another goes to Teacher's desk to get help. Teacher and he confer. Noise is louder now.

10:55. Two boys raise hands. Two others stand next to Teacher. One girl pats his back as he bends over. She giggles.

11:00. Teacher: "O.K., put language books away, please!" He giggles as a girl asks him a question. Pupils put books in desks. Teacher: "Take a couple of minutes here. Girl with the blue hair, get up. Stretch a bit." Loud laughter from the class. Teacher: "Get up and stretch." Most of the class stands. Two boys continue writing at their desks. A boy and girl push each other. The smallest boy in the class stands alone and looks on as two girls wrestle.

At the end of the observation period on this day the Observer wrote, "I feel that the pupils are truly fond of Mr. Jeffries. They enjoy laughing together; not at somebody, but *with* each other." Of course, we might question the last in view of the jokes about Rita and the earlier one about the size of Bob's head. At any rate, there seems little doubt that, like Mrs. Thorndyke, Mr. Jeffries is a love object to his children. In the present observation segment, one little girl strokes his back, and he giggles with another one in a private joke during the lesson. Everybody, including the teacher, has a wonderful time. Frequently, however, the noise gets so loud that Mr. Jeffries has to shout and the students cannot hear. Suddenly at 10:45 he scolds the children for not accomplishing anything, even though he has permitted the disorder and noise to increase. At 11 o'clock the children are pushing and wrestling, but Mr. Jeffries ignores it. The following week, during a particularly hilarious and noisy arithmetic lesson, when the children can barely hear what is going on, a girl takes a boy's paper, tears it up and throws it into the wastebasket; but the teacher laughs, the class pays no attention, the paper is fished out and taped together, and the lesson continues.

About five weeks later the Observer was in this classroom when Mr. Jeffries was out sick and a substitute was an duty. The room was in its usual noisy state when the principal walked in and stood in the back of the room for a few minutes. No change took place in the class, but the principal bent over one of the little girls, embraced her, whispered something to her, then turned to the Observer, said, "Fine bunch of gals here," and left. Thus, in his behavior the principal reinforces the emphasis on impulse release at deeply gratifying levels. *Teacher, principal, children, and community are one continuous cultural system.*

As the school year entered the last month, evidence began to appear that impulse release and noise had reached a point beyond the endurance of the *children*, for the children, particularly the girls, began spontaneously to *shush* the class:

> 10:40. The children have just finished singing. Teacher says, "Get paper, eraser, pencil." There is a loud buzz at this command, and a girl says, "What's the paper for?" Teacher says, "Now don't go wild just because you sang. Your pencils don't

have to be so sharp." Observer notes that a bunch of youngsters is storming the pencil sharpener as Teacher says this. *Someone shushes the class.* Teacher says, "Fill this out the same as yesterday." He passes the sheets out very carefully, dropping the correct number on the first desk of each row. "Today's date is the eighth of May," says Teacher. "Sorry you're so noisy. Don't open your books till I tell you. Just fill out the first page. This is a reading test." The class reads in silent concentration.

11:01. The test is over. Teacher starts to issue instructions for the next activity and a girl says to the class, "*Shush!*"

11:06. A girl goes to the teacher's desk for help in spelling. He spells a word aloud as she writes, leaning on his desk for support. A girl walks by John and smacks him playfully. He gets up, walks by her, smacks her on the back soundly and sprints away. Teacher says, "I notice that most of you have finished your papers promptly. I'm very pleased. Now devote your time, the next fifteen minutes, to your spelling." A girl says, "*Shush!*" There is a loud buzz. Observer notes that this shushing has occurred several times today, *only from the pupils.*

These observations drive home the point made earlier, that responsibility for maintenance of order has shifted in such a way that the children determine when controls shall be set in motion. In the last observation, the children's efforts to hold the social structure together become overt; but throughout the term, the teacher's interest in order is so slight, he so often ignores the racket in his room that the conclusion is inescapable that the children have set their own limits because the teacher has abdicated.

INTERVIEWS WITH TEACHERS

The first section of this paper was devoted to direct observation and interpretation of teacher-pupil interaction. In the interpretation of observations, however, there is always the problem of whether the observer is "imposing his own ideas" on the data. Mindful of this difficulty, I interviewed the teachers on the subject of their ideas about classroom discipline two years after the original observations were made. The original observations of Mrs.

Thorndyke were made by me; those of the other two teachers were made by my students. I give excerpts from Mrs. Olan's interview first. She says:

> In this day and age the children have more tensions and problems than when I first taught. In the one-room schoolhouse in which I first taught the children came from calm homes. There was no worry about war, and there was no TV or radio. They led a calm and serene life. They came to school with their syrup pails for lunch buckets. Children of today know more about what is going on; they are better informed. So you can't hold a strict rein on them. It is bad for children to come in and sit down with their feet under the seat: you have to have freedom to get up and move around. When they do this they are more rested and have a greater attention span. . . .
> Children need to enjoy school and like it. They also need their work to be done; it's not all play. You must get them to accept responsibility and doing work on their own.

Thus, Mrs. Olan feels that children have severe inner tensions that must not be held in close rein because it is not good for them. In answer to the question, "What would you say is your own particular way of keeping order in the classroom?" she explains simply and movingly how she manages her children:

> Well, I would say I try to get that at the beginning of the year by getting this bond of affection and a relationship between the children and me. And we do that with stories; and I play games *with* them—don't just teach them how to play. It's what you get from living together comfortably. We have share times—that's the time a child can share with the teacher; and he gives whatever he wants to share: a bird's nest he has found; a tadpole that he and his dad got. Sometimes he may simply tell about something in his life—that his grandmother fell down and broke a leg and is not at home. . . . These are the things that contribute toward this discipline. Another thing in discipline: it took me a long time to learn it, too—I thought I was the boss, but I learned that even with a child, if you speak to him as you would to a neighbor or a friend you get a better response than if you say, "Johnny, do this or that." If you say, "Mary, will you please cooperate, you are disturbing us; we want to finish our reading," rather than

just giving a command, they feel they are working with you and not just taking orders.

Mrs. Olan is aware of what she is doing: love is the path to discipline through permissiveness, and school is a continuation of family life in which the values of sharing and democracy lead to comfortable living and ultimately to (Mrs. Olan's own interpretation of) discipline.

> With primary children the teacher is a mother during the day; they have to be able to bring their problems to you. They get love and affection at home, and I see no reason not to give it in school.
>
> If you have the right relationship between teacher and child or between parent and child he can take harsh words and the things you say in the right spirit; and if you don't have that bond of affection, he just doesn't take it.

To Mrs. Olan, mother of a 21-year-old son, children are warm little pussy-cats, and you quiet them the way you do kittens. For example, in answer to the question, "Do you think children tend to be quieter if the teacher is affectionate?" she said:

> If a teacher has a well-modulated voice and a pleasing disposition her children are more relaxed and quiet. Children are like kittens: if kittens have a full stomach and lie in the sun, they purr. If the atmosphere is such that the children are more comfortable, they are quiet. It is comfortable living that makes the quiet child. When you are shouting at them and they're shouting back at you, it isn't comfortable living.

Two years before this interview, observation had made clear that Mrs. Olan was no "boss," but lodged much responsibility in the children. She clarifies the matter further:

> It means a great deal to them to give them their own direction. When problems do come up in the room, we talk them over and discuss what is the right thing to do when this or that happens. Usually you get pretty good answers. They are a lot harder on themselves than I would be; so if any punishment comes along, like not going to an assembly, you have group pressure.

As I was about to go, Mrs. Olan spontaneously remarked, "My children don't rate as high [on achievement tests] as other children; I don't push, and that's because I believe in comfortable living."

Mrs. Thorndyke's response to the interview was entirely different from Mrs. Olan's. Mrs. Thorndyke has no children of her own, and we have seen how outgoing she is to her little third graders, patting and stroking them. However, when I talked to her about how she ran her class, she sounded like a strict though benign disciplinarian, who hardly ever touched her pupils. The youngsters need "strong guidance," she said, and from the very first day have to be taught "who the leader is," meaning, of course, Mrs. Thorndyke. Demonstrative affection, in her opinion, is only for kindergarten and first grade; by the time the children get to her, Mrs. Thorndyke said, it should "level off." Thus, if we relied only on what she told us about herself, we would have no sound idea of what Mrs. Thorndyke was really like. If there were no direct observations of her with her children, we would think of her as a "schoolmarm" who, while laying down the law, was at the same time somewhat sensitive—rather at the mechanical "social skills" level—to children's emotional needs.

Since Mrs. Thorndyke's responses in the interview made me wonder whether her view of the teacher's role had changed or whether she was merely unaware of what she was doing, I decided to ask her permission to observe her again and she graciously consented. Her position as a teacher had changed in the intervening two years: according to new school regulations, superior students had been placed in special classes with special teachers, leaving Mrs. Thorndyke, among others, with only the slow children; and these had "a very short attention span," as she put it rather regretfully. As one watched her with these pupils, the most striking feature of her behavior was her *enormously increased mobility* in the classroom as she responded to the children's requests for help. Whereas previously, for example, as Mrs. Thorndyke walked around the room helping children in language skills, she had been able to spend more time with each child as she assisted him in his work, now she was in the midst of a constant silent clamor of hands as these children of lower IQ sought her help again and again. Whereas two years before she *sauntered* around the room, now she rushed, and though this did not prevent her from touching, tapping and stroking them in an affectionate way, her contacts were more ephemeral. There was also a pervasive air of irritation and fatigue in her behavior. However, a striking phenomenon had entered to change the situation in an even more dramatic way: this was David, a disturbed boy with a "hopeless" mother and a "no account" father. Mrs. Thorndyke said that as long as she kept David close to her, she could help him better and keep him under control. He sat close to the front of the room near her desk, and when the other children were sitting at their places reciting, she sometimes had David right beside her at her desk. Some extracts from the record of one observation period will show what the relation was between Mrs. Thorndyke and David:

> Her hand is on David's head. He takes her hand. Now her hand is on his head again.
>
> 1:35. Now she is over near David again; he takes her hand and puts his face against it. She puts her hand on the head of Bobby. Now she touches David again; he holds her hand.
>
> 1:45. David takes her hand, really her whole arm, and holds it for about 30 seconds as he puts his face against it. She calls on him to read and he does. He has her hand again.
>
> 1:50. She is near David again and gives him her hand. He kisses it, fondles it, nuzzles it.
>
> 2:40. David is sitting close to the teacher while the rest of the children are at their seats reciting in the language skills lesson. David is a very beautiful boy. Mrs. Thorndyke puts her hand on David's arm and pats it and he places his fingers on her arm. They are like mother and child. He reads rather well. She strokes and fondles his face like that of a beloved child.

Mrs. Thorndyke says that David "needs affection" and there is no doubt that he is getting it from her. I would be inclined to say that if David could only stick with Mrs. Thorndyke long enough, it would help him. Meanwhile, one becomes aware of the fact that this restless child is held in check by his teacher's affectivity. One would be inclined to say that where affectivity is not dictated by the heart as a way of controlling middle-class children, "common sense" might suggest it. Meanwhile, the problems involved in using this as an *over-all* technique have already been pointed out.

Finally, with respect to the apparent discrepancy between what Mrs. Thorndyke does and what she says she does, I would say that she is unaware of her own behavior along the dimention of "physical conatct with children."

Two years after he was observed for one semester in a sixth-grade class by one of my students, Mr. Jeffries was principal of the school in which he once was teacher. His passionate involvement in teaching and in children easily won me. The following are some excerpts from a very long and thoughtful interview. He says,

> The very first day, I introduce myself to the children and tell them about myself. I use my family a great deal. I talk about my boy and about my daughter. I tell them about certain of my experiences, just to give them an understanding that "here is an individual."

In this way he begins to draw closer to the children. He becomes almost one with them. Speaking of himself, he says,

> They know the teacher's a friend with whom they can exchange jokes and banter. But if the teacher says, "Come on, we must get to this or that," they say to themselves "We must do it." Maybe they say, "He's a good Joe, a good guy, so let's get the job done."

Mr. Jeffries is like Mrs. Olan in that he sees himself as working out the "criteria" for classroom management and discipline with the children in a democratic way, and he lets the children set their own punishments when they get into serious trouble, like fighting in the schoolyard. Mr. Jeffries' long explanation of how he goes about letting the children set their own rules cannot be reproduced here, but, actually, what he does is guide the children in the course of a discussion to the acceptance of his own ideas of what the "criteria" for classroom management should be.

We have seen that Mr. Jeffries' own room is a buoyant, noisy milieu. "You can't hold children in a tight rein," he says, "no more than you can hold a racehorse in a tight rein. A racehorse needs freedom and so does a child." As a matter of fact, Mr. Jeffries fears that if you hold a child in during class he will somehow break loose and "stomp" on somebody, just like a racehorse that breaks out into the fans at a steeplechase, as he put it. Children are "God-given individuals" and have a right to get up and walk around whenever they please. He says that since in this way they may find their way to an encyclopedia or a map, motility is closely related to creativity. To Mr. Jeffries, "a quiet classroom is a dead classroom" where "the children are not thinking or are afraid to think." A stranger walking into his room, he says, might think it a "riot" or that "mayhem was being committed," but he simply would not understand the basic thinking behind Mr. Jeffries' management. Furthermore, "A classroom with affection can be an awfully happy and joyous one. A quiet classroom may be an awfully fearful situation for someone."

Love, demonstrativeness, freedom, mobility, creativity, noise and thoughtfulness go together, as Mr. Jeffries sees it. He is literally afraid of quietness and restraint.

In reviewing these findings, it is important to bear in mind that *the first section of this paper was compiled before the interviewing was done, and has not been altered in any way since.* With this in mind, it can be seen that what Mrs. Olan and Mr. Jeffries *say* about what they do and why they do it confirms both observation and interpretation. In Mrs. Thorndyke, we are dealing with a person who is unaware of her affectional responses to the children.

SUMMARY AND CONCLUSIONS

Today our emphasis on creativity and spontaneity goes hand in hand with culture-weariness—a certain tiredness and disillusionment with impulse restraint, and a feeling that the Self has been sold down the river to the pirates of production, consumption and war. In these circumstances, permissiveness with children, an attitude that had been gaining strength before World War II, has invaded many phases of work with children, so that in some middle-class suburban public schools, there is a great relaxation of controls, and the teacher who is often most highly regarded is the one who lets the children be "free." These teachers are trying to be good teachers: like devoted public servants they are performing their duties as the community requires them to do. The surging impulses of the children whom they are "permitting," however, are threatening: when they are turned loose on a substitute or one one of their fellows, they can be terribly destructive. In these circumstances the teachers handle the children in accordance with their own roles in the culture of contemporary America, and in response to their own inner needs. Women teachers in these schools often manage by making themselves love objects and by making the children feel guilty. The one man in our sample played the role of one type of American *buddy-daddy*, exercising what little control there was by making himself loved the way this kind of modern American daddy is loved, and by occasionally issuing, like any suburban daddy, a peremptory command for order, the effects of which rarely lasted more than a few minutes.

Though in the very act of being released, the children's impulses are narcotized, in most cases it is not enough: the children "climb the walls" anyway. A consequence of this is impairment of the efficiency of the teachers and fatigue and obstruction of learning; for in the midst of constant turmoil, the children's capacities to hear, to concentrate and to absorb are interfered with. This explains the interesting phenomenon of the sixth graders' assuming responsibility for order in the class by *shushing* when the teacher does nothing. As a matter of fact, it would appear that under the conditions of spontaneity, as understood in this portion of Suburbia, noise and disorder destroy the very thing educators would foster.

In the broader cultural context the classroom is the children's first important experience with the administrative structure of the society. It is their first contact with what is fundamentally an impersonal mechanism for getting the culture's business done. But on the other hand, the children are prepared by the erotized atmosphere they encounter for the buddy-buddy, "false personalization" which Riesman has described for American institutions. The boys in particular will become an executive part of the impersonal structures—businesses, government bureaucracies—within which, in line with contemporary ethos, every effort is made to mix business with libido. From this point of view, life in public elementary middle-class schools of Suburbia is a preparation for work in a libidinized social structure which is at the same time basically impersonal and which pivots on "social skills."

Because of its necessary brevity, this paper is scarcely even an introduction to a single dimension of the cultural dynamics of learning. In these schools there is a great variety of ways of managing, and I have discussed but three teachers. In a limited sense, however, they present a view of one important problem: how our teachers manage under the pressure of an ideology of permissiveness and spontaneity which makes their task difficult.

In some of these rooms we get the picture of the immature yet strong egos of children manipulating a social structure which has been practically handed over to them, yet never letting it disintegrate, never actually stepping into chaos. For them this is a training in what has become known in other aspects of our culture as the art of "brinkmanship": a training in holding together in a relatively shapeless social field.

In order to round out the picture somewhat, it seems necessary to point out that the urban public elementary schoolrooms we have studied are entirely different from those discussed here. In those schools, the children are held under rigid control by the teacher, there is little talking that is not specifically permitted, the children stay in their seats, and the rooms are quiet. On the other hand, the atmosphere is also more impersonal, more attention seems to be given to rote procedures, and spontaneity is at a minimum.

In conclusion I should like to re-emphasize the fact that all of the teachers I have known in Suburbia are thoughtful, dedicated, normal human beings, trying to find within themselves the resources to deal with a dictum handed down, while at the same time they have received little instruction in how to do it. This being the case it would be wrong to make teachers the scapegoats of any adverse feeling that might be generated by the spectacle of classroom turmoil, for teachers are the instruments of their culture, as we all are.

12——*George D. Spindler*

The Role of the School Administrator

INTRODUCTION

The way in which a school is administered has a great deal to do with the kind of social and educational institution it is and can become. The principal is the crucial administrative middleman who translates school system ideology and policy into action at the local level, intercepts and transmits sentiment from the classroom teachers and from pupils and parents back to the central office, and makes decisions that directly affect the way education and cultural transmission will be carried out in the classroom. This chapter focuses on the role of the school principal, and the multiplicity of factors—cultural, organizational and psychological—that affect it.

The *role* of the school principal can be given a simple definition: *those expectations and directives for behavior connected with the position of school principal.* But like all simple definitions of complex processes this one covers a lot of ground. Expectations and directives do not originate in a vacuum. They stem from various audiences, each with different, frequently conflicting expectations and criteria for desired behavior. And each of these audiences has its place in the social system within which the role becomes meaningful. So any one role, particularly a crucial middleman's role, becomes the focal point of the whole system—considered from the vantage point of that particular role.

Not only are there various audiences with particularistic expectations that may be in conflict with each other and that must be mediated by the administrative middleman; there are also generalized cultural values that operate in the context of the school. These values are a part of the American way of life, but receive varying degrees of commitment from various segments of the public. They may constitute areas of agreement insofar as they are a part of the core of American culture. Or they may represent areas of conflict insofar as various audiences place priority on some but not all available values built into the general patterning of American culture.

But the occupant of any given role in any particular social system is not a passive agent. People occupy the positions toward which role expectations are directed. People not only occupy these positions, they *react*. No role can be played exactly the same way by any two individuals. The expectations directed toward them are perceived, interpreted, and put into action in ways that only approximate the original character of the expectations as defined by the audiences viewing the actor in the role—in this case the principal. So personality differences, individual attitudes, values and skills must be considered.

The complications do not end here. There are not only audiences with various expectations and cultural values eliciting varying degrees of commitment, but there is a formal organization, in this case the school system. This system has a definite table of organization, with defined responsibilities at each level. More important, the organization can be said to have certain *needs*—certain conditions of existence that must be secured and maintained if the organization is to function and fulfill its obligations within the framework of the larger society. These needs affect the ways in which the expectations of various audiences can be acted upon by the people carrying out the various roles subsumed by the organization. All organizations of comparable size will have similar "needs", but every organization, like every person, will have its own version of these needs.

Beyond these forces that affect the character and function of the principal's role, there are various unpredictable, or idiosyncratic, determinants. The history of a particular school, of a particular community, of a particular neighborhood or school district within the community, will often have much to do with setting the limits of action. And the massive forces of disjunctive social, tech-

nological, and cultural change characterizing American society
are constantly disturbing the orderly fulfillment of role expectations.

What has been said so far constitutes an organizational chart
for the rest of this paper. Each of these major dimensions of the
context within which the school and the administrator of the
school must operate will be analyzed in greater detail and at two
concomitant levels of abstraction. One level will be concerned
with a refinement of the broad principles already stated. The other
will explicate these principles as they apply to single cases.

Much of the case material drawn upon in the forthcoming
analysis was gathered over a period of several years in extended
studies by a Stanford School of Education research team consisting of an educator, a psychiatrist, an anthropologist (the author),
and various assistants representing these and other behavioral
sciences. During this period over fifty case studies were made of
school administrators and their schools, superintendents and their
school systems, and teachers and their classrooms, in a variety of
communities. Thanks are due to the Rosenberg Foundation for
major financial assistance, and to the school systems studied, both
for their most helpful cooperation and for supplementary financial
assistance.

EXPANSION OF BASIC PRINCIPLES

Cultural Values and Conflicts

The American culture is notable for the conflicts woven
into the fabric of its value system. This is not surprising in view of
the medley of cultural backgrounds from which the American
population originated, and in view of our rapidly changing culture. But these conflicts complicate the administrator's role.

If we take only a few areas of American belief and attitude,
the conflict-permeated nature of our culture and its value system
becomes clear.

Thrift—saving for a rainy day	Mortgaging one's future in order to obtain the fruits and the symbols of success early.
Importance of the Individual and his achievement	The "cult of the average man".
Belief in the equality of man	Racial and minority group prejudices; institutionalized inequality of opportunity.
Suspicion of intellectuals and scientists	Over-valuation of the "expert"; "a better world through science."
Belief that there are no fixed technological limits and that change is good in itself	Conservatism about adapting new social or political techniques for achieving change.
Belief in hard work as good in itself—the need to validate one's self by success attained by hard work	Concept of leisure as a measure of the good life; the high value placed upon recreation.

Many more specific value conflicts could be added to the list. The papers by Dorothy Lee and Jules Henry in this book suggest others. The contrasts between *traditional* and *emergent* value patterns described by the author in chapter 7 are an explicit statement of a profile of conflicts that directly affect the school administrator's role. It is difficult to predict how these values will be represented by specific groups or audiences in a specific educational community. Any one individual may embrace several conflicting values in his own system, or certain groups in the community may be committed to one or the other side of a conflicting set. The traditional versus emergent dichotomy seems to have fair predictive power with respect to the educational viewpoints held by various segments of the public (McPhee, 1959) and in the curriculum choices made by undergraduate college students (King, *et al.*, 1961). We can be sure that the context within which the school administrator must work will be characterized by conflicting value commitments that will bias perception and influence judgments made by members of school boards, PTA groups, teachers, pupils, and all other personnel engaged directly or peripherally in the operations of the school. Education is a goal-oriented activity. It is purposeful. And the criteria applied to it by everybody are value-oriented criteria.

The administrator's role is a balancing *role*. The administrator, and particularly the school principal, is caught squarely in the midst of the value conflicts that swirl around his position and the activity of the institution that he administers. His job is in large part that of maintaining a working equilibrium of at best antagonistically cooperative forces. This is one of the reasons why school administrators are rarely outspoken protagonists of a consistent and vigorously profiled point of view. Given the nature of our culture and social system, and the close connection between the public and the schools he cannot alienate significant segments of that public and stay in business. He must play his role to the satisfaction of many audiences simultaneously that are using different and potentially conflicting criteria of his performance. Perhaps it is only because there are certain core values of the kind described by Rhoda Métraux in chapter 6 that cross-cut areas of conflict is it possible for the school administrator in American society to maintain any working equilibrium at all.

Audience Expectations

One of the standard procedures of the Stanford research team that studied teachers in their classrooms and administrators in their schools was to ask respondents representing various groups to rate the individuals we were studying with respect to a wide variety of specific behaviors. The items on the form for school principals included such aspects of the administrative role as relations with teachers, ability to communicate with the central office, handling of public relations problems, and so on. These rating responses were also followed up by direct interviews. One phenomenon that became apparent early in the study and stayed constant throughout was that of consistent variation in ratings supplied by the different audiences. Administrators in the superintendent's office tended to perceive the case (a school principal) differently than school principals did; and principals in turn differed in their perceptions of the same individual and his operations from teachers, and teachers in turn from parents or other members of the lay public.

These differing perceptions are not usually a simple projection of the value system of the respondent, because there are certain consistencies in the perceptions shared by members of each audience. This seems to indicate that the respondents representing these various audiences are influenced by the demands of *their* roles in the perception of those of others.

For example, in one study (Sharpe, 1956) that is consistent in its results with others done by the team, the evaluations of specific school principals indicated that teachers rated an *open attitude towards change* on the part of their principal most highly, while members of the central administrative staff rated *communication* (between central staff, teachers, parents and vice versa) most highly, and paid least attention in their ratings to an open attitude towards change (in curriculum, school management, and so on) on the part of the principal. Teachers also regarded deviations (in the actual behavior of the principal) from their conception of appropriate human relationships between principal and teaching staff as most detrimental to morale, whereas central administrative staff perceived deviations in other areas of behavior on the part of the principal as most serious (see also Shipnuck, 1954).

The perceptions of the teacher and those of the central staff concerning the school principal and his role, as described above, are functions of the role relationships of the members of these audiences within the system in which they are all operating. Teachers in their situation want a principal who will guide them, or at least reinforce them, to educational innovations, but in a human, friendly way. Central staff administrators want a principal to keep them informed about what is going on, and want their directives to be communicated to the teachers and interpreted to the public. These behaviors are respectively most important to

the members of these audiences because they contribute to the
security of the roles and functions the members of the audience
groups must carry out within the framework of the organization.
The school principal must act appropriately in terms of the criteria of performance applied by both the audiences above and
below him in the hierarchy of the organization.

Another study (Fishburn, 1955) was concerned with the
rank order ascribed to various aspects of the teacher's role by administrators occupying a number of different positions in the
organization, and teachers—divided into groups by age, experience
and academic field. The teacher sample as a whole ranked "mediator of the culture" substantially above any other dimension of
their role. This means that they felt that a most important aspect
of their role responsibility was to create a situation where pupils
could learn appropriate attitudes and standards of behavior that
would enable them to get along well in the society in which they
lived. The next role dimension in rank order was "director of
learning." That is, they felt that transmission of the subject matter and academic skills was the next most important aspect of their
role. And thirdly, they felt that "guidance and counseling"—helping pupils to solve their personal problems (insofar as they are
related to learning in school)—was also very important.

The administrator sample as a whole (including both school
principals and central office staff) differed markedly from the
teacher group in its perception of the teacher's role. They ranked
"mediator of the culture" lowest in a hierarchy of six possible
dimensions. They also ranked "director of learning" and "guidance and counseling" as much less important than did the teacher
group. The role dimension that the administrators ranked as of
greatest importance was "liaison between school and community."
The next ranking role dimension was "member of the school community," and the next, "member of the profession." This means
that the administrators perceived as most important those aspects
of the teacher's role that directly relate to the administrative function—maintaining equilibrium among the various and potentially
conflicting audience groups that surround the school and school
system in the community.

The results of this study (and it is entirely consistent with our other long-term observations in the research project) emphasize again the conflict-permeated nature of the environment in which the school principal must function. Not only is he the mediator of relations between the various potentially conflicting audience groups within the school, the community the school serves, and the society at large (as general cultural value conflicts penetrate into his area of responsibility), he must also mediate potentially conflicting perceptions of what the teacher is supposed to be doing that originate within the ranks of teachers and administrators in his own professional community. It is particularly relevant here that the school principals expressed intermediate rankings of teacher role dimensions more frequently than did central office staff. That is, the principals more frequently recognized the relative importance of the mediator of the culture and director of learning role dimensions than did central office staff, who were inclined to see the teacher's role more exclusively in terms that were most relevant to the administrative function. The conflict-permeated nature of the situation is further emphasized by the fact that teachers differ among themselves in their perception of their roles. For example, younger teachers tend to rank the mediator of the culture and liaison between school and community dimensions as particularly important, while older, more experienced teachers tend to rank the director of learning and member of the profession dimensions as most important. Younger teachers are probably more idealistic about their roles, and tend to take on broad and perhaps unrealistic responsibilities. Older teachers come to feel that their job is to teach children the subject matter and promote learning skills. We are not concerned here with who is right or wrong. What is important for our purposes is the fact that again the school principal's role is complicated by potential conflicts between the perceptions of various audiences within the system of interactions that he has to pull together into a working equilibrium.

The Community

Much of what has already been said bears directly upon the nature of the community in which the school principal operates. All American communities will contain audience groups that view the principal's behavior in ways that conflict along the lines described in greater or lesser degree. But every community, and every school district within the community, has a history that furnishes a complex set of antecedents for administrative action.

In one community typical of others studied by the Stanford research team, the situation was complicated by the fact that an explosive post-war growth had changed the situation radically, but the administration was oriented to the power groups and cultural characteristics remaining in the community from the prewar period. This middle-sized town had been a suburban "bedroom" community for a nearby metropolitan center. It was characterized by an extremely high economic level. Its social, economic, and political outlook was conservative, and its interaction patterns were stable. These characteristics did not entirely disappear with the postwar boom. But they were inundated by a flood of industry and of military bases that changed the social, economic, and ethnic composition of the community radically. The virtually "private-school" relationship between the schools and the districts they served was, in most cases, destroyed, but the lines of communication between school administration and the social elite of the community were not. The problems of school management, both in the central office and in individual schools, were obviously complicated by the rapid and disjunctive change that had overtaken the community.

In another larger community studied by the team a somewhat similar situation existed. But in this community the prewar structure had contained more diverse social and ethnic groups. It was more heterogeneous and therefore the strain of accommodation to new environmental forces was not quite as acute. The complicating factor here—other than sheer expansion—was that the major ethnic group undergoing assimilation before the war was Italian and after the war it became Mexican. One might think that a school system that had already digested a large minority group of (at that time) low economic and educational status would be able to handle another without severe strain. Most of the older teachers in the system remembered the Italians well and were extremely proud of the rapid adaptation they had made, with the help of the school, to the American way of life and particularly to the American system of achievement. They expected the same things from the Mexicans, at the same time that they harbored latent feelings of prejudice towards the Mexicans that they did not towards the Italians. The latter were, after all, a population derived from a European culture, and they did not suffer the stigmata of high racial visibility. The Mexican children, in contrast, originated largely from areas in Mexico where the social and economic level was not only comparatively very low, but where the cultural background was decidedly different. They also suffer the experience of prejudice because they are not only socially but physically differentiated from dominant European-American groups, due to the strong Indian inheritance present in many Mexican immigrants. The procedures that had worked well with the Italians did not work at all with the Mexicans, and the relationships between teachers and pupils were complicated by the latent prejudices of the teachers.

The job of the school principal in this community was made difficult by these circumstances. Schools that had no, or very few, Mexican pupils before the war had a majority (over fifty percent) of Mexican children attending by 1955. The older teachers compared them unfavorably with the Italians of an earlier period. Younger teachers were confused and upset by the attitudes of the more experienced teachers. Administrators tried desperately to find ways of mollifying their teachers and at the same time educate the children of the large, semi-literate or non-literate, Mexican population.

In another community, much smaller in size than the other two and of quite a different character, the postwar growth period created a special kind of conflict situation. Before the war the area of the community had been strictly rural, with ranches, estates, and fruit orchards the dominant mode of land use. Much of the land was owned by the wealthy in large parcels of 500 to 3000 acres. Some of it was owned and worked by small ranchers and orchardists—some of Italian and a few of Spanish-American origin. Within the area of what was to become a high socio-economic level suburban community there were also several long-established small enclaves of retired people of modest means and of week-end cottages in the hills occupied intermittently by escapees from nearby cities.

Immediately after the war the area began to fill with people. The first to come were individualists seeking escape from the standardized conformity of the flat-land tracts or from the crowding of metropolitan life. They bought as much land as they could afford and built substantial houses some distance from each other. Together with the owners of large estates, they resist new roads, new subdivisions, and most of what comes under the ubiquitous term "progress"—sometimes including new schools. Shortly after the arrival of this group came the new subdivisions—largely of the "one-acre minimum" type. Each subdivision has its special character. One stresses riding and hiking trails and two-to-ten acre plots. Another stresses the "living in Crestview Heights is a measure of your success" appeal, with the one-acre minimum, but no other concessions to "rural atmosphere." Another established its claim just before the one-acre-minimum code went into effect and offers a community swimming pool, community square dancing, paved roads, sewers (rather than septic tanks—a most accurate index of "rurality"), and a high interaction rate between neighbors living in expensive houses built within whispering distance of each other.

Each of these groups has its own particular style of life and, to some degree, its own value system. The beleaguered estate owners remain aloof excepting as they see their sizeable economic interests threatened by rising taxes, highways cutting through their lands, or school-site condemnation procedures. They tend towards a conservative socio-political outlook and a traditional conception of what the school should do. The small ranchers and orchardists keep on with their established activities, hoping that when they have to sell they can get a good price from the subdivider. They are basically rural in their orientation and tend also towards a traditional view of the functions of the school. The residents of the former week-end cottages or small homes once occupied by the retired of modest means are a heterogeneous group. Many of them are young married students attending nearby colleges and universities, others are skilled laborers, or semiprofessional people who are escaping from the dull conformity (to them) of flat-land tract life like the first post-war wave of individualistic freedom seekers, but who lack their economic means. A few of the elderly retired linger on in their homes. These people—the students, the escapers, and the retired—present no consistent profile of opinion about the schools, but they are consistent in being dissident and individualistic. The extremes of radical progressivism and experimentalism, and of radical conservatism and traditionalism will both be found within the structure of sentiments of this bloc of the population. The "status-seekers" occupying the basically metropolitan suburban areas with the one-acre minimum include successful professionals and business executives. Their educational attitudes vary on the traditional-emergent continuum previously described but tend to be characterized consistently by a strong achievement-drive-success orientation. They want homework and higher mathematics to start in the first grade. They want their children to be equipped to get ahead even faster and farther than they did. The "exurbanites" who built on the two-to-ten acre plots tend to emulate the large estate owners, and maintain a fairly consistently conservative view of most things, including the school and its functions.

But all of these separatistic communities and enclaves are administered together in one school subdistrict. It is not surprising that the area is regarded as an administrative "hot spot"! The cauldron of public sentiment about how the schools should be managed; what should be taught at what grade level with what methods—is always seething. Loyalties to certain administrators form among teachers and parents, and are invoked in vigorous combat with critiques. The school board sessions are stormy, and characterized by accusation and counter-accusation. Every new school bond is seen as a plot by some, and a minimal necessity by others. Epithets fly about in public meetings when indignant citizens rise to their feet to expound upon educational policy. Letters are written to the editor of the newspaper. People are accused of being "beatniks," "radicals," "pinkos," "squares," and "radical conservatives" or downright "reactionaries". Styles of life as well as expressed opinions are cited as evidence—so that a woman who shops in shorts (even Bermuda shorts) and sandals

runs the risk of being typed as at least a beatnik by some. Prominent men send out mimeographed letters to the public describing
people and issues in a manner just short of libel. In this community, if it can be called a community, the administrator's role
is more than that of "balancing"—he becomes a whirling dervish
in a mad attempt to mediate relations among pluralistic elements
in a variegated public that has not lived long enough together to
have learned how to cooperate, even antagonistically. His image
therefore becomes so blurred that he seems to stand for everything
and for nothing, and is consequently little more than a stimulus
for dark and accusatory projections from most of his audiences.

Each of these three communities has its particular character due to its particular history. Each presents unique problems
for the administrator within the broad framework of problems
common to all American communities. Each of them makes its
contribution to the consistent picture of conflicts and varying
audience perceptions that is the working environment of the
school administrator.

The Formal Organization

All organizations of any considerable size share certain basic
characteristics (Selznick, 1949, 1953; Spindler, 1948, 1951;
Etzioni, 1961). This tends to be true even when the cultural context is varied because large-scale organizations must manage personnel and resources in some orderly way. This means that all
such organizations will be characterized by centralization of
authority, by an ordered hierarchy of offices with certain responsibilities and duties attached to them, by formalized lines of
communication within this ordered hierarchy, and by some agreement within the ranks of its responsible personnel regarding the
purposes of the organization. School systems, particularly the
larger metropolitan unified school districts, are no exception. The
character of this organization must be taken into account in a
multidimensional analysis of the role of the school principal,
because it constitutes a crucial aspect of his working environment.

All large-scale organizations share not only the above-named
aspects consequent to the task of ordering personnel and resources

into a functioning system, but also share certain "necessary conditions of existence" that we can call "needs" if we remember that the organismic analogy implied is only an analogy. All organizations need security—that is they must maintain mechanisms of defense against potentially disruptive environmental elements and forces—so that they may continue to exist in order to achieve their goals.

Organizations need stability in the lines of communication among the ordered ranks of offices, and between the surrounding environment and responsible officers, so that policy and decision-making can be made on the basis of accurate information, and so that once made, decisions will be communicated to those whose responsibility it is to see that they are executed.

Organizations need stability and continuity of relations with informal cliques and working groups, and in informal lines of communication that activate the formal structure of purposes and decisions. A formal organization is more than a table of organization. It can operate only because people occupy the roles laid out in the charter, and people usually resist being treated solely as means to an end. Therefore the informal, person-to-person relations and communications within the framework of the formal structure are what "make it go," and therefore there must be a fairly high degree of stability in these informal relations if the formal organization is to perform its tasks efficiently.

All large-scale organizations also need continuity of policy and its determination. The central leadership cannot shift its policy arbitrarily under the usual conditions of operation. The offices and the people occupying them within the hierarchy must have an outlook and set of commitments that permit consistency, and when policy shifts they must know in what direction it is going, and in American organizations, usually *why*. Therefore organizations of the kind being described can be said to need *homogeneity of outlook*. The conception of purposes and legitimate means to attaining them must be shared throughout all levels of the hierarchy of offices. Of course it is never absolutely, uniformly shared. Variations in outlook characterize each group within the system, according to the needs of that particular group, but these variations must occur within a broad framework of agreement or there is no coherent, stable, defensible organization.

It is apparent that the formal organization—the large unified school district or urban school system—within which the school administrator operates is in itself one of the most important determinant forces affecting his role. Many of his actions that seem arbitrary or even nonrational from the viewpoint of teachers, parents, or other audiences more or less peripherally involved with the formal structure of the system are dictated by his position as an officer of the organization. This commitment on the part of the administrator therefore not infrequently creates conflict between the administrator and these audiences, but even so it seems apparent that the formal organizational structure constitutes one of the few constants in the professional role of the administrator. It is helpful to the administrator when teachers understand the nature of this influence upon their administrator's behavior.

But the dynamics of formal organizations, when applied to specific situations, are not as straightforward and uncomplicated as the general description above may make them seem. For example, in one system studied by the Stanford team the central administration was faced with an adjustment to a rapidly changing community much like the first one discussed previously. There had been continuity of leadership—the superintendent of schools had been in office for more than two decades and had managed to keep his organization sufficiently flexible to meet new conditions, even though his administration could not avoid lingering commitments to the conservative elements of the community that had been the dominant group in the prewar period. Understandably, the foundation stone of his administrative policy was to maintain good public relations—to reduce as much as possible the inevitable friction between groups and audiences representing the old and the new, the upper socio-economic groups and the lower, the unions and the industrial managers. Curriculum development took a secondary, though important position in policy determination and action issuing from it. The superintendent's system was also characterized by an unusually high degree of autonomy and decentralization—every school and its principal was considered an independent unit operating within the general confines of the system. Under these conditions a high degree of understanding and homogeneity of outlook with respect to policy was required of school administrators, so they would know how to act when conditions demanding action arose in terms appropriate to agreed-upon general policy.

A new appointment to a crucial principalship was made in this system. The principalship was crucial because the school in question had become a public relations problem. Its district lines had been drawn during a previous period and had not taken into account an unpredictable growth pattern that almost overnight put upper-middle social status high-achievement-oriented groups in the same district with a lower status industrial labor population. These two segments of the population demonstrated different educational needs and wanted educational policies that were definitely in conflict with each other's.

The appointment was made of a young and relatively inexperienced principal to fill the post vacated by an "old timer," with instructions to "keep the people happy." The principal took these instructions seriously, of course, and attempted to form workable liaisons with the warring parent factions. He was most sensitive to public opinion and attempted to take it into account. But trouble developed quickly. The teachers in this school felt the strong need to make curriculum changes and solve pressing problems of relationships with different kinds of children. They conceived of the principal as a person who should be primarily concerned with these necessary changes and problems. But they came to see the principal as primarily concerned with the community outside the school and oriented towards the needs of the central administration—the superintendent's office and his staff within the formal organization of the school system. Dissatisfaction resulted and the principal's security was placed in jeopardy. The principal himself was put in a most difficult position. While attempting to satisfy central administration and organizational needs he alienated his teaching staff. But he did not end by satisfying central administration either. An unwritten understanding, constituting part of the administrative policy of the school system, was that a principal should exhibit sufficient flexibility to know when to break a rule set down by the superintendent's of-

fice; when to deviate from an official directive or instructions issuing from general policy. The principal, inexperienced and com-
mited to solving a specific public relations problem, overlooked
the necessity of satisfying staff and educational requirements even
when this action might not be directly in line with efforts to solve
the public relations problem. The end result was dissatisfaction
and disturbance on all sides without anyone really being "at fault"
in the usual sense of the term. The unfortunate situation was the
consequence of a complex set of interacting pressures created in
part by the attempt of the formal organization, activated in the
offices of central authority, to adapt to the forces in the environment that threatened one of its segments. The school principal's
role was decisively affected as the dynamics inherent in the situation unfolded.

A further example will contribute to an understanding of the
vital function that the formal organization of the school system,
and particularly its definition and manipulation of policy, has in
determining the milieu within which the school administrator
operates.

In one community studied (Tilden, 1953), certain decisions
made subsequent to the building of a new high school decisively
affected, in an unanticipated manner, the roles of the school principals in the system and their relationships to the superintendent's
office. The community was characterized by a high degree of
sectionalism, with an elite power group, a Mexican-American section, a vegetable-growers area, a mercantile class, a Marine Corp
base, and Negro industrial workers. Before the time of the study,
however, it had been a less heterogeneous and more stable community. During this earlier period a laissez-faire policy concerning school attendance districts had been followed. Crossing of
district lines to attend certain schools had been permitted, and
principals had been instructed to make their own judgments within
wide latitudes concerning transfers of students from one school
to another.

When the new high school was built in a low status socio-
economic area of the community a new policy had to be adopted.
Anticipating that many students in the attendance district of the
school would want to (or their parents would want them to)
transfer to one of the high schools in a higher socio-economic

area, the administration decided to alter its established policy, and adopted one of no transfers. Principals of elementary schools that were to send their graduating students to certain high schools according to attendance district lines were instructed to make no commitments, screen cases carefully, and send the most aggressive parents to the superintendent's office.

This policy change had some unanticipated consequences—as policy changes taken in adaptation to environmental pressures usually do. The school system, like the one described in the previous example, was characterized by a high degree of decentralization of authority. Each school in the system was considered a separate and semiautonomous unit. Administrative decisions by principals in these schools had long been based upon this fundamental understanding. The old laissez-faire policy had helped maintain the security of the school system in the environment of that community. The new policy was designed to do the same thing, and it did, but it changed the relationships between principals, central authority, and public. Where before the policy change the principal could make his own decisions in a basic area of public relations, he could now no longer do so. New responsibilities were laid upon the central office and particularly the superintendent, and the principal lost important authority. This shift in responsibility did not stop with attendance matters but had ramifications throughout other areas of authority and responsibility. The centralization of authority was increased, and the degree of autonomy enjoyed by the separate schools of the system decreased. The principal's role therefore underwent a significant change as a result of the adaptation of the formal organization to the changing community forces.

Personality Factors

As stated in the introduction to this chapter, roles are filled by people, and people not only act in terms of expectations issuing from various audiences and in terms of commitments to organizational structures—they *react*. And this reaction is not only a product of situational forces; it is also a product of the unique personality of the person filling the role. This unique personality can never have full expression in any one role, and many individuals never find fulfillment even in the multiplicity of roles one may play in a complex, segmentalized society. But the expectations connected to any role are responded to selectively —emphasized, distorted, or obfuscated—depending always to some degree upon the particular, idiosyncratic *needs*, perceptions, and skills characterizing a single individual.

One principal studied in his school environment faced a large and heterogeneous faculty involved in some very difficult professional problems. The school had rather suddenly acquired a disproportionately large Mexican-American population. All of the problems attendant upon this event were full-blown at the time of his ascendancy to the position as principal of the school. One of the most serious problems had to do with discipline. Mexican children are usually no more (or perhaps they are even less) inclined to create discipline problems than any other group, but many of them had been alienated from the school and its authorities by very unfortunate educational experiences. This alienation process arose out of a number of factors and is not the subject of our discussion at the moment. The reader can understand some of its dimensions by reading Chapter 8, "The Transmission of American Culture." The point is that this principal faced a situation where the faculty was "up in arms" about classroom control, spotty attendance, molesting of children, tardiness, and so forth. The latent hostilities of many of the faculty towards the Mexican-American group, and in some cases towards children in general, had been activated and were running rampant. Committees were formed to work out petitions to the superintendent concerning discipline. There was strong support within some elements of the faculty for a corporal punishment clause in the teachers' code, so that a misbehaving child could be spanked by the teacher (with one other person present). The central administration of the school district would accept no such measure and charged the principal with the responsibility of seeing to it that none such were taken.

This in itself is not an unusual bind for the school principal to be placed in—caught squarely between two opposing forces. What complicated the issue here was that this particular principal could not tolerate hostility of any kind. Autobiographic and psychological test material taken from him showed clearly that his own dependency relationships with his parents, and particularly with his siblings, had never been completely worked out. He suppressed feelings of hostility and aggression on his own part, and was seriously threatened when he perceived such feelings on the part of others. He was not at all suited to the role he had to play in this particular situation. There was a discipline problem in the school. True, it had been exaggerated by the evolving sentiments of the teachers and their latent hostilities, but there was an obvious, operational problem. But rather than working directly on the problem itself, he alienated his faculty from him by denying the validity of their perceptions of the situation and reiterating the stand of the central administration. Nothing constructive could be done until he mastered his own defensive feelings and faced the issue squarely. His unique personality directly affected the way he could and did play the role of principal.

In another case a woman was appointed to a vacated principalship. This school had operated for many years under the leadership of a woman principal who had formed very close personal relationships with most of her faculty. They looked to her for defense from the demands of central office staff and parents alike. Partly because of this defensive relationship the school had become defined as a public relations trouble spot. Parents had frequently been alienated because the principal seemed always to communicate the feeling, when trouble arose, that the teacher was always right. The central office staff was unhappy because the parents were unhappy. So the new appointee was charged with the task of bringing the parents back into a favorable equilibrium at the same time that she obtained and reinforced good working relationships with a teaching staff that had learned to expect an unusually high degree of friendly support from their principal.

This would not have been an impossible, or perhaps even particularly difficult, task for some principals. But it was extremely difficult for her. Psychological projective test responses, autobiographic content, and observational data indicated that she was uncertain and anxious, and that she assumed a rather austere professional demeanor to cover up her internal feelings. This is, to be sure, not unusual among comparatively inexperienced principals (or teachers) but it was a marked characteristic in her case. She also suffered from feelings of isolation—that as a woman she

had embarked on a rather lonely career—that were not reduced
by her mode of life, living as she did in an apartment alone and
sharing little in the way of social life with others. Added to these
personality tendencies was her very intense achievement drive.
She wanted to succeed, she told herself, more than she wanted to
be "happy," and she worked very hard at it. She was indeed a
very competent professional educator, with a wide and well-de-
veloped range of specific skills and good judgment on strictly
pedagogical matters.

Her unique personality configuration made it impossible for
her to meet the expectations of her various audiences—central administration, teaching staff, and parents—in this particular situation. Her teacher audience particularly expected a relationship
from her that she could not give, so they perceived her as unap-
proachable and "cold." Her parent audience, already negatively
conditioned towards school administration, did not find reas-
surance either. The central staff, while impressed with her high
professional competence in the formal aspects of her role, became dismayed by her failure to resolve the public relations problem and by the emerging alienation of her teaching staff. They
were also surprised to find that she tried to follow their directives
too literally—probably as a compulsive defense against her own
anxieties and fear of failure. Eventually she resolved her personal
problems, and her innate good sense and high professional competence then allowed her to make an unusually good adjustment
to the role of administrator; but the process was painful and
created some nearly disastrous consequences in the system of
relationships because her personality configuration did not match
the requirements of her role.

But lest we conclude that personalities and roles must be
exactly matched in order for success to ensue, let it be said that
there are some personality types that seem to be able to remake
the role to suit their personalities—even the sensitive school principal's role. For example, in one school studied in a large metropolitan system the principal was a man in his late thirties who
brought an unusually colorful personality to the position. He had
a vigorous temper and was not above using four-letter words to

express it, even in heated arguments with the superintendent and his staff about policy matters, but he was equally inclined to forgive and forget. He was known to drink immoderately at times, but never around students. He liked horse racing and wagered frequently. He wore very unconservative sports coats and drove a low-slung foreign car. He was extremely popular with a majority (though not all) of his faculty, students, and public audiences. Transgressions on the expectations of ordinary propriety (as applied to the school administrator) were forgiven with an almost prideful smile and a "Well you know Jack!" comment. Other principals viewed him as well with affectionate lenience and asked each other how he "got away with it." As a matter of fact, it is not easy to answer that question. Possibly it was because he did attend to all necessary administrative matters with keen intelligence and unusually good judgment despite all of his apparent deviation from the conforming ideal of the school principal in American society, and at the same time he managed to create an aura about himself into which less colorful people could project their own wish-fulfillment needs to be a little more free of dull obligations to be eminently respectable. He covered himself concerning the obligations of his professional role, and then proceeded to test the limits of the public image connected with the peripheral aspects of this role. Perhaps he managed to keep out of trouble as a school principal despite his deviations because he had an unusual sense of what those limits really were! Not everyone has this sixth sense. And perhaps not everyone needs to deviate as much as he did.

The Ideal Principal

As we near the end of this analysis of the school principal's role and the multiple factors that affect it, the reader may take comfort in being instructed as to what the school principal *should* be. An exhaustive study (Sharpe, 1956) was made of the opinions and perceptions of all of the teachers and administrators in a metropolitan school district. Their responses were combined to determine the configuration characterizing the ideal elementary school principal. I quote from this study:

The ideal principal is a 38 year old man, who is reasonably attractive, who dresses fairly conservatively, and who comes from the same ethnic or racial stock as his teachers but not necessarily from the same stock as the pupils in his school. He enjoys a socio-economic status higher than that of his pupils but not higher than that of his teachers. He has high prestige in the community, where he exerts a strong influence. His social position is above the community average, and he is regarded as a member of the upper middle class. His administrative skills follow this rank order from high to low: (1) Human relations; (2) teaching and educational techniques; (3) community and public relations; and (4) administrative techniques. He acts, in discharging his duty, in such a way that a high degree of communication between his teachers and himself is realized. He is regarded as an intimate member of his school group but he is expected to maintain some social distance between himself and his teachers. He has an open attitude toward change but he is not overly active in promoting it. He creates a permissive, democratic atmosphere in his school yet exhibits sufficient domination to make clear to his teachers that he is the leader who is in charge of their activities.

The analysis of the school principal's role presented in this paper should serve to forewarn the reader that potentially conflicting audience perceptions are subsumed in this statement of the ideal type. But insofar as there is an agreed-upon image shared by members of the different audiences, the one presented should approximate it. The alert reader can discern for himself those pivotal points in this image where conflicts in expectations are most likely to occur. He can also see that this image is in most of its dimensions a direct projection of core American cultural values concerning achievement and the nature of leadership. The *balancing* aspects of the role also becomes abundantly clear.

CONCLUSION

This analysis of the role of the school administrator has attempted to show how various forces issuing from generalized cultural values, audience expectations, pressures created by the formal organization of the school system, and by the unique characteristics of the community and its history interact to form the total set of expectations determining the principal's role. It has also attempted to show how the personality of the principal is a factor of considerable importance. It is granted that specific situations make for a wide (but not infinite) variety of possibilities and that no analysis will be able to take them all into account. But these are some of the most significant dimensions that need to be considered in any given case.

It is crucial to engage with all of these dimensions if the complex middleman's balancing role of the school principal is to be understood. No one scientific discipline concerned with the study of human behavior could supply all of the techniques and concepts needed in the analysis. Cultural anthropology, sociology, social psychology, and clinical psychology each contributed to the procedures of analysis and conceptualization employed. Not all analytic problems of educational structure and process need be approached in this multidisciplinary manner, but some do, and school administration is one of them.

References

Etzioni, Amitai, ed., 1961, *Complex Organizations, A Sociological Reader*. New York: Holt, Rinehart and Winston, Inc.

Fishburn, Clarence E., 1955, *Teacher Role Perceptions in the Secondary Schools of One Community*. Unpublished Ed.D. dissertation, School of Education, Stanford University.

King, Stanley H., Charles E. Bidwell, Bruce Finnie, Harry A. Scarr, 1961, *Undergraduate careers: Alternatives and Determinants*. Unpublished M.S. paper read before the 56th Annual Meeting of the American Sociological Association.

McPhee, Roderick F., 1959, "Individual Values, Educational Viewpoint, and Local School Approval." *Administrator's Notebook*, VII, No. 8, Midwest Administration Center, University of Chicago.

Selznick, Philip, 1949, *TVA and the Grass Roots: A Study in the Sociology of Formal Organization*. Berkeley, Calif.: University of California Press.

————, 1957, *Leadership in Administration; A Sociological Interpretation*. New York: Harper & Row, Publishers.

Sharpe, Russell, 1956, *Differences Between Perceived Administrative Behavior and Role Norms as Factors in Leadership*. Unpublished Ph.D. dissertation, School of Education, Stanford University.

Shipnuck, Murray E., 1954, *Perceived Hostility in Administrator-Teacher Relationships*. Unpublished Ed.D. dissertation, School of Education, Stanford University.

Spindler, George D., 1948, "The Military—A Systematic Analysis." *Social Forces*, 27: 83–88.

————, 1951, "The Doolittle Board and Coöptation in the Army." *Social Forces*, 29:305–310.

Tilden, Charles H., 1953, *Administrative Adaptation to Social Forces*. Unpublished Ed.D. dissertation, School of Education, Stanford University.

13——Fred H. Werner

Acculturation and Milieu Therapy in Student Transition*

The study of student culture in colleges and universities offers excellent research opportunities to those interested in anthropological problems of cultural dynamics and transmission, acculturation and the relationship of the individual to his society. Extensive research on the impact of higher education upon undergraduates has been carried on for the past five years by sociologists and psychologists, but student culture seen in terms of acculturation dynamics has been virtually ignored by cultural anthropologists.

Concerted efforts by these sociologists and psychologists has resulted in the empirical verification of the usefulness of the "culture concept" as a way to discuss collegiate behavior. Modal overt and covert value orientations of students, professors, and administrators clearly affect the educational process at a particular college or university.

This chapter will deal primarily with the reactions of a group of students to a dramatic change in their cultural environment. The students belong to a religious organization of a major Protestant denomination at a southern university, hereafter designated, "Transitional University." The students are from rural southern and religiously conservative backgrounds, and in the course of the paper, it will be suggested that some of the psychological reactions displayed by individuals to their contact with a large urbane

* This paper was given in a shorter form at the Southwestern Anthropological Meeting, University of California, Santa Barbara, Goleta, California, April 1, 1961.

educational community parallels the responses and adaptations of individuals in non-Western societies caught in the binds of an abrupt acculturation process.

RESEARCH METHODOLOGY

During a three-month period, data on the Religious Center was collected by interviewing and participant-observing. Individual interviews with the Religious Center's Director and more active students were arranged. I was also a participant-observer in a Center study seminar on the novels and philosophy of Albert Camus and attended a number of Center functions. Interviews with student leaders at not only Transitional University but the nearby State University and a land grant college for the applied sciences gave a basis for comparison of regional collegiate patterns. Historical documents pertaining to the development of Transitional University were read. Participation in deliberations of a faculty-student-administration committee discussing student life was a source of additional information.

RATIONALE

Contemporary research into the nature and dynamics of American colleges and universities is less than a decade old. One finding substantiated by a series of independent studies suggests that a complex self-selection process by students themselves takes place. This process enables the individual to select an educational institution where he will not only be academically successful but where the dominant cultural press of the institution will be essentially congruent with his acquired home and community expectations. In other words, there is an attempt by the student to maintain a sociocultural-psychological system. However, the conflict begins to develop when we realize that faculty and administrative members in the United States see their role as transmitting some information that will alter the students' behavior. Whether the goal is to civilize the students by developing and refining the power of the intellect, perception or feeling, or by deliberately introducing a new range of sensibility or a new world-view, the idea of change—as in most American institutions—seems to be imbedded into the covert value systems of faculty, administrators, alumni, and the general public conception of the function of education (Clark and Trow, 1962).

This tension between preferences of the students themselves and the educational institutions can be illustrated by using Transitional University and its cultural subunit, the Religious Student Center, as examples. The students and the University are regarded in this paper as symptomatic of more general processes and problems that are to be found at educational institutions. By its uniqueness (being more an exception than a rule to modal religious campus organizations), the Religious Student Center becomes easier to study ethnographically and, for me, the cultural distance is greater than it would be probably among a comparable group in the northeastern United States.

TRANSITIONAL UNIVERSITY

To be somewhat more specific, Transitional University in the past thirty years has been becoming a more secularized academic institution, though its public image in the South is that of a religiously oriented university. The faculty is becoming increasingly a heterogeneous mix. About fifty percent of the students come from outside of the South. The student body tends to be drawn from the middle-class or higher. In contrast, the thirty active members of the Religious Center are southerners, rural, intellectually inclined, and from religiously conservative or fundamentalist homes. Clearly a disparity exists between the *ethos* of the University and sociocultural backgrounds (and one can infer the psychological patterning) of the Center's students. This is the classic acculturation situation.

While many faculty members deny categorically having a "metaphysic," the very nature of the subject matter, its internal logical consistency or structure—whether in the humanities, social or physical sciences—communicates a codification of reality. In a sense, it does not matter what the student studies intensely. Whether history, symbolism, higher or lower Biblical criticism, existentialism, non-Aristotelian logic or mathematics, non-objective art, the contemporary novel—a new world of ideas is presented to the student in the daily classrooms. For example:

In history class, students meet Western civilization in greater complexity and with a greater time depth than they had ever known.

In English, they learn what "symbols" are.

In Religion, there is higher and lower Biblical criticism.

In psychology, the unconscious is discussed.

Then too, there is the theory of relativity, and for some, there is the first look at non-objective art. A new world of ideas is presented in the daily classrooms and in encounters with students who are unlike themselves.

Many of these ideas, these "facts" about the world, are anxiety provoking. For the majority of students in colleges and universities in the United States, at least, a dichotomy exists between what has been taught in familial and community experience and what is formally taught in the University curriculum. In defense of traditional ways of responding to experience, students at colleges and universities have developed and elaborated rituals —behavioral patterns designed to cushion a student from the cultural and epistemological implications of his studies. From college generation to college generation the student culture is transmitted. With a few notable exceptions—Reed, Swarthmore, possibly Harvard, and others—student culture at most educational institutions is a protective reaction to the stresses of what might otherwise be a too rapid acculturation process. As sociologists Clark and Trow (1962) of the Berkeley Center of the Study of College Peer Groups have suggested, the nation's colleges and universities must face a central and serious problem of student boredom, hostility and indifference to learning, and the irrelevance of their associations and relationships to education. In my opinion, this phenomena can be viewed as a psychocultural reaction, having parallels in all kinds of societies throughout the world. Students will be heard to describe themselves and others as being "apathetic," a word found frequently in the literature of acculturation. What is commonly called "apathy," "the sophomore slump," "ennui," "compulsive campus activities," and "meaningless diversion" seem to me to be manifestations of "acculturation shock" in students whose core values, their basic understandings of the world and its meaning, have been challenged and are undergoing some form of redefinition.

Acculturative Types

Anthropological literature of culture change tells us that there are several ways in which groups and individuals respond to acculturation (Spindler, 1955; Voget, 1956; Wallace, 1956). At Transitional University, the Student Religious Center is only one of a series of expressions of this. Other patterns can be briefly summarized in an acculturation typology:

1. *Passive Withdrawal Type*: These are the bored bridge players, compulsive television viewers and movie-goers, isolates and passive observers. In their extreme reaction to classes and their educational environment, they may flunk out of school. Innate intelligence is usually sufficiently high to become an unsatisfactory causal explanation.

2. *Reactive Type*: These students try to encapsulate what they have been taught in the classroom with the cultural attitudes derived from family and community. They prefer *the past* to *the present* or *the future*. At Transitional University, the pattern could be seen in the sentimentality of one fraternity over the "Spirit of Robert E. Lee" and the Civil War, or in an incipient "back to God and prayer movement," which I was told had about ten members.

3. *Compensatory Type*: These students repudiate their earlier belief systems in what might be described as almost an irrational denial. Though the content of their new world-view may be seemingly quite different, the underlying personality structure has changed little. Religious zeal, for example, may be converted into dogmatic scientism.

4. *Adaptive Type*: Most undergraduates would probably be classified under this category. The course content is integrated to some degree into the life-ways of the individual, but by and large

a pattern of cultural continuity has been predominately maintained. While more tolerant and open to experience, these students regard their University education mainly as vocational training.

5. *Cultural Revisionist Type:* These students, more representative of the students associated with the Student Religious Center, often restructure their world-view. But even more important, there seems to be a restructuring of the individual's "cognitive mazeway," to use Anthony Wallace's phrase (Wallace, 1958). Considerable anxiety and discomfort accompanies the process of readjustment. For these students the University experience is a break in the cultural continuity of their lives, to a degree unmatched by the majority of their student peers who selected a university in their own image from the first.

The Religious Center as a Milieu Therapy Unit

It has been my contention that the idea of a subtle disorientation within the individual (though also expressed on the group level) as a result of the impact of the curriculum and the collegiate cultural press helps us to understand the pattern of student behavior. In this section, I shall consider the implications of the Student Religious Center as a functioning "milieu therapy" unit for its members.

"Thinking is a case of active uncertainty set against conviction or unquestioning assurance," writes Dewey (1959). Before entering college, the Center's students had many unquestioning beliefs about the world. Over the months and years of college, the simple, easily definable general categories appropriate enough to handle experience in a small southern town no longer held the new experiences and information acquired at the University. On the one hand, the new information could not be denied; on the other hand (from the point of view of some of the students) there was more "experience" than the major categories could handle.

In order to illustrate the tensions between the old belief system and the new ideas transmitted by the University setting, I shall quote one student who was trying to resolve the conflict

between what she knew about mathematics from her undergraduate training and her religious belief

She told me this:

> I always enjoyed doing math. This was the thing I liked most,
> but when I got to my senior year, I started questioning so many
> of my beliefs, because in math, it seems to me, you start at a
> certain point, and you go by logical deduction from one to the
> next, and you have to prove everything and what you can't prove
> then you say is not true. And when I started to think about this
> in terms of other things besides math and my studies I started
> to think of this in terms of Life. I came to the realization I could
> not prove the existence of God, and this rather upset me because
> I had been brought up in a religious home and had been taught to
> believe in things like that. . . .

Her reaction was a feeling of shame for having lost her
faith. At the Center, she was learning about symbolism, and when
I last spoke to her, seemed to be less literal minded about these
matters.

If psychotherapy ". . . consists of the verbal labeling and resorting to such preverbal categories, so that they may become
accessible to the forms of symbolic or linguistic manipulation
characteristic of adult problem solving," then the Student Center
functions as a psychotherapeutic experience for its student members (Bruner, Goodnow, Austin, 1956):

1. The Religious Center offers a highly permissive environment to students who come from culturally constricted backgrounds. Students are urged to "drop their social masks" and "be"
their "real selves." Conversations at the Center among the students take on a grim intensity. "But what is the meaning of life?"
I heard one student ask another. Some reply was given. "Is that
all?" the first student questioner answered.

2. In seminars, drama groups, publications, the accent is on
"how do you (the individual) feel about this" in contrast to
"what have you been told about this." This key question of feeling is, of course, a conventional psychiatric one.

3. Among the religious workers in the South, there seems to
be an adaptation of the writings of Buber, Bultmann, Niebuhr, and
Tillich. Albert Camus' novels and Viktor E. Frankl's *From Death-*

camp to Existentialism are widely read. What existentialism seems to offer the southern student is a countervailing approach to salvationist-revivalism that seems so much a part of southern rural Protestantism.

4. "Engagement in the human situation" rather than passive observation is regarded as a desideratum at the Religious Center. Personal responsibility for one's action is an expression of this. Personal decision in the face of criticism by the majority must still be made. Thus, the Student Center leaders were among the crucial number who participated in one of the first sit-in demonstrations of last year's series. And it is interesting furthermore to note that initially (for several weeks) the lunch counter demonstrations had a religious quality about them. Several weeks later, the tone of the lunch counter demonstrations clearly shifted as the more articulate student politicians evolved political rationalizations for such activity.

What is happening to this small number of students at the Student Religious Center is a basic realignment of their traditional religious and culturally derived ideas to a more contemporary intellectual framework. The traditional adjustment that the academically most able seem to make is accompanied by decisions to leave the South for graduate training in a large eastern urban educational center. There, the ideas of the Center are reinforced by the secularized and individuated life of the city. But without the milieu therapy implicitly taking place at the Student Center, this transformation of basic values would be even more difficult. Thus, the Religious Center is functioning as a transmitting and mediating agent between the acculturating students from the mid-South and emerging national and world values.

References

Bruner, Jerome J., J. Goodnow, G. Austin, 1956. *A Study of Thinking*. New York: John Wiley & Sons, Inc.

Clark, Burton R., and M. Trow, "Determinants of College Student Subculture," in T. M. Newcomb and E. K. Wilson, eds., *The Study of College Peer Groups* (to be published in 1963).

Dewey, John, 1959, "Natural History of Thinking," quoted in K. Pribrim, "On the Neurology of Thinking," *Behavioral Science*, 4: 265–287.

Spindler, George D., 1955, "Education in a Transforming American Culture." *Harvard Educational Review*, XXV, 145–156.

Wallace, Anthony F., 1956, "Revitalization Movements." *American Anthropologist*, 58:264–281.

Voget, Fred W., 1956, "The American Indian in Transition." *American Anthropologist*, 58:249–263.

14——*Solon T. Kimball*

Cultural Influences
Shaping the Role
of the Child*

It seems somewhat incredible that anything new or different could or should be said or written about children so soon after the close of the 1960 White House Conference on Children and Youth. The thoroughness with which the experts and the interested were solicited to participate reflects credit upon the abilities of the Conference organizers. From these efforts came an outpouring of articles from dozens of contributors covering nearly every conceivable aspect affecting youth. Their authors ranged the gamut of professional, religious, organizational, social, and intellectual segments of American life. Only one group seems to have remained unsolicited in this search for wisdom, namely, youth itself.

This type of oversight is not uncommon in the traditional American procedure of examining institutions and social problems. Those who are most directly affected by the preparation of a program are the ones most likely to be overlooked in the formulation of policy or of its instrumentation through organization. Patients, prisoners, or students are seldom consulted in the operation of hospitals, prisons, or schools. Perhaps this is as it must be, but then, again, perhaps those who suffer or benefit from the effects of the exercise of responsibility by others might also make a contribution, if it could be remembered to ask their participation.

That this remark is not completely gratuitous will become apparent as the analysis of the role of children in our society is developed in the next several pages. Possibly an understanding of

* Reprinted from "Those First School Years." *The National Elementary Principal,* Vol. XL, No. 1 (September, 1960) pp. 18–32, with permission.

its relevance may well be the most important contribution which can be made to those who are charged with the responsibility of formal education in the early childhood years. But first, it is necessary to establish at least some minimum justification to add one more statement to this recent flood of analyses and opinion by those judged most competent to speak on the subject.

An attempt to rationalize or clarify disagreements and confusion among the experts might serve as a legitimate excuse for further treatment. Actually, differences in interpretation are surprisingly minor. The confusion is more a matter of indigestion, due to the quantity of data, than of methodological deficiencies. For this reason, such justification as is offered must be upon conceptual grounds, that it is possible through reorganization and re-examination from a different set of assumptions and with different objectives in mind to extract more meaning from the available data than has yet been achieved.

The initial step in this process is to shift our focus away from the subject, in this case children, to the environment—physical, psychical, social, and cultural—which surrounds and influences the child in his development. This emphasis does not exclude examination of the subject: it simply recognizes the interdependency between the individual and the systems of which he is a part or representative. Precedence for this procedure has been well developed in the natural sciences. Within anthropology, for example, although culture constitutes the central focus of study, it can be objectified only as individuals are examined. Contrariwise, when we come to study personality, we assume that it reflects a mirror image of the cultural experiences of the individual.

Following these introductory comments, we can now turn to an examination of the role or roles assigned to children in our society.

FORCED ABANDONMENT OF CHILDHOOD

Although it is seldom stated in this way, the major role of the child *qua* child is to submit to and assist in the activities and processes which prepare him for adult status. The extreme dependency of early infancy permits no choice in the selection of the external environment in which the initial learning occurs. Later when, presumably, the child has developed some rational discrimination in his response to demands placed upon him, it is too late for him to make effective protest. He has already internalized the emotional set of a system which requires that he eventually abandon the thought and habit ways of children and substitute those of the adult world.

However rewarding the culture of childhood, that of the grown-up world is continuously and persistently presented as more rewarding and desirable, and childhood is defined as a transitory and to-be-abandoned stage of life. No matter how entrancing, the never-never world of Peter Pan turns out to be just that, a fantasy in which childhood is forever threatened by pirates symbolizing demanding adults who must eventually win the age-old struggle between old and young. Although James Barrie allows the illusion of a different solution, both child and adult know that his ending is founded in the realm of dreams.

This forced abandonment of childhood in which, if it is successful, the child is a willing participant, represents the first of a sequential series of tragedies which each individual encounters on the road of life. No matter how sentimental or protective adults may be, the gradual and sometimes forcible destruction of the innocence of childhood is a necessary function of the relationship between adult and child. The latter is not the only one who suffers in this abrupt destruction of childhood certainties. The transition also demands its costs of the adult. The mother's mixed emotion of anguish and pride when her "baby" first enters school is repeated later when her child, turned young adult, leaves home for marriage, college, or the world of work. She may also carry a sense of guilt because of the contradictory desire to both hold and eject, and guilt because there can never be assurance that one has done enough or that what one has done has been right. There is solace in believing that one has done the best he could, but doubt may also nag the conscience.

The male response to these crises is different only in degree, and both parents share the knowledge that they have been parties to a failure, concealment, or perhaps even deception in communicating to the growing child what the world is really like. This conspiracy of silence is in part a function of the inability to articulate the realities; in part, it is an attempt to continue the protective role assumed during infancy; and, in part, it is a result of the parents' own unwillingness or incapacity to face the realities of their own lives. The delusion they have perpetuated, the illusion they have lived under and passed on to their children, should not be assessed as deliberate. Not that adults and parents are blameless, for they are not. The offense with which they may be charged is the same one as that which they first permitted and then prohibited, that of innocence.

The adult world is no more free of fantasy and illusion than is that of the child. The Walter Mittys are everywhere among us. Shaw's *Pygmalion* expresses a contemporary version of the Cinderella story. Our devoted adherence to romantic love as a necessary prerequisite to marriage and adult responsibilities of family and parenthood is real enough, but do we not deceive ourselves when we act as if erotic love is the panacea for the tough job of cementing relations between men and women in domestic functions?

These beliefs, and similar ones in other spheres of life, sustain us through bitterness, tragedy, and boredom. They are undoubtedly a necessary aspect in our kind of cultural world and as such should not, even were it possible, be either dispelled or destroyed. Our sin is that we let them delude us, that we insist upon maintaining an innocence of realities. Perhaps there is no simple way to explain why this is so, but probably these tendencies are linked with the generalized guilt which our culture so successfully inculcates during that period of defenseless infancy. If so, then it is all the more apparent why we can understand the child's role only by examining the nature of the world surrounding him. In that quest, we turn to a brief look at the distinctive aspects of the American family in its metropolitan middle class manifestations.

THE AMERICAN FAMILY SYSTEM

We can begin by examining how labels are used to describe and perhaps also obscure. There is some advantage but also danger in using apt phrases or slogans such as "the whole child." There is the tendency to treat such slogans as statements of objectives and to assign to the words themselves some magical quality which through their repeated utterance may produce the condition desired. There is also a failure to understand that, in most instances at least, the slogan—and the movement which it represents—is an after-the-fact situation. That is, that the conditions which permit some approximate realization of stated goals called for in the slogan are, in fact, already existent. An example will illustrate the point.

The now shopworn label, "the family of togetherness," generated a profusion of slogans which served the special interests of varied groups. Some were self-seekers in their commercialization of this theme. Others were genuinely altruistic in their desire to promote the better life through encouraging praying together, playing together, learning together, and similar activities which, if performed as a family, might somehow enrich and fulfill life. The image of this family type is that of parents and their dependent children. The representation does not include grandparents, other relatives, or neighbors. In technical language, this is the "family of procreation," the biological and nuclear family typical of American society. Neither slogans nor exhortations created it and the definition of the roles of its members has been set by conditions which do not include the effects of conscious propaganda. Its natural history and functions differ from and may be contrasted with other types of family systems such as the stem, joint, or extended.

The succinct and penetrating analysis by Arensberg of the small family type—its historical antecedents, gradual modifications and evolution within the specific conditions of American society, and internal structure—permits one to establish a relation between scientific analysis and popular movements and their accompanying slogans. From his evidence, it is possible to demonstrate that what many conceive to be new approaches or discoveries are, in fact, only an emergent awareness by professional practitioners in education, health, and welfare of already prevalent characteristics of family life. Thus those who advocate democratic family life, togetherness, permissiveness, child-centered education, and individuation are less the creators of new progressive movements in family life and education than they are publicizers of an existing state of affairs. Of the American small family type Arensberg writes:

> . . . The imperatives of our family system, basing the small household on the conjugal pair, isolating that pair to free them to command their own destinies and satisfactions and to confer on them nearly complete and untrammeled authority over minor children (except where the state and community limit them), are not easy ones. Nor is the task our educational ideal assumes a simple one: to prepare each and every man and woman to be in adulthood spouse, parent, householder, and family head all at once. These imperatives of our present small, conjugal type of family, with its minimum of kinship entanglement and support, ideally require each person to find a mate for himself, to love that spouse, to share the upbringing of children with him or her, to maintain a household with him, to find chief emotional identification in the little family growing up around this spouse and partner freely chosen and freely retained (Arensberg, 1960).

Anthropologists know of no other family system which places such heavy responsibilities upon so few. In other times and places, the burden of obligations to succor and protect, to share and alleviate the tensions which arise from internal difficulties or external threat are diffused through kin and the institutions of community. In contrast, the American family in both its ideal and actual state stands nearly alone. And if this imperative, rooted in historical continuity and contemporary conditions, applies to the family as a unity, it also applies to the individuals who comprise the unity. They, too, have been taught the necessity of standing alone. Nor does the child in his period of dependency escape the requirement. If, by circumstance, he no longer contributes economically to the whole, as in an earlier agrarian period, his total burden is not thereby lightened in some degree. The responsibility he now shoulders is, if anything, heavier and more difficult than before.

STANDARDS OF ADULTHOOD

The course which begins in infancy inevitably leads through childhood and adolescence into adulthood. This progression can be viewed in part as the result of natural processes, in part as the consequence of training received from parents, peers, and teachers, but in even larger measure as directed, purposeful, and at times aggressive activity of the child himself. If the question were asked, "Is not this the universal process of acquiring adulthood in all cultures?" the answer given could not be an unqualified affirmative. The major difference is found in the early inculcation in the American child of certain standards of self-performance, the full realization of which will be achieved simultaneously with maturity. Later on we shall show that this expectancy proves to be an illusion which is, nonetheless, also transmitted to each succeeding generation.

First, however, the problem of what these standards are and how they become internalized and are maintained should be examined. Some observation establishes that a parent comforting a hurt child often urges that he behave like a little man and stop his crying. In hundreds of other instances in the life relationship of parent and child, each time the former holds up adult behavior as superior there is implicit in the action a denigration of child behavior and an affirmation of superior adult standards. When boys are told, "Done like a man!" the implications of the praise for the action performed are quite explicit. Has anyone ever intended praise when he exclaimed, "You act like a child!" And when older people do childish things, we call them senile or foolish.

Just when and where do we, in our multi-faceted relations with children, ever really judge their behavior except against the measure of progress they exhibit in the acquisition of adult standards? Irrespective of the steps by which the process is initiated, it is not difficult to observe the relentless insistence upon acquiring adult standards. If, by chance or intention, parents and teachers should abandon this aspect of their role, they would then have, to this extent, abandoned their function as adults.

The other part of the problem posed earlier, the question of what should be included under any listing of adult standards, was answered in large measure by Arensberg in his enumeration of the imperatives of our family system. Within this framework, however, there are certain specificities that need to be mentioned and their relevance elaborated if we are to grasp the role of the child.

It is generally accepted that family, school, and church transmit a greater portion of the cultural heritage to the child than do other agencies. What, then, among the many things which adults expect the child to learn, may we count as significant? The broad categories include skills for handling, knowledge for understanding, and feelings for evaluating the things, persons, and ideas which are encountered in the business of living. These requirements are so universal, however, that their generality does not help us much. If we look at some of the requirements imposed upon the individual in the American cultural system and then examine these in their relation to the family and respective roles within it, we shall encounter those specific traits which have been idealized for all members of the society.

Commitment to Change

The central and perhaps most crucial commitment of American civilization is to the inevitability and, in most instances, the desirability of change. The activities and events of everyday life are interpreted through such terms as "progress," "advancement," and "development" within the context of the never-constant environment in which we live. If the individual is to be successful in this type of society, and the promise of success is one of the imperatives which moves him, he must at least keep up with the times. Even those not motivated by promises of success know that stagnation is penalized. For the individual, this imperative means that he must be continuously poised to take advantage of opportunities for advancement. In fact, he must actively seek and, if possible, modify the environment to insure that situations favorable to him present themselves. Favorable chances and maneuvering avail nothing if there is resistance to

working in new surroundings with new people and possibly learning new skills for new activities.

The successful meeting of new demands requires, first of
all, readiness to abandon the present whether it be locality, associations, or activity. Under such circumstances, it is unwise to
invest too deeply either emotionally, professionally, or financially,
for the wrench which change demands may require a sacrifice too
great to make. The easy fashion in which Americans establish
and abandon new relationships disconcerts Europeans who accuse
us of emotional superficiality. Their projection of values hardly
explains the situation, nor are they likely to understand the necessity of such behavior as a function of our commitment. And the
more deeply imbedded guilt with its corollary of tragedy they
utterly fail to comprehend.

Self-fulfillment

These imperatives of mobility, independence, adaptability, and the capacity for continued growth represent, in one
sense, subsidiary aspects of a more central requirement, that of
competence, wisdom, and maturity. But fulfillment in the context
of perpetual change contains a contradiction incapable of resolution. Final achievement is impossible because the objectives themselves are not fixed. They expand, recede, or are modified as the
conditions within the system are changed, changes to which the
individual in his progression also contributes. There can be no
ultimate in the world view of those who adhere to the concept of
an ever-expanding system. One might suppose that these circumstances would breed frustration and defeat but apparently this
occurs rarely since one is taught to accept striving as a lifelong
necessity.

Perpetual Optimism

Finally, the role must be performed in a mood of perpetual hopefulness, a trait which has also been set by the culture.
The extent to which this mood has been integrated into the events
of daily life may be met in many contexts. The language of salu-
tation reveals the extraordinary extent to which we have carried

our insistence upon a positive and optimistic approach to the world. No matter how we really feel, we are obligated to meet the world with a sunny disposition. Our conventional "Good day" has no relation to the actual state of the weather nor do our replies to inquires about our well-being have relation to the actual situation. The response of "Fine," or one of its many variations, expresses how we ought to be. Any other admission is incorrect. The child learns this ritual language and the accompanying values in his earliest years. He is taught to condemn whining, complaining, crybabies, and pessimists. We should also like to deny that pain, evil, and death exist, and although we are forced to recognize them we assign them only marginal status. We would like to believe that all beings are basically good and should be trusted, a character quality which sometimes causes others to accuse us of being naive. These optimistic and positive traits found expression in the 1920's in the ringing slogan of Coué, "Day by day in every way I am getting better and better!"

Our culture demands that we maintain this euphoric facade in our own perception of the world and our place in it. Furthermore, we demand that our children acquire and exhibit the same psychological posture. Obviously, at times, this optimistic perceptual screen through which we interpret the events of the world must lead to some distortions in our apperception of reality. The truth is that, on occasions, the situation we find ourselves in, individually or collectively, is damned bad. But our "natural" optimism carries us through with the belief that tomorrow or next year will be better, that all things work out for the best, it's always darkest before the dawn, and so on through the dozens of aphorisms which give expression to the same point of view. The fact that events usually do turn toward the better lends credence to the belief.

It is my contention that the configuration of beliefs that we have been examining is a necessary corollary to the central value of self-fulfillment. To deny, in any degree, that societal conditions are not improving (through change) or that individual incapacitation prevents further growth is to admit that this keystone (self-fulfillment) upon which the structural unity of purpose in life has been erected is faulty—denies, then, the very basis of the American's conception of himself in his life role.

It should be apparent now why it has been necessary to examine these interconnections before we could turn to the direct study of the role of the child. The American small family, relatively isolated in its activities from other communal institutions, with the insistence upon the capacity for independence and mobility of its members, building and maintaining in each person the psychological posture of perpetual optimism with its corollary of self-fulfillment, taken as a whole and as functionally interdependent with other cultural systems, provides the conditions within which the role of the individual is defined.

Under such circumstances, the role of the child is as much central to the continued functioning of the whole as is the role of any other family member. A mutual dependence exists between children and their parents since the latter seek some portion of their own fulfillment through their children. In part, they fulfill themselves by providing a sheltering environment which expresses and enforces a temporary dependence. The dependency relationship, however, contains both contradiction and conflict for eventually, as both child and parent know, the independent and mobile condition must be claimed by or forced upon the child since adulthood is a necessary step for continued growth. This brings us to the point where we can more adequately conceptualize the child's role.

PROGRESSION INTO ADULTHOOD

Those who propose two alternative ways of viewing the child, namely, either as a miniature adult or as an undeveloped person but possessing the capacities for achieving maturity, may come to conclusions that distort reality. There is no intention to pose a conundrum by saying that the child is neither and both. For example, most children by the time they have reached the age of three or four have already learned a number of important adult skills. They walk, talk, control the elimination of bodily wastes in socially acceptable ways, and have developed habits, points of view, and skills around sleeping, eating, and their relations to a limited number of other persons. Childish ways may still adhere to some of their activities, but any realistic appraisal of the contrast between behavior in the first year of life with that of the fourth must grant that in some directions adult standards have been successfully transmitted. By six or seven, some children are judged precociously mature. For most children, however, the period of development coincides with physical growth, except that in our society the dependence is maintained for a much longer period because of the requirement for formal training through post-adolescent years.

Thus, at a very early age the child acquires some of the requisite skills of an independent individual. To this extent, he has cleared some hurdles which test for adult competency. In other areas, he remains dependent, undeveloped, and not yet capable of unguided mobility. We again restate the point made earlier that the fundamental role of the child is to become an adult. All his activities are either contributory or incidental to this end. The progression is partly a function of physical and neural growth, partly a function of the social and cultural environment within which the child learns, but it is continuous although uneven.

PRESSURES ON CHILDREN TO BE ADULT

The responsibility parents feel for converting their children into adults is so great that they impose a rigorous regime upon them during their dependent years. The intensity of parental concern reaches into every aspect of child behavior. It is expressed by an overconcern and overdirection of the child's activities. All types of special "opportunities" for developing skills are sought out. One manifestation has been the downward extension of formal schooling to pre-kindergarten classes.

The reality eventually became sloganized in the phrase "child-centered." Whatever excesses have been committed in home or school by adults who abdicated responsibility because of this doctrine, their behavior never violated the fundamental principle that children must be turned into adults. The freedoms given the child in activity or temperament were never justified on the grounds that these would permit him to remain a child; it was because this freedom ensured a healthier, better-adjusted adult. In effect, child-centered dogma was an unwitting device for putting ever-greater pressures upon the child. In its rationale, the adults deluded both themselves and the children they tended because it was never explained that this was a long-term transaction with an expected profitable pay-off at the end.

Perhaps we should be more explicit about the pressures to which the child is subject. The cultural context within which these appear is, of course, that children cannot just be allowed to grow up; they must be wisely directed. The justification is based upon the great latent "potential" in the unformed young which is waiting to be realized. Only as the potential is realized can the child fulfill himself and fulfillment is a function of adulthood, not childhood. What is not made explicit to the child and is probably perceived by only a few parents and teachers is that their own role is dependent upon child accomplishments. Under these conditions, the child carries a heavier burden of responsibility in the proper performance of his role than that placed upon the young in any other society.

The child is expected to grow not only into an adult but into a successful one. The definition of the latter is, of course, adult determined. Success must be found in career, in marriage, in family, in community, and in one's personal life. The adult believes and the child comes to accept early that the route to these objectives can be reached through training. The apparatus through which much of this training is transmitted is the formal educational system. It is here that performance is judged by agreed-upon standards and a preliminary preview of the future seen. Hence, the parental pressures on the child for academic striving.

BARRIERS TO ADULTHOOD

Unfortunately, there are several conditions which inhibit and limit the child's efforts in acquiring that experience necessary for adulthood. The culturally isolating centripetence of metropolitan life reduces enormously the opportunities for significant cross-group experience. The capacity to make social adaptations cannot be learned in the severely limited urban enclave or homogeneous suburb. Emphasis upon personal adjustment is probably related to the narrow range of inter-personal experiences and the ultimate necessity to rely upon oneself. The poverty of cultural variation must have a serious distorting effect on capacities for comparative perception. Vicarious experiences provided by fantasy or documentary in television, cinema, drama, or literature are no substitute and cannot be truly comprehended unless there is a substantial comparative understanding from which these can be interpreted. Situations portraying romantic love, the vicissitudes of family life, or the struggle for power may be dramatized in African, Asian, or American settings but the meaning is reduced to horizons found in Scarsdale, Plainville, or Little Rock.

In spite of our insistence upon cultural pluralism and the tolerance of deviancy, the danger of cultural diversity remains a powerful threat. Is it possible that the social isolation of the small American family intensifies the internalization of its values, manners, and behavior to the exclusion of differing standards? Forced as it is to depend largely upon its own resources, this may be an expected consequence. In any event, family restrictions present another hazard in the child's struggle to grow up. These are found in the nature of the relationships between old and young and the sexes and exhibit emotional correlates. Informed observers agree that not all is well in our family system (Line and King, 1956), and yet what degree of credence should we give to those who see our children as guilt-ridden and hostile? Does the American mother exhibit the black widow spider tendencies as described by Philip Wylie? To what extent have males abdicated their role in the squeeze of demands between wife and job and to what extent are they delinquent in claiming their sons for manhood?

Perhaps these questions really have no answers. Yet they have been repeatedly asked and answered by those with ready replies. The concern should be evidence enough that the child finds himself in a confused and hence difficult position. There seems little doubt, however, that there has been both an increase in pressure upon the child from home and school and at the same time a diminution in his opportunities and hence his ability to act independently. This combination is bound to produce serious trouble.

POSTSCRIPT

Parents and teachers are particularly susceptible to exhortations by "experts" on child rearing and child life. Their position requires that the specialist appear authoritative. And we should be tolerant of their necessity to change emphasis and direction from time to time. But parents and teachers cannot forgive themselves nor can they be forgiven by their children for the consequences of following ill-advised fads of the moment. Our attitude toward the expert should be one of hesitant caution— once bitten, twice shy. The doctrine of the 1950's which extolled the virtues of the democratic family with its security through love, its togetherness, its permissiveness, and its equalitarianism is now being modified. Although the new doctrine of the 1960's has not yet been fully formulated, we may anticipate some of the line. The avant-garde has already abandoned the term "democratic" in its application to family life. Only those who lack sensitivity to the outmoded continue to champion what is dying, not family life but a style of exhortation about it.

Perhaps Bronfenbrenner (1960) is right when he suggests that he detects a cyclical trend toward "explicit discipline techniques of an earlier era" but adds that the most important forces redirecting "both the aims and methods of child training in America emanate from behind the Iron Curtain." Achievement has begun "to replace adjustment as the highest goal of the American way of life." He foresees that guidance counsellors, parents, and even youth itself will do their part to prepare "youngsters for survival in the new competitive world of applications and achievement tests."

Sputnik may have provided the dramatic incident which

focused our attention upon competitive achievement in education but the seeds had been sown long before. Parental pressure upon their children in high school to compete through college entrance examinations for the scarce commodity of quality higher education is no new phenomenon. The band wagon for this new party line of achievement is gaining momentum. Those who disputed adjustment as the central goal of child training were labelled "anti-democratic." Those who question achievement may be considered "anti-American." Such are the caprices of the spin of the wheels of fortune.

The serious question which should concern us all is that of the consequences of the compulsive pressures which are now force-feeding the process of turning children into adults but at the same time extending the period of dependency.

References

Arensberg, Conrad M., 1960, "The Family and Other Cultures." *The Nation's Children.* New York: Columbia University Press, pp. 60–61.

Bronfenbrenner, Urie, 1960, "The Changing American Child." *Reference Papers on Children and Youth.* Golden Anniversary White House Conference on Children and Youth, Inc.

Line, William, and Margery R. King, 1956, "Cross Cultural Research." *The Journal of Educational Sociology.* 29:281–291.

15 —— *Martin B. Loeb*

Social Role and Sexual Identity in Adolescent Males: A Study of Culturally Provided Deprivation*

This paper arises out of a study of young teen-agers done at the request of the American Social Health Association. The goal has been set as finding some socially approved ways of preventing further increases in the venereal disease rate among adolescents.[1] Our approach has been to study those young teen-agers—junior high school students—who are considered "good," whose behavior is acceptable to self and to the community. Out of this we hope to identify those strengths and sources of strength which contribute to their behavior. The results of this larger study will be recorded elsewhere. I am here concerned with one result of the study to date, namely, that young teen-age boys have few opportunities to develop that sense of identity which can serve them in forming an adequate and appropriate set of adult masculine roles.[2] This deprivation will be viewed against historically developed norms and against the opportunities provided for girls of the same age.

Role theory provides a basic theoretical approach. One may look at a role as a set of mutually expected behaviors, within a known reference group, around a more or less clearly defined

---

* Published here for the first time with permission of the author.

[1] William Kimball, Mary Kimball, and Len Glass, University of California, Los Angeles, are collaborators on this project.

[2] See the works of Erik H. Erikson for a discussion of the concept of identity (1950, 1959).

situation, such as family or school. But another dimension must be added to the standard conception of role, and this is *development* that leads to a consideration of the function of any given role as preparation for later roles. Adolescent role behavior may therefore be described partly in terms of the immediate expectations of all persons involved in situations and relationships in which adolescents participate. In addition, roles assumed by the adolescent may also be seen in terms of their functional preparation for adult roles anticipated by self, others, and the community.

The basic question is: What are these young people doing and how does what they are doing prepare them for the taking on of satisfactory masculine and feminine roles in adult life? This question obviously involves more than overt behavior. We must deal psycho-socially with the sense of identity in terms of masculinity and femininity.

Let us look for a moment at a young teen-age girl in our American urban core culture. Some time shortly after the tenth year the girl undergoes physical changes which must somehow be explained to her and the public in terms of being female. Now quite overtly the girl may identify with the mother. Conversely, both negatively and positively the mother identifies with her daughter. At the onset of menarche the girl usually begins to learn to assume responsibilities of femaleness or, to put it another way, she begins to learn how to live up to the expectations of the feminine role both socially and emotionally. One sees this girl in various situations learning to become a woman, which is in itself a role complex that is multifaceted but not unclearly stated. It is a very usual and simple thing for these girls to tell us that they are going to grow up to become wives and mothers, and we see them practicing for these roles by housekeeping, baby sitting, shopping, and dressmaking. They organize formal and informal social affairs at which they practice the feminine side of courtship, social controls, being a proper hostess. We see the beginning of a complicated identity formation in a variety of games of solitaire in which the girls try out their given names with boys' surnames. Particularly, we see in the behavior of the adolescent girl the development of a variety of social and emotional approaches—each one appropriate to different and specific situations. They are, in

Dr. William E. Henry's term, developing an aptitude for "affective complexity."[3] As suggested above, they are enacting a variety of adolescent roles in more or less conscious preparation for adult roles. This complexity and goal-oriented behavior is not only found in overt and conscious statements made in interviews but is also seen in response to projective tests. These girls have many experiences with many models to guide them towards a satisfactory set of adult roles.

In contrast, the boys have few models to guide them and few developmental landmarks to remind them that they are on the road to adulthood. They have few experiences that they can relate clearly to any notion of being an adult. Their father is physically and emotionally distant except for those occasions when the father reverts to being a boy and turns up as his son's pal. Most other male figures in his life have supervisory functions such as teachers and playground supervisors, and generally operate in a manner designed to please the more or less organized mothers in the community. In early times the younger boys had models of the older boys, but today both school and leisure time activities are organized by strict age grades. There are relatively few situations or arenas in which boys may participate with each other in the school, home, and playground. Behavior demanded of them in each of these situations does not require much differentiation. We see each of these boys developing a singular way of coping with most situations that they meet. Following Dr. Henry, we might term this "affective simplicity," which infers a narrow set of emotional approaches to the many different situations faced in modern life. Simplicity is exemplified by the boys' dress habits, which tend to be the same uniform for all occasions. Girls, on the other hand, dress and feel different for many different occasions.

Very few boys at this age can tell us anything specific about their life goals or what they are doing about them. Certainly no

---

[3] W. E. Henry (1956.) As I understand Dr. Henry's conceptualization of "affective complexity," it is that ability to have a variegated emotional armamentarium so that different and somewhat separable affectional constellations can be called on for different and separable situations. Dr. Henry claims that this is necessary for modern urban living and is testing his hypothesis in a study of successful aging that is being carried on by the University of Chicago, Kansas City, Mo.

boy has yet told us that he is going to grow up to become a husband and a father, and few of them know any evidence of "The tangible promise of a career."[4] The approved experiences socially provided do not have much specificity either for a "career" or for a sense of masculinity.

Our theoretical approach has led us to define masculinity as a combination of calculated risk taking, a feeling of mastery, and a sense of work. (These in various combinations are the themes of the favored TV westerns.) Traditionally, these qualities have been tempered by the women folk. The affective simplicity of this masculinity is obvious, but there was a certain virility in our cultural past and it can still be seen in the TV western. In the everyday life of the young adolescent today, this simplicity has been sterilized by taking out as much risk as possible, by denying opportunities and rewards for the development of mastery, and by diffusing the sense of work. It is possible that we are developing a socialization process to produce an affectively complex man to fit the mood of modern civilization. But we have not as yet succeeded and we leave the young adolescent boy deprived.

Let us look at the adolescent boy in a variety of arenas of experience. In the home there are few experiences to teach or reinforce masculinity. The father is preoccupied with his job, but he does not bring into the home many of the essential qualities of his work. Most boys studied do not have any real understanding of their father's job and have never seen him at work. Household chores are not clearly marked as masculine or feminine. The mother is the dominant model and goal-setter. Her notion of masculinity is "a gentleman." Risk is minimized. Fathers are encouraged to participate with their sons but more at the son's level and not the father's.

In the school most of the teaching is done by women and the men are in general doing what the women, teachers and mothers, approve. There is constant supervision. The sense of work is not particularly enhanced. There is little provision for a sense of ac-

---

[4] Erik H. Erikson (1950). "The sense of ego identity, then, is the accrued confidence that the inner sameness and continuity are matched by the sameness and continuity of one's meaning for others, as evidenced in the tangible promise of a 'career.' "

complishment. There are few difficult demands that are meaningful in the sense of a masculine identity.

After school, the boys either "mess around" in peer groups or
play on supervised playgrounds. These activities are highly age
graded, like those in school, so that the only model readily available is the supervisor, who is not likely to present a picture which
would offend the most prudish mother. Outside the playground,
the restrictions on activities in urban America become more volu-
minous and detailed. Any look at juvenile court law and the local
ordinances will show that no adolescent boy can avoid commit-
ting some delinquent or legally disapproved act at least once a
day. Adolescent boys and girls believe (and they have good
cause) that most adults think all adolescents are delinquents. Aggression is frowned upon most strongly, but loitering and con-
gregating are also considered to be bad. It is said in the community
we have studied that anytime "half-a-dozen old women" disap-
prove of something, the city council will pass an ordinance. For
example, no playing of percussion instruments is allowed on the
beaches in many areas.

Jobs may be seen as another arena for the development of
masculine identity. However, a combination of the Child Labor
Laws, local ordinances, and school system regulations makes jobs
for teen-agers scarce and cumbersome. Employers shy away from
employing adolescents. Most of the boys in our study want to get
jobs but most of them feel that it is too difficult. Furthermore,
most of them see jobs as a way to earn money for their own pleasure and do not see it as practice for adult roles. It is not necessary
that they should see work as practice for adult roles in order for
work to be effective, but this lack of goal orientation is important
and if goal orientation is lacking in the job situation, it is an indication of the pervasiveness of this lack. The school, parents, employers, and others all combine to thwart goal orientation in
career lines. With the feeling of uncertainty of what the future
holds, they impose rather than induce a moratorium (Erikson,
1956) on the young adolescent boy. Vocational guidance, for example, turns out to be a way of postponing career decisions rather
than promoting it. The guidance is diffuse and so the goals are
unclear. The general precept, "don't make up your mind now—

there's lots of time," not only interferes with the sense of work but with the notion of risk taking and of mastery.

This situation is highly exacerbated by the present Selective Service regulations. Even in young adolescents there is a sense of frustration—of the uselessness of making long-term plans. This is shared by the significant adults—parents, teachers, and potential employers. Selective Service has no definiteness in it. It is a lottery and for most youngsters cannot be figured out. A combination of anxiety about making mistakes and a sense of futility lead the boy to live in a state of "being" rather than "becoming." The latter state is much more characteristic of girls.

Let us look at two highly condensed, typical cases in the study.

JANE EASTON

Jane is fourteen and lives with her mother and father in an apartment in a lower middle-class neighborhood. Her father is self-employed and her mother has for the past year been a sales clerk in a five-and-ten-cent store. Prior to this she was at home.

Her family is very important to Jane. She says, "I wouldn't want any other mother and father . . . they're just strict enough and they don't go to extremes on anything. If there is anything that . . . we're bothered with . . . we discuss it." She values their opinion and although she doesn't always agree with them, she feels they have her interests at heart, trust her, treat her fairly and according to her age. Complaints are minimal in regard to her family. She says on the Sentence Completion Form, "I FEEL FUNNY WHEN . . . my parents embarrass me in front of my friends." Although she did not complete "SOMETIMES MY MOTHER . . . ," she expressed some dissatisfaction with her mother working, expressing pleasure at the times when she stays home. At these times Jane enjoys both her mother's company and less responsibility for housework. She is responsible for cleaning the house twice a week, some of the cooking, and doing dishes. Although cooking is not required of her, Jane enjoys it and her father does the dishes when she cooks.

The family shares some activities such as going to shows and visiting friends and relatives. Two years ago they spent the summer in Oregon. Her parents expect her to have fun and enjoy life, and Jane in turn tries to live up to their expectations of her. Shame is an effective method used by her parents for controlling her behavior.

Although she says most of her friends own their own homes, Jane claims she is happy living in an apartment. Until this year they lived in a smaller apartment and Jane slept in a roll-away bed in the living room. Now she has her own room, a regular teen-age hideaway with a record player and feminine things all over the room, and she enjoys having her girl friends over.

Jane states her family does not have a lot of money but feels they have always had enough. She gets a "fair" allowance and asks her parents if she needs extra money. She earns some money baby sitting and spends most of it on clothes. She has increasing freedom in choosing her own clothes, although she values her mother's judgment and says, "I've always liked the clothes that she picked out for me. She knows what I like."

Jane is in the ninth grade and was a straight A student in the eighth grade. She finds homework rather interesting but dislikes the time it takes from other things. She feels guilty if she does not do her homework and feels it is worth working for high grades. She likes teachers who can control the class and make school interesting. A teacher can make her change her behavior, just as her mother does, by making her feel ashamed. She says, "Getting an education is a necessity to have a more rewarding life," and she hopes to go to college or to nursing school. She talked her parents into letting her drop accordion lessons, which she had taken for four years, joined the dramatic club at school, and hopes to get into the girls' service league. She enjoys sitting out on the lawn talking with her girl friends between classes.

Jane has one particular friend with whom she has been quite close for over a year and she goes with her to many activities, such as beach parties, picnics, and installations of Job's Daughters. There are several girls in this group and none of them date much. During the ninth grade Jane started dating and became friends with a different group of girls, particularly one girl who was voted cutest and most popular in her class. Dating quite a bit more than the other girls in her former group has resulted in Jane's estrangement from this group, except for the one close friend and her sister. She has attended a few slumber parties and since having her own room, she has had one at her own home. She also gave a dinner party and has entertained mixed groups several times.

Although the Sentence Completion Forms were completed before she started much dating, it gives some idea of her values:

> DATING is terrific when you're with someone you like.
> KISSING A DATE is something very special if you like the date.
> WHAT TEEN-AGERS LIKE TO DO MOST IS to have fun and friends.
> MAKING OUT is fun if you don't do it in public or at parties.
> AT PARTIES I like to have fun and forget about school.
> GOING STEADY is fine if you like the person and if you're in your last year of high school.
> ON A DATE I always try to be a good date for my date.

Her relationship with her date as a friend is more important to her than is the opportunity for exploring the realm of sex. However, since her first kiss and first steady dating, which occurred during her ninth-grade year, she has shown much more awareness of and interest in sex. For contrast, these Sentence Completion Form items completed sixteen months later show some of these changes:

> DATING is a good way of getting away with friends from studies and troubles.
> KISSING is relaxing as well as a good way of communicating feelings.
> WHAT TEEN-AGERS LIKE TO DO MOST IS have a good time.
> MAKING OUT is fine as long as it doesn't get out of hand.
> AT PARTIES I let myself go and have a good time.
> GOING STEADY is okay before engagement but if it is before that I THINK it ties a person down too much.
> I THINK MASTURBATION MIGHT be a good way of getting away from the need of sex relations with the opposite sex.
> SEX is necessary.

Jane feels it has always been easier for her to talk with boys than with girls (although she has close friends and apparently talking with them has been no problem), and this is an advantage to her in becoming acquainted with potential dates. She is not at all reluctant to enter into a conversation with boys while most of her girl friends hang back. This is a source of some friction with her girl friends.

An older cousin who is very popular in Jane's high school is a model for her, although there is little contact between the two girls. The cousin is attractive and quite popular, and Jane is actively striving in the same direction.

At the earlier interview Jane expressed ignorance in the realm of sex but was not concerned and felt she would acquire the knowledge when she needed it. She felt it would probably come from school, never mentioning her mother in this connection. She defined sex as follows: "I don't know, I think that sex is the feelings between a boy and a girl and how they use these feelings." She feels boys should respect girls and modify their behavior accordingly when girls are around, with the implication that they can behave quite differently if no girls are present.

Menstruation was not unexpected—she had seen movies in school. About it Jane says, "MENSTRUATION is a part of being a lady and having a baby." Sixteen months later she said, "It can be quite a nuisance at times."

During this school year Jane went almost steady for several months with a very mature boy in her class. Her awareness of sex and knowledge about it increased during this time, with much conversation between the two of them, as well as the experience of going out without adults since either her date or another couple had use of a car. This allows a greater amount of freedom in boy-girl relations, although Jane's sexual interaction is still limited.

As far as work is concerned, Jane's experience is limited to some baby sitting. She says, "I WANT A JOB THAT I will be happy with and pays well." She would also prefer one that gave her contact with people so she could work and talk. She adds, "GETTING A JOB means money and will relieve my parents of a little of my expenses," and "WORK is pretty necessary in life." In terms of the future she thinks about being a nurse, but this seems pretty far off to her now.

Religion does not seem to be a problem to the Eastons, although the mother is Lutheran and the father Catholic. Jane considers herself a regular church goer, has been baptized a Catholic, and confirmed, and speculates that she will marry a Catholic, although she adds about marrying a non-Catholic, "If I loved him enough I would." "If the man I marry is satisfied with his church, why I'll even go to his church." They never eat meat at home on Fridays, although Jane sometimes forgets when she is away from home. About God she says, "I couldn't live without Him."

Jane is gradually moving out of the home and more into the peer group as the base for evaluating her experiences. Home values are still quite important to her, but popularity and fun are becoming increasingly important. She is resisting more the duties at home which interfere with time with peers. As for the peers themselves, she draws a dichotomy between the "nice" and the "cheap" kids. She likes clean, attractive girls who "act their age" and boys who treat girls with respect. She dislikes both boys and girls who act childish, who are dirty (physically) or cheap. She disapproves of swearing, smoking just to show off, and people who neck in public. She wants to have many friends and be liked. "THE WORST THING THAT COULD HAPPEN TO ME would be not to have any friends."

Age is very important to Jane. She is eager to grow up because she will be able to have a job, understand herself better, and have more dates and more fun. She feels things have gotten better as she has gotten older. She puts a high value on people who "act their age."

Being a girl is important to Jane. Advantages are that one is sought instead of seeking, a girl can wear a greater variety of clothes, and she likes feminine clothing.

In summary, here are some of Jane's central values in life as they developed and changed during this eventful year.

1. HOME . . . Jane is very explicit in her statements of the importance of her family. Home is the place where she feels secure and valued, the base from which she is increasingly moving outwards. It has gained importance in providing her with a room of

her own, a place where she can express herself and bring in her friends. She gains support from her parents in gradually having more freedom and independence, in choosing clothes, in expanding the area of her activities, in dating and hours away from home. Her home experiences have given her a feeling of life's dealing with her fairly.

2. SEX . . . Being a girl has been satisfying to Jane, and her increasing relations with the opposite sex have contributed to her picture of herself as a desirable female. Her desire for expressing affection with the opposite sex without the pressure of her own sex awareness is enabling her to develop satisfactory heterosexual patterns of behavior and control. She feels sex is natural but has some ambivalence about how much can be expressed without conflicting with her feelings that much sexual behavior is "cheap." With increasing dating activities clothes are becoming ever more important, and the desire for a job to relieve her parents of some of her clothes expenses is greater. Besides clothes, other feminine interests are in decorating her room, cooking, and entertaining.

3. ACTIVITIES . . . Social activities are becoming increasingly important to Jane. Activities with peers are drawing more time away from her household and school work. Besides increased dating, she is moving more into school and peer centered activities and is making positive efforts to become more popular with both boys and girls. School is still important in terms of living up to the standard of which she is capable and which her folks expect of her, standards which she has internalized. Activities with her girl friends involve shopping, slumber parties, and planning entertainment for both boys and girls. There is also a great deal of visiting at friends' homes, often to spend the night. Many of these activities are in the direction she will move as she becomes an adult.

JOHN WEST

John is a fourteen year old boy living with his family —father, mother and younger brother—in a nice house situated in a good lower middle-class neighborhood. The father is a production foreman and the mother works part-time in a child-care center.

The family enjoys doing things together, such as sharing regular vacations and their favorite spectator sport events in season. Everything goes well with his younger brother, though they have occasional conflicts and fights. John likes his family, enjoys doing things with them, but he has a few complaints. John feels that sometimes he has to do too much housework and occasionally he leaves the house when his parents argue at dinner time. He expressed his feelings about the arguments in the following story response to a picture; "The boy snuck out of the house because he couldn't stand to hear his Mom and Dad fighting, and was picked up by the officer because it was after curfew. This reforms the mother and father and they don't fight anymore."

John is an A to B student in school, but often student government activities, social life, and organized sports take so much time that he has difficulty keeping up these grades. His favorite subjects are a foreign language (a choice in part influenced by a man teacher whom he admires), science, and sports.

John is an unusually sociable boy, in fact so much so that we suspect that he may fear or dislike being alone. His predominant mode of life seems to be activities with others—parties, sports, school extracurricular activities, dating, and "messing around" with other boys, meaning doing nothing in particular, just being with one or a group of boys talking, walking some place (more exciting at night), playing records, eating or just hanging around together anywhere. John associates often and freely with groups of boys and with two or three close boy friends, individually or in a small group. Occasionally he gets involved in free-for-all fights among boys in the school neighborhood or in places of entertainment where adolescents gather; these fights fascinate him and he strongly feels he is compelled to defend those he sees as the underdogs in these conflicts.

To a greater extent than most boys his age John is involved in the dating and general heterosexual complex; girls are very important to him. Some of his responses on the Sentence Completion Form illustrate these points very plainly:

> DATING to me is the staff of life, but it is second to studies.
> KISSING is something I like to do very much.
> WHAT TEEN-AGERS LIKE TO DO MOST IS to go to a good party.
> MAKING OUT is considered by most teen-agers as a must, and there is hardly anyone in school that hasn't.
> AT PARTIES I like to have fun with girls, but I try to keep anything drastic out.
> BEING ALONE with a girl is a pleasant feeling.
> GOING STEADY can be fun, but you shouldn't ask every girl you go with.

With guilt-ridden overtones, John discussed the desirability of having sexual intercourse, but he says that it is something he would not do with any girl he knows well. He apparently holds the double standard of sex as defiling the female only, but to some extent sees sexual relations with any girl as wrong—sex is desirable but dirty.

While John is well aware of a money problem, for himself as well as his parents, he, along with the great majority of boys and girls, does not yet make the significant tieup of money, work—career—adulthood. In the past he has earned a little money here and there in the neighborhood and his parents have supplied him with the funds for his current needs. Now he sees his greatest money problem as finding some steady source of it, such as a regular part-time job, in order to first save enough to buy a car and second to keep it running. He is rather ambivalent about work itself. And this Sentence Completion Form item expresses this well:

> WORK is something you have no choice in doing, but I would rather accomplish something than do nothing.

Further, he is vague about a career or any path to it now, except through school studies in an indirect way. He expresses a general interest in being a technician, or especially something in science, such as a rocket technician. We do not mean to imply here that this boy seems overly dependent on his parents or irresponsible in regard to money; he expressed satisfaction in being able to buy some of his own clothes and felt this made him appreciate them more.

In the area of religion John and his family seem, like many Americans, to be nonreligious or disinterested rather than anti-religious or atheistic. The parents went to church until, in John's words, they became involved in so many activities that they dropped out completely. When he awakens Sunday morning, John sometimes feels he should go to church, but seldom makes it. However all religious aspects of life are not absent from his mind. He has speculated about reincarnation, is impressed with the amount of pain people unavoidably go through in life (such as having babies, war, "sentimental" pains and just everyday pains), and wants to be forgiven before he dies for some of the things he has done to hurt others.

Perhaps we can sum up this brief study of John West by listing what seem to be his central values in life as he sees it and lives it now.

1. HOME . . . While he doesn't express this value directly as one of the really big things in his life, we can safely say that home is so important that he takes it for granted, though it is increasingly becoming a home-base of operations for school, girls, and peer activities, rather than the all important center of life of the young boy. He still sees home as an all important source of support, materially and psychologically, though he is now entering the period of decreasing nurture and increasing separation from home.

2. SEX . . . is a strong focal point of activity, feeling, and thought. It draws him increasingly into pairing and party activities with girls; it stimulates great genital drives, secondarily engendering feelings of desire for sexual fulfillment, fear and guilt; it increases his need for money, helping to start him along the work-career paths; and perhaps most importantly of all, it is probably his strongest area of masculine identity expression and formation.

3. SOCIAL ACTIVITIES . . . This is probably the most important single value area for this boy. Popularity and social life are very important to him, we might say almost his source of life judging from the following response to the Thematic Apperception Test picture of the man apparently climbing (or descending) a rope.

> This is a picture of a man in ancient Greece who is participating in the Olympic games and is doing the rope climb to see how fast he could go up for an hour before a timing glass of sand was through. He lives till he's won all the events and is given a Laurel wreath that shows he is the winner of the Olympic games and is made a great hero. And he lives off of public food and money the rest of his life because he's such a great hero.

The importance of social activities to him is evident in his extensive and intensive activities with peers and parties, with school government and organized sports, and even in his interest in defending the underdog in free-for-alls.

4. CAR . . . At this time obtaining and becoming able to drive a car, preferably his own, is a material goal that probably mobilized this boy, and many others, more than any previous goal in his life. The car will involve him more deeply with getting money, girls, peers, and independence from parents.

5. SPORTS . . . A large amount of time and interest are spent in a few sports activities, including participation in organized sports away from school as well as in school sports and activities attended with family and friends.

6. SCHOOL . . . More of his waking time during the school year is probably spent in school activities than any other one place. This he sees as important for the social life and for the education that he needs so as not to become a "ditchdigger."

These two cases can virtually speak for themselves. Where Jane has a variety of experiences and experiencing, John has somewhat fewer types of experiences and a narrow repertoire of experiencing. Where Jane is future oriented, John tends to be present oriented. Where Jane has goals, John has avoidances.

CONCLUSION

The results of the study have many implications for education. Primarily we see the need of providing experiences for young boys that allow for developing a masculine identity without requiring recourse to fighting and whoring or futile and un-satisfying dabbling. Our culture provides one more or less satisfying activity for boys when they reach 16, namely, the motor car. It is by all counts the most sought after item and activity. It is the one generally provided facility for expressions of independence, risk taking, mastery, and work.

If we are correct in our analysis then not only working class boys are deprived, as Albert Cohen says, but most boys are.[5] Lower-class culture may provide more outlets for the develop-ment of masculinity, although lower-class masculinity is often seen as delinquency. Despite this, middle-class boys may end up with more serious if more diffuse problems.

On the other hand, our culture may be in the process of re-defining masculinity in a way which would fit better into the modern urban world. This new man would be affectively complex, he would show creativity rather than mastery, be organizationally oriented rather than risk taking, and work would be a means to, rather than a source of, satisfaction. For this to happen many values and traditional conceptions of the male role will have to be redefined, and in the meantime the young male is left without a clear sense of emergent masculine identity.

References

Cohen, Albert K., 1955, *Delinquent Boys: The Culture of the Gang.* New York: The Free Press of Glencoe.
Erikson, Erik H., 1950, *Childhood and Society.* New York: W. W. Norton and Company, Inc.
———, 1956, "The Problems of Ego Identity." *Journal of the American Psychoanalytic Society*, IV:56–121.

---

[5] Albert K. Cohen (1955). One of the implications of his last chapter, "The Delinquent Solution," is that for lower-class boys there is a solution to a problem faced by all adolescent boys. Delinquent girls tend to be sick and delinquent boys tend to be problem solving. Our study supports this implication.

————, 1959, *Identity and the Life Cycle. Psychological Issues,* Vol I, No. 1, Monograph 1. New York: International Universities Press, Inc.

Henry, William E., 1956, "Affective Complexity and Role Perceptions: Some Suggestions for a Conceptual Framework for the Study of Adult Personality" in John S. Anderson, ed., *Psychological Aspects of Aging.* Washington, D.C.: American Psychological Association, Inc.

Part III

Education Viewed
Cross-culturally

Preview

It is in this section, "Education Viewed Cross-culturally," that the comparative framework that has been implicit up to this point is made explicit. The general concern in all of the chapters is with cultural transmission, as in the preceding section, but in Part III the cultural context is varied dramatically. Within this broad focus on cultural transmission in diverse cultural contexts there are three major themes. The first is the relationship between education in the early years of life and the special problems of the adolescent years. The second is education in social environments where rapid culture change is taking place. The third is the relationship between social structure, education, and modal personality.

Margaret Mead orients us toward the most consistent differences between our educational process and assumptions and those of the relatively homogeneous folk societies. She considers a number of differences, such as the emphasis on teaching in our society and the emphasis on learning in folk societies. Her characterization seems apt and is applicable in varying degrees to other comparisons between our own and many other societies where the culture is relatively more stable and homogeneous than ours.

Dorothy Eggan for the Hopi and Spindler for the Menomini show how even as the emphasis, methods, and immediate purposes of education shift, there is continuity through the life experience of maturing individuals. But what happens in later childhood in these two societies is not a simple, linear projection from what happens in early childhood. There is a complementary, balancing relationship between the two. Early childhood experience prepares the way and makes it possible for the more strict and demanding education of later childhood to take effect without resentments or latent hostilities developing to interfere with the commitment of the individual to the value system and the social system in which these values are functional. There is a consistent reinforcement of norms for behavior in both cases, and this reinforcement becomes consistently more compressive as the child becomes a young adult. The result in the cases of both the Hopi and the Menomini is a highly controlled adult personality, even though this personality type operates in two very different social systems that have in common little more than an emphasis on limiting aggression in interpersonal relationships. Of particular significance to us is the fact that Hopi and Menomini youngsters are enabled by their traditional educational systems to move into adult roles without the distressing antecedent ambiguities and conflicts of the adolescent period in our society.

In our culture the usually latent hostilities towards adult, and particularly parental authority, accumulated through the years of early and middle childhood experience are expressed most violently during the adolescent period. We cope with this crucial educational period by allowing adolescents to isolate themselves in their own peer group. This peer group develops its own cultural norms and values, antithetical in varying degrees to adult cultural norms and values. As parents, teachers, and other authority figures, we can exercise little control over adolescents because there are few reinforcing, supportive social institutions or cultural patterns in our society for such control. And we provide no clear-cut mechanism for the change of identity that must take place as adult roles are assumed, or for its announcement.[1] As a conse-

---

[1] I have found Ward Goodenough's published lecture, "Education and Identity," in *Anthropology and Education*, Frederick C. Gruber (editor), The Martin G. Brumbaugh Lectures, Fifth Series, Philadelphia: University of Pennsylvania Press, 1961, particularly useful as I have thought about the problems of adolescent education.

quence many adults suffer from delayed adolescence, and most adolescents fear adulthood. The cultural transmission process is interfered with at a most crucial time, and the continuity of society is threatened with each new generation.

In his chapter in Part II, Martin Loeb states his documented hypothesis that adolescent males in our society lack clear-cut male models and the institutionalized means of emulating them. As a consequence many young males lack purpose and self-identity. This is another and closely related consequence of our failure to cope adequately with the adolescent period. Adult males in most societies take major responsibility for the instrumental roles that keep public institutions running. A society in which young males lack a consistent sense of identity and commitment to adult values is in serious trouble. One obligation of the educational system in all societies is to see that this does not happen.

The chapters by Hart, Watkins, and Reverend Ong tell us how the education of the adolescent is managed in certain societies with radically different ideas of correct educational procedure than our own. Hart's chapter contrasts pre- and postpubertal education, and emphasizes the discontinuity between the two with respect to degree and kind of compression. Watkins tells us what takes place in the West African "Bush" School. He interprets these educational activities as purposeful attempts on the part of adults to transmit essential features of the cultural heritage and induct the individual to the hardship and responsibility of adult roles. Reverend Ong's chapter shifts the focus from the folk cultures of West Africa, Australia, and Native North America, and brings us closer to the Euro-American cultural stream. But we find that two cultures as remote from each other as the Tiwi and late Renaissance European and English conduct initiation rites for very similar reasons.

These three chapters all stress the compressive, strict severity of adolescent education, and by implication where it is not made explicit, this severity is in considerable degree discontinuous with the permissive laissez-faire of early training. The educational situation in these societies is therefore somewhat different than in the Hopi and Menomini cases, where a certain continuity of educational experience is maintained. But in even these cases of mild and consistent compression into the mold of the adult role, certain events transpired during puberty to tighten the hold of the society upon the individual and announce the change in identity that is taking place.

All five of the societies described appear to have handled the problems of adolescent education with greater success than we do. But at the very moment when we arrive at the insights this kind of comparative perspective can give us, we must realize that simplistic transfers from one cultural setting to another are always dangerous. On the basis of these and other cases in the literature, we know that societies tighten their hold upon the individual most decisively and dramatically at puberty where adolescence is preceded by such factors as a prolonged period in middle childhood relatively free of educational constraints or where male children in particular have been under the exclusive care of women. In societies where education is more continuous from birth to puberty, where children in middle childhood do not run in unsupervised packs but interact with members of an extended family or household and have direct observational access to both male and female adult roles, education at puberty is likely to take a less dramatic and restrictive form.

These relationships raise the question: What would be the function of stringent and dramatic education for adolescents in our society? In the societies described, the educational treatment at adolescence is for the purpose of insuring the continuity of culture and, particularly, the continuity of the value system. As Hart makes clear, its purpose is to make dedicated adult citizens out of callow youths. A really efficient educational system—one that transmits the value system from generation to generation—stabilizes the culture around these continuous values. Perhaps our problem is that we have never really decided what our values as a national society are, and nowhere is our poverty of meaningful and shared goals more apparent than in the confused manner in which we handle the transfer from childhood to adulthood. We have trusted to luck, hoping that each new generation could somehow find its way and would eventually take on the responsibility of maintaining the social order. This has resulted in a new kind of dynamism—a potential for change that is probably greater than that of any other human society, past or present. But increasing numbers of young men and women remain disenchanted with our adult values, and stay in the never-never-land of beatnik, or beach, or car-cult culture too long or become real enemies of society, looking for kicks wherever and however they can find them, irrespective of how destructive they are to the welfare of others. Is the answer a new kind of education for adolescents—and particularly for adolescent males—one that separates the sexes and applies strict and dramatically reinforced male-oriented discipline to the boys? Or is the answer that we must re-establish the responsibility of the family, so that by the time adolescence is reached it is safe to let young people form their own club and initiate new members into it in their own way because the core values are so ingrained by that time that we are sure of them?

Melford Spiro shows us another way: Where the central issue of handing on the values of a society is handled by a collective educational system in a communal village in Israel, thus producing as educational products people who are motivated to perpetuate a certain way of life. There is continuity here and little disruption at puberty, because children live in a dormitory together from the time the mother and child leave the hospital after the birth, seeing their parents for only short periods during the week. It appears that this is an effective system of education as measured by the desire of new members of the society to maintain the social order. Must our educational system go collective as urbanization increases and families are less able to take responsibility for citizenship education? These questions are left unanswered in this preview and by the articles in Part III. But these analyses by anthropologists have made it possible to ask these very significant questions with new dimensions built into them and have provided some empirical cases about which to think.

Margaret Mead's chapter on "Cultural Factors in Community-Education Programs" marks a shift in emphasis in Part III. She gives us a convincing exposition of the bases for anthropological thinking about and attitudes towards induced culture change, in which community education programs may play implementing roles. She challenges the assumption that gradual change is least upsetting and argues for the validity of rapid transformation as the goal in induced culture change. In doing so, she combines knowledge about the processes of cultural transmission with knowledge about acculturation and culture change. Her paper therefore marks a shift in emphasis but one that is by no means discontinuous with the preceding analyses. The great significance of her analysis is apparent in view of the responsible position of the United States in a world where the emerging shape of transformation in the technologically undeveloped societies will determine whether our own democratic society can survive.

Jack Fischer's article is a completely unique case study of education in an induced culture change situation and of the conflicts between interests and values of donor and recipient groups. The case study is unique not only because the process is viewed from the perspective of the indigenous population, but because the people inducing the change are not ourselves but the Japanese. The change in emphasis marked by Mead's analysis is in this way carried into an unexpected dimension, but one that is critically relevant. Fischer's case demonstrates that the problems encountered in community-education programs in induced culture change situations are not a unique consequence of our culture in interaction with others but are a consequence in large degree of the situation in which technologically advanced cultures interact with technologically undeveloped cultures as change is brought about.

Bernard Siegel provides a fitting conclusion to Part III in his substantial and revealing survey of the educational process and its functional interrelationships with social structure and ecology in two rural Japanese villages. His paper is unique in its scope as a case study in this book and brings new dimensions into the perspective of education in its cultural context in a complex, non-Western, and changing society.

16———Margaret Mead

Our Educational Emphases in Primitive Perspective*

In its broadest sense, education is the cultural process, the way in which each new-born human infant, born with a potentiality for learning greater than that of any other mammal, is transformed into a full member of a specific human society, sharing with the other members a specific human culture. From this point of view we can place side by side the newborn child in a modern city and the savage infant born into some primitive South Sea tribe. Both have everything to learn. Both depend for that learning upon the help and example, the care and tutelage, of the elders of their societies. Neither child has any guaranty of grow-up to be a full human being should some accident, such as theft by a wolf, interfere with its human education. Despite the tremendous difference in what the New York infant and the New Guinea infant will learn, there is a striking similarity in the whole complicated process by which the child takes on and into itself the culture of those around it. And much profit can be gained by concentrating on these similarities and by setting the procedure of the South Sea mother side by side with the procedure of the New York mother, attempting to understand the common elements in cultural transmission. In such comparisons we can identify the tremendous potentialities of human beings, who are able to learn not only to speak any one of a thousand languages but to adjust to as many different rhythms of maturation, ways of learning,

* Reprinted from *The American Journal of Sociology*, XLVIII, No. 6. May, 1943, 633–639, by permission of the The University of Chicago Press. Copyright, 1943, University of Chicago.

methods of organizing their emotions and of managing their relationships to other human beings.

In this paper, however, I propose to turn away from this order
of comparison—which notes the differences between human cultures, primitive and civilized, only as means of exploring the proc-
cesses which occur in both types of culture—and to stress instead
the ways in which our present behavior, which we bracket under
the abstraction "education," differs from the procedures characteristic of primitive homogeneous communities. I propose to ask,
not what there is in common between America today and a South
Sea culture which recently displayed a Stone Age level of culture,
but to ask instead: What are some of the conspicuous differences,
and what light do these differences throw upon our understanding of our own conception of education? And, because this is too
large and wide a subject, I want to limit myself still further and
to ask a question which is appropriate to this symposium: What
effects has the mingling of peoples—of different races, different
religions, and different levels of cultural complexity—had upon
our concept of education? When we place our present-day concept against a backdrop of primitive educational procedures and
see it as influenced by intermingling of peoples, what do we find?

I once lectured to a group of women—all of them college
graduates—alert enough to be taking a fairly advanced adult-
education course on "Primitive Education" delivered from the first
point of view. I described in detail the lagoon village of the Manus
tribe, the ways in which the parents taught the children to master
their environment, to swim, to climb, to handle fire, to paddle a
canoe, to judge distances and calculate the strength of materials. I
described the tiny canoes which were given to the three-year-olds,
the miniature fish spears with which they learned to spear min-
nows, the way in which small boys learned to calk their canoes
with gum, and how small girls learned to thread shell money into
aprons. Interwoven with a discussion of the more fundamental
issues, such as the relationship between children and parents and
the relationships between younger children and older children, I
gave a fairly complete account of the type of adaptive craft behavior which was characteristic of the Manus and the way in
which this was learned by each generation of children. At the

end of the lecture one woman stood up and asked the first question: "Didn't they have any vocational training?" Many of the others laughed at the question, and I have often told it myself as a way of getting my audience into a mood which was less rigidly limited by our own phrasing of "education." But that woman's question, naïve and crude as it was, epitomized a long series of changes which stand between our idea of education and the processes by which members of a homogeneous and relatively static primitive society transmit their standardized habit patterns to their children.

There are several striking differences between our concept of education today and that of any contemporary primitive society;[1] but perhaps the most important one is the shift from the need for an individual to learn something which everyone agrees he would wish to know, to the will of some individual to teach something which it is not agreed that anyone has any desire to know. Such a shift in emphasis could come only with the breakdown of self-contained and self-respecting cultural homogeneity. The Manus or the Arapesh or the Iatmul adults taught their children all that they knew themselves. Sometimes, it is true, there were rifts in the process. A man might die without having communicated some particular piece of ritual knowledge; a good hunter might find no suitable apprentice among his available near kin, so that his skill perished with him. A girl might be so clumsy and stupid that she never learned to weave a mosquito basket that was fit to sell. Miscarriages in the smooth working of the transmission of available skills and knowledge did occur, but they were not sufficient to focus the attention of the group upon the desirability of *teaching* as over against the desirability of *learning*. Even with considerable division of labor and with a custom by which young men learned a special skill not from a father or other specified relative but merely from a master of the art, the master did not go seeking pupils; the pupils and their parents went to seek the master and with proper gifts of fish or octopus or dogs' teeth persuaded him to teach the neophyte. And at this level of human culture even close contact with members of other

[1] This discussion, unless otherwise indicated, is based upon South Sea people only.

cultures did not alter the emphasis. Women who spoke another language married into the tribe; it was, of course, very important that they should learn to speak the language of their husbands' people, and so they learned that language as best they could—or failed to learn it. People might compliment them on their facility or laugh at them for their lack of it, but the idea of *assimilating* them was absent.

Similarly, the spread of special cults or sects among South Sea people, the desire to *join* the sect rather than the need to make converts, was emphasized. New ceremonies did develop. It was necessary that those who had formerly been ignorant of them should learn new songs or new dance steps, but the onus was again upon the learner. The greater self-centeredness of primitive homogeneous groups (often so self-centered that they divided mankind into two group—the human beings, i.e., themselves, and the nonhuman beings, other people) perserved them also from the emphasis upon the greater value of one truth over another which is the condition of proselytizing: "*We* (human beings) do it this way and *they* (other people) do it that way." A lack of a desire to teach *them* our ways guaranteed also that the *we* group had no fear of any proselytizing from the *they* groups. A custom might be imported, bought, obtained by killing the owner, or taken as part of a marriage payment. A custom might be exported for a price or a consideration. But the emphasis lay upon the desire of the importing group to obtain the new skill or song and upon the desire of the exporting group for profit in material terms by the transaction. The idea of conversion, or purposely attempting to alter the ideas and attitudes of other persons, did not occur. One might try to persuade one's brother-in-law to abandon his own group and come and hunt permanently with the tribe into which his sister had married; physical proselytizing there was, just as there was actual import and export of items of culture. But once the brother-in-law had been persuaded to join a different cultural group, it was his job to learn how to live there; and you might, if you were still afraid he would go back or if you wanted his cooperation in working a two-man fish net, take considerable pains to teach him this or that skill as a bribe. But to bribe another by teaching him one's own skill is a long way from any practice of conversion, although it may be made subsidiary to it.

We have no way of knowing how often in the course of human history the idea of Truth, as a revelation to or possession of some one group (which thereby gained the right to consider itself superior to all those who lacked this revelation), may have appeared. But certain it is that, wherever this notion of hierarchical arrangements of cultural views of experience appears, it has profound effects upon education; and it has enormously influenced our own attitudes toward education. As soon as there is any attitude that one set of cultural beliefs is definitely superior to another, the framework is present for active proselytizing, unless the idea of cultural superiority is joined with some idea of hereditary membership, as it is among the Hindus. (It would indeed be interesting to investigate whether any group which considered itself in possession of the most superior brand of religious or economic truth, and which did not regard its possession as limited by heredity, could preserve the belief in that superiority without proselytizing. It might be found that active proselytizing was the necessary condition for the preservation of the essential belief in one's own revelation.) Thus, with the appearance of religions which held this belief in their own infallible superiority, education becomes a concern of those who teach rather than of those who learn. Attention is directed toward finding neophytes rather than toward finding masters, and adults and children become bracketed together as recipients of conscious missionary effort. This bracketing-together is of great importance; it increases the self-consciousness of the whole educational procedure, and it is quite possible that the whole question of methods and techniques of education is brought most sharply to the fore when it is a completely socialized adult who must be influenced instead of a plastic and receptive child.

With social stratification the possibility of using education as a way of changing status is introduced, and another new component of the educational idea develops. Here the emphasis is still upon the need to learn—on the one hand, in order to alter status and, on the other, to prevent the loss of status by failure to learn. But wherever this possibility enters in there is also a possibility of a new concept of education developing from the relationship

between fixed caste and class lines and education. In a static society members of different caste or class groups may have been
teaching their children different standards of behavior for many
generations without any essential difference between their attitudes toward education and those of less complex societies. To
effect a change it is necessary to focus the attention of the members of the society upon the problem, as conditions of cultural
contact do focus it. Thus, in Bali, until recently the high castes
were sending their daughters to the Dutch schools to be trained as
schoolteachers because it was pre-eminently important that learning should be kept in the hands of the high castes and profoundly
inappropriate that low-caste teachers should teach high-caste children. They felt this strongly enough to overcome their prejudices
against the extent to which such a course takes high-caste women
out into the market place.

As soon as the possibility of shift of class position by virtue
of a different educational experience becomes articulately recognized, so that individuals seek not only to better their children
or to guard them against educational defect but also to see the
extension of restriction of educational opportunity as relevant to
the whole class structure, another element enters in—the relationship of education to social change. Education becomes a mechanism of change. Public attention, once focused upon this possibility,
is easily turned to the converse position of emphasizing education
as a means toward preserving the status quo. I argue here for no
historical priority in the two positions. But I am inclined to believe that we do not have catechumens taught to say "to do my
duty in that state of life into which it has pleased God to call
me" until we have the beginning of movements of individuals
away from their birth positions in society. In fact, the whole use
of education to defend vested interests and intrenched privilege
goes with the recognition that education can be a way of en-
croaching upon them. Just as the presence of proselytizing religions focuses attention upon means of spreading the truth, upon
pedagogy, so the educational implications of social stratification
focus attention upon the content of education and lay the groundwork of an articulate interest in the curriculum.

Movements of peoples, colonization, and trade also bring education into a different focus. In New Guinea it is not uncommon to "hear" (i.e., understand without speaking) several languages besides one's own, and many people not only "hear" but also speak neighboring languages. A head-hunting people like the Mundugu-mor, who had the custom of giving child hostages to temporary allies among neighboring peoples, articulately recognized that it was an advantage to have members of the group be well acquainted with the roads, the customs, and the language of their neighbors, who would assuredly at some time in any given generation be enemies and objects of attack. Those who took the hostages re-garded this increased facility of the Mundugumor as a disad-vantage which had to be put up with. But the emphasis remained with the desirability of learning. Today, with the growth of pidgin English as a lingua franca, bush natives and young boys are most anxious to learn pidgin. Their neighbors, with whom they could trade and communicate more readily if they knew pidgin, are not interested in teaching them. But the European colonist is interested. He sees his position as an expanding, initiating, chang-ing one; he wants to trade with the natives, to recruit and inden-ture them to work on plantations. He needs to have them speak a language that he can understand. Accordingly, we have the shift from the native who needs to learn another language in order to understand to the colonist who needs someone else to learn a language so that he, the colonist, may be understood. In the course of teach-ing natives to speak some lingua franca, to handle money, to work copra, etc., the whole focus is on teaching; not, however, on techniques of teaching, in the sense of pedagogy, but upon sanc-tions for making the native learn. Such usages develop rapidly into compulsory schooling in the language of the colonist or the con-queror, and they result in the schools' being seen as an adjunct of the group in power rather than as a privilege for those who learn.

Just as conquest or colonization of already inhabited countries brings up the problems of assimilation, so also mass migrations may accentuate the same problem. This has been true particularly in the United States, where education has been enormously influ-enced by the articulate need to assimilate the masses of European immigrants, with the resulting phrasing of the public schools as a means for educating other peoples' children. The school ceased to be chiefly a device by which children were taught accumulated knowledge or skills and became a political device for arousing and maintaining national loyalty through inculcating a language and a system of ideas which the pupils did not share with their parents.

It is noteworthy that, in the whole series of educational emphases which I have discussed here as significant components of our present-day concept of "education," one common element which differentiates the ideas of conversion, assimilation, successful colonization, and the relationship between class-caste lines and education from the attitudes found in primitive homogeneous societies is the acceptance of discontinuity between parents and children, even if the actual teacher was not a parent but a maternal uncle or a shaman. Modern education includes a heavy emphasis upon the function of education to create discontinuities—to turn the child of the peasant into a clerk, of the farmer into a lawyer, of the Italian immigrant into an American, of the illiterate into the literate. And parallel to this emphasis goes the attempt to use education as an extra, special prop for tottering continuities. Parents who are separated from their children by all the gaps in understanding which are a function of our rapidly changing world cling to the expedient of sending their children to the same schools and colleges they attended, counting upon the heavy traditionalism of slow-moving institutions to stem the tide of change. (Thus, while the father builds himself a new house and the mother furnishes it with modern furniture, they both rejoice that back at school, through the happy accident that the school is not well enough endowed, son will sit at the same desk at which his father sat.) The same attitude is reflected by the stock figure of the member of a rural school board who says, "What was good enough for me in school is good enough for my children. The three R's, that's enough."

Another common factor in these modern trends of education is the increasing emphasis upon change rather than upon growth, upon what is done to people rather than upon what people do. This emphasis comes, I believe, from the inclusion of adults as objects of the educational effort—whether effort comes from missionaries, colonizers, conquerors, Old Americans, or employers of labor. When a child is learning to talk, the miracle of learning is so pressing and conspicuous that the achievement of the teachers is put in the shade. But the displacement, in an adult's speech habits, of his native tongue by the phonetics of some language which he is being bullied or cajoled into learning is often more a matter of triumph for the teacher than of pride for the learner. Changing people's habits, people's ideas, people's language, people's beliefs, people's emotional allegiances, involves a sort of deliberate violence to other people's developed personalities—a violence not to be found in the whole teacher-child relationship, which finds its prototype in the cherishing parent helping the young child to learn those things which are essential to his humanity.

We have been shocked in recent years by the outspoken brutality of the totalitarian states, which set out to inculcate into children's minds a series of new ideas which it was considered politically useful for them to learn. Under the conflicting currents of modern ideologies the idea of *indoctrination* has developed as a way of characterizing the conscious educational aims of any group with whom the speaker is out of sympathy. Attempts to teach children any set of ideas in which one believes have become tainted with suspicion of power and self-interest, until almost all education can be branded and dismissed as one sort of indoctrination or another. The attempt to assimilate, convert, or keep in their places other human beings conceived of as inferior to those who are making the plans has been a boomerang which has distorted our whole educational philosophy; it has shifted the emphasis from one of growth and seeking for knowledge to one of dictation and forced acceptance of clichés and points of view. Thus we see that the presence of one element within our culture—a spurious sense of superiority of one group of human beings over another, which gave the group in power the impetus to force their language, their beliefs, and their culture down the throats of the group which was numerically, or economically, or geographically handicapped—has corrupted and distorted the emphases of our free schools.

But there has been another emphasis developing side by side with those which I have been discussing, and that is a belief in the power of education to work miracles—a belief which springs from looking at the other side of the shield. As long as the transmission of culture is an orderly and continuous process, in a slowly changing society, the child speaks the language of his parents; and, although one may marvel that this small human being learns at all, one does not marvel that he learns French or English or Samoan, provided that this be the language of the parents. It took the discontinuity of educational systems, purposive shifts of language and beliefs between parents and children, to catch our imagination and to fashion the great American faith in education as creation rather than transmission, conversion, suppression, assimilation, or indoctrination. Perhaps one of the most basic human ways of saying "new" is "something that my parents have never experienced" or, when we speak of our children, "something I have never experienced." The drama of discontinuity which has been such a startling feature of modern life, and for which formal education has been regarded in great measure as responsible, suggested to men that perhaps education might be a device for creating a new kind of world by developing a new kind of human being.

Here it is necessary to distinguish sharply between the sort of idea which George Counts expressed in his speech, "Dare the School Build a New Social Order?" and the idea of education as creation of something new. Dr. Counts did not mean a new social order in the sense of an order that no man had dreamed of, so much as he meant a very concrete and definite type of society for which he and many others believed they had a blueprint. He was asking whether the teachers would use the schools to produce a different type of socioeconomic system. His question was still a power question and partook of all the power ideas which have developed in the long period during which men in power, men with dominating ideas, men with missions, have sought to put their ideas over upon other men. His question would have been phrased more accurately as "Dare the schools build a different social order?" The schools of America have these hundred years been training children to give allegiance to a way of life that was new to them, not because they were children to whom all ways were new, not because the way of life was itself one that no man had yet dreamed of, but because they were the children of their parents. Whenever one group succeeds in getting power over the schools and teaches within those schools a doctrine foreign to many of those who enter those doors, they are building up, from the standpoint of those students, a different social order. From the standpoint of those in power, they are defending or extending the old; and, from the moment that the teachers had seriously started to put Dr. Counts's suggestion into practice, they would have been attempting by every method available to them to extend, in the minds of other people's children, their own picture, already an "old" idea, of the sort of world they wanted to live in.

It is not this sort of newness of which I speak. But from those who watched learning, those who humbly observed miracles instead of claiming them as the fruits of their strategy or of their superior teaching (propaganda) techniques there grew up in America a touching belief that it was possible by education to build a new world—a world that no man had yet dreamed and that no man, bred as we had been bred, could dream. They argued that if we can bring up our children to be freer than we have been— freer from anxiety, freer from guilt and fear, freer from economic constraint and the dictates of expediency—to be equipped as we never were equipped, trained to think and enjoy thinking, trained to feel and enjoy feeling, then we shall produce a new kind of human being, one not known upon the earth before. Instead of the single visionary, the depth of whose vision has kept men's souls alive for centuries, we shall develop a whole people bred to the task of seeing with clear imaginative eyes into a future which is hidden from us behind the smoke screen of our defective and irremediable educational handicaps. This belief has often been branded as naïve and simple-minded. The American faith in education, which Clark Wissler lists as one of the dominant American culture traits, has been held up to ridicule many times. In many of its forms it is not only unjustified optimism but arrant nonsense. When small children are sent out by overzealous schoolteachers to engage in active social reforms—believed necessary by their teachers—the whole point of view becomes not only ridiculous but dangerous to the children themselves.

Phrased, however, without any of our blueprints, with an insistence that it is the children themselves who will some day, when they are grown, make blueprints on the basis of their better upbringing, the idea is a bold and beautiful one, an essentially democratic and American idea. Instead of attempting to bind and limit the future and to compromise the inhabitants of the next century by a long process of indoctrination which will make them unable to follow any path but that which we have laid down, it suggests that we devise and practice a system of education which sets the future free. We must concentrate upon teaching our children to walk so steadily that we need not hew too straight and narrow paths for them but can trust them to make new paths through difficulties we never encountered to a future of which we have no inkling today.

When we look for the contributions which contacts of peoples, of peoples of different races and different religions, different levels of culture and different degrees of technological development, have made to education, we find two. On the one hand, the emphasis has shifted from learning to teaching, from the doing to the one who causes it to be done, from spontaneity to coercion, from freedom to power. With this shift has come the development of techniques of power, dry pedagogy, regimentation, indoctrination, manipulation, and propaganda. These are but sorry additions to man's armory, and they come from the insult to human life which is perpetuated whenever one human being is regarded as differentially less or more human than another. But, on the other hand, out of the discontinuities and rapid changes which have accompanied these minglings of people has come another invention, one which perhaps would not have been born in any other setting than this one—the belief in education as an instrument for the creation of new human values.

We stand today in a crowded place, where millions of men mill about seeking to go in different directions. It is most uncertain whether the educational invention made by those who emphasized teaching or the educational invention made by those who emphasized learning will survive. But the more rapidly we can erase from our society those discrepancies in position and privilege which tend to perpetuate and strengthen the power and manipulative aspects of education, the more hope we may have that that other invention—the use of education for unknown ends which shall exalt man above his present stature—may survive.

17——— Dorothy Eggan

Instruction and Affect
in Hopi Cultural Continuity[*][1]

Education and anthropology have proved in recent years that each has much of interest to say to the other[2] for both are concerned with the transmission of cultural heritage from one generation to another—and with the means by which that transmission is accomplished. And although anthropology has tended to be preoccupied with the processes of cultural *change*, and the conditions under which it takes place, rather than with cultural continuity, it would seem, as Herskovits has said, that cultural change can be best understood when considered in relation to cultural stability (Herskovits, 1950:20).

Both education and anthropology are concerned with learned behavior, and the opinion that early learning is of vital significance for the later development of personality, and that emotional factors are important in the learning process, while sometimes implicit rather than explicit, is often found in anthropological literature, particularly in that dealing with "socialization," "ethos" (Redfield,

* Reprinted from the *Southwestern Journal of Anthropology*, 12, 4, 1956, 347–370, with permission.

[1] The substance of this paper was originally presented to the Society for Social Research of the University of Chicago in 1943, and subsequently enlarged in 1954 at the request of Edward Bruner for his class in Anthropology and Education. Discussion with him has greatly clarified my thinking on the problems examined here. Some elimination and revision has been made in order to include references to recently published work and suggestions from Fred Eggan, David Aberle, Clyde Kluckhohn, David Riesman, and Milton Singer. But intimate association with the Hopi over a period of seventeen years has given me this perception of the Hopi world.

[2] See, for example, Mead, 1931, pp. 669–687; Mead, 1943, pp. 663–639; Whiting and Child, 1953; Spindler (ed.), 1955.

1953), and "values." From Mead's consistent work, for instance, has come a clearer picture of the socialization process in a wide variety of cultures, including our own, and she examines early "identification" as one of the problems central to all of them (Mead, 1953). Hallowell, too, speaking of the learning situation in which an individual must acquire a personality pattern, points out that "there are important affective components involved" (Hallowell, 1953:610), and elsewhere he emphasizes a "need for further investigation of relations between learning process and affective experience" (Hallowell, 1955:251). Kluckhohn, writing on values and value-orientation, says that "one of the severest limitations of the classical theory of learning is its neglect of attachments and attitudes in favor of reward and punishment (Kluckhohn, 1951:430). And DuBois states explicitly that, "Institutions which may be invested with high emotional value because of patterns in child training are not ones which can be lightly legislated out of existence" (DuBois 1941:281).

In fact, increasing interaction between anthropology and psychiatry (which has long held as established the connection between emotion, learning, and resistance to change in individuals) has in the last decade introduced a theme into anthropology which reminds one of Sapir's statement that "the more fully one tries to understand a culture, the more it takes on the characteristics of a personality organization" (Sapir, 1949:594).

Psychologists, while perhaps more cautious in their approach to these problems, since human emotional commitments—particularly as regards permanency—are difficult if not impossible to examine in the laboratory, emphasize their importance in the learning situation, and frequently express dissatisfaction with many existing methods and formulations in the psychology of personality. The shaping factors of emotion—learned as well as innate —are stressed by Asch (1952:29) in his *Social Psychology*, and focus particularly on man's "need to belong." He feels that the "psychology of man needs basic research and a fresh theoretical approach." Allport speaks of past "addiction to machines, rats, or infants" in experimental psychology, and hopes for a "design for personality and social psychology" which will become "better tempered to our subject matter" as we "cease borrowing false notes—whether squeaks, squeals, or squalls . . ." and "read the score of human personality more accurately" (Allport, 1951:168–9). And Murphy, starting with the biological foundations of human learning, particularly the individual form this "energy system" immediately assumes, examines man as psychologically structured by early canalizations in which personality is rooted, to which are added an organized symbol system and deeply ingrained habits of perception, and suggests that the structure thus built is highly resistant to change. He says that, "The task of the psychology of personality today is to apply ruthlessly, and to the limit, every promising suggestion of today, but always with the spice of healthy skepticism," while recognizing "the fundamental limitations of the whole present system of conceptions . . ." as a preparation for "rebirth of knowledge" (Murphy: 926–927).

Anthropologists as well as psychologists are aware that any hypotheses in an area so complex must be regarded as tenuous, but since the situations cannot be taken into the laboratory, there is some value in taking the laboratory to the situation. Progress in these amorphous areas can only come about, as Redfield has said, by the mental instrument which he has called a "controlled conversation" (Redfield, 1955:148)—this discussion, then, must be considered a conversation between the writer and others who have brought varied interests and techniques to the problem of resistance to cultural change[3] (DuBois, 1955). It begins logically with a recent paper on "Cultural Transmission and Cultural Change" in which Bruner discusses two surveys (SSRC, 1954: 973–1002, Keesing 1953; Also Spiro 1955:1240–1251) of the literature on acculturation and adds to the hypotheses presented in them another which he finds relevant to the situation among the Mandan-Hidatsa Indians. As stated in his summary paragraph we find the proposition: "That which is learned and internalized in infancy and early childhood is most resistant to contact situations. The hypothesis directs our attention to the age in the individual life career at which each aspect of culture is transmitted, as well as to the full context of the learning situation and the position of

---

[3] Of particular interest in this problem is this paper of DuBois' and the discussion following it. See also Dozier's (1954) analysis of the interaction between the Hopi-Tewa and Hopi; compare Dozier, 1955.

the agents of socialization in the larger social system" (Bruner, 1956a: 197).

This proposition will be further extended by a consideration of the *emotional* commitment involved in the socialization process among the Hopi Indians; here the "conversation" will be directed to emotion in both teaching and learning, and will center around resistance to cultural change which has been remarkably consistent in Hopi society throughout recorded history *until the Second World War brought enforced and drastic changes.*[4] At that time the young men, although legitimately conscientious objectors, were drafted into the army. Leaving the isolation of their reservation, where physical violence between adults was rare, they were rapidly introduced to the stark brutality of modern warfare. In army camps alcoholic intoxication, an experience which was the antithesis of the quiet, controlled behavior normally demanded of adult Hopi on their reservation, frequently brought relief from tension and a sense of comradeship with fellow soldiers. Deprived of the young men's work in the fields, many older people and young women were in turn forced to earn a living in railroad and munition centers off the reservation. Thus the gaps in the Hopi "communal walls" were, for the first time, large enough in numbers and long enough in time—and the experiences to which individuals had to adapt were revolutionary enough in character—so that the sturdy structure was damaged. It is emphasized, therefore, that in this discussion *Hopi* refers to those members of the tribe who had reached *adulthood* and were thoroughly committed to their own world view before 1941. Much of it would not apply as forcefully to the children of these people, and would be even less applicable to their grandchildren.

The major hypotheses suggested here, then, are:

> (1) That the Hopi, as contrasted with ourselves, were experts in the use of *affect* in their educational system, and that this element continued to operate throughout the entire life span of each

---

[4] An evaluation of these changes has not been reported for the Hopi, although John Connelly is working on the problem; see Adair and Vogt, 1949, and Vogt, 1951, for discussions of Navajo and Zuñi reactions to the war and postwar situation.

individual as a *reconditioning* factor (Herskovits, 1950: 325–326, 491, 627); and

(2) That this exercise of emotion in teaching and learning was an efficient means of social control which functioned in the absence of other forms of policing and restraint, and also in the maintenance of stability both in the personality structure of the individual and the structure of the society.

These hypotheses may be explored through a consideration of (a) the early and continued conditioning of the individual in the Hopi maternal extended family, which was on every level, an inculcation of *interdependence* as contrasted with our training for *independence;* and (b) an early and continuing emphasis on religious observances and beliefs (also emphasizing interdependence), the most important facet of which—for the purposes of this paper—was the central concept of the Hopi "good heart."[5]

If we examine the educational system by which a Hopi acquired the personal entity which made him so consistently and determinedly Hopi, we find that it was deliberate and systematic (Pettit, 1946; Hough, 1915:218). Students of Hopi are unanimous on this point but perhaps it can be best illustrated by quoting one of my informants who had spent much time away from the reservation, including many years in a boarding school, and who was considered by herself and other Hopi to be an extremely "acculturated" individual. In 1938 when she made this statement she was about thirty years old and had brought her children back to the reservation to be "educated." Said she:

> It is very hard to know what to do. In the old days I might have had more babies for I should have married early. Probably some of them would have died. But my comfort would have been both in numbers and in knowing that all women lost babies. Now when I let my little son live on top [a conservative village on top of the mesa] with my mothers, I worry all the time. If he dies with dysentery I will feel like I killed him. Yet he *must* stay

---

[5] The concept of the Hopi "good heart" as contrasted to a "bad heart" which is *Kahopi*, has been documented by every student of Hopi known to the writer, in references too numerous to mention, beginning with Stephen (written in the 1890's but published in 1940) and Hough in 1915. But the clearest understanding of this and other Hopi concepts may be had in Whorf, 1941, especially pp. 30–32.

on top so the old people can teach him the *important* things. It is his only chance of becoming Hopi, for he would never be a *bahana* (White).

The education which she considered so vital included careful, deliberate instruction in kinship and community obligations, and in Hopi history as it is seen in mythology and as remembered by the old people during their own lifetimes. The Hopi taught youngsters fear as a means of personal and social control and for the purposes of personal and group protection; and they were taught techniques for the displacement of anxiety, as well as procedures which the adults believed would prolong life. Children were instructed in religious lore, in how to work and play, in sexual matters, even in how to deal with a *bahana*. Good manners were emphasized, for they were a part of the controlled, orderly conduct necessary to a Hopi good heart.

Constantly one heard during work or play, running through all activity like a connecting thread: "Listen to the old people—they are wise"; or, "Our old uncles taught us that way—it is the *right* way." Around the communal bowl, in the kiva, everywhere this instruction went on; stories, dream adventures, and actual experiences such as journeys away from the reservation were told and retold. And children, in the warmth and security of this intimate extended family and clan group, with no intruding outside experiences to modify the impact until they were forced to go to an alien school, learned what it meant to be a good Hopi from a wide variety of determined teachers who had very definite—and *mutually consistent*—ideas of what a good Hopi is. And they learned all of this in the Hopi language, which, as Whorf has made so clear, has no words with which to express many of our concepts, but which, working together with "a different set of cultural and environmental influences . . . interacted with Hopi linguistic patterns to mould them, to be moulded again by them, and so little by little to shape the world outlook" (Whorf, 1941: 92).

Eventually these children disappeared into government schools for a time, and in the youth of most of these older Hopi it was a boarding school off the reservation where Indian children from various reservations were sent, often against their own and their parents' wishes.[6] Here White teachers were given the task of "civilizing" and "Christianizing" these wards of the government, but by that time a Hopi child's view of the world and his place in it was very strong. Moreover, trying to transpose our concepts into their language was often very nearly impossible for them, since only Hopi had been spoken at home. Examining Hopi memory of such a method of education we quote a male informant who said:

> I went to school about four years. . . . We worked like slaves for our meals and keep. . . . We didn't learn much. . . . I didn't understand and it was hard to learn. . . . At that time you do what you are told or you get punished. . . . You just wait till you can go home.

And a woman said:

> Policemen gathered us up like sheep. I was scared to death. My mother tried to hide me. I tried to stay away but the police always won. . . . Then we were sent up to Sherman [in California]. . . . It was far away; we were afraid on the train. . . . I didn't like it when I couldn't learn and neither did the teachers. . . . They never punished me, I always got 100 in Deportment. . . . I was there three years. . . . I was so glad to get home that I cried and cried . . . , glad to have Hopi food again, and fun again.

As children, the Hopi usually solved this dilemma of enforced education by means of a surface accommodation to the situation until such time as they were able to return to their own meaningful world. For, as Park has said, man can "make his manners a cloak and his face a mask, behind which he is able to preserve . . . inner freedom . . . and independence of thought, even when unable to maintain independence of action."[7] In other words, because the inner core of Hopi identification was already so strong, these children were able to *stay* in a White world, while

---

[6] See Simmons, 1942, pp. 88–89, for an excellent description by Don Talayesva of the government's use of force in the educational policy of this period; and pp. 134, 178, 199, and 225 for some of the results of this policy. Cf. Aberle, 1951, for an analysis of Talayesva's school years and his later reidentification with his people.

[7] Park, 1950, p. 361. Cf. Kluckhohn, 1951, pp. 388–433, who points out that values continue to influence even when they do not function realistically as providers of immediate goal reactions.

still *living* in the Hopi world within themselves.[8] And while for some there was a measure of temptation in many of the things learned in White schools so that they "became friendly with whites and accepted their gifts,"[9] the majority of these older Hopi acquired a White education simply as a "necessary accessory";[10] they incorporated parts of our material culture, and learned to deal with Whites astutely, but their values were largely unaffected.

If we now examine more closely the pattern of integration through which the Hopi erected a communal wall[11] around their children we find in their kinship system the framework of the wall, but interwoven through it and contributing greatly to its strength was a never-ending composition which gave color and form, their religious ceremonies and beliefs.

Let us first contrast briefly the affect implicit in the way a Hopi born into this kinship system experienced relationships and the way in which Western children experience them. In the old days it was rare for a growing primary family to live outside the maternal residence. Normally each lived within it until the birth of several children crowded them out. And in this household each child was eagerly welcomed, for infant mortality was high and the clan was always in need of reinforcement. Thus, in spite of the physical burden on the biological mother, which she sometimes resented, the first strong *clan* sanction which we see in contrast to our own, was the absolute need for and desire for many children. From birth the young of the household were attended, pampered, and disciplined, although very mildly for the first several years, by a wide variety of relatives in addition to the mother. These attentions came both from the household members and from visitors

---

[8] Cf. D. Eggan, 1955, on the use of the Hopi myth in dreams as a means of "identification."

[9] Simmons, 1942, p. 88, and compare pp. 178, 180.

[10] Bruner, 1956b, p. 612, indicates that his Mandan-Hidatsa informants were quite conscious of this "lizard-like" quality of protective coloration in White contacts.

[11] Stephen, 1940a, p. 18, says that the Hopi "describe their fundamental organization as a people" by "designating their principal religious ceremonies as the concentric walls of a house." The concept is extended here to include the entire wall of "Hopiness" which they have built around their children.

in it. In no way was a baby ever as dependent upon his physical mother as are children in our culture. He was even given the breast of a mother's mother or sister if he cried for food in his mother's absence. True a Hopi saying states that a baby is made "sad" if another baby steals his milk, but it has been my experience that these women may risk making their own babies sad temporarily if another child needs food.

Weaning, of course, when discussed in personality contexts means more than a transition from milk to solid food. It is also a gradual process of achieving independence from the comfort of the mother's body and care, of transferring affections to other persons, and of finding satisfactions within oneself and in the outside world. Most people learn to eat solid food; many of us are never weaned, which has unfortunate consequences in a society where *individual* effort and independence are stressed. The Hopi child, on the other hand, from the day of his birth was being weaned from his biological mother. Many arms gave him comfort, many faces smiled at him, and from a very early age he was given bits of food which were chewed by various members of the family and placed in his mouth. So, for a Hopi, the outside world in which he needed to find satisfaction was never far away. He was not put in a room by himself and told to go to sleep; every room was crowded by sleepers of all ages. He was in no way *forced to find satisfactions within himself;* rather these were provided for him, if possible, by his household and clan group. His weaning, then, was from the breast only, and as he was being weaned from the biological mother, he was at the same time in a situation which *increased* his emotional orientation toward the intimate in-group of the extended family—which was consistent with the interests of Hopi social structure. Thus, considering weaning in its wider implications, a Hopi was never "weaned"; it was not intended that he should be. For these numerous caretakers contributed greatly to a small Hopi's faith in his intimate world—and conversely without question to a feeling of strangeness and *emotional insecurity* as adults in any world outside of this emotional sphere. The Hopi were often successful outside of the reservation, but they have shown a strong tendency to return frequently to the maternal household. Few ever left it permanently.

In addition to his extended family, while a Hopi belonged to one clan only, the clan into which he was born, he was a "child" of his father's clan, and this group took a lively interest in him. There were also numerous ceremonial and adoptive relationships which were close and warm, so that most of the persons in his familiar world had definite reciprocal relations with the child (Eggan, 1950: Chap. II; Simmons, 1942: Chaps. III, IV). Since all of these "relatives" lived in his own small village, or in villages nearby, his emotional and physical "boundaries" coincided, were quite definitely delimited, and were explored and perceived at the same time. It cannot be too strongly emphasized that the kinship terms which a Hopi child learned in this intimate atmosphere were not mere verbalizations—as, for instance, where the term "cousin" among ourselves is sometimes applied to someone we have never seen and never will see. On the contrary, each term carried with it definite mutual responsibilities and patterns of behavior, and, through these, definite emotional interaction as well. These affects were taught as proper responses, together with the terms which applied to each individual, as he entered the child's life. This process was deliberately and patiently, but unceasingly, worked at by every older individual in the child's surroundings, so by the time a Hopi was grown kinship reaction patterns were so deeply ingrained in his thinking and feeling, and in his workaday life, that they were as much a part of him as sleeping and eating. He was not merely told that Hopi rules of behavior were right or wise; he lived them as he grew and *in his total environment* (Henry, 1955) (as contrasted to our separation of teaching at home, in school, and in Sunday school) until he was simply not conscious that there was any other way to react. Note that I say *conscious!* The unconscious level of feeling, as seen in dreams and life-history materials, and in indirect behavior manifestations (jealousy and gossip), often presents quite a different picture. But while ambivalence toward specific persons among the Hopi—as with mankind everywhere—is a personal burden, the long reinforced conditioned reaction of *interdependence* on both the emotional and overt behavior level was highly uniform and persistent (See Whorf, 1941:87, Aberle, 1951:93–94, 119–123). Perhaps the strength of kinship conditioning toward interdependence which was conveyed in a large but intimate group, living in close physical contact, can be best illustrated by quoting from an informant:

My younger sister——was born when I was about four or five, I guess. I used to watch my father's and mother's relatives fuss over her. She didn't look like much to me. I couldn't see why people wanted to go to so much trouble over a wrinkled little thing like that baby. I guess I didn't like babies as well as most girls did. . . . But I had to care for her pretty soon anyway. She got fat and was hard to carry around on my back, for I was pretty little myself. First I had to watch her and joggle the cradle board when she cried. She got too big and wiggled too much and then my mother said to me, "She is *your sister*—take her out in the plaza in your shawl."

She made my back ache. Once I left her and ran off to play with the others for a while. I intended to go right back, but I didn't go so soon, I guess. Someone found her. I got punished for this. My mother's brother said: "You should not have a sister to help you out when you get older. What can a woman do without her sisters?[12] You are not one of us to leave your sister alone to die. If harm had come to her you would never have a clan, no relatives at all. No one would ever help you out or take care of you. Now you have another chance. You owe her more from now on. This is the worst thing that any of my sisters' children has ever done. You are going to eat by yourself until you are fit to be one of us." That is what he said. That is the way he talked on and on and on. When meal time came they put a plate of food beside me and said, "Here is your food; eat your food." It was a long time they did this way. It seemed a long time before they looked at me. They were all sad and quiet. They put a pan beside me at meal time and said nothing—nothing at all, not even to scold me. My older sister carried——now. I didn't try to go near her. But I looked at my sisters and thought, "I need you—I will help you if you will help me." I would rather have been beaten or smoked. I was so ashamed all the time. Wherever I went people got sad [i.e., quiet]. After a while [in about ten days as her mother re-

---

[12] In a matrilineal household and clan, coöperation with one's "sisters" is a necessity for the maintenance of both the social structure and the communal unit.

membered it] they seemed to forget it and I ate with people again. During those awful days Tuvaye [a mother's sister] some-times touched my head sadly, while I was being punished, I mean. Once or twice she gave me something to eat. But she didn't say much to me. Even she and my grandfather were ashamed and in sorrow over this awful thing I had done.

Sometimes now I dream I leave my children alone in the fields and I wake up in a cold sweat. Sometimes I dream I am alone in a desert place with no water and no one to help me. Then I think of this punishment when I dream this way. It was the worst thing I ever did. It was the worst thing that ever happened to me. No one ever mentioned it to me afterward but——[older male sib-ling], the mean one. I would hang my head with shame. Finally my father told him sharply that he would be punished if he ever mentioned this to me again. I was about six when this hap-pened, I think.

This informant was about forty when she related this incident, but she cried, even then, as she talked.

Nor was withdrawal of support the only means of punish-ment. There were bogey Kachinas who "might kidnap" bad chil-dren, and who visited the mesas sometimes when children were uncoöperative; thus the "stranger" *joined effectively* with the clan in inducing the "ideal" Hopi behavior. But children *shared* this fear, as they also frequently shared other punishments. Dennis has called attention to the fact that a whole group of children often shared the punishment for the wrong-doing of one (Dennis, 1941:263). This method may not endear an individual to his age-mates, but it does reinforce the central theme of Hopi belief that each person in the group is responsible for what happens to all, however angry or jealous one may feel toward siblings.

Before we examine the religious composition of the Hopi "communal walls," we might contrast more explicitly the emo-tional implications of early Hopi conditioning to those experienced in our society. From the day of *our* birth the training toward *independence*—as contrasted to *interdependence*—starts. We sleep alone; we are immediately and increasingly in a world of compara-tive strangers. A variety of nurses, doctors, relatives, sitters, and teachers march through our lives in a never-ending procession.

A few become friends, but *compared with a Hopi child's experiences*, the impersonality and lack of emotional relatedness to so many kinds of people with such widely different backgrounds is startling. Indeed the disparity of the relationships as such is so great that continuity of emotional response is impossible, and so we learn to look for emotional satisfaction in change, which in itself becomes a value (Kluckhohn and Kluckhohn, 1947:109). In addition, we grow up aware that there are many ways of life within the American class system; we know that there are many choices which we must make as to profession, behavior, moral code, even religion; and we know that the values of our parents' generation are not necessarily ours. If the permissive intimacy in the primary family in our society—from which both nature and circumstance demand a break in adulthood—is too strong, the individual cannot mature so that he can function efficiently in response to the always changing personalities in his life, and the always changing demands of the society (Riesman, 1955, Mead, 1948: 518). He becomes a dependent neurotic "tentative between extreme polarities (Erikson, 1948:198; Murphy, 1947:714–733). But precisely because the permissive intimacy, as well as the punishing agencies, in a Hopi child's life were so far and so effectively extended in his formative years he became *interdependent* with a larger but still definitely delimited group, and tended always to be more comfortable and effective within it. His self-value quickly identified itself with the larger Hopi value (Hallowell, 1955: Chap. IV; Erikson, 1948:198, fn), and to the extent that he could continue throughout his life to identify with his group and function within it, he was secure in his place in the universe.

We have now sketched the situation which surrounded the young Hopi child in his first learning situations, and contrasted these with our own. For descriptive convenience this has been separated from religious instruction, but in the reality experience of the children—with the exception of formal initiation rites—no one facet of learning to be Hopi was separated from others. To understand the meaning his religion had for a Hopi one must first understand the harsh physical environment into which he was born. While it is agreed that it would not be possible to predict the

character or the social structure of the Hopi from the circumstances of this physical environment,[13] it is self-evident that their
organized social and ritual activities are largely a response to it.
And such activities are at once a reflection of man's need to *be*,
and his need to justify his existence to himself and others. If those
who doubt that the forces of nature are powerful in shaping personality and culture were confined for one year on the Hopi
reservation—even though their own economic dependence on
"nature" would be negligible—they would still know by personal
experience more convincing than scientific experiments the relentless pressure of the environment on their own reaction patterns.
They would, for instance, stand, as all Hopis have forever stood,
with aching eyes fastened on a blazing sky where thunderheads
piled high in promise and were snatched away by "evil winds,"
and thus return to their homes knowing the tension, the acute
bodily need for the "feel" of moisture. When rains do fall, there
is the likelihood of a cloudburst which will ruin the fields. And
there is a possibility of early frost which will destroy their crops,
as well as the absolute certainty of sandstorms, rodents, and worms
which will ruin many plants. These things on a less abstract level
than "feeling" resolved themselves into a positive threat of famine
and thirst which every Hopi knew had repeatedly ravaged his
tribe. Is it possible that the effects of this silent battle between
man and the elements left no mark on successive generations of
individuals? It certainly was the reinforced concrete of Hopi social structure, since strongly conditioned interdependence was the
only hope of survival.

Thus, the paramount problem for the Hopi was uncertain
rain, and the outward expression of their deep need for divine aid
was arranged in a cycle of ceremonies, the most impressive of
which, at least among the exoteric rituals, were Kachina (Earle
and Kennard, 1938) dances. These were, for the observer, colorful pageants in which meticulously trained dancers performed
from sunrise until sunset, with short intermissions for food and

---

[13] Redfield, 1955, pp. 31–32; cf. Titiev, 1944, pp. 177–178; Whorf, 1941,
p. 91; D. Eggan, 1948 (first published in the American Anthropologist, vol.
45, 1943); Thompson and Joseph, 1944, p. 133.

rest. Their bodies were ceremonially painted; brilliant costumes were worn, along with beautifully carved and painted masks which represented the particular gods who were taking part in the ceremony. The color, the singing and the drums which accompanied the dance, the graceful rhythm and intense concentration of the dancers, all combine into superb artistry which is an hypnotic and impressive form of prayer. Ideally, the Hopi preceded every important act with prayer, and with these older Hopi the ideal was apt to be fact. A bag of sacred cornmeal was part of their daily equipment.

In the religious context also, we must remember the intimate atmosphere which surrounded a Hopi child in the learning situation. Here children were taught that if *all* Hopi behaved properly —i.e. kept good hearts—the Kachinas would send rain. It was easy for the children to believe this because from earliest babyhood these beautiful creatures had danced before them as they lolled comfortably in convenient laps. There was a happy, holiday atmosphere throughout a village on dance days, but while each dance was being performed, the quiet of profound reverence. Lying in the mother's lap, a baby's hands were often struck together in the rhythm of the dance; as soon as he would walk his feet were likewise directed in such rhythm, and everybody praised a child and laughed affectionately and encouragingly as it tried to dance. As the children grew older, carved likenesses of these gods, as well as other presents, were given to them by the gods themselves. And as he grew in understanding, a child could not fail to realize that these dancers were part of a religious ceremony which was of utmost importance in his world—that the dancers were rain-bringing and thus life-giving gods.

When first initiation revealed that the gods were in reality men who danced in their stead, a *reorganization* of these emotions which had been directed toward them began, and there is much evidence in autobiographical materials of resentment, if not actual trauma, at this point. For some of them the initiation was a physical ordeal, but for those who entered this phase of their education by way of Powamu there was no whipping, although all initiates witnessed the whipping of those who were initiated into the

Kachina cult (F. Eggan, 1950:47–50, Steward, 1931:59ff.).[14] However, the physical ordeal seems to be less fixed in adult memories than disillusion.

In Don Talyesva's account of intiation into Kachina we find:

> I had a great surprise. They were not spirits, but human beings. I recognized nearly every one of them and felt very unhappy because I had been told all my life that the Kachinas were Gods. I was especially shocked and angry when I saw my uncles, fathers, and own clanbrothers dancing as Kachinas. . . . [But] my fathers and uncles showed me ancestral masks and explained that long ago the Kachinas had come regularly to Oraibi and danced in the plaza. They explained that since the people had become so wicked . . . the Kachinas had stopped coming and sent their spirits to enter the masks on dance days. . . . I thought of the flogging and the initiation as a turning point in my life, and I felt ready at last to listen to my elders and live right (Simmons, 1942: 84–87).

One of our informants said in part:

> I cried and cried into my sheepskin that night, feeling I had been made a fool of. How could I ever watch the Kachinas dance again? I hated my parents and thought I could never believe the old folks again, wondering if gods had ever danced for the Hopi as they now said and if people really lived after death. I hated to see the other children fooled and felt mad when they said I was a big girl now and should act like one. But I was afraid to tell the others the truth for they might whip me to death. I know now it was best and the *only way to teach* children, but it took me a long time to know that. I hope my children won't feel like that.

This informant was initiated into Powamu and not whipped. She was about thirty when she made this statement to the writer.

Another woman, from a different mesa, speaking of her initiation into the Kachina society, said to me:

---

14 The Powamu society is coördinate with the Kachina society and furnishes the "fathers" to the Kachinas on dance occasions. At first initiation parents may choose either of these societies for their children. It is reported that on First Mesa Powamu initiates were whipped, but my Powamu informants from both Second and Third Mesas were not whipped.

The Kachinas brought us children presents. I was very little when I remember getting my first Kachina doll. I sat in my mother's lap and was "ashamed" [these people often use ashamed for shy or somewhat fearful], but she held out my hand for the doll. I grabbed it and hid in her lap for a long time because the Kachina looked too big to me and I was partly scared. But my mother told me to say "asqualie" [thank you] and I did. The music put me to sleep. I would wake up. The Kachinas would still be there. . . . I dreamed sometimes that the Kachinas were dancing and brought me lots of presents. . . .

When I was initiated into Kachina society I was scared. I heard people whisper about it. . . . Children shook their heads and said it was hard to keep from crying. . . . My mother always put her shawl over my head when the Kachinas left the plaza. When she took it off they would be gone. So I knew they were gods and had gone back to the San Francisco mountains. . . . My cere-monial mother came for me when it was time to go to the kiva [for initiation] and she looked sad [i.e., serious]. She took most of the whipping on her own legs [a custom widely practiced among the Hopi]. But then I saw my father and my relatives were Kachinas. When they took their masks off this is what I saw. I was all mixed up. I was mad. I began to cry. I wondered how my father became a Kachina and if they [these men, including her father] would all go away when the Kachinas went back to the San Francisco mountains where the dead people live. Then when my father came home I cried again. I was mad at my parents and my ceremonial mother. "These people have made me silly," I said to myself, "and I thought they were supposed to like me so good." I said that to myself. But I was still crying, and the old people told me that only babies cry. They kept saying I would understand better when I got bigger. They said again that the Kachinas had to go away because the Hopi got bad hearts. and they [the Kachi-nas] couldn't stand quarreling, but they left their heads behind for the Hopis. I said why didn't they rot then like those skulls we found under that house? They said I was being bad and that I should have been whipped more. . . .

When children asked me what happened in the kiva I was afraid to tell them because something would happen to me. Anyway I felt smart because I knew more than those *little* children. It took me a long time to get over this sadness, though. Later I saw that the Kachinas were the most *important thing in life* and that chil-

dren can't understand these things. . . . It takes a while to see
how wise the old people really are. You learn they are always
right in the end.

Before we try to find our way with the Hopi to an "understanding of these things" we must examine their concept of the
good heart which functions both in their kinship system and religion to maintain the effectiveness of the "wall of Hopiness." Of
greatest significance in all activities among these people, and
particularly in their religious ceremonies, is the fact that everything of importance is done communally. Thus each individual
who has reached maturity is responsible *to* and *for* the whole community. The Hopi speak of this process as "uniting our hearts,"
which in itself is a form of prayer. A slight mistake in a ceremony
can ruin it and thus defeat the community prayer for rain; so too
can a trace of "badness" in one's heart, although it may not be
visible to the observer. Thus their religion teaches that *all* distress—from illness to crop failure—is the result of bad hearts, or
possibly of witchcraft (here the simple "bad heart" must not be
confused with a "Two-heart," *powaka*, witch), an extreme form of
personal wickedness in which an individual sacrifices others, particularly his own relatives, to save himself (Titiev, 1942; Aberle,
1951:94).

This concept of a good heart in *conscious contradistinction*
to a bad heart is of greatest importance not only in understanding
Hopi philosophy but also in understanding their deep sense of
cultural continuity and their resistance to fundamental change. A
good heart is a positive thing, something which is never out of a
Hopi's mind. It means a heart at peace with itself and one's fellows.
There is no worry, unhappiness, envy, malice, nor any other disturbing emotion in a good heart. In this state, coöperation, whether
in the extended household or in the fields and ceremonies, was self-
less and easy. Unfortunately, such a conception of a good heart
is also impossible of attainment. Yet if a Hopi did not keep a good
heart he might fall ill and die, or the ceremonies—and thus the
vital crops—might fail, for, as has been said, only those with good
hearts were effective in prayer. Thus we see that the Hopi concept
of a good heart included conformity to all rules of Hopi good con-

duct, both external and internal. To the extent that it was internalized—and all Hopi biographical material known to the writer suggests strongly that it was effectively internalized—it might reasonably be called a quite universal culturally patterned and culturally consistent Hopi "super-ego."[15]

There was, therefore, a constant probing of one's own heart, well illustrated by the anguished cry of a Hopi friend, "Dorothy, *did* my son die as the old folks said because my heart was not right? Do *you* believe this way, that if parents do not keep good hearts children will die?" And there was a constant examination of one's neighbors' hearts: "Movensie, it is those——clan people who ruined this ceremony! They have bad hearts and they quarrel too much. That bad wind came up and now we will get no rain." Conversation among the Hopi is rarely censored, and the children heard both of these women's remarks, *feeling*, you may be sure, the *absolute belief* which these "teachers" had in the *danger* which a bad heart carries for everyone in the group.

In such situations, since human beings can bear only a certain amount of guilt,[16] there is a great game of blame-shifting among the Hopi, and this in turn adds a further burden of unconscious guilt, for it is difficult to love properly a neighbor or even a sister who has a bad heart. However, in the absence of political organization, civil and criminal laws, and a formal method of punishment for adults, this consistent "tribal super-ego" has maintained, throughout known history, a record almost devoid of crime and violence within the group,[17] and it has conditioned and ever *reconditioned* a Hopi to feel secure only in being a Hopi.

---

[15] See Piers and Singer, 1953, p. 6, where Dr. Piers defines "Super-Ego" as stemming from the internalization of the punishing, restrictive aspects of parental images, real or projected.

[16] See Dr. Piers' definition of guilt and of shame (Piers and Singer, 1953, pp. 5, 16). Hopi reactions are not classified here either in terms of guilt or of shame, since, as Singer points out on p. 52, an attempt to do so can confuse rather than clarify. In my opinion, both shame and guilt are operative in the Hopi "good heart," but it is suggested that the reader compare the material discussed here with the hypotheses in *Shame and Guilt*, particularly with Singer's conclusions in chap. V.

[17] Cf. Hallowell, 1955, chap. IV, on the positive role anxiety may play in a society.

For through the great strength of the emotional orientations conveyed within the kinship framework and the interwoven religious beliefs, young Hopi learned their world from dedicated teachers whose emotions were involved in teaching what they believed intensely, and this in turn engaged the children's emotions in learning. These experiences early and increasingly made explicit in a very personal way the values implicit in the distinction between a good heart and a bad heart. For public opinion, if intensely felt and openly expressed in a closely knit and mutually dependent group—as in the case of the child who left her baby sister alone—can be more effective potential punishment than the electric chair. It is perhaps easier to die quickly than to live in loneliness in a small community in the face of contempt from one's fellows, and particularly from one's clan from whence, as we have seen, comes most of one's physical and emotional security. Small wonder that the children who experience this constant pressure to conform to clan dictates and needs, and at the same time this constant reinforcement of clan solidarity against outsiders, are reluctant as adults to stray too far from the clan's protective familiarity or to defy its wishes.

There was much bickering and tension within the clan and village, of course, and it was a source of constant uneasiness and ambivalence among the Hopi.[18] But tension and bickering, as I have indicated elsewhere, "are not exclusively Hopi"; the Hopi see it constantly among the Whites on and off the reservation. What they do *not* find elsewhere is the *emotional satisfaction* of belonging intensely, to which they have been conditioned and reconditioned. For, as Murphy says, "It is not only the 'desire to be accepted' . . . that presses the ego into line. The basic psychology of perception is involved; the individual has learned to see himself

---

[18] In a short paper it is impossible to discuss both sides of this question adequately, but these tensions, and a Hopi's final acceptance of them, are discussed in D. Eggan, 1948, particularly pp. 232–234. Cf. Thompson and Joseph, 1944, chap. 16, where Joseph speaks of fear born of the internally overdisciplined self in Hopi children, and its role both in adult discord and social integration. See also Thompson, 1945, for hypotheses regarding the integration of ideal Hopi culture. Aberle (1951) discusses various tensions in Hopi society; see especially p. 94. All authors, however, call attention to the compensations as well as the burdens in Hopi society.

as a member of the group, and the self has true 'membership character,' structurally integrated with the perception of group life" (Murphy, 1947:855; Asch, 1952:334–335, 605). Actually the Hopi clan, even with its in-group tensions and strife, but with all of the advantages emotional and physical it affords the individual, is one of the most successful and meaningful "boarding schools" ever devised for citizenship training.

In this situation, where belonging was so important, and a good heart so vital to the feeling of belonging, gossip is the potential and actual "social cancer" of the Hopi tribe. It is devastating to individual security and is often senselessly false and cruel, but in a country where coöperation was the only hope of survival, it was the *servant* as well as the policeman of the tribe. Not lightly would any Hopi voluntarily acquire the title Kahopi[19] "*not* Hopi," and therefore not good. Throughout the Hopi life span the word kahopi, *kahopi,* KAHOPI was heard, until it penetrated to the very core of one's mind. It was said softly and gently at first to tiny offenders, through "Kahopi tiyo" or "Kahopi mana" to older children, still quietly but with stern intent, until the word sometimes assumed a crescendo of feeling as a whole clan or even a whole community might condemn an individual as *Kahopi.*

It is true that we, too, are told we should keep good hearts and love our neighbors as ourselves. But we are not told that, if we do not, our babies will die, *now, this year!* Some children are told that if they do not obey the various "commandments" they learn in different churches they will eventually burn in a lake of hell fire, but they usually know that many of their world doubt this. In contrast, Hopi children constantly *saw* babies die because a parent's heart was not right; they *saw* evil winds come up and crops fail for the same reason; they *saw* adults sicken and die because of bad thoughts or witchcraft (to which bad thoughts rendered a person more vulnerable). Thus they learned to *fear* the results of a bad heart whether it belonged to themselves or to others. There were witches, bogey Kachinas, and in objective reality famine and thirst to fear. Along with these fears were taught mechanisms for the displacement of anxiety, including the

---

[19] See Brandt, 1954. In his study of Hopi ethical concepts, *Kahopi* is discussed on p. 92.

services of medicine men, confession and exorcism to get rid of bad thoughts, and coöperative nonaggression with one's fellows, even those who were known to be witches. But the best technique was that which included all the values in the positive process of keeping a good heart, and of "uniting our hearts" in family, clan, and fraternal society—in short, the best protection was to be *Hopi* rather than *Kahopi*.

It is clear throughout the literature on the Hopi, as well as from the quotations given in this discussion, that in finding their way toward the goal of "belonging" Hopi children at first initiation had to deal with religious disenchantment, resentment, and with ever increasing demands made by their elders for more mature behavior. These factors were undoubtedly important catalyzing agents in Hopi personality formation and should be examined from the standpoint of Benedict's formulations on discontinuity (Benedict, 1948: 424–423). Here we must remember that shock can operate either to destroy or to mobilize an organism's dormant potentialities. And if a child has been *consistently* conditioned to feel a part of his intimate world, and providing he still lives on in this same world; it seems reasonable to suppose that shock (unless it were so great as to completely disorganize personality, in which case the custom could not have persisted) would reinforce the individual's *need* to belong and thus would tend to reassemble many of his personality resources around this need.

If the world surrounding the Hopi child had changed from warmth to coldness, from all pleasure to all hardship, the discontinuity would have indeed been insupportable. But the new demands made on him, while more insistent, were not unfamiliar in *kind;* all adults, as well as his newly initiated age-mates, faced the same ones. He had shared the shock as he had long since learned to share all else; and he now shared the rewards of "feeling big." He had the satisfaction of increased status along with the burden of increasing responsibility, as the adults continued to teach him "the important things," and conformity gradually became a value in itself—even as we value nonconformity and change. It was both the means *and* the goal. Conformity surrounded the Hopi—child or adult—with everything he could hope to have or to be; outside it there was only the feeling tone of rejection. Since there were no bewildering choices presented (as is the case in our socialization process), the "maturation drive"[20] could only function to produce an ego-ideal in accord with the cultural ideal,[21] however wide the discrepancy between ideal and reality on both levels.

And since the Kachinas played such a vital role in Hopi society throughout, we must consider specifically the way in which the altered faith expressed by informants gradually came about after the first initiation (Aberle, 1951:38–41). First, of course, was the need to find it, since in any environment one must have faith and hope. They also wanted to continue to believe in and to enjoy that which from earliest memory had induced a feeling of pleasure, excitement, and of solidarity within the group. A beginning was undoubtedly made in modifying resentment when the Kachinas whipped each other after first initiation; first, it was again sharing punishment, but this time not only with children but *with adults*. They had long known that suffering came from bad hearts; they also knew, as indicated above, that something must be done about bad hearts. The Kachinas whipped to cleanse the bad hearts implied by disobedience to the rules of Hopi good conduct and then whipped each other for the same reason; thus there was logic in an initiation which was actually an extension of an already established conception of masked gods who rewarded good behavior with presents but withheld rain if hearts were not right, and who sometimes threatened bad children (Goldfrank, 1945: 516–539).

Another reorganizing factor explicitly stated in the quotations was "feeling big." They had shared pain with adults, had learned secrets which forever separated them from the world of children, and they were now included in situations from which they had previously been excluded, as their elders continued to teach intensely what they believed intensely: that for them there was only one alternative—Hopi as against Kahopi.

---

[20] See Piers (in Piers and Singer, 1953, p. 15) for a discussion of the maturation drive.

[21] Erikson, 1948, p. 198, fn: "The child derives a vitalizing sense of reality from the awareness that his individual way of mastering experience (his ego-synthesis) is a successful variant of a group identity and is in accord with its space-time and life plan."

Consistent repetition is a powerful conditioning agent and, as the youngsters watched each initiation, they relived their own, and by again sharing the experience gradually worked out much of the bitter residue from their own memories of it, while also rationalizing and weaving the group emotions ever stronger into their own emotional core—"It takes a while to see how wise the old people really are." An initiated boy, in participating in the Kachina dances, learned to identify again with the Kachinas whom he now impersonated. To put on a mask is to "become a Kachina," and to coöperate actively in bringing about the major goals of Hopi life. And a girl came to know more fully the importance of her clan in its supportive role. These experiences were even more sharply conditioned and directed toward adult life in the tribal initiation ceremonies, of which we have as yet only fragmentary knowledge. Of this one man said to me: "I will not discuss this thing with you only to say that no one can forget it. It is the most wonderful thing any man can have to remember. You know then that you are Hopi. It is one thing Whites cannot have, cannot take from us. It is our way of life given to us when the world began."

And since children are, for all mankind, a restatement of one's hopes to be, when these Hopi in turn became teachers (and in a sense they had always been teachers of the younger children in the household from an early age), they continued the process of reliving and rationalizing, or "working out" their experiences with an intensity which is rarely known in our society except, perhaps, on the psychoanalytic couch. But the Hopi had no psychiatrists to guide them—no books which, as Riesman says, "like an invisible monitor, helps liberate the reader from his group and its emotions, and allows the contemplation of alternative responses and the trying on of new emotions" (Riesman, 1955:13). They had only the internalized "feeling measure" and "group measure" explicit in the concepts of Hopi versus Kahopi.

On the material level, the obvious advantages of, for instance, wagons versus backs were a temptation. And to the extent to which White influences at first penetrated to these older Hopi it was through this form of temptation. But outside experiences usually included some variation of hostility, scorn, or aggression, as well as a radically different moral code, and these were all viewed and reinterpreted through the Hopi-eye view of the world and in the Hopi language, so that a return to the familiarity of the Hopi world with its solidarity of world view and behavior patterns *was experienced as relief*, and increased the need to feel Hopi, *however great a burden "being Hopi"* implied.

In summary, the hypothesis here developed, that strong emotional conditioning during the learning process was an instrument in cultural continuity among the Hopi, is suggested as supplementary to that of early learning as being resistant to change. It further suggests that this conditioning was *constantly* as well as *consistently* instilled during the entire lifetime of an individual by a circular pattern of integration. For an individual was surrounded by a series of invisible, but none the less solid, barriers between himself and the outside world. To change him, influences had to breach the concentric walls of social process—as conveyed through the human entities which surrounded him and which were strengthened by his obligation to teach others—and then to recondition his early and ever increasing emotional involvement in Hopi religion, morals, and mutually dependent lineage and clan groups, as well as those attitudes toward White aggression which he shared with all Indians.

In 1938 one old Hopi, who in his youth had been taken away from his wife and children and kept in a boarding school for several years, said to me:

> I am full of curiosity; a great *bahana* [White] education would tell me many things I've wondered about like the stars and how a man's insides work. But I am afraid of it because I've seen what it does to folks. . . . If I raise a family, clothe and feed them well, do my ceremonial duties faithfully, I have succeeded—what do you call success? . . . [And again, while discussing fear in connection with a dream, his comment was] Well, yes, we are afraid of *powakas* [witches] but our medicine men can handle them. Neither your doctors nor your gods can control your governments so you have more to fear. Now you are dragging us into your quarrels. I pity you and I don't envy you. You have more goods than we have, but you don't have peace ever; *it is better to die in famine than in war.*

As the old man anticipated, enforced participation in modern warfare soon replaced instruction for Hopi citizenship, and the concentric walls were finally seriously breached. But for these older Hopi the walls still enclose "our way of life given to us when the world began."

References

Aberle, David F., 1951, *The Psychosocial Analysis of a Hopi Life-History*. Comparative Psychology Monographs, 21:1–133. Berkeley and Los Angeles, Calif.: University of California Press.

Adair, John, and Evon Z. Vogt, 1949, "Navaho and Zuni Veterans: a Study of Contrasting Modes of Culture Change." *American Anthropologist*, 51:547–561.

Allport, Gordon W., 1951 ,"The Personality Trait," in Melvin H. Marx, ed., *Psychological Theory: Contemporary Readings*, pp. 503–507. New York: The Macmillan Company.

Asch, Solomon E., 1952, *Social Psychology*. Englewood Cliffs, N.J.: Prentice-Hall, Inc.

Benedict, Ruth, 1948, "Continuities and Discontinuities in Cultural Conditioning," in Clyde Kluckhohn and Henry A. Murray, eds., *Personality in Nature, Society, and Culture*, pp. 414–423. New York: Alfred A. Knopf, Inc.

Brandt, Richard B., 1954, *Hopi Ethics: a Theoretical Analysis*. Chicago: The University of Chicago Press.

Bruner, Edward M., 1956a, "Cultural Transmission and Cultural Change." *Southwestern Journal of Anthropology*, 12:191–199.

———, 1956b, "Primary Group Experience and the Process of Acculturation." *American Anthropologist*, 58:605–623.

Dennis, Wayne, 1941, "The Socialization of the Hopi Child," in Leslie Spier, A. Irving Hallowell, and Stanley S. Newman, eds., *Language, Culture, and Personality: Essays in Memory of Edward Sapir*, pp. 259–271. Menasha, Wis.: Sapir Memorial Publication Fund.

Dozier, Edward P., 1954, *The Hopi-Tewa of Arizona*. University of California Publications in American Archaeology and Ethnology, 44:259–376, Berkeley and Los Angeles, Calif.: University of California Press.

———, 1955, "Forced and Permissive Acculturation." *American Anthropologist*, 56:973–1002.

DuBois, Cora, 1941, "Attitudes toward Food and Hunger in Alor," in Leslie Spier, A. Irving Hallowell, and Stanley S. Newman, eds., *Language, Culture, and Personality: Essays in Memory of Edward Sapir*, pp. 272–281. Menasha, Wis.: Sapir Memorial Publication Fund.

———, 1955, "Some Notions on Learning Intercultural Understanding," in George D. Spindler, ed., *Education and Anthropology*, pp. 89–126. Stanford, Calif.: Stanford University Press.

Earle, Edwin, and Edward A. Kennard, 1938, *Hopi Kachinas*. New York: J. J. Augustin, Publisher.

Eggan, Dorothy, 1948, "The General Problem of Hopi Adjustment," in Clyde Kluckhohn and Henry A. Murray, eds., *Personality in Nature, Society, and Culture*, pp. 220–235. New York: Alfred A. Knopf, Inc.

———, 1955, "The Personal Use of Myth in Dreams," in "Myth: a Symposium," *Journal of American Folklore*, 68:445–453.

Eggan, Fred, 1950, *Social Organization of the Western Pueblos*. Chicago: The University of Chicago Press.

Erikson, Erik Homburger, 1948, "Childhood and Tradition in Two American Indian Tribes, with Some Reflections on the Contemporary American Scene," in Clyde Kluckhohn and Henry A. Murray, eds., *Personality in Nature, Society, and Culture*, pp. 176–203. New York: Alfred A. Knopf, Inc.

Goldfrank, Esther, 1945, "Socialization, Personality, and the Structure of Pueblo Society." *American Anthropologist*, 47:516–539.

Hallowell, A. Irving, 1953, "Culture, Personality, and Society," in *Anthropology Today: an Encyclopedic Inventory*, by A. L. Kroeber and others, pp. 597–620. Chicago: University of Chicago Press.

———, 1955, *Culture and Experience*. Philadelphia: University of Pennsylvania Press.

Henry, Jules, 1955, "Culture, Education, and Communications Theory," in George D. Spindler, ed., *Education and Anthropology*, pp. 188–215. Stanford, Calif.: Stanford University Press.

Herskovits, Melville J., 1950, *Man and His Works: the Science of Cultural Anthropology*. New York: Alfred A. Knopf, Inc.

Hough, Walter, 1915, *The Hopi Indians*. Cedar Rapids, Iowa: The Torch Press.

Keesing, Felix M., 1953, *Culture Change: an Analysis and Bibliography of Anthropological Sources to 1952*. Stanford, Calif.: Stanford University Press.

Kluckhohn, Clyde, 1951, "Values and Value-Orientations in the Theory of Action: an Exploration in Definition and Classification," in Talcott Parsons and Edward A. Shils, eds., *Toward a General Theory of Action*, pp. 388–433. Cambridge, Mass.: Harvard University Press.

———, and Florence R. Kluckhohn, 1947, "American Culture: Generalized Orientations and Class Patterns," in *Conflicts of Power in Modern Culture*. 1947 Symposium of Conference in Science, Philosophy, and Religion, Chap. IX.

Mead, Margaret, 1931, "The Primitive Child," in *A Handbook of Child Psychology*, pp. 669–687. Worcester, Mass.: Clark University Press.

———, 1943, "Our Education Emphases in Primitive Perspective." *American Journal of Sociology*, 48:633–639.

———, 1948, "Social Change and Cultural Surrogates," in Clyde Kluckhohn and Henry A. Murray, eds., *Personality in Nature, Society, and Culture*, pp. 511–522. New York: Alfred A. Knopf, Inc.

———, 1953, *Growing Up in New Guinea*. A Mentor Book, publ. by The New American Library, New York; first publ., 1930, by William Morrow & Company, Inc.

Murphy, Gardner, 1947. *Personality: a Biosocial Approach to Origins and Structure*. New York: Harper & Row, Publishers.

Park, Robert Ezra, 1950, *Race and Culture*. New York: The Free Press of Glencoe, Inc.

Pettit, George A., 1946, *Primitive Education in North America*. University of California Publications in American Archaeology and Ethnology, 43:1–182. Berkeley and Los Angeles: University of California Press.

Piers, Gerhart, and Milton B. Singer, 1953, *Shame and Guilt: a Psychoanalytic and a Cultural Study*. Springfield, Ill.: Charles C Thomas, Publishers.

Redfield, Robert, 1953, *The Primitive World and Its Transformations*. Ithaca, N.Y.: Cornell University Press.

———, 1955, *The Little Community: Viewpoints for the Study of a Human Whole*. Chicago: The University of Chicago Press.

Riesman, David, 1955, *The Oral Tradition, The Written Word, and the Screen Image*. Founders Day Lecture, no. 1, Antioch College, October 5, 1955.

Riesman, David, in collaboration with Reuel Denney and Nathan Glazer, 1950, *The Lonely Crowd: a Study of the Changing American Character*. New Haven, Conn.: Yale University Press.

Sapir, Edward, 1949, "The Emergence of the Concept of Personality in a Study of Cultures," in David G. Mandelbaum, ed., *Selected Writings of Edward Sapir in Language, Culture, and Personality*, pp. 590–597. Berkeley and Los Angeles, Calif.: University of California Press.

Simmons, Leo W., 1942, *Sun Chief: the Autobiography of a Hopi Indian*. Publ. for The Institute of Human Relations by Yale University Press, New Haven, Conn.

[SSRC] Social Science Research Council Summer Seminar on Acculturation, 1954, "Acculturation: an Exploratory Formulation." *American Anthropologist*, 56:973–1002.

Spindler, George D., ed., 1955, *Education and Anthropology*. Stanford, Calif.: Stanford University Press.

Spiro, Melford E., 1955, "The Acculturation of American Ethnic Groups." *American Anthropologist*, 57:1240–1252.

Stephen, Alexander MacGregor, 1940, *Hopi Indians of Arizona*. Southwest Museum Leaflets, no. 14. Highland Park, Los Angeles, Calif.: Southwest Museum.

Steward, Julian H., 1931, "Notes on Hopi Ceremonies in Their Initiatory Form in 1927–1928." *American Anthropologist*, 33:56–79.

Thompson, Laura, 1945, "Logico-Aesthetic Integration in Hopi Culture." *American Anthropologist*, 47:540–553.

Thompson, Laura, and Alice Joseph, 1944, *The Hopi Way*. Indian Education Research Series, no. 1. Lawrence, Kan.: Haskell Institute.

Titiev, Mischa, 1942, *Notes on Hopi Witchcraft*. Papers of the Michigan Academy of Science, Arts, and Letters, 28:549–557.

———, 1944, *Old Oraibi: a Study of the Hopi Indians of Third*

Mesa. Papers of the Peabody Museum of American Archaeology and Ethnology, Harvard University, vol. 22, no. 1.

Vogt, Evon Z., 1951, *Navaho Veterans, a Study of Changing
Values*. Papers of the Peabody Museum of American Archaeology and Ethnology, Harvard University, vol. 41, no. 1.

Whiting, John W. M., and Irvin L. Child, 1953, *Child Training
and Personality: a Cross-Cultural Study*. New Haven, Conn.:
Yale University Press.

Whorf, B. L., 1941, "The Relation of Habitual Thought and Behavior to Language," in Leslie Spier, A. Irving Hallowell, and
Stanley S. Newman, eds., *Language, Culture, and Personality: Essays in Memory of Edward Sapir*, pp. 75–93. Menasha,
Wis.: Sapir Memorial Publication Fund.

18———George D. Spindler

Personality, Sociocultural System, and Education among the Menomini

Every society tends to favor certain personality types. This is a matter of common sense. The heroes of myth, folklore, and literature display this idealization. Best selling English and best selling American novels stress different personal qualities in their heroes and heroines, and different qualities of excitement (Cooper, 1955). Hopi mothers tell their children not to be "ka-hopi", and they have an ideal in mind against which they contrast undesired behaviors and traits. American mothers tell their little sons, "Stand up for yourself—don't let him push you around!" and they have an image of the man they want their sons to grow up to be in the back of their minds.

What is not so clearly a matter of common sense observation, though social scientists have written about it for some time, is that a given kind of social system *requires* certain kinds of psychological structures in people in order to make the social system work.[1] As Erich Fromm has made so clear, the problem is how people in a given society come to want to act as they have to act if the social structure is going to function properly, and at the same time find gratification in acting this way (Fromm, 1941; 1949).

---

[1] I have been particularly influenced by Fromm (1941), Weber (1930), Kardiner (1945), Linton (1945), Riesman (1950), Parsons (1955), Merton (1949), Parsons and Shils (1951), and Inkeles (1954). Readers who would like to examine some recent reviews of the problems involved will find the following useful: Inkeles (1958), Kaplan (1957), Parsons (1961), Hsu (1961). The casebook assembled by Cohen (1961) is particularly notable for its scope and its organization of relevant materials.

This chapter is concerned with the ways in which certain aspects of the personality structure modal among the native-oriented personnel of the Menomini Indian community interact to maintain, and at the same time are maintained by, the sociocultural system of that group, and how this personality structure is created through educational experience. My purpose is not only to analyze the Menomini situation, because this situation is in itself interesting, but also to treat it as a case that will illustrate crucial relationships that have significant implications for other cases, including our own. It may seem to some readers that a small, homogeneous, enclaved group of native-oriented Indians is too far removed from the heterogeneous, worldly complexity characterizing school populations in our society. One should never, it is true, make the error of assuming that a one-to-one correlation will obtain between any two unlike situations, and particularly this is true for projections from tradition-oriented enclaves to complex changing societies. It is also true that due to the loss of certain aspects of the sociocultural system and the small number of people in the group the native-oriented Menomini are very homogeneous. Therefore a high degree of uniformity between culture and personality can be expected. What I wish to strive for in this analysis is *understanding;* understanding of dynamic relationships that can serve as starting points for analysis of similar relationships in other settings, just as the clinician can use his understanding of an individual personality in a unique setting and with unique problems to understand other personalities in different settings and with different problems. The virtue of the small, homogeneous, enclave situation is that the relationships can be understood relatively easily. Understanding these relationships can serve as a significant step towards formulation of working hypotheses for study of more complex cases, taking into account the ambiguities inherent in those situations.

DEFINITIONS OF CONCEPTS

"Social system" and "cultural patterning" have been combined in this chapter under the term *sociocultural system.* By "social system" I refer to the ordering of people into statuses and roles, such as in positions of authority and in kinship categories; the interaction occurring between people occupying these positions; the alignment of groups in equivalent, superordinate, or subordinate, positions of power, prestige, and responsibility; and the structuring of activities by economic and subsistence needs. By "cultural patterning" I refer to a wide range of directive, or prescriptive, orientations, varying from highly specific directive patterns such as ritual and verbalized belief, through values of all levels of specificity, to broad thematic orientations. I regard specific cultural directives for behavior as implemented through roles connected with statuses ordered by the social system, and thematic orientations and values as merging into the area normally designated as "personality structure."

By "personality structure" I refer to the organization of emotional and intellectual resources characteristic of individuals. I do not regard this organization as fixed, or as necessarily even stable, under certain conditions. Where sociocultural continuity is maintained, and the demands upon the individual in social interaction therefore exhibit continuity, the personality will also exhibit continuity, excepting in cases of severe mental illness. When sociocultural conditions change the individual struggles to adapt to these conditions, and in so doing, the organization of his emotional and intellectual resources changes. This changing, adaptive, organization will, however, exhibit certain broad continuities with the previously stabilized personality—this is what anthropological studies of psychological process in culture change situations indicate (Mekeel, 1936; Thompson, 1948; Hallowell, 1951; Spindler and Spindler, 1957). This psychological organization develops out of interaction with people (parents, teachers, peers) as cultural agents who are carrying out roles provided by the social system and cultural patterning of their group, but who are modifying these roles constantly as adjustments are made to various situations and as they are interpreted by the individual cultural agent. The developing child encountering these agents identifies with specific persons and specific roles, as perceived through his experience. He internalizes certain directives structured into these roles and merely acknowledges others—depending upon the stringency of their demands, the emotional investment given them by the cultural agents he encounters, and the role relationship existing between the individual and these cultural agents. He also *reacts* to these directives—both as he encounters them and after they are internalized— frequently at a "preconscious" or "subverbal" level of interaction within his own psyche. His reactions, his "acknowledgments," and his internalization as well as the responses to his behavior that he perceives in others are the material out of which his personality structure develops. His personality is therefore a dynamic and sometimes delicate equilibrium of forces. Dramatic changes are sometimes possible in this organization because changed conditions call latent forces in the personality to the fore. The personality equilibrium is dependent to a large extent upon the kinds and intensity of conflicts in directives encountered during socialization, and the ways in which the individual's reactions to culturally patterned directives are interpreted by the cultural agents he encounters.

The "modal" personality is that organization of emotional and intellectual resources, created out of the process of "encounter," exhibited most frequently by members of a group. It need not characterize a numerical majority, since subgroups where different personality structures are functional and complementary to each other are a part of most social systems. Nor do we need to deal with the whole personality structure. The features of this organization that are most relevant (most functional) in the particular sociocultural setting are of the greatest interest to us in the kind of analysis this chapter pursues. These features will be shared more widely among the members of a group than any one whole personality type can be. I follow Inkeles (1954, p. 980) in calling these features together the "socially required personality," but depart from his logic in regarding the characteristics thus subsumed as potentially empirically modal (statistically derivable) in a group, rather than as inferable largely from the "collective policies and products" of social institutions.

The concepts described above will be applied in the analysis to follow without extensive restatement or qualification. I am taking the liberty of compressing "social system" and "cultural patterning" into *sociocultural system* for purposes of this analysis. The rationale for this follows from the definitions provided; since cultural patterning is implemented in social interaction through roles attached to statuses provided by the social system and socialization occurs through encounters with cultural agents playing these roles, it seems justifiable to merge the two concepts. For other purposes they would have to be kept separate. The three dimensions that will be used in the rest of this discussion are therefore: *sociocultural system, socially required modal personality*, and *education*. The latter term includes the encounters between growing children and cultural agents acting out roles that lead to the development of the socially required personality.

THE MENOMINI COMMUNITY

Today the Menomini are a divided people. Numbering about 3000 tribal members, they occupy an area in the woodlands of Wisconsin approximately 400 square miles in extent. Until April of 1961 this was a reservation, set aside for the Menomini and supervised by the Federal Government. Today this area is a separate county in the state of Wisconsin, because the Menomini have been "terminated"—all federal control has been removed and the Menomini are on their own. They are a divided people because not all members of the tribe have moved at the same speed towards assimilation into the dominant American sociocultural system. Some of them, a group I have termed "elite acculturated" in previous publications (Spindler, 1955), appear to be totally assimilated. They wear business suits and sports clothes, drive new cars, live in substantial homes, and earn their living in managerial or supervisory capacities in the lumber and mill industry from which the bulk of the Menomini make their living. Others are equally assimilated, but earn their living by working at semiskilled or unskilled jobs lower on the socio-economic scale of the dominant society. Still others are socioculturally "transitional." They are suspended between traditional and modern forms of behavior and belief. Some of these people are struggling for advancement on dominant American terms. Some are socially and psychologically disorganized and engage in activities that get them into trouble with the law. Some are apathetic, and vegetate. All of the transitionals suffer from much cultural loss and little cultural gain. Another group on the reservation, a very small one, belongs to the Peyote Church. This group is systematically deviant from the rest of the Menomini, both socioculturally and psychologically (Spindler, 1952; Slotkin, 1952), and have joined the church as a way out of the transitional dilemma. There remains yet another group, also small, but very significant—the native-oriented group. Numbering approximately seventy persons, including all ages and both sexes, this group carries on an attentuated, yet recognizable version of the traditional Menomini culture. The ancient Medicine Lodge still functions intermittently. The Dream Dance membership holds its annual seasonal rites and frequent "song services." Ghost feasts for the dead, naming ceremonies for newly born children, ritual sacrifices for inherited guardian spirits are observed. Kinship usages dictated by traditional conceptions are operating, though not intact. And particularly important for our purposes—the concepts of the universe and of the proper state of human affairs—are maintained and acted upon as living conceptions.

It is this native-oriented group, living in the main together at one end of the Menomini area, that I will describe within the framework of concepts developed on previous pages. There will be no attempt to reconstruct the totality of the traditional Menomini way of life, though occasional reference to changes in the culture of this group will be made. The group will be discussed as a living entity, in a present-day environment, where a personality type that is markedly different from most types encountered in our society is modal to the group because it is socially required.

The Native-oriented Menomini Personality

After a year away from our friends in the native-oriented group we[2] returned, full of anticipation and excitement

---

[2] By "we" I mean my wife, myself and our (then) ten-year-old daughter. In other contexts "we" will refer to my wife and myself, having collaborated on all phases of the research. We started field work with the Menomini in 1948 and continued working each summer through 1954. We have visited the Menomini for short periods of a week or two since then in 1957, 1959, and 1961.

at the prospect of seeing the people again and participating in the ceremonies and dances. We had been doing research in the area for three full summers by then, and during the last summer had become intimately familiar with individuals in the group. We had gone cherry-picking with them to Sturgeon Bay, eaten their food, entertained them at our camp, attended Dream Dance services, and even danced with them for the tourists.

Then we had gone away, back to the university, and back into what seemed then to us a tight, conventional routine. We had thought all winter long about the forests and streams, the people and the excitement of doing field work among them, and now we were back again. After establishing our camp on a lake nearby, we drove to the native-oriented community called *Zoar*. No one was in sight at the houses close to the main highway where it cut through the dense forest, so we turned up one of the dirt roads leading back to the clusters of quonset style, board and roofing paper houses, bark wigwams, and log cabins in which the people lived. As we approached one of these clusters near the Zoar community hall where the Dream Dance rituals were held, we saw a group standing and sitting about. Some of the men were playing poker on a blanket spread on the ground. Others were kibitzing. We parked our car, got out, and tried to walk casually, not run, into the circle of what we perceived as old friends who would greet us with the enthusiasm of long-lost members of the family. But we had forgotten what the native-oriented Menomini were like! Expressionless faces greeted us. Some even turned away, as though preoccupied with other matters more interesting. Only the children stared, but quietly. I walked over to the group of people clustered around the poker game and joined the kibitzers. Ranks opened so I had a place to stand and a clear view of the game, but otherwise no special notice was taken of my arrival. I stood across from a man about my age with whom I had, I felt, formed an especially close friendship, and who had been enormously helpful to me in my research in the past. He continued with his game, taking no notice of me whatsoever. I began to feel acutely uncomfortable. Perhaps there had been a long winter of gossip about the white strangers who had invaded their privacy for too long. Perhaps we were suspect of witchcraft, or at least of bringing bad luck. Finally, after several minutes of paranoid fantasy on my part, my friend Nepenahkwat[3] glanced up, smiled quietly, and said calmly, "Hello George, I see you made it." And then continued with his game.

We stayed for several hours that afternoon. During the first hours we gradually became aware of the fact that the people were glad to see us, that they had thought about us during our absence, and that they had looked forward to our return. We also re-established our timing and role-taking in social interaction with native-oriented Menomini. We realized again that these were different people, with a different psychology, and a different set of norms for proper behavior. Overt emotionality is not displayed. The loud, overstated greeting normal for the situation in our own society would not only have been in very bad taste according to Menomini standards, but it would have been virtually impossible for a native-oriented Menomini adult, properly educated and formed in the traditional framework, to act that way even if he had, conceivably, wanted to.

Another summer we returned to find nearly everyone in the native-oriented group gone. We later found out that they were gathering ferns from the forest to sell in nearby towns for the making of floral displays and funeral wreaths. We turned here and there on the back roads hoping to find someone who had stayed behind. Smoke curling up from one of the shacks announced that someone had. We tapped on the door, and the voice of a woman who had formed the same relationship with my wife as Nepenahkwat had with me came through the plank door, "Come in." We entered and found her sitting by a table. A small child sat playing quietly on the floor. Another lay in the bed, covered with blankets. Her oldest boy was off with the others picking ferns, as we discovered later. A new baby lay on the bed, heavily swaddled. Our friend smiled, "We wondered when you were coming." And after a moment of silence, "It's too bad all the others are gone, but they'll be back next week."

We sat down and chatted about things for about a half an hour. During this time we both began to feel somewhat uneasy.

---

[3] Where Menomini names or terms are used I will approximate the phonetic spelling with standard letters.

Our friend did not seem quite as relaxed as we remembered her to be. Then the child on the bed began to cry restlessly. She got up slowly and walked hesitatingly to the bed to stroke her daughter's head. Then turned to us almost apologetically to say, "She's got some kind of illness. She's hot, and she hasn't kept anything down for two days." We did what we could—gave the child a little aspirin—and offered to take her in to the hospital to see the doctor. Then it dawned on us that last year there had been no baby and that the one swaddled in blankets looked virtually new-born. "Yes. She's new. She came three days ago." Then the story came out.

Our friend's husband had gone on one of his long trips to a neighboring reservation several hundred miles away. In the meantime our friend had borne her fourth child during his absence and while everyone else was gone. She was isolated. She had no car and could not walk to the highway to get help. Her five year old daughter had become ill. There was no food left in the house. She said all of this quietly, with none of the hysteria or blaming that would have been normal for a woman in similar circumstances in our world. She merely stated the facts. Of course we immediately took action, and the crisis passed.

She retained her emotional control under what seemed to us to be a most trying situation. But it is not exactly correct to say that she "retained her emotional control." The hysteria that would have mounted over the long hours of isolation and misery in a white woman in our society was never there in the first place, so she was not "controlling" it. She was fearful, but she feared the realities of the situation. She did what she could, and then she did what other Menomini have done in similar circumstances—she waited. She was not sure that something would happen to solve her crisis, but she let fate take over when she had done what she could within her framework of doing. She displayed a quality that we can call *equanimity under duress*. She also displayed a dependent, waiting attitude towards fate, and what it might bring. She had made a sacrifice of food and tobacco to the Dream Dance drum for which she was the keeper, and that rested in its coverings on a special bench on the eastern side of her kitchen, where the light of the new day would touch it each morning through the nearby window. So she had reason to hope that the spirits might take notice of her predicament and take pity on her. Apparently it worked, from her point of view, as it had many times in the past.

As her brother had told me one time, "Yah, that's the way it is. I'm one of those guys that have not much, but I've got those drums there. [He kept two in his house.] It seems the last minute I always get something. That's the way it was with my Dad too. Somebody was always bound to bring him something. That job I got in the woods, it's a low salary job. They got better jobs, those others, but they're always out of everything before I am. They have to come over here—we always have something. My wife sees that, she says, 'Even though they get more, they only have to come over here, and ask us for something'."

This characteristic attitude, or quality, of waiting, of quiescent expectancy, we may term, following Louise Spindler (1962), "latescence." The term stands for a complex of related qualities —passivity, quiescence, receptive expectancy. It is the key theme to much that characterizes the modal personality of the native-oriented Menomini personality, and I will demonstrate later on that it is a *socially required* quality. This pervasive feature of personality is most fully developed among the adult women of the group. They are fully participating members of the group in all of its activities, but they do not take the instrumental, public roles of leadership in religious ceremonies or subsistence activities. They are therefore more subdued in their social behavior than are the men, and the latescent quality is most apparent. But it is shared by both sexes in degrees appropriate to their roles.

The quality of *equanimity under duress* is closely related but not identical to latescence. The stoic quality that makes equanimity possible (or vice versa) makes for endurance. Passive, quiescent, waiting expectancy is an important part of the Menomini ability to endure privation and hardship, but latescence is based on the expectancy that if the proper rituals are performed the fates will provide—unless the fates decide otherwise—while *equanimity under duress* is part of a survival drive, which takes into account the realities of the situation and makes it possible to retain the necessary emotional balance even when the reality conditions are very threatening.

The other quality apparent in these descriptions of behavior is that of marked control of expressive emotionality. I have already indicated that this is not really a correct statement of the actual state of affairs, but the English language does not afford us exactly descriptive terms. In any event, the characteristic conveyed by the description of our reception by the native-oriented group is congruent with the other qualities described above. It is another facet of the same configuration but of a somewhat different order. We may regard it as a product of the other two qualities described, and it is the most easily observable.

This reduction of overt emotional response is very apparent in all interpersonal relationships in the native-oriented group. The interaction rate is so low that coming fresh from tense, high-speed urban society one is thrown completely off his pace for a time. The interviewer is likely to find his questions left in the air for minutes, while the subject sits quietly thinking over his response. Loud voices are most uncommon. A group of twenty native-oriented Menomini can sit in a small room carrying on conversations without the noise level ever reaching the point when one has difficulty hearing his friend—unless his voice is so low as to be almost inaudible, and there are long silences that no one attempts to fill with talk. Silence is not embarrassing. Ordering people about, even children, is not done. Even pointing a finger at someone is considered in poor taste—one points with one's lips. Asking direct questions of anyone is distasteful. One always approaches matters indirectly. "There may be someone here who is unhappy about something," not "What's eating *you?*" Direct criticism of others is not expressed, either in their presence or behind their backs. One might say to another person about someone else, "There could be some people here that don't do just right. Sometimes they could have enough to get along on but they try to get it from someone else." Brusque and discourteous behavior is extremely rare. People go out of their way to avoid arousing ill feelings on the part of others.

Another quality of the modal personality in this group is that of *autonomy*. No one is his neighbor's keeper. The mild and covert resentment expressed about people who come to "borrow" food, indicated in the statements quoted previously reveals this quality to a certain extent. But it goes much farther than this. When a ceremonial gathering is to be announced a *skapewes* (messenger) is appointed. He travels about from house to house, passing tobacco to those who should be notified, and telling them the time and place. But the tobacco is not given to the "head" of the household or family. It is passed to *every person who might be expected to come;* to man and wife, to brother and sister, to each older child. Collective notifications are never given; even when people from another tribe are to be notified it is necessary to travel to the places where they live and pass tobacco to each individual. The same principle applies to transportation. People are expected to arrange their own. Even old people may not be taken care of in this regard, and an old man of eighty, who is important to the conduct of the ceremonial because he is the only one who knows the ritual, will have to stumble across the fields and through the dark woods to the gathering by himself, unless a member of his household happens to be coming to the gathering and the old man is standing by the car when it starts. This is not *individuality*, as we conceive of it. Members of this group conform closely to the norms of the group. Part of this conformity is to be autonomous. No one is anyone else's "boss." No one is responsible for anyone else's welfare, other than in those areas of reciprocation dictated by kinship obligations. No one, not even a father by his own son, can be discredited because of the actions of another.

The modal qualities of the personality structure of the native-oriented Menomini most directly relevant to the interdependent relationship between sociocultural system and personality structure are, in summary: *equanimity under duress, latescence, control of overt emotionality and aggression,* and *autonomy*. This does not exhaust the list of qualities that are exhibited modally among the native-oriented Menomini. For example, a sense of humor is marked. Old *Kimeyowan* attended a tribal council meeting called to discuss the budget for the next year. There was a lot of criticism of past expenditures voiced by the more vocal transitionals and acculturated personnel (who have moved out of the framework of traditional culture and who therefore respond to different norms with different psychological resources). Much of the criticism was directed at a substantial expenditure for installation of heavy machinery to move logs from the collecting pond into the mill, and particularly of a heavy cable suspended across the pond, from which logs were snagged and pulled over to a lift. The debate ranged long and acrimoniously. *Kimeyowan*, who spoke no English, listened to the interpreter and noted the heat of the debate. Finally he arose, thereby signaling that he, a respected old man from the "conservative element" (as the sophisticated acculturated personnel viewed him) wished to speak. He spoke briefly and without an overt trace of feeling:

> There has been much talk about the money that has been spent. Many people seem unhappy. I do not know much about these things, but I see what is going on. Now let it be said that I do not understand the purpose that our brothers had in installing that cable. But I have noticed that it has some use. This fall, as the leaves began to drop from the trees, the birds were all lined up on it, wing to wing. For them it is a good thing, because it gives them all an even start on the way south.

His comment brought down the house. The issue passed, but the budget-makers had something to think about.

This quality of humor, which is constantly apparent in day to day interaction, is not directly a part of the complex of features that have been described. But like other similar, peripheral aspects it does not detract. In fact, it may serve an important function in that it serves as a release of any tensions built up by the constraints imposed upon expressiveness, and particularly the expression of aggression. This becomes especially apparent in the relations between a man and his father-in-law and brother-in-law. Ribald and grotesquely humorous remarks are passed between them and by one about the other. It is a way of diverting aggressive feelings that would otherwise disrupt or destroy the desired state of interpersonal relations—even between in-laws. I have made a particular point of this because I wish to make it clear that in this kind of analysis it is not necessary to account for *all* features of an empirically derived modal personality. We are concerned with those features which are *socially required* in the most crucial degree.

The alert reader will wonder how we know that the qualities described are modal in the native-oriented group. The answer is that we observed and interacted with the members of this small group over a period of years, with visits of two or three months each year. We recorded our observations carefully, keeping records of the kinds of behaviors that have been described. We know how each person in the group acted in a wide variety of situations over a long period of time. This is the essential feature of anthropological field work, and there is no substitute for it.

Besides applying what anthropologists call the "participant-observer" technique, we also administered the Rorschach Projective Technique (the "inkblot" test) to seventeen adult males and eight adult females, and collected life histories from two of the males and four of the females in the native-oriented group. We are fully aware of the many problems concerning the validity of interpretations for the Rorschach, even in our own society, and acknowledge that the problems are compounded by cross-cultural usage. In this particular application, however, the Rorschach seemed to produce results that were entirely congruent with our other extensive observations, and "made sense" with respect to the sociocultural demands in the situation. I will summarize briefly what the Rorschach tests showed to be the modal personality patterns for the native-oriented Menomini. I will not discuss the methods or rationale of interpretation. The interested reader may find these in other publications (G. Spindler, 1955; L. Spindler, 1962; L. and G. Spindler, 1958).

The modal personality revealed by the Rorschach responses is sharply limited in its range and modes of expression, An adequate number of responses by usual standards was given by each subject, but there is a marked tendency for the range of content to be narrow and for various stimulus properties of the inkblots to be used very selectively. The perceptual field can therefore be described as narrow. The responses that are given within this narrow field cannot, however, be described as "rigid," as one would expect them to be if respondents from our own society were thus "constricted." That which is used is used flexibly. Overt emotionality is not displayed. (This is a very consistent feature.) Responses are careful, and obvious features of the blots, such as bright color, are rarely used in favor of more subtle features, such as achromatic shading. The action quality of human figures in movement is passive. Human figures are rarely projected as doing anything but "sitting," "standing," or "facing that way." Motives for human action are not imputed. Animal figures are most frequently projected as being in action, such as "eating," or "climbing a tree," or "sneaking along through the brush," or "looking out from behind a tree." They are rarely perceived as engaged in aggressive action, such as attacking another animal. The concentration on animal figures is such, however, that we may describe the perceptual structure as zoomorphic. There is little content that we could describe as "morbid." The passivity and the quiescent quality of responses is not hopeless or depressive. The intellectual functions are adequate—there are virtually no distortions or breaks in reality. There is little drive to produce more than is necessary to complete the task as perceived. No native-oriented respondent asked, "How many responses do most people give?" as many acculturated respondents did. Once a response is given it is regarded as a problem solved, and there is little point in solving it again for the sake of accumulating a "good score."

In summary, the typical native-oriented personality revealed in Rorschach responses appears to be highly introverted, sensitive to the environment but able to maintain equilibrium despite its variations, not achievement-oriented, lacking generally in overt emotional responsiveness and exhibiting a high degree of rational control over it when it does appear, motivated more by biologically-oriented "survival" drives than by self-projective fantasy, intellectually uncomplicated but reality based and adequate in terms of its setting, lacking in rigidity, without evidence of the usual forms of anxiety, tension, or internal conflict. It is apparent that the personality profile derived from analysis of Rorschach responses is congruent, though not identical, with the focal orientations of personality derived from analysis of behavior in the environment. What the Rorschach adds is a clear estimate of the psychological homogeneity of the native-oriented group, a substantial indication of the lack of achievement orientation (at least in terms most meaningful in our society), a very valuable indication of the low anxiety level that is characteristic despite the "constriction" that might lead us to other inferences on the basis of personality dynamics in our society, and useful supplementary confirmation of many other features of personality that can be inferred from behavior-in-situ, such as the low degree of overt emotional responsiveness. It is equally relevant methodologically that the Rorschach did not tell us about other important features inferred from analysis of ordinary behavior. For instance, the Rorschach told us nothing about *autonomy*, and this is a crucial feature with respect to personality function in the framework of the sociocultural system.

The patterns of response to the Rorschach described are accurate descriptive statements for the majority of the native-oriented respondents. In this instance, therefore, "modal" is equivalent to "majority." This is *the* typical personality structure. The group is psychologically very homogeneous. This is the case, I hypothesize, because the present native-oriented Menomini group is a small remnant enclave. Probably the more aggressive members of the group have been drawn into transitional categories and are on their way to being acculturated. Both in terms of population aggregate and in terms of selective process this group probably exhibits a narrower range of personality characteristics than could have been true in the aboriginal society. This makes the case more dramatic, for purposes of our analysis, than would normally hold for whole functioning societies, but it helps to make the interrelationships I hope to draw out more clear-cut. We are dealing with a "pure," or "ideal," type situation, and this is helpful for purposes of illustration.

The Sociocultural System

With the modal personality structure for the native-oriented Menomini established it is now time to describe the sociocultural system that provides the framework within which this personality is functional. There is a conceptual problem involved that has frequently gotten in the way in other attempts to do the same thing. The dividing line between what is culturally directive and what is psychological is difficult to maintain. The prescriptions *for* behavior are apparent in much behavior that has been described. But this is the case because these prescriptions have been internalized by the people behaving, and this is precisely what this discussion is about. I have tried to avoid excessive contamination of the psychological inferences by dealing with *adult* behavior, that is consequent to the internalizations that take place during the encounters with cultural agents in the socialization process, and I have cited Rorschach responses because though they are influenced by culture they are not identical with it, since there are no direct antecedents for the experience of taking a Rorschach (responding imaginatively to culturally ambiguous inkblots) in Menomini life. This section of the chapter will deal with subsistence activities, religion, the structure of authority and social control, and ceremonial organizations that provide the framework of meanings within which the native-oriented Menomini act.

Though much has changed in the environment of the Menomini during recent decades, the subsistence activities of the native-oriented group exhibit a certain continuity. Their way of life was always one of seasonal and intermittent activity to gain a living from the forests, streams, and lakes. They had small gardens before the white man came in which they grew squash, beans, and corn, but they were basically hunters and gatherers. They also made extensive use of the resources of lakes and streams, particularly of sturgeon and wild rice. Because of their horticultural and maritime habits, it was possible for them to live in villages for a part of the year, for their environment was quite productive as a rule during the summer months, and there was always the wild rice harvest in the fall. But during the harsh winters the people resumed the nomadic, hunting life that represents the basic subsistence pattern of all the northern forest tribes. During this time it was not possible to live together in villages. Each extended family or small band went on its separate way, hunting over a territory defined by usage, and the threat of starvation was always present. The Menomini, like the Ojibwa, knew well the *Windigo*, the cannibal spirit that rode the howling northern winds during the winter months.

Today the people no longer gather in villages in the summer

and fragment into nomadic bands in the winter, and yet their life retains a nomadic and intermittent character. Some of the men in the native-oriented group work with logging crews in the forest, but this work is intermittent, depending upon the season of the year, the depth of the snow, and the "cut" needed to keep the sawmill operating. All of the men and boys fish and hunt. Most families go to pick cherries, potatoes, and strawberries, in season, for white farmers and orchardists in Wisconsin and Michigan. A few baskets, paintings, bas-relief carvings, and particularly beadwork, are sold to tourists. Many individuals and families pick ferns and evergreen boughs. A fast worker can make ten to fifteen dollars per day in season. A few people go to Minnesota to gather wild rice each year.

Hunting is an important source of meat, and most men spend long hours in the woods. The dense forests of the Menomini area still shelter deer, bear, and partridge, and the many lakes float their share of ducks and occasional geese. Skill in hunting is highly valued. One man who is regarded as an excellent hunter shot thirteen bears in five years and averages about seven deer a year. The technique most used is to take position near a deer run or watering place, or sometimes by a salt lick set out to attract game. Once in position a man may wait for his quarry for a whole day or night with hardly a movement. When food runs low a man will go out to stay until he kills something. One man stayed out four days, with only a half a loaf of bread and a pound of salt pork for provisions.

The method of hunting is in sharp contrast with that employed by most white hunters. The whites select an area where there is good cover and a number of them "drive" the area. The frightened game moves ahead of them, to be shot by hunters posted at strategic points where they can cover a certain area. This method is foreign to the native-oriented Menomini. Each man hunts for himself. He settles down and waits for the game to appear rather than forcing it out. When he kills, the meat is not distributed piecemeal to all the members of the group, or even to his relatives. His in-laws, if nearby, will receive a sizeable chunk. If there is a seasonal rite for the Dream Dance or a meeting of the Medicine Lodge, he will contribute his meat to feed the participants, but otherwise he and his immediate family consumes it as rapidly as possible. Or he may sell it to a white man and use up the money just as quickly.

Life in this mode has its ups and downs. People still go hungry, though no one starves today. But from the white man's point of view there is little security. There is rarely food in the house for more than a very few days ahead. No one has freezers or food storage lockers. And work is intermittent. The typical pattern is to work hard at cherry-picking or greens-gathering for a few weeks. When that is finished there is money for food and a few bottles of beer for awhile. Then there is no point in working. Work in itself has no value. There is nothing to "get ahead" towards, from their point of view. As long as there is enough to eat things are fine, and when the food runs out something "always comes along," if one can wait long enough to see what it will be.

It is apparent that the qualities of personality described are functional in this setting. "Equanimity under duress" is a good quality to possess in an intermittent and seminomadic subsistence economy. "Autonomy" is apparent in the lack of organized co-operation in economic endeavor. "Latescence" makes it possible for one to wait for the game to come rather than drive it out, or wait expectantly, rarely hopelessly, for the next thing to turn up that will put food in the pot. Of course it is possible to argue that they do not have to do things this way. After all, Wisconsin is a more or less civilized state. But if they did not live this way, the native-oriented Menomini would cease being native-oriented. It is their way of life and has continuity into the past.

Religion and ceremonial organization

The native-oriented Menomini have now, and have had for some time, ceremonial organizations that maintain religious commitments and require public participation. Less obvious is the individuality that underlies these forms of group worship and is more consistent with the most ancient forms of religious behavior. Until recently, every normally socialized Menomini went through the *Mesahktoway* (Great Fast) at puberty. Preparation for the Great Fast began during early childhood with short fasts of a day or two and instruction in the properly humble state of mind. When the individual felt ready for the ordeal and had received proper instructions from an elder, he or she went off, with a charcoal-blackened face, into the woods, to a tiny bark wigwam already constructed for this purpose. One stayed alone, quite cut off from all human contact, and with no food for periods ranging up to ten days or even two weeks. During this time the initiate was supposed to banish all thoughts from the mind excepting those concerned with the purpose of the fast—to receive a vision and through this experience find the source of the power, in the form of a guardian spirit, that would guide and keep him through his whole lifetime. His attitude must be humble, supplicatory, so that the powers would take pity on him and notify him of their interest. If he was successful, the Golden Eagle, the White Bear, the Buffalo, or one of the many other spirit powers that resided in one of the layers above the earth, usually but not always in animal form, would appear before him. The Golden Eagle would take the supplicant on his back and fly over the forests and lakes, pointing out natural features that were significant in Menomini mythology. The Buffalo might chase him over rough terrain to the point of exhaustion, and he would fall face down into a sacred pool from which he might drink the source of life. If he was unsuccessful, he might either receive no notification from the spirits, or be visited by one of the creatures inhabiting the strata below the earth, such as *Mishkeneebec,* the Horned Hairy Serpent. If unsuccessful, he tried again after a lapse of some time. If he was visited by one of the underworld creatures for the fourth time, he was doomed to live a tragic life as a witch that used bad medicines to harm others, or as one who some day would murder a loved one.

In any event, what happened during the Great Fast determined to a considerable, though, of course, not absolute degree, what the initiate would be in his present lifetime. Whether a man would be a good hunter, a ceremonial leader, a woman a good mother and wife, or a witch, was decided by the events at that time. Most significantly, the individual's access to the power pool through his guardian spirit—the all-permeating, universal sacred power in living things and inanimate objects alike—was defined at this time. By observing the proper rituals at the proper times one could maintain this access. But not all the powers were equally accessible, and not all guardian spirits were equally powerful. If a man or woman failed in some pursuit, he or she could not be personally blamed by others or by oneself. His or her power was not strong enough.[4]

Today there is only one person left alive who had the Great Fast and received its benefits, though until very recently there were a number of old people still living who had.[5] But this does not mean that either in spirit or in specific forms the culture pattern is dead. All adults in the group had fasted for short periods as children. Some received notifications from the spirits in these preparatory fasts and ritually observe the relationship thus formed. Others have inherited both the powers and obligations of ritual observance from departed relatives, and the same attitude and relationship is maintained and reinforced by the rituals and beliefs connected with the *Nemeheetwan* (the "Dream Dance") and its sacred drums.

The events and attitudes described seem bizarre and unreal to the white man, with his rationalistic objective view of the universe. But in the tradition-oriented Menomini framework so much is so different. The separation between mind and body, man and animal, spiritual forces and material forces, natural and supernatural that is so much a part of our thinking is simply absent in the Menomini framework of belief and rationality. The dream experience itself is a dramatic indication of this difference. In talking with the people about these affairs I would frequently use the word "vision" to describe what one sees and experiences under these conditions. I was often, but gently corrected, "A white man might say that, but this was no 'vision,' this happened." The term

---

[4] Where I describe those features of traditional Menomini culture that are now quite attenuated in the patterns of the native-oriented group, I use both the memories of the older people in the group and the ethnographies written about the Menomini when the traditional culture was comparatively intact. For a fairly complete bibliography on the Menomini see Spindler (1955). I have found Hoffman (1896) and Skinner (1915) particularly useful.

[5] The one old man in the group who had experienced the Great Fast died recently, but I take the liberty of the "ethnographic present" in this instance.

"dream" was more acceptable, for they had many dreams and knew that one is directly involved with the events in a dream— that it *seems real*, so real that even whites awake wondering if it really happened.

For the Menomini dreaming is a very significant activity. No dream is casually dismissed. The individual usually tries to find the meaning in the dream, but if he is unsuccessful he talks about it with an elder who has great powers and who by virtue of his nearness to the end of life is close to what we would call the "supernatural." The interpretation placed on the dream experience can foretell a significant event, provide revelation concerning life, death, and sacred powers, or dictate a specific course of action ranging from how to make a special drumstick or beadwork design to how to prevent one's husband from running off with another woman. Even songs are acquired in dreams. In fact, I feel quite secure in saying that we did not observe any significant innovative behavior or important individual decision-making among native-oriented Menomini that was *not based on a dream experience and its interpretation*. The same receptive dependence upon "supernatural" power seems to be operating as in the acquiring of and relationship to the guardian spirit.

One must literally be a "dreamer" (passive, receptive, quiescent) to get along in this society. And the autonomous character of the relationship between individuals and "power" is apparent. Each has its own experiences and carries out his own rituals. It is also apparent that the ability to retain one's equanimity under duress is functional in the requirement to fast in isolation. While the Great Fast is no longer possible, the fasts required of young children reinforce this ability.

The *Nemeheetwan* is the major ceremonial organization still operating among the native-oriented Menomini.[6] The ritual centers upon a large drum, about 30 inches in diameter, about 10 inches deep, and constructed of rawhide stretched over a circular wooden

---

[6] An excellent account of the Dream Dance is given by J. S. Slotkin (1957) who studied this ceremony during the period of our work. This account in this chapter is based upon our own field work; but my knowledge of the ritual and its symbolic meanings has been amplified by reading Dr. Slotkin's monograph.

frame. There are four such drums in the native-oriented group. The head of the drum is painted red, to symbolize the dangerous spirits, and blue, to symbolize the good spirits—corresponding to the dualistic concept of the universe held by the Menomini— with a yellow line bisecting these two colors to symbolize the course of the sun and the right path of life. The sides are decorated with beadwork in the form of symbols denoting the origin of the rite.

Each drum has a number of offices, which are related to each "leg" of the drum—one for each of the four directions of the compass. There is a drum owner, a man in the older age group, who retains major responsibility for the conduct of the ceremonies in which it is used. He is the authority on proper ritual, and he is supposed to look out "like a father" for the people occupying offices connected with his drum and their families. "He sits there just like God, and watches what we do. If we do anything wrong (in the ritual) he is supposed to tell us. He is supposed to look out for us too, and not be stingy with anything." There is also a "keeper" for each drum who maintains the drum in his home in its sacred wrappings, keeps a lighted lantern near it at night, and is responsible for its care.

When a "song service" (which may be held any time) or a seasonal rite is being conducted, from four to eight men sit around the drum, singing in chorus and hitting the drum in unison. The drum has a deep and resonant tone that is exhilarating, if deafening—especially in the confines of a small room. The floor, windows, and human bodies vibrate with every beat. The people claim that the service makes them "feel good," that they forget their worries and troubles. Indeed, the ritual is a means of renewing power. "The old man in the drum," *kemehsoman*, is the intermediary between man and spirits, particularly *kesemanetow* (roughly—"Great Spirit," an Ojibwa loan word). When the drum is hit, its voice, symbolized by a small bell suspended on a wire inside the drum and most apparent in the deep voice of the drum itself, notifies the spirits through *kemehsoman* that the ceremony is being held and asks for their "blessings." "When that drum is hit, his (*kemehsoman's*) voice is sent all over, in all four directions, to all those spirits. *Kesemanetow* hears that and gives us what we ask for. That old man in the drum gets those messages out." It is believed that in order to keep group and individual access to sacred, life-giving power intact, it is necessary to hold the seasonal rites and frequent "song services." Without this access to power, "bad luck" will ensue. Through the medium of the rites and proper ceremonial sacrifices (mostly of tobacco), the drums are a means of renewing power and therefore securing good luck, as well as revitalizing the spirits of the participants.

The drums are also a source of individual powers, particularly for the "drum keeper" who has the drum in his house, and cares for it. The relationship is virtually identical to that once maintained with the guardian spirit gained through the Great Fast, usually through the medium of a sacred bundle representing that spirit, and with the relationship now maintained with individual, inherited guardians. I will let a member of the group speak for himself.

> Well, about the *Nemeheetwan*, I believe in that my whole life. I know what they preach is true, I proved it myself. It is the religion I am trying to get hold of . . . the Medicine Dance (*Mitawin*) is just about gone now.
>
> They preach lots of things, like my old aunt, they tell me this, and they tell me that. Especially about tobacco. That takes the lead. Anything you do, you got to have tobacco. Just the plug kind—it goes farther that way. I'll tell you, for instance, if you're going out hunting, if you're keeping a drum, and you have some tobacco cut up in fine pieces, you put it by the drums, and you smoke some yourself. Well, I done that, and I asked him (*kemehsoman*) what I'm going to do, just like I was talking to an old man. I would say to him, "I want your help." Like one time I was staying over to Kimeyowan's place, and it happened that his wife and I was home alone. I was doing my chores, hauling wood and filling the water bucket. About four o'clock I told her, "I'm all set, I'm going out hunting." She says, "Oh well, that's good." Well, I had some tobacco, and I cut it up and put it in the tobacco boxes (ceremonial wooden bowls associated with the drum) and lit some of it in two pipes. I smoked first one, then the other. And I talked to that drum, like if I was talking to you. I'd say, "I'm going out. I'm going to try to get some meat. Would you mind helping me out?"

The night before he had a dream. He was out hunting and two deer approached him. One of them said "I thought I'd tell you, that fellow (the other deer), he just gave you his life." This dream prompted his decision to go out hunting the next evening. In order to insure the prophecy and to take advantage of the offer of the deer to "give up his life," my friend had made the sacrifice to the drum in order to notify the powers of his and the deer's decision, and to secure the "luck" (the power) to perform the deed successfully.

He went out hunting after the sacrifice to the drum. He waited by a salt lick for several hours until it was almost too dark to see any more. Finally two deer approached the lick. One of them threw up his head, startled probably by the scent of the man, and bounded off in the brush. The other started to run, then stopped and turned towards my friend. He shot this one, the one that gave him his life in the dream the night before, through the heart. "That's happened many times. I'd ask for help . . . I'd get it. I believe to this day that it's this way. I asked for that deer, and I got it."

The native-oriented Menomini system of belief is encapsulated in this sequence of events just described. The dependence of the individual upon revelation through dreams. The importance of keeping one's access to power intact. The dependence upon the power thus gained for success in all the ventures of life. The quiescent, waiting, expectancy that if the proper rituals are observed "fate" (as we might term it) will provide. The autonomous character of the relationship between these powers and the individual, all of this is clear.

The other ceremonial organization—the *Mitawin* is of less importance today than it was only a few years ago. Meetings are held infrequently, not more than once every other year. The major purpose of the ceremony is to prolong life and keep health. The ritual is complex, and the rites last four days, involving the efforts of numerous participants and particularly of elders who know the ritual and its meanings. The characteristic Menomini individualism underlies the complex elaboration of the ritual. Each member of the lodge must possess a medicine bag. These bags are inherited, or made under sacred conditions by an elder. An otter, mink, weasel, or other animal skin serves as the bag. It is kept whole, with all exterior parts of the animal intact. Inside the abdomen and in the hollows of the legs and skull are kept small packets of medicine made from roots and herbs, each for a specific, curative purpose. The powers of the bag must be kept intact by ritual observances, both in and outside the setting of the lodge ceremonies. Individual members and their bags have different powers. The relationship between the individual and sacred power is consistent with the the terms of this relationship in other spheres of Menomini religious and ceremonial life. The Medicine Lodge is an association of medicine men (and women) who join together occasionally in ceremony. The relationship between the socio-cultural system and the socially required personality is somewhat less direct with respect to the *Mitawin* than in other settings described, but there is nothing in this setting to detract from the main thesis and the individualistic aspects of it support the thesis.

The structure of authority and social control

No one has the right, on the basis of position or prestige, to exercise direct authority over another, not even a father over his son. Children are given their earnings from the dances put on for tourists to spend as they will. A child of five years may sell his carefully made, bead-decorated buckskin costume on his own and keep the money thus gained. There is love and honor in traditional Menomini marriage, but no "obeying." Strong men do not order weak ones about.

There is virtually no "leadership" in our sense of the word. One day a group of native-oriented personnel were sitting about after an afternoon of dancing for tourists at a nearby "woodland bowl." It had been suggested that it would be helpful to have a battery-operated loud-speaker system for the master of ceremonies to use in his announcements to the assembled crowd. A white man had offered to sell one of them for fifty dollars. The group was faced with the decision—should or should they not buy it? Everyone sat quietly, saying nothing. A man of about forty years who was the intermediary between the group and the proprietors of the "bowl" and the owner of the loud-speaker system said, "What does the group think?" No one spoke for a long time. Someone finally said, "Well sometimes those people can't hardly hear." An indistinguishable murmur or two emitted from the assemblage— neither in agreement or dissent—or so it seemed to me at least. Another period of quiet waiting. Another question by the intermediary, "Well, what does the group think?" Another murmur or two. And so it went for some time. So long that the white man, who was waiting in his car for their decision, came over. "Well, what's the answer? Do you want to buy it or don't you? I can't wait all day." No response. In exasperation he stomped back to his car. "This man, he wants to know. What does the group think?" the query came again. No arguments, no open discussion, a few half-voiced murmurs. The people standing and sitting around left to attend to other business. Had a decision been reached? I thought not, but I was wrong. The intermediary went over to talk to the white man. He said somewhat apologetically, "I guess the people don't want to spend the money." How did he know? Apparently there had been no sentiments expressed in favor of the proposition other than the comment that "those people can't hardly hear." The absence of general consensus was enough. No "leader" would try to coerce or convince others that a given course of action was best, even though the intermediary thought, as I knew he did in this instance from other discussions with him, that a loud-speaker system was essential.

The elders know the rituals; have greatest access to the spirits and their powers and, therefore, have potential for both beneficent and harmful behavior; can prophesy with their dreams; and are the authorities for questions on kin relationships. They are therefore "leaders" in a sense. No man under sixty could pretend much knowledge or experience in these matters, but not all men over sixty are leaders. The oldest man in the group (in his eighties) is the highest authority on these affairs. He is also the only Menomini alive who can claim to have gone through the Great Fast. But even he does not exert authority, as such, over others. For example, he once took some liberties with the Dream Dance Drum of which he is "owner," kept by a younger man in his own home. To be a drum "keeper" is to be entirely responsible for the care and maintenance of it. Not even the owner is supposed to remove it to use in a ceremony without the direct knowledge and permission of the keeper. Under the pressure of unusual circumstances that arose in the absence of the drum keeper, the old man removed the drum from the keeper's house to use in a ceremony. Upon learning of this, the younger man was quite disturbed and made a few very indirectly critical statements to others concerning the old man's action. At a ceremony some time later the old man arose to make a short speech. "My children, I am good to you. I care for you all the time. I pray for you to the Great Spirit. I cure you when you get sick with good medicines. Now somebody here does not feel good about things somehow. Now, all right—I did not take that drum away from anybody. I did not want to hurt anyone's feelings—that is all I have to say." Even with his high status as an authority on all things important in the traditional framework of the native-oriented group, and even with his great capacity for good or evil because of his access to great powers, he did not and could not exercise direct authority over another younger man charged with an inviolable responsibility. And in his indirect apology, he exhibited his concern about possibly having given offense for seeming to have exercised an authority he did not have. Not in our observations extending over a decade have we ever seen an exception to the mode of leadership described.

In a system of this kind social control must function in indirect and subtle ways. The ways of the native-oriented Menomini can be categorized as follows: by indirect gossip—the drum keeper said enough about the old man's "indiscretion" so that the old man was brought to make a virtual apology; by reward—the old man can cure the ill and intercede for the people with the powers; by dreams—many times people had dreams that were publicly interpreted as prophecies of dire results for drinking, desertion, and failing to keep up ritual observances; by witchcraft—the constant threat that socially deviant behavior will result in the use of sorcery by the injured party.

This last means of social control—witchcraft—is one of the most dramatic and one of the most effective. Any old man or woman is presumed capable of acting as a sorcerer, given enough provocation. That is one of the reasons why the drum keeper was so careful about what *he* said. All of his comments were very

indirect and quite subtle. He did not want to offend the old man
—not only because being so aggressive as to give offense is not
a part of his personality, but because it would be dangerous to
do so. On the other hand, sorcery against another man is not something to be activated casually, even by a powerful old man. The
powers directed at another can rebound against one's self. The
evil powers are not entirely predictable, and are not infrequently
overcome either by another witch's evil power or by another
person's essentially beneficent guardians. The younger man was
a drum keeper. The power in the drum, or rather symbolized by it
and made accessible through it, might be stronger than the old
man's power. So there are checks and balances operating. But the
fear is there.

Another elder said, as part of the life story he was telling me,
"Then my Father started preaching about religion . . . what to be
afraid of. 'Maybe you live for quite awhile. If you don't, it is because you will shorten your life if you get in wrong.' That's how
I was afraid, even right up to today; afraid I might get somebody
mad. Some Indians have some bad medicine, and this bad medicine
travels at night. Like a devil it can work." A young mother said,
"You should never hurt old men's feelings . . . your child might
die." Another, said "If people dress better than the rest or think
they are somebody, they have to watch out. . . ." The recognition of witches and witchcraft as a fact of existence is a persistent
theme in autobiographies, gossip, and behavior. There is no doubt
that it is a powerful sanction against deviant behavior operating in
the native-oriented system of social control.

In view of this, it seems strange that *anxiety* is not a pervasive
force in the modal native-oriented Menomini personality and behavior. We could find no evidence that it is—in everyday behavior, in Rorschach responses, or in autobiographies. In some
communities of Indians sharing the same cultural fund as the
Menomini, like the neighboring Ojibwa (Hallowell, 1955), there is
real anxiety. With the Menomini there is *fear;* fear of what is
discerned as a realistic threat—a part of the surroundings in which
the people live—and this fear can be accepted and endured, as the
"fear" of hunger is. But the Menomini world view is essentially a
supportive one. The same fates that guide the daily life of ordi-

nary mortals will destroy the powers of the sorcerer if he abuses that power. Witchcraft is a bad thing. As one father told his son, "I don't want you to go around looking for bad medicine . . . just good medicine. All the Indians look for medicine to help out to live. Go out and hunt for medicine, to help you get well when you are sick, and to help you live good." Few people want to inherit a "witch bag." It is a most dangerous possession because it must be "fed" by killing or causing illness once a year. If one does use it, the sorcery can rebound. If one does not, the evil powers may get dissatisfied and kill or maim the holder. But in the absence of overt social controls exercised through positions of secular power, sorcery and the threat of sorcery is functional as a means of controlling or preventing behavior that is potentially disruptive in interpersonal relations and to the values embedded in the way of life. The controls over expression of emotions, particularly of aggressive feelings, that are a part of the personality make it possible to live in this sociocultural system. And the threat of sorcery reinforces these controls in the personality at the same time that it vests elders, who are committed to the status quo, with awesome powers (L. Spindler, 1952).

In this and all human societies, underlying all means of social control is the structure of motivations and controls characteristically present in the socially required personality. I hope that I have demonstrated that equanimity under duress, latescence, control of overt emotional expression, and autonomy are socially required in the native-oriented Menomini group. Indeed, without these particular qualities it is difficult to conceive of this sociocultural system existing at all. In the last section I will describe the means through which this kind of personality is created.

The Educational Process

Personality is formed and education occurs as the growing child encounters cultural agents acting in the various roles and statuses provided by the social structure of his society. In the native-oriented Menomini "society," the social system is now and was always fairly simple insofar as statuses and roles are concerned. There are, for example, adult males and females, babies, sib-

lings, kinship designations, ceremonial leaders, old people, secular leaders, and occupational statuses and roles. Each of these
categories of status and role are further refined into specific
statuses and roles in social action. Some old people are witches,
some are grandparents, some are both. Some adult males are
fathers, others are possible fathers-in-law, and so forth. But
even with these complications, one very important circumstance distinguishes the situation of the Menomini child from that
experienced by ours—the Menomini child encounters cultural
agents in all of the roles and statuses provided by his society
early in his education experience. By the time he is five years
of age, probably before, he is at least dimly aware of all of them.

This difference is most apparent in the many isolated, nuclear,
suburban familes in our society where preschool children are left
most of the time in the care of one person—Mother. Father tends
to be a rather shadowy figure, gone most of the time, introjecting
occasionally and not infrequently as a disturbing influence when
he does. Young children, even of school age, know very little or
nothing about what Father does. His occupational role, that role
which is instrumental in giving him and his family subsistence, luxuries, and status in our work and success-oriented society, is nearly
a complete blank to his children. Disciplinary roles, as well as
rewarding and loving roles, are left much of the time to Mother.
Children become so wrapped up in her, and she in them, that the
relationship can be described as one of "personality absorption."
(Green, 1946) That the sharp discontinuity between home and
school, and between home and *life*, as the child encounters more
and more people who are not mothers, should create behavior
problems in many growing children and residual psychological
problems in many more adults (particularly males) who have gone
through the process, is not surprising. Even when personality absorption does not occur between Mother and children, and where
Father has some real substance, the discontinuity between the
nuclear family home group and the rest of the world is such that
a child has great difficulty in learning enough through his encounters with parents and siblings to enable him to get along without considerable anxiety in his encounters with other people

occupying statuses and behaving according to role prescriptions for which there are no antecedents in his early experience.

There are discontinuities in Menomini education and experience too. Children do attend schools run by white men and women with very different ideas about proper behavior than the children's parents have. Later on even children from the native-oriented group will begin thinking of how to make a living in a world dominated by a sociocultural system not only different but mostly antithetical to the premises of his own. But these discontinuities are not a part of the educational experience of the native-oriented group as such, even though they are a fact of contemporary life. The problems of adaptation to these problems of discontinuity and conflict are a closely related, but separable subject that I cannot deal with in this chapter. I will only say that there is a native-oriented Menomini group in existence today because the educational experience for children in that group is so effective that it is successfully refractive in many cases to the impact of the educational experience contrived by agents of the dominant society. We also have evidence from our extensive sample of Menomini at all levels of acculturation that adults who have undergone a tradition-oriented socialization experience, including the learning of the Menomini language, rarely (possibly never) are psychologically transformed even though they may, as adults, take on specialized occupational roles and acquire the necessary accessory behaviors to get along in today's world.

Part of the effectiveness of traditional Menomini education is that aspect with which this discussion began—children early in their experience encounter all of the statuses and roles constituting in their arrangement the social structure of their society. Menomini education is also effective, I believe, because these encounters are nearly all favorable to the child, and, as a consequence, he develops very little by way of recalcitrant or ambivalent feelings towards adults or what they would have him learn (in sharp contrast to our own situation). And Menomini education is also effective because at a certain stage in the child's development most of the latent learning he has acquired about the values and ethics of his group up to that time is made highly explicit and given a great deal of verbal reinforcement. These three dimensions of educational experience, and others related closely to them, provide the format for the rest of the discussion in this section.

When a male baby is born his penis is pinched by an old woman in attendance, usually one of his grandmothers, so that it will not grow to abnormal size and so that he will be able to control his passions when he grows to maturity. Doubtless this act has little direct effect on the child, but it is symbolic of a point of view that is applied systematically. The child's first direct experience with restraint is with the swaddling cloths and blankets in which it is wrapped. The cradle board is no longer used, but children are enfolded in several layers of cloth, and are usually placed in a blanket that is folded in such a way that it can be tied at both ends and suspended as a hammock. Even on hot days babies are enclosed in this manner, sometimes with only the head and face peeking out of the tightly folded blanket. The effects of such constraint are not fully understood, and it is true that in other tribes where cradle-boarding is still the custom and the child is even more tightly confined, babies seem to learn to crawl and to walk normally and at the usual times. In any event, the constraints imposed appear to be consistent with the requirements of Menomini culture.

Other than in the specific respects just described, however, children in the native-oriented group are treated with tolerance and permissiveness. They are nursed whenever they are hungry or whenever they fret. Weaning is gradual, and even children in the walking stage may be given the breast if they are ill or uneasy, and if there is milk. Toilet training is carried out casually. Children are encouraged to "hold back" when they can understand the reasons for doing so, but no particular fuss is made if they do not succeed. Menomini mothers are puzzled by the concern displayed by whites over such matters.

Until the child can run about by itself, the mother, a grandmother, or an older sibling is always nearby. Infants and young children are held a great deal. Fathers and older brothers as well as mothers walk about holding children in their arms, even when talking with strangers. Apparently it is assumed that everyone likes to hold babies, because during a conversation the holder of a baby will hand it over to the person with whom he or she is talking without asking if the recipient of the frequently rather damp bundle wants to hold it. But despite the supportive holding of babies by almost everyone there is little demonstrative fondling, hugging, or kissing. Babies are frequently held facing away from the holder. And the interaction rate in general between adults and young children seems low to the white observer. In short, there seems to be a consistent, supportive relationship at a low level of overt affectivity.

Punishments are rare. No adult in the native-oriented group remembers being whipped as a child, and none of them whip their children now. "They used to be good to me, never scold me, and I used to be good that way too. I never went through anything like being hit on the face . . . like I saw one white man do to his kid. He hit him right on the mouth, like he was a man," as one fifty year old man said. Another man in his thirties related, "I don't remember ever getting a real switching. Oh maybe just a little bit on the legs, that's all. When I didn't mind, like maybe I cried for some little thing, or they can't make me be still, or maybe I didn't listen to my ma, then maybe I got a dipper full (of cold water) in the face. Then I had to listen!" The attitude of adults towards children and the conception of proper treatment seems clear in the following:

> I remember how nice and quiet my uncle used to talk to me, so I always listen to what he say, and try to do what he want. So one time we took a boy (they had no children of their own). He was mean, used to run around, his parents treated him bad, but we treat him like my uncle treated me. We keep him clean . . . get food what's good for him. If he like something to eat, we get that for him. We try to keep him around us all the time. We think he get better if we treat him like that. After a while he did. He minded good, listened, try to do like we say.

This same man, while giving me his autobiography, reminisced about his school experience.

> One time at school they hit me with a strap doubled over while I lay across a chair. He hit me as hard as he could, and he count up to twenty-one. When he count nineteen I didn't squeal yet,

but them last two, they kinda made me say 'ow'! But they couldn't make me cry. Then my partner, they took him. I tell him, "Indian don't squeal. Don't do like I did." I guess I was never used to that treatment.

Children are always present when anything is going on. When a Dream Dance is being held, all of the children down to the smallest baby are in the room where the service is conducted. Adults are tolerant of potential disruptions that would disturb whites in similar circumstances. A baby that starts fretting when a prayer is being offered or a tobacco sacrifice being made is held gently, given the breast, or carried out of the room without any visible tension or anger on the part of the mother or other attendant who carries it out. Very young children are encouraged to take some part in the affair. Toddlers dance, held at first by their upraised arms by an older brother or sister. One eleven year old boy was given a regular place around the drum. He used his drumstick to help the fast-moving and highly synchronized beat, and tried to join in the rather complex and very quick-tempo songs. His beat was a little ragged, and his singing was far from being a positive contribution to the chorus, but the men carrying out the service treated him like a full member of the ritual group. His careful and self-conscious attempt to replicate every move and posture of the men, even the facial expressions, was an impressive demonstration of how learning occurs in this group. His youngest brother, aged three and one half, ran over to him one night shortly after he took his place at the drum. The eleven year old promptly found a stool for him and gently sat the child on it next to him. The little boy sat on the stool quietly, absorbed by the activity, while two choruses were sung. Then he became restive and started to run about the room. His older brother got up, took him by the arm and rather firmly sat him down again upon the stool. The little boy, unaccustomed to such firm treatment by his brother, started to sob quietly—apparently fighting for control but not quite achieving it. Finally his brother took him by the hand, and with a very solicitous look upon his face, led him out of the room. The next time a song service was held the little boy sat again upon the stool by the side of his older brother, but this time he stayed there quietly for about an hour, then got up and walked carefully over to his mother's side and climbed upon the bench beside her. At subsequent services he took the same position by his brother during the early part of the evening. He had learned something too. Seven years later he sat with his brother, now a young man, at the same drum, but now he had his own drumstick, and tried to sing, like his brother had before at the age of eleven. This is the way roles are learned in the native-oriented group and why the way of life of this group persists in the face of intensive pressures for change from the outside world.

Children are respected in the native-oriented group. This respect is clear in the way their earnings as part of a dance troupe that puts on shows for tourists are regarded. The money is theirs to spend as they will. Respect is also shown in the special observances for children. During the first year of life each child must be given a name. An elder is requested to give the name, and it is bestowed at a feast given by the parents for as many people as they have food and place for. The elder gives the matter serious thought, sometimes mulling it over for several months. Then after the food is consumed he rises with the child in his arms and gives a talk, giving the name and explaining why it is selected and asking the spirits for a long life for the child. Sometimes the name is given in recognition of some special characteristic the elder believes he sees in the child. Other times the name of a deceased person is given in recognition of the possibility that his spirit has been born again in this child. This event is of great importance, because if a child is not pleased with his name he may depart to the spirit world from whence he came. Children are carefully watched to see if they are at ease with their name. If one stands quietly in the midst of play, as though preoccupied with some inner distress, the parents will take the child to an elder who will attempt to talk with it to see whether it has the right name. Children are close, like old people, to the supernatural, to the great power that pervades all things, and from which man receives life and energy. So the character trait we have called autonomy—one aspect of respect for the individual—is reinforced by a belief system.

This respect and concern for children extends through all the years of growing up. When a boy kills his first game—no matter how small or large it is—a feast is held to celebrate this event and his praises are sung by all present. And this attitude extends to everyday matters. The little girl who fills her pail with wild blackberries is praised—but never in such a manner as to imply that she did better than someone else. When the boys and girls hop around the dance area in imitation of the adults, all the Menomini present whoop and clap as though the children had done something quite marvelous. Menomini adults seem to be able to treat children supportively without "possessing" them.

The native-oriented Menomini believe strongly in the power of the spoken word. As soon as children can understand, adults are constantly "putting a bug in your ear," as one young man expressed it. There are several different ways of putting a bug in. In the old days there was a regular cycle of stories and myths told through certain times of the year. Usually some elder who was both powerful and wise would establish a special reputation as a good story-teller. He would hold forth by his hearth on certain evenings, and parents would bring their children to hear him. Older people in the present group remember these story-telling times when as many as twenty children might be listening at the same moment. There were two major types of stories. One type consisted of stories about various wizards and heroes and their exploits; stories of war, hunting, love, ghosts, and magic; and stories about "how the skunk got his stripes," or "how the crane got the black ring around his neck." They are remembered by the older and middle-aged people even today as most entertaining. The stories had many dramatic props—a magic canoe that could go by itself, the kettle that never became empty, the dog's bones that came to life to save its master, the flaming arrow that came from nowhere to save the hero, "little god boys" that could pass through rocks and performed mischievous acts. The other major type included the cosmogonic myths—the origin of the Menomini; the nature of the stratified universe and the beings in it; and particularly the *Manapus* cycle, myths about the culture hero of the Menomini who was part hero and part buffoon. This latter category of stories were told in a more serious vein, usually to older children, and during a period of weeks when the cycle would not be interrupted.

Certain themes are constant in these tales and myths. The hero is helpless without his dream-bestowed and ritually-maintained power, and he may lose it by abuse, neglect, or lack of constraint. On the other hand, the hero is particularly successful only because he has acquired a certain power. In contests between great shamans, one of the contestants may realize and admit that his power is not strong enough to withstand that of the other so he gives in without further struggle. The individual is dependent upon this power as something beyond himself—something gained by him through proper behavior. The heroes, particularly in the Manapus tales, are vulnerable. Though Manapus is capable of great and miraculous deeds, he can be outwitted at times by the fox, the beaver, or even the duck. He can do very stupid things and seem more like a fool than a hero at times, but despite his fumbles and buffoonery, he manages to retain his character. A good man is brave, respects the rights of others, and does not arouse antagonisms; he lives quietly, observes the sacrifices required to maintain good relations with the powers; and he is modest, even-tempered, and guards himself against undue pride.

Today the children do not have the opportunity to hear these same stories and myths told in their fullness by a gifted story teller. Much of the content has been lost and there are too many interferences, such as going to school. But all children in the native-oriented group hear stories even now. They are told more casually, and the content is attentuated, but the themes are recognizable. For example, one night a man in his late thirties was telling his children about a great hunter. He always got his bag full of ducks. He went out to his favorite spot and waited for the ducks to fly in during the half-light moments of dawn. Suddenly there was a rush of wings as a flight settled in before his hiding place. He rose to shoot but slipped and fell, discharging his shotgun harmlessly in the air. The ducks all rose in a flurry of beating wings. But one big black duck stayed on the water. The great hunter reloaded his gun and shot the unfortunate laggard. To his consternation he saw that he had shot his own hat, which had flown off his head when he fell down, and it floated, crownless and tattered, on the surface of the water. The great hunter went home, disgusted. That evening, as though to remind him of his ineptness, a large crane flopped past his house by the river, wearing the brim of his hat around his neck. Now every time he sees the ring-necked crane he is reminded of his clumsiness on that morning.

Grandparents still tell children "bedtime stories," and the adults in the group remember when their grandparents told them stories. "Grandmaw told us kids a story every night before we went to sleep. First thing next morning she would ask us what the story was about. If we couldn't tell her, she would tell the same story again the next night. She would do that until we could tell her what the story was about." What Grandmaw was looking for was the moral point of the story, "that we shouldn't offend anybody's feelings," or "not to envy what someone else has got."

Adults seem to always be ready to point out a moral to children. One little boy stood by the window looking longingly out at the blizzardy landscape. "Gee, I wish it would clear up so I could go out and play tomorrow," he said. The next day dawned with a bright sun and he could go out. But before he did, his mother pointed out that he had asked for that the day before and this showed that one should never wish for things unless one really wanted them to happen. Frequently the moral point will be made with a proverb. "He who brags bites his own tail." "People who mind others' business get long noses." "One who talks too much will get a big mouth." "He who spits at him gives him his life."

Constraint is taught directly. One young woman said:

He, my father, did right and treated all people the same. He was kind to everybody. Even the children today brag about my father. My father always made us sit everytime we ate anything. He said the food wouldn't do no good otherwise. He said we would be just like horses, running around and eating, and our food wouldn't do us no good. We had to sit a while after we ate to let our food digest. We could never talk very much while we was at the table. He didn't even like us to stretch or things like that after we ate. I used to think my Father was awful hard on us, but I can see now, that he was just tryin' to raise us right and teach us the right things to do. So I keep tellin' my children the same things as my father told us.

Children are taught to be quiet and not ask a lot of questions. "Sit quiet like a stone, and let thoughts come to you. Think about a leaf in a pool." Children are taught to be generous and respect old people: "Father said, 'Live in peace. Be good to every person. If you live somewhere . . . if you have something to eat . . . feed him . . . even though there is only one meal in your house, feed him anyway, especially if it's an old lady or an old man.' "

Moral instruction is formalized in the "preachings" that every Menomini child is supposed to receive from an older person, usually a grandparent, starting at about age eight. Grandparents have already played a very important role in the child's education before that time. Children spend almost as much time with their grandparents (particularly on the mother's side) as they do with their parents, and sometimes considerably more. Menomini mothers have always claimed a rather high degree of freedom. They dance, help collect greens and ferns, hunt and fish, travel, and to increase freedom of movement children will sometimes be left with grandparents. The attachment to the older people on the part of the children is usually great, but it is given a special character by the respect towards and fear of old people as retainers of great supernatural power. Children are taught never to irritate old people, not to stare at them, or talk loudly around them. They are told to fill their pipes, run errands for them, and never hurt their feelings. All old people are potential witches. So children listen well to their grandparents. When the child has reached the eighth year, it is believed that he is no longer likely to want to go back to the spirit world. His own spirit is satisfied with the treatment it has received. So it is now time to lay out the virtues he is expected to acquire and live by in a more directive fashion than heretofore. This preaching continues, with content appropriate to age and role, until the youngsters are married.

Grandmothers tell young girls that they will be getting married someday. They should look after their husbands, keep their clothes well, put good food on the table, not be lazy around the house. They should avoid love potions to get or hold him, because these potions are dangerous and may kill him, or cause him to become so jealous that he will kill her. They are told that a menstruating woman is dangerous, that when she menstruates the first time she will be given utensils of her own to cook with, and that she should stay away from men and children during her menstrual period thereafter to avoid causing them to become ill or die. She is told about the penalties of loose sexual behavior, and that when they are married their husbands can tell "if they have been good." Later on they are also instructed concerning "medicines" that can cause abortion if used during the first few weeks of pregnancy. They are also told to avoid gossiping, talking too much, and minding other people's business. They are told to treat everyone the same way, and particularly to treat their husband the same way whether he is drunk or sober.

Grandfathers tell young boys to be generous, to feed old people. They tell them not to boast of their exploits or abilities, and never to envy someone else's. They are cautioned about looking for bad medicines and are told to keep away from menstruating women. They are told about their obligations to in-laws and their responsibilities to any guardian spirits they may have inherited. They are cautioned about sex and the diseases that can come as a result of dalliance. They are told to treat their wives well and cautioned about the danger that sorcery may be directed at them by the wife's parents if they do not. They are told to mind their own business and never to talk carelessly about important things like religion or the spirits.

In the old days, this period of being "preached to" would have been climaxed by the puberty fast, followed by an intensive period of instruction on the esoteric and sacred aspects of Menomini belief. Individuals who received unusual guardians or vision experiences would be given prolonged and specialized instruction, with all of the details of ritual and cosmogonic rationale, by an old man who was one or another kind of "medicine man." As indicated before, today the puberty fast is no longer possible, and even though there is continuity in the way individuals maintain sacred power and the expectations people have concerning it, the loss of the puberty fast is a serious blow to the efficacy of the native-oriented educational system. Adolescent education is the weakest link in the process today, and it is during adolescence that young people frequently move away from the native-oriented group into the transitional and acculturation-oriented groups in the Menomini community. Sometimes they return to the native-oriented group after several years of experience with an essentially antithetical way of life and the rebuffs any Indian receives as he attempts to move into our social system. More frequently they stay away—psychologically unreconstructed but making partially successful social and economic adaptations to the different way of life. The native-oriented group is shrinking but shows surprising strength in view of the predictions made by every student of Menomini culture since 1890 that the Menomini culture would disappear completely during the next decade or so. I believe that this ability to survive is directly traceable to the effectiveness of the educational system I have described.

The reasons why the system is so effective were made partially explicit in the beginning of this section, and I hope that they have become clearer as the description of education proceeded. Autonomy, equanimity, latescence, and emotional control are taught as character ideals, as values to aspire to in personal conduct. These qualities are taught in the way young children are inducted into more advanced roles, in the things children hear elders saying at ceremonials, in the moral points underscored again and again by parents and grandparents with a definite point of view, making observations and reinforcing behavior in different contexts as events occur that lend themselves to such interpretation. They are taught in myths and stories told now in attentuated but recognizable form. They are revitalized and encapsulated in highly explicit preaching by respected and feared mentors during the period of most intense development just before and into early adolescence.

But the relationship between the Menomini sociocultural system and modal native-oriented Menomini personality is not merely reflexive. Children do not simply grow up to exhibit the socially required personality because they are told to do so. They grow up this way because there is no reason for them not to. Children in this society do not grow up resisting what they are being taught or the cultural agents doing the teaching. The encounters they have had with cultural agents during the early years of experience have been more than favorable—they are designed to make children feel "at home," to make them want to stay. Children are treated with tolerance and supportiveness. It is true that these are qualities in varying degrees characteristic of many non-literate groups, but Menomini children are treated with special respect. Respect, even for children, is probably characteristic of social systems exhibiting a high degree of individual autonomy. In the Menomini case this feature is emphasized and reinforced by the belief that children and old people possess the greatest power and are closest to the supernatural. To be sure, this respect does not result in complete permissiveness. There is gentle, constant, consistent discipline in the restraints with which children are surrounded, and in the constant urging toward morally desirable behavior.

Though subject to gentle constraints, Menomini children are supported, and rarely threatened by authoritarian demands or crude violations of their person in the form of physical punishment. All encounters with cultural agents during the early years of life are favorable to the child. As a result he is open, receptive to learning, and *to becoming what his preceptors want him to be.* The early years of relaxed supportiveness in treatment of children are therefore not discontinuous with the later years of greater constraint and moral discipline. These earlier years are essential as groundwork for what comes later, but the personality structure resulting would be very different without the constraint, the discipline, and the explication of basic moral principles of the later period.

Certain other aspects of the educational process and its effects are more subtle. As Dr. Loeb's paper has made clear, one of the serious problem areas in our education of children is that of sex role identification. This is particularly acute where the mother must take over much of the disciplinary as well as the love-reward role in the nuclear family. Intense emotional relationships between mother and children are formed, and these relationships are marked by ambivalence where the mother is carrying out roles that are in part quite contradictory. The problem is made more acute because there is no escape from it, for either mother or

children. These tight and tense as well as intense emotional relationships between mother and children are fertile grounds for
neurotic dependency, particularly because when the father inter-
rupts this relationship and demands his share of attention from his
wife, the children—especially male children—are likely to resent
his intrusion, and this further interferes with identifications that
should be formed with him and with the male role. Ambivalence
towards both male and female cultural agents identifiable to children as parent surrogates (such as school teachers) is often fostered
by our familial arrangements, and results, I believe, in considerable
displacement of hostility toward adults responsible for education
which interferes with the learning process from kindergarten
through graduate school.

In the native-oriented Menomini situation this constellation of
relationships and resultant feelings do not occur. The mother-
child encounters are at a low level of interaction, with little
eroticism.[7] Exclusive dependency on the mother is impossible also.
The child encounters many other cultural agents very early and
is "mothered" by the father as well as disciplined, and disciplined
by the mother as well as "mothered." The child also frequently,
meaningfully, and early encounters the highly respected grandparents. The relationship formed out of these encounters is even
less loaded emotionally than the one formed with parents. It is
rewarding and supportive, as are those with parents, but the intense (and tense) emotional ties formed between mother and child
in our nuclear suburban families are most unlikely in the Menomini
grandparent-grandchild relationship. Nor can the Grandmother
even offer the erotic rewards of nursing, and there is little competition for her favors between grandsons and grandfathers. The
electric quality of the sexual-emotional triangles and constellations apparent in our nuclear families between young parents and
young children, and in a very muted way, even in the parent-
child relationships in Menomini families, is virtually totally absent

---

[7] I am indebted to John Whiting for numerous insights concerning
parent-child relations and the relationship of later educational experience
to them. His writings on various phases of the processes are numerous, but
two are particularly relevant here. (J. W. M. Whiting, 1958, 1960)

in the grandparent-grandchild "family." Perhaps some of our problems are due to the fact that because of our extreme mobility, both spatially and socially, we do not usually exploit grandparents as educators and caretakers of young children.

These relationships between children, parents, and grandparents help to explain why the native-oriented Menomini can conform to the constrictive demands placed upon them by their sociocultural system—in fact, why they can internalize these constraints without anxiety as a by-product. The guilt and self-doubt, as well as the ambivalent feelings towards parental authority, that issue from the relationships described as occurring frequently in our own society are simply never developed. Guilt and self-doubt are created out of hostility that at first has an outside target but is then inverted because the target becomes unavailable. Children must love their parents, particularly their mothers, in our nuclear family situation, because there are few others to love, or to love them. And yet there is cause for hostility, sometimes intense (if temporary) hate, in the relationships frequently occurring in this family type. This hostility is turned back upon the self because the love relationship must be kept. Anxiety and guilt feelings result. The child must love what he sometimes hates, so he must be wrong. A native-oriented Menomini child is rarely, if ever, put into this "double bind." He can conform to and eventually internalize the norms of his way of life without feelings of hostility, or of self-doubt and guilt, to interfere.

CONCLUSION

I would like to feel that a system of this kind would endure forever, but the powerful industrial-political forces for change towards a sociocultural system and a character type more suited for aggressive, competitive, exploitive human relationships are inexorable. The Menomini way of life is doomed despite its staying power, as are hundreds of others formed over millennia as man groped his way along various and dramatically different paths to separate solutions to the problems of human existence. The native-oriented Menomini know that their way is threatened. They fight to retain it. With self-conscious determination parents say of their children, "We have to try to get 'em on our side. They're Indians and they'll always be Indians." But the older people know that doomsday has come. I would like to end this chapter by letting an old man tell of this in his own way.

> It is tradition for us to teach our children what has been taught to us. I am an old man. I am telling my son, the only one I have. But when I tell him anything, he will not believe me. He believes in the white man's way. But he is an Indian, and full-blooded.
>
> We have come to the crossroads. There came to us one time when I was a boy another white man, that has written down records. What that white man predicted, I still remember. He was talking to my old people. There were many of us there and we listened to him.
>
> He told my father then; "This is your boy. When you die, your boy is coming to the same place as you are now. If he has inherited the same wisdom he will be prominent as you are. But there are not many who will remember these things. Someday it will be gone."
>
> That is now a reality. Soon there will be no one to represent the place of the old people.
>
> My son disregards these things because we are changing to the white man's road. He has no regard for the sacred things I was taught to preserve. He looks upon them as relics.
>
> He has no disrespect for me. The things he disregards he does not think of as sacred. He has no understanding that there are two sides to these things. When I think of his future . . . he is alone in the world with no understanding of life . . . of the old Menomini way. He is trying to make a poor copy of the white man's civilization. He will never know anything himself, even if I were to teach him.
>
> It is as that white man said. Now you have come to me, like this man did with my father. But sometime a man will come to my son and he will know nothing.[8]

---

[8] The white man was Alanson Buck Skinner, who wrote prolifically and well on the Menomini in the 1910s and early 1920s. This is an excerpt from an autobiography, given in Menomini and translated by Robert Deer, my interpreter.

References

Cohen, Yehudi, 1961, *Social Structure and Personality: A Casebook*. New York: Holt, Rinehart and Winston, Inc.

Cooper, Kenneth C., 1955, *Individuality in the U.S. and English Cultures*. Unpublished M.A. thesis, Stanford University.

Fromm, Erich, 1941, *Escape From Freedom*. New York: Holt, Rinehart and Winston, Inc.

————, 1949, "Psychoanalytic Characterology and Its Application to the Understanding of Culture," in S. S. Sargent and Marion W. Smith, eds., *Culture and Personality*. New York: The Viking Fund.

Green, Arnold, 1946, "The Middle Class Male Child and Neurosis." *American Sociological Review*, II:31–41.

Hallowell, A. I., 1951, "The Use of Prospective Techniques in the Study of the Socio-psychological Aspects of Acculturation." *Journal of Projective Techniques*, XV:27–44. Also in A. I. Hallowell, 1955, *Culture and Experience*, Philadelphia: University of Pennsylvania.

————, 1955, "Fear and Anxiety as Cultural and Individual Variables in a Primitive Society," and "The Social Function of Anxiety in a Primitive Society," in A. I. Hallowell, *Culture and Experience*. Philadelphia: University of Pennsylvania.

Hoffman, Walter J., 1896, *The Menomini Indians*, Bureau of American Ethnology, 14th Annual Report, Washington, D.C.

Hsu, Francis, 1961, "American Core Value and National Character," in F. Hsu, ed., *Psychological Anthropology: Approaches to Culture and Personality*, Homewood, Ill.: Dorsey Press, Inc.

Inkeles, Alex, 1958, "Personality and Social Structure," in R. Merton, L. Brown. *Sociology Today*. New York: Basic Books, Inc.

————, and D. J. Levinson, 1954, "National Character: The Study of Modal Personality and Sociocultural Systems," in G. Lindzey, ed., *Handbook of Social Psychology*, Vol. II. Reading, Mass.: Addison-Wesley Publishing Company.

Kaplan, Bert, 1957, "Personality and Social Structure," in J. B. Gittler, ed., *Review of Sociology, Analysis of a Decade*. New York: John Wiley & Sons, Inc.

Kardiner, Abram, 1945, *The Psychological Frontiers of Society*. New York: Columbia University Press.

Linton, Ralph, 1945, *The Cultural Background of Personality*. New York: Appleton-Century-Crofts, Inc.

Mekeel, H. S., 1936, "The Economy of a Modern Teton-Dakota Community." Yale University Publications in Anthropology, No. 6. New Haven, Conn.: Yale University.

Merton, Robert K., 1949, *Social Theory and Social Structure*, New York: The Free Press of Glencoe.

Parsons, T., and R. Bales, 1955, *Family Socialization and Interaction Process*. New York: The Free Press of Glencoe.

————, 1961, "Social Structure and the Development of Personality," in B. Kaplan, ed., *Studying Personality Cross-Culturally*. New York: Harper & Row, Publishers.

————, and E. A. Shils, 1952, *Toward a General Theory of Action*. Cambridge, Mass.: Harvard University.

Riesman, David, Nathan Glazer, and Reuel Denney, 1950, *The Lonely Crowd: a Study of the Changing American Character*. New Haven, Conn.: Yale University Press.

Skinner, Alanson B., 1915, *Social Life and Ceremonial Bundles of the Menomini Indians*. Anthropological Papers of the American Museum of Natural History, Vol. XIII, Part I. New York.

Slotkin, John S., 1952, *Menomini Peyotism*. Transactions of the American Philosophical Society, Vol. 42, Part 4, new series. Philadelphia: American Philosophical Society.

————, 1957, *The Menomini Powwow*. Milwaukee Public Museum Publications in Anthropology, No. 4, Milwaukee Public Museum.

Spindler, George D., 1952, "Personality in Menomini Indian Acculturation." *Psychiatry*, 15:151–159.

————, 1955, *Sociocultural and Psychological Processes in Menomini Acculturation*. University of California Publications in Culture and Society. Vol. V. Berkeley, Calif.: University of California.

————, and Louise Spindler, 1957, "American Indian Personality Types and Their Sociocultural Roots." *The Annals of the American Academy of Political and Social Sciences*, 311: 147–157.

Spindler, Louise, 1952, "Witchcraft in Menomini Acculturation." *American Anthropologist*, 54:593–602.

————, 1962, *Women and Culture Change: A Case Study of the*

Menomini Indians, Memoir 92, American Anthropological Association.

——, and George D. Spindler, 1958, "Male and Female Adaptations in Culture Change" *American Anthropologist,* Vol. 60: 217–233.

Thompson, Laura, 1948, "Attitudes and Acculturation." *American Anthropologist,* 50:200–215.

Weber, Max, 1930, *The Protestant Ethic and the Spirit of Capitalism,* trans. by T. Parsons, New York: Charles Scribner's Sons.

Whiting, John, R. Kluckhohn, and A. Anthony, 1958, "The function of Male Initiation Ceremonies at Puberty," in E. Maccoby, T. Newcomb, and E. Hartley, eds., *Readings in Social Psychology.* New York: Holt, Rinehart and Winston, Inc.

——, and B. Whiting, 1960, "Contributions of Anthropology to the Methods of Studying Child Rearing," in P. Mussen, *Handbook of Research Methods In Child Development.* New York: John Wiley & Sons, Inc.

19———C. W. M. Hart

Contrasts between
Prepubertal and
Postpubertal Education[*]

GENERAL INTRODUCTION

This chapter represents an attempt to use the body of
generally accepted anthropological information as a baseline for
considering the educational process. It might be paraphrased as
"the educative process, anthropologically considered." I assume
that "anthropologically considered" is equivalent to "cross-culturally considered," and I assume that education refers to any
process at any stage of life in which new knowledge is acquired or
new habits or new attitudes formed. That is, I have taken the question which forms the core problem of this volume and tried
to develop a few generalizations about that problem from the
general anthropological literature. But it follows that since they
are anthropological generalizations their usefulness to education
is a matter of opinion. All I claim for them is the old basis upon
which anthropology has always justified its preoccupation with the
simpler societies, namely that by studying the simpler societies we
gain perspective and proportion in really seeing our own society
and from that better perspective comes better understanding of
common human social processes. I hope that the material contained in this chapter will at least enable the readers interested in
education to see our own educative process in better perspective

*Reprinted with minor revision from *Education and Anthropology*, George D.
Spindler, Editor, with the permission of the Publishers, Stanford University Press; copyright 1955 by the Board of Trustees of the Leland Stanford Junior University.

and help them separate what is distinctively American in it from what is general-social and general-human.

My starting point is a distinction that is made by Herskovits. In his chapter on education in the book called *Man and His Works* (1948) he finds it necessary to stress that the training of the young in the simpler societies of the world is carried on through two different vehicles. The child learns a lot of things knocking around underfoot in the home, in the village street, with his brothers and sisters, and in similar environments, and he learns a lot of other things in the rather formidable apparatus of what is usually called in the anthropological literature the initiation ceremonies or the initiation schools.

Herskovits stresses that initiation education takes place outside the home and is worthy to be called schooling, contrasts it with the education the child receives knocking around the household and the village long before the initiation period begins, and decides that the main feature of the latter is that it is within the home, and that it should therefore be called education as contrasted with schooling. There he, and many other writers on the subject, tend to leave the matter.

This tendency, to leave the problem at that point, is rather a pity. Further exploration of these two contrasting vehicles for training of the young will pay rich dividends, and it is to such further exploration that the bulk of this paper is devoted. But before going on, certain unsatisfactory features of Herskovits' treatment must be mentioned. To suggest, as he does, that pre-initiation education is "within the home" is misleading to people unacquainted with the character of primitive society. While initiation education is very definitely outside the home and—as we shall see later—this remoteness from home is a very essential feature of it, it does not follow that the other has to be, or even is likely to be, "within the home." The home in most primitive societies is very different indeed from the connotation of "home" in America, and the type of education to which Herskovits is referring takes place in every conceivable type of primary group. The young child in primitive society may be subjected to the learning process in his early years in his household (Eskimo), or in a medley of dozens of households (Samoa); his parents may ignore him and leave him to drag himself up as best he can (Mundugumor); he may be corrected or scolded by any passer-by (Zuñi); his male mentor may not be his father at all but his mother's brother (many Melanesian cultures); and so on.

I do not intend to explore the social-psychological results of this variety of primary-group situations; all I mention them for here is to demonstrate how misleading it is to lump them all together as comprising "education within the home." About the only things they have in common is that they all take place in the earlier years of life and they don't take place within the formal framework of initiation ceremonies. I propose therefore to call all this type of education by the title "preinitiation" or "prepuberty" education (since most initiation ceremonial begins at puberty or later), and the problem I am mainly concerned with is the set of contrasts that exists between what societies do with their children in the preinitiation period and what is done with them in the postinitiation period. In other words Herskovits' distinction between education and schooling becomes clearer and more useful if they are simply called prepuberty education and postpuberty education.

One further explanatory comment is necessary. Not all primitive societies possess initiation ceremonies of the formal standardized type that anthropology has become familiar with in many parts of the world. How "schooling" or postpuberty education is handled in those primitive societies which lack initiation ceremonies and what the results of such lack are for the adult culture are interesting questions, but they are outside the scope of the present paper. What we are concerned with here is the set of contrasts between prepubertal and postpubertal education in those numerous and widespread societies which include formal initiation ceremonies in their set of official institutions.

PREPUBERTAL AND POSTPUBERTAL EDUCATION—HOW DO THEY DIFFER?

If attention is directed to the ways education is carried on in the prepuberty and postpuberty periods in a large number of simple societies—viz., those "with initiation ceremonies"—some very impressive contrasts begin to appear. They can be dealt with under four heads—(1) Regulation, (2) Personnel, (3) Atmosphere, (4) Curriculum; but the nature of the data will require us to jump back and forth between these four divisions, since they are all interwoven.

1. *Regulation.*—Postpuberty education, in such societies, does not begin until at least the age of twelve or thirteen, and in many cases several years later than that. By that age of course, the child has already acquired a great deal of what we call his culture. How has he acquired the things he knows at the age of twelve or thirteen? The traditional anthropological monographs are said to tell us little or nothing about "early education." I suggest that the reason the older literature tells us so little that is definite about the early prepubertal training of the children is basically for the same reason that we know so little about preschool education in our own culture, or did know so little before Gesell. Until the appearance of *The Child from Five to Ten* (Gesell and Ilg, 1946), the information on the preschool "enculturation" of the American child was just as barren as the anthropological literature. Whether Gesell has really answered the question for the American child and whether a Gesell-like job has been done or can be done for a primitive society are questions which need not concern us here except to point up the real question: Why is it so rare to find clear information as to what goes on in the learning process during the preschool years, in any culture?

One possible answer is that preschool education is rarely if ever standardized, rarely if ever regulated around known and visible social norms.[1] It is an area of cultural laissez faire, within very wide limits of tolerance, and society at large does not lay down any firm blueprint which all personnel engaged in "raising the young" must follow. If, instead of asking for a "pattern" or "norm," we ask the simpler question, "What happens?" it seems to me that the literature is not nearly so barren of information as has

---

[1] *Editor's note:* Nonanthropologist readers should be aware of the fact that Dr. Hart's statements concerning the lack of uniformity in prepubertal child training would be contested by many anthropologists, though the same ones might accept his basic position that in comparison to pubertal and postpubertal training the earlier years of experience are *relatively* less structured and less subject to the pressure of public opinion.

been argued. It tends to suggest that anything and everything happens in the same society. For instance Schapera's account of childhood among the Bakgatla is pretty clear: "The Bakgatla say that thrashing makes a child wise. But they also say a growing child is like a little dog and though it may annoy grown-ups, it must be taught proper conduct with patience and forbearance" (Schapera, 1940). As Herskovits has pointed out, this mixture of strict and permissive techniques is also reported for Lesu in Melanesia by Powdermaker, for the Apache by Opler, and for the Kwoma by Whiting (Herskovits, *op. cit.*). This list can readily be added to.

There is no point in counting how many cultures use severe punishment and how many do not. The explicit statements of the fieldworkers just cited are at least implicit in dozens of others. Do the natives beat their children? Yes. Do they fondle and make a fuss over their children? Yes. Do they correct them? Yes. Do they let them get away with murder? Also yes, All this in the same culture. I repeat that it is pretty clear what happens in the prepuberty years in the simpler societies. Anything and everything from extreme punishment to extreme permissiveness may occur and does occur in the same culture.

The fieldworkers do not tell us what the pattern of early education is because there is rarely any one clear-cut pattern. What each individual child learns or is taught or is not taught is determined pretty much by a number of individual variables. A few such variables are: interest or lack of interest of individual parents in teaching their children, size of family and each sibling's position in it, whether the next house or camp is close by or far away, whether the neighbors have children of the same age, the amount of interaction and type of interaction of the particular "peergroups" of any given child. The number of variables of this type is almost infinite; the child is simply dumped in the midst of them to sink or swim, and as a result no two children in the same culture learn the same things in the same way. One, for example, may learn about sex by spying upon his parents, a second by spying upon a couple of comparative strangers, a third by getting some explicit instruction from his father or his mother (or his elder brother or his mother's brother), a fourth by listening to sniggering gossip in the play group, and a fifth by observing a pair of dogs in the sexual act. Which of these ways of learning is the norm? Obviously none of them is, at least not in the same sense as that in which we say that it is the norm for a person to inherit the property of his mother's brother, or to use an intermediary in courtship, or to learn certain important myths at Stage 6B of the initiation ceremonies.

In asking for a uniform cultural pattern in such a laissez faire, anything-goes area, we are asking for the inherently impossible, or at least the nonexistent. There are, of course, some cultural limits set in each society to this near-anarchy: there will, for example, be general outrage and widespread social disapproval if one family shamefully neglects its children or some child goes to what is by general consensus regarded as "too far," but such limits of toleration are very wide indeed in every society. The household is almost sovereign in its rights to do as much or as little as it likes —that is, to do what it likes about its offspring in the *preschool* years. The rest of society is extraordinarily reluctant everywhere to interfere with a household's sovereign right to bring up its preschool children as it wishes. And most primitive parents, being busy with other matters and having numerous children anyway, leave the kids to bring each other up or to just grow like Topsy.

There are other strong lines of evidence supporting this judgment that prepuberty education in the simpler societies is relatively so variable as to be virtually normless. One is the self-evident fact which anybody can verify by reading the monographs, that no fieldworker, not even among those who have specifically investigated the matter of child practices, has ever found a tribe where several reliable informants could give him a rounded and unified account of the preschool educational practices of their tribe comparable to the rounded and generalized picture they can give him, readily and easily, of the local religion, or the folklore, or the moral code for the adults, or the local way of getting married, or the right way to build a canoe or plant a garden. This difference can best be conveyed to an anthropologist audience, perhaps, by contrasting the sort of answer fieldworkers get to such questions as "Tell me some of your myths," or "How do you make silver ornaments?" or "How do you treat your mother-in-law?" with the answer they get to a question like "How do you bring up children?" To the former type of question (not asked as crudely as that, of course) the answers will come (usually) in the form of norms—stereotyped and generalized statements that don't differ a great deal from one informant to the next, or, if they do so differ, will always be referred to a "right" way or a "proper" way: the "right" way to build a canoe, the "proper" way to treat one's mother-in-law, the "correct" form of a myth or a ceremony, and so on. Even in the type of sentence structure the answers come in, they will have this official character—"We do it this way" or "It is our custom here to do thus and so"—and often in case of conflicting versions an argument will develop, not over what the informant himself does but over whether what he says is "right" or socially sanctioned as "the right way."

But given the opportunity to perform a similar generalized descriptive job upon "how children are or should be brought up," informants fail dismally to produce anything of this kind. They either look blank and say little or nothing, or come up with a set of empty platitudes—"All boys should be brought up good boys," "They should all respect their elders," etc.—which clearly have no relation to the facts of life going on all around the speaker; or (most common of all) they fall back onto their own life history and do a Sun Chief or Crashing Thunder sort of job. That is, they give in endless and boring detail an account of how they individually were brought up, or how they bring up their own children, but they clearly have no idea of whether their case is typical or atypical of the tribe at large. And the anthropologist equally has no idea of how representative or unrepresentative this case is. This happens so constantly that we are left with only one conclusion, namely, that if there is a cultural tradition for preschool education (comparable with the cultural tradition for religion or for tabu-observance or for technology), then the average native in a simple society is completely unaware of what it is.

This same conclusion is also supported by another line of evidence, namely, the complete change that comes over the picture when we move from prepuberty education to postpuberty education. Postpuberty education is marked in the simpler societies by the utmost degree of standardization and correctness. At puberty the initiation rituals begin, and perhaps the most universal thing about these is their meticulously patterned character. Every line painted on a boy's body, every movement of a performer, every word or phrase uttered, the right person to make every move, is rigidly prescribed as having to be done in one way only —the right way. A wrongly drawn line, a misplaced phrase, an unsanctioned movement, or the right movement made by the wrong person or at the wrong time, and the whole ritual is ruined. They belong to the same general type of social phenomena as the English Coronation ceremony or the Catholic sacrifice of the Mass; there is only one way of doing them, regardless of the individuals involved, namely the "right" way. By contrast that meticulously patterned feature throws into sharp relief the haphazard, permissive, and unstandardized character of the education that *precedes* the time of puberty.

2. *Personnel.*—So far, then, our stress has been on the unregulated character of primitive preschool education. Certain further things become clearer if at this point we switch our attention from the focus of regulation to the focus of personnel—i.e., from the question of whether the education is controlled and standardized to the question of who imparts the education. Anthropologists are coming more and more to realize the importance of the "Who does what?" type of question in field work, and perhaps nowhere is it so important to know who does what than in the area we are discussing. From whom does the child learn in the simpler societies? As far as the preinitiation years are concerned the answer is obvious: He learns from his intimates, whether they be intimates of a senior generation like his parents or intimates of his own generation like his siblings, cousins, playmates, etc. In the preinitiation years he learns nothing or next to nothing from strangers or near-strangers. Strangers and near-strangers are people he rarely sees and even more rarely converses with; and, since learning necessarily involves interaction, it is from the people he interacts with most that he learns most, and from the people he interacts with least that he learns least.

This is so obvious that it needs little comment. But one important point about intimates must be made. In all cultures it appears as if this "learning from intimates" takes two forms. The child learns from his parents or other senior members of his family and he also learns from his play groups. And the interaction processes in these two situations are different in several important respects. The parents are intimates and so are the members of the play group, but there is the important difference that parents, to some extent at least, represent the official culture (are the surrogates of society, in Dollard's phrase), while the play groups do not. All the work upon play groups in Western society has tended to stress what autonomous little subcultures they are, each with its own social organization, its own rules, its own values. The family is a primary group, but one which is tied into the total formal structure of the society and therefore subject to at least some over-all social control. The play group is an autonomous little world of its own, whose rules may be, and often are, directly at variance with the rules of the home or of the wider society.

If, then, as suggested above, it is true that in most societies—simple or modern—each household is allowed a great deal of freedom to bring up its children pretty much as it chooses, and if this wide degree of tolerance leads in turn to a wide variation in the ways in which the culture is presented to different children, then obviously such variation is enormously increased by the role of the play group. Even if we were told of a culture in which all households standardized their child-training practices, it would still fall far short of being convincing evidence of a standardized child-training situation because of the great amount of knowledge which children in all cultures acquire without the household or at least the parents being involved in the transmission process, namely the knowledge which the child "picks up somewhere."

Once we recognize the influence of this second group of intimates on how the child acquires certain aspects of his culture, the case for wide variation in early child training is greatly strengthened. There seems to be no evidence that would suggest that the play group in simple societies functions in any notably different way from the way it functions in modern societies, but unfortunately we have few studies of the "subcultures" of the playworld in other than Western cultures. Among child psychologists dealing with Western cultures, Piaget in particular has some findings that are relevant to the present discussion (Piaget, 1929, 1932). These findings tend to show that at least by the age of ten or eleven the child has become empirical and secular in his attitudes toward rules and norms of play behavior, partly because he has learned by that time that each primary group has its own rules, so that there is no "right" way, no over-all norm—at least for children's games such as marbles—for all play groups to conform to. Piaget, of course, is describing European children, but primitive children spend at least as much time in unsupervised play groups as European or American children, and since their preschool period is certainly many years more prolonged, there is no apparent reason why this conclusion of Piaget should not have cross-cultural validity.

However, I am not trying to develop a theory but merely to follow through some of the difficulties that are hidden in the simple statement above that preschool learning is between intimates. There are different sorts of intimacy because of the child's dual relation to his home and to his playmates, and some of his culture is mediated to him by each. We don't know nearly enough about degrees of intimacy, and we may be forced by further research to start making classifications and subdivisions between the different sorts of intimate relationships (different "levels" of primary groups?) to which the child in any culture is exposed in his preschool years. Even if we do, however, the fact still remains that in his preinitiation years the child in primitive society learns nothing from strangers or near-strangers. And this leads to the second comment under the head of Personnel, which is that in his *postpuberty* education in contrast to that of *prepuberty* he *has to* learn from strangers or near-strangers and cannot possibly learn from anybody else. When puberty arrives and the boy is therefore ready for initiation (or the girl for marriage), his family, his siblings, his gangs, his village, all the intimates to whom his training or learning has been left up to now, are roughly pushed aside and a whole new personnel take over his training. Who these new teachers are varies from culture to culture, but a very common feature is that they be nonintimates of the boy, semistrangers drawn from other sections of the tribe (opposite moieties, different districts or villages, hostile or semihostile clans, different age groups, and so on), people with whom he is not at all intimate. Who they are and what they represent is made painfully clear in the ritual. An actual case will help to make clear the nature of the transition.

Among the Tiwi of North Australia, one can see the traumatic nature of the initiation period in very clear form, and part of trauma lies in the sudden switch of personnel with whom the youth has to associate. A boy reaches thirteen or fourteen or so, and the physiological signs of puberty begin to appear. Nothing happens, possibly for many months. Then suddenly one day, toward evening when the people are gathering around their camp-fires for the main meal of the day after coming in from their day's hunting and food-gathering, a group of three or four heavily armed and taciturn strangers appear in camp. In full war regalia they walk in silence to the camp of the boy and say curtly to the household: "We have come for So-and-So." Immediately pande-monium breaks loose. The mother and the rest of the older women begin to howl and wail. The father rushes for his spears. The boy himself, panic-stricken, tries to hide, the younger children begin to cry, and the household dogs begin to bark. It is all terribly simi-lar to the reaction which is provoked by the arrival of the police at an American home to pick up a juvenile delinquent. This simi-larity extends to the behavior of the neighbors. These carefully abstain from identifying with either the strangers or the stricken household. They watch curiously the goings-on but make no move that can be identified as supporting either side. This is par-ticularly notable in view of the fact that the strangers are strangers to all of them, too, that is, they are men from outside the encamp-ment, or outside the band, who, under any other circumstances, would be greeted by a shower of spears. But not under these cir-cumstances (see also Hart and Pilling, 1960).

In fact, when we know our way around the culture we realize that the arrival of the strangers is not as unexpected as it appears. The father of the boy and the other adult men of the camp not only knew they were coming but have even agreed with them on a suitable day for them to come. The father's rush for his spears to protect his son and to preserve the sanctity of his household is make-believe. If he puts on too good an act, the older men will intervene and restrain him from interfering with the purposes of the strangers. With the father immobilized the child clings to his mother, but the inexorable strangers soon tear him (literally) from his mother's arms and from the bosom of his bereaved family and, still as grimly as they came, bear him off into the night. No society could symbolize more dramatically that initiation necessitates the forcible taking away of the boy from the bosom of his family, his village, his neighbors, his intimates, his friends. And who are these strangers who forcibly drag the terrified boy off to he knows not what? In Tiwi they are a selected group of his senior male cross-cousins. To people who understand primitive social organization that should convey most of what I want to convey. They are "from the other side of the tribe," men with whom the boy has had little to do and whom he may have never seen before. They belong to the group of men who have married or will marry his sisters, and marriage, it is well to remember, in primitive society is a semihostile act. As cross-cousins, these men cannot possibly belong to the same clan as the boy, or to the same territorial group, and since only senior and already fully initiated men are eligible for the job they will be men in their thirties or forties, twenty or more years older than he.

By selecting senior cross-cousins to conduct the forcible separation of the boy from the home and thus project him into the postpuberty proceedings, the Tiwi have selected men who are as remote from the boy as possible. The only thing they and he have in common is that they are all members of the same tribe—nothing else. If, then, we have stressed that all training of the child in the prepuberty period is carried on by intimates, we have to stress equally the fact that the postpuberty training has to be in the hands of nonintimates. Anybody who is in any way close to the boy—by blood, by residence, by age, or by any other form of affiliation or association—is *ipso facto* ineligible to have a hand in his postpuberty training.

I selected the Tiwi as my example because the case happens to be rather spectacular in the clarity of its symbolism, but if one examines the literature one finds everywhere or almost everywhere the same emphasis. Those who prefer Freudian symbolism I refer to the initiation ceremonies of the Kiwai Papuans (Landtmann, 1927), where during initiation the boy is required to actually step on his mother's stomach; when Landtmann asked the significance of this he was told that it meant the boy was now "finished with the place where he came from" (i.e., his mother's womb). Van Gennep has collected all the older cases in his classic *Rites de passage* (Van Gennep, 1909), and no new ones which invalidate his generalizations have been reported since his time.

I therefore suggest two reasonably safe generalizations about initiation rituals: (*a*) The rituals themselves are designed to emphasize in very clear terms that initiation ceremonies represent a clear break with all home, household, home-town, and friendship-group ties; and (*b*) as a very basic part of such emphasis the complete handling of all initiation proceedings, and initiation instruction, from their inception at puberty to their final conclusion often more than a decade later, is made the responsibility of men who are comparative strangers to the boy and who are thus as different as possible in their social relationships to him from the teachers, guiders, instructors, and associates he has had up to that time.

3. *Atmosphere*—It should now be clear what is meant by the third head, Atmosphere. The arrival of the strangers to drag the yelling boy out of his mother's arms is just the spectacular beginning of a long period during which the separation of the boy from everything that has gone before is emphasized in every possible way at every minute of the day and night. So far his life has been easy; now it is hard. Up to now he has never necessarily experienced any great pain, but in the initiation period in many tribes pain, sometimes horrible, intense pain, is an obligatory feature. The boy of twelve or thirteen, used to noisy, boisterous, irresponsible play, is expected and required to sit still for hours and days at a time saying nothing whatever but concentrating upon and endeavoring to understand long intricate instructions and "lectures" given him by his hostile and forbidding preceptors (who are, of course, the men who carried him off to initiation, the "strangers" of the previous section). Life has suddenly become real and earnest and the initiate is required literally to "put away the things of a child," even the demeanor. The number of tabus and unnatural behaviors enjoined upon the initiate is endless. He mustn't speak unless he is spoken to; he must eat only certain foods, and often only in certain ways, at fixed times, and in certain

fixed positions. All contact with females, even speech with them, is rigidly forbidden, and this includes mother and sisters. He cannot even scratch his head with his own hand, but must do it with a special stick and so on, through a long catalogue of special, unnatural, but obligatory behaviors covering practically every daily activity and every hour of the day and night. And during this time he doesn't go home at night or for the week end or on a forty-eight-hour pass, but remains secluded in the bush, almost literally the prisoner of his preceptors, for months and even years at a time. If he is allowed home at rare intervals, he has to carry all his tabus with him, and nothing is more astonishing in Australia than to see some youth who the year before was a noisy, brash, boisterous thirteen-year-old, sitting the following year, after his initiation is begun, in the midst of his family, with downcast head and subdued air, not daring even to smile, still less to speak. He is "home on leave," but he might just as well have stayed in camp for all the freedom from discipline his spell at home is giving him.

The preoccupations of anthropologists with other interests (that of the earlier field workers with the pain-inflicting aspects of the initiations, and the recent preoccupation with early physiological experiences) have directed attention away from what may well be the most important aspect of education in the simpler societies, namely the possibly traumatic aspect of the initiation ceremonies. From whatever aspect we view them their whole tenor is to produce shock, disruption, a sharp break with the past, a violent projection out of the known into the unknown. Perhaps the boys are old enough to take it in their stride and the experience is not really traumatic. If so, it would seem that primitive society goes to an awful lot of trouble and wastes an awful lot of man-hours needlessly. Actually we don't know what the psychological effects of initiation upon the initiates are. All that can be said safely is that judged by the elaboration and the minuteness of detail in the shocking and disruptive features of initiation rituals, they certainly appear to be designed to produce the maximum amount of shock possible for the society to achieve.

This may suggest that our own exaggerated concern with protecting our own adolescents from disturbing experiences is quite unnecessary. If the grueling ordeal of subincision, with all its accompanying disruptive devices, leaves the young Australian psychologically unscathed, we needn't worry that Universal Military Training, for instance, will seriously upset the young American. But perhaps something in the prepuberty training prepares the young Australian and makes him capable of standing the trauma of the initiation period.

4. *Curriculum.*—What is the purpose of all this elaboration of shock ritual? Ask the natives themselves and they will answer vaguely, "to make a child into a man." "Occasionally a more specific verb is used and the answer becomes, "to teach a boy to become a man." What is supposed to be learned and what do the preceptors teach in the initiation schools? Perhaps the most surprising thing is what is not taught. It is hard to find in the literature any case where the initiation curriculum contains what might be called "practical subjects," or how to make a basic living. (There appear to be certain exceptions to this generalization, but they are more apparent than real.) The basic food-getting skills of the simpler peoples are never imparted in the initiation schools. Where practical subjects are included (as in Polynesia or in the Poro schools of Liberia and Sierra Leone), they are specialized crafts, not basic food-getting skills. Hunting, gardening, cattle-tending, fishing, are not taught the boy at initiation; he has already learned the rudiments of these at home in his intimate groups before his initiation starts. This is a surprising finding because of the well-known fact that many of these people live pretty close to the starvation point, and none of them manage to extract much more than subsistence from their environment. But despite this, the cultures in question are blissfully oblivious of economic determinism, and blandly leave instruction in basic food production to the laissez-faire, casual, hit-or-miss teaching of parents, friends, play groups, etc. When society itself forcibly takes over the boy in order to make him into a man and teach him the things a man should know, it is not concerned with teaching him to be a better hunter or gardener or tender of cattle or fisherman, even though the economic survival of the tribe clearly depends on all of the adult men being good at one or another of these occupations. The initiation curricula cover instead quite a different series of subjects, which

I am tempted to call "cultural subjects"—in either sense of the word "culture."

Of course, there is much variation here from tribe to tribe and region to region, but the imparting of religious knowledge always occupies a prominent place. This (in different cultures) includes such things as the learning of the myths, the tribal accounts of the tribe's own origin and history, and the performance, the meaning, and the sacred connections and connotations of the ceremonials. In brief, novices are taught theology, which in primitive society is inextricably mixed up with astronomy, geology, geography, biology (the mysteries of birth and sex), philosophy, art, and music—in short, the whole cultural heritage of the tribe. As Pettit has pointed out (dealing with North America, but his statement has universal anthropological validity), the instruction in the initiation schools is "a constant challenge to the elders to review, analyze, dramatize, and defend their cultural heritage" (Pettit, 1946). That sentence "review, analyze, dramatize, and defend their cultural heritage" is very striking, because you can apply it equally aptly to a group of naked old men in Central Australia sitting talking to a novice in the middle of a treeless desert, and to most lectures in a college of liberal arts in the United States. It serves to draw attention to the fact that, in the simpler societies, the schools run and manned and controlled and financed by the society at large are designed not to make better economic men of the novices, or better food producers, but to produce better citizens, better carriers of the culture through the generations, people better informed about the world they live in and the tribe they belong to. It is here finally, through this sort of curriculum, that each adolescent becomes "enculturated," no matter how haphazard and individualized his learning and his growth may have been up to now. It is through the rigidly disciplined instruction of a common and rigidly prescribed curriculum that he assumes, with all his fellow tribesmen, a common culture. This is where standardization occurs in the educational process of the simpler societies. Everybody who goes through the initiation schools, generation after generation, is presented with the same material, organized and taught in the same way, with no allowances made for individual taste or choice or proclivity, and no substitutions or electives allowed. When we realize how stand-ardized and rigid and uniform this curriculum is, it should help us to realize how variable, how un-uniform, how dictated by chance, accident, and the personal whims of individual parents, in-dividual adult relatives, and the variation in peer and play groups is the "curriculum" on or in which the individual child is trained during the long impressionable period that precedes puberty.

GENERAL CONCLUSION

The above discussion has, I hope, provided the basis for some helpful generalizations about education in primitive so-cieties, or at least has opened up some new avenues for further exploration. The main points of this discussion may be summed up as follows:

1. There are typically (though not universally) in primitive societies two sharply contrasting educational vehicles, the pre-school process, lasting from birth to puberty, and the initiation procedures, beginning around puberty or a little later and lasting from six months to fifteen years. These two educational vehicles show some highly significant contrasts.

2. From the point of view of regulation, the preschool period is characterized by its loose, vague, unsystematic character. Few primitive societies follow any set standards or rules on how chil-dren shall be brought up. It is true that there are frequently, per-haps usually, pretty clear rules (which are actually followed) telling mothers how to hold a baby, correct methods for suckling or weaning, and standardized techniques of toilet training (though I suspect some of these are nothing but copybook maxims), but outside the "physiological areas of child-training" (which there-fore have to bear all the weight the Freudians put upon them), it is rare indeed to find in primitive cultures any conformity from family to family or from case to case with regard to anything else in the child's early career. This is not, of course, to deny that there are differences from culture to culture in the degree to which children are loved and fussed over or treated as nuisances or joys.

I am not questioning the fact, for example, that the Arapesh love children, whereas the Mundugumor resent them. What I am re-iterating is that there is still a wide variation not only possible but inevitable in conditioning and learning between one Mundugumor child and the next.

3. If this view is correct, it raises certain interesting possi-bilities for theory. Because of the heavy Freudian emphasis in the literature on child training in recent years, there exists a strong and unfortunate tendency to talk of child training as if it were co-terminous with swaddling, suckling, weaning, and toilet-train-ing practices. But these "physiological" areas or "bodily functions" areas are only a small part of the preschool education of the primi-tive child. Even if in primitive cultures the physiological areas of child training are relatively standardized (and this is by no means certain), there is no evidence that the nonphysiological areas are. On the contrary, the evidence points in the other direction. Among adult members of the same society there may be, for ex-ample, great variation in apparent strength of the sex drive, or in the overt expression of aggressive or passive personality traits (Hart, 1954). Where does such "personality variation" come from? From childhood experiences, say the Freudians. I agree. But in order to demonstrate that personality variation in adult life has its roots in early childhood experiences, it is necessary to show not that childhood experiences are highly standardized in early life and that child training is uniform, but that they are highly variable. How can we account for the self-evident fact of adult personality variation by stressing the uniformity of standardization of childhood training? Surely the more valid hypothesis or the more likely lead is to be found in those aspects of child training which are not uniform and not standardized.

4. So much for the preschool training. But there is also the other vehicle of education and youth training in primitive society, the initiation rituals. The initiation period demonstrates to us what standardization and uniformity of training really mean. When we grasp the meaning of this demonstration we can only conclude that compared with the rigidities of the initiation period, the prepuberty period is a loose, lax period. Social scientists who find it necessary for their theories to stress uniformity and pressures

toward conformity in simple societies are badly advised to take the prepuberty period for their examples. The natives themselves know better than this. When they are adults, it is to the happy, unregulated, care-free days of prepuberty that they look back. "Then my initiation began," says the informant, and immediately a grim, guarded "old-man" expression comes over his face, "and I was taken off by the old men." The same old men (and women) who sit around and indulgently watch the vagaries and idiosyncrasies of the children without correction become the grim, vigilant, reproving watchers of the initiates, and any departure or attempted departure from tradition is immediately reprimanded.

5. Who are the agents of this discipline? Primitive societies answer in loud and unmistakable tones that discipline cannot be imposed by members of the primary group, that it has to be imposed by "outsiders." The widespread nature of this feature of initiation is, to my mind, very impressive. Making a boy into a man is rarely, anywhere, left to the family, the household, the village, to which he belongs and where he is on intimate terms with people.[2] The initiation schools are directed at imparting instruction that cannot be given in the home, under conditions as unlike home conditions as possible, by teachers who are the antithesis of the home teachers the boy has hitherto had. The symbolisms involved in the forcible removal from the home atmosphere; the long list of tabus upon homelike acts, homelike speech, homelike demeanor, homelike habits; the selection of the initiators (i.e., the teachers or preceptors) from the semihostile sections of the tribe—all tell the same story, that the turning of boys into men can only be achieved by making everything about the proceedings as different from the home and the prepuberty situation as possible. Everything that happens to the initiate during initiation has to be as different as it can be made by human ingenuity from the things that happened to him before initiation.

----

[2] In the original draft of this paper I mentioned the Arapesh as one of the few exceptions. At the Stanford conference, however, Dr. Mead pointed out that while it is true that initiation in Arapesh is carried out by intimates, they wear masks. To me this correction of my original remark dramatically emphasizes the main point. The Arapesh social structure is such that there are no "strangers" to use for initiation; therefore they invent them by masking some intimates.

6. This becomes pointed up still more when we remember that what is actually being taught in the initiation schools is the whole value system of the culture, its myths, its religion, its philosophy, its justification of its own entity as a culture. Primitive society clearly values these things, values them so much that it cannot leave them to individual families to pass on to the young. It is willing to trust the haphazard, individually varied teaching methods of families and households and peer groups and gossip to teach children to walk and talk, about sex, how to get along with people, or how to be a good boy; it is even willing to leave to the individual families the teaching of how to hunt or to garden or to fish or to tend cattle; but the tribal philosophy, the religion, the citizenship knowledge, too important to leave to such haphazard methods, must be taught by society at large through its appointed and responsible representatives.

In doing this, society is asserting and underlining its rights in the child. The fact that, for example, in Australia it is a group of senior cross-cousins, and elsewhere it is men of the opposite moiety or some other specified group of semihostile relatives, who knock on the door and demand the child from his mourning and wailing family, should not be allowed to disguise the fact that these men are the representatives of society at large, the native equivalents of the truant officer, the policeman, and the draft board, asserting the priority of society's rights over the family's rights in the child. Clearly in every society there is always a family and there is always a state, and equally clearly both have rights in every child born into the society. And no society yet—Western or non-Western—has found any perfect way or equal way of adjudicating or harmonizing public rights and private rights. The state's rights must have priority when matters of citizenship are involved, but the assertion of the state's rights is always greeted with wails of anguish from the family. "I didn't raise my boy to go off and get subincised," wails the Australian mother, but he is carried off and subincised just the same. "I didn't raise my boy for the draft board or the school board," says the American mother, but her protests are of no avail either. It is an inevitable conflict, because it arises from the very structure of society, as long as society is an organization of family units, which it is universally. The only solution is to abolish the family or abolish the state, and no human group has been able to do either.

7. The boy is not ruined for life or a mental cripple as a result of the harrowing initiation experience, but is a social being *in a way he never was before*. He has been made aware of his wider social responsibilities and his wider membership in the total society, but more important in the present context, he has been exposed to a series of social situations in which friendship counts for naught, crying or whining gets one no place, whimsy or charm or boyish attractiveness pays no dividends, and friends, pull, and influence are without effect. The tribal tradition, the culture, treats all individuals alike, and skills and wiles that were so valuable during childhood in gaining preferential treatment or in winning approval or avoiding disapproval are all to no avail. He goes into the initiation period a child, which is a social animal of one sort, but he comes out a responsible enculturated citizen, which is a social animal of a different sort.

8. Primitive societies, then, devote a great deal of time and care to training for citizenship. They make no attempt to even start such training until the boy has reached puberty. But once they start, they do it thoroughly. Citizenship training in these societies means a great deal more than knowing the words of "The Star-Spangled Banner" and memorizing the Bill of Rights. It means exposing the boy under particularly stirring and impressive conditions to the continuity of the cultural tradition, to the awe and majesty of the society itself, emphasizing the subordination of the individual to the group at large and hence the mysteriousness, wonder, and sacredness of the whole individual-society relationship. In Australia, the most sacred part of the whole initiation ritual is when the boys are shown the *churinga*, which are at the same time their own souls and the souls of the tribe which came into existence at the creation of the world. Citizenship, being an awesome and mysterious business in any culture, cannot be imparted or taught or instilled in a secular atmosphere; it must be imparted in an atmosphere replete with symbolism and mystery. Whether it can be taught at all without heavy emphasis on its otherworldliness, without heavy sacred emphasis, whether the teaching of citizenship can ever be a warm, friendly, loving, cosy, and undis-

turbing process, is a question I leave to the educators. Primitive societies obviously do not believe it can be taught that way, as is proved by the fact that they never try.

9. One last point, implied in much of the above but worth special mention, is the rather surprising fact that technological training, training in "getting a living," is absent from the initiation curricula, despite its obvious vital importance to the survival of the individual, of the household, and of the tribe or society. Mastery of the food-obtaining techniques by the children is left to the hit-or-miss, highly individualistic teaching processes of the home, to the peer groups, and to the whimsies of relatives or friends. The reason for this omission from the socially regulated curricula of the initiation schools is, I think, pretty clear. In the simpler societies there is nothing particularly mysterious, nothing spiritual or otherworldly about getting a living, or hunting or gardening or cattle-herding. It is true that there is apt to be a lot of magical practice mixed up with these things, but even this heavy magical element is conceived in very secular and individualistic terms. That is, it either works or doesn't work in particular cases, and each man or each household or clan has its own garden magic or cattle magic or hunting magic which differs from the next man's or household's or clan's magic. Dobu, for instance, is a culture riddled with garden magic; so is that of the Trobriands, but each group's magic is individually owned and comparisons of magic are even made between group and group. For this reason, garden skills or hunting skills, even though they include magical elements, can still safely be left by society to the private level of transmission and teaching. Public control, public supervision is minimal.

This leads to two further conclusions, or at least suggestions. (1) On this line of analysis, we can conclude the primitive societies, despite their marginal subsistence and the fact that they are frequently close to the starvation point, devote more care and attention, *as societies*, to the production of good citizens, than to the production of good technicians, and therefore they can be said to value good citizenship more highly than they value the production of good food producers. Can this be said for modern societies, including our own? (2) This relative lack of interest in standardizing subsistence-training, while insisting at the same time on standardizing training in the ideological aspects of culture, may go a long way toward enabling us to explain the old sociological problem called cultural lag. Everybody who has taken an introductory course in social science is acquainted with the fact that change in technology is easier to achieve, and takes place with less resistance than change in non-technological or ideological fields. I do not suggest that what we have been talking about above offers a complete explanation of the culture lag differential, but it may at least be helpful. I would phrase the relation between culture lag and education like this: that because prepuberty education in the simpler societies is loose, unstructured, and left pretty much to individual household choice, and because such laissez faire prepuberty education typically includes food-getting techniques and the use of food-getting tools (spears, harpoons, hoes, etc.), the attitude toward these techniques and tools that the child develops is a secular one and he carries that secular attitude toward them into his adult life. Hence variations from or alternatives to such tools and techniques are not resisted with anything like the intensity of feeling with which variations from or alternatives to ideological elements will be resisted. From his childhood, the boy believes that in trying to get food anything is a good technique or a good tool, provided only that it works, and he is familiar too with the fact that techniques and tools differ at least slightly from household to household or hunter to hunter. Therefore, as an adult he is, in relation to food-getting techniques and tools, both a secularist and an empiricist, and will adopt the white man's gun or the white man's spade when they are offered without any feeling that he is flouting the tribal gods or the society's conscience. The white man's ideology, or foreign importations in ideology, are treated in quite a different way. They are involved with areas of behavior which have been learned not in the secular, empirical atmosphere of the home and the play groups, but in the awesome, sacred atmosphere of the initiation schools, wherein no individual variation is allowed and the very notion of alternatives is anathema.

To avoid misunderstanding, a brief comment must be made about societies like that of Polynesia and the "schools" of Africa such as the Poro, where specialized technical knowledge is imparted to the adolescent males in special training institutions. The significant point is that in such societies ordinary food-getting techniques (fishing in Polynesia, gardening in West Africa, cattle-tending in East Africa) are still left to the haphazard teaching methods of the individual household, whereas the craft skills (woodcarving in Polynesia, metalworking in the Poro) are entrusted to vehicles of instruction in which apprenticeship, passing of exams, standardized curricula, unfamiliar or nonintimate teachers, heavy emphasis on ritual and the sacred character of the esoteric knowledge which is being imparted, and the dangers of the slightest variation from the traditional techniques of the craft are all prominent. In such societies, despite the inclusion of some technology in the "schools," basic food-getting techniques remain in the common domain of the culture and are picked up by children haphazardly—only the special craft knowledge is sacredly imparted. (Even as late as Henry VIII's England the crafts were called the "mysteries," the two words being apparently interchangeable.)

To conclude then, we may pull most of the above together into one final summary. In primitive society there are two vehicles of education, the prepuberty process and the postpuberty process. No Western writer has ever succeeded in contrasting them as much as they need to be contrasted, because they are in every possible respect the Alpha and Omega of each other. In time of onset, atmosphere, personnel, techniques of instruction, location, curriculum, the two vehicles represent opposite poles. Everything that is done in or through one vehicle is the antithesis of what is done in the other. Standardization of experience and uniformity of training is markedly present in the post-initiation experience: it is markedly absent in the prepuberty experience of the growing child. If this is accepted as a base line, it has very important implications for the whole field of personality studies, especially for those studies which seem to claim that personality is very homogeneous in the simpler societies and for those allied studies which allege that child training and growing up in primitive society are very different from their equivalents in modern Western cultures. It is suggestive also as a base for attempting to answer a question that nobody has yet attempted to answer: Why do individuals in simple cultures differ from each other so markedly in personality traits, despite their common cultural conditioning? And it furnishes us finally with another link in the complicated chain of phenomena which exists between the problem of personality formation and the problem of culture change.

All these things are brought together, and indeed the whole of this paper is held together by one single thread—namely, that childhood experience is part of the secular world, postpuberty experience part of the sacred world. What is learned in the secular world is learned haphazardly, and varies greatly from individual to individual. Therefore no society can standardize that part of the child's learning which is acquired under secular circumstances. My only claim for this paper is that the use of this starting point for a discussion of primitive education enables us to obtain some insights into educational and cultural processes which are not provided by any alternative starting point.

References

Gesell, Arnold, and Frances L. Ilg, 1946, *The Child from Five to Ten*. New York: Harper & Row, Publishers.

Hart, C. W. M., 1954, "The Sons of Turimpi," *American Anthropologist*, 56:242–61.

———, and Arnold R. Pilling, 1960, *The Tiwi of North Australia*. New York: Holt, Rinehart and Winston, Inc.

Herskovits, Melville J., 1948, *Man and His Works*. New York: Alfred A. Knopf, Inc.

Landtmann, Gunnar, 1927, *The Kiwai Papuans of British New Guinea*. London: The Macmillan Company.

Pettit, George A., 1946, "Primitive Education in North America," *University of California Publications in American Archaeology and Ethnology*, XLIII, 182.

Piaget, Jean, 1929, *The Child's Conception of the World*. New York: Harcourt, Brace & World, Inc.

————, 1932, *The Moral Judgment of the Child*. London: Kegan Paul.

Schapera, I., 1940, *Married Life in an African Tribe*. London: Sheridan House.

Van Gennep, Arnold, 1909, *Les rites de passage*. Paris: E. Nourry. Translated paperback edition, 1960, University of Chicago Press.

20——*Mark Hanna Watkins*

The West African
"Bush" School*

The social anthropologists and the sociologist consider education in its broadest aspects to be coterminous with the cultural process in which, over successive generations, the young and unassimilated members of a group are incorporated by their sharing of the social heritage. Education from this point of view thus is directed by the group in the daily interaction of its members as well as by specialized functionaries or subgroups, and in the process the cultural patterns are transmitted and the socially accepted values realized.

The social values of a group are those phenomena which it recognizes as constituting the active or potential factors in the promotion of its welfare or which, when not properly controlled, create dysphoric conditions. Thus there are, on the one hand, positive social values, as food, shelter, health, and the fundamental necessities of life, as well as other socially desirable ends defined by the culture, and, on the other hand, negative social values, as crime, disease, death, witchcraft. These constitute in a large measure the social environment and determine the characteristic activities of a society. It is in relation to them that we may therefore speak of the function of education. This function is not to be confused with purpose, although in social life the two are often closely related; for the function of anything is simply what it does, and we speak of the function of objects which have no purposes, as, for example, that of the sunlight. Moreover, in attempting to achieve the goals which are proposed, a people often attain quite

* Reprinted from *The American Journal of Sociology*, XLVIII, No. 6, 1943, 1666–675, by permission of the University of Chicago Press. Copyright, 1943, University of Chicago.

different ends, as in the case of the teacher who, desirous of creating friendship, makes two boys embrace after a fight, but only intensifies their enmity; or of the Volstead Act, which created a wave of vice and crime instead of a nation of temperate citizens.

Hence, while the function of social life, in general, is that of passing on the cultural heritage, it may be recognized that not every social example is worthy to be copied and preserved. Every group struggles to maintain only its ideals, along with the technology and skills needed for providing subsistence. Thus, while education is identical with life in a particular society, it is obligatory that in every group there should be imposed upon certain institutions the duty of making deliberate efforts toward fostering the best in the cultural heritage, in regard both to the objective world of materials and techniques and to their subjective counterpart of sentiments, interests, and attitudes. In short, the incidental educative function of social life is supplemented by a more or less self-conscious purpose, superimposed upon one or more fundamental institutions or carried out by a special educational organization. This purpose involves the conservation, extension, and transmission of all the culturally accepted values and ideals to the succeeding generations so as to insure their continuity as they are defined in the local group and thus to perpetuate its life. There generally is required a more or less special emphasis determined by national or local aims. There also are the problems of adjusting the group to the larger world in which it lives and of accommodating the individual so that his efforts to realize his wishes may not conflict too seriously with the needs of his society.

The formulation of an educational program for any group therefore is dependent upon two general factors: the nature and needs of the child, which determine the methods of procedure, and the nature and needs of the society, which determine the goals.

In the very simplest societies, as that of the Andaman Islanders, the Sakai of the Malay Peninsula, an Eskimo village, or other similar groups, informal education, in which the individual learns incidentally by direct participation and imitation, is relatively adequate for social continuity. The learning that goes on under such conditions is genuine; for the patterns of life are presented to the individual in their immediate setting, and what he learns is close to his interests and put into direct use; in fact, he learns by doing. In such a society where there is only a meager differentiation of vocations, with no complex technology, and in which the system of beliefs and practices is comparatively simple, the gap between the growing child and the adult world is relatively narrow and may be spanned without a long period of special preparation. Here the inculcation of the social values is achieved with a minimum of self-conscious purpose; that is to say, it is not abstracted from the daily life. In more complex social orders, where only the general designs of life are accessible to the young, the educative process must take on some degree of specific and separate organization; the social heritage must be broken up into assimilable portions and simplified, so that education as a purposive endeavor becomes differentiated from the educative function of daily life. Some form of specialized educational institution develops, and the passing-on of selected social ideals takes place in a relatively distinctive and artificial environment. But this differentiation entails certain problems, for the social values tend to become somewhat impersonal to the learner, are not immediate and vital in character, and are likely to be hidden in symbols. In such a situation learning may degenerate to mere acceptance of preformulated matter, to rote memory without understanding or responsibility. It becomes more and more difficult to relate the experiences acquired under such formal circumstances to those obtained in direct association, to distinguish between intrinsic and mediate values, and for the learner to understand the mediate values associated with his contemporary activity.

From the foregoing remarks it would appear that the adequacy of any deliberate and formalized educational system may be tested by considering the extent to which it is representative of the cultural heritage and its achievement in so relating the activities of the more or less specialized environment to those of the practical social world of which it is a part that the two may be contiguous.

It seems permissible and profitable to describe and study the "bush" school of West Africa on the basis of this framework, although that educational system may not be regarded as formal on a par with the schools among westernized peoples. The "bush" school, as will be seen, has the characteristics of a deliberate and purposive procedure in a specialized environment.

The training of youth in West Africa is accomplished through one of the types of secret societies common in the area. In these societies, as in many other affairs, the sexes are segregated. The name which is now in general usage for the boys' society is *poro* —in the Vai language, *póló* or *póró* (with open *o*).[1] This form, or some dialectic variant of it, is found over a relatively wide area in Liberia, Sierra Leone, and other areas over which the Mandingo languages are spoken. The name for the corresponding girls' society is *bondo*, Vai *bòndó* (*o* closed), or, more correctly, *sàndì* (with open *i*). There is little variation in the organization and activities of these societies as they occur among the Mende, Vai, Kpelle, Krima, Gola, and other related groups. The description given here refers to them as they are established among the Mende and Vai, the data being obtained primarily from Miss Fatima Massaquoi, a native Vai student at Fisk University, including notes in correspondence with her brother, Mr. S. Ciaka Massaquoi, of Pendembu, Sierra Leone. *Poro* seems to be a generic term which once was and still may be applied to the societies without regard to the sex of the participants and which includes similar associations among men and women, the adult group being political and civic rather than distinctively educational in aim.

> The most widely distributed and probably also the oldest name of the society is *poro*, strictly speaking, *polo*, thus with open *o* in both instances. Dapper, in the seventeenth century, called it *paaro*, so that perhaps the stem originally contained an *a*. (Westermann; 236).

---

[1] For sake of economy, the few native (Vai) words included have not been transcribed in phonetic script, with the exception that the tones are shown by the grave accent (for low) and the acute accent (for the high register). There are at least three significant tonal distinctions (tonemes) in this language, but the middle tone does not appear in any of the words employed here. The vowel qualities have been described briefly in parentheses following the first occurrence of each word. The Vai *a* is invariably a low back vowel, while *i*, *e*, and *o* may be open or closed. A colon following a vowel indicates that the vowel is long. The consonants have practically the same qualities as in English.

The adult groups are not strictly germane to the subject presented here and therefore may be omitted.

The original meaning of the word *poro* is not known clearly. Westermann, (1921:236n) quoting two other authors, makes the following statement:[2]

> Wallis (p. 183) says *poro* means literally "law" or "one word"; also Alldridge, *A Transformed Colony* (p. 194), speaks of "the order of the Poro or law." If this translation is not etymologically correct, it is nevertheless expressive of the power of the *poro* for legal discipline.

These societies are of fundamental importance in the local culture, and every youth, male or female, must receive such training before being considered worthy to assume the responsibilities of an adult. With the growing influence of Mohammedanism, Christianity, and European culture, the significance of the *poro* in native life is waning, along with detribalization and the general modification of aboriginal culture.

The boys' society or school may be described first. In the Vai language, the specific name for this institution is *bélì*, and a person who has been inducted into it is known as a *bélì kàì*, "initiated man." (The *e* of *bélì* is open, the *i* closed; in *kàì* the *a* is a low back vowel and the *i* is closed.)

The sessions of this school are not held in the towns or villages proper, but a permanent place is selected in the forest not far distant from the principal or capital town of a chiefdom or district. This special section of forest is called *bélì fìlà* (*fìlà* pronounced with closed *i*, low back *a*), "*bélì* forest," and is never used for other purposes, although all the structures are burned at the close of each term. Every district or subchiefdom has its own school and special reserved forest for the purpose.

Once boys have entered the forest, they are at no time allowed to return to the towns until their training is complete; nor under any circumstances are female visitors tolerated. No one except

---

[2] The writers quoted by Westermann are Braithwaite Wallis, "The Poro of the Mendi," *Journal of the African Society*, IV (1904–5), 181–89, and T. J. Alldridge, *A Transformed Colony: Sierra Leone as It Was and Is* (London, 1910).

members of the society is permitted entrance to the area. If uninitiated persons approach it, they must make their presence known so that none of its secrets will be exposed. If a man trespasses, he will be initiated, while a woman under such circumstances will be killed. During the period in which the school is in session the forest is said to be the special possession of the principal official of the institution, and not even the chief is permitted to enter without the permission of this man. Thus, in a physical and spatial sense, the "bush" school is a special or distinctive environment.

The principal official of the school is the *dá zò:* (*a* low back, *o* closed and long), "the leader who stands at the mouth or head," who is endowed with wisdom and mystic power in a superlative degree. He has a majestic status in the society, is respected by the chief and elders of the tribe, and is honored with intense devotion by the youth of the land. In personal characteristics he must be chivalrous, courteous, public-spirited, law-abiding, and fearless. He must have a full knowledge of all the native lore, arts, and crafts, must be well versed in the history and traditions of his people and an authentic judge of all matters affecting their welfare. Other men of good repute who are specialists in various fields of activity serve as his assistants and as teachers of the novices.

For the institution among the Kpelle the characteristics and role of the leader have been described in the following words:

> The grandmaster, *ñamū*, is, of course, a human being and is known as such by the members. At the same time, he possesses attributes which raise him above the merely human. He himself is immortal; that is, his death is kept a secret, and the choice of the successor takes place in the strictest secrecy and in the narrow circle of the outstanding members; and he has the power to kill people and restore them to life. This refers, of course, actually to the secret sojourn of the *poro* youths in the *poro* bush and their later re-entrance into the community of village companions. They are thought of as having been dead and restored to life, actually swallowed by the grandmaster and reborn, which, however, the usual popular opinion quite generally conceives of as the ability of the *ñamū* to revive the dead.
>
> It is only natural that the imagination of the folk is vigorously occupied with the *ñamū* and attributes to him the supernatural. He is

seen surrounded by the beings [people] in the village, since he moves about just as other people, but he also flies through the air. Thus near Densu [place name] there is pointed out a large, slender tree with fantastically projecting boughs, on which the *ñamū* takes rest when on his journeys through the air on which he meets the grandmistress of the *sande* society.

On his visits to the towns the grandmaster always makes his appearance surrounded by a group of initiated, who protect him from strange glances [glances of the uninitiated]. He generally goes unclothed. Only to the initiated is he visible: upon his appearance in the village all the uninitiated—women, children, and strangers—must retire to the huts and close the doors.

On festive occasions the *ñamū* wears a gala costume which consists of wide trousers extending over the knees; a short-sleeved, close-fitting waistcoat; and a headdress which is a type of cylindrical hat made of small metal plate, ornamented on the upper portion of the front with the head of a plumed raven [*Hornraben*], and trimmed with cowrie shells and white otter or ape fur; over the brow a white band; around the neck a large ruffle made of projecting leather pieces (leopard and antelope skin), three to five centimeters wide and ten centimeters long, trimmed with white fur and cowrie shell; a medicine bag and other magic hung around the neck; in one hand a large fan decked with many pieces of skin underneath and little bells above and in the other hand a horse-tail or cowtail.

A *ñamū* can conduct several schools at the same time—as many as three—which often are located some distance apart. In this case he spends alternately some time in each one and intrusts the remaining part of the development to his assistants, one of whom always carries out the inspection of a school. The journeys of the *ñamū* from one school to another are kept secret, and the students learn hardly anything of his absence; therefrom originates the belief that he may be in several places simultaneously and is bound to no locality. Often agreements are made between various headmasters for the purpose of conducting a course interchangeably. The headmasters then hold a conference in the capital of the oldest, and the latter presides. (Westermann: 238–240).

The period during which a session is to be held is determined by a council consisting of the leader, his assistants, and the elders of the tribe. The term in length varies from group to group.

Among the Gola, in the old days, the session is said to have had a duration of from four to eight years; among the Krima, or Krim, it was three to five years; while among the Mende and the Vai the time was from two to three years. Westermann gives the length of the term as recorded by himself and others for a number of tribes. His figures vary from two months among the Kru to ten years for the Temne, although he adds the statement that "many of the figures given above may be more ideal than actual" (Westermann: 234–235).

At present, under the influence of new ideas and the gradual Europeanization of the region, there is a general desire for opportunity to acquire knowledge which the "bush" school alone cannot provide, so that the periods have been progressively reduced. Thus the term among the Vai and the Mende is now approximately eighteen months only, while it is about two years among the Krima and from two to three years among the Gola.

When the time arrives for the school to convene, parents who wish their boys to be initiated make known their desires to the tribal elders, who in turn inform the paramount chief. The latter passes the information on to the leader and other officials of the school. Then the news circulates rapidly throughout the land, and the boys begin to gather, coming in from all parts of the chiefdom. There is no established regulation covering the age limits for membership. However, it is generally believed that human beings are more tractable and teachable when young than when fully mature, so that boys are expected to enter usually between the ages of approximately seven to nineteen years. In exceptional cases, however, the authorities do not generally object.

At the beginning of the session all the boys who have not been circumcised already are given this treatment. The number of boys who are circumcised at this time is dependent upon the age distribution, as the older ones will have received the operation prior to entrance. It appears that in years before the influence of the West was so great, most of the novices were quite young and consequently were uncircumcised at the opening of the term.

Circumcision constitutes a sanitary measure, although there were no social diseases before the coming of the Europeans. It is thought, however, that less dirt will be accumulated when the skin of the male organ has been excised. An uncircumcised man, more-over, is considered to be a weakling and is despised as an inferior being.

After the circumcision rites a period of time is allowed for the healing of the wounds. Then a feast is celebrated so that the boys may be given opportunity to know one another as well as to be-come acquainted with the teachers. The women prepare food for this festival, but they are not permitted to bring it into the school.

Now begin the specific forms of training. The boys are divided into groups according to their ages and aptitudes and receive instruction in all the arts, crafts, and lore of native life, including a variety of games and sports, such as swimming, canoeing, hunting, trapping, acrobatic stunts, dancing, sing-ing, drumming and the playing of other musical instruments, wres-tling, climbing, etc. These are for the purpose of physical develop-ment, the acquisition of fundamental skills, the sharpening of the wits, and appreciation for native art. It is by this means that the char-acter is molded and a youth is prepared to take his place among the generation of adults. Moreover, the continuation of all these traits is insured. The first instruction involves a series of tests in order to determine individual differences, interests, and ambitions (to see what the boys can do) and an acquisition of the funda-mental knowledge which every adult is supposed to know. Later, opportunity for demonstration of special ingenuity, skills, and originality is afforded. A youth who shows special aptitude for weaving, for example, is trained to become a master of the craft; while those who show distinctive skill and interest in carving, leatherwork, dancing, "medicines," folklore, etc., likewise are developed along these specialized lines. This early training also includes work in the erection of the structures which are used while the session lasts. The buildings constructed for the school are sufficiently numerous to constitute one or more towns. All the laws and traditions of the tribes are taught, as well as duty to the tribal chief, tribe, and elders, and the proper relations to women. Training is given in the recognition and use of various medicinal herbs, their curative powers, and various antidotes. Also, the secrets of wild animals are taught—how they live, how to recog-nize their spoor, and how to attack them.

All this training is tested out in the laboratory of "bush"-school life. For example, instruction in warfare is accompanied by actual mock battles and skirmishes. The boys are separated into various "towns" similar in location and arrangement to those in which the general population is or has been distributed. These towns must be barricaded, defended, and attacked. Previous wars in which the tribe has been engaged are re-enacted, the boys of one group playing the role of the people under attack at a certain time, while those of another act the parts of the enemies. The ruses which the enemy employed are gone over carefully, and the attackers must carry them out with precision and dexterity. Some of the attacks are made on rainy nights, when the inhabitants are asleep; others are made when there are festivals, when the "men" are in the fields, the actual situation, with all the preoccupations, distractions, and surprises of some known war, being re-created. All this is possible because the forest is sufficiently large, covering several square miles. All the buildings, fields, and activities are the responsibility of the boys after they have received their instructions. They must live in these towns, work the fields, and carry on all the activities of normal tribal life, at the same time preparing to defend their possessions or to make attacks according to the assignment which they have received and the account which the instructors have given of the previous war. Sometimes a lapse of two or three months may occur before the plans can be executed. This makes the situation all the more genuine. The defenders are informed of the errors in judgment and tactics which were formerly committed in actual combat, and the battle is conducted upon the basis of the previous life-situation. Then the entire war game is replayed, the defenders having learned what the shortcomings were and how to correct them, and the "enemy" making special effort to succeed in the face of the new improvements in defense. In these battles all the obstacles with which the people were once confronted in such crises are recreated. Some of the boys play the roles of women and children who must be guarded and defended, who constitute the impediment of a human cargo. The "enemy" attempts to capture and enslave these "women" and "children" just as is done in normal warfare, for it is not the custom to kill women and children in military combat.

Thus, although the "bush" school is conducted in a special environment—i.e., in one which is differentiated from the general social milieu—the degree of artificiality is not so great as it often is under the conditions of formal education among peoples of European and American cultures. The greatest amount of dissimilarity between the school situation and that of native life in the towns and villages would seem to be the absence of certain distractions in the school—the removal from normal family ties, from the direct influence of mothers and kinsmen, who tend to condone the frailties of the youths. This does not seem to constitute a disadvantage or to seclude the activities in an ivory tower. In fact, there is a general notion among these people that there should be some form of counterbalance to the intimate association between children and their immediate parents (those of the simple or biological family), for under such conditions they will be cajoled, indulged, and petted too much and in this way not prepared for the sacrifices incidental to normal social life beyond this narrow circle. For this reason, children are distributed often among the more distant relatives for various periods of time. The requirement that life in the "bush" school must involve withdrawal from such contacts appears to be an application of this fundamental principle. Indeed, a child is not expected to enter a "bush" school in which his close relative has a position of authority.

Life in the secret society is a complete *rite de passage* from the helplessness and irresponsibilities of childhood to citizenship in a world of adults. Thus a youth acquires a new name in the *béli*, according to his rank in the group and his achievements. He retains this name for life, and it is always applied to him by those who have been initiated in the school. Uninitiated persons may not use it. This latter form of life, it may be seen, is developed gradually within the confines of the institution. Entrance to the society is a symbolic death for the young, who must be reborn before returning to family and kin. Those who die from the strenuous life are considered simply not to have been reborn, and their mothers are expected not to weep or grieve for them.

It may be seen that life in the "bush" school is not a tranquil experience but rather a thorough physical, mental, and moral test in which unsuitable traits are eliminated, the individual either undergoing profound modification or meeting his death. It is said that abnormal characters experience no rebirth; weaklings, freaks, and homosexuals do not return. This has elicited some disturbance among the missionaries and humanitarians, but it should cause no lack of elation for the Hootons (See Hooton, 1937), for the natives feel that those who cannot endure the test are no loss to society.

Yet a boy is proud of his "bush"-school days, and he reflects over them with fond remembrances. At the completion of the session the chief is informed privately, and he then (as during the whole period) visits the society only in the role of a private citizen. A day or two after his return he sends his representatives to meet the leader and the authorities in a highly ceremonious manner. The boys make a number of demonstrations, covering a day or more. Then there are various examinations administered by the representatives, after which they return to the chief and elders, who are informed of the impressions received. At this time preparations are made for the ceremonial return of the boys to the town. This is usually considered to be of great tribal, and in some instances intertribal, importance.

A type of pavilion is erected within the chief's compound for the reception of the boys; or, if the chief's court is sufficiently large, it may be decorated elaborately for the purpose. After all these preparations have been completed, the chief and his retinue meet with the leader and the officials of the society, when the formal presentation or return of the forest to the ruler and elders is made. This does not usually occur in the forest itself, and only responsible male citizens are present. Great speeches are made, and sentiments of appreciation are expressed to the leader. After these ceremonies the leader rises, thanks his chief and elders in a brief speech, and finally kneels before the chief (the boys of the school following his example) and, with the palm of his right hand resting on the ruler's knee, makes a statement somewhat as follows: "I pledge loyalty to you and to my tribe. Now I give back your forest. Here am I, and here are your boys." This is followed by great shouting, rejoicing, and the sounding of drums. The chief, sitting in his official chair of state (formerly a stool), lays hands on the leader and replies, "Thank you. I bid you rise." Following this, the chief is escorted to his compound with all the pomp and circumstance befitting a great ruler.

By this time the parents and relatives of the boys, the general public, friends and acquaintances from far and near, have assembled in the town in order to witness the arrival of the boys. The latter, having been ceremoniously washed and having rubbed chalk or clay on their bodies, splendidly clad in their "bush" uniforms, each bearing a long staff, are lined up near the town awaiting the signal to enter. Suddenly the report of a musket or sound of the tribal drum is heard, and amid great shouting and rejoicing the boys begin rushing immediately into all parts of the town, gazing furiously in all directions as if they were warriors anxiously in search of booty.

According to tradition, the boys have the right at this time to beat to death any animal which may be encountered as they rush about the town. Some parents deliberately leave such animals as sheep, goats, and fowl at their doors so that the boys may kill them in this manner. Wealthier people may leave even cattle for this purpose. There are at least two native explanations for the custom. One is the idea that the boys, as warriors and adventurers being permitted to enter the town, have the freedom to plunder therein, while the other notion is that they must be given the privilege to demonstrate publicly their manly and courageous spirits. It is said that at present animals other than fowl are rarely left exposed to such destruction.

After this period of license the youths are lined up again and led to a stream, where they take baths and dress in their best clothing. Then they are taken back to the "bush" quietly and secretly by way of a different route. Next they march in orderly and peaceful manner, to the accompaniment of the native guitar, drum, and singing, applauded by the jubilant and anxious spectators, to the pavilion erected for them. In this place they are met once more by their relatives and friends and enjoy the companionship of the distinguished men of the tribe. Gifts are bestowed upon them by relatives and friends. While quartered in this pavilion, they are not permitted to raise their hands to their mouths, but each is fed from a dish by a special servant, for they are considered to be babies, newly reborn. They are retained in the building for four or five days, during which time there are great feasts and much rejoicing. They have many great privileges and may call for and receive the best that can be afforded. This may constitute a burden on their proud parents, who, if they are poor, even incur debts in order to please their boys. In some instances years of preparation are required before a boy can be initiated, so heavy is the cost. This may delay the time until the boy almost reaches full manhood, or even later. However, this expense is connected entirely with the aggregation rites, as there are no fees for attendance in the school.

After these rites have been concluded and sentiments of appreciation have been expressed to the leader, chief, and elders, the boys are returned without ceremony to their parents and are finally taken to their respective homes. They are now full citizens of the society, with legal rights and responsibilities equal to those of all adults. Before being worthy of great leadership, however, a youth must have further experience in the civic and political societies, of which there are five grades.

The elaborate ritual of aggregation fulfils the function of giving effective public expression to the social sentiments associated with the cultural values which the school preserves, enlarges, and passes on to the young people. These rites are therefore educative, for it is through public expression that the sentiments are kept alive and made contagious. The behavior has inherent motivation, as it is bound up intimately with certain basic elements of human nature, such as pride, display, and heroism. Thus the activities of this group are contiguous with those of the general social order, and the *bélì* may be regarded as an effective educational institution—judged of course, in the light of its cultural setting.

Attention may be directed now to the sister-organization. No great detailed consideration of it seems necessary here, for in organization and operation the *sàndì*, or "society for girls," is parallel to the *bélì*. However, it is not conducted so far from the town or in so great a space as is the latter. The inclosure for the *sàndì* consists of a large fence constructed of giant forest wood, neatly plastered on both sides with clay and surrounding a spacious campus. It is usually built near one end of the town and, if possible, near a river, so that the girls may wash and bathe without having to go very far and expose themselves to public gaze. Within are constructed several temporary buildings, according to the number of inmates; and, as in the case of the school for boys, the entire structure is burned at the close of the session. The buildings and campus are the *bòndò* proper, indicating privacy, while the society itself is the *sàndì*.

The heavy construction work is done by men, after which everything is given over to the women and the men have no further concern with the institution. It is considered to be a capital crime if a man should gain knowledge of the activities or interfere with the deliberations.

At the head of the society is the *zó: bà*, "the big *zó:*," whose position, as that of the chief official of the boys' group, is hereditary. She represents the spirits of the female ancestors, who have left the institution and all the cultural values to their descendants and who are with the latter in the school. She is usually a woman of more than middle age, established in the society, and in position to break her ties with the home and domestic responsibilities during the term of the school. As a representative of the ancestral spirits she may undergo a metamorphosis and become what has been called by Europeans "the dancing devil," due to the fact that she, or a younger substitute, dances on certain occasions completely concealed by a large mask and special dress. There may thus be two persons with this title—the one who rules the school and the other who dances in the form of the spirit. The division may be necessary because the leader may be too old for the strenuous exercise required by the dance. In any case the identity of the masked dancer can never be revealed, as she is symbolically a spirit. There is a special attendant who follows the dancer, continuously praising and giving thanks to the spirit for the benefits which have accrued to the group. This attendant carries a mat, as the dead are wrapped in mats for burial. The active leader is merely the spirit having taken corporeal shape. In all these respects she is similar to the leader of the boys' society.

Next in rank to the leader is an official called the *léì gbà* (with open e), who holds the position of vice-leader or assistant leader. Then comes the *léì gbà kpó* (with open o). These constitute the leadership of the group and are called "mothers" by the girls. In addition, there is another woman, the *mámbái* (with closed *i*), who supervises and is responsible for the cooking, washing, and general domestic affairs. Among the girls the oldest or first initiated also holds an official position. She is a type of student leader, who calls the girls together for various activities; decides, in consultation with the adult women, the program of work and recreation; and assigns the girls to various groups for these activities. She must be highly respected by her fellow-members, and she takes the lead in every important affair.

There is some uncertainty as to the time during which this society holds its session. It may very well be that the period is practically the same as that of the society for boys (which is the notion of our female informant, who herself was initiated but did not remain for a complete term). She estimates the term as varying from three to seven years, but her figures for both groups are higher than those of her youngest brother, who says: "In no case do girls remain in the *sàndì* or *bòndò* for more than one year; this term has from ancient times never changed." By way of comparison, Westermann's figures for the Kpelle groups may be cited. He states that the *póró* in this tribe has a term of six years, while the *sàndì* term is only three years (Westermann: 234, 256). The differences between the social responsibilities and status of males and females may constitute an argument in favor of a briefer session for the latter.

There is not much ceremony at the beginning of the *sàndì*, although the girls must undergo clitoridectomy. It appears that the age for entrance is about the same as that for boys and that the actual time of joining likewise may vary according to circumstances.

This institution is very clearly maintained for the purpose of preparing a girl to assume her place as a wife and mother attached primarily to the domestic unit in the social order. The girls are said to be spirits, as all unborn children are, and they smear their faces with a preparation of white clay so as to simulate spirits. This clay must be replenished and replaced when washed off until the session is concluded. It is symbolic of membership in the *sàndì*, along with a necklace consisting of a small horn-shaped fruit shell in which a red berry is placed and a string of beads made of cylindrical pieces of wood and worn around the waist. These are removed at the ceremonial washing of the novices at the end of the term.

The girls are instructed in all domestic affairs, such as cooking, the various ways of preserving food, the collection of non-poisonous mushrooms, medicinal herbs and lore, the preparation of cosmetics, spinning, embroidering, the care of children, and the elements of being good mothers and capable wives, as well as in dancing, singing, story-telling—all that which a native woman is expected to know. Like the boys, they receive new names according to their position and accomplishments in the society; and, like the boys, the weaklings may not experience rebirth.

The aggregation rites are very much the same as those at the close of the society for boys, including the special reception hall, the feasting and rejoicing (except, of course, that the girls do not rush about the town and "plunder" it as the youths do, nor do they bear staffs or wear "bush" uniforms). Upon graduation, in most instances, they are ready for marriage, although in the case of very young girls the marriages may not be consummated physically for some time. Also the girl, unlike the boy, until she has reached middle age or thereabout does not venture to offer her hand in greeting the leader of the school in which she was initiated, even for years after the session has closed. She usually bows in deep respect, resting the palm of her right hand on her knee. The leader responds by placing her hands lightly on the subordinate's shoulder.

The *sàndì*, which so closely parallels the *bélì*, seems to possess the same educational characteristics and suitability as the latter, and both may be rated on equal terms.

It may appear that much of what has been described more closely approaches the ideal native cultural pattern than what is carried out in actual practice. This is no doubt true; but it would not seem to invalidate the conclusion that these institutions, considered in relation to the cultures of which they are a part, are more genuinely educative and efficient than many of the formal schools of occidental culture. There are no cultural lags and "useless knowledge" stored in symbols remote from the contemporary social order. Some of the activities and subject matter of the "bush" school may be rejected on the basis of the standards of modern civilization, but the system should be considered with sympathetic appreciation before missionary or other efforts are made to modify it fundamentally; for no criticism so severe as that which has been made of the French educational system of the recent past (and which seems largely applicable to many of our present-day schools) can readily be made of the native youth trained in the *póró* or of this institution in relation to its cultural milieu. It has been said of the French system that

> the primary danger of this system of education—very properly qualified as Latin—consists in the fact that it is based on the fundamental psychological error that the intelligence is developed by the learning by heart of text-books. Adopting this view, the endeavour has been made to enforce a knowledge of as many hand-books as possible. From the primary school till he leaves the university a young man does nothing but acquire books by heart without his judgment or personal initiative being ever called into play. Education consists for him in reciting by heart and obeying (Le Bon 103–104).

The experience which is gained in the "bush" school would seem to be far less spurious.

References

Alldridge, T.J., 1910, *A Transformed Colony: Sierra Leone as It Was and Is.* London: Seeley and Co., Limited.

Hooton, Earnest A., 1937, *Apes, Men and Morons.* New York: G. P. Putnam's Sons.

Le Bon, Gustave, 1908, *The Crowd.* London: T. F. Unwin.

Wallis, B., 1904–1905, "The Poro of the Mendi." *Journal of the African Society*, IV:181–189.

Westermann, D., 1921, *Die Kpelle.* Göttingen, Germany: Vandenhoeck & Ruprecht.

21————Walter J. Ong, S.J.

Latin Language Study as a Renaissance Puberty Rite[*]

I

The reasons why any particular society follows the educational curriculum which it does follow are always exceedingly complex. Because, in being a preparation for the future, it is inevitably a communication of what is available from past experience, education is always primarily a traffic in this experience and only secondarily a matter of theory. The theories concerning the handling of this experience never quite compass the actuality and totality of the experience itself. They are generally rationalizations, after-thoughts, however valuable or venturesome they may be under certain of their aspects.

This is true of education today, and it was true of education during the Renaissance. To be sure, no one bristled with educational theory more than Renaissance man. He had often very definite ideas as to what should be done to produce the proper sort of courtier or soldier or scholar or even ordinary bourgeois. Yet his theories never quite came to grips with everything in the pedagogical heritage.

Such is the case particularly with the Renaissance teaching of Latin. Depending on how much or how little he was influenced by the humanist tradition, the Renaissance educator thought of Latin as bringing students into contact with the ancients, whom Erasmus had declared to be the sources of practically all human knowledge. But quite independently of this theory, the Renais-

* Reprinted from *Studies in Philology*, LVI, April, 1959, 103–124, with permission.

sance educator was also compelled to teach Latin because the books in use, contemporary as well as ancient, were books written in Latin or translated into Latin. These included the books on language and literature, on "philosophy" (which meant, besides logic, physics and what we might best style general science, inextricably interwoven with psychology and snatches of metaphysics), books on medicine, law, and theology, not to mention books on military science, botany, alchemy, physiognomy, geography, and on every other more or less learned subject. This unacknowledged reason for teaching the language—the fact that pupils had to be able to read it, write it, and think in it—in actuality outweighed all other reasons through the Renaissance period.

This fact also made the teaching of Latin inevitably different from the teaching of Greek or Hebrew, although in the upper reaches of humanist theory these two languages were recommended for study at least as urgently as Latin. The humanists' own encomia of Greek and Hebrew, from Erasmus to Ramus and beyond, together with institutions such as the nominally trilingual colleges of Louvain, Salamanca, and Alcalá, attest the existence of this equal theoretical esteem for Greek and Hebrew and of a desire to implement the theory. Yet Renaissance Greek and Hebrew are sorry failures compared to Renaissance Latin. They produce no perceptible literature at all. When someone, such as Poliziano, writes epigrams in Greek, this achievement—or, perhaps better, this tour de force—is completely overshadowed by the bulk of the same author's Latin writings. And the currency of Hebrew never even remotely approximated the extremely limited currency of Greek.

As compared with the other "classical" languages, the Latin of the time thus has a viability which is not at all accounted for by humanist theories and attitudes regarding the ancient world. To understand the practices of the Renaissance educator we must look beneath his theories for other things, for the psychological and social drives, for the complex of psychological and social stresses and strains and compulsions to which he is heir and which register in his performance. Here I should like to single out for attention some patterns in the Renaissance teaching of Latin which manifest certain of these complexes and suggest that the Renaissance teaching of Latin involved a survival, or an echo, devious and vague but unmistakably real, of what anthropologists, treating of more primitive peoples, call puberty rites.

II

There is a vast literature on puberty rites, but a brief summary of some of their features will suffice to make the necessary points about Renaissance Latin language teaching and study.[1] Peoples of simpler culture have, virtually universally, a systematic ceremonial induction of adolescent youths into full participation in tribal, as opposed to family and clan, life. These rites have certain more or less well-defined characteristics. The individual being initiated is established in a special "marginal environment" so that the puberty rites are accurately styled by A. van Gennep *rites de passage*. The past of the individual is considered to be cut off, and certain excesses—license, theft, arson, violence—are often allowed. This sense of a break from the past may be dramatized, for example, when the home of the boy destined to undergo the rites is invaded by those who are to initiate him and who tear him forcibly from the company of the women, and sometimes physically from the very arms of his mother, who puts up a show of resistance, half conventional and half real. During the period of initiation the boy is made to do many things that are hard, often, it appears, simply because they are hard. In some cases, special taboos are enforced. Thus a boy may not touch his own body any-

---

[1] See Hutton Webster, *Primitive Secret Societies* (2d ed. rev.; New York: Macmillan Co., 1932), pp. 20–73; A. E. Jensen, *Beschneidung und Reifezeremonien bei Naturvölkern* (Stuttgart, 1933); Arnold van Gennep, *Les rites de passage* (Paris: E. Noury, 1909), pp. 93–164; Goblet d'Alviella, "Initiation (Introductory and Primitive)," *Encyclopedia of Religion and Ethics*, ed. by James Hastings (Edinburgh: T. and T. Clark, 1914), VII, 314–19; Charles W. M. Hart, "Contrasts between Prepubertal and Postpubertal Education," in *Education and Anthropology*, ed. by George D. Spindler (Stanford, California: Stanford University Press, 1955), pp. 127–45, and the discussion by various persons which follows, pp. 145–62; etc. See also Hutton Webster, *Taboo, a Sociological Study* (Stanford University, California: Stanford University Press, 1942), p. 109 n. For a brilliant, if somewhat precious and erratic, extrapolation on a theme relevant to puberty rites, see José Ortega y Gasset, "The Sportive Origin of the State," chapter i in his *Toward a Philosophy of History* (New York: W. W. Norton and Co., 1941).

where with his hands, but only with a stick—if, for example, he wishes to scratch himself. An atmosphere of continual excitement is cultivated to enlist the youth's interest. As Nathan Miller states it, "Put on edge through ingenious torments, sleeplessness, and nerve-racking frights, the candidate becomes keenly sensitive to the power of his preceptors and indelible, life-long impressions are made."[2]

The role of the preceptor is important, for the puberty rites are essentially didactic, "the chief vehicle to link generations in the transmission of the culture complex."[3] The climax is reached in the inculcation of lessons in tribal law, morality, and tradition. Bushman puberty rites, for example, feature religious dances in which animal masquerades predominate. Over all these presides the belief that the youths must be made by their preceptors to assimilate their lessons the hard way. Among the Bechuans, the boys in a state of nudity engage in a dance during which the men of the village pummel them with long, whip-like rods while asking such questions as, "Will you guard the chief well?" or "Will you herd the cattle well?"

Needless to say, because they incorporate youth into the tribe rather than into the family, puberty rites involve sexual segregation. The rites for boys are for boys alone. There are comparable rites for girls, but we are concerned with the boys alone here, for, generally speaking, it is boys alone who are taught in Renaissance schools, or who are given a systematic formal education. There are some few rare references to school education for girls in the Renaissance,[4] but commonly the girls of the time learned what

---

[2] Nathan Miller, "Initiation," *Encyclopedia of the Social Sciences*, ed. by Edwin R. A. Seligman and Alvin Johnson, VIII (New York: Macmillan Co., 1937), 49–50.

[3] *Ibid.*

[4] See Norman Wood, *The Reformation and English Education* (London: George Routledge and Sons, Ltd., 1931), 77–78, 181–82; cf. *ibid.*, pp. 3–7, 28, 159ff. Cf. Carroll Camden, *The Elizabethan Woman* (New York and London: Elsevier Press, 1952), pp. 44–50; Ruth Kelso, *Doctrine for the Lady of the Renaissance* (Urbana, Ill.: University of Illinois Press, 1956), pp. 58–77, esp. pp. 66, 68, 73 (girls' reading to be in the vernacular); A. F. Leach, *The Schools of Medieval England* (2d ed.; London: Methuen and Co., 1916), pp. 88–89.

reading and writing they learned outside the schoolroom, in the privacy of the home.

Puberty rites are thus ceremonial inductions or initiations of the youth into extra-familial life which involve a sense of break with the past (a "marginal environment") together with segregation from the family and from those of the other sex, and chastisement under the direction of elders for didactic purposes. Any system of schooling which separates boys from girls and is carried on outside the home will, of course, to a greater or lesser extent involve all these things, with the possible exception of chastisement. And it is common knowledge that in the school from early Greek and Roman times well through the Renaissance, chastisement was definitely involved. Thus any formal education through the Renaissance might well tend to activate the complex of behavior on the part of preceptor and student characteristic of puberty rites, and, indeed, almost any conceivable educational procedure outside the home will to some extent do the same thing. The coincidence of various forms of hazing with schooling everywhere is ample evidence of this fact.

The point of this article is that, although there are these general connections between school education and puberty rites, in Renaissance times (and to a great extent through the Middle Ages, as these led into the Renaissance) the status of Latin encouraged in a special way the development of a puberty rite setting and puberty rite attitudes in the educational activity of the time, and incidentally, that traces of these attitudes can be found in the few places where Latin lingers on the educational scene today. This is thus an attempt to explore certain of the complex social implications of Latin as a learned language.

These social implications were large. For when Latin passed out of vernacular usage, a sharp distinction was set up in society between those who knew it and those who did not. The conditions for a "marginal environment" were present. Moreover, the marginal environment was one between the family (which as such used a language other than Latin) and an extra-familial world of learning (which used Latin). The fact that the marginal environment was primarily a linguistic one only heightened the initiatory aspects of the situation, for the learning of secret meanings and means of communication is a common feature of initiatory rites. It is through ability to communcate that man achieves a sense of belonging.

III

The cleavage between the vernacular world and the Latin world did not coincide with the division between literacy and illiteracy, but it did coincide with the division between family life and a certain type of extra-familial life and with a division between a world in which women had some say and an almost exclusively male world. Literacy could be, and frequently was, acquired at home, often under the tutorship of women in the family. But this literacy, which can be distinguished from "learning," was commonly restricted to ability to read and write the vernacular. Schools often prescribed that a boy be able to read and write at least the alphabet as a requirement for admission,[5] for it was the business of the school proper to teach, not reading and writing, but the Latin language. This medieval and Renaissance situation still registers in our vocabulary, where elementary schools are called not reading and writing schools but grammar schools—the "grammar" here referring historically to the teaching of beginners' Latin, which was Latin grammar. This situation meant that, in general, girls, who were educated at home and not in schools, could be quite literate without having any effective direct access at all to the learned world, which was a Latin-writing, Latin-speaking, and even Latin-thinking world. There were only occasional exceptions such as Hroswitha, Lady Jane Grey, Margaret More, and Queen Elizabeth—or perhaps Shakespeare's Portia—to ruffle the masculine sense of self-sufficiency. Because their sex was so committed to the vernacular, women could become—as Raymond W. Chambers and others have shown they did become—both a major audience for English literature and some of its chief patrons.

Closed to girls and to women, the schools, including the uni-

---

[5] For example, the statutes of Canterbury School and St. Paul's School so prescribed in the sixteenth century—Wood, *Reformation and English Education,* p. 3.

versities with their own "schools" (*scholae* or classrooms), were male rendezvous strongly reminiscent of male clubhouses in primitive societies. At the top of the academic structure, in the universities, with the exception of doctors of medicine, who at Paris, for example, were allowed after the year 1452 to marry and continue as regents,[6] teachers through the Middle Ages and the Renaissance (and in many universities much later than the Renaissance) were obliged to remain unmarried so long as they continued active teaching, and this whether or not they were clerics in the ecclesiastical sense at all. Peter Ramus, his erstwhile secretary and biographer tells us, often spoke about marriage but decided to forego it because if he had married he should have had to resign as principal of the Collège de Presles and as a university master.[7]

Somewhat mysterious in its origins and implications, this specially closed environment of the universities was maintained by a long apprenticeship or bachelorship (common to medieval guilds of all sorts) terminating in the *inceptio* or inaugural act of teaching. Today the *inceptio* is echoed really but faintly in the now wholesale ceremony known by the mystifying name of commencement, and words surviving on university diplomas, *periculo facto* or "having undergone the (requisite) danger or trial," bear witness to the old feeling that education was an initiation. But in helping to maintain the closed male environment the psychological role of Latin should not be underestimated. It was the language of those on the "inside," and thus learning Latin at even an infra-university level was the first step toward initiation into the closed world. Earlier groups of learned men—the Academy, the Stoa, the schools at Alexandria—seem never to have achieved the close-knit, jealously guarded internal organization of the university. It seems not irrelevant that they did not have a secret language to nourish their *esprit de corps*.

The humanists, who for various reasons often thought in terms of a home-centered system of education, were hard put to

---

[6] Hastings Rashall, *The Universities of Europe in the Middle Ages*, new edition edited by F. M. Powicke and A. B. Emden (Oxford: Clarendon Press, 1936), I, 446.

[7] Nicolas de Nancel (Nancelius), *Petri Rami . . . vita* (Paris, 1599), pp. 58–59.

find a substitute for the closed male environment of the school. One recalls the embarrassment of Erasmus, More, and Ascham when they speak of rearing a youngster in a home where he would hear the proper use of language at an early age. These educators of course mean the proper use of the Latin language—they are giving no thought to the vernacular at all—and they are visibly nonplused by the fact that this means that the youngster will be in the company of women, since it had proved impossible, even for the humanists, to have homes without women in them. Roger Ascham speaks rather glibly of the way in which Tiberius and Caius Gracchus were brought up in the home of their mother Cornelia, where "the dailie use of speaking were the best and readiest waie to learne the Latin tong."[8] But Ascham here is not merely resorting to humanist piety by preferring a classical example to a current one. He is bowing before historical fact. There were no current examples, and could be none. We can be sure that no English mothers cooed to their children in the language native to the mother of the Gracchi, and thus we find Sir Thomas Elyot more realistically stating, "After that a childe is come to seven years of age, I holde it expedient that he be taken from the company of women, savynge that he may have, one yere, or two at the most, an auncient and sad matrone attending on hym in his chamber."[9]

Sir Thomas pleads here that this arrangement will remove the child from temptations against chastity. However, although this reason might conceivably at times apply with reference to servant girls or other attendants, the separation of the child from his own mother which Elyot seems to envision here, and which families such as Sir John More's practiced (his son Thomas grow up in Cardinal Morton's household), is here generating its own special warrant in humanist educational aims. In cultivating the young boy's ability to speak Latin, women, not being part of the Latin world, were commonly of no use to a child after the age of seven,

---

[8] Roger Ascham, *The Scholemaster*, ed. Edward Arber ("English Reprints"; London, 1870), p. 28. Subsequent references here are all to this edition.

[9] Sir Thomas Elyot, *The Boke Named the Governour*, ed. by Henry Herbert Stephen Croft (2 vols.; London, 1883), I, 35 (Book I, chap, vi).

for this is the age when Elyot and others prescribe that a boy begin to learn and to speak Latin—and, for that matter, Greek as well. The difficulty was that if there were too many women around, the child would speak English, not Latin. He would slip back into the vernacular family circle instead of being forced out already at this tender age into the world of the "tribe," of men. We are faced here with a rather precocious appearance of the puberty rite situation around the age of seven, but the humanists favored precociousness and promoted it when they could.

Sir Thomas More and others, more realistic, would try to remedy the situation by educating the women of the household, making them not only literate but learned (that is, in Latin). But their efforts would meet with no large-scale success. For some mysterious reason Latin was tied up with schools, and by the time it became accessible to women generally in schools, it had practically disappeared as a medium of communication. Even in its present attenuated form Latin has never been assimilated in the curriculum for girls' schools as it has in certain curricula for boys'. One suspects that something of what it stood for, and in a certain degree still stands for, cannot be assimilated. It is a matter of record that the women students who today matriculate at Oxford or Cambridge Universities, where some classical tradition remains fairly strong, are almost invariably less well prepared in Latin than the men matriculating from the English public schools. Curricula are the product of complex and fugitive forces, but the forces are real and cannot be gainsaid.

IV

Flogging was a common practice in the schools of antiquity, as we know, for example, from St. Augustine's rueful remarks in the *Confessions* about his own boyhood experiences.[10] The fact that school pupils were all boys of course encouraged rule by the rod. In the Middle Ages not only does this environment and rule persist, but there is evidence that the specifically

---

[10] St. Augustine, *Confessiones,* Lib. I, cap. ix, in *Opera omnia,* Vol. I ("Patrologiae cursus completus," Series prima [Latina], ed. J.-P. Migne, XXXII; Paris, 1841), cols. 667–68.

initiatory cast of the punishment grew more intense and evident. This is made abundantly clear by Leach, who collects stories about the flogging in school of boy aspirants to monasteries which accompanied the early stages of initiation into monastic life, and quotes from Ælfric's *Colloquy* the "highly characteristic" question which Ælfric has his typical master put to his typical pupils: "Are you willing to be flogged (*flagellari, beswungen* or *swinged*) while learning?"[11] To this the boys—in this case not monastic aspirants— answer at once that they prefer flogging to ignorance. The question, answer, and setting suggest the initiation practice among the Bechuans mentioned above. The boy must acknowledge the equation of learning and flogging, and thereby face courageously into learning as into an initiation, something of itself taxing and fearsome.

Renaissance educators did not, on the whole, abate the ferocity of medieval or ancient school punishment. Pictures of Renaissance classroom activity, such as Pieter Brueghel the Elder's engraving "The Ass at School," feature bundles of switches as regular classroom equipment. "Advanced" ideas on education did not necessarily entail diminishing physical punishment. Whereas an earlier tradition had, in Erasmus' phrase, tended to regard pupils as merely small-sized men, the Renaissance educator was often quite sensitive to the immaturity of his charges and to the psychology of child education. But for him psychology included the use of the birch. In Thomas Murner's *Mnemonic Logic* (*Logica memorativa*, 1509, etc.), which in an extremely "progressive" fashion purveys the otherwise terrifying logic of Peter of Spain in the form of a logical card game, one of the woodcuts of "cards" features a master holding three bundles of switches.[12] These, we are told, are to suggest the three questions, "What? What kind? and How many?" used in handling enunciations, for, as Murner explains, it is with the aid of the switches that the answers to these questions are extracted from the pupils. Switches serve as mnemonic devices in both the real and the allegorical orders.

---

[11] Leach, *The Schools of Medieval England*, pp. 81–82, 89.

[12] Thomas Murner, *Logica memorativa, Chartiludium logice, sive Totius dialectice memoria; et Nonus [i. e. novus] Petri Hispani textus emendatus, cum iucundopictasmatis exercitio* . . . (Strasbourg, 1509), fols. Bv{sup}v{/sup}-Bvi{sup}r{/sup}.

It is well known that the Renaissance Jesuit plan of education provided for a *corrector* for the "little boys" (in effect, those still studying Latin) to "keep them in fear," although the plan registers an oblique protest against beating as compromising good teacher-pupil relations, for it provides that this *corrector* never be one of the Jesuit teachers but either a person specially hired to do the beating or another student.[13] We should not suppose that punishment in Renaissance schools was always mild. Nicolas de Nancel, Peter Ramus' biographer and erstwhile pupil and secretary, a physician who goes into biographical detail with a whimsical clinical objectivity, reports that Ramus, who was a highly successful educator with "advanced" ideas, often punished his pupils in savage outbursts of temper, not only whipping but also kicking them until they were "half dead" (*semineces*) although— and Nancel adds wistfully here, "for this he must be praised"— during all this process he never swore.[14]

However, although Renaissance reliance on physical violence as a teaching device was not new, the connection of this punishment with Latin teaching acquired a greater urgency. This was due to the greater prestige of Latin established by the humanists, but also to an increasing divorce between Latin and extra-curricular life and communication. In the Middle Ages, for casual communication between scholars, young or old, Latin was unblushingly vernacularized. Hence the venture into Latin, while a break with the past, was a relatively less violent break. For the humanist, only "correct" classical Latin should be spoken, even by small boys beginning the language. The break with the past thus reached a kind of maximum in the Renaissance, and the sense of the Latin school as a special marginal environment reached its greatest intensity. The break with the past—that is, with the vernacular of one's childhood—was further enhanced by the concurrent growth of vernacular literature and its greater and greater independence of Latin which marked the Renaissance period.

---

[13] See the documents in George E. Ganss, S. J., *Saint Ignatius' Idea of a Jesuit Universiaty* (Milwaukee, Wisconsin: Marquette University Press, 1954), pp. 26, 309, 331.

[14] Nancel, *Petri Rami . . . vita*, p. 60.

V

In the Renaissance the association of violence with teaching takes another special and interesting turn, for the Renaissance educator appears aware of the teaching environment not only in terms of the violence sometimes resorted to on the side of the teacher but also in terms of the courage which he hopes to develop in his pupils. This emphasis seems connected with the tendency of the humanist educator to think of educating his pupil as a whole person. Humanist teachers frequently functioned less as members of teachers' unions or university faculties than as *familiares* or even employees of bourgeois or noble families. Hence they show an interest in the pupil's total upbringing not so often met with in the medieval university, where all pupils were by definition (if not always in actuality) mere apprentices learning the more or less highly specialized teaching trade.

The new interest manifests itself in the many courtesy books and in the various *rationes studiorum*, or works on educational procedure, which were turned out in the humanist tradition and which connect in many ways with the courtesy literature. In this setting, where educational objectives are formulated under the more or less direct influence of well-to-do or noble households, concerned with family tradition and prestige, there flourishes the Renaissance cult of "glory" and there develops the curious interest in the epic poem, together with the typical Renaissance view that such a poem is the highest creation of the human mind and consequently the normally preferred focus of literary (as apart from oratorical) study. By the same token there develops, under the concurrent influence of Plato's *Republic*, a keen interest in courage (which makes the glorious epic hero) as an express objective in the education of boys.

It has not been sufficiently remarked how much Renaissance poetic and other language study finds itself wandering from the consideration of poetry or language to the consideration of courage, or of its opposite, softness or effeminacy. In part this common deviation is undoubtedly due to the fact that in the Renaissance generally poetry tended to be exclusively a matter for education at what we should consider the secondary-school or even the elementary-school level. With our present upper-division courses and graduate courses in poetry and literature, we are likely to forget that the ordinary Renaissance student finished his rhetoric and poetry in his early teens and went on immediately to "philosophy" and shortly after, if he continued his formal education, to medicine or law or theology.[15] On his own initiative or in some more or less special circumstances a student could study literature at an advanced level, and in the later Renaissance students, in Great Britain at least, tended to linger on in Latin for a longer time, but, by and large, literary studies in the Renaissance were for youngsters. In the mid-sixteenth century Peter Ramus had explained how his students had finished not only rhetoric (together with what poetry was included in this "art") but philosophy as well by the age of fifteen.[16] Rationalizing about the existing situation, Ramus states that poetry is taught at a very early age because the logic in it is diluted and thus assimilable by the tender youthful mind, unable to absorb the more concentrated logic of philosophy.[17]

This statement that poetry respects young boys' weakness is, of course, another way of saying that it gets them over the weakness. The Jesuit savant Martin Antonio Delrio a few years later will explain how the lowly humane letters toughen the young boys who suffer from too great tenderness in age and mind, preparing them for the weightier disciplines of philosophy, medicine, law, and theology. He goes on to add that not only poetry, but drama, history, oratory, and literature generally should be studied only by young boys, not by adults, whose sole concern with these things should be to edit texts for boys—Delrio is here apologizing for his own preoccupations, for these remarks of his occur in the preface to his collection or "line-up" (*syntagma*) of Latin trag-

---

[15] See Ganss, *Saint Ignatius' Idea*, p. 45. The curriculum and students' ages here outlined may be taken as fairly representative of Continental practice generally, since the Jesuit program of studies was conceived on an international basis and drawn up by pooling international educational experience.

[16] Peter Ramus, *Oratio de studiis philosophiae et eloquentiae coniungendis*, in Peter Ramus and Omer Talon (Audomarus Talaeus), *Collectaneae praefationes, epistolae, orationes* (Marburg, 1599), pp. 248–50; Peter Ramus, *Pro philosophica Parisiensis academiae disciplina oratio*, in his *Scholae in liberales artes* (Basle, 1569), cols. 1019–20.

[17] Peter Ramus, *Oratio initio suae professionis habita* (Paris, 1551, p. 31.

edies, which turn out to be entirely Senecan.[18] The idea that Seneca is exclusively for children may strike us as amusing and might have seriously upset even the Stoic Seneca himself, but Delrio's views represent one standard Renaissance position, supported chiefly by two considerations. First, in the actuality of the curriculum, if literature was to be studied at all, it had to be studied in the early years of school, for literature was used in the schoolroom chiefly to perfect the boy's competence in Latin so that, as soon as possible, he could move on to philosophy and the sciences. This was not Erasmus' ideal, but then Erasmus' ideal of an education terminating not in philosophy and science but in language and literary study, with theology itself cast in a grammatical rather than a philosophical mold, was never effectively realized.

A second consideration moving Delrio would have appealed to Erasmus: Seneca was a stern Stoic moralist and could thus be counted on to make the young boy manly and courageous. At this point we are reminded of the tendency of Renaissance educators to assimilate to the linguistic portion of the curriculum not only literary works of Stoics such as Seneca or his nephew Lucan, but also more properly philosophical works, such as the *Enchiridion* of Epictetus, which appears in a great number of Renaissance editions, often together with the *Tabula* of Cebes. The somewhat aphoristic character of the philosophy of the *Enchiridion* made it a congenial adjunct of rhetoric, which often cultivated the epigram. But, more than this, its strong moral and ascetical bias fitted the Stoic philosophy to the puberty-rite mentality which we have been considering here as connected with language study. Epictetus' was a toughening philosophy in a way that Aristotle's was not.

The Renaissance humanist could be disturbed by the plausibility of the charge that literature, and poetry in particular, was actually soft or effeminate, so that, being purveyed to youngsters at the very age when they should be maturing in manliness (the puberty rite attitudes clearly evince themselves here), it actually

---

[18] Martin Antonio Delrio, *Syntagma a tragoediae Latinae* (Antwerp, 1593), Preface, fols. *3ᵛ, **1ʳ. A translation of Delrio's Preface by Richard G. Wittmann is available in typescript at St. Louis University on application to the present author.

only weakens him. This is the burden or background not only of Ramus' opinion that poetry has little "logic" in it but also of Gosson's attack on poetry, revealed by his charge, taken up by Sidney, that poetry is "the schoole of abuse." Although Gosson's principal concern is not poetry taught in schools but drama seen in the playhouses, his resort to the school symbol not only in his title but constantly through his argumentation—"I have been matriculated my selfe in the schoole [i.e., of the stage], where so many abuses flourish. . . . I should tell tales out of Schoole, and be Ferruled for my faulte. . . . Liberty gives you head [i.e., in the playwright's world, conceived of as a school], placing you with Poetrie in the lowest form"[19]—leaves no doubt that the case for or against drama and literature generally is to be adjudicated in a pedagogical frame of reference: Do these things serve to make boys men (or men more manly)? Sidney works in this same frame of reference when he asserts that he knows *men*—the word is deliberately pointed and is Sidney's own—"that even with reading of *Amadis de gaule* (which God knoweth wanteth much of a perfect Poesie) have found their hearts moved to the exercise of courtesie, liberalitie, and especially courage."[20]

In Gosson and Sidney the connections between poetry, courage (or the lack thereof), and the education of young boys are suggested rather than explicitly dealt with. But in specifically educational treatises connected with the courtesy tradition they come definitely to the fore and show some of the real grounds for the Renaissance educator's preoccupation with the hero and with glory—these grounds being in this case associated with the proper toughening of the youth in his initiation into extra-familial society.

Thus in Book I, chapter x to xvi, of *The Boke Named the Governour* (1531) where Sir Thomas Elyot treats the scholastic curriculum of his youthful pupil, it is striking that at every juncture where he mentions the age of the boy, he brings in courage or

---

[19] Stephen Gosson, *The Schoole of Abuse,* ed. by Edward Arber ("English Reprints"; London, 1869), p. 24.

[20] Sir Philip Sidney, *The Defence of Poesie,* in *The Complete Works,* ed. by Albert Feuillerat (Cambridge: The University Press, 1922–26), III, 20; cf. *ibid.,* 28.

"corage" for explicit comment.[21] At seven, we are told, the child begins grammar, but not in too great detail, for too detailed grammar "mortifieth his corage" (chap. x). Up to his thirteenth year, "the childes courage, inflamed by the frequent redynge of noble poetes, dayly more and more desireth to have experience in those things that they so vehemently do commende in them they write of" (chap. x). After fourteen, and some study of oratory and cosmography, it is time, says Elyot, "to induce a childe to the redinge of histories; but fyrst, to set him in a fervent courage, the mayster . . . expressinge what incomparable delectation, utilitie, and commodite shall happen to emperours, kinges, princis, and all other gentil men by reding of histories" (chap. xi).

The connection of literature (Latin) with toughness of moral fiber is here explicit, and this toughness of moral fiber goes with physical toughness as well. Thus, says Elyot, "for as moche the membres by movying and mutuall touching do waxe more hard," physical exercise must be insisted upon for boys, "specially from the age of xiiii yeres upwarde, in whiche tyme strength with courage increaseth" (chap. xvi). However, by the time the boy comes to the age of seventeen, a different emphasis must be given, for at this age "to the intent his courage be bridled with reason, hit were needful to rede unto him some warkes of philosophy, especially . . . morall" (chap. xi).

The picture is here complete. By seventeen the child has become something of a man, his courage has been proved and he must now practice what one practices after crossing the threshold of maturity, namely, control. For our present purposes what is of interest is the absolute coincidence in the ending of language studies and the ending of emphasis on developing and proving courage. Both mark the ending of a period of initiation. Courage or "corage" (heart-iness, strength of heart) designates for Elyot something definitely connected with the process of maturing, not merely with high spirits, although it would include this. And this strength of heart is communicated by the study of literature— that is to say, of Latin literature (with some smattering of Greek).

It is true that Elyot is interested specifically in educating a

---

21 All quotations from Elyot are from the edition cited in n. 9 above.

"governor," or, as he puts it elsewhere, a "gentleman," one who rules or at least is part of the ruling class of a *respublica*. Still, his program of Latin and Greek studies for his governor-to-be is basically no different from that of Renaissance schools generally, where it would presumably inspire the same kind of "courage" in the sons of merchants and tradesmen as in prospective governors. In showing how the typical ideal Renaissance educational program built around Latin is suited to nobles—the fighting class, who, above all, must pass through the puberty rites ("Will you guard the chief well?" ask the Bechuans)—Elyot is revealing something of the way this program was felt as operating. In books such as Elyot's the humanists set out to show that even the nobles should be educated men—which, from one point of view, means that the humanistic study of Latin was a good and desirable substitute for more barbaric practices of initiation. In this context, how could it be entirely dissociated from such practices?

A cluster of forces sustaining and sustained by the Renaissance cult of the epic hero and of the epic can be seen here. This view of literature as inculcating "courage" both nourishes and feeds on the cult of the hero and his "glory" which the epic fosters. This cult, which affected governors and governed alike, has far-reaching and mysterious roots in human history. At this point we can only indicate that the position of Latin in Renaissance culture, the way in which this Latin was taught, the things it was supposed to do to the pupil, and the interest in the epic which by the seventeenth century in Western Europe amounts almost to a frenzy are not unrelated phenomena.

It is true also that Elyot's focus on courage in his educational plan is related to a similar focus in Plato's *Republic*, the major source for much that was explicit in the Renaissance cult of courage. However, the point here is not whether or not Elyot has assignable sources but rather where such sources strike root in his thinking—for not everything that Plato said manages to root itself in Renaissance educational theory or practice. What interests us here in Elyot is the association of courage with language study, and in particular with Latin. The study of Greek for Plato's pupil involved no break with the past. For Elyot's pupil, the study of classical languages did. The Renaissance environment for Platonic ideas was different from the original Greek environment.

Moreover, because of the attitude toward the classical languages peculiar to the humanist tradition, for Renaissance boys the learning of Latin represented, like the passage through puberty rites, not only something difficult but precisely a transit from ignorance to tribal wisdom, that is, to the accumulated wisdom of mankind. This wisdom was thought of as stored behind doors linguistically controlled from the inside. "In the Greeke and Latin tong," writes Ascham, "the two onlie learned tonges, which be kept not in common taulke but in private bookes, we finde alwayes wisdome and eloquence."[22] In any generation the wisdom of the past, which is not only the matter communicated to neophytes in puberty rites but a major item in all formal education, may be thought of as "situated" somewhere. The only point we are making here is that Renaissance man regularly located this somewhere in linguistic terms.

The connection of the teaching of Latin and of literature with puberty rites is further manifest to us, if it was not manifest to Renaissance educators themselves, when these educators explicitly discuss the problem of physical punishment. In the long dialogue on the pro's and con's of corporal punishment with which Roger Ascham opens his famous educational treatise, *The Schoolmaster*, he provides glimpses of issues relevant to our present subject which he never really fully exposes. Some pupils have recently run away from Eton, we are told in the course of this dialogue, "for fear of beating," and the discretion of schoolmasters is called into question because they may flog to punish "weakenes of nature rather than the fault of the Scholer," thus actually driving boys from learning.[23] This seems a clear indication that, whether it should be or not, punishment is felt by some masters as advisable for reasons other than the encouragement of formal learning.

We note further on in the dialogue that Master Mason and Master Haddon vastly enjoy reminiscing about schoolboy escapades (one recalls that in puberty rites the ordinary rules of behavior are often suspended and outlawry is regarded with approval). Master Mason proves "very merry with both parties, pleasantly playing with shrewd touches [trials—i.e., of the schoolmaster's patience] of many cours'd [flogged] boys and with the small discretion of many lewd schoolmasters," and Master Haddon remarks that "the best Scholemaster of our time [we know that he refers to Nicholas Udall] was the greatest beater."[24] Masters Mason and Haddon here plainly speak not as scholars but simply as men who had "gone through" the *rites de passage* and who look back on such experiences, with their aura of lawlessness, as trials which others should perhaps go through not so much for learning's sake as simply to prove their prowess as members of the "gang" and to achieve a sense of belonging. This is a line of argumentation which Ascham, like earnest educators today, does not like, but the fact that it is used and reported testifies to an existing state of mind.

Ascham himself suggests that native ability, not attributable to their experience of Udall's birches, might account for the success of Udall's pupils and leaves no doubt that he himself is against flogging as a device for teaching Latin. He himself does not state that there were other things besides the mere learning of Latin in the back of Renaissance educators' minds when they beat their boys. Yet the fact that there were, that the flogging served the purpose—unstated, unformulated, but real—of initiating boys into a tough, man's world, as suggested by Masters Mason and Haddon, is curiously confirmed by the example which Ascham himself brings forward to prove that beating is not necessary. The example has become classic. For it is an example not of schoolboy or budding young gentleman, but that of a girl, none other than the young Lady Jane Grey, whom Ascham, to his delight, found one day reading Plato's *Phaedo* while the more boisterous members of her family were out hunting.

Lady Jane was at great pains to explain how nice a person was her teacher, "Master Elmer," by comparison with her straitlaced parents, by whom she was constantly "so sharplie taunted,

---

24 *Ibid.*

so cruellie threatened, yea, presentlie some tymes with pinches, nippes, and bobbes."[25] Ascham does not pause to note that, rather than straightforwardly contrasting schooling based on kindness with schooling based on physical punishment, his example really contrasts the romantic world of a maturing young girl with the rough-and-tumble world his society prescribed for young boys. Despite Ascham's attempt to make something else out of his example, what is remarkable about Lady Jane is not that she is not being flogged—Master Elmer certainly could not have flogged her—but that she is studying the classics *instead* of hunting. This suggests that Lady Jane's approach to literature was somehow radically different from that of the ideal Renaissance gentleman, who liked both the classics *and* hunting. Had not Ascham himself written a treatise on the use of the longbow?

The *rites de passage* prescribed for the Renaissance gentleman were to initiate him into an aggressively competitive man's world. For Lady Jane, too, the study of literature was a kind of *rite de passage*, an initiation into a new world ahead and a break with the past. But the break-through was at a different point. It opened out upon a pleasant, fanciful, romantic world. As a *rite de passage* the study of literature here meant to a girl something different than to a boy. One made the *passage* to Lady Jane's world precisely by staying away from the hunt, just as the medieval lady, intrigued with vernacular romances, had done. One thinks of the Green Knight's lady in *Sir Gawain and the Green Knight*, or perhaps even of Paolo and Francesca.

I do not wish to pass on the relative merits of the two worlds, that of literature-and-hunting and that of literature-and-Master-Elmer, or to speculate as to where in the dialectic between the two we are at present situated, but only to point out that they can engender a dialectic because they represent different and opposed positions. In view of this fact, however, it seems not entirely irrelevant that *The Schoolmaster*, never published during Ascham's lifetime, is presented to Sir William Cecil and to the world by a woman, who writes the preface, Ascham's widow, Margaret. Nor does it seem entirely irrelevant to this dialectic

---

[25] *Ibid.*, p. 47.

that corporal punishment and the stress on Latin in school have, pretty generally, been disappearing in modern times with the emergence of co-education.

VI

This study has been a sketch of certain forces at work in the Renaissance attitudes toward Latin, toward literature, and toward education. It could be elaborated indefinitely, and no doubt refined in many ways, by exploiting more and more examples, of which there is certainly "copie" in Renaissance documents. Here we have limited ourselves to samplings from better-known sources, chiefly British. Perhaps further development is worth while, perhaps not. In either event, we can sum up or present conclusions.

First, I have not sought to maintain that Renaissance educators explicitly thought of Latin study as a puberty rite. They had no definable, abstract idea of what a puberty rite is or was—and neither, for that matter, do the primitive peoples whose puberty rites we have taken as a term of comparison. Renaissance educators, like primitive peoples and like ourselves, have no rationalized explanation for everything they do. They do certain things because they feel these things should be done, finding reasons for them afterwards if at all—and, if they are observant and honest, often being surprised at the reasons which turn up on close inspection.

The basic conclusion is that when Latin, in which learning was encoded, became by the time of the Renaissance a "dead language—a language which, however widely used, was divorced from family life—initiation into the language of learning became more than ever a *rite de passage*. Thus, when other Renaissance courses were being labeled "methods" and "systems," Comenius finds it natural to describe his course in Latin and other languages as a "door"— *Ianua Linguarum*. Thus, in a Western society destined to become progressively more humane in its educational procedures, the status of Latin helped maintain the relatively violent puberty rite setting, a sense of existence on a threshold, within a marginal environment (associated with forced seclusion from the company of women and to a certain extent from one's own family), in an atmosphere of continuous excitement and of that aggressive competition or *aemulatio* which, toned down or outlawed in modern de-Latinized coeducationalism, was a key principle of most Renaissance education.

The complex of attitudes, not new but concentrated with new urgency around language study, helps explain (although I do not wish to suggest that it entirely explains) the frenzied fascination with epic poetry (most of which was in Latin during the Renaissance), with the courageous epic hero (given to war much more than to love-making), which epic theory, and with courage itself, which marks linguistic studies in the period when Renaissance Latin education was having its full effect on society.

Seeing Renaissance Latin teaching in the psychological framework of the puberty rite helps us to explain much in the later trajectory of Latin teaching. In the nineteenth century, when Latin was on its way out as the core subject of the curriculum, educators produced the theory that Latin "strengthened" or "toughened" the mind. This theory, which is still met with today, has been labeled new,[26] and it was new in the sense that earlier educators had not explicitly advanced it. But the complex in which Latin was normally taught had associated the language in a special way with some sort of toughening. Were not nineteenth-century educators, and are not the few twentieth-century educators who repeat their words today, merely giving voice to a vague feeling which has its roots in the psychological setting of the Renaissance Latin school—the feeling that the teaching of Latin, independently of the communication of the ability to read the language (the immediate aim of Renaissance Latin teaching), had somehow to do with toughening the youngster for the extra-familial world in which he would have to live?

Translated, this means the feeling that a boy's education was basically a puberty rite, a process preparing him for adult life by communicating to him the heritage of a past in a setting which toughened him and thus guaranteed his guarding the heritage for the future. Latin had indubitable connections with the past, and

---

[26] See Ganss, *Saint Ignatius' Idea*, pp. 210–11, 219 ff.

it was hard, indeed all the harder as motivation waned when real use for the language began to wane. This association of Latin with a toughening marginal environment of a puberty rite type was sufficient to keep Latin in its place as the basic discipline forming the prep school character, with its twin emphases on Latin and physical hardihood (modulated eventually into good sportsmanship.)

The perspectives proposed in this paper are, of course, suggestive rather than complete, but they open the way, I believe, to a better understanding of some curious and important momentums developed by past ideas and practices. And, since it is impossible to study the past without reference to the present, they suggest matter for reflection—forward-looking, let us hope, rather than nostalgic—concerning the twentieth-century situation. Where are the *rites de passage* for youth today? Does a technological society have any? Should it have any? If so, what should they be?

22——Melford E. Spiro

Education in a
Communal Village
in Israel*

The agricultural communes in Israel, known as *kib-butzim* (sing., *kibbutz*), are characterized by the absence of both private property and the profit motive, by a high degree of communal living, and by a social and economic ethic whose basic principle is: "from each according to his ability, to each according to his need." Another unusual characteristic of *kibbutz* culture is its system of education, known as *chinuch meshutaf*, or "collective education," a system in which children are reared in communal children's dormitories. Since there are many variations in this system, this paper will restrict itself to Kiryat Yedidim, the name I shall give to the *kibbutz* in which this research was carried out.[1]

The founders of Kiryat Yedidim were Eastern European Jews who had rebelled, among other things, against the differential status of the sexes and against the traditional family structure of both their Jewish and European cultures. The traditional family, they felt, was characterized by the subjection of the wife to her husband and by the subservience of the child to the father. Moreover, they charged, the division of labor that characterized the family and which, in turn, was a reflection of the broader social system, confined the woman to the home, relegated her to the role of housewife, and precluded her participation in the economic,

* Reprinted from *The American Journal of Orthopsychiatry*, XXV, 1955, 283–292, with permission.
[1] The field research on which this paper is based was conducted in Kiryat Yedidim in 1951–52, and was made possible by a grant from the Social Science Research Council.

cultural and political life of the community. These "evils" they proposed to exclude from their new society by abolishing the so-called "double standard"; eliminating the marriage ceremony; creating communal institutions—a communal kitchen, dining room, laundry, etc.—which would free the woman from her role as housewife and enable her to work in the larger *kibbutz* economy; and by instituting a system of "collective education" which would free the mother from the responsibilities of child rearing and at the same time would remove the child from the patriarchal authority of the father.

I am not unaware of the unconscious motives that might have prompted such a system. In this paper, however, I am concerned exclusively with conscious motives and manifest meanings as they are found *today*. With this qualification in mind, it may be stressed that Kiryat Yedidim is a child-centered society *par excellence*. Measured by any criterion, whether it be the investment of money, of energy, of time or of love, the child is king in the *kibbutz*. He is—as he was in the East European Jewish culture in which the founders of Kiryat Yedidim grew up—"the parents' crown."[2] We may now turn to an examination of the system of "collective education."

Four days after giving birth in the hospital, the mother returns with her infant to the *kibbutz*. Here the child is placed in the Infants Dormitory where, with 15 other infants ranging in age from four days to approximately one year, he remains in the charge of a head nurse and two full-time assistant nurses. These nurses, like all other personnel in the educational system, are *kibbutz* members who, for the most part, have received specialized training. Since the infants are not taken to the parental rooms until they are six months old, almost all their physical needs—with the exception of nursing—and many of their emotional needs as well are satisfied primarily by their nurses.

This does not mean that parents play an inconspicuous role in the life of the infant. The mother breast feeds the child—beginning with six scheduled feedings a day and gradually tapering off until he is weaned at eight months—and at the same time, she plays

---

[2] Mark Zborowski and Elizabeth Herzog, *Life Is With People* (International University Press, New York, 1952), pp. 308–330.

with him, changes his diaper, and tucks him into bed. Hence, it is not unlikely that the *kibbutz* infant has as much opportunity for interaction with his mother as has the infant raised in a private home. The father, of course, sees the infant only after work. During this visiting hour, and during the free visiting hours on Saturdays and holidays when both parents visit their infant together, the dormitory, as well as its front lawn and porch, is filled with adults romping and playing with their infants.

The first important change in his life occurs at six months, when the infant may be taken by his parents to their room for an hour every afternoon. The second important change occurs at about one year when he is moved from the Infants Dormitory to the Toddlers Dormitory, where he must learn to adjust to a new building, one new nurse, many new (and slightly older) children, a new routine and new disciplines. It is in the Toddlers Dormitory, which includes two nurses and eight children, that the child is gradually toilet trained, is taught how to feed himself (a process which had begun in the Infants Dormitory) and learns to interact with his age mates. It is at this age, moreover, that the child may stay with his parents for two hours in the evening (since he goes to bed at a later hour) and may stay with them on Saturday. I shall have more to say about parents and children later.

Between the ages of two and three the group acquires a nursery teacher, in addition to its nurse. This teacher, like the nurse, cares for the physical and emotional needs of the children, but she is primarily in charge of their social and intellectual development. At about four years the children encounter another important change—kindergarten. This involves moving into a new building, acquiring (sometimes) a new nurse and nursery teacher and enlarging the original group of 8, by addition of another group so as to include 16 members. This enlarged group, or *kevutza*, will remain together until its members enter high school.

The institutionalized aspects of the children's lives are similar throughout this early period. The children in each dormitory rise at the same time and have a free play period before breakfast. Breakfast, like other meals, is eaten by the group in its own dining room. After breakfast there is usually an organized activity supervised by the nurse or nursery teacher. These activities include various games, art (drawing, dancing, sculpting, etc.), listening to stories told by the teacher, hikes, tours through the animal barns, etc. This is followed by a midmorning snack, after which there is either a free play period or a continuation of the organized activity. After lunch the children nap for two or three hours (depending on their ages), and when they waken they change into their "good clothes," are given a snack, and spend the rest of the afternoon in either free or organized play. Supper is eaten early so that the children may be ready when their parents upon their return from work come for them. After returning to the dormitories with their parents in the evening, the children are given showers by their nurses, who tuck them into bed, usually tell them a story or sing them a song, and kiss them goodnight before departing. The children are left alone until the following morning, except for a periodic check by the night watchman.

After spending a year or two in the kindergarten, the group (*kevutza*) passes into the " Transitional Class" where, for one year, the children receive their first formal intellectual training before moving into the grammar school. School marks an important transition in their lives for a number of reasons: it is the beginning of their serious intellectual training; it expands their interactional group to include many more children, as well as children who are both older and younger than their own age mates; and it introduces them into formal responsibility and work. Each child devotes an hour a day to a regular work assignment, such as cleaning the dormitories and classrooms, setting tables in the dining room, and working in the school's vegetable garden or poultry run. Instruction in the school, which is based almost entirely on the project method, is conducted in an informal manner. Children have a voice in choosing the curriculum; they call the teacher by her first name; there are neither exams nor grades and passing is automatic—no one fails.

At the completion of the sixth grade, at the age of 12, the children graduate into the combined junior-senior high school. This, too, is an important transition in their lives for at least three reasons, in addition to the intellectual one. 1) The children for the first time encounter important male figures other than their fathers. Heretofore nurses and teachers have all been female; now teachers are primarily male, as are the youth group leaders and the "educators"—the teachers who are the advisers to each *kevutza* and who serve as its moral and ideological mentors. 2) The *kevutza* is split up, and the children form new groups comprised of children from the cities and from other *kibbutzim* as well as from Kiryat Yedidim. This is the first time that the children must interact intimately with "strangers." 3) The children begin to work in the *kibbutz* economy (from 1½ to 3 hours a day, depending on their ages) together with the adult members of the *kibbutz*. Hence, by the time they graduate from high school they have had experience in almost every branch of the economy and can elect to work in the branch which most interests them.

The high school curriculum reflects the self-image of Kiryat Yedidim as a socialist society of farmer-intellectuals. There is practically no vocational or "home economics" influence in the entire curriculum. The emphasis, instead, is on the humanities, science and the arts, with much emphasis on the social implications of knowledge. In both intensity and breadth this curriculum is more like that of a European Gymnasium or a very good American private school than that of the average American public school.

While still in high school the children are not viewed as members of Kiryat Yedidim itself, membership in which can be attained only through election, and not by birth. They are members, instead, of the *chevrat yeladim*, or the "children's society," which has considerable power. It elects a student council, plans its own social programs, has a large voice in the planning of curriculum, exercises punitive power over recalcitrant and antisocial members, and even has the power—which it has exercised at least once—of expelling those of its fellows who are particularly obnoxious.

Before examining some of the results of this educational system, we must briefly describe two important psychological areas which have been neglected in this discussion thus far—sex and interpersonal relationships. From birth until graduation from high school, both boys and girls live in the same dormitories. Until they enter grade school boys and girls not only eat, play and sleep together, but they shower together and use the toilet facilities simultaneously. The identical patterns characterize behavior in the grade school, except for the discontinuance of the simultaneous use of the toilet facilities, and in high school, where joint showers are discontinued as well. The taking of joint showers was practiced in the high school in the past, but it was abolished by the students themselves, with the influx of students from outside the *kibbutz*, who brought with them the sexual values of the larger culture. Sexual education begins in the nursery when the children are taught, literally, about the birds, the bees and the flowers, and continues in the grade school with instruction in human biology, and in the high school with specific instruction in sex. Living on a farm, moreover, provides the children with the informal education which comes from observing barnyard animals.

Sexual behavior, in the form of attempted sexual intercourse, has not been observed among preschool children. Other manifestations of child sexuality are permitted by the nurses, with the exception of bisexual sleeping, which is not seldom attempted. Prohibitions of sexual behavior from, roughly, prepubescence through early puberty are not necessary, since the children themselves prefer to remain in unisexual groups, between whom there is sometimes marked hostility.

By middle adolescence boys and girls begin to display heterosexual interests. *Kibbutz* culture, it will be remembered, is entirely "enlightened" concerning sexual matters. There is no taboo on premarital sexuality, and there is considerable experimentation before marriage. Nevertheless, Kiryat Yedidim frowns on adolescent sexuality, not because of puritanical attitudes, but because it is felt that the encouragement of sexual relationships would serve to deflect the students' interests and energies from their (more important) intellectual, ideological and social activities. If a couple is obviously in love, however, the high school authorities do not interfere with their activities. The high school program, with its all-morning classes, afternoon work and evening study, as well as its many social, artistic, political and intellectual activities, in effect, leaves little time or energy for sexual activity. *Kibbutz* adolescent culture, incidentally, does not include such patterns as dating, social dancing, make-up, smoking, drinking, expensive or fancy clothes.

It should be noted, finally, that neither sexual behavior nor marriage has taken place between individuals who, together, have gone through this system of education. When questioned about this avoidance pattern the *sabras*[3] point out that they view each other as siblings, so that such relationships are perceived *by them* as incestuous.

The other area of psychological significance that demands some description is the relationship between the child and the most important persons in his life—his peer group, parents, and parental surrogates. If only because he spends most of his time with them, a child's nurses and teachers are parental surrogates in every sense of that term. They are responsible for the satisfaction of almost all his physical needs; they teach him most of the culture patterns he will have to employ to satisfy his social needs; finally, they institute most of his disciplines and hence are important in both the creation and satisfaction of his emotional needs.

But however important a role the nurses play in the child's development, both objectively and subjectively considered, the parents remain crucial figures in the child's life—at least in his early years. For most parents of young children, their day is but a prelude to the afternoon hours which they spend with their children. These hours are sacred, and nothing is allowed to interfere with them. In the summer parents and children play games, romp on the grass, visit the barns, stroll through the fields. In the winter when they are confined to their rooms, they play, read, listen to music, talk. It is little wonder that the children are eager to be with their parents. In the dormitories they are subject to the various disciplines imposed by the nurse and, at the same time, they must share her love with all the other children in the group. In the parental rooms, on the other hand, they monopolize the attention of their parents, they are seldom disciplined, and they are indulged to the point where the adults themselves say that the children are "spoiled." Hence, until the children enter high school they view their parents, as the latter view themselves, as affectionate comrades in whom one confides and with whom one maintains intimate bonds. This relationship, much to the bewilder-

---

[3] *Sabra* is the term applied to any native-born Israeli. In this paper it will be used to refer to any native of Kiryat Yedidim.

ment of the parents, changes shortly after the children enter high school. They visit their parents less frequently—sometimes not more than once or twice a week—and the intimacy that characterized their earlier relationship is often replaced by psychological distance.

The third group of psychologically significant persons in the child's life is his peer group. Almost all the activities, experiences and belongings of the child are shared, either voluntarily or under compulsion, with these age peers. It is little wonder that the children are obviously ambivalent to each other, and that their interaction may suddenly shift from warmth and cooperation to bitterness and aggression, and back again, many times a day. Children, moreover, though eager to leave the group in order to join their parents in the afternoon, are for the most part just as eager to leave their parents in order to join their group in the evening. As the children grow older, however, some of them complain about the lack of privacy which dormitory living imposes; and many of the high school graduates, when they become members of the *kibbutz*, seem to withdraw into the privacy of both their rooms and themselves—as a reaction, perhaps, against the previous pressures of group living.

Evidence from both interviews and tests is available for a quantitative check on this qualitative picture. Since this paper is concerned with the conscious and the manifest, we shall examine only the results of the Bavelas Moral Ideology and Stewart Emotional Response tests, which yield information on that psychological level. After the children were asked, as part of the Bavelas test, to name those good things they could do for which they would be praised, they were asked to name the persons who would do the praising. For both the younger children (ages 6–11) and the older children (ages 12–17), the most frequent response category is "the group" (and specifically, the peer group) in contrast to children from other societies for whom "parents" is almost always the most frequent response. For both younger and older children the second and third most frequent responses are "parents" and "parental surrogates" (teachers and nurses) respectively. In both cases these two responses are almost identical in frequency, and in both cases the sum of the latter two is less than the frequency for the first category.

In other words sensitivity to peer-group approbation seems to be of greater importance in the socialization process than sensitivity to the approval of authority figures. It should be stressed, however, that the youngest respondent was six years old. It is my impression that for the children under six, parents and parental surrogates would have loomed much larger than the peer group.

The children were then asked to name those things for which they would be blamed, and to name those persons who would do the blaming. To the latter question, "parents" is the least frequently mentioned response, a not unexpected finding in the light of what we know about the parent-child relationship. The most frequently mentioned response varies according to age, which again is predictable in terms of this culture. For the younger children, "parental surrogates" constitute the most frequently mentioned category while "the group" is the category with the highest frequency for the older children, those whose basic disciplines have already been learned. From these data it may be concluded that (a) for children over six years of age, and on a conscious level, parents play a smaller role in the socialization process than is played by either parental surrogates or by the group; and that (b) the influence of the group increases with age.

Since the family seems to play a minimal role in the socialization process, it is instructive to discover the role it plays in the wider emotional life of the child. With the same reservations mentioned above, evidence derived from the Emotional Response test may be presented here. Combining the responses to the questions "What is the best thing that could happen to you?" and "On what occasions have you been happy?" we discover that 13 per cent of the responses of the younger children and 10 per cent of the responses of the older involve family members, a finding which is in sharp contrast to the corresponding figures of more than 50 per cent for the children of both an American Middle Western white community and certain Southwest Indian tribes. If, on the other hand, the *kibbutz* responses to the questions "On what occasions have you been angry?" "ashamed?" "afraid?" are compared with the responses of the Middle Western and Indian communities, we discover that while none of the responses of the younger *kibbutz* children, and only 1 per cent of those of the older involve family members, approximately 50 per cent of the responses of the Mid-western and Indian children involve family members. These figures seem to confirm what we might have inferred from the cultural data alone: that the *kibbutz* family plays a smaller role in the emotional life of the child over six than is the case in other societies, but that the role that it does play is almost exclusively positive. That is, contributes to the child's euphoric, but not to his dysphoric emotions. There is, moreover, some evidence which suggests that the positive role of the parents is greater than it appears. Although the mere presence of parents is not mentioned by any of the children as a cause for happiness the temporary absence of parents constitutes 10 per cent of the younger children as a cause for sadness, and permanent absence constitutes 15 per cent of the responses of the older children as the worst thing that could happen to them.

I should like now to examine to what extent, culturally viewed, this system of collective education has been successful. From the cultural point of view the success of the educational system of any society is to be measured by the degree to which it has produced members who are motivated to perpetuate the culture of their society, and by the extent to which it has developed in its members the kind of character that is consistent with the values of that culture. In short, a well-educated person, from a cultural point of view, is a person who, to paraphrase Fromm, wants to do what he ought to do—the "oughtness" being defined by his culture.

On both scores the system of "collective education" has been successful. In the first place, in its entire history not one person born and raised in Kiryat Yedidim has left it. The children have many opportunities to learn of non-*kibbutz* life in books and movies and in their many visits to the cities. Moreover, every high school graduate must live in the city for at least one year before deciding to be a candidate for membership in the *kibbutz*, and some have even traveled abroad. Nevertheless every child of Kiryat Yedidim has chosen, upon attaining adulthood, to remain in Kiryat Yedidim. This fact is, of course, amenable to varied and conflicting interpretations; the *sabras* themselves explain it by saying that socialist living is superior to other forms of living. What is important, however, is not the interpretation of this fact, but the fact itself: collective education has been successful in producing people who wish to perpetuate their culture despite much competition, as well as hostility, from the outside. We must now discover to what extent they have the character structure to do so.

Of the many psychological characteristics necessary for the survival of *kibbutz* culture the following are among the most important: identification with the group, a sense of security within the group, the absence of intense acquisitive drives, the absence of intense "success" strivings, a willingness to assume social responsibilities. Since the Moral Ideology and Emotional Response tests yield information on these points we shall examine the test results of the oldest *sabras* (ages 18–28) for evidence on these points. These *sabras* are full-fledged members of the *kibbutz*. It should be emphasized again that these results deal exclusively with conscious attitudes.

Since social control in the *kibbutz* is a function primarily of group identification, it is important to know to what extent the *sabras* possess this characteristic. This may be inferred from data already presented which revealed that even the young children are more sensitive to the opinions of the group that to those of individuals or of the family. And this sensitivity to the opinion of the group becomes more intense with age, as the responses of the oldest *sabras* reveal. I am assuming, of course, that one is sensitive to the opinions of others only if he identifies with them (i.e., he is a member of their group or he would like to be a member of their group).

That the *sabras* experience great security within the *kibbutz* is also abundantly clear. An examination of their responses reveals that Kiryat Yedidim itself, or some group within it, is responsible for only 15 per cent of the sadness responses, 0 per cent of the fear responses, and 0 per cent of the "worst things" responses. These data seem to indicate that "collective education" produces persons who find great security in *kibbutz* culture. It is little wonder that they are loath to exchange it for another.

Kibbutz culture would not long survive if the desire for personal acquisitions were a strong drive in the *sabras*. This is not the case. The acquisition of material objects accounts for 0 per cent of their happiness responses, and for 6 per cent of their "best things" responses. The lack of material objects, moreover, accounts for 0 per cent of their sadness responses, 4 per cent of their anger responses, and 0 per cent of their fear, shame, and "worst thing" responses. It is understandable, in the light of these data, that personal acquisition is not mentioned even once as an act worthy of praise. It seems abundantly clear that "collective education" has succeeded in inculcating in the *sabras* the values of *kibbutz* culture with respect to personal acquisitions.

Kibbutz culture would not survive if personal "success," as that term is understood within the context of western capitalism, were to become dominant in its members' hierarchy of values. And, as a matter of fact, this concept is not to be found at all in any of the *sabra* responses. This is not to say that personal achievement or ambition is not an important motive in their lives, as indicated at least in these tests. Thirty-two per cent of the happiness responses, 17 per cent of the "best thing" responses, and 20 per cent of the "praiseworthy" responses are concerned with personal achievement. But an examination of these responses reveals that they involve the attainment of a goal, or the mastery of a skill, as a pleasurable end in itself, rather than as a means to the attainment of some competitive goal. In short, there is little, if any, expressed desire to "succeed," in the sense of outdoing one's fellows. Here again, "collective education" has been successful.

Kibbutz culture, finally, can survive only if the members of the *kibbutz* are highly motivated to work for the welfare of the entire society. The *sabras* seem to have acquired this drive. They have learned, as measured by their responses to the question "What are the things you could do for which others would praise you?" that prestige is attained primarily by behavior which benefits others. For the youngest children, who are in process of learning the cultural norms, the most frequent response to this question is "generosity" with either assistance or goods. For the oldest group, which, presumably, has already learned the cultural norms, the most frequent category of response is "social responsibility," i.e., doing those things for which the group as a whole will benefit.

The same pattern emerges in the responses to the question "What are the things you could do for which others would blame you?" For the youngest group, in the midst of the socialization process, aggression is the most frequent response; for the oldest, who have already internalized this norm, "social irresponsibility" is the most frequent response category.

In other words the *sabras*, who, as we have already seen, are highly sensitive to public opinion, believe that the most effective technique for acquiring the acclaim of one's fellows is to assume a large share of social responsibility. And this is exactly what is demanded in a society which has a minimum of formal leadership patterns.

It is apparent, on the basis of these tests, that "collective education" has been successful in developing those attitudes which are necessary for the survival of a communal society. Whether it develops a character structure which may be labeled "healthy," "normal," "integrated," etc., is a question which time does not permit my discussing here. I hope to be able to answer this question in the future.*

---

* *Editor's note:* For further reading on education in the *kibbutz* see Melford E. Spiro, with the assistance of Audrey G. Spiro, 1958, *Children of the Kibbutz.* Cambridge, Mass.: Harvard University Press.

23——Margaret Mead

Cultural Factors in Community-Education Programs*

THE CHANGING CLIMATE OF OPINION

The sciences which deal with human behavior are peculiarly interwoven with the political and moral climate of opinion within which they develop and are peculiarly sensitive to changes in that opinion. To understand the extent to which cultural anthropology can attest to a scientific background for the practice of community education, it is necessary to visualize the changing world situation which has obtained since the latter part of the nineteenth century, particularly the decisive changes introduced by World War II. The behavioral sciences have been developing rapidly owing to the introduction of new models and new methods, and the questions which they have been asked to answer have altered drastically. Moreover, the living materials available to these sciences have assumed new forms, such as societies in the process of rapid transformation, studies of brainwashing, a proliferation of cults, or factories completely converted to automation. Also, these studies of new situations of change have made it possible to reinterpret some of the less-satisfactory cultural records and psychological experiments of the pre-World War period.

Up to World War II, community education, whether it was imposed by military force, transplantation of populations, monastic

* Reprinted from *Community Education,* Nelson B. Henry, Editor, National Society for the Study of Education, 58th Yearbook Part I, 1960, 66–96, with permission

orders, or gentle doctrines of local participation, was primarily something that was done *to* or *for* some people *by* some other more advanced people desirous of raising the cultural level of the less advanced. Implicit in these various endeavors was the idea of raising the cultural level of a local population within limitations but not raising it as high as that of their mentors. The assumption was made that, along with backwardness, illiteracy, low agricultural skill, superstitious and magical practices about health, and inferior forms of social organization, there went various other forms of inferiority which could be remedied. Depending upon the nature of the assumptions about the people to be benefited and the people who did the benefiting, the level to which the recipient population was to be raised would be differently conceived. So, slavery might be seen as a temporary and appropriate state for a recently Christianized savage, whereas manumission would become the correct procedure, once the slave, or his children, had received a "Christian" education. Contradictions between regulations which rigorously segregated natives and Europeans might be justified by the general state of hygiene, skin infections, and living habits of the bulk of the population; and yet members of this same group, wearing clothes and carrying pocket handkerchiefs, might be admitted to university or court circles in Europe. The prevalence of racial theories of inferiority could be invoked in order to give more opportunities to the hybrid members of a population, to limit the opportunities to their full-blood relatives, or to ban whole populations from opportunity.

Throughout these varying devices, by which people temporarily occupying positions of superiority explained their positions, there ran corresponding variations in the remedies proposed and the rate of change believed to be possible. When the emphasis was on the soul, a few years or even a moment of conversion might entitle the simplest savage to a place in heaven. If the emphasis was historical, then possibly many generations of "experience with free institutions," for example, would be demanded before any sort of equality with the present advanced state of the donors could be expected. If nutrition and health were heavily invoked, then often it would be regarded as hopeless to do very much with adults, undernourished and diseased from childhood, but great hopes could be held out for a change in one generation. But, however conceived, there was a consistent degree of patronage from those who tried to educate toward those whom they educated and whom they conceived of as *in need* of education, for the sake of church, or state, or for their own welfare. These needs were usually seen as unrecognized by the recipients, who therefore had to be induced to admit them by a great variety of methods, preaching and proselytizing, demonstrations, "finding local leaders," permitting converts to buy little pigs cheaper, or near-coercion in sending the younger generation away to school. Even those efforts which relied on community co-operation were instigated from outside or above, and the local community had to be "stimulated to want" change.

In a historical context, it is not surprising that the older literature concentrated on negative elements, such as how to overcome resistance to changes in living habits, and how to combat the dangerous effects of social disorganization and individual breakdown. In explanation of these unfavorable results of induced change, several theoretical positions have been used, such as the intractability of habit, the painfulness of new learning, and the primacy of early childhood learning, on the psychological side, and the importance of the whole pattern of culture, on the anthropological side.

The effects of the type of psychological thinking characteristic of the first half of the century, with the enormous new knowledge about childhood and with the growth of animal experiments on learning, inevitably weighted the scales in favor of early experience, endangered by later disruption. And without taking the extreme position taken by Laura Thompson in the 1940's at the close of her study of American Indian acculturation, namely, that the American Indian still lives in a primordial pattern of relationship to nature and his fellow men, most anthropologists still emphasized the contrasts between older patterns of culture, whether they were considering the peasant peoples of Asia and northern Africa, the dwellers in small European enclaves in the Balkans, the Hebrides, the aboriginal primitive—that is preliterate—peoples of North and South America, Africa south of the Sudan, Oceania and the Arctic, or the immigrant groups—Poles, Algerians, South

Italians, Slavs, Japanese, Tamils—who moved in large numbers from one country to another and resisted, at least in the migrating generation, the culture of the country to which they moved. In both these theoretical assumptions—the potency of earlier over later learning, and the potency of an achieved cultural whole over new patterns—there was the assumption that adults not only learned differently from children but also could not be expected to learn as much, or as completely, something that was new.

Community education is primarily concerned with teaching adults. Thus, nonliterates are taught to read; poor farmers to farm better; mothers who let flies cluster on their babies' eyes to put their babies under netting; peasants who keep their money under the mattress to use banks; people who had no form of co-operative corporate action to work on committees, organize boards of directors, take and delegate responsibility. When the emphasis is upon changing the immediate physical circumstances, there is usually less attention given to the children in the scheme than where community education and community development are seen as laying the groundwork within which the next generation can be brought up differently, fed, clothed, disciplined, and taught in a way which their parents have not been. But whether the goal is to change poor farmers into good farmers, to teach adults to read the 1,300 commonest Chinese characters, or simply to introduce the adults to the idea that their children should be allowed to go to school instead of tending sheep, pigs, or younger children, it is today still a form of education directed toward adults. A few experiments, based on a recognition of the role children in the United States have had in changing the attitudes of their foreign-born parents, have been tried where the school was the focus of change, but this was primarily just another way of pressuring adults into doing something good for them. From the New Deal experiments and the related experiments in India, Mexico, the Middle East, and Greece, in which fully formulated democratic participation patterns were artificially, although devotedly, stimulated, to the lack of faith of the Soviet leaders in the re-educability of adults of the wrong mentality and the resulting penalization and liquidation of millions, to the more recent Chinese Communist attempt at an intensive reformation of adults, the mid-twentieth-century community-education movements have worked with a concept of an adult, preformed in conservative ways, unanxious to change, who formed an obstacle to social advancement.

It is important to note that there were also groups of those interested in the welfare of the peoples being subjected to this process who formed a countermovement, stressing a people's right to maintain their historical culture, no matter how backward; the superiority of a whole, traditionally patterned way of life, however simple, over the fragmentation of "modern mass society"; the beauty of handicrafts as compared with machine manufactures, or natural dyes over chemical dyes; and the security given to the individual by the rituals of kin and clan, planting and harvest, which he lost when he became a resident in a Westernized city. Under this heading fall attempts to provide scripts for small indigenous languages, to revive ancient languages, to revive or nourish languishing handicrafts, to encourage the simple life of the village as leading to greater faith in God, to maintain native costumes and folk dances—activities which have been instigated from the point of view of religion, art, and the humanities, as opposed to the technological emphases of the agricultural expert, the sanitary engineer, and the economic planner. The contrast between these points of view comes out sharply in the discussions about alteration of ancient scripts, like Chinese, Japanese, and Arabic. The advocates of change and improvement point to the need for simplified orthographies which do not implicate an immense system of reference to a historical literature available only to scholars. The opponents of change point to what has happened in Turkey, for example, where, with the changes in the written language, the young Turk gained access to the science of the West but lost his connection with his old tradition.

So the advocacy of any set of principles "basic to community education," which must also be referred to the behavioral sciences, must be put in this setting of the moral and political attitudes toward change, the experiences of one-sided change on which our theories were built and the particular state of the sciences of psychology and anthropology.

World War II created a new over-all political position as people in every part of the world began to realize the advantages and the accessibility of those "goods," material and immaterial, toward the desire for which so many different agencies had attempted to direct them in the past. Whether it was powdered milk on the shelf of a remote country store in the southeast of the United States or the availability of atabrine in New Guinea, where only quinine had been available before, or the presence of planes, field hospitals, outdoor film showings, in a thousand ways, through the behavior of individuals, the experience of organization, and the presence of machines and other goods, the peoples of the world learned to aspire to the products of Western science. Literacy centers turned from attempting to bribe or seduce a few "leaders" to turning away the queues that formed at their doors. Naked savages, the pig fat washed off, and speaking through two interpreters, marched into government centers in the highlands of New Guinea, saying they had built a hospital and a school and would like to have a doctor and a teacher tomorrow morning. Villagers in remote islands of Indonesia set to work to build roads and bridges, in intended imitation of modern techniques but without the necessary technical knowledge for such work. In mountain and jungle the people who would formerly have been the resisting, conservative objects of community education became its initiators.

There has also been a shift in the availability of energy to instigate and carry through the changes involved in introducing literacy in a population of which 50 or 90 per cent are illiterate. In the past, the exigencies of church, or state, or party, and, individually, the moral commitment of monk, missionary, official extension agent, or party organizer were the channels through which energy was mobilized. When the efforts were unsuccessful and conservatism and "resistance" defeated these aims, the situation in which "long contact with the oppressed whose lot one is powerless to ameliorate breeds a subtle contempt" became one more reinforcing factor in separating the improved from the improvers. Today, the energy is provided by those who in the name of their village or tribe, their class, their sex, or their nation are demanding literacy, medicine, technical skill, and new social institutions. The resistance which they meet to their demands, in turn, tends to invest those who they think should help them with an aura of resentment, which is also potentially divisive.

It is possible to trace the history of education from an emphasis on learning, in which the student sought out the teacher, to the emphasis on teaching which came with a greater complexity of skills than parents and apprenticeship could handle. From the primitive pattern of taking a present to the man one hoped would teach one or one's children, we have shifted to forcing children and adults to learn and attempting to equip the schools with techniques and sanctions to make them do so. Community education developed as one facet of this second pattern. Just as universal childhood education has been directed toward making other peoples' children acquire some, but not all, of the skills available to the children of the privileged and powerful within a society, so community education has been devoted to making the adults of other countries, other regions, or other classes learn part, but not all, of the skills available to the donor nation, region, or class. As the shift has come between the desire of the donor group to educate, to the desire of the other groups to catch up, a new inequality between the two groups has been introduced. But this time it is not an underestimation of the recipients, as too inferior to be able to learn all that the more advanced group has to teach. The new interpretation of the relative positions of donor and recipient has come from phrasing the state of the donor culture as static, and that of the recipient group as dynamic. The people of underdeveloped countries are to work very hard to catch up, and no allowance is made for the fact that the donor cultures, whether they may be those of the Western world or the entrepreneurial core of business and governmental leadership in India, for example, are also changing very rapidly so that most of the adults in the technologically advanced groups hold traditional beliefs as hampering to their roles in regional or national planning as, for example, is the belief that painting blood and feathers on a carved wooden image will improve the crops in local community development.

So instead of equipping the personnel of community-education efforts with the most advanced projections of what medicine or communication is likely to become in the next half-century, too often they are given sixteenth-century phrasings of religion and nineteenth-century schoolbook models. This, of course, has not been universally so; many programs have drawn on the most advanced *techniques* of education, and use of film strips, films, radio, giant projection screens, and teacher-selection devices. But too often this tapping of the rapidly moving sections of our own culture has been limited to techniques; twentieth-century electronics devices to teach nineteenth-century methods of child care, anthropomorphic representations of germ theory to teach people who are fully ready to grasp the implications of the most modern psychosomatic medicine, medieval pre-Columbian religious geography to people who then have to reconcile the medieval concreteness about heaven and hell with their experience of modern submarines and airplanes.

It is within this climate of opinion and of historical and contemporary practice that the behavioral sciences began to make contributions to the theory and practice of social change. Just as World War II marked the shift from people who had to be thought of as resisting change to people who were expecting and demanding too much change, so World War II also provides a convenient boundary line in the development of scientific theories of change.

PRE-WORLD WAR II ANTHROPOLOGICAL APPROACHES

The cultural anthropologist, working with the peoples who were having various types of experience with the attempts of outsiders or factional leaders to change their traditional cultures in the directions which government, missionaries, and modernizers wished to go, was specially sensitive to the disruption produced by such changes. It was his scientific task to try to record, and reconstruct when possible, the untouched pattern of the life of an American Indian, or African, or South Sea tribe before "contact." Contact was the word for the dramatic meeting of peoples with highly developed cultures and peoples who, because of the accidents of history, had preserved ways of life which were primitive and lacked a written language of any sort. Every change—the introduction of a mission or a school, or indentured labor which took the men away to work—further complicated the anthropologist's task and "spoiled" his material. Furthermore, he saw the effects of induced change and so was particularly ready to identify the incongruences and destructiveness of this external grafting of new upon old.

During this period the use of the science of cultural anthropology made two contributions to community-education programs: (a) It helped break down the image of a great mass of savage, illiterate, superstitious peoples clustered in jungle, mountain, and desert, whose major characteristic was their ignorance of our culture, and helped establish the fact that each of these peoples of the world had a historical tradition of its own, a cherished way of life, a "cup from which they drank their life," as old as our own. (b) It helped establish the importance of differences among peoples and a recognition that methods of education for change must be developed in connection with the special attitudes of the different groups. It was concerned about whether a group preferred to follow conspicuous leaders or men behind the scenes, what would trigger wider change, which deeply rooted religious beliefs were significant for some particular change, where appeals to pride or fear of the death of children or the destruction of fertility of the land were appeals to values of central importance in a given culture. It served to focus attention on the need to study not only the situation and needs of the community, such as a rift between returning soldiers and a village population, or which diseases were endemic and which sanitary practices would have to be changed, but also the need to study the culture of the group, whether they were Navajo or Burmese, Mexican Indians or village Greeks. Emphasis was placed upon the wholeness of the cultural pattern and the disruptive effects of a change which threw one part of the pattern out: as when firearms led to the disappearance of the buffalo; the introduction of factory-made cloth destroyed the weaver's handicraft and status; mission teaching upset the authority of the garden magician; the acceptance of a new religion led to a lopsided development of black magic; the introduction of sheep as men's property upset the previous balanced matrilineal ownership of land and agricultural products; the mission teaching about forbidden degrees of marriage wrecked a social system based on cousin marriage; the elimination of pagan holidays led to a change in food consumption and so to undernourishment; or the introduction of a head tax necessitated all the young men going away to work. Anthropologists pointed out that each of these changes was related in a special way to a particular culture and that if an agency wished to introduce a change, start a school, or build a hospital, a knowledge of the whole cultural pattern of the particular tribe or area was necessary.

From the pre-World War II anthropological work came, then, the following principles:

1. Each human culture is unique and, although cultures in the same area of contact will show important similarities, each must be respected as embodying the whole way of life of a people within which they were able to perpetuate their society. Although cultures may be arranged on a scale in regard to any single feature or clusters of features, no scale has been found which would make it possible to arrange them in rank order when the whole pattern is considered. The recognition of each culture as comparable, in this way, with every other culture provides a basis on which cultural change, community education, or community development must proceed with mutual respect for the cultures of each group involved in the process of change. As a later insight, it was recognized that the culture of the donor group, involving as it does a complete pattern, must also be taken into account just as much as the culture of the recipients, and in the culture of the donor or teaching group there will be found traditional and irrational elements comparable to those found among the people of the less-developed area. So we have the very different histories of the relationships of Catholic Spaniards or Portuguese and Protestant Northern Europeans to African slaves and indigenous American Indians; of frontier Czarist Russians who lived on quite different terms with Lapps than did the Danes; and the colonial attempts of British, Dutch, and Americans, who established yet very different forms.

2. There is no evidence that there is any difference in the capacity to learn, to innovate, and to transmit culture among any of the existing human stocks, all of whom are members of one

species, capable of fertile matings, and possessed of the same general range of capabilities. Thus, differences in race should not be regarded as having any significance unless they have been given social significance. If an Australian aboriginal child has accepted an estimate, held by whites and aborigines, that all aboriginal children are inferior, this will influence his achievement in school; or if Negro American boys have given up hope of competing successfully in the labor market, this may show itself as an apparent loss of capacity for intellectual maturity. Comparably, if a people living in a tropical climate have defined their rate of possible activity as low because of the climate, this may keep their activity low; and moving them to a cooler climate may step it up. Again, there is no evidence that the culture of ancestors with whose culture one has had no contact will have any influence on a child reared in another society. "Gallic" wit, "Negro" rhythm, "Anglo-Saxon" stolidity, "Oriental" mysticism are examples of the kinds of cultural characteristics which have been mistakenly attributed to race and expected to survive several generations after cultural transmission is interrupted.

The recognition of these principles meant, in practice, that when anthropologists were asked to advise on programs of change, they insisted on a complete cultural study being made of the people involved in the program. In the course of such studies the anthropologists were reimpressed with the disruptive effects of the change which had already occurred, such as the loss of tribal unity, of a sense of dignity, of motivation, of a sense of security, as well as in the economic and social confusion which accompanied the fragmentation of the old culture. The advice with which they came up was: *know each culture in detail, make changes as slowly and carefully as possible, and work on equivalences between old and new cultural forms.* For example, study the shaman before you introduce a physician, the local midwife before you introduce a public health nurse, and provide a pig as a substitute victim before forbidding headhunting. These findings based on a quarter of a century of active interest, research, and applied anthropology still permeate the thinking of many anthropologists and are responsible for other members of community-development teams, especially the economists, seeing the anthropologist as the defender of the old, the one whose task it is to put a carefully calibrated brake on change by providing details of probable resistance on the part of any given people. The other part of the anthropological role, as specialist in the full content of the local culture, has been given a great deal of lip service but less recognition.

THE SITUATION DURING WORLD WAR II

World War II presented anthropologists with a whole series of challenges in which speed was an important consideration. The older recommendation that an intensive and complete study be made of the whole culture of any group before any advice could be given was impractical. During this period there was a demand for answers to questions about the organization of partisan units behind enemy lines, the selection of personnel from little-known Asiatic groups, the provision of food for evacuated or just-liberated peoples, the design of programs of block organization in large cities, guides for GI's in Moslem countries, instructions for pilots downed in the New Guinea bush, orientation courses in how to establish liaison between American and English staff officers, strategy for getting bills for reinforced flour through a U.S. state legislature, methods of persuading American-trained doctors to use local substitutes for absorbent cotton—a hundred and one diverse requests, all of which demanded a knowledge of the culture of some particular group. This stimulated the development of new methods for generalizing anthropological theory to meet such situations.

To meet the demand that a complete study of the local culture pattern be made, new principles were advanced:

1. In preparing to transmit to members of another culture, or to individuals within one's own culture who embody another version of that culture (members of another region, class, sex, generation, or occupational group), it is first important to recognize that there will be a cultural difference, grossly perceptible when one group is European and the other Eskimo or Indian. It is

also important to note that this is much harder to perceive between groups with the same physical appearance within the same national unit. This cultural difference, furthermore, will be systematic and will be found to run through many aspects of life: the way parents treat their children, employer-employee relations, and how audiences deal with actors, or how teachers manage their pupils. For the need to know a large number of small details which seem unrelated, it is now possible to substitute higher-level generalizations which subsume the details from which they were abstracted.

2. In preparing to transmit any practice or theory from a donor cultural group to a recipient cultural group, one useful device is to strip the new practice or idea down to universals, to attempt to provide only the core, which is free from particular emphasis. For example, in teaching nutrition—kinds of food, number of meals, and ways of preparing foods carry a great deal of cultural baggage from the particular historically developed habits of the donor group that has developed the science of nutrition. Instead of insisting on particular culturally limited styles of food use, students can acquire knowledge of the nutritional content of food, ways of assaying it, and ways of assaying the biological status of those who subsist on it. It is possible to teach principles of the conservation of vitamins during preparation of indigenous foods or principles of combinations of different nutrients within periods of time that allow them to be reconstituted within the pattern of the recipient group. These have been called "stripped universals"; they are sometimes called "culture-free," but this is misleading, for they bear the imprint of a high development in Western culture, and they are simply stripped down to the point where they are cross-culturally viable, applicable to a diet of dates, fish, or legumes, to cooking in earth ovens, clay pots, or pressure cookers, to three meals a day or five. Although the emphasis to date has been on members of teams who go out to teach how to strip techniques down in this way, we may expect that the sophisticated spokesmen of the recipient groups will also demand that those who come to teach them consider what and when to strip. For example, the vice-chairman of a Council of Navajo Indians, making plans for enlisting in their attack on tuberculosis the help of a school of public health, said, in his sanctioning speech: "Medicine covers a

wide range, at one end the white man has more knowledge about drugs, while at the other end, the Navajo has more knowledge about treating special types of mental illness; in the middle group we must work together!" The request that the campaign against tuberculosis should be free of local American preoccupations, such as the perils of "kissing babies," would be a logical corollary of such an attitude.

3. In the reclothing of such a stripped universal in forms appropriate to the receiving culture, it is not necessary, nor even desirable, to place this responsibility on a foreign specialist in that culture. A more reliable method is to provide for ways in which members of the recipient group work with the bare principles, the new materials, the new techniques and, acting as members of their own culture, incorporate the new ideas within the traditional patterns. These principles accord, of course, with the more widely recognized desirability, which has been stressed by the social psychologists and community organizers, of a people always participating from the start in any program which involves their own lives.

4. After the world-wide repercussions of World War II, it is necessary to contemplate a kind of culture change which will make some members of every culture world-mobile in one generation, speaking some of the world languages—English, Chinese, or Russian—in which the principal scientific and humanistic achievements of mankind are available, and for which translation is available at international conferences. (Although this was stated as a principle in the handbook which we prepared for UNESCO in 1950, it was still at this time regarded as unfortunate that this would mean such very rapid change, as rapid change was still regarded as much more disruptive than slow change.)

THREE CASE STUDIES

Today we have, for the first time, comparable and careful studies of peoples who have been changing, both through practices initiated from within and programs of change induced and directed from outside and above. This makes it possible to evaluate different kinds of effort. I can draw on my own years of anthropological work to give time and depth and, at the same time, illustrate several kinds of total situations. All of these are examples of drastic contact between very primitive groups and modern Western society. Contact with traditional, unindustrialized but highly developed societies, such as in Indonesia, or contact between the urban educated and the peasant and the proletarian in both Western and traditional societies present less drastic but comparable problems—such as the consequences of induced change and of spontaneous change, what kind of learning can be expected of adults, what kind of models are needed, what are the conditions for transformations rather than piecemeal changes.

The Samoans of American Samoa, 1925—

In 1925 the Samoans of Eastern (American) Samoa were a politically sophisticated people, with a culture in which religion was subordinated to social organization, with a simple technology, an adequate food supply, and few indigenous diseases. They were organized into autonomous local groups, who combined in purely ceremonial ways into larger units, and they had the good fortune to be missionized by the formally congenial London Missionary Society, Congregationalists who were not given either to extremely complex ritual practices or to evangelistic types of religious intensity. After a century of contact, during which they were Christianized and became literate in Samoan, they had for a quarter of a century been governed by the U.S. Navy as a part of a Naval Station, where the emphasis had been placed on good medical care, formal good relationships, and keeping the islands free of civilians whose activities might have disrupted the even order of events. Within this regime, the felicities of which were largely a matter of historical accident, the Samoans had developed a stable new level of culture. They grew copra which the government marketed for them, and the funds were available for village projects such as a whale boat, piped water, a roof for the church. They had preserved their own house forms, open pavilions with thatched roofs and coral rubble floors; but for the traditional bark

✦

cloth they now had cotton sheets, mosquito netting, and European-type pillows; the new bedding was still wrapped in a pandanus mat and stored in the rafters. Kerosene lanterns had replaced strung candle nuts as a source of light; they had charcoal irons; matches, soap, starch, kerosene, sugar, tea, ink, pens, pencils, paper, cloth; hand sewing machines had been added to the usual consumption goods. The guest house of the chief of each village boasted enough European furniture, cutlery, and crockery to serve a correct European meal to a visiting missionary or government officer. They were 98 per cent literate in Samoan, and a few individuals in the local police, the local pastorate, and nursing and medical corp knew English. There was no pidgin; people who knew only a few English phrases spoke them correctly. They were completely Christian, and practices abhorrent to missionaries and government, such as the power of life and death which a head of a household had had over members of his household or the public defloration of a bride, had been discontinued. The space into which promising young men could move had been widened by the jobs provided by the mission, the educational system, police and medical care, clerical jobs in the port, the foreign mission field among the peoples of New Guinea. Occasional trips away from the islands as entertainers or stewards on yachts provided a little overseas adventure. Very occasionally a member of the American Navy took a bride from the islands or married and attempted to stay there.

Their Christianity was an effective compromise between their aboriginal ideas of human relationships and those of the missionaries. Premarital chastity was expected of the groups of school girls who lived in the pastors' houses or in boarding school; otherwise one did not become a church member until after marriage. Combined with the high level of literacy was the Samoan disapproval of precocity; each class waited for advancement until its slowest member had completed the work, and this effectively blocked roads to higher education. The training of the nursing, medical, pastoral, and teaching groups had been adjusted to a simple level of literacy and a simple, clear pattern of practice, well integrated within the economy of each village, which provided for their daily subsistence.

Analysis of this system showed that from many points of view it was ideal. Older, more burdensome technologies—like making bark cloth—had lapsed. Where the older technology was adequate and simple, like in the use of the earth oven, the use of banana leaves as dishes, and the older forms of house and furniture, it had been kept. Their literacy was fully adequate to the new social and technical skills which they were using. Ability to read the Bible and to read government orders, combined with a knowledge of the necessary social etiquette of entertaining European visitors and wearing European dress while at the same time preserving their own basically democratic and formally hierarchichal system, gave them a sense of dignity vis-á-vis the Western world.

But the weaknesses in the system are also warning signs in any technical-assistance program which relies on this type of local and protected cultural syncretism. The introduction of medical care has greatly increased the survival rate, and the birth rate did not suffer the decline which sometimes comes when a primitive people lose their zest for living, so the population increased beyond the economic capacity of the fishing, agriculture, and copra-growing potentialities of these tiny islands. During World War II, some five thousand U.S. troops were stationed in Samoa, wage labor on a large scale superseded the former type of co-operative household and community activity; after World War II, the departure of the big Navy installation and the installation of a very modest civil administration in keeping with the climate of opinion of the modern world, left the islanders with a feeling of impoverishment and isolation. Whereas the few individuals who had gone abroad before World War II had made very good adjustment, the group of young Samoans who followed the Navy to Hawaii found adjustment as wage laborers in a modern city much more difficult; the pride which had sustained them in their contacts at home became a source of touchiness and liability to insult in the more complex environment. In 1956, the Navy, in a recruitment program, found 84 young men who were able to meet their tests—including English, which had been a school subject for many years—among the 150 who were anxious to leave the islands.

The compromise adjustment between aboriginal Samoan life and the core of Western religious and medical ideas, combined with literacy, was not adequate to deal with disaster—with the inroads of a large group of servicemen and a money economy, with an increase in population, and with immigration as workers into a more complex society. The Red Cross had to step in. One element had been missing, in the established, synchronized society —the expectation that Samoans would become mobile members of a world community, with all adults able to meet the requirements in a modern urban industrialized society—if necessary—and some members prepared for a university education and participation in the world intellectual and political scene.

A Plains Indian Tribe in 1930: The "Antlers"

The Samoan situation represents a high point of historical good fortune, a bountiful food supply, a healthy people, and a fortunate congruence between the style of the mission and governing group and the local culture. Most culture contacts between very primitive peoples and modern cultures have not been so felicitous but have produced compromise cultures, much less stable than the Samoans' and more vulnerable to outside pressures. Such a culture was that of the group of buffalo-hunting North American Indians, whom I have called the "Antlers" because when I studied them in 1930 there was so much that was painful and damaging to report.[1] These Indians had led a seasonally divided life, hunting in small groups in the winter, planting and harvesting in villages in spring and fall, and engaging in a large buffalo hunt in the summer. The scale of the buffalo hunt was itself a result of the post-Columbian importation of the horse, so that a very recent flamboyant cultural development was ushered in by the introduction of firearms, the coming of the fur trader, and the extinction of the buffalo. As American settlement pushed westward, a part of the Antlers' original territory was assigned to them as a reservation, thus permitting them to remain in a familiar environment. Under government administration and financing and mission pressure, they gave up their old way of life as a hunting, raiding, and only partly horticultural people and became nominally Christian, adopt-

---

[1] Whereas in writing about the Samoans I had only to change the names of individuals to protect their privacy when I reported intimate details of their personal or political lives.

ing the square frame house which the government provided, a slender standard of furniture and modern dress, and began farming. The earlier forms of political organization in which the position of chiefs had been validated by distributions of property, including horses taken in raids, buffalo robes, and meat obtained by hunting, was gone. The dress which became standardized, although based on factory-made materials, marked both men and women as Indians and sharply distinguished them from their white American settler neighbors. The earlier religious ceremonial had shrunk to a few observances for love magic and sorcery, and a Peyote cult, in which mystical experience is obtained by eating mescal, incorporating some Christian and some aboriginal elements, provided the religious framework for life. A few individuals had been sent East to school and came back speaking good English to act as interpreters for the group.

But the land on which the Antlers had lived, a generous section of which had been give to each adult male, was some of the best farming land in the United States. Settlers continued to press west looking for land; meanwhile, the pattern of farming for which the government had provided houses and equipment had never really taken hold among a people where horticulture had been women's work. So a new way of life developed, in which the Indians leased their farmland to white settlers and lived on the rent, supplemented by the gardening and food gathering of the women, while the men devoted their time to social gatherings which preserved an attenuated but recognizable stamp of the old culture. The children were sent for a few years to large government boarding schools, where several tribes were mixed together, where they did a large amount of manual work with equipment they would never see again, learned the barest rudiments of English, and returned to the reservation to forget most of what they had learned. A way of life defined as Indian had become standardized, based on federal protection and federal subsidy, setting a permanent barrier between the Antlers and the people of the wider society. There was no definition of any future to which they could aspire, and there were still old men to tell of a more glorious past. Under the guise of preserving their identity, their culture, and their land, they had been immobilized, no longer able to adapt constructively to new events and new inventions as they had when the horse had been introduced just a few generations before.

Then came a genuine land rush. Under the original federal grants, individual Indians now owned and could sell their land; there was a reversal of the federal policy which had sent their children to boarding schools, which meant the children had to attend local schools. So at the period when I studied them, the thin, economically unstable adjustment was disintegrating—malnutrition, disease, gambling, family instability, and drunkenness were becoming ever more prevalent as their economic resources diminished with the sale of more and more land. This disintegration has continued, until in 1953 the withdrawal of federal protection left the "reservation" entirely without any police protection at all. Their situation was vividly described as follows in September, 1957:[2]

> The landless adult Antlers of today do not realize that it was the government which built the good houses their fathers used to live in and that their fathers owned the land because the government for twenty-five years would not let them sell it. They think wistfully of their fathers as greater men than they are and look back on their fathers' time as a kind of "Antler golden age," which has vanished because, they, the sons, are mysteriously a lower order of men.
>
> No wonder they think so. Today, large fertile areas of their reservation have passed into the hands of white owners, and good corn is growing on them. Some land remains to Antler individuals and the tribe, but the Antlers, with a few magnificent exceptions, do not farm that either. They lease it to white farmers and, themselves, live below subsistence level on the lease money. The good frame houses that the government built for their fathers in the Antler golden age still stand on the reservation. Some of them are in excellent repair, painted, curtained, and cheerful; these have passed into the hands of non-Indian farmers along with the land. Others are grey for lack of paint, have front steps missing and doors broken; these are the ones which remain in Antler ownership. Most of those who do not live in these decaying farmhouses live in rickety little homes in the joyless town which is the center of the reservation. Their land, if worked by the Antler instead of

---

[2] Adapted for purposes of preserving anonymity.

by white leaseholders, could support many of them. In certain cities, which are within commuting distance of the reservation, there is employment to be had by earnest seekers. Family income would be low, but it would be higher than that now obtained from leases, aid to dependent children, old-age assistance, and borrowing.

Hating the social apathy which they themselves recognize, not knowing how to extricate themselves from it, most Antlers eye outsiders with sullen distrust and fear each other. Those they elect to govern them in their own tribal council they turn upon savagely. Perhaps, feeling a great need to strike out at something, they put people in office in order to have a target for their stones. There has been no law enforcement on the Antler reservation since 1953 when, under Public Law 280, the responsibility for this passed from the federal government to the state. The reservation is, literally, lawless. The Antler tribal chairman speaks publicly and often about the desperate need for the state to be forced to assume its obligation to its Indian taxpayers. He does not speak, however, about the tragic breakdown in human behavior which underlies the lawlessness and which no mere law-enforcement officer can control. He is aware of this breakdown, is working to stay it with all his power, but could never bring himself to attribute it publicly to his own people.

Any visitor who spent a week in "Rodner" would feel its impact. He could not fail to hear the endless, obsessive, ingrown gossip about adultery and dishonesty. He could not fail to see drunken parents, neglected children, youthful violence sometimes ending in bloodshed, and deliberate cruelty to animals.

In contrast to the Samoans, the original way of life of the Antler had been destroyed, a new way imposed, the occupations and preoccupations of the men had been destroyed, the old political structure had gone, and the Antlers had been frozen in a position of dependency, with patterns of living—dress, speech, manners—which cut them off from the wider life around them without protecting them from the drink, gambling, motorcars, etc. Their children were unable to compete in school, and no measures were taken to compensate for their difference in background. If at this point a community-education program had been introduced, it would have been terribly handicapped by this long history of

broken, reassembled, and rebroken economic and cultural adjustment, which each Antler now embodied in a mixture of resentment, inferiority, and arrogance. The community energy which
can be tapped when a people wish to get new weapons and new
tools would have had to be tapped long, long ago. The period of
enthusiastic factionalism over whether to embrace the white man's
ways was over. The possibilities of a native religious revival cult
to carry them forward had passed, and the Peyote cult had become a routine religion, not, as one old man put it in 1930, "Something the next generation won't need because they will be able
to *read* the Bible." The Antlers stand as an example of people
who had attained within the contact situation a position where
they were culturally incapacitated to make any of the kind of efforts on which community-education and community-development plans must rely and in which their sense of identity, as individuals and as members of a group, was a hindrance in every
way. There was no group leadership, no belief in a future, no belief in themselves to which it was possible to appeal.

The Manus of the Territory of New Guinea

The Manus of the Admiralty Islands are an example of
culture contact which occurred a century later than that of the
Samoans, but inititially under the rather comparable conditions
of German penetration by missionary, trader, and administrator.
Unlike the Samoans, the people of the Admiralties spoke many
languages. Relations between villages, even within linguistic
groups, were marked by continuous fighting and trading, each
group being dependent upon other groups either for fish or vegetables, utensils, tools, and raw materials. Without political organization other than that of big men who validated their position by playing an entrepreneurial role in organizing exchange of
goods, European penetration brought village after village under
control. Warfare was suppressed; a limited trade based on native
desire for steel, cloth, beads, and tobacco was introduced. A pattern of indentured labor was set up, based on taking adolescents
away from their villages to work on distant islands, with a strip of
cloth as their only clothing, rice with a tin of meat as their ration,

and a few pounds and some trade goods all they had to show for it at the end. A *lingua franca* grew up, called *pidgin English* (now called Neo-Melanesian), based on Melanesian grammar and a predominantly English vocabulary. The Germans discouraged the native from learning German and helped to standardize *pidgin English* as a language. The Protestant missionaries tended to learn one small local language and then, as new linguistic groups were converted, to teach mission teachers a limited literacy in this language in which there was nothing to read except the Bible and a hymnal. The Catholic missions worked in *pidgin English* which gave a territory-wide type of literacy but, again, kept the natives in a linguistic enclave.

With World War I, the German territories in New Guinea and the Bismarck Archipelago fell to the Australians and were established as a mandate under the League of Nations. A regime consciously designed to protect native rights was introduced, a few schools were established, more stringent rules in regard to indentured labor were set up, medical patrols were combined with training local medical assistants in simple first-aid skills, and a fairly stable situation prevailed for the years of the mandate, which ended with the Japanese conquest of the islands in World War II.

Here again was a regime which was consciously benevolent, protected native lands, prevented traders from giving credit for which land could be seized, and prevented overt physical cruelty from white man to native. There was a native constabulary—as in Samoa—and natives became skilled as supervisors of labor, captains of small schooners, etc. But the gulf between the level of any white man and any native was fixed and appeared absolutely uncrossable. Where the Germans had brought Samoan wives with them, and sometimes had married or taken natives of the territory as mistresses, a rigid racial line was now drawn, under which old settlers with a quarter of Samoan ancestry were made to smart. Natives might become teachers or catechists, but not ordained members of the clergy. No native sat at the same table with a white man (except possibly in some remote missions) or walked beside a white man down the street of a town. A caste system developed, based on both racial differences and the primitiveness of the villages from which the laborers came and to which they returned—villages where people sat and slept on the ground, wore hardly any clothes, chewed betel constantly and spat out the acrid saliva, ate lice out of their hair, and had very recently been cannibals, head-hunters, and grave robbers. Government control meant a cessation of warfare, the partial elimination of diseases like hookworm and yaws, paths cleared between villages, taxation, sometimes a rear-rangement of the houses of a village, and the maintenance of courts in which quarrels could be resolved. Mission influence meant the substitution of a very rudimentary concrete type of religious belief and a few rituals for earlier beliefs, usually with a fair amount of local black magic surviving, clothing for the upper part of women's bodies in church, as well as a contempt for their own past savage ways and for un-Christianized natives.

Between 1928 and 1938, I studied five of these New Guinea peoples, and in 1953 I returned to restudy one of them, the Manus, who, under the stimulus of World War II conditions, were re-ported to have wrought a transformation in their culture. In 1928, the Manus were just half a generation from warfare and the prac-tice of selling victims to cannibals, not yet Christianized; they had incorporated only steel, a little cloth, beads, and tobacco from the white man's world. In 1946, under the combined influence of a very gifted leader named Paliau and a typical New Guinea Cargo cult—in which the return of the ancestors bringing them at once all the wealth of the white man is promised in return for the de-struction of all native property—the Manus transformed their cul-ture into a crude but recognizable version of the twentieth century. They had redesigned their social organization, set up a crude democracy within a group of thirty-three villages now politically unified into a movement, emancipated women, set up skeleton schools, hospitals, courts, customs, and banks. They then clamored for teachers, doctors, and an administration-sponsored local govern-ment scheme for which they would not have been expected to be ready for years.

This movement was conceived in a desire to have political and social equality with the white man, in the newly acquired belief that the native was capable of acquiring full equality with the white man, that just as the American Army had made the African "all right," so that he spoke and thought as well as dressed and ate and moved like a white American soldier, so the natives of New Guinea, having come late into their social inheritance, could also become full and complete participants in the modern world. It is clear from old records that this sudden desire for imitation was not unique but has happened many times before in history, when a people have met another people whose level of civilization is perceived to be higher. But gradually the honeymoon has faded off into discouragement as the eager imitators found that the newcomers admitted them as souls into their heaven but not as guests at their table, as workers but not as husbands of their daughters; on the national level, their chiefs might be invited to a coronation, but, in between, they were people with whom one did not mix or marry.

But the Paliau movement of the Manus took place after World War II in the new climate of opinion in the world; Paliau was taken to Port Moresby and told about co-operatives and baby clinics, instead of being executed for treason or goaded into an armed uprising. The policy of the party in power in Australia, which had continued the mandate, as a trust, was in favor of encouraging native leadership, community development, literacy. So, in spite of tremendous difficulties, a break with the mission, and conflict with local white men, the new society has survived, and the New Way has swept everyone along with it, grandparents as well as grandchildren.

The detailed analysis of this extreme and successful transformation, which was possible because I could study the same village and the same individuals whom I had known as children, suggests that their success was due to a variety of circumstances, some fortuitous and unrepeatable, others which can be incorporated into world-wide programs. The fortuitous events were exposure to large-scale models of Western society, in the American, Australian, and, to some extent, Japanese armies, the special gifts of Paliau, and the peculiarity of the local culture of the Manus people who formed the core of the movement. Manus culture was extraordinarily pragmatic, experimental, oriented toward flexible, skeptical, intelligent response to the external world, and the Manus found American ways of thought particularly congenial. As in Samoa there had been a fit between the Congrega-

tionalist form of religion and the Samoan form of village autonomy, on the one hand, and the Naval hierarchical formality and the
Samoan hierarchical formality on the other; so here also was a
specially good fit.

But leaving aside the historical accidents, the Manus success
can also be laid to its initiation by the people themselves; to the
completeness with which they changed the whole pattern of
living habits so that old parts were not there to compromise the
new; to the fact that the whole people moved together, preventing
the usual break between generations; and to their sudden sense of
their own capacity to do anything that the white man could do.

Their future is not only dependent upon world events completely beyond their control, such as the advance of Communism
in the Pacific, changes in the political climate of opinion in Australia, and shifts in the price of wool and of copra, but also by two
more immediately relevant conditions. The first of these is emphasis on their local identity, as Manus, rather than upon becoming
citizens of New Guinea, participants of the Commonwealth, and
in the world. This emphasis can be laid at the door of the administration which tried to "contain" the Paliau movement and so
made it local and chauvinistic. The second inimical condition is
the refusal to teach literacy first in Neo-Melanesian (as pidgin
English had now been renamed in accordance with the new climate
of opinion), as a basis for literacy in English. A combination of
circumstances, namely, the attitude of Asian and African members
of the United Nations toward any *lingua franca* which can be regarded as a "slave language," the attitude of Australians sensitive
to any bastardization of English, the old guard in the missions
who invested heavily in local languages—these attitudes resulted
in an insistence that English (for which there are neither teachers,
texts, nor any local readiness) be taught immediately in the schools.
Experiment has shown that English can be very easily incorporated if the children, who already speak Neo-Melanesian, learn
to write in it, just as the enormous experience in Indonesia, during
the Dutch administration, showed the value of becoming literate
first in a language which was spoken. As Manus, rather than as
citizens of New Guinea, bound to their own territory and interested in "becoming more" rather than going on to higher educa-

tion and a role in the country, foiled in their hope of becoming literate in a world language in which they might listen to broadcasts and read books and magazines, these people who have themselves taken a giant step into the world may also be thrown back into a partial, self-defeating adjustment.

OUR PRESENT STATE OF KNOWLEDGE

In the post-World War II period, anthropological theory has been able to draw upon the new climate of opinion, in which the "haves" of the world were recognizing as never before their obligations to the "have nots" and in which the demand from those who lacked literacy, medicines, agricultural techniques, community organization, and the facilities for dignified participation in the larger world exceeded the eagerness of those who were able to impart the knowledge and techniques which were demanded. We have had the benefit of anthropological restudies of communities studied a quarter of a century before, of the reports of many kinds of technical-assistance teams, of the experience of the newly freed colonial countries, of the extraordinarily diverse experience of Israel, and to a lesser extent, of the methods used in the countries which have recently come under the sway of Soviet Communism. These experiments and experiences have been utilized in new ways in response to the theoretical position called "action research" developed by Kurt Lewin which recognized the advantage of a continuous interaction between theoretical and experimental work and attempted to apply the theory so developed, so that records of what happened when the attempts were made become part of the developing body of theory. Furthermore, post-World War II anthropological field research has been specifically directed to some of the problems of purposive and controlled change, so that the results have been more relevant than was the case when anthropological work was done within the framework of pure science alone.

From the anthropological field research and analysis of the last decade a new set of principles is emerging:

1. The comparability of all human cultures, which has been

one of the basic assumptions of cultural anthropology, is not only a statement which exacts respect from all those involved in the processes of change but has more profound implication. Each viable human culture, whether that of a handful of Eskimos or of a nation of fifty million people, must be seen as a system which contains provision for all "normal" human beings who are born within it, with the recognition that, as we make technical and ethical advances, more previously discarded individuals, such as the blind, the deaf, the cerebral palsied, will be included within the communication system of the culture. Furthermore, as the range and kind of individual differences discernible in populations of any size are assumed to be of the same order, a language or any other part of the whole system of a culture which has been developed by one human group can be learned by every normal member of another human group. So children of any stock learn as their first language any language with equal proficiency, the stupid child learning less well than the bright, of course, but no language as a system presenting greater problems than another to to the naïve learner.

2. Rapid change which is pattern change, in which a whole culture is transformed, may be less traumatic than slow, uneven change, which separates generations, the sexes, members of the family, work life from home life, manners from material culture, and results in fragmentation of life and faulty adjustments. Groups, primitive or peasant, who have a clear, coherent cultural tradition may be able to change their entire way of life in a very few years, carrying the entire community, grandparents, parents, and grandchildren with them, and take on a new way of life, provided they are presented with living models of the new culture. (This has been true of the rapid transformation of the culture of immigrants moving to the United States who were scattered as single families within the American scene.) Just as remaining in a familiar habitat within a large community practicing the old culture holds back change, so the more complete the change, in material and nonmaterial ways, the more rapidly is needed adjustment facilitated.

Rapid change can have the advantages over slow change that are found as between someone who moves to a new country but only picks up the language slowly and haphazardly, as compared with someone who makes a tremendous effort to acquire the entire pattern of the new language and a large vocabulary immediately after arrival, which will in turn facilitate his making a living and participating in the life of the new country.

But because it is the across-the-board change in pattern which is the essential here, a smaller change, if it is across the board, is more desirable than a larger but more uneven type of change. It would be better for a primitive, jungle-living group to develop a pattern roughly comparable to that of a handicraft society, in which a higher standard of living involving furniture and new types of sanitation is provided by local labor, than for them to move directly to a wage economy where their wages have to buy imported, rare, and expensive factory-made goods. It would be better for a desert-dwelling Arab to learn to live in modern urban fashion and perform an unskilled task than to learn to handle complex oil machinery while preserving the living habits of a tent dweller.

3. Survivals of earlier types of culture, as special festivals, semi-legal medical practices, obscure magic, and "folk remedies," do not, as was formerly believed, help to cushion the changes brought in through community education. These may be festering points of maladjustment, preserving as they do parts of a culture which is no longer appropriate.

So the general principle which can be derived from our post-World War II experiences is in favor of rapid transformations, conducted by the group of people making the change and not under coercion or persuasion. These changes should come as a result of their own initiative with what technical help can be provided in which the emphasis is upon a level of change which can be accomplished thoroughly and efficiently, in all parts of the culture, rather than upon attaining peaks of literacy or industrialization—which are unsupported by the rest of the culture.

ADULT CAPACITIES TO LEARN

From this post-World War II work there has come also a new evaluation of adult learning, a recognition that adults, in any

culture, have learned to be human, have learned about language, social organization, tool-using, and the family; and they have learned
that learning a second language, a new form of social life, a new
set of tools, is profoundly different in kind from the first learning
of a child. Cultures will differ very much in the extent that there is
a belief that adults can learn, a recognition that knowledge of
one system can increase rather than decrease one's ability to learn
another, and in the kind of learning experience which is given a
child. In community education it is important to discover which
parts of the cultural life of any people are seen as concrete and im-
mutable and which parts are seen as interchangeable. So some
people, including many American children, are taught their language as if it were the only real language and the speech of others
were an inferior translation, in which case they find it difficult to
learn another language. In the same way a people may believe
that their food habits, their sex habits, their method of classification of time, space, plants, and animals, and their forms of selecting leaders or resolving a quarrel are "true" or "right." Whenever this is the case, they have to unlearn and relearn instead of
making a simple transformation, such as is made by a cosmopolitan
and literate European who moves from Vienna to Paris and assumes that, as a matter of course, he will converse in French, find
a different cuisine, and discover different expectations in etiquette.

Many peoples, especially primitive peoples who have lived
close to others with different customs, are sophisticatedly aware
that their culture is simply "our way of life" and are extraordinarily well equipped to make a transformation from a very primitive system to a complicated one. Conversely, some missionary
groups have been able to preserve the pattern of the religion or
the style of democracy which they were propagating, while dropping out non-essentials in content, and so accomplishing a reverse
transformation from complex to simple.

The success of the team members who go as Americans or as
members of the UN technical-assistance teams of the UN agencies
depends on their ability to see their own cultural practices, including sanitary habits and ethical insistences, as simply one set in a
series which had varied over time and varies now among contemporary peoples. If an agricultural specialist or specialist in literacy
techniques believes that the way he uses a knife and fork, a tooth-

brush, soap and towel, holds a pen, sits on a chair, or wears clothes is intrinsically more "natural," "righter," and "truer" than the way in which other peoples manage these things, then no amount of conscious good will and tolerance will make the technical help that is offered really palatable to the receiver. The counterpart of these rigid members of civilization is sometimes found among a people who have just become more civilized and view the ways of their immediate ancestors with horror. Such rigidity can often be broken down by wider experience among the admired models from civilization—that is, contemporaneous comparisons. The rigidity of the modern expert can sometimes be loosened up by a serious look at his own history, finding out how recently separate drinking cups replaced the tin cup, and how recently the tomato, now a source of vitamin C, was regarded as poison and as a love apple to be placed on the mantelpiece as an ornament. If, to such exercises, it is possible to add experience of some very recent change which has made some honored and habitual piece of behavior outmoded and insanitary, for example, the disappearance of pocket handkerchiefs and linen napkins as sources of reinfection, the necessary flexibility may be provided.

In most such cases, some element of shock is necessary, as, for example, the culture shock which trains anthropologists to view other cultures with objectivity. But there are hazards here also, as in the case of the young European pediatrician who suddenly realizes the plight of a mother accustomed to bearing many children but caring only for the few who survive and who now, owing to improved public health practices, is confronted with the support and care of nine or ten children. Faced with this unmanageable situation, the pediatrician came to doubt his whole medical mission, to doubt the very values which were most wanted and needed by the people he was caring for. When a technical-assistance expert has been rigidly and dogmatically convinced of the absolute superiority of his methods, under any and all circumstances, the very rigidity of the belief makes a violent conversion against it possible.

The greatest guarantees of the necessary flexibility in the teacher or technical expert who comes from the donor culture to help the recipient culture are a recognition that he or she is also part of a changing culture and a determination to help people join a moving procession and to cut in as near the head of it as possible. If the people who are being developed belong to an old, highly complex culture which is fully capable of accepting the most abstract ideas the West has produced, the emphasis can be on stripping our most modern ideas down to essentials. If, on the other hand, the people are so primitive that a complete transformation of their culture on some more complex model is necessary, then the emphasis should be on giving them as up-to-date models as possible. If they have had a long traumatic history of half-realized change, coupled with self-identification as inferior, then it is necessary to send them better teachers and to expend higher-level skill than in either of the other two cases. The smoothing-out of great discrepancies in knowledge, in skill, in self-image in one generation requires in every case more imagination, more skill, and more dedication than is necessary to teach those adults within their own culture who have made no change in class or country. Too often it has been the misfits and the failures who have been available for work in the backwoods, on reservations, and overseas. A recognition that this is a field which should command the most gifted will be a next step in our concerted effort to make all members of the human race co-sharers in our growing knowledge of how to live on this planet and beyond it.

24——— J. L. Fischer

The Japanese Schools
for the Natives of Truk,
Caroline Islands*

INTRODUCTION

There is an abundance of official and semi-official reports of schools for dependent people in various parts of the world which emphasize the administrator's picture of the school system: the value and nature of the physical plant, aims, curriculum, enrollment and attendance, etc.[1] However all actual educational systems include two major parties: the teachers and the taught. The latter are all too often ignored. Our purpose in this paper therefore will be to discuss the operation of the former Japanese school system for the natives of Truk, Caroline Islands, viewed as the product of an interaction between two major forces: the official government policy and the native culture.

Some description of the educational system of the former Japanese Pacific mandate, which included Truk, has appeared in English as a part of general studies of the mandate government (Clyde, 1935; Yanaihara, 1940). While these descriptions do not concentrate specifically on the schools in Truk, the data came

* Reprinted from *Human Organization*, 20, 1961, 83–88. Society for Applied Anthropology, and the New York School of Industrial and Labor Relations, Cornell University, with permission.

[1] There would be little point in citing examples of such studies, as they are mostly of regional significance. Included would be many publications of colonial and national departments of education, as well as UNESCO, and secondary publications based mainly on data from these and other official sources.

mainly from official sources, directly or indirectly, so the authors were forced to be concerned largely with the official educational policy and programs. These were similar throughout most of the mandate and Truk is not atypical.

Another quite different source of published information about the Japanese schools on Truk is found in the life histories of some natives of Romonum I., Truk, published by Gladwin. Here the opposite emphasis—on the native side (Gladwin and Sarason: 1953) —is present. Since Gladwin was interested in the psychology of the natives, he does not discuss the schools as such but simply records certain incidents in the scholastic history of his informants which they happened to remember in the course of giving a general life history.[2]

In this paper we shall try to put the Japanese and native sides together, using information from the authors cited above as well as other information gathered personally in the Caroline Islands, during the years 1949–53, while I held the position of District Anthropologist and later Internal Affairs Officer, for the present U.S. government of what is now the Trust Territory of Micronesia.[3] During this period, data about the schools were acquired from native informants, from limited Japanese official reports and regulations, and from inspection of the old school sites and buildings themselves.

Needless to say, it would have been highly desirable to have questioned some of the former Japanese teachers and officials. This was not possible, since our Navy, for security reasons, repatriated all persons of Japanese nationality at the end of the war. However, there may be an advantage to the weighting of the

---

[2] Thomas Gladwin, Unpublished field notes, 1947. Gladwin's life histories as published are somewhat abridged to eliminate material which is redundant or superfluous for the study of the personality of his informants. Some of the omitted material deals with native experiences in the Japanese schools. Gladwin has kindly provided me with access to his full life histories for the purposes of this study.

[3] I was actually on Truk for about fifteen months in 1949–50, after which I transferred to Ponape, about 380 miles to the east. On Ponape I was able, however, to learn more in general about the Japanese schools for natives, and also continued to work on Trukese culture with informants drawn from the sizable immigrant colony there.

data on the native side for once, since the balance is the other way around in most reports of schools for dependent peoples.

HISTORICAL BACKGROUND

To most Americans the name of Truk,[4] if it means anything at all, suggests an impregnable Japanese naval base which was left to "wither on the vine" in World War II. However, before the Japanese military development, Truk had a native population of about 10,000 people. These people or their descendants are still there today, now under a United Nations trusteeship administered by the United States. To the islanders, the fortification of Truk toward the end of the Japanese rule was a violent but transitory stage of history which has now passed, leaving little to show. The era of Japanese peacetime administration between the two World Wars, however, is still recalled by those who experienced it as a time of relative prosperity and progress. We shall be concerned below mainly with the operation of the schools during this settled peacetime era, roughly 1924 to 1939.

Geographically and culturally Truk and the rest of the Carolines are classified as part of Micronesia, "the small islands." Truk is not the name of any one island but applies actually to a cluster of about a dozen high islands of habitable size. No island is more than a few miles long and the total land area amounts to about 37 square miles, but the islands are located in the middle of a large, reef-encircled lagoon about 40 miles in diameter.

European traders and whalers in the Carolines in the nineteenth century considered the natives of Truk to be especially hostile and treacherous, so they largely avoided it in favor of allegedly more hospitable places, such as Yap, Ponape, and Kusaie. Consequently Truk was the last high island group in Micronesia to be brought under the control of a large modern nation. Until the beginning of this century, the people of Truk were divided into a number of independent, frequently warring communities, of

---

[4] For more detailed information and bibliography on the history and culture of Truk, consult J. L. Fischer, and A. M. Fischer (1957).

which there were several to an island two or three miles in length. This disorderly state of affairs, which was considerably aggravated by the introduction of foreign firearms and liquor, was suddenly and efficiently terminated in 1904 when the German government, which had bought the Carolines from Spain shortly before, sent in a warship which collected several hundred rifles and carried off a few disruptive chiefs to exile on another island. Beyond establishing law and order and guaranteeing the personal safety of foreign missionaries and traders, the German government did little during its brief stay on Truk.

In 1914 when World War I began, only ten years after effective German occupation of Truk, the Japanese promptly declared war on Germany and easily occupied the lightly garrisoned German island possessions in Micronesia: the Carolines, Marshalls, and northern Marianas. The islands were governed initially by a military administration, but at the Versailles peace conference arrangements were made to put them under a League of Nations mandate. Therefore the Japanese, along with other mandatory powers, were under international pressure to establish a civilian administration with certain obligations to protect the interests of the native inhabitants. The transfer to civilian authority was completed in 1922, and economic, medical, and educational programs for the natives gained momentum after this date.

The Japanese, like the Germans, divided the Carolines into administrative districts governed from centers located on some of the more populous high islands. Under the Japanese, Truk—more specifically Dublon or Tolowas Island—was established as an administrative center. (Previously, under the Spanish and Germans Truk had been governed, rather nominally, from Ponape, 380 miles to the east.)

EDUCATIONAL SYSTEM OF THE JAPANESE MANDATE

The Japanese administration followed a policy of starting their educational and other socio-economic programs for the natives at the district centers and spreading outwards. The government school system for natives was initiated by establishing a three-year elementary school near the district administrative center on Dublon Island. This school was staffed by Japanese male teachers with Trukese assistants. The latter at first served as interpreters and helped with the discipline. Students were selected on a quota basis from the various islands of the lagoon. Apparently only boys were selected at first, although girls were soon added.

Eventually other three-year elementary schools were established on the other large islands of the lagoon and on one of the Mortlock Islands, a group of atolls to the south of Truk, while a higher elementary school of two additional grades was established at the district center on Dublon Island for selected graduates of the lower schools. Lower school attendance was then made compulsory within Truk Lagoon.

A further step on the educational ladder was eventually provided with the establishment of a trade school for carpenters at Koror, Palau, a thousand miles to the west. Promising graduates of the higher elementary schools were selected from all over the mandated territory to attend this school. Later a small agricultural school was established on Dublon Island, Truk, and, after the Japanese started to alienate "undeveloped" native land for colonization, a surveyor's school was established in Palau.

The purpose of the schools for natives, judging from both reported policies and the Japanese school regulations (South Seas Government Office, 1939) was to civilize the natives and make them into loyal and economically useful citizens of the Japanese empire. While there was theoretically no limit to the higher education which the native child with sufficient ability and financial support might obtain, in actual fact only a minority of Trukese children attended the fourth and fifth grades, and only a minority of those completing fifth grade obtained further education at the vocational schools. Apparently no Trukese native obtained any academic education beyond fifth grade, except incidentally along with vocational training. The system was geared in effect to produce a supply of general laborers and domestic servants who understood the Japanese language, plus a small elite of skilled laborers and petty officials.

The chief subject in the prescribed elementary school curriculum was the Japanese language, spoken and written. Officially language work was supposed to occupy half of the teaching time; arithmetic about a quarter; and miscellaneous subjects, such as gymnastic exercises, singing, handicraft, ethics, and geography, the remainder. According to reports of students the actual emphasis on the Japanese language was if anything even greater than this. While the official curriculum prescribed the teaching of the more common Chinese ideographs as well as the Japanese *Kana* syllabary, few, if any, native students could be said to be literate in Japanese to the extent of being able to read a newspaper by the end of fifth grade. Certainly none could read the regulations promulgated by the South Seas Government Office; and these regulations were not translated, except sometimes orally and in summary by rather confused native interpreters.

The pronunciation of spoken Japanese by Trukese elementary school graduates left much to be desired. Apparently no native students learned to pronounce the letter *h*, nor to distinguish between the voiced and unvoiced consonants, so that, for instance, the Japanese words *aji*—"taste" and *hachi*—"bee" would be pronounced identically.

The Japanese schools did not try to teach reading or writing in the native language, although some Trukese learned these skills from the Western Protestant and Catholic missionaries. Starting even before German rule, the missionaries had translated parts of the Bible and prepared hymns and other religious materials in Trukese, and continued to teach reading and writing in the native tongue to such children as would come to them.

It is only proper to point out that the official emphasis on teaching the Japanese language was no doubt conceived to be for the benefit of the natives as well as for their rulers and potential employers. For any nonreligious subject there were no suitable instructional materials in the native language. Trukese is only one of a number of mutually unintelligible languages in the mandate, each with a small number of speakers, so translation and publication of textbooks would have been difficult even if contemplated. Moreover, the natives themselves wanted to learn Japanese, and in view of the small number of grades open to the average student even the considerable time devoted to studying Japanese could be argued to be less than optimum.

In the higher grades the official curriculum emphasized agriculture somewhat more—four hours a week in fourth and fifth grades (South Seas Government office, 1939). According to native students this meant mostly working in a vegetable garden for the teachers and was not regarded by the students as education. The average Trukese, in fact, does not regard green vegetables as fit for human consumption.

Instruction in mathematics was limited to simple addition, subtraction, multiplication, and division. Graduates of fifth grade were officially supposed to know how to work with fractions but I received the strong impression that few of them did. Some Protestant mission-school graduates, on the other hand, could work out the most elaborate problems in fractions on paper but had no idea of what they meant; they could not use fractions, for instance, to figure out how much the trader owed them for their bag of dried coconut meat.

The physical plant of the government schools consisted of the school building itself (classrooms and storerooms), and quarters nearby for the teacher or teachers. The school buildings were designed and built by the Japanese government, although native contributions of building sites and labor were evidently sometimes encouraged. The school buildings were of substantial contruction; more substantial, one might argue, than was needed in the mild climate of Truk.

No provision was made to feed or house the students at the elementary schools (except for some meals provided for a time at the Dublon school). Students from other islands in the lagoon were expected to find distant clan relatives or friends of the family with whom to board and lodge. Students who had trouble finding a place to stay would sometimes end up with the local chief, who was no doubt under considerable informal pressure from the government to assist in this respect. Students could obtain some food to take back with them on weekend visits home. However, since breadfruit, taro, and fish, the native staples, spoil rapidly, these supplies would not last the whole week and off-island students would be dependent on their local hosts for the balance of the school week.

The school site was generally large enough to have an athletic ground of some sort. Some of these grounds were large enough for baseball fields. Baseball became quite popular in Truk in Japanese times and English baseball terms are still prononunced in a Trukese modification of a Japanese accent by the men who attended Japanese schools.

Japanese methods of instruction of native children relied heavily on drill and rote memory. The first item in an official curriculum description of arithmetic for first grade, for instance, is "recitation and writing of the numbers up to 100"; for second grade the corresponding item is the same for numbers up to 1000. For the subjects most emphasized, i.e., language and arithmetic, constant drill is probably especially efficient in the early stages of mass classroom instruction.

Many of the children feared the instructors, who tended to be rather harsh disciplinarians. In life histories collected by Gladwin (1947) and myself, references are made to children being frequently beaten, slapped, or "hit on the head with a small stick" for being lazy in their school work or giving incorrect answers. More severe beatings and other punishments are reported for more serious offenses such as unauthorized absences or fighting with other children. One of Gladwin's informants reports (Gladwin, 1947; Gladwin and Sarason, 1953) twice being made to stand out in the sun for several hours. This same informant reports being slapped until his face was "covered with blood" by one of the Trukese assistant teachers for making an unauthorized trip to his home island. On this particular occasion the Japanese teacher intervened and stopped the beating, but only to substitute standing in the sun.

Very likely the corporal punishment experienced by the native students was more severe than would be administered to pupils in the Japanese homeland. We no doubt think of these punishments as something that would not be administered by American teachers but parallel examples could be cited from accounts of American Indians (Kluckhohn and Leighton, 1946) describing their white teachers. The severity of the punishment in both cases can be attributed to the relatively small danger of effective protest by the children or their parents for any injury short of serious maiming, and also especially to the numerous frustrations in the teacher's job. In the case of Truk, frustrations occurred partly because of the inherent difficulties of teaching small children in a language not their own about a culture not their own, but also because of the lack of motivation of most of the Trukese students.

EFFECTS OF TRUKESE CULTURE
ON PUPIL BEHAVIOR

The native social structure and school experiences both contributed to low pupil interest in school work. For one thing, Truk is a rather cooperative culture where much emphasis is laid on modesty, submissiveness, and helping one's kinsmen. A child who shows off his superior knowledge in school exposes himself to the ridicule of his comrades for his "haughtiness" (Trukese *nama-nam tekia*, more literally "thinking high").

Perhaps even more important, nature is fairly kind in Truk and children have traditionally been allowed to spend their time playing, with few demands on them for concentrated effort in subsistence labor or otherwise. Serious applied effort, physical or intellectual, is hardly expected of people until middle age.

Those children who were from other islands found themselves removed from their families and were generally quite homesick. Several of Gladwin's informants tell of inventing stories about sick or dying relatives in order to get excused from school for extra visits home.

The dislike of being away from home was often aggravated by fears about the community in which the school was located. Only a few years before the founding of the school system, it will be recalled, the various communities of Truk Lagoon were independent and often at war with each other. The peace imposed by the Germans and maintained by the Japanese was appreciated by most people, but they had good reason to wonder just how friendly the intentions of their neighbors across the channel or around the point were. The hostilities of the adults were reflected in small-scale fights between gangs of boys from different communities. When the teacher was not looking, fights between boys of different communities often broke out at school. This is mentioned by all the Trukese men who give accounts of any length. Younger boys from a community off the island on which the school was located were in an especially difficult position, and were subject to regular bullying.

The problems of off-island pupils with respect to food and housing have already been alluded to. While the Trukese are fond of visiting and are quite casual about where they sleep, they typically exhibit a strong concern about getting enough food, more so even than would seem to be justified by the environment. In any case, it is not hard to understand the resentment of the chiefs and others who were asked to feed and lodge strange students from other communities without compensation from the government or the students' families. It does not seem unreasonable that the "hosts" should have hoped to get a certain amount of labor after school hours from these free boarders. At the same time the reluctance of the hosts to feed the students liberally provoked considerable anxiety at times in the latter, and the demands of the hosts on the students to help pay for their food by working after school had a similar effect on children who had little to do at home except to amuse themselves. Parents were often sympathetic with these problems of their children at school and sometimes assisted them in fabricating excuses to present to their teachers.

Another distraction to the older students was the tolerance of early sexual activity characteristic of Trukese culture. Truk is among those Oceanic cultures which have the charming notion that the beginning of menstruation in girls is an effect, sooner or later, of loss of virginity. Since the prescribed minimum age for entering school was eight years and an age of nine or ten was common, many of the students reached puberty in their fourth or fifth year of school and became deeply involved in romantic affairs with their schoolmates of opposite sex or with other age mates in the community.

An excerpt from the life history of one of my male informants illustrates this situation:

Eventually I got to fourth grade and I started to become stupid. I no longer knew a thing, so to speak. For that was when I started to be concerned with women and started to get women. . . . And I also started to smoke cigarettes. . . . And I was all filled with thoughts of women but my thoughts of school were rather small. I used to return to my own island and I met many women and they liked me very much. I thought I would give up school . . . just because of my interest in women. I would stay away for a week or two at a time.

The informant was nevertheless not expelled from school and was eventually straightened out by his mother's brother, after his grades had dropped markedly.

No doubt increased sexual interest at puberty can interfere with scholastic achievement in large urbanized societies as well. The point to be noted here is that Trukese culture maximized this interference by regarding early sexual activity as normal and healthy, whereas modern European cultures would tend to limit heterosexual contact and stigmatize sexual intercourse immediately upon reaching puberty as precocious and unhealthy.

It would be wrong to give the impression that every Trukese was unalterably opposed to the Japanese school system. Many adults recognized the usefulness of a speaking knowledge of the Japanese language in dealing with government officials, police, and traders, and in getting odd jobs to get cash which would buy cigarettes, rice, and other luxuries for oneself and one's family. The chiefs especially recognized the value of getting promising young relatives through school and into minor local government posts to serve as buffers between the Japanese and the native community.

Some of the more capable and ambitious students eventually came to recognize these advantages of a Japanese education for themselves. In addition, some of the more adventurous boys in the higher elementary school cherished the hope of getting to visit distant places by their school work. They hoped good studying might lead to their acceptance in the Carpentry School at Palau, or to a job as labor foreman in a mine or plantation on some far island.

Although most academic subjects held little intrinsic interest for the Trukese there was some interest in vocational subjects. Most notably, carpentry was traditionally a highly respected craft in Truk, and Japanese style carpentry was respected by both students and adults, both for its technical superiority and its association with the ruling group. Most parents, however, were reluctant to have their children go out of Truk Lagoon to attend school and it is my impression that most Trukese students who actually got to the carpentry school in Palau, a thousand miles away, were orphans with no intimate close relatives to restrain them.

LONG RANGE EFFECTS OF THE SCHOOLS

After graduation the fate of the students varied. The most common fate for graduates of the first three grades, and especially the girls, was simply to return home and forget much of what they had learned, if indeed they had ever learned it. However a sizable minority got menial jobs with the government or private firms or individuals, or went on to two more grades of higher elementary school. In any of these events the start in learning the Japanese language was of use to them. Eventually, during the war, all able-bodied Trukese men were conscripted for military labor and any knowledge of the Japanese language they had helped them at this time, although the peacetime curriculum does not appear to have been directed specifically to the requirements of military labor.

Those students who had gone on successfully through fifth grade, especially the boys, were in greater demand as personal servants, government interpreters, assistant teachers, policemen, native village secretaries, labor foremen, and the like. These graduates generally had a working knowledge of spoken Japanese and enough knowledge of the written language to keep simple records or prepare simple reports, mostly in *kana*. They were by no means all reliable workers—the schools seem to have developed ingenuity in making excuses for absences and the Trukese are great visitors— and periods of employment often alternated with periods of living on their own land, but they did constitute a sort of trained labor supply which was available to be drawn on.

A few of the higher elementary graduates went on to vocational training, principally the Carpentry School at Palau. Graduates of this school were capable of constructing sizable Japanese-style wooden buildings without supervision and some of them are still doing this.

In assessing the results of the Japanese school system for natives the intention here is neither to criticize nor praise the Japanese mandate administration but simply to call attention to some of the major effects of the school from the viewpoint of the principal parties—the Japanese government and their Trukese wards—and to suggest some of the chief factors producing these effects.

The evaluation of these effects is, of course, different depending on the viewpoints involved. Three viewpoints seem especially important: that of the Japanese administration, that of the native community, and that of the students as individuals. The Japanese administration had two principal goals, which were regarded as closely related: the politico-economic integration of the natives into the Japanese empire and the advancement of the natives by civilizing them. The native community had the goals of securing more favorable treatment from the Japanese officials and commercial firms, and of acquiring greater articulateness, which might be used either to gain assistance for desired changes or to resist disliked innovations. Further, individual graduates might have special personal goals of their own which their education helped them to obtain.

The Japanese government was achieving fair success in its goal of making the students and the native community a functioning part of the Empire. The large number of students who did not go beyond third grade should not be taken as an indication of the failure of the system from the Japanese point of view. The schools were intended to proceed by progressively selective stages and produce a small native elite, which would then help modify the native society with government support. In this aim the government was reasonably successful, given the time which they had for operation, and the small amount of acculturation at the beginning of the Japanese period. This integration into the culture of the Empire took place not only through native employment under the Japanese, but through certain changes in the ways in which the

Trukese lived among themselves. Election of local officials was introduced, for instance, and, on the material side, it was largely thanks to the Carpentry School graduates that, at the end of World War II, the Trukese were able to utilize abundant scrap military lumber to eliminate the old style grass huts—esthetically pleasing to the anthropologist but damp and drafty—and to replace them by more livable modified Japanese-style houses. In changes such as this the goals of teachers and students tended to coincide.

But the native goals, both community and individual, were at times opposed to the goals of the mandate government. On such occasions the education served the natives equally well to manipulate Japanese into acting against general government policy. For instance, one accomplished graduate told how he used his knowledge of Chinese characters to forge a liquor purchase permit to which he was not properly entitled, and how he flattered a policeman and bribed him with a chicken to avoid arrest for drunkenness. He probably could have done neither of these successfully without having gone to school.

Some individual natives also used their education to obtain favors for themselves which were against the general interests of the native community. In land disputes or political appointments interpreters sometimes managed to bring about decisions favorable to themselves or their families of which the community at large disapproved. The Japanese government disapproved of such behavior, of course, as well as the native community.

Community as well as individual interests were pursued with the aid of education received by the public school graduates. The same informant who forged the liquor permit and bribed the policeman told me of participation in a strike of workers who were helping to build an airfield. Evidently the idea of an organized strike was received via the Japanese language from certain private Japanese citizens, and was thus to an important degree dependent on the education of some of the workers. Such a strike was certainly not in the interests of the government nor even, perhaps, in the interests of the individual Japanese who told the Trukese about the existence of strikes. The strike was, in fact quickly and forcibly suppressed by the officials in charge with the aid of the police, ostensibly with no concession to the strikers, although it may have had some hidden effect in warning the overseers not to push the Trukese workers too far. I do not wish to imply that the idea of a strike could not have arisen spontaneously without diffusion from Japanese through educated natives, but I would recall that, as already mentioned, the Trukese even today have strong local loyalties to their own particular village and lineage, and do not easily cooperate with Trukese from other parts of the group. I believe, therefore, that the conception and execution of the strike of airfield laborers was materially hastened by the education some of the laborers had received, although certainly there would have been no strike at all without a strong conflict of interest between employers and employed.

The interpreters, jailers, and assistant policemen employed by the Japanese government consisted almost entirely of public school graduates chosen for their ability to speak some Japanese. While there are many accounts of how these individuals used their special positions for personal ends, there are also reports that many of them were secretly responsive to the recognized Trukese leaders in the performance of their duties as well as to their Japanese employers. It is said that they often served as spies on the government for the Trukese community, and communicated information between the community and prisoners whom the community wished to support, thus enabling witnesses and accused to fabricate consistent alibis. Education, as colonial powers have often discovered, can be a two-edged sword.

CONCLUSION

In the above discussion the role of the Trukese culture and values in the actual operation of the Japanese schools for natives in Truk has been especially stressed. This is partly unavoidable because of the fact that the data were mostly collected in Truk after the end of the war when, as mentioned above, the Japanese personnel involved had been repatriated and dispersed, and most official records lost. However, there is also a theoretical justification for the emphasis on the native culture. Too often discussions of directed culture change in underdeveloped areas proceed on the unstated naïve assumption that the only important dynamic factors are the goals and plans of the initiating group; that the behavioral differences between the initiating group and the group to be developed are principally a matter of information and perhaps also technological equipment, which, once supplied by formal education or other means, will automatically result in a harmonious and productive relationship between the two groups. The very term "underdeveloped" implies that something desirable is not there and the principal question is how soon "it" gets there.

Perhaps it is only necessary to state this assumption to see its absurdity, but the application of this insight can only be achieved by constantly bearing it in mind and considering it repeatedly in a variety of concrete situations. All human groups and individuals have, of course, their own particular interests and values. Even if we grant, as I would, that these have an ultimate biological foundation and are basically similar, their persistent concrete manifestation and balance often differ significantly from group to group. And even where two groups have very similar interests, the interests may conflict if attached to different particular objects. Thus, for example, practically all Trukese share a similar strong local and lineage loyalty, but to a variety of particular places and lineages which are in competitive conflicting relationships. And, if the Japanese had succeeded in weakening these narrow loyalties and in substituting a wider national loyalty, this might still have turned out to be a pan-Trukese or pan-Micronesian loyalty, rather than a pan-Empire loyalty.

It is hoped that apart from any local historical contribution this paper may make it will illustrate the importance, in studying trans-cultural education and other directed culture change, of considering not only the goals of the initiating culture and institution but of considering also the goals and values of the recipient group in interaction with the goals of the initiators, sometimes impeding them, sometimes hurrying them along in a continuous process. From a practical point of view this means that to develop an underdeveloped area for the greatest benefit of all concerned, including developers and those being developed, it is not enough simply to supply missing information and technological equipment, under an assumption of community of basic interest between the parties involved. Nor is the problem of difference of interests and values to be solved simply by labelling certain new interests and values—those of the politically or economically more powerful group—as more "civilized" or "progressive." Rather, the particular interests and values of the group to be developed and the relation of these to those of the assisting group must both be examined, and the new knowledge (and equipment) must be introduced and applied in such a way as best to serve multiple and often partly conflicting interests, interests which may conflict both *within* the local society and *between* the local society and the assisting group.

It would, of course, be unreasonable and impractical to demand that all possible conflicts of interest and values involving the concerned parties be determined in advance and a resolution of them be formulated before establishing schools or providing other assistance to a dependent or depressed group. Conflicts of interest cannot always be foreseen in detail, and in any case require careful, repeated, and detailed attention. But without such attention we can certainly predict that the results of the educational process will be something other than those intended by the initiators, and may "backfire" on the initiators, as the example of Truk shows on a small and at times amusing scale. And if strong conflicts of interest are simply ignored and a rational compromise is not arranged and maintained, the effects of educational and technical assistance may even operate to the net major detriment of the assisting group.

References

Clyde, Paul H., 1935, *Japan's Pacific Mandate*. New York: The Macmillan Company.

Fischer, J. L., and A. M. Fischer, 1957, *The Eastern Carolines*. New Haven, Conn.: Human Relations Area Files.

Gladwin, Thomas, 1947, Unpublished Field Notes.

Gladwin, T., and S. B. Sarason, 1953, *Truk: Man in Paradise*. New York: Viking Fund Publications in Anthropology, Vol. XX.

Kluckhohn, Clyde C., and D. Leighton, 1946, *The Navaho*. Cambridge, Mass.: Harvard University Press.

South Seas Government Office, 1939, *Nan' yō-Chō Hōrei Ruishū* Compendium of the Regulations of the South Seas Government Office. Tokyo: Government Printing Office.

Yanaihara, T., 1940, *Pacific Islands Under Japanese Mandate*. Oxford, England: Institute of Pacific Relations.

Social Structure, Social Change, and Education in Rural Japan: A Case Study*

INTRODUCTION

In this essay I shall attempt to depict some dimensions of the educational process inherent in the fabric of life in two Japanese village areas. Insofar as data permit I shall also indicate certain important relations between schools and teachers on the one hand, and community and cultural transmitters on the other. The goal that I have in mind is to analyze what the young learn from diverse, potentially competing models—in whatever appear to be structurally significant units, like the household, age groups, and so on—with respect to values, moral concepts, expectations, and aspirations. I have ignored many important technical concerns of the professional educator, such as school curriculum, effectiveness of periods allocated to the teaching of various subjects, language learning (so crucial in Japan), or financing and administration of the schools because they involve another order of problem. Nevertheless it should be clear that the school does not exist in a vacuum, and that its aims and methods, which are complexly determined and put into effect are linked in subtle ways with the

* At the time of writing I was engaged as consultant to a research project on postwar education in Japan, energetically and ably conducted by members of the Faculty of Education, Tokyo University, under the direction of Professor Tokiomi Kaigo and supervision by Assistant Professor Morihiko Okatsu. More specifically I reviewed much of the literature on the structure of rural communities, in an effort to discover significant relations between the school and other agencies of cultural transmission. I am greatly indebted to Mrs. Kazuko Fujimori, student of education at Tokyo University, for her invaluable services as translator and general assistant.

aims and methods of other agencies of transmission in the community. Because these educational forces are more readily comprehended on the small scale of hamlets and villages in Japan, I have chosen to draw in some detail upon the results of a recent study well suited to this purpose and not yet generally available.

At the outset it will perhaps be useful to put such an approach within the context and scope of research on matters of educational concern in Japan since the war. There is actually a respectable body of literature published in English by the Japanese Ministries of Education and Agriculture, UNESCO, The Committee for Democratic Education in Japan, as well as by American scholars who have specialized in studies of Japanese education, to inform the interested layman about the history of education. It covers such subjects as the remarkable achievements in the development of universal education during and after the Meiji Restoration; subsequent experimentations relating to developing goals of Japanese society; integration with the war effort; Occupation reforms; and the early aftermath of these reforms. In Japan itself educational research since the turn of the century has been divided into three main divisions: teaching methods, philosophy of education, and the history of education. Each of these fields emerged in response to ever-increasing exposure to and assimilation of Western educational theories and practice; each in turn has fed into the others. In addition to these branches of research, sociology, psychology, and, in one major university, anthropology came to be represented in faculties of education.

The substantive content of Japanese classrooms is not so very different from that of their American counterparts. How it is taught might be and so might conceptions of what are more appropriate subjects for males or females at different ages, modes of learning, encouragement or not of discussion, the manifest and latent purposes of different learning activities. Some of these are questions that should be directed to the study of school and classroom as subsystems, a conceptual approach which, after an abortive beginning, has largely lain dormant in the face of attention paid to political, economic, and social issues in relation to educational aims and programing.

Japanese educators evidence the same kinds of anxiety as their

American colleagues over the relation between skills and special knowledge taught and the needs of a highly complex technologically oriented society. Shall they produce a society of engineers or of scientists and in what proportion? What kinds of mathematics should be taught, when, and how? What role should humanism and broad scholarship assume in training for emerging leadership? How most effectively can the goals of the modern industrial organization be met in the context of greater individual dignity? These are some of the urgent questions, and they strike at the heart of traditional and changing outlooks.

Other problems primarily affect urban families and youth. The most poignant of these, perhaps, centers around the whole system of higher education which has been least affected by postwar reforms. A young man's future can still be largely determined by the particular university he enters (if any). With the small number of students that can be accepted, the factors that enter into his chances for success may go far back to the choice of school in the early grades. A private school in Tokyo with an exceptionally good reputation in this regard even requires an examination for entrance at the kindergarten level! The pressures to succeed in school are thus enormous, and success or failure is most sensitively reacted to in terms of personal and family worth. What happens to those young men and women who are admitted is yet another critical area that, at present, affects only a small number of rural youth.

There is no doubt that the concern uppermost in the minds of educational scholars is the problem of the political control of educational policy. This in turn is closely related to the anxiety felt in recent years over the abrogation of local control of education and the resumption of centralized control by the education ministry. To many mature graduate students other approaches, such as natural history studies of the transmission process, appear to be of minor importance as long as the spectre of central government control—with all its dread overtones of repressive and narrowly directing pressures of yesteryear—hangs like a Damocles sword over the head of the nation. This issue is actually complex, and it is perfectly arguable that either local or centralized control can be used for or against any specific set of aims considered to be in the public good. The fact is that there were many reasons why locally elected boards first established in 1948, with functions largely conceived after their American model, failed to win general support. They all tend to add up to inexperience, misconceptions of responsibilities, the weight of traditional hierarchical and power relations, and, in the early days, the activities of Communist party members in the Japan Teachers Union. At any rate, taking advantage of inefficiencies that plagued the early efforts at local control, the Diet has passed or attempted to pass a number of new Laws:

(a) In 1956 a law was passed by which members of boards of education were to be nominated by prefectural governors or village mayors, and were to be put under the control of the ministry of education.

(b) In the same year the approval of textbooks became much stricter as a result of legislation introduced (although not passed) for the purpose of prohibiting free selection of textbooks by schools and by placing control over the selection in the hands of each prefectural board of education.

(c) In 1958 the national standards of elementary and lower secondary school curricula were revised. According to this revision, moral education as a special subject was reintroduced; government regulation of minimum allotments of school hours became more strict. Courses of study issued by the ministry of education became the legal standard of curricula instead of being mere recommendations and advice for teachers as before.

These developments are viewed with alarm by democratically oriented and politically nonconservative elements, and understandably so. But it makes a dispassionate consideration of many educational concerns a difficult thing to achieve. One might like to see empirical studies conceptualized in terms of educational policy in action at the level of specific schools or school systems. These would help to specify the weight which must be attached to the many factors that find their way to teacher-pupil interaction at the classroom level, including the Japan Teachers Union, government stated aims, teacher recruitment and teacher-training experience, textbook use, local board composition and actions, and parental expectations.

Considerations of this sort, however, bring us back once more to the social and cultural maps of the two contrasting village areas in Saga Prefecture and their implications for cultural transmission. The remainder of this chapter will be largely devoted to this analysis.[1]

NAO AND HONJO VILLAGES [2]

Nao is a farming village located in an isolated mountainous region, approximately fifteen kilometers from Saga City. The three adjoining hamlets of the larger community selected for investigation consist of about twenty households respectively. Rice cultivation is the basic occupation, and the raising of persimmons (for drying) is the only important subsidiary crop grown as a cash commodity. Non-farmers comprise only about ten percent of the total adult population and consist of a day laborer, a doctor, a lumber carrier, and a few other semiskilled and skilled workers. The average size acreage under cultivation per household is only 4.6 *tan* or approximately one and a half acres of terraced fields.

Although they are surrounded by mountains, the inhabitants

[1] This discussion is based upon a field study directed by Teigo Yoshida, Assistant Professor of cultural anthropology at Kyushu University, in collaboration with Assistant Professor T. Yano and Mr. F. Kobayashi. Research extended over a period beginning in the spring of 1955 until the spring of 1960. It is part of a larger research project on moral education conducted by the staff of the Research Institute of Comparative Education and Culture, Kyushu University. Part of the information available to me was derived from one published report (Yoshida, 1960a). Part of it was derived from a recent draft of an unpublished paper kindly made available to me by Dr. Yoshida (1960b). Some of the information was also communicated to me personally in response to specific questions put to Dr. Yoshida on several occasions.

[2] "Village" is the translation used here for *mura*, the modern rural administrative unit. With recent administrative reorganization a village may consist of many smaller compact *buraku* communities, which we shall henceforth translate as "hamlet." The hamlet today retains its character as the fundamental local group in the Japanese countryside.

of these *buraku* make only limited use of forest products, and there is no house that makes a livelihood by depending upon forestry. By comparison with agricultural villages of the plains areas this district has always been characterized by petty farming. To alleviate the poor economic situation a home industry of Naogami paper making was introduced in the middle of the Edo period, and by 1928 had grown to be the most important subsidiary industry. Nowadays, in the face of competing larger enterprises, this small-scale home manual industry has declined greatly and has almost become extinguished. At present only seven houses in the three *burakus* still engage it it, whereas the production of dried persimmons has become the most significant subsidiary industry, accounting for ten to thirty percent of all cash income. Unfortunately the production of persimmons has also been decreasing recently owing to damage by blight and harmful insects. Charcoal making, vegetable cultivation, and cultivation of dried mushrooms have been attempted in turn—unsuccessfully—and now dairy farming has been started with guarded hopes and expectations.

The land reform successfully carried through during the Occupation period had several effects and led to somewhat different contemporary conditions among the several hamlets. For example, in one hamlet a former large landowner lost his land completely, so that now there is no dominant landholder. Discrepancies in size of holdings, while not so great as in prewar times, still affect the distribution of power in the other two hamlets. In one, 53 percent of households are devoted to full-time farming; in another, only 17 percent; and in the third, 67 percent. These differences are associated with varied emphases in other structural changes noted. Rationalization of agricultural techniques in the three communities has been limited in large measure by mountainous conditions that are unsuited to the use of machines.

In contrast with Nao, the two hamlets studied in Honjo village are located in the plains region about two kilometers from Saga City. They consist of 25 and 35 households, respectively. Although Honjo has recently been incorporated under the municipal administration of Saga, all but two households in one hamlet and in the other are farm houses. The principal crops grown are rice and wheat, supplemented by the raising of chickens, pigs, and milk cows; 15 percent of the families manufacture straw goods. The average area under cultivation is almost twice that of Nao. Thus level of wealth, productive output, and the flat nature of the terrain have combined to facilitate the introduction of various agricultural machines as well as other innovations.

The ecological variability and associated social-cultural differences within and between the two villages reflect on a small scale the considerable heterogeneity of community structure in rural Japan.

The structure of production and work, here as elsewhere, embodies important values of the person, particularly conceptions of what kind of formed person is valued and the shape of valued behavior. In Saga hamlets local consciousness and social indoctrination before the war was influenced with and beyond family and kin relations by cooperative patterns of mutual aid. These relations took the form of an exchange labor system (called *temagae*), irrigation control, purchase and use of farm machines, and the provision of nonproductive services. All of these patterns still exist, but their importance has diminished in both regions. Probably as a result of differences in degree of isolation from Saga City, the inhabitants of Nao hamlets made far less use of hired labor than did those of Honjo (6 percent in the former as against more than 20 percent in the latter). Today 25 percent of labor used in rice planting in the Nao region and 50 percent in Honjo consists of hired wage workers.

In Nao, which is the more conservative in this respect, *temagae* between neighbors amounts to ten percent of all labor hours expended (half of what it was in prewar times), whereas *temagae* between relatives in different hamlets has increased twofold. The earlier norms for such cooperation, as expressed in questionnaire responses, still support the *temagae* system to a degree that is inconsistent with actual relations in productive activities.

Effective hamlet controls on the other hand still prevail in both sets of communities as a result of present patterns of land ownership and forms of water supply. Most land—as much as between 50 and 100 percent in respective communities—is owned by families living within the hamlet. In Nao, water is abundant so that the management of water supply constitutes no problem. Each hamlet has established a reservoir that is controlled by a local committee, and improvements or repairs are carried on through assigned cooperative work. No one outside the hamlet (including kinsmen who assist in other *temagae* exchanges) is employed in this activity, since responsibility for same is limited to farm owners.

In Honjo communities adult men continue to cooperate in a long standing practice of removing soil from creeks, which extends over a period of from a week to ten days. This work facilitates irrigation and recovers fertilizer, and still continues to be undertaken on a hamlet-wide basis. Each household is expected to supply one able-bodied adult man to take part in this work; if the farm is larger than average, it should supply two persons; and in addition all unmarried young men must lend their assistance. The more favorable position of agriculture since the war, coupled with a comparatively restricted water supply have combined to maintain this important hamlet function. For different reasons, therefore, compact local communities in Nao and Honjo continue to exert moral coercion on a hamlet-wide basis.

Rational changes in technology in Honjo date back to 1921 when water mills were abandoned and irrigation machines were introduced. In 1935 communities also purchased machines for removing soil from the creeks. This had no effect upon the norms of cooperative work participation, although in fact it led to a great decrease in the labor contributed by elder men—not, however, in that of youths. The repair of pumps and cleaning waterways for irrigation continue to be practiced on a hamlet-wide basis as before. These two kinds of machines thus were purchased collectively by all farmers in the hamlet in accordance with size of land holdings; the larger the acreage under cultivation, the more a household was requested to contribute.

Other agricultural machines, particularly motor-driven cultivators and cutters, have been purchased and used collectively either by extended patrilocal families—a main family (*hon-ké*) and branch family or families (*bun-ké*)—by affinal relatives, or by neighbors who are not related by kinship. One significant effect of technological change in Honjo, when viewed in relation to other factors such as increasing attractiveness of agriculture and the small loss of young adult males through emigration, therefore, has consisted in reinforcing moral-political and kinship ties of the small hamlet.

In certain other respects, however, technical innovations have resulted in important social changes which are functionally linked with attitudes towards formal education and potential conflicts between parents, teachers, and children. The introduction of machines facilitated a reduction in time and energy allocated to manual labor which in turn enabled the promotion of a more diversified economy. Furthermore, the introduction of machines, the growth of subsidiary occupations such as stock raising, and innovation in techniques and management of farming have largely originated with young men in their thirties rather than with the older men who have traditionally wielded power. Consequently the social power of the old men (*genro*) has gradually declined in relation to the rise of power of the middle-aged men (*churo*). The dynamics of age-groups will be further discussed below. We may simply note at this time that social power of the *genro* continues to prevail in Nao (though not equally in all hamlets), and that it is strongest in that hamlet where the least number of youths have left the community and where the present older generation never engaged in experimental diversification of productive activities.

In nonproductive activities the mutual aid system operates almost in the same degree in the two areas: *temagae* assistance in building a house or thatching a roof; in helping a woman in and just after childbirth; in giving a farewell feast for a bride-to-be by her age mates; in the introduction of a bride to the groom's community by housewives; in a farewell feast for a bridegroom celebrating his passage from the "youth group" to "middle-age married men's group"; and in preparations for a funeral. In most of these situations traditional patterns still obtain in Nao and Honjo hamlets.

Local consciousness within the hamlet today is further inculcated, but in different ways, in both areas through respective systems of community financing. The hamlet in Nao owns a forest land and community public money (*muragane*) as common property. The *muragane* income is derived largely from the selling of forest products (trees or bamboo) and from public subsidy provided by the local government for repairing roads or bridges. The income from these sources is used to defray expenses of public works such as repairing roads or bridges. Part of it is allocated for loans to poor farmers or to farmers who have suffered serious losses by fire. At present the common forest land and hamlet monies are indispensable for support of village life in Nao.

Honjo hamlets, on the other hand, lack common properties. Local expenses are borne by assessments levied against all households of the community as well as by a certain return of taxes from government sources. Depending upon the hamlet, households are divided into a number of levels based upon land holdings, and monies are collected either once a year or whenever needed. Income from the rice field belonging to the Shinto shrine, over and above what is necessary for shrine festivals, is sold and may come back to the common fund of the hamlet. Overwhelming approval is given to this method of financing, although it means that hamlet expenses are borne by the people in contrast to financing from common lands as in Nao.

Sanctions applied to traditional coercive activities reflect again the complex asymmetrical support of village sentiment and shaping of the individual in Nao and Honjo. Thus traditionally in Nao, households that failed to send a representative to assist on cooperative endeavors (such as road and bridge repairing, cleaning of irrigation ditches) were fined a certain amount, which was added to the common fund of the hamlet; if a woman came in place of a man, the household was fined 30 percent (her labor being considered equivalent to 70 percent of a man's). These fines still prevail and are firmly enforced. In Honjo, on the other hand, the penalty system came to be weakened around 1930, after which time no discrimination was made in terms of the sex and age of the labor contributed. Today headmen will receive a fine when it is voluntarily contributed, but no penalty is coercively imposed upon households that do not donate to the communal labor pool. Decline in this village function can be traced rather directly to the introduction of labor saving machines.

Thus the political system in relation to community services shows a much greater weakening of hamlet integration in Honjo as compared with Nao. National youth and women's organizations penetrating to the local level and functionally related to agricultural development are also more numerous and important in the former area, and are inversely correlated with the decline of sanctions (consistent with a decline in this respect of local autonomy).

In more purely symbolic activities, however, the situation tends to be reversed, shrine festivals having declined more in the isolated villages than in the hamlets closer to the city. Regular visits to shrines by individuals follow the same pattern—more than twice as many visitants being received in Honjo buraku as compared with those of Nao. Certain other ceremonial observances that have been abandoned in Nao—the children's fire festival, for example—continue to be held in Honjo. Yoshida suggests that the persistence there of a hamlet-centered folk belief system is probably a function of greater wealth due to increase in rational agricultural practices and the somewhat larger size of the shrine fields. These are undoubtedly important enabling factors, but they do not explain the continued orientation to collective sentiments in the face of changes in land tenure that have led to increasing individuation of households. The fact is that strains created by national concerns and institutions have, if anything, resulted in reinforcement of local concerns in certain significant ways, especially by increased attractiveness of life in the hamlet community. In Nao itself one hamlet exhibits greater local consciousness than the others. The communal bath continues to be used; the old age group is more powerful and directs folk rituals and festivals more frequently than elsewhere; and inhabitants more uniformly stress the importance of common properties. In this case it is not by choice that moral imperatives of the village persist, but it is rather a consequence of restricted occupational opportunities. Only 6 percent of farmers engage partly in wage work outside the community, the rest being full-time farmers. Postwar land reform also led to a lowering of the economic standard of living, thus requiring more cooperation and symbolic reaffirmation of traditional relationships and morality. Those who must seek work outside leave the village permanently.

The hamlet remains the largest significant unit in the daily life of the individual. The constraints, expectations, and values that are transmitted through participation in its activities are still important models of behavior and for the development of the social person. The changes that have been observed and that in turn affect educational processes must be viewed initially from this vantage point.

The age-sex system within the hamlets themselves provide further models for the shaping of moral formation and the teaching process: between older and younger members of the same generation and between generations. Since the aim here is to clarify patterns of formation of the young, attention will be focused upon youth groups; *genro* (old-age groups) and *churo* (middle-age groups) will be discussed particularly in relation to the former.

Young Men's Associations

Young men's associations in Nao and Honjo have traditionally played an important role in disciplining and teaching norms of behavior to new members. There are two such groups. One is the *seinen-kumi* indigenous to the hamlet. The other, called *seinen-dan*, is a chapter of a national youth organization established by the government in Saga Prefecture in 1924 as a deliberate educational instrument. Although established on the basis of different principles (members in the *seinen-kumi* were recruited automatically as part of the local rites of passage), both have played important roles in young men's activities. Until 1930 in Honjo and until the end of the war in Nao, the members of the *seinen-kumi* had the responsibility of preparing for the festival of the tutelary god, maintaining vigilance over the proper conduct of each other, and determining the schedule of farm labor for mutual aid enterprises. The *genro* and *churo* in fact regulated some of these activities as a result of their control over financial matters. Nevertheless the *seinen-kumi* exercised a fair measure of independence over its own proper sphere. In addition to its formal responsibilities it was also expected to discipline its members in basic collective values: avoiding quarrels and disputes, obedience to elders and nonparticipation in symbolic privileges of adults (smoking was specifically forbidden to the young).

The *seinen-kumi* was an effective agency of the cultural integrity of the *buraku* whereby intragroup quarreling was strictly controlled while internecine disputes with other buraku tended to be encouraged. Thus the collective life of youth cultivated hamlet consciousness and played a dominant part in the molding of desired kinds of persons through informal training and sanctions.

In Nao since the war, the *seinen-kumi* has changed considerably in the discharge of its functions and even in its structure. Age distinctions within the group have largely disappeared and many of its collective activities have been abandoned. It ceases, for instance, to organize mutual aid or to take effective charge of the festival of the tutelary god. The dissolution of the formal system of *seinen-kumi* is directly related to recent economic and social changes discussed above. The hamlets in this mura have suffered a substantial loss of youths, who have either gone to work part time or permanently elsewhere, or who entered a higher school in another community to prepare for occupational opportunities outside their native region. Those who remain, therefore, are few in number so that apart from any natural loss of interest they cannot effectively discharge their former functions. *Seinen-kumi* have not entirely ceased to exist and in fact exhibit some vigor in the most conservative villages, but qualitatively the system has changed. Perhaps the most important point to observe is that its disciplinary and directive functions have disappeared. Traditional annual events are now enjoyed as recreation rather than as solemn duties. In Nao *seinen-kumi* no longer acts as an effective intermediary reinforcing agency in the transmission of hamlet norms.

In principle *seinen-kumi* activities in Nao hamlets embody the traditional aims and directives of the village community. *Seinen-dan*, on the other hand, links youth interests with outside concerns and is best reflected in a course for the young called *seinen-gakkyu* and in the formation of 4H clubs (an American innovation introduced through the national Ministry of Agriculture). In the two buraku studied (where it has taken root), *seinen-dan* operates as the chief source of innovations and reforming of subsidiary enterprises to supplement reduced farm income. In one buraku it was sufficiently important as to have undermined seriously *genro* political control, but in the most conservative village where *seinen-kumi* has continued to be most active there is no such experimentation and the old men have retained their former functions.

In practice there has been a considerable intertwining of functions in that many of the youths in all but the most conservative village belong to both groups, and reforms are instituted sometimes in the name of the one, sometimes of the other. On the whole *seinen-dan* in Nao occupies a more important position as an organ of future more radical reform and of the penetration of external pressures.

The youth groups of Honjo, despite mechanization and urban stimuli, are more active in all ways than those of Nao. In the first place there are more youths in Honjo *buraku* where there is more land available and land reform acted as a strong incentive to make of farming a desired way of life for the new generation. With mechanization and progressive improvement in agricultural techniques the young also acquired new skills more readily than the old and hence their labor was at a premium. Although the number of children supported through high school (beyond the present nine years' compulsory education) has been increasing in both areas, their motivation is quite different. The boys in Nao are encouraged to attend school in order to leave the native village and qualify for a job in the city; those in Honjo are sent to high school or agricultural higher schools so that they may return and add to the growing stock of agricultural skill and knowledge.

Honjo youths not only contribute thus to family welfare—and indeed have changed its character—they continue to be important at the hamlet level itself. One of the determinants of strong membership in youth groups today is the indispensable role they play in operating the machines now used for raising soil from the creeks. This alone has acted as a strong deterrent against the dispersal of the group. In addition, they are responsible for opening and closing the irrigation dam (an unnecessary function in Nao) and for selling coal to families in the village. In both areas youths cooperatively repair roads, clean irrigation ditches, and so on, but the efficiency of such activities has declined sharply in Nao because of the shortage of youths.

The youth groups in Honjo hamlets are not only more active in matters requiring technical services, but they are also more energetic participants in shrine festivals. It is the older and middle-aged married householders in Nao who attend the ceremonial feast held annually in the local shrine; in Honjo persons of all ages actively participate. Greater prosperity and wealth of the farms as well as the larger size of the rice field belonging to the hamlet shrines make this possible. The strong inculcation of hamlet consciousness and local welfare is an important motive for this observed lively interest in the festival.

Sixty percent of youths in Honjo are affiliated with the *seinen-dan* as compared with 30 percent in Nao. Branches of other nation-wide associations such as women's clubs also function more actively in the former area, providing a broader channel of communication with other hamlets and with concerns of the larger Japanese community. The siphoning off of youths in Nao in effect strengthens local barriers to external stimuli, whereas in Honjo the recruitment of able young men into the community provides an innovating force that acts as the nucleus of continuing, even revitalized, hamlet identification and development. It is no accident that a communal ritual, like the farewell feast given for young men who marry and move into the middle-age category, is still punctiliously observed in Honjo but has virtually disappeared in Nao.

As we have seen, youths upon marriage assume new age as well as marital roles, and pass successively from vigorous adulthood (*churo*) to old age (*genro*). Traditionally, interaction between these age levels took place within the context of the structure of authority and power relations—in the family and community. Advancing age is a sensitive barometer of hierarchical status and is reflected in the relation between household and local government. In Nao the position of headman in the hamlet is filled by rotation among the househeads of the community; in Honjo buraku he is selected biennially through discussion among the ranking householders (rank being determined on the basis of a combination of wealth, age, intelligence, and ability). The job is a taxing one, putting such claims upon the time of the incumbent that in one Honjo hamlet nobody would accept the position; in the spring of 1960 the people had to resort to voting—by household heads—in order to formalize a sense of responsibility.

Headmen in both areas initiate such important local activities as cooperative labor and the collecting of monies for hamlet expenses. They also act as intermediaries between community and outside local government. In most Nao hamlets the headman are still selected from the *genro* where real political and social power

lies. In all Honjo hamlets, however, it is the *churo*, or middle-age group that has become dominant. This group itself is now differentiated into an older and younger *churo*, a reflection of the different relation of older and younger vigorous adult men to technological change. Within the two middle-age groups, the younger is more preoccupied with agricultural improvements, the elder with the political and governmental affairs of the village. The tensions observed between members of these two groups derive from the threat that the older men feel about their status in the face of potential power open to their younger age-mates who are now introducing new agricultural techniques.

Corresponding to their increased social status (proportionate to their exclusive command of new desired skills), *churo* men increasingly fill the position of household manager; men in their thirties are frequently farm managers in Honjo, so that they tend to exercise power in family life to a far greater degree than in Nao, where the elder men still enjoy this prerogative. Elders in the latter hamlets are still an important repository of traditional knowledge and teachers of the young in basic skills, whereas in Honjo hamlets the dynamics of agricultural life make each successive older generation relatively obsolete. Insofar as training and standards of conduct are linked to the social structure, the new authority of relevant experience has both corroded people's convictions about valued persons and begun seriously to alter the structural principles upon which those convictions are based.

Family and Household

Finally, in this brief analysis we come to a consideration of family and household which are the basic unit of life in the hamlet. The family system in Japan has been the subject of extensive investigation by numerous Japanese and other scholars.[3]

---

[3] A bibliography of studies by Japanese scholars dealing with various dimensions of family structure since the war has recently appeared in the *Journal of Social Science*, June, 1960, pp. 185–254. It contains the impressive number of over 200 items for this period alone. We should have to add to this list analyses of family and kinship that form part of the many community studies available. One of the best of these in the English literature is to be found in R. Dore (1958), Chapter 8.

It is not possible here to treat this important subject with the attention to the varied forms, historical antecedents, and ecological determinants that it deserves. Systematic comparison and generalization from the many community studies published is not yet available. For the past three hundred years or so—since the Tokugawa Period—there does appear to have emerged a normative patrilocal household with three generations under one roof. In certain regions, where local circumstances favored it, this unit grew by extension to embrace a corporate patrilineal kin group composed of a stem family and one or more branch families (what Japanese sociologists refer to most frequently as the *dozoku*). "There is, so to speak," Cornell asserts, "a natural form of the household in Japanese peasant society [Cornell]."[4]

In Saga Prefecture the extended patri-family (stem-branch, *dozoku*) which elsewhere in Japan acts as a corporate productive unit is very weak. In the Nao district in earlier days branch families used to be established by second or third sons whenever this was feasible, with the first son receiving 70 percent of the property (including land) and the second son 30 percent. As farm lands became increasingly smaller by such division it became difficult to create new branch families. Indeed, in the most mountainous areas there was not enough land from the first to manage as full-time farms for all families. Analysis of the careers of graduates after compulsory education reveals that from the Taishow period (1912) onward second and third sons tended to follow some occupation other than agriculture. Whereas 60 percent carried on the father's occupation, most of the other sons left the village to obtain a new job; about a third of the latter continued to reside in the Nao area (but in some other hamlet) and to obtain employment on another farm. The several household heads interviewed in each hamlet studied affirmed that as their houses did not have the "power" to form a new branch family they wished their son(s), sometimes even first sons, to complete as high a school grade as possible. This amounts to a kind of succession by education.

The norms of family succession embody the principle of responsibility for all family members who once formed an integral

---

[4] We are not concerned here with the differences in family and household that obtain between rural dwellers and the traditional elite.

part of the household. There is in fact no word in Japanese that exclusively refers to either the nuclear family or household in our sense. The concept of *Ie*, Yoshida thus points out, extends beyond the family in its instrumental functions and supports a moral consciousness that affects training of the young and village loyalties. This is part of what certain Japanese scholars have in mind when they refer to the "familistic" principle. In Nao and Honjo *Ie*, in the sense of family, centers in the household, but it is not thought of simply as a group existing a certain place and time. It traditionally extends along, and is responsible to, a patrilineal line of ascent to past generations. Injunctions for the welfare of the kin group for its continuity and its reputation provide the framework of moral training and role learning. These concerns, we have seen, lie behind decisions about sending children to a school of higher grade and employment, both of which are closely related to family succession.

In Nao hamlets primogeniture is expressed as the norm for succession to the *Ie* (over 60 percent unequivocally expressed this preference). In fact, however, exceptions do occur; when the first son exhibits no talent for farming a second or third son—or sometimes just "some other son"—is selected as successor. The character of the individual children thus is increasingly taken into account, but this procedure still affirms family consciousness in attempting to maintain continuity in the face of unfavorable environmental circumstances. Usually succession means the inheritance both of the position of family head and of the father's estate. Sometimes, however, cases are encountered in which succession to the headship is distinguished from inheritance of farming property. That is to say, sometimes parents expect a son to succeed only to a house. This involves the performance of certain religious services and the duty of supporting one's parents during their old age, without succeeding to the family occupation. Divided succession of this sort occurs rather frequently in families where farming is a part-time occupation and in small scale full-time farms. Hence *Ie* succession is often partly guaranteed by providing educational opportunities for some other occupation or by means of a special fund set aside for one or more children. Only rarely is a property divided and a branch family established, as many individuals ideally prefer. The right of second and third sons to an education fund or to capital for engaging in some business of their own, in the many cases where farm lands are not divided equally, is linked to traditional *Ie* consciousness. The children who move from the natal hamlet carry with them reciprocal responsibilities for the welfare of the local family of orientation. It is still deeply rooted in people's minds that resources should be allocated as rationally as possible in order to preserve both the physical landed identity and the spiritual identity of the family. Norms of family and hamlet are also indivisibly linked; children are expected to be raised so as not to offend standards of conduct of other like-minded families within the community.

In Honjo the situation has been a little less clearly described. There, too, the patrilocal extended family as a corporate productive unit, with patriarchal control vested in a head family, is very weak. For reasons previously adduced—greater amount of available land and increased attractiveness of agriculture combined with wage labor as an occupation—more sons are able to acquire a parcel of land and remain in the village. They tend to establish independent households in such cases rather than to form branches of a corporate entity. They may still share in the responsibility of caring for aged parents, not defame the family name, have concern for its physical continuity, and so on.

School and Community

This sketch of the structural features and value training in two agricultural regions in southern Japan can perhaps be viewed in terms of a congeries of models that participate in shaping and forming the growing individual.[5] In both Honjo and Nao the young have a number of teachers and educators in their midst; they are also influenced in as yet some indeterminate degree by agents and forces outside of immediate local control: faculties of education, the powerful Japanese Teachers Union, and the politi-

[5] Elsewhere I suggested, in thinking about education in the American scene, that Kurt Lewin's concept of "channels" provides one useful framework for generating hypotheses about relations between variables in the transmission process. The present discussion, while much less formal, pursues essentially the same line of reasoning. See Bernard J. Siegel (1955).

cal power struggles on the prefectural and national levels. The latter, as we have seen at the beginning of this essay are large and complex problems in themselves. Little if any research has been directed towards the study of the effects of such agencies upon the quality and character of teaching in specific local contexts, and I shall not attempt to speculate upon these concerns here.

In reflecting upon the training of the young in Saga Prefecture, I have found it useful to make the distinction which Cora DuBois has suggested between *teachers* ("the type of educator that functions in relation to schools") and *educators* (experienced or "formed" individuals who transmit knowledge, attitudes, values, and the like to the "unformed"—outside the institutional context of the school) (DuBois, 1955:91). In one sense, of course, society as a whole may be conceived as a "school," much as Durkheim (1912) in another context conceived of the highly integrated community as a "church." Where the school exists as a physical place, however, with a visible personnel, a publicly stated curriculum, and a specific obligatory duration, it constitutes a definite target for public interaction and concern. Any proper analysis of the transmission of valued means and ends of living, in a country like Japan, therefore, must take into consideration the relation between education and teaching, of the school and community. I should like at this point to suggest the nature of this interaction at Nao and Honjo villages insofar as the data of this study permit.

The school, to begin with, is conceived in this part of rural Japan as a tool—a necessary tool—by means of which certain urgent socio-economic problems are solved. For most families in Nao, high school education (which is not compulsory and for which a small but significant fee is required) provides a distinct advantage to those children who must seek a livelihood outside the hamlet. On the other hand, families of lowest economic status cannot send their sons to high school, a factor which tends to increase wealth differences in each hamlet. Second and third sons, as well as successors to family property and management at all economic levels in Honjo attend high school at a higher rate than the national average (which is about 50 percent). Families from middle and upper economic levels frequently send their second and third sons to a nearby university. A very few students have succeeded in entering the major universities of Kyushu and Tokyo. It is interesting to note that even the poorest families in Honjo aspire (although unrealistically) to send their sons to university, so important are the economic advantages perceived to be for the benefit of the hamlet.

At first blush these observations would seem to call to mind a frequent response to schooling and education in the United States, where many families that have become familiar with statistically supported associations between level of education, income, and occupation adopt a basically instrumental attitude toward formal education. There are important differences, between the two situations, however, which derive largely from a much greater respect accorded the teacher in Japan. This valuation has a long history and is deep rooted. The most recent episode of large-scale foreign influence, at the time of the opening of Japan to the West and the Meiji Restoration in the nineteenth century, led not simply to rational nativistic reaction or self-conscious borrowing on a massive scale to facilitate national cultural survival and international competition. It involved also a great admiration on the part of new leadership of Westerners as teachers. More recently, in the decade preceding World War II, the schools in Japan came to be used as a major instrument for the inculcation of ultranationalist aims of unification. The peasant's conception of the proper form of social life and of the place of all categories and groups of persons within it was in no small measure shaped by a uniform influencing by prestigeful educators.

In both Nao and Honjo today, conflicts of interest between family and school never lead to teacher-parent discussions, overt expressions of hostility, or interested participation in educative councils like school boards or PTAs. There is a strong attitude among the parents in these areas as well as in other parts of Japan that the job of teaching lies wholly within the province of government and professional teachers. However much anxiety might be felt in this regard, parents rely completely upon teachers for stating the aims of education and interpreting them in the classroom. These in consequence are little affected by local orientations. The attitude of respect towards and flow of authority from teachers overrides the more traditional deference to age as a principle of authority and control. In the hamlets studied, several of the elementary school teachers come from local families and command far more prestige than individuals of corresponding age who have gone into other occupations. They also play important leadership roles in the Life Improvement Activities Association (Seikatsu Kaizen Katsudo)[6] and in Public Hall (Kominkan) activities initiated on a purely local basis.

Nevertheless conflicts do exist; it cannot be said that teachers and parents share common ideas about the aims of education. Unreserved loyalty toward the family and strong filial obedience to parents, for example, is no longer stressed in the schools, and local parents feel that teachers do not inculcate enough of this value in the classroom. Instead teachers are inclined to think that the attitudes and ways of thinking of local people are rather "feudalistic" and tend to stress what they conceive to be democratic, individualistic values in the schools. Though they have not so long ago come from it, they tend to look down upon the local culture. Thus teachers, while treated as real members of the hamlet, are somewhat different from other people, as certain farmers feel free to confide. Household heads not infrequently reveal skepticism about teachers, and sometimes find it impossible to accept their leadership on local issues. A native teacher told the principal investigator that he occasionally felt like a stranger in the community. On the other hand, teachers unquestionably are among the most prominent innovators of the hamlet, while their fathers and other householders act as checks to rapid change. This subtle interplay requires more study. In addition, special attention should be paid to the socializing of teachers in the course of their professionalization. Undoubtedly some young men and women will respond more readily than others to new moral concepts in universities and faculties of education (and perhaps as members of the Teacher's Union). The degree of commitment to values assimilated with teacher-role in relation to previously acquired disposi-

---

[6] A chapter of a national organization which is concerned with the health activities, improvement of agricultural techniques, the welfare of women and children, and adult education. Four national ministries—Welfare, Agriculture, Labor, and Education—contribute to its formal programming.

tions to behavior is a matter of great importance to understand. It bears upon the nature, strength, and resolution of conflicts between teachers and other educators in the community; hence upon the degree of consistency or inconsistency in value transmission to the young.

Traditionally in Nao and Honjo age gradations were punctiliously observed as channels for training in obedience, respect for authority, and the organization of many activities. Outside the home organized youth groups before the war were closely supervised by both household elders, government agents, and teachers so that they tended to support and reinforce the monolithic values extending from hamlet to nation. The most conservative hamlet in Nao mura still approaches this norm; teacher-parent disparities in training are completely overridden by parental dominance. Elsewhere, however, the situation is more complicated. Through the *seinen-dan*, as we have seen, are funneled many innovations related to the rationalization of agriculture, fishing, and forestry. Youths from fourteen years of age and upward are trained in techniques of self-government and initiative, but schools and town hall leaders take a lively interest in the implementation of their activities. Teachers who participate in both groups tend to act as innovators and potentially to exacerbate generation cleavages and conflict. Yet it is interesting to note that it is in Nao hamlets, where half as many youths belong to the *seinen-dan* as in Honjo, that adults complain most about the lack of hard work and "easygoing" attitudes of the young. The small inefficient size of a great many holdings have reduced the number of young men who can remain in the community. As a consequence the functions and roles of the remaining few are more ambiguous and far less enthusiastically discharged.[7]

---

[7] These differences between isolated and nonisolated hamlets contrast with what appears to be a more usual development in postwar Japan. Thus Dore asserts that "the solidarity of the hamlet tends to vary roughly in proportion to the degree of its isolation. The more isolated, solidary hamlets are often spoken of as the most "backward"—the strength of community sentiment itself as well as the small degree of urbanization and the prevalence of old customs are considered criteria of backwardness. Yet it seems, paradoxically, that of recent years it is these very "backward" hamlets that often exhibit the greatest innovating zeal. It is in remote fishing and

Adults in Honjo hamlets, on the other hand, cannot fairly complain of unusual laziness (due to demoralization), since youths remain there by choice, energetically pursue their new opportunities, are among the foremost advocates of innovation, and make an important contribution to support of hamlet cooperative values. They need little by way of repressive sanctions to help with soil removal from the creek, irrigation, and the like. Paradoxically, however, the support which parents lend to higher education, partly as a prestige value but more importantly for bringing advanced technical skills to the hamlet, has tended to subvert traditional hierarchical relationships and expand the base of leadership to their own detriment. This has created conflicts not only between the old-age groups and young, but also between old-age and middle-age groups and between upper and lower middle-age groups. As a result of a new kind of education and differently qualified educators, the teachers and schools appear to have a stronger impact upon the young than in Nao where they suffer by competition with older models. This has not led, for reasons adduced, to serious cleavages within the hamlet since farming youths continue to adhere at the same time to hamlet norms. Perhaps the long experience and genius for intensive cooperative forms of social life which the Japanese exhibit will constitute an important vehicle for continued educational reforms (in the broad sense). "One often wonders whether the 'community consciousness of the hamlet,' so often deplored by contemporary Japanese writers as a survival of a feudal age and a mark of the backwardness

---

mountain villages that one often finds the most active and successful family-planning movements, the most earnest young farmers' clubs, the greatest diffusion of rationalized kitchens, the brides' societies which discuss how to get on with mothers-in-law, the agreements to cut down unnecessary prestige expenditure on *rites-de-passage*. The reason is not difficult to seek. In such hamlets, in the Japanese phrase, *matomari ga ii*—they hang together. The more solidary hamlet provides a greater social energy for reforming leadership to work with and can mobilize a greater willingness to cooperate. The slogan "let us make ours a bright (*akarui*) hamlet" has greater appeal, and where it is accepted that each man is his brother's keeper, it is easier to suggest to one's brother's wife that she should not have so many children." (Dore, 959: 386–87.) In the light of the data from Saga we should have to modify this statement to the effect that maintenance of buraku consciousness and values will vary directly (and also lead to dynamic innovation) with any forces that enable the traditional forms of solidarity to persist.

of Japanese social development, is really such a bad thing as they make out [Dore, 1959:387]."

ADAPTIVE FUNCTIONS OF THE SCHOOLS AND EDUCATION

The analysis up to this point has centered upon educational problems within the most important social unit of rural life in Japan, the hamlet. Cultural and social transformations and the reshaping of attitudes and commitments to old or new values sink roots here first of all. Land reform was intended to stimulate individual initiative and dignity and to democratize Japanese village life by the redistribution of productive resources. Changes in these directions have certainly occurred in varying degrees to an extent unthinkable in prewar Japan. But the redistribtuion of wealth also eliminated a major source of chronic, smoldering, intensely felt frustrations by widening the base of local leadership. As tenant dependency upon former landlords was destroyed a growing sense of personal worth began increasingly to assert itself in terms of hamlet solidarity. A great many local citizens felt themselves for the first time to be real members "in good standing" within the buraku. This feeling, in turn, gave renewed strength in all but the most demoralized areas to the collective sentiments and demands of the hamlet and to pressures to conform—to make it a shining example to others.

At the same time life has become far more complicated for the farmer. Instead of being ordered what to raise and how much, he now makes these decisions for himself. He therefore must learn about marketing (and will participate in agricultural cooperatives at least for the handling of rice, but also for silk, milk, tea, mandarin oranges, and so on).

To achieve certain individual and collective goals the modern farmer must learn also how to implement them politically. From one study we are told about farmers who lobbied for the construction of a highway that would lead into the city of Hiroshima. If successful, it would enable them to double their income from vegetables currently produced and also to raise quality cash crops, such as late season tomatoes (Ishino, Iwao, Donoghue: 3). Skill in political maneuvering and motivation to do so are now taught at several levels: in the classroom where individualistic, independent attitudes are encouraged and "democratic personality" is stressed; in women's and youth organizations (part of what is called social education); and in the running of the village and hamlet affairs. Not only in Nao and Honjo areas but in rural Japan generally the effectiveness of this training will depend upon its articulation with character formation processes in family and hamlet (including, importantly, ordinal position within the family), ecological and perhaps other situational factors. In the most conservative hamlet of Nao there have been the fewest inroads; in Honjo many changes have occurred but without destroying the security functions of the tiny local unit.

Given his typically small land holdings, the farmer to be successful as an entrepreneur today must also extend his perspectives to learn about such things as farm credit, interest rates, crop insurance, and taxes. These are forms of special knowledge which most farmers can appreciate but which again put younger adults in Honjo in an advantageous position by virtue of more and superior schooling. On the one hand, the strength of traditional deference to leadership exercised by the more well-to-do (provided they are in other ways "respectable"), coupled with a very high rate of literacy, on the other hand, tend to offset economic and social competition from the young. 91.5 percent of households in Nao hamlets own radios and 79.7 percent subscribe to newspapers. In Honjo 95 percent of the households own radios, 93 percent subscribe to newspapers, and 5 percent subscribe to a monthly agricultural magazine. The last, along with episodes in the lives of movie stars, articles on sport, jazz, and the like, also devotes considerable space to agricultural advice, agriculture in foreign countries, planning of kitchens, and articles on successful model farmers and villages. There are a few television sets in Honjo, none in Nao; books are rarely read in either area. In addition to popular recreational programs the radio provides weather forecasts and some farm news. Information on Cooperative Associations whose educational functions provide another link with the larger national community, is unfortunately not available. From other regions one learns that more successful cooperatives introduce new crops, provide demonstration, organize lecture meetings geared to agricultural improvement, and the like.

The flow of new patterns of behavior and thought from city to country through mass media of communication, school personnel and higher education, the concerns of national ministries of the central government, unions, and the interaction between national, prefectural and village decision-making mechanisms—all of these forces have led to new problems of cultural transmission at the local level. But the changing demands of extremely rapid economic recovery and industrial growth after the war have created yet a different kind of problem, namely, the extent to which education and teaching have adapted today's mobile individuals for urban life. Of the many youths who must leave Nao hamlets for employment elsewhere, for example, one might ask how many are in a competitive position with urban youths recruited into the same labor force; what kinds of social adjustment do they make and how effectively do they participate in civic affairs; whether or not there are differences between urban and rural recruits or between different categories of rural youth themselves; if so, what appears to lie behind them. One might also compare the adaptation of second and third sons who have moved to urban centers with those who have settled in a neighboring hamlet, village, town, or nonurban industrial community.

These matters have only begun to be studied, and research related to them is in its initial stages. At present they can be stated largely as important matters of theoretical and practical concern in the study of education and teaching in the complexity of modern rural life.

Saga Prefecture and Rural Japan

While there is considerable variability within and between Nao and Honjo hamlets in matters pertaining to social structure and cultural transmission, they represent only a part of the general variability to be found throughout rural Japan. Ecological differences, disparate population densities, modes of livelihood (fishing, farming, combined fishing and farming, for example), available alternative outlets for the locally frustrated or disaffected are among the situational determinants of community types and associated educational processes.

At one extreme is a fishing hamlet in northeastern Japan, so cut off even today from communication even with neighboring hamlets that it remains as isolated as one can possibly imagine in modern Japan (Saito, 1955). Only a handful of households subscribe to or read newspapers or magazines, or listen to a radio. Eighty five percent of men and 75 percent of women are natives of the hamlet; the scope of life is so narrow that people rarely visit other buraku of the village, and they still continue an old practice of shopping as a community twice a year at the neighboring town. A combination of stable, limited resources, a growing population, and a virtual absence of escape valves has led to even greater emphasis upon traditional role relations—strong patriarchal controls, symbolic supports of hierarchical arrangements (in language, seating customs), mother-in-law and daughter-in-law conflicts, the exercise of stern repressive controls over hard work imposed on the young. Economic and social dependence upon the buraku has meant that possible sources of educative innovation are almost completely stifled; experimentation is at a minimum. One is reminded of the constricted narrow educational channels by which minds are molded and personalities formed in the most conservative American Indian pueblos.

By contrast, certain villages in a prefecture embracing fertile valleys in the Japanese Alps, noted for its strong emphasis upon educational values and political progressivism, we are told suffer from a shortage of vigorous adult young, who elect in increasing numbers to seek a livelihood in distant cities. Initiative exhibited by teachers in the schools is matched in women's and youth clubs by encouragement to discuss a wide range of current conflicts and problems, from nutritional improvement and technical farm improvement to birth control. The local Council has strong support in its efforts to enrich the curriculum of village life and introduce whatever leaven is necessary to make the modern *business* of farming an attractive way of life.

Each variant in the relation of scale of farming, community

type, changes in environmental characteristics, and interaction with the national society faces its own challenge. Everywhere, however, the Japanese are energetically pursuing a continuing evaluation of the kinds of persons they wish to form and to experiment with techniques and materials by which these goals can be achieved. The demand for special substantive skills—mathematics, science machines, and language, for example—few tend to dispute (except as they clearly challenge entrenched authority). The more human values, the reasons for living as Redfield put it, in Japanese terms they find harder to evaluate.

In 1937 Embree observed as follows about the classroom in Suye Mura:

> Most of the time is taken up with singing, reading, and athletics —all three with a leaven of nationalism. No attempt is made to teach children to think critically either in primary school or in high school. The schoolmaster of the primary school sets as his aim the rules for primary-school education of the department of education in Tokyo, the schoolmaster of the middle school sets as his aim the rules of middle school education of the department of education, and so also for the agricultural school, girls' high school, etc. The schoolmasters vary from the sacred word of the department only on the side of greater nationalism. In rural schools practically all children are promoted every year, the emphasis in teaching being more moral than intellectual. Teachers feel that, if they left some child behind in his class, he would feel very badly about it and that the resulting psychological effect and family chagrin would not be compensated for by any good the child might receive mentally by repeating a school grade. Similarly, at school athletic contests all entrants, not only first, second, and third receive prizes. . . . While occasionally people are shown the virtues of initiative and leadership, they are more often shown the virtues of cooperation, and the good but mediocre child is held out to be superior to the bad but brilliant one. (Embree; 187–188).

Neither in Suye village nor elsewhere in rural Japan could one find teachers or school administrators who deliberately foster this set of attitudes today. Yet an emphasis upon collective solidarity and submergence of the individual will to the welfare of the group—be it family, neighborhood, hamlet, or firm—has become an endemic product of such training. Cooperative sentiments thus form a point of departure at all levels for contemporary experiment, action, and reaction.

From the formulators of educational policy, scholars, and professional educators to the members of a hamlet household one finds differences of opinion on matters of teaching and education in relation to the manifold realities of modern life. These differences are sometimes small, often great, questioned with an open mind or espoused with deeply felt conviction. Perhaps this is the greatest hope in the educational scene of a postwar Japan which is struggling so admirably, if precariously, to evolve a secure tradition newly oriented toward a firm place within the democratic family of nations.

References

Cornell, John B., 1959, "Family, Kin, and Community in Peasant Japan." Paper delivered at annual meetings of the Central States Anthropological Society, Madison, Wisconsin.

Dore, R. P., 1958, *City Life in Japan: A Study of a Tokyo Ward*, Chap. 8. Berkeley, Calif.: University of California Press.

———, 1959, *Land Reform in Japan*. London: Oxford University Press.

DuBois, Cora, 1955, "Some Notions on Learning Intercultural Understanding," in G. D. Spindler, ed., *Education and Anthropology*, pp. 89–126. Stanford, Calif.: Stanford University Press.

Durkheim, Emile, 1912, *Les Formes Eléméntaires de la vie Religieuse*. Paris: F. Alcan.

Embree, John, 1939, *Suya Mura*. Chicago: University of Chicago Press.

Ishino, Iwao, and J. Donoghue, 1959, "The Loss of Peasant Heritage in Japan." Paper delivered at annual meetings of the Central States Anthropological Society, Madison, Wisconsin.

Saito, Yoshio, 1955, "On the Structural Analysis of a Fishing Village. The Case of Miyagi-ken, Ogiku-gun, Onagawa-machi,

Tsukahama-buraku." *Japanese Sociological Review,* 5:24–46.

Siegel, Bernard J., 1955, "Models for the Analysis of the Educative Process in American Communities," in G. D. Spindler, ed., *Education and Anthropology*, pp. 38–61. Stanford, Calif.: Stanford University Press.

Spindler, George D., ed., 1955, *Education and Anthropology*. Stanford, Calif.: Stanford University Press.

Yoshida, Teigo, 1960*a*, "The Social Background of Moral Formation in Mountainous Agricultural Villages: The Nao Area in Saga Prefecture." *Japanese Journal of Education Research*, No. 3, pp. 54–67.

——, 1960*b*, "Cultural Integration and Change in Japanese Villages." Unpublished manuscript.

Index

R

Ramus, Peter, 450, 454, 456, 458
Rashall, Hastings, 450
Raup, Bruce, 96, 113
Read, Margaret, 43, 47, 59, 82
Reconstructionism, 102–103
Redfield, Robert, 33, 72, 74, 321, 323, 334, 349, 558
Renaissance, teaching of Latin during the, 444–466
Research, educational, 66–69
Research techniques, 6–7, 31–34
Riesman, David, 40, 47, 87, 113, 133, 147, 321, 333, 344, 349, 351, 398
Robbins, Florence G., 73, 83
Roberts, John M., 21, 33, 47, 48
Robinson, Francis, 73, 82
Rockefeller Foundation, 173
Roheim, Geza, 99
Role behavior, adolescent, 284–300
Rosenberg Foundation, 64, 236
Rosenstiel, Annette, 58, 64, 83
Rubel, Arthur J., 28, 48
Ruesch, Jurgen, 147

S

Saito, Yoshio, 557, 559
Sakai, 427
Samoans, 35, 42, 73, 138, 401, 494–497
Sapir, Edward, 34, 48, 89, 107, 108, 109–110, 113, 322, 349
Sarason, S. B., 513, 519, 528
Sargent, S. Stanfield, 45, 397
Scarr, Harry A., 257
Schapera, I., 404, 425
Schmidt, W., 89

Schneider, David, 35, 46
Seligman, Edwin R. A., 447
Sellars, R. W., 114
Selznick, Philip, 246, 258
Seneca, 457
Shakespeare, William, 449
Sharpe, Russell, 239, 255, 258
Shaw, George Bernard, 271
Shils, Edward A., 348, 351, 398
Shipnuck, Murray E., 239, 258
Sidney, Sir Philip, 458
Siegel, Bernard J., 48, 62, 74, 83, 307–308, 548, 560
  on rural Japan, 530–560
Simmons, Leo W., 327, 328, 330, 336, 349
Singer, Milton B., 321, 339, 343, 348
Sioux Indians, 35, 73
Skinner, Alanson B., 371, 396, 398
Slotkin, John S., 356, 372, 398
Smith, Marion W., 397
Social class, 105, 106
Social Science Research Council, 467
Social-self-realization, 102–103
Sociocultural system, of Menomini Indians, 351–399
Sorokin, Pitirim A., 89, 92, 98, 114
South Sea culture, 309–310
Spanish-American, Catholic, 21
Spencer, Herbert, 93
Spengler, Oswald, 97, 107
Spier, Leslie, 346, 347, 350
Spindler, G. D., 23, 24, 33, 42, 48, 49, 55, 68, 74, 79, 83, 84, 173, 215, 246, 258, 263, 267, 302, 321, 347, 349, 353, 355, 356, 364, 371,